D0700346

DIRECT ACTION

❋

MEMOIRS OF AN
URBAN GUERRILLA

DIRECT ACTION

✳

MEMOIRS OF AN
URBAN GUERRILLA

ANN HANSEN

BETWEEN THE LINES

TORONTO

AK PRESS

EDINBURGH, LONDON, OAKLAND

Direct Action
Memoirs of an Urban Guerrilla

Every reasonable effort has been made to identify copyright holders. Between the Lines would be pleased to have any errors or omissions brought to its attention.

First published in Canada in 2001 by
Between the Lines
720 Bathurst Street, Suite #404
Toronto, Ontario
M5S 2R4
www.btlbooks.com

Published in the rest of the world
in 2002 by
AK Press
674-A 23rd Street
Oakland, California 94612-1163
U.S.A.
www.akpress.org

U.S. and U.K. CIP have been applied for.

National Library of Canada Cataloguing in Publication Data

Hansen, Ann, 1953-
        Direct Action: memoirs of an urban guerrilla
ISBN 1-896357-40-7

1. Hansen, Ann, 1953- 2. Direct Action (Group) 3. Anarchists — Canada.
4. Terrorists — Canada. I. Title.
HV6430.H35A3 2001   320.5'7'0971   C2001-901905-X

AK Press edition (outside Canada) ISBN 1-902593-48-0

Front cover photograph: Police examine the damage done by a bomb blast to the Litton Systems Canada Ltd. building in Toronto, October 15, 1982. (CP Picture Archive)

Cover design by David Vereschagin, Quadrat Communications
Page preparation by Steve Izma
Printed in Canada by Transcontinental Printing

Between the Lines gratefully acknowledges assistance for its publishing activities from the Canada Council for the Arts, the Ontario Arts Council, and the Government of Canada through the Book Publishing Industry Development Program.

 Canadä

For those who struggle so our planet can flourish;
for those whose names may never be known.

Contents

Preface

During the late 1970s and early 1980s there was in Canada a large anarchist community that was particularly active in the prison abolition, feminist, Native, environmental, and Third World solidarity movements. While still working within these movements, some anarchists began to adopt direct action tactics that went beyond the legal boundaries defined by the state. They took up direct action not because they couldn't control their rage, but as part of a long-term strategy to build a revolutionary movement that would be beyond the control of corporations and the state. An even smaller group within this movement decided to start a guerrilla campaign — going underground to avoid possible arrest and imprisonment. I was part of a guerrilla group that we called Direct Action.

I have reconstructed my story of Direct Action's militant campaign based on my own recollections and using court documents and newspaper articles. Despite my best attempts to tell this story as though I were holding up a mirror to the time period, I do recognize the limitations of my memory, time, and the available documents. Inevitably my account of the details of events, and my presentation of the thoughts and emotions that I ascribe to people, have been guided by and represent my own interpretations.

I have used the real names of the people involved in Direct Action because their participation in these events is part of the public record. But I have changed the names of many secondary characters not only to protect their identities but also because I have re-created conversations, thoughts, and emotions in order to tell a more complete story. One major character, "Wayne Fraser," is a composite based on a real police intelligence officer involved in the investigation and surveillance of Direct Action. I fictionalized his character in order to create a counterpoint to our group's unfolding campaign. The other policemen's actions and characters are also based on real people, but their names too have been changed. "Rose Gibralter" is also a composite character created to provide more information about the popular legal struggle against the construction of the Cheekeye-Dunsmuir power line. I used the real names of the Litton bombing victims and the various anti-cruise missile protesters (chapters 28, 30, 35) because their comments come directly from newspaper articles and are therefore a matter of public record.

Although I have tried to present the details of the main events surrounding the conversations involving Brent Taylor, Doug Stewart, Julie Belmas, Gerry Hannah, and myself as accurately as possible, I have re-created the conversations based on memory. Chapters 38 to 44, however, include largely verbatim conversations taken from transcripts of the RCMP wiretaps provided to us during our trial. Since the stack of papers from the wiretaps is about a foot high, I have had to edit the conversations, but in doing so I tried to remain true to the spirit and intent of the originals. I believe they give the reader a window into the group dynamic.

Chapters 29 and 31, which describe police surveillance, are based on surveillance notes given at the time of our trial to the Crown prosecutor, Jim Jardine, by Corporal Andrew Johnston of the RCMP Security Service. These documents were available to us as part of the legal disclosure that the Crown had to make to our defence lawyers.

Thanks go to Maureen Garvie, my writing mentor, who gave me the confidence to write about these events, and also to all the people at Between the Lines, who gave me total freedom to express myself on a taboo topic that most publishers would want to carefully mould in order to create the "right" message. And a special thanks to Brent Taylor, Doug Stewart, Gerry Hannah, and Julie Belmas. They were not involved in writing this book, but they risked the consequences of acting upon their convictions.

Doug Stewart, 1983, Oakalla
All photos courtesy of the author.

Gerry Hannah, 1983, Oakalla

Julie Belmas and Ann Hansen, 1983, Oakalla

Brent Taylor, 1983, Oakalla

Somewhere
near
Squamish

✳ 1 ✳

January 20, 1983, started out as a normal day in our rather atypical lives. The five of us got up at dawn, loaded our truck, and headed out of Vancouver for our weekly shooting practice in a secluded box canyon near the sleepy coastal town of Squamish, British Columbia. It was the kind of clear and sunny winter day when all living creatures seemed glad to be alive, despite the morning cold. The air was filled with the sound of birds. Down in the strait, pods of black and white killer whales arched through the waves and dark seals lay smiling and basking on snow-covered rocks. The air was so clean and crisp that it was a joy just to breathe it.

We took our usual route along highway 99, which winds like a long black snake up the coast to Squamish and the Mount Whistler ski resorts. The barren, snow-covered cliffs on one side of the highway and the sheer drop into the ocean on the other left little room for driver error. I leaned into the steering wheel and clutched it until my knuckles turned white and the fresh scab on my index finger began to ooze blood. I recalled Brent's dire warning that this little scratch would scar me for life if I didn't take the time to bandage it before we left. The only solace I found was in the comforting sound of our four-wheel drive's huge tires humming soothingly on the slick asphalt turns.

By the time we reached Britannia Beach, about thirty kilometres south of Squamish, I needed a break. We pulled off the highway into a parking lot, stopping at a small gas station and variety store nestled into the cliffs. I stepped out of the pickup, which we affectionately called Bob, and stretched my arms into the air. Gerry and Julie jumped out of the front seat too and immediately started chasing each other around, throwing snowballs and laughing so loud their squeals echoed off the rock faces. Doug and Brent lifted up the glass door of the truck canopy and slid out from the back, where they had been sitting in the freezing cold amongst all the packsacks full of pistols, rifles, shotguns, and ammunition. Doug looked like some handsome soldier of fortune with his dark sunglasses, camoclothes, and military-style haircut. They were still immersed in a debate over the mechanics of converting a Mini-14 from a semi-automatic into a fully automatic rifle.

After buying coffees we piled back into the pickup and continued on our journey to the abandoned logging road and box canyon where we always did our target-practising. As we drove, a punk tune on the radio sparked our attention: "*You call us weirdos, call us crazy / Say we're evil, say we're lazy . . .*"

"Hey, that's the Subhumans!" laughed Julie, turning the volume way up. Until he'd decided to embark on this mission with us, Gerry had been the bass player in the now-defunct punk band. Julie sat beside me, singing along in her abandoned way. She was a stunning young woman with strands of jet black hair falling loosely across her white skin. Her bright blue eyes were animated and alive. On the other side of her, Gerry smiled at her earnest singing attempt.

We had been driving again for about forty-five minutes when on the highway ahead I could see a long line of cars backed up to a standstill, its front end out of sight somewhere around a curve. "I wonder what that's all about?"

"Probably a rock slide," Gerry said. "They're always clearing away debris on this highway."

We reached the last car in the line and came to a stop. Every now and then a car passed in the oncoming lane, indicating that up ahead, at least on the other side, someone was letting traffic through. We sat listening to the blare of the radio as our long file of cars crept forward.

Finally we crawled around a curve and could see the head of the line a few cars forward, where a highway flagman was stopping vehicles and talking briefly to the passengers before sending them on their way. Eventually we were second in line, and we stared, half-blinded by the glare of the sunlight reflected off the glass and metal of the car in front of us, as the flagman leaned inside it. Then he waved the driver off and the car disappeared slowly around a bend.

It seemed to take forever before he waved us on too. Slowly we drove forward, the music from our radio echoing off the mountainside. The stretch of winding highway was now eerily empty except for a helicopter that seemed to be hovering above us. For almost half a kilometre we drove without seeing another car from either direction until we came to a blind curve. As we rounded it, we came to an abrupt halt in front of a huge dump truck parked oddly across both lanes of the highway, though with no sign of blasting or road work going on. In front of the dump truck stood a flagman wearing a bright yellow vest with a large red "X" criss-crossed on his chest. I distinctly remember being struck by this flagman's red hair and clean, chiselled jaw line.

"Doesn't that guy remind you of that cartoon character, Dudley Do-Right?" I laughed nervously to Julie and Gerry. "You know that crazy RCMP guy in the cartoon?" To my surprise, they both agreed.

The flagman held up the "STOP" side of his sign and stepped up to our truck window, motioning for me to roll it down. As I leaned over to turn the handle, I caught a glimpse in my side-view mirror of another dump truck pulling up behind us.

"Is somebody going to move that dump truck or do I have to move it for you?" I was saying lightheartedly when I was struck by the expression on his face. His cartoon smile was stretched tautly, and his eyes were filled with terror, as though my feeble joke was a serious threat.

As his eyes locked on mine, my whole world began to move in slow motion and my insides went numb. He reached in through my open window and grabbed my arm with one hand and with his other opened the cab door. He flung me out onto the ground. I lay in the gravel at the side of the road with the flagman poised on top of me, the barrel of his .38 revolver pressed tightly against my temple. He yelled something in a voice filled with fear to another flagman, who I could see was now crouched on top of Julie on the other side of the road. She lay motionless. I wondered if she was dead.

A shot rang out, so loud it shook me to the core of my being. Then another shot. *They have shot Brent and Doug.* Smoke from the guns filled the air and stung my nostrils and eyes. Suddenly highway crewmen were everywhere, jumping from behind large boulders, running towards us from stands of trees, and leaping over snowdrifts beside the road. They were dressed in the uniform beige coveralls of the Department of Highways, with the exception of the assault rifles they carried, pointed in our direction. As the gunsmoke began to clear, I also saw men wearing camouflage combat fatigues, bulletproof vests, and gas masks. There were even dogs.

It was all so surreal. My brain was incapable of absorbing and deciphering the meaning of these events, but I knew that our little trip up the Whistler highway had taken a terrible turn and life as I knew it would never be the same.

From my spot on the ground I could see the highway crewmen and men in combat fatigues massing in groups around the dump trucks. They yelled to one another in strained voices. Several unmarked cars with men in suits inside pulled up from around the bend. They got out and appeared to take command of the situation. Looking under the truck, I could see Julie lying motionless on the other side. I figured I was the only one left alive.

The man on top of me had handcuffed me. Now he got up, slowly and cautiously, treating me as though I was the one with the gun. "Get up," he ordered. His expression was so tense that I moved very carefully, for fear that, despite the handcuffs, one false move on my part might cause him to shoot me. He patted me firmly all over my body to make sure I didn't have any weapons.

The fact that these were policemen had finally entered my consciousness. I was told to begin walking towards the unmarked cars parked a short way down the road. The winter sun sent heat waves curling off the asphalt, melting images of people in its path. I felt sure they would shoot me before I reached the cars, and no one would ever know what had happened on this isolated stretch of highway. The only witnesses left alive would be the cops and highway men with assault rifles. But, strangely, I was not afraid. My entire nervous system seemed to have shut down. It was as though I was in a slow-motion nightmare that would soon end.

I walked and walked, yet the expected shot did not ring out. Why didn't they shoot me? I looked around. They were everywhere. There must have been a couple of dozen riflemen. If they weren't going to shoot me, my fate was clear. If I continued walking, I would get into that car and be whisked off to prison and to probable torture.

I could change my fate by one simple move. *Run*. I pictured myself beginning to run, and the fear in those men's faces guaranteed me that their reaction, through both instinct and instruction, would be to shoot. It occurred to me that they wanted me to run, so they would have an excuse to kill me. What other reason could there be for choosing such a remote area to make the bust?

Time and space had entered another dimension. Seconds had become hours; movement, incredibly slow. Should I begin to move my legs, *run, run, run*, and guarantee death — or should I continue to walk towards the car and begin the slow death that prison would inevitably be? I listened to the rhythmic crunch of my boots in the gravel and the chirping of a solitary sparrow on a branch somewhere nearby. I don't know what tipped the scale in the direction of life. Perhaps it was the sound of that bird; perhaps the fear of death. Whatever the reasons, I kept slowly walking. Later on there would be many times when I looked back on that moment and wished I had chosen to run.

Then I saw Julie, looking dazed and dishevelled, walking towards the cars. My heart soared and I smiled at her. Then another welcome sound: Gerry asking a cop if he could retrieve a tooth that had been knocked out during the arrest. "That's the least of your worries," the cop said. He opened the car door so Gerry could get in.

So Gerry and Julie were still alive. I looked around for Brent and Doug. To my relief, they were already sitting in one of the cars, staring blankly forward, looking as numb as I felt. Their eyes were bloodshot, and they were covered in sludge, as though they had been dragged through the wet snow on the side of the road. Looking back, I could see poor Bob, our pickup, the doors flung open, the windows of the canopy smashed into thousands of glass fragments strewn all over the road. Later on I would learn that the cops had fired tear gas canisters into the back of the truck in order to pacify Brent and Doug. For me these images became forever frozen in time.

I was directed into a car along with Julie. We sat motionless and speechless, each in our own little world trying to come to terms with what had just happened. I stared at the back of the heads of the two cops sitting in the front seat, murmuring to each other. Two other cars, one carrying Brent and Doug and the other Gerry, pulled out in front of us and began the winding journey back down the road. We were driven along the isolated stretch of highway to the point where the roadblock began. As we went slowly by the line of vehicles, each carload of heads turned to stare at us. Our lives as a public spectacle had begun.

Once my brain was no longer consumed by trying to digest the events taking place, my first thought was of my mother. In the years leading up to this moment, I had conveniently blocked out the possibility that someday she would be exposed to everything I had done and that this would cause her great pain. Now I was overwhelmed with the realization that in a few hours my actions would be front-page news. The headline "Litton Bombers Arrested" (and my name mentioned in the first paragraph) would come screaming out at her, shaking her peaceful existence. The news of my arrest and involvement in English Canada's biggest so-called terrorist activities would no doubt hurt her as profoundly as would news of my death. I fervently regretted that I had not chosen to run and be shot dead, because in the long run my death would probably have been easier for her to cope with than the knowledge that her nature-loving oldest daughter was one of Canada's most notorious "terrorists."

The vision of her sitting in her kitchen staring in horror at the newspaper haunted me. All my good intentions and motives during the past few years would receive no airplay or newsprint; only my actions in their criminal context would be of interest to the mass media. I shook my head and stared out at the waves crashing against the rocks below the highway as our little entourage of police cars wound its way steadily down the road. The three police cars carrying us were escorted behind and in front by unmarked cars. Later I found out that they were filled with SWAT team members in the unlikely event that fellow "terrorists" had plotted a counter-ambush.

But as the reality of our situation sank in, I became aware of a strange feeling of relief that I had never anticipated. It was over. For the past two years we had lived a life normally only depicted in movies and novels, a life that could best be described as a political crime drama. We had lived daily with the threat of death or prison hanging over our heads. We had spent our time either plotting or in the midst of carrying out bombings, robberies, or other related support actions.

The tension of our lives had been relentless. We never took a break, never went to the beach for a day of doing nothing, never took a casual walk in Stanley Park, never slept in or hung about the house lazily reading a book on a rainy day. Our group was on a mission, and we lived each day with the zeal and fervour of people who believed that their every action was so important that the survival of the planet depended on them. If we did go for a walk in Stanley Park, it was to discuss the merits of bombing CF-18s at the Cold Lake Canadian Forces base versus blowing up a bridge in the infrastructure of the Northeast Coal Project. When we went swimming it was for exercise, not leisure. If we stayed home to read a book, it would be a provincial government report on megaprojects in Northern British Columbia. If we slept in, it would be because we had been up until three o'clock the night before practising stealing cars for a future robbery. Urban guerrillas do not take vacations.

Finally it was over. I would not have to get up tomorrow morning and case the Lougheed Mall for the Brink's robbery. Better yet, I did not have to worry about doing the Brink's robbery five days from now. My fate was no longer in my hands, but in the hands of others. In some bizarre way, this was a relief. The moral and political responsibility I had created for myself to carry out these actions in what I believed would be a militant political movement was over, at least for the time being.

Now, facing the reality of prison, I found it strangely comforting to know that the threat of prison no longer existed. I could finally relax and let events beyond my control unfold.

I looked over at Julie, wondering how she was coping. She was only twenty, nine years younger than me. We didn't dare speak because we knew the police would be listening to glean information from every innocuous thing we said. She did not look back at me, but stared out the window at the pine forests whizzing past.

✳ 2 ✳

Julie told me later that she was overwhelmed by the irony of her situation. It was all going to come to an end just as it had begun. She still remembered, as vividly as though it was yesterday, seeing a TV news story two years before about a group of peasant women and children massacred by renegade military men in a church in El Salvador. The pictures of the surviving peasant women and children from the village were burned clearly in her memory. With terror in their eyes, their faces etched with expressions of horror, they stood barefoot before the cameras, their wounds both physical and emotional, open for all the world to see. That newscast was the turning point that had motivated her to take her first political step to join an El Salvador support group.

During our arrest, when a cop lifted her right out of her seat in the truck onto the ground and put a gun to the back of her head, the spectre of the women and children in El Salvador was so terrifying that she lost control of her bladder. Perhaps the comparison between her arrest and the massacre in El Salvador was extreme, but that fact did not make her terror less real. Now, in the police car, she turned her gaze from the white surf below the road to the wire mesh that separated us from the backs of the two policemen sitting in the front seat. Despite her constant self-reminders that this was Canada, not a military dictatorship, and that the likelihood of being killed was remote, images of the cops pulling over and shooting us kept plaguing her. Perhaps the wet spot on her jeans would not be noticeable when we finally reached our destination.

One of the policemen in the front seat was RCMP Corporal Wayne Fraser, who, we found out later, had been part of the investigation from the beginning. Later he said that he deeply resented that his superior, Detective Jean Despaireux, had gone against his advice and chosen to take these terrorists down in the most dangerous of possible situations — in a truck filled with loaded weapons of all descriptions and enough ammunition for a week-long standoff. These people had been under twenty-four-hour surveillance for about three months — surveillance using all sorts of technological and human means. Video cameras had been trained on the house where four of them lived and the apartment of the fifth. The RCMP Security Service's team of "Watchers" had followed them every time they left their homes, and room bugs had been planted in the house's kitchen and bedroom and in the apartment. The police knew their every movement and plan. The RCMP were well aware that these terrorists normally did not travel about the city with weapons, and that the guns and ammo were always locked in the basement. They knew that the group went swimming several nights a week at a local indoor pool, obviously unarmed. Why had they chosen to arrest them in an isolated location and when they were armed to the teeth, with the greatest likelihood of a shoot-out? Could Despaireux really have been so threatened by these people that he wanted to set them up to be killed?

Fraser had close friends in the Force and believed that their lives had needlessly been placed in jeopardy. Sick with worry over the potential consequences, he had not slept all night. Luckily, the takedown had gone as peacefully as anyone could have hoped. He breathed a sigh of relief.

He did not like Despaireux much at the best of times. He looked over at the aging detective, whose hair had gone grey and whose face had taken on the look that it deserved at age fifty-five: cold and mean. They never socialized, but Fraser had heard that Despaireux drank too much and treated his wife badly. Fraser had joined the Force as a young man to do good. It sounded hokey, but he had devoted his life to protecting society from criminals, including people who drank too much and abused their wives, so he found it difficult to work with such a man.

He turned to look at the two young women sitting behind the

wire mesh. Thank God they were finally safely in the custody of the police. They didn't look like your stereotypical terrorists, but he had heard the wiretaps and knew what these people were capable of.

Thank God Rose, his sister, had never got roped in by them. She was involved with some radicals over the building of the hydro transmission line, Cheekeye-Dunsmuir, but he felt quite confident that Rose knew where to draw the line. Still, the two women in the back looked like just about anyone's sisters or daughters. From what he knew about the case, they were from good families, not victims of abuse or poverty, and there was no known explanation or turning point that one could look at and say "Aha! So that's why she decided to go beyond the law!"

He had always felt overly protective of Rose. Perhaps it was because she did sometimes step out of her safe middle-class world, a little too close to the line that separates the good from the bad, the law-abiding from the criminal. A few years ago, as part of his intelligence work, he had attended demonstrations against the Cheekeye-Dunsmuir transmission line. Rose and some of her friends were there, lawfully protesting the construction of the line, but also in attendance was a group of anarchists, well known to the police. Fraser believed that the others were dangerous, particularly to Rose. Over the years Fraser had taken a profound disliking to one of them, a guy named Brent Taylor. Today he felt great satisfaction that he had played an instrumental role in Taylor's capture.

His first encounter with Taylor had come six years before, when he was assigned to watch over the federal leader of the opposition, Joe Clark, who was making a speech at the University of British Columbia. It had been an uneventful afternoon until, unexpectedly, a tall young man lunged from the crowd and smacked Clark in the side of the face with a cream pie. Before the cream had started to drip, Fraser was pushing through the gathering to pursue the culprit. After clearing the crowd, Fraser spotted him only sixty metres ahead. Racing across the university's manicured lawn, his heart pounding, his legs pumping, Fraser was sure he would quickly catch up. He was six-foot-four, an excellent skier and athlete, any criminal's nightmare. But he found himself falling behind. Taylor was also an athlete, with provincial high-school track records to his credit. Unfortunately for him, a bunch of guys were playing rugby on the field, and two of the players went for Taylor as he passed, tackling him to the ground.

Out the car window behind the prisoners, Fraser could see the deep purple of the Tantalus Range. Sometimes he longed for a more innocent world where he wouldn't constantly be exposed to the dark and seamy side of life. When he was younger, he could have made a living as a ski instructor, but his conscience wouldn't let him live a life of superficial pleasure. He was compelled to do something that would make society a better place for his children. On the weekend, though, he would take his wife and kids back up this highway — but in the other direction, to Whistler — and forget about the terrorists, Despaireux, and all the sadness of the streets, to ski and have a good time.

* * *

I looked at the backs of the cops' heads — the one silver, the other black — and wondered what we were in for. Did they know everything, or were we just being busted for the weapons? I hoped the others wouldn't say anything, because maybe, just maybe, this was only about the weapons.

Losing my balance as the police car rocked around the curves brought back a story that Brent had told me when we first met three years before in Toronto. One morning, in 1977, he had heard on the radio that Joe Clark was going to be speaking at the University of British Columbia that day. He shoplifted a coconut cream pie from a supermarket and headed out to the university. When Clark stepped up to the mike, Brent quickly moved out of the crowd and threw the pie at Clark's face. Then he took off — fast, because if there's one thing Brent could do, it was run.

Racing across the university lawn, he was actually widening the gap between himself and his pursuers. "If it wasn't for a bunch of rugby players I had to run past, I would have got away," he boasted. "But once they tackled me, it was game over. A couple of cops ran over and handcuffed me . . . really tight. They put me in their car and drove over to the campus security office. They drove fast enough around the corners that I would fall over in the back seat 'cause my hands were cuffed behind my back and I'm telling you it hurt. They were on so tight I broke into a total sweat. I even asked if they could loosen them, which is something I'd never do today because there's no way they were going to loosen them. That was my punishment.

"Anyway, once we got to the campus security office, they sat me down in the middle of the room, still handcuffed, for an hour and a half. There was absolutely nothing in that room except a cop guarding me by the door and a map of the university and endowment lands with coloured pins in it representing the places where indecent assaults, rapes, flashings, and other stuff had gone on. I stared at those coloured pins and counted them for the entire hour and a half just to get my mind off the pain from those cuffs. Finally they let me go. To this day, my thumb goes numb whenever it's cold."

Brent told me that story in the summer of 1980, when he stopped to visit mutual friends in Toronto on his way to New Hampshire. He was going to participate in an anti-nuclear protest at Seabrook against the construction of the nuclear power station. We had both gone out that night with a group from the *Bulldozer,* a prisoners' support newsletter, to spray-paint slogans on walls informing people that August 10th was Prison Justice Day. We had split up into groups, and Brent and I were paired up quite accidentally.

Separating from the rest, we headed down the deserted downtown streets, looking for perfect blank walls to use as canvases for our graffiti. Toronto at 2:00 a.m. was a black concrete wilderness starkly illuminated by street lights and blinking red stoplights. The only witnesses to our surreptitious activities were a few taxis taking drunks home from the bars and street people with seemingly nowhere to go.

We headed down Spadina Avenue, stopping to spray slogans on walls that would get the most commuter and pedestrian exposure. I had a hard time keeping up with Brent. He didn't walk along — he bounced, as though he had springs on the balls of his feet. He moved easily in and out of the shadows and the light of the street lamps like a cat stalking his prey, working the various walls with his spray can. From his fluid, agile movements I could tell that the danger and excitement of our illegal activities stimulated him. I could almost see his nerve endings bristling.

I wasn't cut from the same cloth. My mind kept conjuring up images of cops lurking around every corner just waiting to bust us. Of course, these forecasts of doom were self-fulfilling, sending adrenalin surging through my body, making my movements jerky, my hands and feet heavy. My instincts were to flee, not confront danger.

After several hours of prowling the streets and leaving our anti-prison messages for the morning traffic, we sat down to rest on a bench in Kensington Market. All the little market stalls were boarded up for the night, but you could still smell the banana peels and tomatoes left squished on the sidewalks. The quiet activity of the late-night scavengers had replaced the noisy hustle and bustle of the daytime shoppers and vendors. A few fat rats scurried in and out of the shadows and alley cats prowled after them, stopping to savour the odd fish scrap rotting on the ground.

Our feet ached, although we were still wide-eyed from the night's excitement. Brent turned towards me for a moment, and I could feel his pale blue eyes on me. As he talked I became aware that my body was vibrating and my breathing sharp. I hoped he hadn't noticed. He was telling me that he lived in a communal house in Vancouver with a bunch of anarchists. I asked him what they did.

"All kinds of stuff. Cause trouble for the powers that be."

For hours we sat on that bench talking about our pasts, our present lives, and plans for the future. Brent's long black hair flew around wildly as he talked. His hands were in constant motion. Although mismatched in emotional mettle for spray-painting, we found that we were definitely cut from the same political cloth, kindred spirits. We had both spent much of our youth working within the left, organizing demonstrations, putting out information, going to rallies and meetings, and doing everything else involved in lives of radical activism.

He stared at his feet for a while in silence. "I'm very burnt out," he said. "Tired of all this useless leftist shit. The government knows that letting the Americans test the cruise missile here is not popular. But it doesn't matter how many demos, letter-writing campaigns and acts of civil disobedience we have — nothing is going to change. The Canadian government is more interested in convincing us that what the American government wants is good for us than it is in fulfilling its own people's wishes."

He looked me straight in the eye. "So, Ann, what do you think?" It's crazy, but my first thought was, "Someday we're going to be lovers and soulmates." Instead I simply said "Yeah," because I was the converted.

Brent left a few days later. We made vague plans to get together that summer at a gathering in the Black Hills of South Dakota, but I never made it. I was busy working for the *Toronto Clarion*, a monthly left-wing paper, and helping put together the *Bulldozer*, but I didn't forget those few days I spent with Brent.

* * *

A few days after I first met Brent, Rose Gibralter was standing in the hot sun waiting to stop a bulldozer on Texada Island in British

Columbia, almost five thousand kilometres away. She had been an active member of the Cheekeye-Dunsmuir Alliance for three years. She was not by nature a rebel, but she had joined the group after becoming outraged at the lack of democratic process in the decision to construct the transmission line — which was no small residential project, but a $1 billion megaproject to construct a 112-kilometre line to run from the B.C. mainland to Vancouver Island. Part of the route would travel through her neighbourhood in Edgmont on the Sechelt Peninsula. She shared her outrage with many other normally law-abiding citizens over the complete lack of consultation on this project. They were worried about the environmental effects of the line, which would cut a huge swath through the countryside, emitting electro-magnetic radiation and requiring the use of dangerous herbicides to prevent undergrowth. Taxpayers in general believed that the costs of the project would ultimately fall on their shoulders.

After three years of attending meetings with B.C. Hydro, protesting in front of the provincial parliament buildings in Victoria, and fruitless pressuring of their MLAs, the activists had finally decided to resort to civil disobedience. Calvin Hill, the spokesperson for their group, had warned Hydro in May 1980 that in the summer protesters would set up camp in the vicinity of the Hydro access road used for the construction of the line. A small number of people representing the different regions would stand in a section of the access road under construction on Texada Island, in the path of machinery as it approached. Rose had volunteered to represent the Sechelt Peninsula.

That day the small group was milling about Calvin, waiting for the symbolic bulldozer to arrive. They were a motley crew: teenagers with rings on their fingers and toes, and in their ears and noses; students energized by the idealism of their youth; and adults in their thirties, children of the sixties, who had integrated into society with jobs, homes, and children — like Rose. Unlike many of her peers, Rose had not abandoned all her youthful idealism in exchange for her comfortable house in the suburbs. She still found time to be active in the community and help organize around causes she believed in. Even though she and her brother had taken very different paths in life — he was a cop and she was a wife and mother — they shared a strong moral constitution.

Rose scanned the landscape, wondering when the bulldozer would arrive. They were going to stand in front of it, preventing any further clearing at least until after their arrests. Hydro had obtained a Supreme Court order allowing the police to arrest anyone who obstructed the excavation company hired to clear the right-of-way. Their actions wouldn't stop Hydro from clearing the land, but Rose hoped that at least Hydro would think twice in the future about pushing through projects without consulting the public.

She did not like the idea of being arrested, but in her mind the protest was not the same thing as breaking the law. They would all plead "not guilty" to public mischief, because God knows they had tried every other possible legal avenue just to have a public hearing. Considering that this project would ultimately be paid for through Canada Pension Plan funds, loaned to Hydro at below-market rates, she and her community were paying for it. The least the government owed them was a public hearing to determine whether or not it was really necessary.

Her brother had been very concerned about the civil disobedience aspect of her work, but, as she had explained to him, the idea was not to have a confrontation with the police but to express opposition to the Hydro project. The police were not responsible for the decision to push it through: they were there to enforce the laws. Calvin and the others had taken great care to explain to the police that this was a matter of conscience, not a matter of breaking the law.

Calvin stood a head above the rest of the group. He was a natural leader and loved it. Rose found herself inexplicably attracted to his tanned, rough, good looks. There was something animal-like about him that stirred her, although she would never act upon her attraction. Suddenly her attention was brought back to reality by the dull roar of a bulldozer coming up over the horizon. She jogged lightly over to the small group of protesters who had formed a line across the path the bulldozer would have to take between the trees. In front of the bulldozer walked a line of uniformed policemen ready to make routine arrests as they had been doing all week. Calvin Hill stood in the middle of the line and the other six stood three on each side of him.

A few days before, on Sunday, August 12, a larger group of twenty-five protesters had encircled the bulldozer. The owner of the excavation company, George Edge, arrived that day to drive the bulldozer. In the ensuing confrontation, one of the protesters had approached a worker with a tape recorder to ask a few questions and the man had grabbed her arm and thrown her tape recorder to the ground. Another worker had grabbed a camera, which one of the protesters was using to document events, and hit him over the head with it. In a final act of defiance, Edge continued to drive the bulldozer through the crowd, striking the ankle of one of the protesters as he passed through. Although the RCMP were about one hundred feet away when all this was happening, they did not intervene. Later they claimed that they didn't see a thing.

Rose prayed that today's would be a more peaceful protest, and her prayers were answered. As the bulldozer approached, the police walked up, handcuffed each protester, and led them off to a waiting van. No one put up a fight, because the object of their blockade was more symbolic than to actually stop the progress of the excavation company. One of the cops helped Rose into the police van, which was almost full of protesters. She shuffled awkwardly through their knees to a small spot between Calvin Hill and another young woman. As she sat down, her thigh brushed lightly against Calvin's leg, but he was so engrossed in conversation that he didn't even notice. Through the dirty little window across from her she stared at the pine forests whizzing past.

Going Underground

In the autumn of 1980 Marion Mueller, visiting from West Germany, stopped by my room in Toronto to ask if I could help her hook up with people involved in the prison abolition movement in Canada. I had spent time in Europe a year earlier, and she had been given my name by people I had stayed with then. I introduced her to the people who put together the *Bulldozer*, then decided to use her visit as an excuse to travel out west and introduce her to Claire Culhane, the bulwark of the prison abolition movement in Canada. Claire was a retired older woman who kept in regular correspondence with dozens of prisoners, both male and female, across the country, championing their causes and fighting for what little rights they had. It was a thankless task with no remuneration. Her only reward was the respect she gained with prisoners and their support groups across Canada and even the United States.

So, not long after her arrival, Marion and I boarded a train for the trip to Vancouver. We had three days to get to know each other to the rhythmic clanking of the wheels on the tracks and the scenery flowing past us. She instantly fell in love with the vastness of the country, and so we spent much of our time in the glass-covered viewing car. Each day we awoke to a new landscape. One day it was the rugged rocks and coniferous forests jutting out of the lakes dotting the Canadian Shield; the next day it was the broad expanse of the prairie wheat fields, ebbing and flowing in the wind like the ocean waves; another day the abrupt sight of the Rockies' sharp peaks. We talked endlessly. Marion was well-educated and politically sophisticated, the product of a long history of European revolutionary development. In North America, communists, socialists, and anarchists were considered fringe elements, whereas in Europe these forms of politics had been institutionalized and long represented by political parties, unions, and even universities.

Marion asked me if I wanted something from the canteen, but I shook my head. Watching her make her way down the narrow aisle, I thought she would make a perfect fugitive or guerrilla because I couldn't imagine anyone more difficult to describe. She was attractive more for her healthy, natural good looks than for any outstanding features. She was of average height and build with mousy brown hair, cut neatly at her shoulders. Her style of dress was conventional and neat, and she never wore colours that were bold or loud. What stood out about her were less immediately obvious qualities — her kindness, gentleness, and wisdom.

When she returned she had orange juice and cheddar cheese sandwiches for both of us. Having never met me before, she was curious about my past. How had I become interested in politics? I found myself trying to explain my political development as a teenager. Like most teenagers growing up in the late 1960s, I had opinions on everything. But unlike many of my peers, I was particularly fascinated with the hippies, absorbing everything I could learn about their ideas and lifestyle from newspapers and magazines. My ambitions along those lines were frustrated by the fact that I lived with my family in a small suburb on the outskirts of Toronto and was still too young to actually become a hippy.

I remember beginning to develop a political consciousness during my high-school years. I had a particularly telling memory about writing an essay supporting the views of the FLQ in Quebec. Since Marion wasn't familiar with Canadian history, I explained to her that the Front de Libération du Québec was an urban guerrilla group of the 1960s; its members fought for the independence of Quebec from Canada using the tactics of guerrilla warfare. At the age of sixteen, I was not intellectually sophisticated enough to base my support for their guerrilla actions in sound political arguments, so in retrospect I assumed that much of my reasoning must have been grounded in a more instinctive support, an idea that had always intrigued me. Marion smiled at that revelation.

As I got older I became more and more interested in politics until by the time I was twenty-five I was consumed by it. I studied Marxism when I attended the University of Waterloo, which led to a brief stint working for the university newspaper, *The Chevron*, which at the time was under the direction of a Marxist-Leninist group. But after a time I became disillusioned with the group's tendency of applying Marxist political philosophy to history, and everything else, like a religion. No political philosophy, however brilliant, should remain stagnant as economic and social conditions changed. Eventually I moved on to become interested in the urban guerrilla groups emerging in Europe during the 1970s as the mass protest movements of the late 1960s were waning. To pursue my new-found interest, I enrolled in the university's Integrated Studies Department, established in the sixties to allow students the opportunity to design their own course of studies. I formulated a plan in which I would travel to Europe for six months to study the groups there first-hand and then, upon my return, present a paper outlining what I had learned. After obtaining my advisors' approval, I was off.

I flew to London, England, not knowing a soul. Since I was charting my own course in the study of modern-day guerrilla groups, I decided the best way to meet their supporters would be through the local left-wing bookstores. After dumping my stuff at a hostel, I headed out for Freedom Press, a large left-wing bookstore in London. As luck would have it, I was rummaging through some militant magazines when a guy came over and started looking through the same section. Eager to meet a local radical, I initiated a conversation, which he no doubt took as a come-on. After I told him my story, he invited me to a pub, ostensibly to discuss my studies. Being somewhat naive, I thought that by virtue of being a radical this man must be a kindred spirit and would thus introduce me to his friends in the left. After a few beers he told me that he was in trouble with the law and if he didn't get some money to flee England before his court date, he would end up in prison. He portrayed himself as a heroic revolutionary, a victim of the justice system who, if convicted, would spend a long time in prison. I tried to find out details about his so-called crime, but he made it clear that it was political in nature and to reveal more would be dangerous and uncool. Despite my naivety, it didn't take long before I began to see through his feeble attempts to find out how much money I had. I didn't have to be too perceptive to guess that he was probably some con stringing me along.

Even though by that point I didn't believe a word he was saying, I was desperate to meet activists. So, after I had laid my cards on the table, he blatantly came up with a proposal to trade money — mine — for an address of some Parisian supporters of the Red Army Faction, the West German guerrilla group. I weighed the odds and decided to take the gamble. The amount he wanted to borrow was minimal and seemed a small price to pay for the possibility of meeting those people in Paris. After a short interrogation on my part to determine if the names and addresses he had were real, I decided they were and handed over the money in exchange for an address.

By that time it was getting late and he said I could spend the night in his nearby flat rather than make the long journey back to the hostel. When I asked about the sleeping arrangements, he reassured me that I would be quite comfortable on the floor. My decision to take him up on his offer was not influenced by alcohol, because I had only drunk a couple of pints of the watery English draft. I was simply tired, and did tend to trust strangers more than I would today.

His "flat" turned out to be a tiny and cold bedsitting room heated by a gas radiator that had to be fed English pence. Since he had no money, his room had not been heated for some time. The comfortable sleeping arrangements turned out to be a narrow bed and a barren wooden floor. To make the situation even more uninviting, he explained that I could sleep on the floor but there was no other bedding available than the single, worn blanket on the bed. Obviously, he had known from the beginning that I would have little choice but to sleep in the bed with him. Considering how late it was, and despite my anger, I decided to sleep beside him, using a pillow as a barrier.

I got into bed with him, fully clothed, and quickly realized — but too late — what a big mistake I was making. Ignoring my protests, he immediately began to grope me. My anger turned to fear when I sensed that if I resisted him forcefully, he might become violent. I really knew nothing about this guy. His true crime might be rape or, worse, murder. In a court of law my decision to just lie there and let him rape me as quickly and peacefully as possible would probably be construed as consent, but I let my instincts guide my actions. After he finished I got up and left. Fortunately I had no physical scars, only a damaged spirit and a great loss of trust in human nature. That was the last I saw of him.

The next morning I hitchhiked to the ferry and crossed over to France, spending the night in a cheap hotel in Calais. By noon the next day I was standing on a boulevard in Paris and looking up at a huge apartment complex. I managed to make my way up to the apartment number that my contact had given me, and knocked on the door. When a young French woman answered, I explained in my high-school French how I had managed to get her address. I was not surprised to learn that neither she nor her roommates had ever heard of the man. But in the end it turned out to be the right place, and they were kind and friendly enough to invite me in. The relationship was somewhat handicapped by both my imperfect knowledge of French and their political opposition to learning English, "the language of imperialism." This was the beginning of a three-month stay in which they grew to trust me implicitly, despite the language barrier, and involved me in all the support work they were doing for the Red Army Faction in Paris.

After letting me go on about myself, Marion interrupted to explain that she had also done support work for the Red Army Faction in West Germany. In North America, even the left knew the Red Army Faction mostly by its media-dubbed name, the Baader-Meinhof gang, named after founders Andreas Baader and Ulrike Meinhof. All that was commonly known about them was that they had kidnapped and killed Hans Martin-Schleyer, a powerful West German industrialist, in October 1977. But in Western Europe a body of people, such as Marion, supported the RAF as Marxist urban guerrillas waging a long-term struggle, in conjunction with Third World liberation movements, against U.S. imperialism. In Europe a body of intellectuals even dared to write theoretical papers discussing the validity of guerrilla group action on the continent. During my stay in France, an Italian university professor, Franco Piperno, applied for political asylum there. His crime appeared to be having helped the Italian Socialist party attempt to negotiate a solution to the 1978 kidnapping of Aldo Moro by the Italian guerrilla group Red Brigades. Specifically, Piperno had been asked to interpret letters written by Aldo Moro while he was being held in captivity by the Red Brigades. However, the ruling Italian coalition of the Christian Democrats and Communists was opposed to negotiating with the Red Brigades, and after Moro's death Piperno was charged with participating in a subversive and armed association. In the absence of any real crime, most of the European left believed Piperno was being persecuted for being a theoretician of the extraparliamentary left. To quash the support for the guerrillas, many European parliaments enacted laws making it illegal to write or distribute information supporting "terrorism." Marion was particularly concerned with the criminalization of ideas because, as a revolutionary, her talent and interest lay more in publishing ideas than in actually carrying out militant actions.

At the apartment in Paris I realized that I was in a unique situation to learn first-hand about the politics and workings of an urban guerrilla group, and I worked passionately putting out leaflets, aiding RAF fugitives, and doing anything else I could. We even travelled to Stuttgart, West Germany, to attend the trial of Klaus Croissant, a German lawyer for some RAF militants, who was accused of passing information amongst his RAF clients and thereby "supporting a criminal association." Although I was absorbing everything around me like a sponge, I was growing disillusioned with the RAF tactics of assassination and the injuries to innocent victims that occurred in some of their actions. It was becoming increasingly apparent that they did not have the necessary popular support that would lead to an understanding of these tactics. I was not convinced that the RAF represented a model that I would aspire to follow.

Despite my criticisms, I had never felt as intellectually and emotionally alive as I did in those six months in Paris. Besides doing support work for the RAF, I dived into whatever political events were unfolding in that city of teeming revolutionaries who seemed to represent every possible stream of political thought. I thrived on the excitement, danger, and intensity of activities that demanded one hundred per cent of my attention. History was not determining our lives — we were determining history! I did not want to go back to Canada.

I remembered attending a huge demonstration on March 23, 1979, organized by a coalition of trade unions protesting unemployment and government plans to reduce the number of workers in the ailing steel industry. My attendance had nothing to do with my support work for the RAF but everything to do with my hunger for political experience. I had never walked in such a large crowd — with over one hundred thousand people it seemed to be one gigantic living, breathing organism. It started off as most demonstrations do, with thousands of people marching together in small interest groups, banding together under similar placards proclaiming a common goal. But as I marched I noticed that the most animated contingent was a group of autonomists who were spearheading the demonstration.

Autonomists were the political version of punks — anarchists who believed in living and acting autonomously from society and the government. Every aspect of their lives reflected their politics. They lived in "squats," vacant buildings they reclaimed as rent-free homes. They shoplifted all their material needs in open defiance of society's laws, and they dressed unconventionally in used clothing acquired at the French equivalent of the Salvation Army and Goodwill stores. Essentially they lived as total outlaws, existing outside the boundaries of legality, rejecting all political parties in an attempt to live the revolution in their daily lives. The demonstration's trade union organizers made obvious, but frustrated, attempts to keep the autonomists under control. They were afraid that the anarchists would not remain peaceful and organized and as a result would cause chaos at the end of the demonstration. Their fears were not unfounded.

The closer we came to the prearranged end of the demonstration, the closer I tried to get to the autonomists. I was attracted to both their energy and philosophy. By the time we reached the end of the march the autonomists had amassed in a group of milling black-clad youth, dressed appropriately for militant actions in crash helmets, ski masks, leather gloves, and even gas masks. Their dress code was obviously geared towards hiding their identity and protecting them from police brutality. The press photographers had also gravitated towards them, sensing that this was where the real news story was going to unfold. But the autonomists were not interested in appearing in the front-page photograph of the daily papers and had come prepared. The first thing they did as the demonstration began to disband was to attack the press photographers, throwing stones and blatantly trying to grab and destroy their cameras.

The police, anticipating problems, had positioned themselves in huge numbers at the end of the demonstration, setting up metal barricades in front of all the streets. I felt my spine tingling with a mixture of fear and excitement as I looked around me at the formidable lines of cops with huge shields, gas masks, and batons at the entrance to every street save one that had been preordained as the dispersal route for the thousands of demonstrators.

Once the autonomists had finished attacking and dispersing the photographers, they began to separate and move off. Even though I was just going with the flow, reacting to events as they unfolded, I was beginning to suspect that the autonomists were indeed quite organized despite their public reputation as the purveyors of anarchy. I followed one group down a street towards the financial district, where they began to smash the huge plate-glass windows of the main commercial establishments. As small skirmishes began to unfold all over the financial district between the police and the autonomists, I noticed that often the looters were normal Parisians who were simply taking advantage of the opportunity to reach in open windows and grab whatever goods they could while the police were preoccupied with the protesters.

After a while the group I was tagging along with became overpowered by the police and began running down the street towards one of the Parisian train stations, the Gare de l'Est, that services the suburbs. We raced down the streets pursued by pairs of cops on small motor scooters, positioned so the cop on the back could use his baton to knock down the protesters. Any unfortunate autonomist who got knocked down in this manner was quickly scooped up by the police officers following on foot and thrown into one of hundreds of paddy wagons driving along behind the action. These skirmishes and retreats to the many train stations were happening throughout Paris.

Once inside the train station, I realized just how organized the autonomists were. No sooner had we arrived in a small group inside than they began to rip metal lockers from the wall and use them as barricades to the entrances, thus prohibiting anyone from getting in or out, both cop and citizen alike. I stood there in awe, surrounded by an odd assortment of black-clad autonomists, who were occupying the huge piles of metal lockers, and normal Parisian citizens, who were walking about casually looting the smashed-in train station stores.

As a testament to their organization, the autonomists had stashed Molotov cocktails and rocks inside the lockers long before the demonstration had begun, and now they lobbed their arsenal at the impotent cops who had surrounded the train station but couldn't deploy tear gas because of the good citizens of Paris who were also inside. After what seemed like hours the cops finally launched a concerted assault on one of the entrances, knocking the lockers aside and shooting canisters of tear gas inside. The autonomists had piles of lemon-soaked bandannas inside their packsacks and began handing them out to the Parisians, who were screaming and trying to get out in a panic. When I tried to escape, just as I got outside a tear gas canister landed right beside me, almost blinding and suffocating me with its gas. An autonomist wearing a protective bandanna leaned over, picked up the canister, and lobbed it back at the cops, then grabbed my arm and covered my face with another bandanna and dragged me out of harm's way. When I was finally able to breathe again, I looked around but my little saviour was gone. It was probably one of the most exciting days of my life.

After that day I had no desire to return home to a country where revolutionaries seemed to be an endangered species. Later I revealed my dilemma to a young West German woman, Sabine Schmidt, an RAF member who was hiding out at our apartment. I explained that I didn't want to go back to Canada because there were no militants there I could relate to. I believed Canada was so far behind France in revolutionary development that the political climate would never be supportive of militancy in my lifetime. I knew that there were all kinds of legitimate and important revolutionary work to be done in Canada, but I now identified as an urban guerrilla and thought I would be isolated and ineffective back home. To fulfil my ambitions and identity, I felt I needed to work with like-minded individuals who shared my passion for revolutionary activity. To illustrate my point I asked Sabine if a feminist wouldn't always be frustrated working on political issues with predominantly male groups, even though working with men was not bad in itself.

Sabine sensed the importance of this decision for me, and perhaps for that reason when she responded she spoke fluent English and didn't force me to speak French — for me, an exhausting exercise because of the constant effort required to find the right words, much less ideas. She advised me to go back and work in Canada. "What would happen if everyone went to places in the world where things were happening just as they wanted?" she asked. "Then nothing would develop in other areas of the world. If most of the revolutionaries in North America came to Europe, the revolutionary development in North America would be stunted — and that is the most important place in the world for revolutionary development. If we can weaken the strength of the economic and political structures in North America, then the liberation struggles in the Third World will thrive and eventually conquer their dictatorships. I think you would be more effective in Canada where you have a personal history you can build on — where you know the language, the people, and the culture. Here, you are a stranger in a strange land."

I didn't know Sabine very well; she was a role model more for who she represented than for who she really was. After weighing her opinion, and after considerable soul-searching, I decided to return to Canada and find some like-minded individuals and do whatever it took, no matter how long, to initiate some militant political activity in the Canadian left.

Meanwhile, as my conversations with Marion continued, our train left the Alberta foothills and began the slow, winding journey through the Rockies. Like many others before me, I'm sure, I was struck by the majesty and vastness of the mountains. In contrast to the cultivated peacefulness of the prairies, the wild nature of the Rockies — the crashing waterfalls, craggy chasms, and the threat of avalanches or catapulting rocks — seemed to rule here in all its unforgiving power. Somehow our little metal cars winding slowly through the valleys seemed so frail and inadequate. Our talk became noticeably more subdued, and philosophical. Finally Marion pointed down to the map nestled on her lap. "It looks like we're heading into the Fraser Valley." The suburbs of Vancouver were not far off.

✷ 4 ✷

After disembarking from the train we took a bus to the address that Brent had given me during our brief encounter in the summer. I hadn't told him I was coming, but he had said he lived with a group of people and assured me I'd be welcome to stay any time I was in town.

As we walked down the residential street he lived on, we noticed prostitutes hanging around the street corners. Most of the houses were in ill repair, and a few were even boarded up. The large, once attractive homes had obviously been deserted by middle-class families and left to fend for themselves as rentals where drug addicts, prostitutes, and poor families tried to survive. Scattered amongst the houses were small industrial buildings and warehouses. I imagined that in another few years certain good citizens would level the houses, ridding the area of the "vermin" and freeing it up for the manufacturing enterprises that already had their toe in the door.

We found Brent's address, a large two-storey house with paint peeling off the wooden siding and flapping in the breeze. Carefully climbing the broken wooden stairs, we rang the doorbell. Miraculously, it worked. The door was opened by a muscular young man with short, neatly trimmed hair. He was wearing a pair of beige shorts and no top. When I took the liberty of introducing myself and Marion as friends of Brent, he did not introduce himself but told us to come in. We walked down a hallway into the kitchen and sat down. The young man disappeared down some basement stairs.

The first thing that struck me about the house was that every square inch of wall space was covered with posters, signs, and slogans. We didn't need a book to read — we could have sat and read the walls for days. Everything was political. Marion and I sat speechless for awhile, reading the different slogans and looking at the pictures, since the young man did not hurry back. I noticed a number of newspaper photos on the wall, apparently from the past of the man who had answered the door. I got up and started reading the fine print to try to discern some information about him. In one photo he was holding a flag at some festival from 1978. Below it was a small article from the newspaper's courts section stating that Doug Stewart had pleaded guilty to the theft of a flag at the Sea Festival. Another showed him with a bunch of other people holding an anti-nuclear banner at a demonstration in 1980. Most of the other newspaper photos of him also pictured him as part of some group at a demonstration or rally. The odd part was that in every photo he wore the same dark sunglasses and beige shorts, even though some were taken years apart. I had to laugh.

Finally he reappeared. "Brent's over at Angie's but he'll be home in a few hours," he said brusquely, then disappeared again downstairs. He was obviously not preoccupied with social conventions. We made coffee and continued to amuse ourselves reading the material on the walls.

About an hour later the door burst open and in came two young women who obviously lived there. They were much friendlier and introduced themselves as Bridget and Saphie.

"Yeah, Brent told us you would be coming sometime," said Saphie, plopping herself down on a chair. Bridget immediately sat down on Saphie's lap, even though there were other empty chairs. "He won't be back for awhile. Do you have anything to do today?" she added, stroking Bridget's hair affectionately.

"I want to get in touch with Claire Culhane," Marion said. "But I'm still tired from the train ride so I think I'll just give her a phone call and rest for the day."

"You can sleep up there," Bridget said. She led us to the living room and showed us a loft built of two-by-fours and plywood. "We usually sleep up there but we're going over to Quadra Island for the weekend. Brent and Doug's rooms are downstairs." The loft spanned half the room, creating a space where at least six people could sleep comfortably. Underneath were old sofas, chairs, and tables that allowed the living room to function as a sitting area as well. Up against the other walls were row upon row of bookshelves that went to the ceiling. In one corner they had converted an old door into a table, which was covered with cut-up magazines and half-finished posters.

"Are you tired?" Saphie asked, looking at me. "Cause you're

welcome to come with me and Bridget to the laundromat if you want."

The chance to get to know Brent's roommates overcame my fatigue. While Marion and I unpacked our clothes and piled them into crates lined up against the walls of the loft, Saphie and Bridget dumped dirty clothes out of other crates onto the floor below. By the time they'd finished there was a mound far larger than the three of us could possibly carry.

"Let's call a cab," Saphie decided. By the time it arrived we were waiting with four huge sacks on the front porch. The frown on the cab driver's face forewarned us that the laundromat better be far enough away to make the trip worth his while. Before we even opened the cab door, he yelled out, "Where to?"

"The laundromat at Broadway and Main," Saphie yelled back. He responded by stepping on the accelerator, leaving us with our small mountain of clothes standing in his exhaust on the sidewalk.

Not one to be discouraged, Bridget jogged off down the sidewalk, yelling that she'd be back in a minute, which she was, with a discarded shopping cart. In this neighbourhood, shopping carts were more prevalent than cars. We loaded up the cart with our bags and proceeded towards the laundromat. We walked along for a couple of blocks exchanging stories until the street took a sharp downhill turn. Without a word, Bridget gave the cart a sharp push and jumped onto its bottom rail. It started coasting swiftly down the street. Saphie and I jogged along beside her until the momentum built up to the point that we were in a flat-out run and then gave up the chase. Bridget was screaming with joy every inch of the way until the cart hit a pot hole and overturned abruptly, leaving a pile of metal and clothes, and Bridget, on the ground. We ran down the hill to see if she was alright and reached her at the same time as a cop in an unmarked car.

"Oh, it's you again," said Saphie with attitude, as she struggled to extricate herself from the pile of metal and clothes. "This is Corporal Wayne Fraser, the local cop who watches over us." The cop did not get out of his car or say anything. He just looked us over and drove off. "What's that all about?" I asked.

"He's some political undercover type who turns up at benefits, demos, and just about everywhere. Everybody recognizes him but I guess he just takes notes in case something ever happens around here," said Bridget flatly, picking up the clothing that had broken loose from the bags.

"One night we were out spray-painting and I had painted something like 'Lesbians Unite!' on a wall, when that guy suddenly appeared out of nowhere," Saphie explained as we loaded our clothes back into the cart. "He grabbed me, took my spray cans as evidence, and wrote out a charge and summons to appear in court for defacing the building. Anyways, I went down to Stan Guenther's office — this lawyer who handles a lot of political cases. He said we could beat it so we went to court. The prosecutor couldn't prove that I didn't own the building because he had no documentation about the owner so I got off on a technicality." She laughed. "I think that undercover cop has had it in for me ever since."

After that little bit of excitement, we continued to the laundromat, did our laundry, and went back to the house, talking and laughing the whole time. I got the impression that Bridget and Saphie could make even the most boring task fun.

As we dragged our bags up the stairs, a faded yellow Volvo pulled in the driveway with Brent and, in the driver's seat, a young woman who looked about my age. I'd already learned from Bridget and Saphie that Angie was Brent's girlfriend or, to be politically correct, partner. It was obvious through the younger women's descriptions that they held Angie in high regard, except for a certain degree of bewilderment over her relationship with Brent. They did not try to hide their preference for women's company, and in fact they firmly believed that men, with all their flaws, drained women of their energy and thus were best left to fend for themselves, at least until they'd learned how to overcome their sexist ways. In their personal lives they had made an exception for Brent and Doug, but as a rule they did not waste any energy on men.

I immediately liked Angie, a response that instantly made me feel a little guilty about coming here because I could not lie to myself — deep inside, my interest in Brent went beyond the political. But from the moment we met, Angie's eyes exuded warmth and she was nothing but kind to me. I had to respect a woman who greeted me with such genuine emotions, knowing I had travelled across the country to stay at her partner's house at his invitation. I think Brent was also aware of this undercurrent of emotion between us, because his eyes did not once meet mine that evening, probably due to a mixture of respect for Angie and a mutual fear that if our eyes did meet they would tell the whole story to the others.

Everyone was hungry, so Brent began preparing dinner. "We're almost out of food," he said, peering inside the empty kitchen cupboards. "We're going to have to rent a wreck and go shopping tomorrow."

Marion had been napping while we did the laundry but now she was up and watching the activities. "If you don't mind, I would like to stay for a few days," she said politely. "So I would like to give you some money for food."

"Oh, we never *buy* food," Bridget laughed.

"What do you mean?" asked Marion, her eyebrows crossed.

"We rent a car from a place called Rent-A-Wreck. They're super-cheap and don't ask for a deposit. Then we get a bunch of us together and drive around and get five-finger discounts," Bridget explained with a big smile. "Know what I mean?"

Marion was not familiar with English euphemisms.

"Shoplifting," I said bluntly.

Brent made an impressive spaghetti, substituting canned beans for meat. He also produced a large salad, which we learned, after swallowing our last bite, was made from lettuce and tomatoes found in garbage bins in the Granville Island Market. Angie explained that some friends went garbaging there daily because a lot of the vendors threw out perfectly good unsold vegetables at the end of the day.

We had finished eating and were sitting around talking about a benefit Angie was organizing when the young man from the basement, Doug Stewart, came in. I had forgotten all about him. He walked in without saying a word and began preparing brown rice. When Marion and I said "Hi," he turned quickly to us and responded in kind, then left the room, presumably until the rice was done.

Even though it was none of my business, I asked why he didn't eat with the others. "Doug has a schedule," Saphie said without a hint of sarcasm. "It's just the way he is. He eats and sleeps at the same time everyday and doesn't feel good if his routine is altered. That's just Doug." I could tell by the tone of her voice that she felt very protective towards him.

"Come on," Brent said, motioning for me and Marion to follow him, leaving Angie, Saphie, and Bridget to continue discussing the details of the benefit. Down in the basement Brent gave what was apparently Doug's bedroom door a quick rap, to which a sullen "Come in" greeted us. The three of us walked in and draped ourselves about his tiny room, but Doug didn't raise his head from his book. "What are you reading?" Brent asked.

"Oh, just some of my old physics books," he answered, still not looking up.

Brent invaded his space by lifting the book off the table even though Doug was still apparently engrossed in it. Oddly enough, Doug was not offended by this intervention.

"This is your third-year university physics book," stated Brent.

Doug smiled for the first time. "That's very observant of you."

"And what are you reading this for?"

"Oh, some electric circuits I'm designing have got me stumped, so I'm just brushing up on some formulas."

Marion and I couldn't help noticing a peculiar set of lights, consisting of about one hundred tiny light bulbs, set up in neat rows, flickering on and off, on a black velvet board. Doug noticed us looking at it and explained that the system was designed to light up the bulbs continually in random patterns. Why was never explained, and we didn't ask.

"I saw a newspaper article on the wall in the kitchen about some anti-nuclear rally you were in?" I said, trying to spark up a conversation.

"Yeah, that was a demo, me and Brent helped organize in April. It was the first anti-nuclear rally in Vancouver and about five thousand people came, which is a lot for this city."

"Have you guys been involved in organizing a lot of rallies?" I continued.

"Oh yeah. There's usually someone from either this house or Angie's involved in any demo or benefit going on in town."

"We're going out postering for Angie's Women Against Prisons benefit tonight. Do you want to come?" Brent asked.

"Naw," Doug said flatly, taking back his book and starting to read again. Since he didn't seem interested in talking, we went back upstairs. After a little while he came back up, got his rice, put a bit of soya sauce on it, and went back to his room to eat. Brent explained that Doug ate an exclusive diet of brown rice and boiled vegetables with soya sauce.

For hours that evening we sat and talked about Women Against Prisons, a group Angie had formed to provide support for women in the local prison and to educate the public about prison conditions. She asked if I wanted to work with them while I was there, which I found flattering since she hardly knew me. Besides suggesting that we go out postering that night, she also invited me to go out to dinner the following Sunday with an ex-prisoner friend of hers. Once a month, she explained, they chose an expensive restaurant, the kind where the staff leave the bill in a tray on the table. Diners frequently put their money on the tray and leave without waiting for change. In Angie's case, she would leave five dollars under the bill, creating the impression of more money below. Then she and her friend would make a hasty exit, to put it mildly. She called it an "eat and run." It was, she said, "The only way poor people could ever eat in a fancy restaurant."

I was becoming increasingly aware that Brent and his friends were modern-day Robin Hoods. I'd never in my life met any group of people who lived a more complete rebel lifestyle than this particular group. They lived and breathed rebellion.

Later that evening we piled into Angie's old Volvo and headed downtown to staple up posters advertising the Women Against Prisons benefit. Marion decided not to go. She would crash early instead so she could meet Claire Culhane in the morning. Besides, she was a German citizen and postering was illegal, which meant she could be sent back to Germany if we were caught. As for the rest of us, after breaking up into pairs we went off in different directions with our piles of posters and staplers. A few hours later we ran out of posters and joined up again at Bino's, an all-night restaurant chain with the attractive allure of the bottomless coffee. We sat in one of the many bright plastic-seated cubbyholes that afforded each group of customers some privacy. Surrounding each table was a low plastic-wood wall lined with green plastic plants. The stark fluorescent lighting accentuated the restaurant's atmosphere, which was far from homey.

Angie had barely sat down when Bridget came in and said she had run out of posters to do the Commercial Drive area, which I found out later was the progressive neighbourhood of Vancouver where all the yuppies, radicals, and feminists lived. Angie immediately stood up and, looking at me, said, "I've got some paper in my car. Do you want to come?" I didn't know where she was going, but I wanted to go.

We drove for a short distance into an area that housed a mixture of low office buildings and old homes converted into apartments. After parking the car, Angie stuffed a huge packsack full of Xerox paper. We walked two blocks from the car before we veered onto the small lawn of an old office building. Angie walked quickly and purposefully up to a ground-floor window that was only a few feet from the ground and, to my surprise, was open half an inch.

Reading my mind, she turned and whispered, "I opened it earlier, just before the building closed."

Glancing around quickly, she clasped the bottom of the window and shoved it open, sliding in as though she had done this a thousand times before. I followed suit. Once inside, she shut the window and then froze, listening for sounds. I could feel the hair on the back of my neck stand on end and, just like the time I was spray-painting with Brent, felt certain there would be a cop hiding around the corner ready to jump out at me.

Angie seemed to be incredibly relaxed yet intensely concentrating on the task at hand. The inside of the office building was pitch black, but she walked purposefully out of the room we had landed in and went down the hall past several doors before darting into a room. As soon as I was in too, she locked the door behind us. From the way she manoeuvred around this office in the darkness, I realized she must have done this work many times before.

She flicked a switch, illuminating a tiny, windowless photocopy room. Without missing a beat, she began pushing buttons on the photocopy machine, causing it to hum. I was completely paranoid, even though there was no way anyone could see us. "Won't someone hear us?" I whispered hoarsely.

"It's just a welfare office. There's never anyone here on Sunday nights," she answered calmly, never pausing from the mission at hand. She deftly removed the paper already in the machine and replaced it with her own, then began making copies of her poster. To me the sound of the machine was a major disturbance, but I managed to control my fear. I didn't want to disturb Angie. At one point the paper jammed, but that wasn't a problem either. She fumbled around with the paper and a few buttons and, in a matter of minutes, we were back in business.

When we were finished she took out what was left of her paper and replaced the original paper, so there was no sign anyone had been there. Half an hour after we'd come in, we were peering out the window again. When Angie decided the coast was clear, she pulled herself up on the sill and slid out the window. Once I was out as well, she closed the window and we walked back to the car. I felt as though I had joined a group of urban hunters and gatherers.

We got back to the house in the wee hours of the morning. Exhausted, I climbed up the wooden ladder to the loft where Marion was sleeping peacefully. I made a bed beside her and in the morning found myself sharing the loft as well with Bridget, Saphie, and Angie.

* * *

It was well past eleven the next day before everyone was up. Marion was dressed and ready to leave for her appointment with Claire Culhane. While I sat sipping away on my first coffee, Saphie was already booking a car from Rent-A-Wreck. I could see there was never a dull moment around the place. "Why don't we just use Angie's car?" I asked.

"Cause if we get caught, they'll ID her. With Rent-A-Wreck, we can use false ID and say that someone else with a licence is driving it. They're still slack, not like one of the bigger car rental companies," explained Saphie. She and Angie went off to get the car.

When everyone finished breakfast, they started gathering up gym bags and packsacks of different sizes. I didn't know exactly what was going on but I emptied my clothes out of my packsack and carried it out to the rental. I was a little disappointed to find that Angie was not going shopping with us: she lived in a different house with a group of women. Through conversations at Bino's the night before, I had learned that some of the women she lived with were lesbian separatists who didn't believe in living or working with men, for much the same reasons as Bridget and Saphie. I figured Angie's relationship with Brent must be very strong to withstand the inevitable criticisms it must draw from her female companions.

Once again a group of us piled into the car. We set out on a route covering at least four large food stores. I had rarely shoplifted before, and in general lacked the nerves of steel required to do anything illegal. At the first store I decided to start out small, perhaps a can of tuna or something. I walked into the store assuming Brent was behind me — at least he had been when we were just outside the store. I walked down the aisles looking for tuna and there he was, in the canned fish section. As I walked towards him, I saw him open his Adidas bag as wide as he could, take his arm and swipe, not just one can, but every can of tuna, salmon, and smoked oysters on the shelf. Within seconds his bag was absolutely full.

He walked swiftly towards me and whispered tersely, "Let me know when the checkout clerk isn't looking in my direction."

I sauntered towards the checkout line, and when the clerk was busy I nodded to Brent. He glanced around to see if anyone was watching, crouched down behind a fruit counter near the door, and slipped out before anyone had even seen him. He must have been in the store less than two minutes. I was so paranoid just watching him that I decided to wait for the next store to make any move of my own.

By the end of the afternoon the four of us had filled the trunk of the car and all our bags with groceries and headed home. So for the price of the car rental — $30 a day — split four ways, we picked up more than $400 worth of groceries, which would easily last a month when combined with the fruit and vegetables picked up from the Granville Market garbage. I'd met a lot of radicals in my young life, but never a group like this one.

Unpacking the gym bags and knapsacks was like opening presents at Christmas. Bridget held up a huge pair of black corduroys. "Look at the cool pants I got! Do you want them, Brent? They're way too big for me."

Brent pulled off his old pants and tried on the new ones right there and then. "These are the first pair of new pants I've had since I left home," he said excitedly.

Over a gourmet dinner, Marion's meeting with Claire Culhane earlier that day inspired a conversation that ended in a final tribute to Claire. Marion toasted the most important revolutionaries, "Those who do the often tedious, day-to-day work that gets no glory or recognition — their only reward coming from knowing that what they are doing is right and will make the world a better place." After our spirited dinner conversation, Brent proposed that Doug and I go out with him to Bino's again. Even though I was feeling a little burnt-out from all the excitement, the prospect of some quiet conversation was appealing.

"So what do you think?" he asked after we had ordered coffees and muffins.

"You've got a great group of friends," I said.

Brent chomped down on a muffin. "There's not enough of us to do anything really militant. Angie, Bridget, Saphie — none of them are willing to leave their scene. As long as the actions allow them to maintain their normal lifestyle, they'll be eager to participate, but anything that carries serious consequences such as prison time, forget it."

As we talked it became clear to me that there was an unspoken understanding between Brent, Doug, and me that we were an inner circle of future militants and that we would only include others who showed a great commitment not just to the theory of militancy but also to a desire to be a militant. "Yeah, there's just the three of us," smiled Doug, "and that ain't enough." I agreed.

"But the way I see it," continued Brent, "there's no reason why we can't get things together like money, ID, and guns, so someday when there's a need, we won't have to waste a lot of time getting that shit together."

"What's the point of getting all that stuff together if there's no foreseeable use for it?" I argued. "People don't develop a revolutionary consciousness in a vacuum. I'm sure if we even did small actions, it would at least cause some debate and the people involved would learn something. Who knows, maybe there's more people out there that want to be active but we just haven't met them yet."

Brent nodded impatiently. "I guess there's no reason why we can't do both. It'll take time to figure out how to get ID, money, guns, and everything else. In the meantime we could do smaller actions with people around town."

"Sure. I got a real beef with that Amax corporation in Alice Arm." Doug pulled out a frayed newspaper clipping from *The Vancouver Sun* and passed it to me.

"Who's Amax?" I was unfamiliar with B.C. political issues.

"It's a molybdenum mine north of Prince Rupert that makes a hard grey metallic element used to harden steel alloys," Doug explained. "Last spring the federal cabinet gave Amax special permission to dump a hundred million tons of toxic mine tailings directly into the ocean up in Alice Arm. That's eight thousand times more mine tailings than the standard federal levels, and the B.C. environment ministry went along with it and also made a decision to let Amax discharge air pollutants twenty-four hours a day. All those tailings are pumped through this huge pipe right to the ocean floor, where the crab and other bottom-feeders digest them and either die or pass on this toxicity through the food chain. That means the Nishga[*] Indians, who live off crab fishing and hunting up there, won't be able to live traditionally any more. The Nass River Valley, where the river flows into the ocean inlet of Alice Arm, is part of the land claims that the Nishga are fighting in court. The Nishga didn't even get a chance to contest this plan to dump the tailings into the ocean until a year after Amax got its

---

[*] Today this is often written as Nisga'a.

special federal permit because the notice for their application was printed in the Prince Rupert newspaper, three hundred kilometres from the Nass River Valley where the Nishga live. Sneaky eh? It's amazing that more people aren't hip to this."

"Maybe some people might be interested in doing a small action around that issue?" I suggested. We fell silent while the waitress refilled our coffee cups. "Angie said something about you having some weapons training." I smiled at Brent.

"Yeah, some," Brent said. "I'm not great but I got some training in the army."

"The army?" I was surprised.

"I told you how I pied Joe Clark in '77. About that time I joined the Seaforth Highlanders of Canada, a militia regiment in Vancouver. I didn't join because I was patriotic but I figured it was the best way to get some basic weapons training. I showed up for their parades every Tuesday night for about a year and then quit. I was getting uncomfortable with them and they were getting uncomfortable with me." He was quiet for awhile, then said, "You know how you can learn a lot of stuff?"

"No."

"Through those right-wing rags, *Soldier of Fortune*. They're put out for all those guys that want to be mercenaries and fight in South Africa against the blacks or even for all those right-wing nuts in the States, but they have a lot of useful technical information about guns, and in the back they advertise all these obscure pamphlets that show you how to steal cars or pick locks or convert semi-automatic guns into fully automatics. We've got a bunch of them back at the house we'll show you."

Doug looked at his watch. "It's just about my bedtime."

"Do you want to hear my idea on getting ID or not?" Brent was getting a bit frustrated.

"Let's hear it," replied Doug.

"To get a driver's licence or social insurance number or any kind of ID, you have to mail away for it and give the government your birth date, mother's maiden name, your middle name — you know, statistics the average person doesn't know about you. That way a total stranger can't just mail away and get a copy of your SIN or driver's licence or birth certificate. It takes a long time to get together a good false ID and you never know when someone is going to need it, so I think it's important that we start work on it now. Okay, so we make up an opinion poll and take it to the university or someplace where they're used to stuff like that, and we stick in a few questions that will reveal the person's maiden name and date of birth, so we can mail away for ID," Brent said.

Doug thought about it for a moment. "Actually that's not a bad idea. Let's make up an opinion poll and go up to UBC and see if it'll fly. I mean, it can't hurt to try."

I spent much of the following week with Marion since she was leaving for the States soon, but I had time left to help design and print a phony opinion poll with Doug and Brent. We did not include any of the others in our plan to acquire phony ID.

True to her word, on Sunday afternoon, Angie phoned the house and asked if I was still up for the Sunday night restaurant outing. I was. I had just finished putting on my cleanest and finest recycled clothing from the Goodwill store when the doorbell rang. I ran to get the door, as excited as I had been on my first high-school date. Angie looked great. Her long, feathered, blonde hair was freshly washed and combed and she smelled of patchouli oil.

I was a very plain dresser, much like Marion. I put on clothes because I couldn't go naked on the streets. Angie, on the other hand, was a work of art. When she walked into our kitchen, even though the walls were all covered with posters and the smell of food permeated the air, her presence dominated the senses. Her pungent perfume and the sound of her numerous arm bangles and ear rings jingling were captivating, and her colourful layered clothing was in sharp contrast to the black lacy blouse erotically exposing her cleavage. I wondered how we could possibly make an unobtrusive exit from a restaurant?

"You look wonderful!" I gasped.

"Ah, these are just a bunch of old clothes from the Goodwill box. Jenny couldn't make it. I hope you're still into it."

I didn't know her friend Jenny so I was actually relieved she wouldn't be there. This would give me a chance to get to know Angie better. We spent most of our time in the company of others, so we rarely got an opportunity to discuss private matters.

We got into her old Volvo and drove to a Greek restaurant. In case something went wrong, we parked a few blocks down the street so that our licence plate number wouldn't be visible from the restaurant. For obvious reasons we chose a window seat close to the door and then scanned the restaurant. It was a Sunday evening and still early, so not very many people were in the place.

"It doesn't look like it's normally busy on Sunday night because they only have one person working here," I noted, looking over at a huge Greek man pouring drinks at the bar.

"I wouldn't worry about it." Angie brushed off my concern. "By the time we finish eating the place will be packed, and the fewer employees the more preoccupied they'll be with the other customers to even notice us." She proceeded to point out the more expensive dishes we should choose from, because, after all, the meal would be free. After a few moments the waiter came over and took our drink order.

"So is Brent driving you nuts with all this guerrilla stuff?" she asked. Perhaps Angie was of the same mind as myself and wanted this opportunity to get to know me better. Perhaps she was not as insensitive to my feelings towards Brent as I thought.

"Well, actually I'm probably as motivated to initiate some militant action as he is." I wanted so much to open up to someone about my feelings towards Brent, and Angie would be that perfect person if only she didn't happen to be his lover. I couldn't think of anyone I wanted to hurt less, but I knew that in the long run, if I continued on this course, inevitably my relationship with Brent would come between us.

"Not me," she said with no sign of jealousy. "If there was a large group of women, that would be different, but I couldn't live in isolation with Brent, Doug, or any other macho types. It would drive me nuts. I have a hard enough time getting along with him as it is and we don't even live together."

"I don't fully understand why I feel so compelled to get involved in militant actions," I revealed. "I should have been born in El Salvador where there's a clear need for women to join the guerrilla struggle. I know my personality is completely compatible with that lifestyle at this point in my life. I also know that it's not the only valid activity for a revolutionary, but I just wouldn't be content putting out a radical newspaper, or organizing benefits or demonstrations."

"You and Brent are very similar in that respect," Angie said, scanning the menu. The waiter had returned with our drinks and took our food order. "I know that after high school his parents pressured him into enrolling at the University of Victoria, but he wasn't happy in school and quit after one semester." She paused to take a drink and I noticed under the lace of her blouse that she had a long black snake tattooed to her arm. "He took a trip to California and got involved with some of those sixties guerrilla types and came back wanting to do the same thing here — that's when he enrolled in the army to get some weapons training. His parents are professors at the University of Victoria, you know."

"Hmm." I tried not to appear too interested in him.

"They don't get along," she said, glancing back at the people sitting at a table behind us, the only others in the restaurant. "I think he had a good childhood in the sense that they had money and didn't abuse him, but they were very critical of him and even more so since he quit university and doesn't work. I don't know what attracts me to him because I would rather be with women, even as lovers. Other than my relationship with Brent, all my energy goes into the women's movement. The problem with the guerrilla stuff is the isolation. I couldn't live with four or five people and never go out to dances, meet new people, or all the other social interactions that make life worthwhile. I think it would be very unhealthy for the psyche."

The waiter arrived with two huge plates of souvlaki. He asked if everything was alright, which of course it was. There was still only one table of diners besides ourselves.

"I can't enjoy life anymore and ignore the devastation going on around us," I said in between mouthfuls of eggplant. "Sometimes I wish I had never become aware of the poverty that the majority of the people on this planet endure and the destruction of the natural world. I don't know why it bothers me so much. If I lived in a cabin in the woods and a lumber company came along and started clear-cutting the trees around me, I wouldn't be able to ignore it and focus on the beauty of the land left around me. I would be completely consumed by anger and the need to stop that kind of destruction. I would be perfectly willing to give up all the conveniences of our modern-day world if I knew it would prevent the further destruction of the forests and pollution of the lakes and air."

"It bothers me too," she said, "and that's why I'm always working in some group trying to raise awareness and change things. But I'm still able to enjoy my friends and have a life."

"I wish I could, but I can't," I admitted. "For example, if I drive downtown and pass a group of happy people strolling down the sidewalk and a homeless drunk guy laying on the sidewalk, I feel nauseous and physically ill from the sight of the homeless guy and it obliterates the picture of the happy group in my mind. That's why I don't feel I can enjoy my life unless I do everything in my power to prevent all this human and environmental destruction."

We had finished our meal and were doodling around with our napkins when the other table of diners got up and left the restaurant.

"Hmm, how the hell are we going to get out of here?" I asked Angie.

The waiter walked over and placed the tray with the bill in front of us and asked if we were going to pay by credit card or cash. Angie said we'd pay by cash. There was a painfully long moment of silence while he waited for us to hand over the money, which gave me the impression that he did not trust us. When it became obvious that we were still not ready to pay, he retreated to his post in the shadows of the bar.

"Normally the restaurants we go to are busy, so after we put the money under the bill we can walk out casually. But I don't like the way he's just standing there staring at us," whispered Angie. I glanced over my shoulder and it was true — he was just standing there glaring ominously at us. He seemed to have grown taller and more muscular in direct proportion to the level of fear growing in my mind. He resembled a hulking monster more than a restaurant waiter.

It was getting close to closing time. To create the appearance of normality we sat and chatted about nothing while we racked our minds for a way out. We did not have the money to pay the bill.

"I don't think we have any choice but to slip some money under the bill and make a dash for it. He's on to us," concluded Angie.

Although I desperately wanted to be the first to leave, I realized the only practical thing to do was have Angie leave first and get the car running so if he did decide to run after me, I could just jump in the car and we'd be off. I swallowed my fear and stated the obvious. "Why don't you go out first, unlock the passenger door, and have the car running?" She agreed. Calmly she pushed back her chair and sauntered out of the restaurant. The door had barely closed behind her when the monster stalked over to our table in what seemed to be three strides. I could not believe how fast he could move for someone so huge.

"Where did your friend go?" he asked in a loud, accusing tone of voice. I wasn't at all prepared for his question and in a timid voice, shaking with fear, said, "Oh, she just forgot her purse. She'll be back in a minute. Maybe I'll have a coffee." I couldn't have come up with a more stupid response if I had planned it. Now his suspicions were confirmed. He knew I didn't have any money and if Angie wasn't back in a few minutes, which she wouldn't be, he would probably grab me and beat me up on the spot. Now I would have to flee for sure. My stupidity angered me so much, I felt like picking up the butter knife and stabbing myself in the heart. But I didn't.

For one monumentally long second he stared into my terrified eyes as if to say, "Now I'm going to get you . . . " But instead he said, "What do you want in your coffee?"

"Cream and sugar, please," I begged.

I turned around and watched him lumber back towards the bar and the coffee pot, which was somewhere behind. As soon as he had gone back as far as he could, I fled. My suspicions regarding his awareness of our intentions were right on the money. The second I pushed back my chair to flee, I could see him out of the corner of my eye beginning to run towards me with his gigantic stride. I was as terrified as if I had just murdered someone in that restaurant and was about to be chased by the victim's family. I knew I couldn't outrun him to the car. As soon as I hit the pavement outside, I noticed a drugstore door open beside the restaurant. Racing inside and down the centre aisle to the back of the store, I ducked behind a display case, oblivious of the other customers. I had tunnel vision that centred down the aisle through the front window of the drugstore to the street. All I remember seeing is the monster racing like a blur back and forth in front of the store.

Since I didn't want anyone in the store to become suspicious and connect my behaviour to the obviously distraught waiter running back and forth in front of the store, I went into a crouched position and pretended I was looking at the greeting cards on the bottom shelf of the display case, while periodically peering around the corner to the street. After what felt like hours, I wasn't seeing the waiter pass by out front anymore. I tiptoed slowly down the aisle, ready to duck at the drop of a hat, and walked gingerly to the door. I peeked outside and, thank God, there was Angie, parked across the street, motioning frantically for me to get in the car. I made a mad dash across the road and leaped in. The second my feet were inside, Angie floored the accelerator and we sped off down the street.

"My God you're lucky!!!" she howled. "If you hadn't ducked

into that drugstore, he would have had you for dinner! He ran back and forth down the street and just before you came out, he went back into the restaurant. All I can say is you got a guardian angel, honey."

With a flood of relieved emotions, we laughed and relived the episode over and over as we drove back towards the house into the dusk of a lazy Sunday evening.

* * *

After Marion left for the United States, Doug, Brent, and I drove up to the University of British Columbia in Angie's car to try out our phony opinion poll on nuclear energy. The poll started out with a series of questions regarding nuclear energy. Then we threw in a few questions about the respondents' ancestry, which led to their birth dates and mothers' maiden names. We had decided that if the person asked about the connection between their opinions on nuclear energy and their ancestry, we would explain that the purpose of the questionnaire was to discover if there was any relationship between people's ethnic background and their opinions on nuclear energy. When respondents seemed suspicious, we didn't put any pressure on them to answer the questions, but it was surprising how many people gave their birth dates and mothers' maiden names. We even asked for the respondent's social insurance numbers if they seemed completely compliant. In just one afternoon we were able to get enough information to apply for several people's birth certificates and SINs.

"This is just great!" marvelled Doug as we drove back to the house from the university. "If only they knew that their ID is going to a good cause."

"I doubt that any of them would want to contribute to some revolutionary cause if they were given the choice," I said.

"Even if we mail away for their ID," interrupted Brent, "we can't apply for their driver's licences here because they probably already have one and it will come up at the licence bureau. If we want a phony driver's licence, someone's going to have to go to Ontario to get one. There's nothing illegal about having a driver's licence in both B.C. and Ontario."

"I'd love to go back to Ontario for a short visit," I offered. "Plus I know a lot of people there, so I could easily get an address where the ID could be mailed."

"Not a bad idea," replied Doug. "We'll pick out a good woman from this lot and mail away for her birth certificate and social insurance number. Then you can take those two pieces of ID to Ontario and write a test for your temporary learner's permit. Then you'll have to go back again later to do the actual test. It'll be worth it in the long run."

"I wouldn't mind seeing Nick again," I revealed.

Neither of them replied to that statement. Not long before I had left for British Columbia with Marion, I had struck up a casual relationship with a young man, Nick Walker. I can't honestly say we were in love but we satisfied each other's needs for intimacy and sex. I didn't love him enough to make commitments that would interfere with my political ambitions, but if I was going back to Ontario to write this driver's test, seeing him would be an added perk.

At the house we went through the polls and picked out people who had not only given us a full name, date of birth, and mother's maiden name, but who also fitted our general descriptions. Then we decided to start looking for places to use as return addresses for our false ID, such as boarding houses or apartments where mail was left on radiators or dropped in open mail slots.

I loved the excitement of our lives during those months. I would wake up in the morning, never knowing exactly what new adventure the day would bring. Routine and predictability were foreign to us. Most people's lives are consumed by the pursuit of necessities such as food, shelter, and clothing. They get up and go to work so they can pay for their home, food, and clothing. By the end of the day it's all they can do to cook supper, clean up the dishes, and put the kids to bed. Then at the end of the week they have forty-eight hours to cram in all their leisure activities before the routine begins again on Monday.

I know most people are content with this lifestyle, because they want to raise families and need the security that homes and steady jobs afford. But we were not like most people. We didn't share the basic values and principles upon which the majority of people based their lives. We were opposed to the consumerism and materialism underlying this society. We didn't aspire to buy homes, wear nice clothes, and work for companies that we generally viewed as destructive and that left very few enterprises where any of us could have worked and been satisfied. We even saw careers in the so-called helping professions such as social work as Band-aid solutions to problems rooted in greed and materialism. How could we help poor people survive when we saw the real solution to poverty as a total revolution of the economic system and the values upon which it was based?

We ardently believed that we were helping people and the environment by spending our days trying to change it radically. We accepted welfare as the least we were owed for our efforts and suffered no pangs of conscience in supplementing our meagre incomes by looting and pillaging Vancouver's various capitalist enterprises. As modern-day Robin Hoods, we plundered the large food and department stores for food and clothing, freeing us up for what we saw as more important missions such as organizing benefits, rallies, and support groups for the various victims of our society.

We found some drop-off locations for our false ID and mailed off the applications for the social security numbers and birth certificates. One of our candidates was a woman named Mary Milne, whose temporary driver's licence I planned to apply for in Ontario, once we received the rest of her ID in the mail. In the meantime I spent the next few months working with Angie in the Women Against Prisons group, attending meetings of an El Salvador support group, and spending long hours at Bino's strategizing with Brent and Doug over our future militant action group.

Angie was quite eager to make a slide show about life in Oakalla women's prison, the provincial jail where B.C. women served sentences of less than two years. She figured the slide show would be a great climax for the upcoming Women Against Prisons Benefit. There was only one snag — we had no photos of life inside the prison and no way of getting any, although the B.C. Elizabeth Fry Society did. We asked if we could get copies of their photos made, but for some reason they would not lend them. Believing this was unfair, we decided that no harm could come of borrowing the photos without permission and returning them unharmed. We found a sympathetic insider who was willing to lend us the key to the Elizabeth Fry office as long as we returned the photos unharmed. We viewed this as simply borrowing the photos, as opposed to breaking in to the building, because we were entering by way of a key. We had become quite creative at accomplishing projects without money or resources.

So late one night we went to the old office building that housed the Elizabeth Fry office and unlocked the main door. We walked up a flight of stairs to their offices on the fifth floor and unlocked the door, only to find that the room containing the photos was locked, and we didn't have that key. Luckily, the offices in this old building had windows above each door allowing for air ventilation, and we decided to take the trim off the window above the door, remove the window, climb in, and then put the window and trim back.

We had come prepared for this kind of problem with a few basic tools in a knapsack. As the tallest, I was standing on a chair, removing the glass from the window, when we suddenly heard a lot of noise and voices. We froze. The commotion was getting closer and closer. Since it was impossible to put the glass and trim back up in a matter of seconds, we quickly grabbed the glass and trim and hid under a large oak desk. We had barely slid under the desk when the door to the Elizabeth Fry office opened and three people came in. Our hearts were pounding so loudly I was sure they would hear them. One of the people walked towards the desk and picked up a metal wastebasket, when suddenly a loud machine came on. I was so startled I inadvertently sat up and banged my head on the desk, but the sound of the machine, which we now recognized as a vacuum cleaner, drowned out the thud. It was the janitorial staff. For a few heart-stopping minutes they cleaned the office. Thankfully they did a lousy job, because if they had vacuumed under the desk we would either have been caught or, if we had lost our minds, have attacked them in desperation with our amateur burglary tools. I don't know how many times I've read in the paper about criminals who, in a panic, have lost all sense of reason and have assaulted or murdered someone in a desperate attempt to escape from a relatively minor criminal situation like the one we found ourselves in.

Once they had finished cleaning and had moved on down the hall, we gathered our wits and, once again, continued on our mission to get the photos. Our main problem would be getting out without crossing paths with the cleaning staff again.

We put the chair back and I managed to hoist myself up through the window into the other room. Even though we made quite a bit of clatter, the noise of the cleaning staff's vacuum cleaner and laughter easily drowned us out as they moved quickly through the offices down the hall.

I didn't have much trouble finding the photos or getting back to the main office. Although we put the trim back up around the window, some of the nails did get bent in the process, so it wouldn't have been surprising if the window fell off the next time someone opened it to get some ventilation. Finally we opened the Elizabeth Fry door and peered down the hall, listening as hard as we could for the cleaning staff. Of course, they had chosen a perfect time to be absolutely silent. We stepped out, locked the door behind us, and moved swiftly down the hall towards the stairwell. As we went past the elevator we saw the reason the noisy cleaning crew had grown so quiet. The elevator lights revealed that they were in the elevator heading down towards our floor — or perhaps towards the ground floor, where we had to go to get out. We breathed a sigh of relief when the lights indicated they were stopping one floor above our destination. With that information, we hurried down the stairwell towards the ground floor, opened the main door, and stepped out onto the street as though nothing was amiss. As we locked the heavy main door behind us, I slumped over in relief. Mission accomplished. We had the photos for our slide show.

Angie got copies of the photos made, but rather than return them the way we got them, we asked our insider friend if she could just put them back herself. Considering how close we had come to being caught, she agreed to do that.

The Women Against Prisons benefit was a big success. Although men could attend, most of the people who showed up were women. We made a point of inviting members of the Elizabeth Fry Society, which ended up creating a private show for us within the public presentation of our slide show. After an hour of wild women's punk music by an all-women's band, the Moral Lepers, the lights dimmed and we presented our slide show, accompanied by an exceptionally radical critique of the prison conditions. Angie and I stood off in a corner with one eye on the slide show and the other on the Elizabeth Fry members.

After the slide show, one of the women from Elizabeth Fry came over to Angie and me and introduced herself. "That was an incredible slide show!" she gushed. "I'm with Elizabeth Fry. My name is Heidi."

"Yeah, it was rabid eh? And I'm Angie."

"It certainly was no holds barred. You know, we have some photos but we could never have made a presentation like yours with such a radical critique of the prison system without jeopardizing our funding. It certainly must have been difficult to get photos from inside the prison." She gave Angie a piercing look, which I interpreted as an attempt to break Angie's bubble of deception. But Angie was not one to break down and confess easily.

Angie nodded. "Yes, it was very difficult getting those photos. You could imagine how dangerous it was to acquire photos of the inside of the prison, especially since we aren't even allowed to visit the prison."

"Why is that?" asked Heidi, her eyebrows raised incredulously.

"I suppose because we are constantly exposing the injustices that go on there," said Angie matter-of-factly.

"Yes. So I imagine it was quite the feat, involving a certain degree of surreptitious cloak and dagger work?" Heidi appeared to be in the mood for sparring. Angie rose to the occasion. She did not melt under pressure and loved a challenge.

"You have no idea how difficult it was," she smiled. "How did you get your photos?"

"Well, as a government-funded organization, we couldn't resort to anything illegal, so we simply asked and Correctional Services gave us some from their archives." Heidi smiled back. "You know they are remarkably similar to yours." Touché, I thought.

"Unfortunately," Angie shot back, "the government would never give us photos or help us because we have a more critical perspective on the prison system than Elizabeth Fry. As you know, the old cliché 'you can't bite the hand that feeds you' holds particularly true in cases where an organization like yours is government-funded."

For a moment Heidi paused and seemed to be deciding whether to stay the course or declare a truce. Finally, in a conciliatory tone, she said, "Congratulations with your show, because the women in the prisons need groups like yours that are free and unencumbered to 'tell it like it is,' as they say." Then, leaning over to Angie, she whispered, "Between you and me, I wish we could give you our photos to use because they are just gathering dust in our office drawers." In a final coup de grace she turned and winked at me with a warm smile on her face. I could tell that the woman had won Angie's respect at this point in the conversation.

"We do play a role," agreed Angie, searching for common ground, "but the women in prison also need the people in Elizabeth Fry. Your organization has to abide by the rules of the prison system and government but I know that within those bounds, you are doing the best you can to represent the prisoners' interests, and without Elizabeth Fry those women would be left without a watchdog inside the system to represent them. At least your parole officers and halfway houses try to implement the philosophy of rehabilitation as opposed to punishment."

"If you need any help in the future, please let me know," Heidi said warmly with an outstretched hand. Angie shook her hand vigorously, and I felt that something good had been accomplished that evening. For the rest of the night, we writhed and shook and danced ourselves into oblivion. Sometimes it was so liberating to lose oneself in the moment.

* **5** *

In early February 1981 I flew back to Ontario. I had only lived in Vancouver for a few months, but so much had happened it felt like years. I liked my new friends so much that I wouldn't have left if it hadn't been a practical necessity.

My family was in Ontario, but I had grown distant from them. To this day I carry a load of shame and guilt for the total disregard I exhibited in my twenties towards a family that had always been supportive and understanding towards me. At the time I would have attributed it to differences in politics and values, but in hindsight I realize the real reason lay in my intolerance for anyone whose views were not similar to mine. I no longer celebrated traditions such as birthdays and Christmas, because I saw them as just capitalist trappings, and so I didn't even phone my family on those occasions. It didn't occur to me that it was more important to acknowledge my family at those times than to cause them to worry and think I didn't care about them.

That said, I didn't phone or visit them during my short visit to Ontario. I stayed with a friend, Jim Campbell, who had taken on the task of putting out the *Bulldozer* on a quarterly basis. I also contacted Nick.

I wondered if I was still attracted to him. Nick was tall with dark hair and strong facial features, but it was not the physical that drew me to people. At that point in my life, I was looking for someone who shared my political passion, someone with whom I could fulfil my ambitions. Nick was a militant theorist who loved nothing better than to write about radical political action and the ideas behind it, but he was not one to act on the theory. He would always be the kind of person who would analyse events after the fact, safely, from a distance. I was drawn to the actors; those who were bold enough to implement the theory that Nick could articulate so well. My attraction for Brent had grown over the past few months and was beginning to surpass my feelings for Nick.

I phoned Nick, and we arranged to see each other over lunch the next day at the Mars, a little restaurant on College Street. Over a huge plate of cheese blintzes, we caught up on each other's activities. I told him all about the Women Against Prisons group, my involvement in the El Salvador support group, and our plans to do some small actions around the Amax mine. I didn't tell him anything about my late-night Bino's meetings with Brent and Doug.

"I've been helping Jim put together the *Bulldozer* and I'm writing letters to prisoners," he explained enthusiastically. "I've had great letters from some political prisoners in the States like Standing Deer and Kuwasi but I'm real excited about this pamphlet I want to put out a couple of times a year. I'm thinking I'll call it *Resistance*. You see, the *Bulldozer* publishes letters from all kinds of prisoners, but it doesn't focus exclusively on political prisoners. I want to put out something about the armed struggle groups in Europe and the States. There's lots of political prisoners all over the world who were part of some militant struggle, and as far as I know there's no paper for them to publish their letters or communiqués in. That's what I want to do."

"That's a great idea," I encouraged him. "I could help by writing my friends in France for information about the RAF and Red Brigades that's been translated into English, and if it's only in French, I think my French is good enough that I could translate it."

We talked about his idea with such enthusiasm that by the time lunch was over, Nick was hinting at visiting Vancouver. I didn't encourage or discourage him because I was confused about my feelings towards him. In the end, I decided that if he did come, we could be friends but I would make it clear that I was not interested in an exclusive love relationship. I just wanted a relationship of convenience with no strings attached.

We spent the night together. As soon as I lay down beside him, his tender, loving embrace stirred me and we made a kind of desperate but comfortable love. When it was all over, we lay wrapped in each other's arms, separated by our own thoughts and, on my part, a sense of loneliness that I could not drive away. After a while, he fell asleep and I sat up on the side of the bed and lit a cigarette. For a time I let myself fantasize that we were revolutionary partners, heroically bound together on an important mission for which we were willing to risk our lives. I imagined we were part of a large movement of courageous young revolutionaries who were willing to risk everything in order to save the natural world from destruction.

I was jarred from my fantasy by the disturbing awareness that my dreams were so different from those of most women my age. Most women at age twenty-six would be sitting here wishing that they could marry this kind, intelligent man beside them and have children and a nice house in the suburbs — or, less conventionally, be partners but have a successful career and family. All my sisters had married their high-school sweethearts, saved their money, had two or three children, and lived in new suburban homes. By all accounts they were happily married to decent men and were contributing members of their communities. Why was I so different?

The blame could not be placed on my family upbringing. I often likened my childhood to the fifties television show *Leave It to Beaver*: a typical, well-adjusted nuclear family. Our family history was spotless. There was no substance abuse, physical abuse, or emotional abuse — my childhood was as idyllic as any I had read or heard about. Maybe that was the problem.

I grew up in Concord, a small town on the outskirts of Toronto. My parents were born in Denmark but emigrated to Canada after the Second World War because Canada was a country where dreams could come true for those who were willing to work hard. With little education but a strong work ethic, my parents managed to obtain the dream: a home, car, and five healthy children. They bought a small house with enough acreage for my father to grow and sell evergreens as a second job to his main employment as a produce manager at a large food store. My mother stayed home and raised the children, sewing all our clothes and cooking all our food. I don't recall ever going to a restaurant as a child with my family. We were a working-class family who worked hard for everything we had.

Our little neighbourhood, bordered by pastoral farms, woodlots, and streams, was far from the social diseases of the big city. Much of my childhood was spent in a fantasy world in which I was a beautiful young tomboy living in the pioneer days on a horse farm. I was always galloping through the fields and across the streams from one adventure to another on my black stallion. Except for the hours I spent in school and talking to my family at dinner, the rest of my waking hours were spent on my fantasy horse, riding through one action-packed adventure after another.

By the time I was a young teenager, the neighbours were asking my mother when was I going to stop running around, apparently aimlessly, in the fields, pawing the air and nickering like a horse.

Eventually I became self-conscious and began to bottle up my fantasy world in my head instead of acting it out in the fields. Every day after school I would go for long walks, lost in dramas playing out in my head, until I came to a place far from prying eyes where I could burst into a gallop and nobody could witness my actions and accuse me of being odd.

I loved the land. I revelled in the smells of the seasons, the feel of the mud between my toes, and the sounds of the creek, the birds, and the wind in the trees. My relationship with nature was so fulfilling that escape into those memories, even today, is the most therapeutic thing I can do to soothe my mind when it's troubled.

Unfortunately this area, just north of Toronto, was slated for industrial development. As I grew older I witnessed the old farms being bought up by developers and left to rot as land prices soared. By the time I was a teenager, parcels of this land were being covered with concrete and transformed into factories. Perhaps it is a testimonial to just how idyllic my childhood was when I say that witnessing this transformation was one of the most disturbing experiences of my youth. It pained and angered me to see the beautiful woodlots cut down and turned into parking lots, and the streams channelled into culverts and diverted into holding ponds for sewage plants. My beautiful pastures, once filled with cows peacefully chewing their cud, were paved over and covered with various industrial plants producing more junk for the city.

During the late 1960s, the ideas of the hippies that I gleaned from newspaper articles put my pain and anger into perspective. Even though the newspapers described the demonstrations and protests of the sixties with a critical spin, I managed to unravel it and identify with these long-haired freaks and long to be part of their movement. I wore blue jeans and grew my hair long. I started to recycle, and I read about the separatist movement in Quebec. In my isolation on the outskirts of Toronto, I began the metamorphosis into a full-fledged hippie.

My mother and father didn't much like what they saw happening to me. Throughout my childhood I had been their star, a nature-loving tomboy who gladly helped around the house, hoed weeds in the evergreens on weekends, and did well in school. In my recollection, there was very little family discord during my pre-pubescent years. Even during my first three years of high school I had above-average grades. I was a cheerleader and was even chosen to represent our school as "Girl of the Week" in a newspaper contest that featured young women from each high school — girls who were both attractive and successful in sports and academics. What was going wrong?

I started arguing with my father about values. I told him I wanted to live in a commune when I left home; he expressed a concern about family heirlooms, since I was the oldest child. I preached endlessly about pollution, the plight of the Indians and Eskimos, my abhorrence of material things, and my concern for the fate of cattle, chickens, and pigs. I hated the industrial development encroaching on our pastoral neighbourhood and wanted nothing to do with a society that could justify it. As intolerant as I was of anyone who didn't share my all-consuming passion for my newfound social consciousness, I idolized and took on as role models the protesters of the sixties. I was a fifteen-year-old hippie, living in isolation on the outskirts of Toronto, just waiting for the opportunity to bust loose and join up with all these kindred spirits that I could only read about in the papers and watch on TV.

Perhaps my idyllic upbringing in this protected enclave far from the blights of the city heightened my sensitivity to the inherent poverty, pollution, and other negative aspects of our society. I had lived a protected childhood, never seeing a homeless drunk, a displaced Indian, or a slaughterhouse. Even now I still don't know why I couldn't accept these blemishes as part of our societal makeup. I don't know why my three sisters and brother were able to mature "normally" and accept social evils as a necessary part of life. Why did I instinctively gravitate towards the "hippie philosophy" of the sixties out there in Concord, miles away from any long-haired social movement?

Now, years later in Toronto, the answers to those questions were still a mystery to me. I sat on the edge of the bed so absorbed in my thoughts that it took the cigarette burning my fingers to bring me back to reality. For whatever reasons, I was a revolutionary intent on finding other like-minded souls to fulfil my ambitions. I knew that Nick could never spark the fire inside me so necessary for a true love relationship.

The next morning I set off looking for a small apartment building in Jim's neighbourhood where I could get my temporary driver's licence mailed and be able to pick it up. After wandering in and out of a few boarding houses, I found one where the mail was just dumped on a radiator in the front hall. I then proceeded to the licence bureau to write my test as Mary Milne.

The rest of my stay in Ontario was uneventful. I received the temporary licence in the mail just before my plane was scheduled to leave. I figured that next year, about the same time, I would come back and take my road test so I would then have a permanent driver's licence under the name Mary Milne.

* * *

A few weeks after I returned from Ontario, we were sitting around the table one morning reading the paper. Brent often sat and read articles out loud, which inevitably led to heated discussions.

"Hey, they finally sentenced those people from the Cheekeye-Dunsmuir Alliance," he said. Then he read aloud: "On March 18, 1981, seven people were sentenced on contempt of court charges relating to standing in front of bulldozers clearing an access road on Texada Island. Calvin Hill was fined $500 and got a six-month suspended sentence. Paula Laurie, John Leus, and Marguerite Mueller were fined $100, with fourteen-day suspended sentences, and Murray Kennedy and Rose Gibralter were given conditional discharges on condition they don't violate the injunction for one year. The case was adjourned against Susan Rising-Moore. B.C. Supreme Court Chief Justice Allan McEachern, in sentencing them, said, "Some otherwise law-abiding citizens sometimes fall into lawlessness over issues that are not as important as they think them to be."

"What a pig!" exclaimed Saphie, who was standing beside the table combing Bridget's hair.

"The Cheekeye-Dunsmuir Alliance has been fighting that battle for three years now, so I guess that's the end of it," Brent said. "By the time their conditional discharges are over a year from now, the line will be built."

Saphie snorted. "Somebody in high places must think the issues are important or they wouldn't have the chief justice doing the sentencing on contempt of court charges."

"I think they want to nip protest against Hydro in the bud right now," explained Brent, "because this is the first of a series of megaprojects that Hydro wants to build over the next ten years, and they don't want to be accountable to a bunch of citizens every time they start one. The government passed the B.C. Utilities Commission Act on the last day of the summer session, which basically gives the B.C. cabinet the power to approve any Hydro project without public hearings. They passed that act after all the hoopla over Cheekeye during the summer to underscore the fact the government is not going to set up mechanisms for the people to interfere with Hydro's plans."

"I remember meeting this Rose Gibralter last summer," Brent said. "She was at some protest in front of the parliament buildings in Victoria. We had a long talk about the Cheekeye-Dunsmuir line. She was a real cool person with kids and a husband, and had been involved in fighting the line from the beginning. She knew they weren't going to win, but she was willing to risk getting arrested and a record in order to publicize the lack of democracy, as she put it, in the decision-making process. But the bottom line for her and the other people there was that they believe in our legal system and the values of our society. So I bet now that they've been convicted, they'll accept the sentencing and end their protest against the construction of the line. The difference between her and me is I don't respect the legal system or government and so I won't play by their rules."

"Yeah. Me neither!" Saphie joined in.

"Have you read Hydro's *Energy Blueprint 1980* that they put out last summer?" Doug asked her pointedly.

"No," she said timidly.

"It's outrageous!" he said with real feeling."Why don't you dig it up Brent, and let her take a look at it."

Brent went into the living room and began rummaging through the pamphlets on the bookshelves. A few minutes later he came back with the *Blueprint* as well as an assortment of pamphlets put out by the Cheekeye-Dunsmuir Alliance and other protest groups. He plopped them down on the table in front of Saphie and Bridget.

Bridget picked up Hydro's *Blueprint*. "Where'd you get this?"

"At the B.C. Hydro office. They have a library with all kinds of information about the history of Hydro, their current projects and plans. I just popped in there one day around closing time and took this one with me," Brent explained.

Bridget began skimming through the pamphlets and paraphrasing parts of them for Saphie. The *Hydro Energy Blueprint* was a ten-year plan calling for four more dams to be built on four northern B.C. rivers, in addition to the construction of the Hat Creek Coal Generating Plant. The need for these megaprojects was based on the belief that the growth of British Columbia's mines and pulp and paper mills would be stunted if B.C. Hydro could not supply them with massive amounts of electricity. The possibility that large amounts of this electricity could also be produced for export to the United States was a virtual footnote.

The Cheekeye-Dunsmuir pamphlet explained that the transmission line was designed to transport power not only to Vancouver Island but also back to the mainland. That possibility aroused people's suspicions that Hydro had long-term plans to someday build a nuclear power plant over there. Initially the Cheekeye-Dunsmuir power line would be fed from the existing Revelstoke dam in northern British Columbia, but eventually it would be linked to the megaprojects outlined in the *Blueprint* through the Site C dam on the Peace River. All these dams would flood some of the province's best farmland and destroy the Native fishing industries in the areas.

The C-D Alliance claimed that the line was not so much a need as a government strategy to turn the Island into an industrial park against the wishes of the public. This claim was based on the belief that nine major industrial firms were already consuming nearly half of the Island's electricity and would continue to be the main beneficiaries of any increased electrical output on the Island. However, the main beneficiary of the potential water contamination from the weed killer 2-4-D, which would be used along the transmission line right-of-way, would be the people living near the line — just as those living near or under the lines would be the real-life beneficiaries of the potential effects of the electro-magnetic radiation emitted from the line. Scientists were still not able to say unequivocally that this level of radiation would not cause cancer.

Bridget put down the pamphlets and tilted her head back to get the most out of Saphie's grooming. I was about to pick up the pamphlets and continue reading, but Doug uncharacteristically fixed his gentle blue eyes on mine and began to speak. I had never heard him speak at such length. This, and his habit of pacing back and forth to work off steam, reflected the passion that B.C. Hydro's plans inspired in him.

In his quick, clipped voice he explained that Cheekeye-Dunsmuir, like all the Hydro megaprojects in *The Blueprint*, would be funded through various forms of taxation by the people of the province, to supply electricity for a few large pulp and paper mills and mines. These companies would, in turn, take the resources from British Columbia but keep the profits for themselves. In the end the people who funded it all would get very little except a few jobs in the construction phase, a ravaged environment, and huge provincial debts, all without any direct say in whether they really needed the projects.

Doug was never short on facts. To prove his point, he explained that Hydro currently had a debt of $5.2 billion, which was sixty-nine per cent of the provincial debt, yet it would still need another $13 billion over the next decade to implement its plans. Where would this $13 billion be coming from? From the people, through taxes. As a Crown corporation, Hydro was getting its money from government-subsidized loans and teacher's pension funds, which were being loaned to Hydro at below market rates. As a result the pensions and loans were not making as much money in interest as they would if they were loaned out on the international money market.

Not only were taxpayers funding megaprojects that would essentially benefit large corporations, but Hydro had set up its rate structure to discourage conservation, so that the need for more megaprojects would remain insatiable. The more electricity a customer used, the less they paid, so industrial customers were paying less per kilowatt hour than residential customers were. So long as Hydro was protected from the higher costs of funding projects, it was unlikely to discourage excessive use of energy or encourage the use of conservation projects such as thermal co-generation and hog fuel.

While Doug was speaking I had been vaguely aware of the doorbell ringing, but since I had my back to the door I couldn't see who it was. There was so much traffic in and out of this house that the doorbell ringing was a non-event.

As Brent was finishing his little speech, I gasped as a set of cold hands wrapped across my eyes. I instantly recognized them as Nick's. He lifted his hands off my eyes, leaned over, and kissed me on the lips. My acute awareness of Brent's presence paralysed me. In Toronto I had been confused about Nick coming here, but now I suspected it was a huge mistake.

Nick stepped in front of me and smiled, waiting for a reaction. I felt as though I was naked. I was sure that everyone in the room could see through my thinly disguised attempt to appear excited and thrilled to see him. Surely they could see my disappointment and fear. "Wow, is it ever good to see you." I tried to smile, but I was dying to get out of the room, away from the audience. Maybe I could muster up some affection in private. "Did you bring a suitcase or anything?"

"They're still out on the porch." He wasn't showing any sign of disappointment in my reaction. Maybe I wasn't naked after all. Maybe nobody could tell I wasn't happy to see him. "I'll get them for you." I jumped out of my chair and fairly ran out the door. Outside I took a deep breath and slowly let it out. I could feel the tension leaving my body as I exhaled. I could hear the others, inside the house, bombarding Nick with excited questions about his work in Toronto. Brent knew Nick from previous trips to Ontario.

After a while Nick came out to see why it was taking me a phenomenally long time to come back with his suitcases. "What's wrong?" he asked innocently. "Are they too heavy for you?"

"No." I answered weakly." I just wanted to give you some space with the others."

"I'm sorry I didn't let you know I was coming earlier," he said, perhaps sensing my discomfort. "Somebody had a ticket to Vancouver they couldn't use. I got it cheap and decided spontaneously to come." To compensate for my cold greeting, I wrapped my arms around him and gave him a warm hug. "Let's go in."

For the rest of the morning we sat around the table with Brent, Saphie, and Bridget, talking about what we had been doing. Doug retreated down into his room again. While Nick told us about his fledgling newsletter, *Resistance*, I tried to figure out how I would deal with his arrival.

Around noon Nick was showing signs of fatigue so I suggested he take a nap in the loft. Nick took me up on the offer and within a few minutes was quietly sleeping. Doug, Brent, and I walked down the street to Bino's and ordered coffees.

"*Resistance* sounds like a great idea," Brent said. "If we ever do any militant actions, it'll be a great pamphlet for our communiqués and discussions about guerrilla action. Do you think Nick would be interested in doing anything militant?"

"He's really not that interested in illegal actions. He's more the analytical, intellectual type. But we could include him in one of those Amax actions we've been talking about. They're not so heavy that they'll scare him, but they'd be a good way of testing him."

"I've been scouting around for a place to pick up some typewriters," Brent said. Our house had an old one, but it was broken, and we didn't know anybody else who had one we could use. If Nick was going to put out *Resistance*, we would have to have a good electric typewriter. Brent said he had found a place we could easily get into at night and pick out what we needed. "What about tonight?" he asked. "It's the perfect action for Nick, and he'd see the need for it since he doesn't have a typewriter to put out *Resistance*."

"I'm not into it," Doug said. "I'm really not interested in these low-level actions or putting out militant rags. Count me in when you're ready to get some dynamite, guns, money, or real action."

"Doug, we can't just come out of nowhere and do some huge bombing," I argued. "There has to be some kind of militant community to support us or else we'll be totally isolated, with no support or people to continue on if we get killed or caught."

"Well, that's fine, but it ain't my bag." Doug had been doing reading on dynamite and how to break into the places — magazines — where they store it. He wanted no part of B and E's. By now I had learned that once Doug made up his mind, there was no changing it.

When we got back from the coffee shop, Nick was eating toast. He was hesitant when I told him about our idea, but agreed to come along since the typewriters were essential to his publishing project.

Around three in the morning we drove past a single-storey office building in a mixed residential and commercial area. We parked a block away and walked to the back of the building. Brent had gone in before closing time and left a washroom window unlocked. While he used a crow bar to pry it open, Nick and I acted as scouts. Brent and I easily squeezed our way in, and Nick stayed outside on watch for a police car or anyone else who happened by. Brent went quickly from one room to the next, carrying typewriters and other miscellaneous office supplies to the washroom window. His philosophy was that once he was stealing, he might as well get as much as possible, since the consequences would be much the same whether you got one typewriter or ten. I ran around beside him with a small flashlight trying to anticipate where he was headed so I could illuminate the way.

Once we had every typewriter in the building, plus staplers, paper punches, and paper supplies piled by the window, Brent slowed down and started rummaging around, more out of curiosity than anything else. I could see we had everything we'd come for, and I was eager to leave. I whispered irritably for him to get the hell out of there. But he only motioned for me to follow him down a hall to what I assumed must be the president's office, since otherwise the whole building consisted of one main room partitioned into many cubicles by moveable privacy walls, surrounded by small rooms used for photocopying, storage, coffee, and washrooms. The only other sizeable room was the one Brent was leading me to.

We opened the heavy oak door and walked up to the main desk. Brent opened each drawer and searched the contents. From the bottom drawer he pulled out a dozen pornographic magazines. He turned and looked at me as if to say "mission accomplished," then proceeded to open each magazine to the centrefold and placed them strategically all over the room, so they'd be the first thing anyone entering the office in the morning would see. Just before leaving, he walked over to a liquor cabinet and grabbed a couple of bottles.

Back at the washroom window he whistled for Nick, whose head appeared out of the shrubs lining the parking lot. Brent motioned for Nick to come to the window. "You're going to have to get the car and park it here," he whispered. "It'd be more danger-ous to carry all these typewriters down the street than to load them into the car here."

At that point it seemed to me whether we made it or not was up to fate. I watched Nick dart through the bushes towards the car. I wiggled out the window so Brent could hand me the typewriters. By the time we had two out, Nick was pulling up in the car, with-out the headlights on. He got out and opened the trunk. In less than five minutes we had the typewriters and everything else loaded in the car. Brent shut the window and hopped into the car and we cruised out of the parking lot, turning on the headlights once we were safely driving down the street. Despite my agnostic beliefs, I said a little prayer of thanks to God for allowing us to get out of that situation safely. There was no harm in prayer.

"So where to?" Brent asked.

"Let's go to Bino's and unwind," Nick said.

My body was still pulsating with adrenalin so I welcomed the idea of a relaxing cup of tea that I hoped might induce sleep. At the restaurant, Brent was chuckling. "When the first people arrive and go into their bosses office in the morning, they'll be exposed to the real man behind the face."

"Do you think they'll laugh and in a sense feel like conspirators in this break-in?" Nick asked with a serious look on his face.

"What do you mean?"

"Do you think that when they walk in they'll be terrified at the sense of violation of their security, or do you think they'll identify with us?"

"I'm pretty sure they'll be horrified their office has been broken into and they'll think, 'This could have been my home these criminals broke into," Brent said.

"I think the degree of amusement they experience at seeing their boss's porno magazines spread all over his office will depend on how well they get along with him — and on whether they have pornographic magazines at home themselves," I added.

"Obviously this was not meant to be some overtly political action," Brent said. "This was a necessary B and E to get typewriters for the community, so you can put out *Resistance* and we can enable people to type up newsletters, posters, or whatever shit they're doing."

"In the long run, the biggest problem people like us are going to have is getting the workers on our side," continued Nick. "They just can't identify with our methods, our goals, or even our lifestyles. As far as I'm concerned, we'll never be able to have any kind of popular resistance to the government if the workers aren't on our side."

I agreed. "We're not just opposed to pollution, nuclear technology, and all that stuff. We're opposed to the entire lifestyle and values of this society. Even the poorest of the poor in North America believe in the capitalist way of life. Everyone wants a car, a TV, and a job. People like us, and there aren't many, don't want a job, not because we're lazy, but because most jobs involve being a part of a company that is essentially destroying the planet."

"Take a pulp and paper mill, for example," Brent said. "I don't want a job that involves having forests cut down so they can be transformed into paper products through some industrial process that pours the waste products into the rivers or incinerates them and pumps them into the air. In the end, most of that paper is used to wrap up millions of consumer products that we either don't need or are obsolete in no time. I could not in good conscience work in a pulp and paper mill."

"What if they replanted the trees, used some kind of anti-pollution devices in the pulp and paper mills, and recycled all the paper products?" Nick asked.

Brent shrugged. "I would reconsider, I guess."

"The problem we have is that workers in our society identify with the values of the owners of the companies and aspire to have their lifestyle," stated Nick. "I'm quite sure if they were given the choice to either live like us or live like the people they work for, they would choose the latter. Unions are fighting for the workers to acquire more stuff, they're not fighting to change the premises upon which this society is based. They are far from revolutionary."

"Is that why you got so involved in the union when you were working as a printing press operator in Toronto?" I asked. "Were you trying to make the union more revolutionary?"

"I guess. Nothing's going to change if we can't get the workers on board. If they are completely alienated from our cause, then we're just blowing smoke into the wind," Nick said.

Brent took another tack. "Even the leaders of liberation struggles in underdeveloped countries couldn't relate to what we're saying, because they're struggling to gain control of their own economies. And once they've got that, they want industry, wealth, and consumer goods for their people. They want what we've already got." He paused. "Our kind of revolution can only happen in North America or Europe, where we've already experienced everything capitalism has to offer. Most of us have TVs, cars. We could get jobs, educations, and all that. We can afford to critique the affluent consumer lifestyle and develop a vision different from anything before. We are not Marxists, communists, or socialists. We are not rooted in the working class. We're rooted in the alienated youth, the older hippies that didn't lose their ideals, the intellectuals who dare to articulate a new philosophy that critiques materialism, technology, and asks 'What the hell is progress anyway?' "

"Well, I have no illusions about being on the brink of an imminent revolution," I said. "I'm in it for the long haul." The three of us sat in silence for a few minutes, letting the conversation settle in our tired minds. I could feel the calming effects of the tea kicking in and wanted to go to sleep. "Let's go home."

It was a rare time to be up. As we drove north down the Kingsway at 5:30 in the morning, the sun was just beginning to peak over the mountains, washing the sky in pastel hues. All the windows of the skyscrapers in the city core were ablaze, reflecting the fiery glow of the morning sun. The streets were empty. A soft breeze pushed stray fast-food wrappers discarded the night before into our path.

I felt so tired. As we pulled up to the house in Angie's old Volvo, a young Native woman came out of the house across the road. Her long dark hair was pulled up in a tight pony tail. Even though it was a cool March morning, she wore a pair of shorts that exposed half her buttocks, and her shirt was tied in a knot under her breasts, exposing her cleavage. Her beautiful features were heavily made up, almost as though she was going to a masquerade party. It was awfully early for her to be heading off to work, but I figured she might have clients who would stop by her corner for a quick blow job on their way to work. She was so thin she must be an addict, I decided, and certainly nothing else would draw someone out to work so early dressed like she was. Yes, I was so tired.

Sometimes I wished I wasn't so obsessed with this idea of being a revolutionary. When was the last time I had spent a day by the ocean or walking in the woods? I felt so far away from those childhood days when I used to gallop wildly through the fields, snorting and pawing the air in ecstasy. If I closed my eyes and concentrated, I could bring back the smell of dry grass and dirt, the sound of bees in the air, and the feel of the sun and wind parching my skin. Why couldn't I ignore the clear-cut mountainsides or the yellow contamination on the banks of the Fraser River? Why couldn't I just get a job on some horse ranch, meet a nice guy, save up some money, and buy a little piece of land where I could make my childhood fantasies come true? I could have a simple cabin, barn, and horses and live like my childhood alter ego.

Was I drawn to this revolutionary mission by a need for danger and excitement or perhaps even some subliminal suicidal attraction? I didn't know. I needed to sleep. That poor Native girl probably had no choice but to be a prostitute. According to the usual statistics, she was probably from a broken alcoholic home where she was sexually abused as a child. With little education and nothing to look forward to but a welfare existence on the reserve, it was understandable that she would end up on the streets of Vancouver, obliterating her memories with drugs and eking out an existence doing the only thing she had ever learned could get her what she wanted.

I had no bad memories to obliterate. There was no reason in the world why I couldn't go to university, get a great job, and be a success. Why was I choosing this path that would inevitably lead to self-destruction with little or no social change as a consequence? My brain was tired. I knew that unlike the Native girl I alone was responsible for choosing this path in life that would lead to my own demise.

But even with these intense doubts I couldn't stop myself from walking up the sidewalk towards the house where I knew I would continue laying plans for militant action. All the articles I had read, all the TV programs I had watched, and all the destruction of nature I had witnessed had laid the unconscious groundwork for a compulsion to complete this mission to fight in every way I could a society that made that Native girl's future inevitable. I truly believe that if there was a God and he or she appeared in front of me and said, "Ann, if you are willing to die, right now, no more animals will become extinct at the hands of man, horses will run free, no more rivers will be cesspools for factories, and no more Native girls will have to be prostitutes," I would willingly have sacrificed myself.

I was no hero. Everyone is willing to lay down their life for someone or something they love. How many mothers or fathers would not lay down their life so their child could live? How many people would not lay down their lives for a place or country they love? I was just tired, and sometimes I wanted to forget and just bask in the beauty of what was left in the natural world. I walked up the sidewalk behind Brent and Nick into the house. Without a word, Nick and I climbed up into the loft and Brent trudged down to his tiny bedroom. Once in bed, I rolled over on my side facing the wall away from Nick. The last thing I remember before dropping off into the black abyss of sleep was Nick gently placing his arm across my back.

✳ 6 ✳

In April 1981, after many late-night meetings at Bino's, we finally got around to doing an Amax action. The issue was not getting a lot of attention in the press, but would have a devastating impact on the Nishga Indians living in Alice Arm. It was also an issue that clearly showed how the legal system was set up to protect the interests of big business as opposed to the principles of justice. To prevent contamination of the marine food chain, the federal government had strict regulations regarding the quantity of toxic mine tailings that any company could legally dump directly into the ocean. But in the case of Amax the provincial government had given special permission to allow a discharge eight thousand times greater than the existing federal standards. The rights of

Amax to dump toxic mine tailings directly into the ocean super-seded the rights of the Nishga Indians to continue their traditional way of life based on fishing and other activities on both sea and land.

We decided to keep the actions small and simple so that people could get involved without having to fear serious prison time as a consequence. We were a small group of five young white people, with no connection to the Nishga other than our good intentions about publicizing their plight.

"What do you think of this fine catch!" Bridget burst in the door one day with a plastic bag full of partially decomposed fish.

"Great." Brent didn't even look up. He was too preoccupied with a boiling pot full of glass bottle jars.

"What the hell are you doing?" asked Saphie, who had come in with Bridget.

"I'm boiling these jars to remove any fingerprints in case the cops take this little action real serious and check." He carefully lifted the pot of boiled jars off the stove.

"I'm going to leave these here to cool off for a while, so don't touch them," he yelled as he headed downstairs. When he came back up he placed an old can of bright red paint and a box of large rocks on newspapers that he had laid all over the kitchen table. The plan was to throw the rocks through an Amax office window, followed by the jars of paint and fish.

Brent handed out pairs of latex surgical gloves to the rest of us. "This is fun. Just like arts and crafts in public school," laughed Saphie.

Carefully we picked out rotting fish parts from Bridget's bag and placed them in the jars, then poured red paint over them until the jars were full. Brent tightened each lid and wiped the spilled paint off the outside of each jar. "What do you think?" he asked proudly, holding up a jar for us to admire.

Doug had come upstairs to make a pot of tea. He was reading Homer's *Iliad* and barely put the book down while he poured water into the pot.

"Well, Doug, what do you think?" Brent asked.

"What can you say about a jar of red paint and fish heads?" he answered. Brent just shook his head in exasperation as Doug turned around and marched back downstairs to his room.

Later that night, after the bars had closed and the revellers had gone home, four of us piled into Angie's car. Angie, who was not in attendance, had said we could use her car as long as we promised to park it several blocks away from the action.

During the months I had spent in Vancouver, a steady diet of small illegal activities had boosted my confidence in our abilities to get away with things. I no longer imagined a cop hiding behind every obstacle and actually found myself feeling quite relaxed out on a mission. Still, a certain level of fear is a good thing in these matters — it keeps a healthy flow of adrenalin coursing through the bloodstream, which tends to heighten awareness. I think I had finally reached this healthy medium.

It was raining lightly that evening, and I loved rainy nights. We rode cosily in the car, peering out of the greasy windshield as the tattered wipers smeared the rain back and forth. Finally we pulled into an alley a few blocks from the Amax office and parked in an oily puddle. I stepped out of the car and into the puddle, mesmerized for a second or two by the beautiful purple ripples that my footsteps made. Three of us — the other stayed behind to watch the car — walked quickly down the sidewalk towards the large windows of the office building. Once we got there we quickly glanced around, thankful for the rain because it would make visibility poor for any unexpected spectators. With the way all clear, one of us threw a heavy rock through the window. The sound and sight of the heavy glass smashing down were terrifying. Besides that, the second the rock went through the window, an ear-shattering alarm started resonating. I found my knees going weak and my hair standing on end. So this was the feeling that some people found addictive. Not me.

I threw my jars of red paint and fish through the gaping hole. The others followed suit. Huge hunks of dead fish clung to the wall in the thick red goop. All of us, I think, wanted to race at breakneck speed back to the car, but instead we forced ourselves to walk quickly so that we wouldn't draw attention. Once we were all safely inside the car, our driver pulled out and started off towards home. We could still hear the alarm resounding over the roar of Angie's car.

The action went smoothly and quietly, but unfortunately did not garner any publicity. "That's a drag," Brent said the next morning after he had meticulously gone through the newspaper. We had phoned in a statement after the action. "I guess the papers decided our communiqué wasn't worth printing — probably because Amax refused to confirm that anything happened, to prevent bad public-

ity. Hey, does anyone want to go to the Smiling Buddha tonight?"
Two bands, the Subhumans and Dead Kennedys, were playing that
evening in a Rock Against Radiation benefit.

"Naw," said Bridget slowly. She looked over at Saphie, who was
lying on a bench pressing a weight bar over her head. "I don't
know how you can do that in the morning."

"I've got to build up my muscles for hockey," Saphie huffed.
"We have a practice this afternoon."

"I wouldn't mind going to the benefit," I said. "Maybe Nick and
Angie want to go."

Brent looked over at me. "Yeah, two nice radical couples going
out for a couple of beers on a Friday night."

I spent the rest of the day shoplifting food with Angie. She was
eager to go to the benefit. Later that evening, Brent, Nick, Angie,
and I drove to Chinatown. The Smiling Buddha was a derelict bar
on a side street between a number of failing Chinese restaurants
frequented by east-end drug addicts and prostitutes. It had become
an infamous punk bar where bands of notoriety along the west
coast played and every punk band in Vancouver tried their first gig.
It was an exciting place to go, not only for the music but also
because one gig out of five was busted by the cops for underage
drinking and open drug use.

In the early 1980s punk was the music of rebellion, replacing
the co-opted rock music of the 1970s. Kids who came to the Buddha had parents who had grown up in the late fifties and the sixties listening to rock 'n' roll and the Rolling Stones and Bob Dylan.
Growing up, these kids had heard lots of rock on the radio and
family stereo. By the early 1980s, the rebellious lyrics of the sixties
bands were in sharp contrast to the lifestyles and images of the
now-wealthy, aging musicians. There was something poignantly
hypocritical about a forty-five-year-old millionaire in designer
jeans singing about "a rollin' stone, with no direction home." These
musicians were no longer capable of expressing the feelings and
aspirations of a generation of kids who had grown up in a later
era.

The parents of the punk generation had grown up after the
Second World War on a steady diet of hope and possibilities in an
age in which idealism was still possible. There were plenty of jobs
and money. But when the Vietnam War began to take its toll on
American youth it also awakened young people's consciousness to
the social ills that threatened their dreams of an ideal society.

Rachel Carson's 1962 book *Silent Spring* warned that human beings could destroy the planet through pollution. The civil-rights movement underscored how, even in the mid-sixties, the blacks' right to vote existed in theory only, and the birth-control pill sparked women to become sexually liberated and demand equal opportunities in the workforce.

The baby boomers fought for their ideals and in many ways won. They helped bring the war in Vietnam to an end. Blacks won the right to vote, and schools were desegregated. In 1965 the *Voting Rights Act* abolished mandatory literacy tests and "poll taxes" — which had previously prevented the majority of blacks in the Southern States from voting — as a prerequisite to the vote. Women were no longer forced to have large families and stay home and care for them. But the struggles of the sixties did not result in a revolution. Corporate America learned how to co-opt the opposition and fine-tune the capitalist machinery. A lot of money could be made by selling things the baby boomers wanted, like health food, blue jeans, recycled products, and rock concerts. A few sacrifices had to be made, but in the end the machine ran more smoothly than ever.

The Vietnam War ended, anti-pollution laws were enacted, and affirmative action programs were implemented to make up for a long history of discrimination against both women and people of colour. But underneath these token changes, nothing really changed. A horse of a different colour is still a horse. The struggles of the sixties did not change the economic system or the values it was based on. Corporate and political leaders driven primarily by greed and power hid behind the sacred motives of profit and material growth.

The parents of the punk kids were wooed into complacency through slick marketing of the illusion that corporate America was moving towards a society free of pollution, with equal opportunities for all. Both men and women could drive to their corporate offices in their BMWs listening to the sounds of Bob Dylan or the Rolling Stones. On weekends working women could don their Birkenstock sandals and shop at the local health-food franchise or choose "natural" products from row upon row of packaged "green" products in the supermarket. Now women had the choice to work out of the home, although that choice was becoming more and more a choice for the rich, since the traditional home and car and two or three kids now seemed to take two working parents to acquire and maintain. But underneath these illusions, the driving force of the economy remained unchanged: profit at all cost.

Unlike their parents, the punk kids had grown up learning about pollution, nuclear war, and birth control since public school. They had also been taught not to talk to strangers or to stray far from their yards, because perverts and dangers were everywhere. The same public park that in the 1960s had conjured up images of children playing innocently on swings and in sandboxes was now a potentially lethal place where children were supervised closely in case they found a dirty syringe in the sandbox, or that man sitting on the park bench exposed himself — or, worse, kidnapped the children.

At school these kids were pushed to make decisions about their future careers by the age of twelve so they would end up in the right stream that would lead to well-paid jobs for the privileged few who could afford to go to university. They would have no childhood memories of playing unsupervised at the local creek or scrub baseball games in the cow field. Instead, they would remember sitting in their bedrooms playing computer games or attending some organized sport supervised by a team of adults.

The kids at the Smiling Buddha were the ones who had become jaded or tired of the constant supervision and control of the adult world. They were often the ones who didn't come from families that could afford the expensive education so essential for a job. As their music so frequently reminded us, theirs was a world of no future, no hope. Their music was filled with warnings of suicide and death, cries of anguish, despair, and anger.

As we stepped into the Buddha, a local Vancouver punk band called the Subhumans was playing "Fuck You," written by Gerry Hannah.

You call us weirdos, call us crazy
Say we're evil, say we're lazy
Say we're just the violent type
Kind of dumb, not too bright
We don't care what you say — fuck you
You tell your friends we're really sick
Short-haired fags on a commie trip
And you should know 'cause you're so cool
Number one, nobody's fool
We don't care what you say — fuck you
Well, come on, man, you better jump right in

This is one game that everybody's in
Don't care where you've been, don't care how you look
It's hell's fire, man, you're in, you gotta cook
We don't care what you say — fuck you.

A huge disco ball made up of hundreds of shards of mirror turned around and around, reflecting coloured lights around the room. It gave the dark room full of thrashing teenagers an eerie look. It was as though someone had put on a disco record but had set the speed to 78 RPM instead of 45, and everything was wound up into a frenzy of wild dancing, with the exception of the disco ball rotating serenely around and around.

We began weaving our way across the room, sweaty bodies leaping up and down and throwing themselves against each other in an aptly termed slam dance. As we neared the old wooden stage, set about three feet above the floor, I noticed teenagers pulling themselves up onto the stage and then throwing themselves with abandon into the mass of bodies writhing below them. This reminded me of an exercise, designed by psychiatrists, in which one person falls backwards, trusting that their partner will catch them before they hit the floor. But in this case the exercise had reached the ultimate form in which the individual had to trust a mass of strangers, who were not at all concentrating on the activity.

I was at least seven years older than most of the crowd and had never been to a punk bar before, so all of this was new to me. Brent and Angie were also older, but they seemed to know everyone — they organized many of the benefits and gigs where the bands played. We finally found a spot at a table up against the wall where I could sit and watch the spectacle. It reminded me of some tribal purging of the soul in which the participants lose consciousness and let all their repressed feelings escape through movement. Various visible body parts were pierced; noses, ears, eyebrows, breasts. Many people were covered in tattoos. The dancers wore old clothes that I presumed were from the Salvation Army or Goodwill store — certainly not designer clothes from the mall. As they danced, some of them ripped pieces of their clothing until they were wearing only shreds of sweaty T-shirts and pants. What the dancers lacked in dress colour, they more than made up for in hair colour. Every fluorescent colour I hated was represented; flamingo pink, phosphorescent green, and orange streaks running through hair-sprayed black spikes. It was spectacular, as though we had stepped off the street into some time warp where the 1970s disco ball threw its coloured pinpoints of light slowly around a room full of writhing tribal primitives whose hair had been attacked by futuristic, fluorescent spray bombs.

Angie and Nick had left their seats and melded into the mass of bobbing bodies. Brent and I sat quietly staring off into the crowd. I found myself fantasizing that this group of disillusioned kids could someday turn into heroic revolutionaries and channel their anger and despair into something constructive. I could never imagine any of these marginalized kids walking down the sidewalk, briefcases in hand, on their way to their starkly clean corporate offices. Instead I envisioned them finding strength in fighting a system that left them no future, no hope. I figured becoming revolutionaries was the only positive future for kids who would otherwise end up as drug addicts or prisoners if they continued on the path they were now following.

I was startled out of my reverie by Brent pushing his chair back and yelling "Julie!" Out of the crowd of moshing kids appeared a young woman of eighteen or so with short jet black hair and light blue eyes. When she saw Brent, her face lit up. She was stunningly attractive and alive. So many of the other young women here cultivated — or genuinely felt — jaded or, worse yet, dead inside. Julie exuded life. "Brent! What are you doing here?"

"Oh, just a night on the town," he told her.

"Why don't you sit down?" I asked.

"Sure. This is great, eh?" Her voice bubbled with enthusiasm.

"Yeah," said Brent with equal enthusiasm. "You going to the El Salvador meeting next week?"

"Sure. I made a neat poster you gotta see. That's Gerry!" she yelled, pointing up at the bass player on the stage.

"I know him. We've done lots of benefits with the Subhumans," Brent yelled back. "Where are you staying?"

"At my sister's for a while. She was in a bad car accident so I'm helping her out. Maybe I'll bring the poster over to your house tomorrow. Anyways, I'll come over and talk to you guys when they stop playing."

After she left, Brent told me all about her. "She's great — probably the most political and rabid punk in here. She's been going to the El Salvador support group and seems the most enthusiastic person in the group. I'd like to see her get involved with us. She'd dig it."

When the band put down their instruments, Julie jumped up

on the stage and gave the bass player a big kiss. He was a tall, lean young man with a clean jaw line. Even from a distance, I could see he adored her. After she kissed him, she jumped back off the stage and joined a group of women. His eyes never left her.

Brent noticed me watching them. "Gerry helped start the Sub-humans a few years ago. They're the most political punk band in Vancouver. He's a good guy." Gerry must have had ESP because at that very instant he turned in our direction and saw Brent. Gerry waved, jumped off the stage, and strode over to us.

"Hey Brent, how's it going?"

"Not bad. What's happening?"

"I was going to say the same thing to you," Gerry said, laughing.

"You and Julie should come over to our house sometime." Our conversation was interrupted by the singer, whose name I learned was Wimpy. He motioned for Gerry, who said he'd see us later. We spent the rest of the evening at the Buddha. Angie and Nick mingled comfortably with the punk kids and danced while Brent and I sat quietly at our table.

* 7 *

B y the look on his face, I could tell that Brent was as surprised as I was when Julie and Gerry actually did show up at our door the next evening. They were dressed in matching leathers, heavily adorned with metal chains, bracelets, and earrings. Julie had circled her light blue eyes with a thick layer of black mascara, giving her an almost Egyptian look. I wished I had the courage to dress as exotically.

"Hi!" Julie beamed with what I assumed was her characteristic enthusiasm. "Me and Gerry were just driving around and I thought I'd drop over and show you the poster I designed for the benefit."

She carefully pulled out a poster from a large black portfolio and laid it out on the table. Stepping back, she cocked her head this way and that, looking at it from different angles. I peeked over her shoulder, and even though I wasn't much of an art critic I could tell that it was well-balanced, and the black silhouettes of helicopters, peasants, and churches were impressive. "That's really good!"

"She took a semester of art at Douglas College," said Gerry, putting his arm around her shoulders proudly. "But she's got natural talent."

"Yeah," Julie said. "I had to quit, 'cause I just didn't have the money and my family don't have the money to pay for it either. Maybe next year. I don't need a degree to do art anyway, eh Ger? I'm working at Woodlands for awhile. I might go back."

"What's Woodlands?" asked Brent.

"A home for handicapped kids. My mom worked there, but when her arthritis got real bad she had to quit."

"You'd never recognize Julie when she goes to work," laughed Gerry.

"I'm good at changing my appearance," Julie added. "If I take off my makeup and put a little barrette in my hair and wear some straight clothes, you wouldn't recognize me on the street."

"How'd you like the gig last night?" asked Gerry.

"It was great," said Brent.

"I couldn't believe how young some of the kids were. I recognized some from my old high school, Burnaby North. We started that band, what, in '78, after I quit school in Grade 11. Wow, that's three years ago. I'm an old man!" Gerry laughed easily. "It's funny cause there was an article in the paper today about some guy escaping from Matsqui prison. The photo of the prison looked just like Burnaby North High. Identical. The only difference is the prisoners know why they're there!"

We all chuckled with Gerry.

"Did you know that Gerry's mom named him after a missionary — Gerald? He was brought up to be a preacher. He just turned out to be a preacher with a different message. He writes a lot of the lyrics for the Subhumans, you know," Julie said proudly, poking Gerry in the ribs.

"Julie!" He jumped out of her reach. "I really got to go to practise. If you want to stay here, I could pick you up on the way back?" She looked over at us and Brent nodded.

After Gerry left, we sat around and talked politics for awhile. "Ann's going to get a FAC," Brent told her.

"What's that?"

"A firearms acquisition certificate — a permit to buy a gun. You have to have one. Basically you fill out a form so the cops can check to see if you have a record, but I don't think I could get one since I have a small record. Plus I pied Joe Clark in '77 and that'll be on my record too. If Ann buys a shotgun, we should all go up in the mountains target-practising sometime?"

"That'd be great." Julie beamed. I gave Brent a piercing look meant to convey disapproval in no uncertain terms, but he avoided my gaze. I thought it was premature for him to tell Julie about the possibility of my buying a gun and, even worse, to invite her out target-practising without discussing it with Doug and me first. To make matters worse, he suggested she should consider getting a FAC. "You never know when a gun may become necessary."

Julie didn't say much but I could tell by her expression that she respected Brent and considered everything he said with great gravity. As the evening progressed, the conversation became even more outrageous, as far as I was concerned. I would have left but felt obligated to stay just to monitor the situation. Brent pulled out the newspaper clipping about the Amax action and asked Julie if she had seen it. She knew nothing about Amax so he proceeded to educate her about the issue. Thankfully Gerry arrived to pick her up before Brent had got to the point of inviting her to participate in anything.

The second the door had closed behind them, I laced into him. "What the hell are you doing? You hardly know her and you're inviting her out target-practising?"

"Relax," he said in a patronizing voice that infuriated me. "I've been talking to Julie about politics for months now, every time there's an El Salvador meeting. She's a lot cooler than you think. Anyway, how do you expect to get anywhere if you don't include people in activities that test their will to become militants?"

"Well, I think you should at least ask me and Doug before you start including her in anything." I left the room and went downstairs and knocked on Doug's bedroom door. I heard a gruff grunt, which I assumed was an invitation to enter.

He was lying on his bed immersed in a heavy book by the nineteenth-century political theorist Nechayev, who espoused the controversial belief that political assassinations are an effective means of bringing about social change. I was in no mood to discuss the book. "Doug, have you ever met Julie and Gerry?"

"Yeah, I know who they are, but I can't say I know them." He still hadn't stopped reading his book.

"Doug — I'm pissed at Brent because Julie was just here and he told her I was getting a FAC, invited her to go out target-practising when I get a gun, and showed her the Amax article. She'd be a fool if she didn't figure out we did it. As far as I'm concerned that's way too quick to get someone we hardly know involved, especially considering he didn't even ask us first."

Doug finally looked up at me. "That's not cool."

"I want to have a meeting about it right now before Brent gets the impression he can just make these kinds of decisions unilaterally."

"Sure," Doug said, sitting up on the bed.

I went back upstairs and asked Brent to go downstairs with me. My intensity seemed to amuse him. He took his time making a sandwich, which only further fuelled my anger, and then came down.

"So what's the problem?" he mumbled through a mouth full of bread.

"Ann says you've been talking too much to Julie," stated Doug.

"Well you guys might not know her, but I've spent a lot of time with her and she's real interested in doing stuff. How are we going to get anyone involved if we don't invite them?"

"I've met Julie and Gerry at a few gigs and I'm not impressed with their political maturity," Doug said. "How old are they?"

"Julie's about eighteen and Gerry's twenty-one, I think," Brent said. "I'd like to ask Julie if she wants to do this next Amax action. It's not heavy and it'd give you guys a chance to get to know her. How else are we going to know if we want to work with her?"

"Like I said, I'm not impressed with what I've seen of them," Doug went on. "They're a couple of punk kids who say a lot of rabid shit, but I'm not convinced they know what they're talking about or that they've thought of the implications of acting on anything they say. They might talk about trashing places and 'fighting the pig,' but I doubt they have any idea what that really means." I agreed with Doug.

"How are they going to learn anything about political issues if we don't talk to them?" Brent argued. "And if there's no opportunity to do any actions, they'll never think through the implications."

The conversation carried on late into the night until Doug and I eventually capitulated, to a degree. We agreed to invite Julie to participate in the next Amax action. But Brent agreed to isolate her involvement to Amax and for the time being not to discuss our future plans with her or Gerry.

At the next El Salvador meeting Brent mentioned to Julie the possibility of doing a small Amax action in Vancouver, and she responded with unqualified enthusiasm. We decided that she and I would do the casing for the action. Since Amax was on the third floor of a small office building, we would have to visit their offices several times to see when the employees left for the day.

Late one Friday afternoon Julie dropped over to our house so that we could prepare for our expedition. She brought a suitcase full of clothes and makeup. I soon discovered that she considered herself an expert at camouflage. I was impressed with the level of thought she had given to this mission, and I readily gave up control over decisions related to our disguises. She explained that we should look like secretaries if we were going to hang around the offices, so that no one would find our presence there suspicious. The clothes she had for me were from her sister's wardrobe. Unfortunately her sister was about a foot shorter than me, so what should have been a knee-length skirt became a miniskirt on me. A beautiful silk blouse that would have fit her sister loosely became a skin-tight body shirt compressing my breasts upwards and outwards so that the first and only thing anyone looking at me would see was my cleavage. Since I didn't own a bra, Julie suggested that I wear her sister's, which only accentuated what was already overexposed.

I knew that Julie was doing a much better job at dressing us than I could have, but even she was somewhat out of touch with normal secretarial garb. Her fashion experience had come more in the realm of punk leathers, garish makeup, and transforming Sally Ann clothes into in-your-face punk fashion. So when she took on this task, her experience couldn't help but influence the finished product. Instead of a subtle pink lipstick hue, we sported bright red lip gloss that I suspected would glow in the dark. The black mascara encircling our eyes probably made us more attractive to males of the raccoon species than those of the human. To make matters worse, I never wore mascara so I found it impossible to avoid rubbing my eyes and smearing the black goo all over my face. In the end we went tottering out of the house in our high heels, looking less like secretaries than we normally did in our respective punk and hippie garb.

The first judgement on our disguises came as we carefully sauntered down the sidewalk. A couple of construction workers repairing a roof across the road yelled at us, "Slum sluts!" Not to be deterred, Julie shrugged off their insults by thrusting a finger at them and whispering to me that those guys would mistake any secretaries in this end of town for hookers.

All the way downtown on the buses, people stared at us. Julie seemed oblivious to them and remained proud of her handiwork. I didn't dare tell her how embarrassed I was that all those eyes were focusing on my cleavage. By the time we got to the office building, my feet had swollen up so much inside the high heels that I couldn't have got them off without a pair of garden shears. In the elevator a couple of businessmen snickered at each other when they thought we weren't looking — they might have been wondering whom we were servicing on their floor. Despite Julie's good intentions, our disguises served a purpose opposite to that intended. Few people in the Amax offices could forget the day when two prostitutes came up to their floor.

Still, we did manage to learn that on Friday afternoons workers disappeared like clockwork by 5:00 p.m., and a week later five of us sprang into action. As usual one of us stayed in the car as the getaway driver while the rest of us went up to the office. One person, acting as a lookout, hung around the stairwell where she could also observe the elevator. Another stood within view of the lookout to pass along word of any intruders. The remaining two of us began spraying "Amax Kills," "Fight for Survival," and "Resist Corporate Greed" in huge bold strokes all over the office walls. The bright red paint dripped eerily down the white office walls, leaving the ominous impression that there was more to come.

On our way out of the building we stopped and taped a communiqué inside a newspaper box. Then we stopped a safe distance from the action to call the daily newspaper to let them know where we had stashed the communiqué. Just in case someone else got the message before a reporter did, we made their work easy for them by reading it over the phone. "*Amax was attacked by persons outraged over the company's molybdenum mine in northwestern B.C., where at least 90 million tonnes of toxic mine tailings will be dumped into Alice Arm . . .*"

The next morning a short article and a photograph of the painted slogans appeared in the newspaper, claiming that "yahoos" had been responsible for the attack.

"Do you think they got the symbolism of the red paint"? Bridget wondered.

"Oh yeah," Brent said. "They didn't write much, but it'll keep the issue alive a bit longer. Maybe some of the environmentalists around town will do something to help the Nishga out."

Julie had spent the night at our place. From what I could tell, she had thoroughly enjoyed the action. "We should do another one! There's no way they should be allowed to get away with that shit!"

Doug looked up from his book at her and raised an eyebrow sceptically. "What do you mean?"

"I'd love to go to Victoria and do something they can't ignore. But this time I think we should hit the Ministry of the Environment and expose them — show they aren't doing anything to protect the environment in Alice Arm. Plus it would be fun."

"That's a good idea." Brent seemed to be cultivating Julie as his protegé.

I must admit that some of the appeal of doing these actions was the sheer excitement of it all. For a group of young people, going to political meetings, writing pamphlets, organizing rallies, and writing letters could get boring. Although we were genuinely concerned about the pollution caused by the toxic mine tailings and the fate of the Nishga Indians, we enjoyed advertising their plight through these trashings more so than through the traditional pamphlet-distribution and letter-writing campaigns. We also liked the immediate results. We felt like we were really doing something ourselves as opposed to appealing to the government to change the laws. In fact, we were opposed to the whole proposition of appealing to the government because we saw it as part of the problem. From our perspective, it was the government that was facilitating the actions of the Amax mine. We believed that the interests of the government and Amax were one and the same: to make greater profits for the mine and thus provide a greater tax chunk for the government. The Nishga's interests did not fit into this equation. We believed the government saw them as just another tax burden, contributing nothing to the economy.

Trashing gave us a sense of power. We were acting directly against "the enemy" in such a way that we could not be ignored. For someone like Julie, who was bright and wanted answers, these actions fulfilled her needs. We were educating ourselves around the issue and talking about it until we were well aware of the facts, and then we were doing something about it . . . now. It was fun. It was exciting. We were standing up against the powerful in society to protect the weak.

We didn't know any Nishga personally and had never tried to find out how they would like their predicament handled, so we didn't know if they appreciated our "actions." And we felt we didn't have the time to educate and change society and wait for large numbers of people to agree with us. But even though we weren't Nishga, we identified with them as victims of society's values. We too were poor, albeit out of choice. We too hated the unrestricted polluting of the natural world, which we likened to the rape and pillage of the land. In this respect, we identified with the Nishga and thus felt justified in acting on their behalf.

We soon came to a consensus around another Amax action. Doug wasn't interested. He was more focused on our long-term plans and spent much of his time learning more about dynamite, guns, and timing devices. He wasn't a social creature and didn't enjoy spending time getting to know more people, which the rest of us believed was a prerequisite to building a larger group of militants. So he wasn't with us when, early on the morning of May 10, 1981, six of us piled into Julie's bright red sedan for an overnight camping trip to somewhere near Victoria on Vancouver Island.

We were in great spirits, looking forward to the trip as more of a social occasion than a serious political action. In preparation we had spent the previous day on a shoplifting spree, picking up tents, sleeping bags, and food. If there were any questions about Julie's nerve in regards to carrying out small illegal actions, they were soon dispelled. She proved to be a bold shoplifter who had honed her skills for years before making our acquaintance. She enjoyed shoplifting to the point of being compulsive. I remember many situations when we had to remind her not to shoplift when we were already involved in a more serious illegal activity. Both Brent and Julie found it difficult to pass up any five-finger discounts.

On the ferry we headed for the upper decks for the one-and-a-half-hour ride. That day is still memorable for the beauty of the May sunshine bouncing off the waves as we cut a swath through the Strait of Georgia heading for the Island. Accompanying us all the way across was a flock of sea gulls diving in and out of the wake, picking up garbage that the ferry unloaded from its canteen. About an hour into the ride a school of black and white killer whales suddenly appeared from the depths, arching in and out of the water around the ferry. We were all out on deck, leaning over the rails to catch the spectacle of the whales performing for us. It appeared to me as though the whales thought of the ferry as some arthritic comrade who couldn't keep up with them or perform their tricks. They breached the sea, blowing water in the air and apparently mocking the inability of the ferry to do anything other than swim a straight line. They accompanied us until we could see the outline of the small island town of Nanaimo on the horizon. Then, as suddenly as they had arrived, they turned and disappeared into the depths from which they had come.

After getting off the ferry we drove towards Victoria, looking for a park where we could camp for the night. Goldstream Provincial Park was not far from the wealthy Victoria suburb of Oak Bay, where Brent had grown up. His parents still lived there, but we decided not to pay them a visit. His father was a professor of education at the University of Victoria and his mother had been an English professor but had left that position to sell real estate. After graduating from high school with above-average marks, Brent had enrolled in the University of Victoria but had quit after one semester to travel to California. He was more interested in "the university of life, majoring in modern guerrilla groups," than he was in the more traditional university fare. His parents were not proud of their son's chosen lifestyle and remained on bad terms with him.

After pitching our newly acquired top-of-the-line tents, we lit a small campfire and sat around talking late into the night on rotting cedar logs that gave off a woody perfume in the moist temperate climate of the rain forest. On the west coast of Canada, the moisture-laden winds blowing off the Pacific Ocean drop their rainy burden as they rise through the cool mountain air of Vancouver Island and the Rockies. This climatic phenomenon results in near-rain-forest vegetation. The smoke from our fire wafted through the dense canopy of Douglas fir, hemlock, and cedar boughs above us.

The next morning we got up early and drove into Victoria. We didn't actually have a plan, so we were improvising as we went. After reconnoitering the Ministry of the Environment in Victoria, we drove downtown to see what we could find to use in our action. Brent ran across some signal flares in a boat store and "liberated" them. Over coffee in a downtown restaurant, we decided to keep it simple, using our signature jars of red paint but, in this case, also dramatizing the action with the signal flares. We returned to our campsite and spent the rest of the afternoon preparing for the action.

The provincial Environment Ministry was in a one-storey building in a desolate area on the outskirts of Victoria, so we didn't have to worry about witnesses. Around two in the morning we cruised slowly by the building, scanning the area for activity. "Maybe somebody should get out and throw stones against the window to see if there's a security guard inside," Julie suggested. I thought this was a good idea. We pulled over into a parking lot, letting Brent out to check the building. While he crept across the lawn into the bushes, we stayed in the car and put on our latex gloves and toques. From where we were sitting we couldn't see the front windows of the building, but we could see Brent kneeling in the bushes not far from the front. He threw some pebbles against the window, which would presumably cause a reaction inside if there was a security guard, but after about ten minutes the building remained dark and lifeless. He came back to the car and we went into action.

Julie stayed behind the wheel, ready to drive off the second we returned. Racing across the front lawn of the building, we threw a volley of large rocks against five ground-floor plate-glass windows. Instead of causing the glass to rain down in a million noisy pieces, the rocks left a series of neat gaping holes in the centres of the windows. Perhaps it was some kind of shatterproof glass. Two of us carefully took aim and threw our jars of red paint through one of the holes. Unfortunately, the room was very large and so the jars didn't hit a wall and smash but landed on the carpeted floor and rolled harmlessly off in different directions. It was difficult under the circumstances to get enough velocity for the jars to reach the walls because we had to take such careful aim just to get the jars through the hole. If it hadn't been for the flares, the action would have been a failure. But the flares turned the event into a front-page spectacle that surprised even us. As we lit each flare and threw them one by one through the hole, they began to sizzle like sparklers on firecracker day, then suddenly shot bright red flames off into all kinds of crazy directions, until they finally fizzled to the floor, billowing clouds of red smoke in their dying moments. In seconds the large open office space of the Ministry of the Environment was filled with thick red smoke from which crimson flames shot up periodically. It was like a huge "little red schoolhouse firecracker" display, and it would have burnt the building to the ground if not for an efficient sprinkler system that went into effect seconds after the flares landed. Throughout the room, huge circles of water spun from the sprinkler jets in the ceiling. We were so mesmerized by what was going on that we remained frozen to the spot until Julie snapped us out of our spell by beeping her horn. We raced to the car. As we sped off towards downtown Victoria, I looked back through the rear window and noticed that one of our group had spray-painted "AMAX KILLS — GOVERNMENT APPROVED" in huge black and red letters on the building wall, leaving no uncertainty as to the motive for the action.

"That was amazing!" gasped Julie. "Will it burn the building down?"

"I hope not," I said. Our group wasn't yet prepared for anything like that, and both Brent and I, at least, knew it. If all we did was break a window and spread some red paint around and a few flares caused some smoke damage, the cops wouldn't be motivated to spend a lot of time and money catching us. But if the building burned down, the cops would come under a good deal of pressure to track us down. Our group wasn't yet prepared for a full-scale detective pursuit.

We drove back to the campsite quietly immersed in our own thoughts, mulling over the gravity of our situation. New fears had definitely put a damper on our initial excitement over the night's events. Back at the campsite, we lit a small fire and sat around going over our next course of action.

"I don't think we can make any decisions until we read the papers in the morning and find out how much damage we did," Brent said, poking at the embers. "If we burned the building, we might want to stay a few days until the heat dies down. If not, we could leave in the morning."

"Are we going to claim this action?" Julie asked.

"Oh yeah," said Brent emphatically. "But let's see what happened first."

We woke up the next morning at the first sound of fellow campers lighting their fires and making breakfast. In the midst of an atmosphere of early morning bird calls, fires crackling, and the smell of smoky bacon wafting through the air, it was hard to imagine that anything bad could happen to us that day. We dressed quickly, piled into the car, and headed into Victoria to pick up the morning paper. Sure enough, on the front page was an article about the damage done to the Ministry of the Environment building. Apparently there was only smoke and water damage and a few burns in the carpet. There was no mention of the jars of red paint, although we were quite sure that the cops would have taken note of those clues.

After a discussion in the car, we decided to go to the university and use a typewriter in the library to make up a communiqué. After mailing it to the media outlets in Victoria and Vancouver, we would take the ferry back to Vancouver that evening.

As we went about the tasks at hand, I noticed that Julie's mood had changed dramatically. Before the action she had been bubbly, talkative, and eager. Now she was sullen. I asked if she'd had second thoughts about participating in this action, but she brushed off my concerns and explained that she was just tired and worried about her dog, Rex, who was alone in her sister's apartment. I had the feeling she hadn't considered the possibility that anything could go wrong or that she could go to prison. It dawned on me that she had put all her faith and confidence in Brent and me, believing we would protect her from anything bad. I think she still had a child-like attitude towards us as being almost like parents who were all-knowing and all-seeing. I told myself that the next time I was alone with her, I would have a talk with her about personal responsibility and put the idea in her head that Brent and I were not immune to making mistakes, and as a result she would have to think things through herself to be sure she was prepared for the worst. If we were caught the authorities wouldn't treat us as kids carrying out fun little pranks, but as adults who had committed serious crimes, with prison time as a consequence.

We caught the six o'clock ferry back to Vancouver. By the time we had settled down on the viewing deck, we felt relaxed about the action. We hadn't left fingerprints, and we were confident that no one had witnessed anything. I kept my eye on Julie, and when she took a seat by the window I went over to sit beside her. "So how did you like it?"

She didn't turn to look at me, but continued gazing out at the water. "It was great," she said without a lot of emotion.

"Are you worried about getting caught?"

"No. I'm just tired and I miss Gerry and Rex. I wish Gerry could have come, but he's not into this kind of stuff. He wants to quit the band and move up into the Chilcotins and build a cabin," she said quietly. "I'm not ready to settle down, and I really do want to do political shit to stop the pigs from totally destroying the earth."

"Well, that's great," I said in a consoling tone of voice. "But I just hope you realize that Brent and I do make mistakes. I'm just a little concerned that you look up to us too much."

She immediately took offence and snapped, "I think for myself, you know. I don't look up to anyone blindly. I know what I'm doing." Turning back to the window, she continued staring across the water.

"I didn't mean to insult you, but you just seemed awfully quiet once you realized that we might have burned the building down."

"Well, we should have thought of that," she said, still not looking at me. "It's my fault too for not thinking that the flares would obviously start a fire. It was just stupid. But next time, I'm going to make my opinions more clear."

I had not intended my heart-to-heart conversation to turn into a confrontation, and I had not anticipated that she would take my concerns defensively. I became aware that Julie's perceptions of herself, as a strong woman with independent views, were in sharp contrast to mine of her as an innocent young woman easily influenced by others.

The rest of our trip back to Vancouver was uneventful. In the next day or two our communiqués reached their destinations and were mentioned in small articles in the back section of Vancouver's two daily papers, *The Province* and *The Sun*. Even though we did not connect the three Amax actions through the use of a name for our little group, the papers did this for us by again labelling us "yahoos," a description we found demeaning. We didn't expect the authorities to like us, but we did want to be respected and taken seriously, and the term "yahoo" definitely did not fill that bill.

✳ 8 ✳

The one thing we were lacking was a vehicle. We could borrow Angie's, but she lived in a different house and worked on different projects than the people in our house. We could rent cars for shopping expeditions, but travelling out of town was a problem.

Ever since the publication of Hydro's *Blueprint 1980*, grassroots groups had been forming all over British Columbia to organize opposition to the various megaprojects outlined in it. One such group was the Hat Creek Alliance, which was organizing a Survival Gathering in the summer. It was an event we wanted to attend. The Hat Creek Alliance was a loosely knit coalition of residents and Native people from northeastern British Columbia in the area surrounding the Hat Creek watershed, where Hydro planned to build a $5 billion coal-fired hydro-generation plant. The coal would be strip-mined from open coal pits, then transported by conveyor systems for transportation to the power plant.

Everyone from our house wanted to go, but we didn't have access to enough vehicles to transport us all, which would mean travelling by bus. Besides this, there were many times I found life inconvenient without a car. Unfortunately, living off welfare did not leave me with any extra money at the end of the month for buying one, so I started thinking. One by-product of living a lifestyle of illegality was my newfound criminal mindset. Combining that with regular discussions about the technicalities of crime led me to think of robbing a place to get the money for a vehicle. I couldn't do this by myself, so I mentioned my idea to Doug and Brent in one of our nightly Bino's meetings.

"We need a vehicle and I'd like to buy one," I began.

"That's a good idea," agreed Brent.

"The only obstacle is money. I'd like to do a robbery," I said.

"What?" said Brent incredulously.

"You heard me. I want to do a robbery."

A long spell of silence followed while Brent and Doug mulled over this idea. "The idea of doing a robbery appeals to me," Doug said. "But I really don't need the money that bad. I'm sure I'm going to have to do some robberies eventually if we're going to carry out our plans, but I'm not going to rush into one now."

Brent also decided to pass on the idea. He was notoriously thrifty and didn't particularly need money. He was the only person I've ever met capable of saving large amounts of money while collecting welfare.

During this period we had included in our Amax actions a number of people who were interested in militant actions but drew the line at moves that could potentially result in substantial prison time. One of these people was a young man named Hector, who moved into our house in the spring of 1981. We had known him for a while and he had often complained about his lack of money and indicated his interest in robberies. The frequency of these conversations increased after he was cut off welfare. I had never taken Hector all that seriously, but now that I knew Doug and Brent were out of the question for a robbery, all his comments came to mind.

"How would you feel if I approached Hector?" I asked sheepishly. I figured they would immediately veto the idea because we had never included Hector in any of our serious guerrilla discussions. "I think he'd be better than Julie and Gerry to work with on something serious. Actually this would be a perfect opportunity to work with him more to see if he would be interested in political stuff beyond trashing."

Once again there was a long silence while they digested this idea. "If you do a robbery, it's not a political action that would affect us," Doug said. "So I think it's your decision. If you trust him enough to put your life in his hands, go for it." Brent nodded in agreement.

"If you do a robbery, you'll need to steal a couple of getaway vehicles," said Doug, always the pragmatist. "I don't want to know anything about this robbery or be a party to it, but this would be an opportune time to test our knowledge of all that stuff we've been learning from those books." He was referring to *In the Steal of the Night*, an obscure pamphlet we had ordered from *Soldier of Fortune*. Although the pamphlet was advertised as intended for repossession experts who had to recover vehicles that people had forfeited payments on, many people ordered them for less legitimate purposes.

Reflecting our middle-class backgrounds, Doug, Brent, and I used books and libraries as resources for learning criminal skills — as opposed to the real-life resources of other criminals. With so much to learn, we had decided to focus on the various skills required to be effective urban guerrillas. Doug had completed a three-year science degree, majoring in math and physics at UBC (with a first-class average), so he specialized in areas requiring a knowledge of electronics. He also studied explosives. Brent specialized in robberies, break-ins, and the acquisition of sensitive information, and I took on the task of learning how to steal cars and pick locks.

Before discovering *In the Steal of the Night*, I had gotten the idea of hot-wiring cars from watching television crime dramas, and I went to the library to study wiring diagrams of the various car manufacturers. I discovered that recent car models had locking steering columns that prevented thieves from driving off with the stolen car even if they could get it running by connecting the wires under the hood or dashboard and circumventing the ignition. Since any car we stole would be used in the course of a serious political action, we didn't want to be driving an older and less reliable model.

Always one step ahead of the anti-theft devices designed by the car manufacturers, thieves would pull out the steering column ignition, which in turn would break the steering column lock. There were two ways of doing this. The method used by most criminals was to buy an ignition puller, or slammer, a device you screw into the ignition lock. Then you slam a metal block against the puller's handle until the ignition is forced out of its housing. This technique is loud and unpredictable. Sometimes the puller would just break the tumblers in the lock.

The other method, which we got from *In the Steal of the Night*, was quiet and appeared more dependable. This involved ordering "fingers," small metal rods specially designed so you could insert them into the ignition cylinder. Then, by turning a bolt, you could, using leverage, slowly pull out the ignition and break the steering column lock. We had ordered the fingers and practised using them on ignitions we bought from a car wreckers, but we had never actually used them "in the field."

We decided it was premature to get Hector involved in learning our car theft skills, but since I was determined to do a robbery Brent and Doug would help steal the cars. After that they would drop out of the picture, leaving Hector and me to use them in our robbery.

Before heading out to steal a car, we decided to look for a common vehicle to decrease the odds of being pulled over by the police. Brent learned that about fifteen cars were being stolen in Vancouver and its suburbs every night. With an average of one hundred stolen cars per week, it was unlikely that the police would have the time or memory to check every car they passed that fit the description of a car reported stolen two or three weeks earlier. We decided to look for a neutral-coloured Pinto, the most common car on the road in 1981, and then we'd park it on side streets for a few weeks before driving it around. We would have to move it from street to street periodically to minimize the possibility of neighbours reporting a suspicious car parked for days in their neighbourhood.

Finally we were ready to test our skills. We borrowed a car and began our night when everyone else was asleep, around 2:00 a.m., cruising around the residential downtown neighbourhoods. At that time a large number of low-rise apartment buildings had small underground parking lots without locking garage doors or security. We decided these would be ideal locations, because we could leave a lookout just outside the parking lot, and once we were inside no one would see us.

Since we had a particular car and location in mind, it took a long time to find what we were looking for, but finally we did — a white Pinto in an underground parking lot. Doug was crouched down in some bushes outside while Brent and I were inside. The whole atmosphere was spooky and conjured up images from a number of horror movies. In my overactive imagination, underground parking lots at night are more often associated with stalking and murder scenes than with convenient places to park a car. I felt less like a fearless criminal predator than the potential victim of some violent property owner. I knew from reading the newspaper that victims of property crime could assume heroic personalities when confronting the perpetrator of a crime against their property. Most people are willing to risk their life for $50 in the till of their store. I was sure they'd do no less to rescue their old Pinto from the hands of some evil car thieves.

Brent and I quickly jogged over to the Pinto parked in the shadows of the dimly lit parking lot. The sounds of our feet padding on the cement and even our breathing were amplified by the echoing effect of the cement walls. To make matters worse, our ears were more finely attuned to sound than normal, because the only contact we had arranged with Doug, our lookout, was a whistling signal. Once we reached the car I pulled out the Slim Jim, another criminal tool, used to open the car door lock. The Slim Jim is basically a metal ruler with a hook on the end that slides down between the glass window and the car door panelling. Once it's in there, you pry around until you hit a lever connecting the door handle to the locking mechanism. It's a quiet operation, but because of the echoing acoustics underground it seemed loud to us. As I poked around with the Slim Jim, Brent focused on the stairwell leading to the apartments above and listened for Doug's warning whistle from outside. Within a few seconds I heard a loud click and the door button popped up.

I grinned at Brent and opened the door. Once inside the car, I set about the task of inserting the fingers into a ridge around the ignition, a task made infinitely more difficult by the latex gloves I was wearing. Unfortunately, the fingers are so small and delicate that they require a steady hand to use properly. In practice sessions at home they were easier to use because there was plenty of light and my hands weren't shaking violently. Now I kept dropping them on the car floor and found it difficult to insert them in the dim light of the parking lot. I vowed that when this was over I would figure out a less intricate method of extracting an ignition.

Finally the fingers were in. I took my wrench and turned the bolt that applied opposing pressure against the steering column and ignition until I heard the sound of metal cracking. Out came the ignition! But I had no time to celebrate — at that exact split second the ear-shattering blast of a horn filled the parking lot — amplified as the sound resonated and bounced back and forth off the concrete walls and floor of our huge cement cell. An anti-theft car alarm!!

I didn't bother trying to recover the little metal fingers. We just ran out of the parking lot. Doug was still faithfully kneeling in the bushes, and as soon as he saw us we all ran down the block to our car. There was no point walking: at three in the morning we were the only people on the street and thus the only suspects related to the resounding car alarm that could be heard for blocks. As we drove off we decided to take the rest of the night off and try again some other time.

"I left the finger thing in the car!" I gasped as we drove slowly towards home.

"Did you get the Slim Jim?" asked Brent.

"Yeah. I didn't like those fingers anyway."

"Thank God we didn't leave any prints," sighed Brent.

It was a bad start to our experience in car theft, but in the end it forced us to invent a better ignition-extraction method. Brent took the principles that the finger device was based upon and invented his own tool. It was simple but ingenious. Over the next few days he busied himself exploring hardware stores and found that a self-tapping metal screw could be turned into the tumblers of the ignition keyway. Then a metal cylinder attached to the screw would press against the steering column, forcing the ignition out as the screw was turned deeper into the keyway.

A few nights later we headed out again, looking for another Pinto. Unfortunately, unless the owner put a warning sticker on the windshield, we had no way of knowing in advance if a car had an anti-theft device. Again we toured the underground parking lots and found another Pinto, again a white one. Even though I felt even more paranoid the second time around, this car did not have an anti-theft alarm and everything went smoothly. As soon as I had the ignition out, I inserted a screwdriver in the hole where the ignition had been and turned on the car. It roared to a start in the cavernous underground. Brent jumped in beside me. It was still too early to smile, but we turned on the headlights and cruised slowly up the ramp to the outdoors. As we passed Doug, our head-lights caught his face beaming in the bushes. He walked quickly down the block to our parked car and followed us towards the neighbourhood we had designated as the place to leave the "hot car" for a few days until its description as a stolen vehicle was less prominent in the minds of the Vancouver police.

A few days later I took a bus to the neighbourhood and walked casually down the residential street with the goal of moving the car to a different area. I wasn't wearing the "disguise" Julie had devised for our Amax casing but I had made a point of dressing in nondescript clothes so no one would remember seeing me if the car was ever found. As I walked towards the place we had parked it I craned my neck in anticipation — and yes, it was still there.

I walked past the car once, glancing around to see if it was staked out. This idea was totally paranoid, because cops don't have the time to stake out every stolen vehicle they find, unless, maybe, they find one used in the commission of a serious crime. But I was still new at this work and I tended to err on the side of caution. I walked once around the block planning out how I'd get in and start the car without arousing suspicion. It was a hot summer day, so the gloves that I'd have to use to open the door to avoid leaving fingerprints might draw attention. As I got up to the car, I looked around with my eyes, trying not to move my head too much. I took a glove in the palm of my hand and opened the car door without making skin contact. Once inside, I put on my gloves, stuck a screwdriver into the gutted ignition and turned it on. The car sprang to life. For a few seconds I let it idle while I surveyed the area for nosy neighbours. With none in sight, I stepped on the gas and drove off towards the area we had decided to leave it in next.

We figured that a cop probably wouldn't pull me over as long as I wasn't violating any traffic rules. I had driven a few miles when it occurred to me to check the fuel gauge. Sure enough, it was almost on empty. Damn! I started looking around for a self-serve. When I found one I realized the gloves might draw unwanted attention on a hot, sunny day. I parked beside the pump and put the glove in my palm again and opened the door. As I stepped out, a car pulled in beside me. I had to open the lid to the fuel tank before I could put the gas in, which meant using the glove again. The guy in the car beside me looked over and I smiled at him as attractively as I could, figuring my smile might distract him from noticing the glove in my hand. It did. He smiled back. I put the gas nozzle in the tank and filled it up, all the while smiling moronically at him. As soon as he went up to pay for his gas, I quickly started the car with the screwdriver and drove off.

✳ **9** ✳

I n the short time since Hector had moved into our house, we had become good friends. He was a dedicated environmentalist with an impressive academic background. Like Doug, he had majored in math and physics at UBC, but had difficulty resolving the contradiction between the prevailing environmental philosophy of the scientific community and his own more radical views. Hector did not want to use science and technology to alter the environment to make it more profitable for humankind if this meant harming nature in any way.

The similarities between Hector and Doug were uncanny. Besides sharing degrees in math and physics, both were solitary individuals, thriving on self-imposed routines. If the world could be one giant equation with predictable outcomes following the laws of mathematics, they would have been a lot more comfortable. However, people, like life, are a combination of paradox and reason, chaos and order. Underlying Doug's and Hector's attempts to impose order on their lives were two emotionally intense characters fighting to escape from those very same restrictions. I think that's why they were attracted to people who could draw them out of their own intellectual prisons. Both men had an affinity with Brent, who went to great pains to involve them in wild, spontaneous events.

We moved the Pinto around for a few weeks before Brent and Doug dropped out and I brought Hector into the plan. Now that we had a getaway vehicle, the reality of doing a robbery kicked in. We began to lay down our plans with great excitement, analysing every aspect of the future robbery as though it were a topic for a doctoral thesis.

We decided it was paramount that nobody know about our plans other than the two of us. We also wanted to eliminate risk and avoid anyone getting hurt, as much as possible under the circumstances. That ruled out banks, because they had the most security and the fastest police response time and were usually located in heavy traffic areas. After analysing countless possibilities, we decided "the take" from a Cineplex theatre would probably have the most money for the least risk. A Cineplex on a Saturday would have a couple of matinees plus evening showings of several movies. All the moviegoers paid cash, and a lot of them also bought popcorn and drinks, again with cash. Our decision was made easier when a friend innocently let slip that the Cineplex where she had once worked counted the money at the end of the night after all the moviegoers had left, and then walked with it to a local bank deposit box.

After dissecting every aspect of the potential robbery, we realized that the most likely cause of anyone getting hurt would be desperation or heroism on the part of "the victim." We were confident that we could control ourselves. We decided that to prevent chaos at the scene our instructions had to be absolutely clear and concise, leaving no doubt in the victim's mind that we were serious but that no harm would come to them if they obeyed us. We decided that we would carry, and show, a gun: that would deter any heroics such as fighting back. Our gun would also deter the victim from entertaining thoughts of escape, which could result in unpredictable actions and make the situation much more dangerous for all involved. If the victim did decide to be a hero, we planned to abort the robbery and do whatever we had to do to get away, short of killing anyone. It certainly wasn't worth killing anyone over a sum of money.

After laying the ground rules, we began casing the few Cineplexes in the Greater Vancouver area. We reasoned that our possibilities for a successful robbery without injuries to anyone were fairly high compared to those of the average criminal because we were taking the time to thoroughly case the various target locations and we had enough money to get by on indefinitely. Most robberies are committed by desperate people who act quickly without thorough planning. They don't have control over themselves or the situation, so the whole event becomes completely unpredictable.

* * *

Although my initial motive for doing a robbery was to buy a van to go to the Hat Creek Survival Gathering, it didn't look as if we could carry off the theft in time. The van I had in mind belonged to Alah, a big blond man of Lithuanian descent who did a lot of work for various environmental causes. Luckily, Alah wanted to go to the Gathering, so on a Friday morning in early July 1981 everyone from our house except Doug piled into the van and headed up the Trans-Canada Highway towards the Hat Creek Valley, two hundred kilometres northeast of Vancouver, near the town of Ashcroft.

The first part of the trip was a beautiful drive along the Fraser River, which flows from the mountains, creating a vast flat flood plain before it reaches the ocean. After speeding north along this straight stretch of highway for a couple of hours, we began a winding journey following the Fraser River into the mountains. As we headed into the mountains, the serene nature of the river changed to a violent whitewater, surging through the rocky chasms it had formed in the sides of the mountains. Alah's mood changed just as dramatically as the river when the driving became quite treacherous once we reached the mountains. The highway, blasted into the sides of the Fraser River canyon, hung perilously close over the jagged rocks and white foam of the churning river below. After another hour we veered off the Trans-Canada and took another route heading into the B.C. interior, where the landscape was much drier and the mountains were worn down into large hills. The climate in this area was desert-like because most of the moisture that the winds had picked up on their journey across the Pacific had been dropped on the west side of the mountains. By the time the winds reached central British Columbia they tended to be dry, picking up moisture instead of dropping it.

Alah relaxed as he drove along the twisting highway surrounded by sandy hills dotted with rocks and coniferous trees. Here and there we even spotted tumbleweed rolling across the barren landscape. The relaxed atmosphere was much more conducive to conversation than the earlier part of the drive.

"You know what's going to bug me about this gathering?" Brent said to no one in particular. "There's going to be all these little groups fighting to protect their own interests. There'll probably be some people here from the Cheekeye-Dunsmuir Alliance, Indians from the Cache Creek and Lillooet bands, white environmentalists from Vancouver — that's us — and maybe some people from up north who are fighting against the Site C or the Stikine-Iskut dams. They'll all be united against B.C. Hydro as the one common enemy, but I don't know if anyone is going to present the bigger picture."

"What do you mean?" asked Alah.

"Well, the problem with Canadian radicals is they don't have a revolutionary analysis, so they organize around one issue after another instead of putting their particular issue into a national and international perspective," Brent said. He went on to talk about how people on the left would be further ahead if all the different groups were organized and fought against a common enemy instead of each group fighting their own battle in isolation from the others. At that time people across the country were organizing to fight against megaprojects planned by provincial governments and companies. People in Ontario, for instance, were organizing against the construction of a nuclear power plant at Darlington, a half-hour drive east of Toronto; and people in Quebec had been organizing against the James Bay hydroelectric project for the past half-decade or so. But, Brent argued, "There's no national continuity, no connected analysis or practice by these separate groups. We'd be a lot more effective in Hat Creek if, for example, we were linked up with people in Ontario and Quebec."

For Brent, and the rest of us too, it all went back to Canada's historical economy based largely on the export of natural resources. The job of the various provincial governments had always been to make it possible for the private sector to extract natural resources, and one of the ways the government did this was by providing the infrastructure — the electricity, roads, bridges, water, all the things the companies needed to actually cut down the trees and mine the minerals. That infrastructure sometimes intruded on the life of the average person. For example, dams would destroy the natural habitat that the Native people depended on for their traditional lifestyle of hunting and fishing. Some of the megaprojects of the various provincial utilities would destroy the agricultural land of the farmers or alter the flow of a river that a town was dependent on.

Alah nodded. "Yeah, I guess all across Canada the Indians, the environmentalists, and other interest groups basically want the same thing: more direct public accountability and control over the decision-making involved in planning these megaprojects."

As a group I think we all believed that it was our job as a radical contingent at meetings like this gathering to inject a more national strategy into the grassroots movements against B.C. Hydro.

The talk in the van went on — at times with all of us, it seemed, trying to make our points at once — until Bridget noticed a little cardboard sign saying "Hat Creek Gathering" stapled to a post. A big black arrow pointed to a dirt road winding away from the highway. Alah slammed on the brakes and backed up to the road we had almost missed.

The discussions ended as we bumped noisily along the pot-holed road. After a few miles we followed another sign pointing to a trail better suited to all-terrain vehicles. Huge weeds grew in the median between two tire tracks. We drove slowly along the trail until we came upon long lines of decrepit cars and pickup trucks parked on both sides of the tracks. Obviously, the Gathering had not attracted a lot of high-income earners.

Stumbling out of our rusty old van, we put on our packsacks and carried our coolers down a hiking trail through the woods until we could hear voices and smell the smoke of campfires. The Gathering was situated in a clearing beside Hat Creek in a valley surrounded by high rolling hills, sparsely blanketed in coniferous trees, with huge boulders jutting out here and there. After breathing stale city air for so long, we found it instantly invigorating to fill our lungs with the moist valley air.

I dropped my pack on the ground and walked over to the creek. The area was truly breathtaking. Even though the region surrounding the Hat Creek was dry, during the past few millennia the fast-flowing river with the misnomer "creek" had cut a deep, lush valley through the soft hills. The dramatic drop in the elevation of the land caused the water to course rapidly around the rocks in the riverbed. It looked like a great place for whitewater rafting or kayaking.

I knelt down beside the racing current, cupping my hands so I could splash the cold mountain water on my parched skin. As I squatted on my heels enjoying the sensation of wind drying off my face, I noticed two people, a man and a woman, not far downstream and chatting quietly. I did a second take at the man because he looked awfully familiar, and it dawned on me that he was the cop who had stopped beside us that first day in British Columbia when Bridget's grocery cart full of laundry had toppled over. Shielding myself from their view by crouching behind the bushes along the riverbank, I shamelessly tried to eavesdrop on their conversation.

"Why were you assigned to something like this?" the woman was asking.

"Rose, it's my job," the man said, "to keep tabs on these groups. Some of the people in them don't abide by the laws of this country and they'll go to any lengths to get their way. They are anything but democratic."

"What about B.C. Hydro? I heard the woman — Rose — retort.

"They're far from democratic." They talked some more in lowered voices until finally I heard "Just be careful who you get involved with" as the man touched her shoulder before leaving to walk slowly back up the trail towards the camp.

With my legs numb from crouching, I got up, stretched, and climbed back up the bank. The people from our house were already busy setting up tents in the clearing. When I told them about my eavesdropping experience, nobody was particularly surprised. It was common knowledge that the police gathered intelligence at most demonstrations and open political gatherings.

Later that evening, after everyone had arrived and set up tents, we cooked our meals on little campfires and then gathered as one large group around a huge bonfire that had been built in the centre of the clearing. As darkness settled over the valley, the orange and yellow flames licking the sky lit up the faces of the sixty-odd people sitting there. I felt warm and cosy, listening to the logs bursting in the heat and sending streams of hot embers up into the black, starry sky. Around the perimeter of the campfire circle, little white points of light flashed on and off in random patterns, much like Doug's lightbulb invention, except these were fireflies. Between the laughter and murmur of pleasant conversation we could hear, off in the distance, the high, yippy sound of coyotes squabbling.

I looked around and tried to read the background of the faces around the fire. A young couple with little children sleeping in their laps sat across from me. He wore faded denim pants, a weathered Stetson, and dusty cowboy boots. His sunburnt face, etched with white lines from squinting into the sun, convinced me that he was a real cowboy, not some wannabe from the city. Beside them sat a stout old man with the same features and weather-beaten face. I guessed he was the cowboy's father. Next to them sat another couple with children who were playing dangerously close to the fire. Their father kept yelling at them, but they didn't seem to hear. He wore overalls and a plaid shirt. Both he and his wife sported matching ponytails tied neatly at the nape of their necks. She smiled serenely at her children, who ran to her every time his yelling reached a threatening level. I figured they were aging hippies who might have moved up here from the city years ago to "get back to the land." Then there was Rose, the woman I had overheard talking to the cop. With her peasant skirt and long hair she also looked like an aging hippie. I wasn't sure if the man beside her was her husband or not, because he was dressed much more conservatively, in clean khaki pants and a blue polo shirt. Even though they had been busy setting up a campsite, not a hair on his head was out of place and his fingernails looked manicured. I decided he was a perfectionist who probably had an office job in the city. My suspicions about their relationship were confirmed when he absent-mindedly brushed an ash off her skirt.

On the other side of the fire, in their own row, sat a small number of Native people, some wearing traditional clothing and others dressed more like ranchers, which they probably were. Even though the Indians talked across the fire to some of the local white people, the fact that they sat separately made me think they still felt like outsiders.

I tired of this solitary game after awhile. The warmth of the fire was like a sedative. Pretty soon I found myself dozing, and so I got up and stumbled through the darkness to our tent, where I instantly fell into a deep sleep.

The next morning after breakfast, the people from the Hat Creek Allicance gave a seminar for everyone in the clearing about B.C. Hydro's plans to build a coal-fired hydro-generation plant and the plans for open-pit coal mining in the Hat Creek Valley. Then we split up into clusters to hear about the effects these projects would have on local people such as Indians, ranchers, and townsfolk. Nick, Brent, and I joined one that would discuss the repercussions for Native people. After listening to the first seminar, I found it painful to imagine what this beautiful valley would look like once the strip-mining started. I looked up into the clear, blue sky and imagined a thick plume of smoke drifting across it from the future coal-fired hydro-generation plant. These plants were notorious for emitting the deadly chemical mix that fell on the earth as acid rain.

Although I found all the information useful and interesting, there was a disturbing pattern here that was repeated in all the critiques I'd read on future Hydro megaprojects. British Columbia could not justify building so many hydro-generation plants over the next ten years for its own consumption, so the logical conclusion was that the province intended to export the electricity for sale to the United States, much like the province of Quebec with its controversial James Bay Hydro Project.

As the afternoon came to an end, Brent struck up a conversation with the Native guy sitting beside him: a tall, muscular man in his forties named Couchee. He had long, scraggly black hair and a few teeth missing, and his skin had the leathery texture that only years of exposure to the sun and wind can produce. He was a man of few words but a lot of big smiles. Much to our surprise, he invited us to go with him for a first-hand look at his traditional fishing camp on the Thompson River.

I felt honoured to be invited to his fishing camp and padded along eagerly behind him to his dusty old pickup truck. Brent, Nick, and I squeezed into the cab and, instead of dominating the conversation in the way we were accustomed to doing with our environmentalist friends, sat in quiet reverence on the journey up the highway along the Thompson River. I had never known any Native people personally and, like so many white people on the left of the political spectrum, I tended to put Indians on a pedestal of spiritual wisdom and harmony with the Earth — a pedestal so high that very few Native people could stay on it for long. We were as guilty of romanticizing Native people as those on the right of the political spectrum were of demonizing them. It seems as though white people are incapable of seeing other races as real people like themselves but have to make them into cartoon characters who are either lazy drunks living off welfare or, on the flip side, spiritual gurus who can do no wrong. My later years of experience with Native people and others taught me that all people, regardless of their origins, are subject to the weaknesses and vices that come with being humans. Being born African, Asian, or Native American does not in itself impart a moral or spiritual superiority. But then I had not yet reached that awareness, and so I took in everything Couchee said as some deep spiritual truth. I hung on his every word. If he had told me to eat worms to gain inner peace, I would have gobbled them up immediately.

His fishing camp was a few miles up a dirt track off the highway that went along the turbulent river. His truck sped along the track in a cloud of dust. Every time we hit a deep pothole at sixty miles an hour, we became airborne and I was sure we would land in the white froth of the river only a few yards to the side of the track. Thankfully Couchee was familiar with both the road and the aerodynamics of his ancient truck. Finally we slowed down and drove towards a small group of plastic tents pitched on a dry, rocky hillside beside the river.

Couchee got out and walked over to one of the plastic tents, where an old woman was busy washing some dirty cups in a bucket on a picnic table. Since he didn't invite us to do anything, we just followed along behind him wherever he went, like three young dogs. It seemed as though a number of families had set up camp here, each living temporarily under a plastic sheet, with a picnic table, some cots, and crates holding their belongings. Not far from the plastic tents were row upon row of wooden drying racks with hundreds of dark pink salmon fillets, drying in the sun. While Couchee stood talking to the old woman, who we later learned was his mother, Nick, Brent, and I wandered amongst the salmon racks breathing in the scent of fish drying in the sun. I couldn't help wondering why we made our lives so complicated earning a living in the city, when all the food we needed was right here for the taking. Of course, I knew it was much more complicated than that, but it seemed to me that there was a point in human history when it hadn't been.

"Hey, come on over here," Couchee yelled from the plastic tent. In the few minutes we had been wandering around the dried salmon, his mother had laid out some food on the table for us. We sat down around the picnic table to eat a delicious spread of store-bought white bread, salmon-egg porridge, strips of dried salmon, and pop. I picked up a long strip of dried salmon and bit into it. I anticipated a leathery, dry texture, but the natural fish oils had kept the flesh succulent even after a long time of drying in the sun.

The plastic tents crackled as they flapped in the breeze blowing across the open hills. The desert-like climate was tempered by the mist blowing up off the rapids of the river just below the camp. The air was surprisingly comfortable, considering it was an exceptionally hot day with no trees to protect us from the unrelenting glare of the late afternoon sun.

We weren't the only ones enjoying salmon. Gliding above the river and occasionally dropping vertically from the sky was a group of bald eagles feasting on the salmon making their way up the perilous river. There were even a few bold eagles half running among the drying racks, scavenging pieces of salmon with their sharp beaks so they could fly off and eat in peace in one of the pine trees that had managed to take root in the sparse earth on the river-bank.

We sat quietly eating, watching the noisy spectacle unfolding around us. A few scruffy dogs of mixed breed amused themselves by trying to guard the drying salmon from the eagles. The eagles raced around the racks, half in flight, screeching viciously at the dogs pursuing them. The dogs barked angrily back, frustrated by these huge birds who could lift into the air just before their jaws could make their mark. It was an interesting dance between these two groups of predators, the eagles and the dogs. The eagles were the more formidable. The dogs, racing around yapping, baring their little white fangs, seemed no threat when one of these huge birds came diving down at them with its yellow hooked beak opened wide in a spine-tingling screech.

Off in the distance we heard a low rumbling. Couchee put down his bread and looked down the river canyon in the direction of the sound. A few seconds later, another predator from the sky arrived — a helicopter with its distinctive rhythmic pounding wings, flying low between the high rock cliffs on both sides of the river. As it approached, the little black dots standing beside the river, which were Native fishermen, quickly disappeared among the rocks.

Couchee explained that it was the Department of Fisheries doing their daily fly-by looking for people fishing. "It's illegal to fish while the salmon are spawning. We say it's our traditional right to fish this river, which our grandfathers have been doing since long before the white man ever arrived. A lot of people depend on the dried salmon for food in the winter."

"Why is it illegal?" I asked.

"The government is trying to blame traditional Indian fisher-men for the dwindling salmon stock," he said, bitterness in his voice. Then he turned to look at me with his tired dark eyes. "Have you ever seen the commercial salmon fishing boats around here? There's hundreds of them all up and down the B.C. coast hauling in thousands of salmon, processing them right on their boats." He explained how there was no comparison between the number of salmon being caught by the commercial fishing fleets and the number that his people were catching with their poles and a few nets along the rivers. "We also need the salmon to survive. In your food stores there are all kinds of fish and meat that people can buy to eat. If you visit the reserves in the winter, a lot of people have no money and subsist on salmon for much of the winter." He bit into a large piece of dried salmon on a hunk of white bread. I watched his jaw muscles knotting up as he chewed it.

I looked back down and saw a dark green Land Rover bar-relling along a dusty track towards the river. Just before it screeched to a stop on the edge of the riverbank, two men in dark green uniforms with rifles leaped out of the truck and raced towards an outcrop of boulders. Moments later, they came out from behind the boulders with a young Indian man wearing a bright red bandanna around his head. We couldn't hear what they were saying, but their actions told the story. One of the men in green carried a bucket he had no doubt found behind the boulders. They took out a pad and wrote something on paper and handed it to the young Indian man, who balled it up and stuffed it in his back pocket and walked away. Then the men got back in their truck and drove up the track to the highway above.

"Those are Department of Fisheries officers. They gave that guy a ticket for illegal fishing. He'll have to go to court and pay a fine," Couchee explained. "The guys in the helicopter pass by here every day and radio down to the guys in the truck when they see some Indian fisherman hiding. Then they boot down there and ticket him. It's a cat and mouse game. Most of the time they have a hard time catching us because we hear them coming and know where to hide. But they usually get lucky at least once a day, like you just witnessed. They won't be back anymore today. That's why a lot of us fish at night now. It's a lot more dangerous but safer in terms of not getting caught. I'm going down to do some fishing. Want to come along?"

Did we ever. He took a long pole with a leather-thonged net attached to the end of it and started walking down the hill towards the river. We walked along behind him. When we got down to the river, I was amazed at just how loud it was. We could barely hear each other talk over the noise of the river hurling itself against and around the huge boulders obstructing its path. Couchee walked down to a flat piece of earth right beside the black water. We stood back, knowing that if we accidentally slipped off that piece of earth we would be instantly sucked into the current and disappear downstream. He motioned for us to come closer, which we gingerly did. In a voice barely loud enough to be heard above the roar of the river, he asked if any of us wanted to fish. That exact spot, he said, had been used by his father, his grandfather, and many generations before him. His family knew that just beyond this spot in the water was a current that was like a highway for the salmon fighting their way upstream. If he put his net in that particular current, he knew that within minutes he would have a thirty-pound salmon flapping inside his net.

He also explained that he had let the occasional white person fish here, but he always tied them to the small cedar tree just behind him so that if they slipped or were thrown off balance by the thrust of the salmon in the net, they wouldn't be swept away by the current before he could rescue them. "If you fall in without this leash, you're never coming back," he said, tying a nylon cord to the tree.

Respectfully declining his offer, we sat back to watch him fish. He stood with his feet straddled wide apart for balance and placed his long pole into the water. Sure enough, we had barely relaxed when his arm muscles went taut like ropes in his effort to lift his pole back out. He leaned back on one leg, and in a powerful motion heaved the net out of the water and over his shoulder, flinging the chinook salmon, writhing for its life, onto the rocks behind him. I looked at the huge salmon flopping helplessly on the rocks. A part of me wanted to run over and throw it back into the water so it could continue on its spawning run. That fish had fought hard against the odds to reach this point, only to be scooped up in the net and then die a slow pitiful death on the rocks. Couchee put an end to these thoughts when he picked up a thick bough lying beside the salmon and clubbed it once on the head.

The three of us sat quietly for a few hours, until it was almost dark, watching Couchee haul in one salmon after another. Each time he mercifully clubbed them on the head before dumping them into a bucket. Finally he put down his pole and walked back to us. He sat down and rolled a cigarette from a pouch of tobacco. Out here, far from the smog of the city, just like the night before the sky was pitch black and covered with pinpoints of light. We sat silently for awhile, listening to the roar of the water pitching in front of us and letting the coolness of the night air refresh our tired bones.

"That river just looks like a big black body of water doesn't it?" asked Couchee, blowing smoke rings into the air. "But to the salmon, it's a road map of eddies and currents that they use in their journey to their spawning grounds. Where I was fishing, there's a current runs against the stream, and the salmon catch that on their trip upstream. That's how they do it. All the way up the river, there's currents flowing in circles and backwashes that the salmon catch so they don't just have to swim straight against the current upstream."

"I wish we could live like this," I said almost inaudibly.

"You could," offered Couchee. "Humans have been around for thousands of years, and it's only been since the industrial revolution that people have become alienated from the natural world. That's only about a hundred and fifty years — a tiny percentage of human history. But people seem to think that the reality of the modern technological age is the only one worth living."

"Do you think we could combine living in harmony with the natural world and yet still have a technological society?" I asked.

"No," he said. "I've heard people say we could use computers in a conserver society, but think of the industrial base necessary just to build a computer chip. To my knowledge, computer chips are basically tiny photographs of electronic circuits burned onto silicon chips and covered in a protective plastic coating. If you think about it, to produce a computer you need mines and copper smelters, plastic and silicon chemical plants, and a transportation network to move these products from the different parts of the globe where they originate. To live in harmony with the earth, this industrial base would have to be pollution-free, all those minerals would have to be replaced, and when the computer finally became obsolete, it would have to be recycled. Take any consumer product and think through the incredible industrial base required to transform the raw materials from the earth to the finished product in your home.

"For thousands of years, many different tribes and races of people have lived on this earth without technology and have had rich cultures with advanced music, art, story-telling, and even science. Of course, no culture has ever been perfect, because humans, as a species, are not capable of perfection — and would we even want that? But just because we have a lot of junk, does that mean this point in human history is superior to any other time?"

I think we all agreed with him — it was something we had all thought about, talked about, but maybe had never heard so well expressed. To gain all the material goods we had at our disposal in North America, we had sacrificed many species of living beings and were destroying the earth in the process. We had forgotten that the earth was our natural habitat and that we couldn't live without it. People were living in cities, like we were, inside their concrete dwellings, isolated from the natural environment and preoccupying themselves with creating even more artificial forms of life — like the computer. We had become alienated from the simple truth that we needed clean air to breathe, water to drink, trees to produce oxygen — all things the earth produces as a matter of course for us to survive; or at least it had done so far.

"No," Couchee said, "the answer to your question is that we can't live in harmony with the earth and continue living in this kind of technological society. You don't need a university degree to understand that simple truth, but with all our intelligence it seems to be the one truth we are trying very hard to hide from. In time that simple truth will become apparent to us when the effects of all this pollution begin to take their toll on the earth."

Soon after that we were piled into Couchee's truck. He gave us a ride back to the Hat Creek Survival Gathering, and along the way, with so much to think about, we didn't say much for a change.

✳ **10** ✳

When we got back to Vancouver I decided it was about time I got my firearms acquisition certificate — or FAC. Hector and I would be carrying out our robbery sometime during the summer, and a gun was part of the plan.

Acquiring a FAC was by no means difficult. It involved going to the local police station and filling out a form so they could check to see if I had a criminal record or history of mental illness. Since I didn't have either, I was given a FAC, which I could take to any gun store and use to purchase a weapon other than a handgun. In Canada purchasing a handgun requires a restricted weapons permit, which involves more stringent criteria than a rifle.

I was not excited about purchasing a rifle. It was simply a necessary prerequisite for being a guerrilla. I had never had any interest in weapons, either on a practical or psychological level. I'm sure there are many people who would entertain fantasies of being an urban guerrilla because deep down inside they would love to have the power inherent in carrying a gun. And there are many people who would like to carry a gun for extra protection in a world full of violent and mentally damaged people. I do have some psychological quirks, but a love of weapons is not one of them. It was just that we had decided that we would need a gun as an enforcer and for protection on the robbery — and we would probably need weapons to help carry out the political actions we were discussing. The more comfortable and proficient we were with weapons, the less likely we would be to panic, pull the trigger accidentally, or aim in the wrong place. At least that was the theory.

I decided on a Ruger Mini-14, a smaller, lighter civilian model of the U.S. military assault rifle, the M-1. About thirty inches long, it could, theoretically, be used for hunting but was more commonly purchased by gun aficionados for target-practice at local gun clubs. The Mini-14 would be too big and cumbersome for us to use in our robbery but, for around $400, we could buy one as a means of becoming more proficient with weapons. After I bought the rifle, we started organizing an expedition to the mountains to try it out. Obviously Brent, Doug, and I would go, but who else? Since Julie and Gerry showed the most interest in our guerrilla politics, and I had put my misgivings on the back burner, we decided they should be the first of our friends to go with us. We figured that in the long run taking people who were supportive of militant politics out target-practising would be a good way of gauging just how interested they would be in putting their politics into practice.

On a beautiful July morning we piled into Julie's car with the rifle, ammunition, and a lunch. We were in good spirits, laughing and feeding off each other's adrenalin. After stopping at a self-serve for gasoline, we drove across the Second Narrows Bridge and up the Capilano hill to Highway 99, which leads to Whistler Mountain. Brent had recalled seeing logging roads running off into the mountains just north of Squamish when he had travelled this highway as a teenager en route to the Whistler ski resorts.

We were babbling away about everything under the sun when Gerry made an announcement that focused our attention. "I'm quitting the Subhumans."

"What!" Brent sounded incredulous.

"That's right, I'm quitting. I'm sick and tired of all the bullshit in the music scene. I've been doing this since '78 and I need a break. I'd really like to build a cabin in the Chilcotins but I don't have the money. Everything takes money."

"Me and Gerry are thinking of going to Jasper in a few months to find jobs and hang out in the mountains," Julie said.

Doug, Brent, and I did not share their enthusiasm for retiring to the mountains. In any case, Brent suggested that Julie should get a FAC and then buy a Mini-14, because he thought they would have a perfect opportunity to hone their shooting skills in the wilderness of Jasper National Park. Julie thought this was a great idea. Gerry remained silent.

As soon as we had passed the pulp and paper town of Squamish, we began looking for logging roads cutting away from the highway. There were lots of them, but we were looking for something specific. We wanted a road that was no longer in use, one that led to an area far enough away from the main highway that our gunshots couldn't be heard.

The mountains all along the route had been clear-cut of their old-growth forests. Some areas were bald, with only stumps of trees sticking out between saplings that had newly taken root. These areas were particularly vulnerable to mud slides in the spring because there were not enough tree roots to hold the soil in place when the spring run-off began. Just that spring there had been a terrible accident when motorists speeding down the curving highway at night had not been able to stop in time to avoid crashing into the rocks below a bridge completely washed out by a mud slide. One at a time the cars had rounded the corner and plunged into the dark abyss below, until someone finally was able to stop in time and get out to warn other motorists coming along. We decided we would have to drive a little more slowly on the way home, when darkness would have set in.

Finding an accessible logging road was not easy because the roads in active use were usually blocked off by some form of chain-link gate or fence, aimed mainly at preventing access to dynamite magazines. The dynamite was used to clear right-of-ways for highways and roads and sometimes to clear paths through rock for loggers' trucks that had to go up into the furthest reaches of the mountains where the trees had been felled. The dynamite was stored in steel magazines built to government specifications. We took note of these logging roads, anticipating that at some future date, it might come in handy to know the location of dynamite magazines.

Several hours had passed since we had left the town limits of Squamish. We had driven up dozens of logging roads and still not found one to our liking. Our gas gauge was dangerously low and not a human habitation was to be found. We continued driving, now with the single-minded intention of finding a gas station, and our prayers were answered. As we rounded another sharp curve a gas station and general store appeared out of nowhere, with a tiny hamlet on a small beach just below.

We pulled over, and while Julie filled up the tank the rest of us went into the general store to buy coffee and chocolate bars. I felt like I was in a Norman Rockwell painting. The store was stocked with everything a person would need to survive. In the winter the hamlet below was probably snowbound so often that it was imperative the general store meet every requirement, from kerosene to candles to snowshoes.

I don't know why, but as I was walking out of this homey place my subconscious dredged up a nickname for it that would stick with all of us for years: "Gary Gilmore's." The name came from a man who, shortly after being released from prison in 1976, robbed and killed a motel owner and a gas station attendant in Utah. He was later executed — at his own request, by a firing squad. At the time I was reading Norman Mailer's book *The Executioner's Song*, about Gilmore, and we were having endless conversations about guns and robberies, all of which probably led me to conjure up the morbid nickname. In retrospect I think our sardonic humour was a way of venting the frustrated anger and bitterness we felt towards society.

After loading up on coffee and chocolate, we continued our search. About fifty kilometres past "Gary Gilmore's" we came upon a logging road that headed up into an area that had not been recently clear-cut. We were getting frustrated and the sun was beginning its descent. We turned off the highway and drove along a winding, potholed trail. Because there was no heavy chain-link fence blocking the entrance we assumed the site had no dynamite magazine, and judging from the height of the weeds growing on the trail we deduced it had not been used for years. The only things keeping the trail from being completely overgrown were faint tire tracks left behind, probably, by hunters using all-terrain vehicles.

After about half a kilometre the road became impassable for Julie's car. We liked the look of the area enough to get out and carry the rifle and ammunition on foot. We thought if it was suitable, we could use the place as a target-practice area for years to come.

The trail ran along the top of a small cliff, bordering a stream that had cut a valley between two small, densely forested mountains. After about twenty minutes of uphill walking, the trail suddenly veered away from the stream and into a box canyon. Nirvana. We could not have dreamed up a better place. The canyon would act as a soundproof box. It would also be a perfect place to camp, with its low-lying vegetation and a mountain stream for fresh water.

It didn't take us long to set up a simple target range. Doug spent some time setting the sights of the Mini-14, while the rest of us admired the deep purple silhouettes of the Tantalus Range from atop the box canyon. It was so beautiful I wished I were building a cabin there instead of setting up a target range. But I knew my awareness of, and stand against, the clear-cut logging practices of the lumber companies would prevent me from enjoying anything like a survivalist lifestyle in these surroundings. The environmental destruction I saw all around me was compelling me to commit my life towards doing whatever I could to stop it.

Finally we were ready. We each took turns standing, feet slightly straddled, with the stock of the rifle resting against the shoulder, slowly squeezing the trigger until it fired thunderously. Fortunately we had brought along huge ear "silencers" that prevented the noise from causing damage to the ear.

Since we had spent the greater part of the day finding the place, we didn't have much time left before dark. When we finished we walked around picking up spent casings and the paper bull's-eyes so we wouldn't leave any evidence of our activities. As we headed back down to the car, I decided guns would never be a hobby of mine. I hated the loud noise, and I thought it must create great anxiety for animals living within earshot. It was a necessary skill that we would have to master, but I could not bring myself to spend my spare time reading the *Guns and Ammo* magazines that Brent picked up.

* * *

Over the past few weeks Hector and I had been diligently scouting possible locations for our robbery. We finally settled on a Cineplex where the manager and another employee carried the Saturday take to a bank deposit chute at the end of the night. Our preparations had been thorough. We had spent several Saturday nights sitting in our Pinto at the back of the parking lot, making sure the night deposit routine was consistent. I had attended a Saturday matinee of *Superman II* just to see how many people went to the movies in the afternoon. We sat in the lot late one Friday night to see if they did a night deposit, which would have an effect on how much money we could anticipate on a Saturday. We took turns sitting there all day Saturday to see if they made more than one deposit per day. We went inside to identify the manager and other employees so we wouldn't accidentally rob moviegoers who might just happen to go to the bank after a late-night movie. We hung around all day to see if there was an armoured-car pickup earlier in the day, which would suggest that the night deposit might just be paperwork. We spent many other afternoons going over every getaway route imaginable.

At first we travelled to the Cineplex by bus and did our surveillance from a bus stop or restaurant that afforded a view of the theatre and bank. But after a while we got lazy and toyed with the idea of driving the Pinto. We had already started using it during the day for household tasks that were legal. By that time the car had been stolen for about a month, and we figured it was unlikely that the police would have this particular white Pinto on their minds if they saw us. Even though it still had its original plates, how often did the cops run plates through their computer for no reason? As long as we didn't do anything to arouse their suspicions, it seemed fairly safe to keep driving it. We just had to be meticulous about following traffic laws — everything from speed limits to the proper use of turn signals — and we had to make sure nothing was mechanically wrong — no malfunctioning brake lights or muffler problems, for instance. As a result we were probably the best drivers on the road, never tailgating or driving too slowly in the passing lane.

Finally we were ready. I was to be the getaway driver, and Hector would do the robbery. Two weeks earlier we had stolen another car that we would use as a first getaway car. Then, after a few blocks, we would transfer to the Pinto. I had shoplifted a black wig, called a "Dolly Parton": it was big hair just like Dolly's, but black. That particular model came in three colours: bleach blonde, auburn, and black. I thought the black seemed the most "natural," although that's an inaccurate use of the word. Unfortunately there had not been much of a selection in the department, especially since I was limited to the wigs that could be shoplifted.

As I dressed I realized how nervous I was. In the preceding days I had managed to block out my fears, but now that we were only hours away from the event I could no longer bury them in my daily routine. My stomach ached, and I know that my eyes were huge. No wonder the little information available about doing crime always advises the perpetrator never to look anyone in the eye before carrying out the act. Even the familiar sound of a knock on the door startled me. Everyone else in the house had gone out. It was only Hector, carrying his gym bag and otherwise looking like a university student.

I smiled at him in an attempt to look calm, but I'm sure he could read the fear in my face. I know I could see it in his. Without saying a word he sat down at the kitchen table and slipped on a pair of latex gloves. Pulling a handgun out of his bag, he unfastened the clip and polished each of the bullets before sliding them into it. We were meticulous in making sure we left no fingerprints on anything. Once he had loaded his gun and clicked on the safety, he asked if I was ready.

"As ready as anyone could be for something like this," I said with a reassuring smile.

We walked the few blocks to the spot where we kept the Pinto. I would only put "Dolly" on after we were in the other stolen car. Driving to that car, we ran over the details of the robbery one more time, reminding one another of things we might instinctively be inclined to do that we should not.

"So what do you do if the guy refuses to hand you the money?" I asked.

"Tell him again and warn him, 'I'll kill you if you don't,' " Hector said. We figured it was better to leave no doubt in our victim's mind that we were serious, in the hope that he would be more co-operative.

"What if he still refuses?" I repeated.

"Then I'll tell him to keep walking and we'll scram." We had decided it was better to abort the robbery than to start any physical confrontation or to fire the gun, which would only draw the attention of other people and thereby increase the risk of getting caught. "So what do you do if you see a cop pull into the parking lot while I'm doing the robbery?" Hector asked.

"I just stay put unless he does something that one hundred per cent indicates he knows there's a robbery in progress." We were both aware of just how easy it would be to overreact to the sight of a cop.

We continued this question and answer exercise until we came to the other stolen car. I got out of the Pinto. Sliding into the seat of the other car, I started it up with a screwdriver and drove towards the Cineplex. A thin veil of perspiration covered my whole body, making my hands slimy inside the latex gloves.

As I neared the Cineplex the streets I would have to turn down on our getaway route jumped out at me. I went down the street where we would leave the Pinto. Hector was already there, waiting. I parked a block away and watched him in my side-view mirror, walking towards me looking just like any university student, swinging his gym bag at his side. Without moving my head, I scanned the area for people and quickly slipped the black wig on my head. He got in with me. We cruised the six blocks to the Cineplex, which was set back off the road with a huge parking lot surrounding it. We parked close to the spot where the manager and one of his clerks always walked en route to the bank.

Even at 11:30 p.m. the street in front of the Cineplex was busy with activity from the restaurants, stores, and residential neighbourhood surrounding it. But to me the cars whizzing down the main street, stopping and starting at the intersection, moved by in a silent blur, irrelevant to the events at hand.

The darkness of the night was in sharp contrast to the bright lights illuminating the activities of the employees cleaning up the snackbar in the Cineplex lobby. Suddenly the lobby exploded with people pouring out of the three movie rooms. Simultaneously my heart started pumping even faster. With each change in scenario, the moment was approaching. The doors of the Cineplex burst open and out poured droves of people, laughing, talking, some sad-looking. They split up into twos, threes, and fours and fanned out all over the parking lot, some even heading towards our car. Hector and I slumped a little lower in our seats, trying to disappear, to become invisible. I watched as a young couple sauntered towards us, holding hands and pecking each other on the cheek. Closer and closer they came. I could have sworn they knew. Surely they must wonder: why were we sitting there? My black big hair was so obviously false! Why was Hector staring straight ahead at the cinema door? I was certain they were going to knock at our window and ask us what were we doing. They were going to call the police as soon as they reached a phone booth.

After the young couple walked past us, I watched them suspiciously in the rear-view mirror as they got into their own car a few spaces behind us. They drove off. All around us cars were pulling out and obscuring our vision of the Cineplex. As each car passed by us, I looked past them so they wouldn't make eye contact and see into my head and know that we were up to no good. Why were they driving so slowly? And why were they all staring at us?

Finally the parking lot cleared and we could once again

concentrate on the lobby and watch for the manager carrying his little brown bag under his arm. From our casing, we had learned that it took about twenty minutes after the last moviegoer had left and the doors were locked before they finished the books and carried the money to the bank. We sat frozen, watching the remaining two women cleaning the snackbar and chatting amongst themselves. Ten more minutes. I took a deep breath.

A couple of teenage boys came walking along, heading towards the front door of the Cineplex, kicking an empty pop can in front of them. "They better get the fuck out of there or they'll fuck up the whole thing," Hector whispered. Each time they kicked the pop can, the clanking on the asphalt made my hair stand on end. They gave it one final kick against the curve and walked up the stairs towards the front doors of the cinema and sat down on a concrete planter. One of the women inside opened the front door and said something to them.

Then something unbelievable happened. Around the corner of the Cineplex, out of nowhere, came a police car. As soon as it appeared it turned on its wailing siren and flashing red lights. Every impulse in my body said "flee!" but Hector whispered "wait." The cop car went fast across the lot towards and past us and came to a quick halt beside the teenagers. Its lights were still revolving, washing our faces in pulsing waves of bright light. After a brief exchange with the cops, the boys hopped off the planter and sauntered off towards the street. The cops waved at the women inside, then turned off their revolving lights and drove off.

Hector and I just looked at each other. *Unbelievable*. Obviously this place was not meant to be robbed. I felt a wave of relief pass over me, only to be replaced by a surge of severe disappointment. I knew that we would have to go through all this anxiety some other time. We drove off, and after parking the stolen car again we went in the Pinto to Bino's for a drink.

"The women in the snack bar must have called the cops to get rid of those kids before the manager did his night deposit," Hector said. "Too weird."

"I think it was a message not to do that place," I said. Hector and I were not normally superstitious, but in this case we decided to go with our instincts and drop it. There was another Cineplex we had also been casing. Instead, we would try that one the following Saturday. It was smaller and on a quieter commercial street, but had a similar routine. We knew that after the last show ended around

11:30 p.m., the manager counted the money and walked along the street for two blocks with an employee to drop the money in the bank's night-deposit chute. We were confident nothing had changed since we had cased the place several Saturday evenings in the past, so all we had to do was go over the getaway route. The only reason we had decided on the first Cineplex was because it was bigger and would probably bring in more money.

The following Saturday evening unfolded just like the previous one. Hector was in the same clothes and I wore my big black hair. We parked the Pinto, then proceeded together in the second stolen car. "Are you nervous?" I asked Hector.

"Nope." His eyes told a different story. Still, if he felt like I did, he was nowhere near as nervous as on the previous Saturday.

Even on a Saturday night the sidewalks and street were quiet in this neighbourhood. We parked in between the Cineplex and the bank, beside the sidewalk where the manager would walk on his way to the bank. In order to watch the Cineplex exit more easily, we sat facing it, but that position would also give the manager the opportunity to see us as he walked towards the bank. Avoiding eye contact as he neared us would be crucial.

Just as we arrived, the movies were over and people were pouring out onto the sidewalk, creating the chaotic activity that we found so nerve-wracking. We found it was impossible, without staring intently at everyone passing by, to be sure the manager wasn't in the crowds of people milling past our car. Even though we felt very uncomfortable, we had no choice but to stare out, because he might just break from his routine and decide to make his deposit early. Mixed in with my feelings of discomfort was a feeling of regret over my decision to shoplift that outrageous wig instead of spending a hundred dollars to buy a more subtle one.

After what felt like hours, the sidewalks cleared and finally were deserted. This was the kind of middle-class neighbourhood where people stayed home after midnight. Hector looked at his wrist watch: *12:15 a.m.* The manager should be coming any minute. Once again my heart was in my mouth. *12:20.* I looked at Hector. He was staring intently forward even though it would be impossible to miss anyone on this desolate street. *12:30.* "Do you think we missed him?" I whispered.

"Not unless someone else carried the money this time," Hector said, glancing over at me. But no one had come out of the cinema since the crowds had cleared.

"Maybe someone else carried the money and left with the stragglers at the end."

"That's possible," Hector said. He had been watching the bank's deposit chute through his side-view mirror and had seen a couple of people make deposits, but nobody that looked like the manager. "I guess he could have had someone else make the deposit tonight."

During the next half-hour, while we sat there, a couple of women left who we assumed were employees, locking the door behind them. Finally Hector walked casually past the cinema to see if there were any lights on inside, stopping briefly to light up a cigarette before coming back. Just before he got in the car, he slipped on his latex gloves. "Lights are out, no one's home," he said with finality. I sighed and turned on the engine.

On the way home, we figured there were two possibilities: they had either not made a deposit or made it earlier. It was that simple. "Let's forget cinemas," Hector said. "Somebody might have noticed us sitting there. If they did make the deposit when all those people were around, then they might have seen us even though we didn't see them. They'll certainly notice us next week if we're there again. How many people sit in a car beside a cinema, two weeks in a row for no apparent reason?" I agreed.

Since there was no panic to get the money, we put the robbery on hold. To avoid suspicion, we parked the second stolen car but moved it around every second day while we continued to use the Pinto on a daily basis for legal activities. The more we used it, the more comfortable we felt driving around in it. As long as we wore the latex gloves and abided by the rules of the road, we felt like we could use it indefinitely.

✳ 11 ✳

Other than casing for the elusive robbery, I was busy working with Angie in our Women Against Prisons group and on my own in a group to inform people about the Hat Creek power project. This second group was made up largely of people from Vancouver who had attended the Hat Creek Survival Gathering as well as people active in the Society to Promote Environmental Conservation (SPEC). I had found out about SPEC after a friend and I were arrested for shoplifting by two store dicks at a Zellers. I was given a conditional discharge with one year's probation, which meant the charge would be erased from my record if I abided by the conditions of my probation — to carry out one hundred hours of community work and remain free of criminal charges for one year. I chose to do my community work at the SPEC offices, doing whatever menial work they asked of me.

Julie and Gerry didn't get involved in the Hat Creek Action Group because they had finally decided to travel to Jasper and work towards acquiring the money to build Gerry's dream cabin in the Chilcotins. Julie wrote Brent diligently while they were gone, and from her accounts it was an ideal period in her life. She got a job working on a road crew and Gerry worked at the Marmot Basin Ski Resort in Jasper National Park. They were able to rent a cabin in the park, transforming the place into a cosy little retreat from their hectic working days.

At first the Hat Creek Action Group meetings were great. We were all of an anarchist bent and quickly came to the conclusion that we should hold a fall conference in Vancouver and invite all the groups across the province fighting against the various B.C. Hydro projects. At the conference we would share information about the various megaprojects and propose a people's inquiry into B.C. Hydro and the role of the government in implementing these projects. We would be advocating direct action in a mass way in the sense that we wanted those affected by the Hydro projects to set up their own people's inquiry, completely independent of the government, to look into B.C. Hydro's megaprojects and decide on their own course of action.

Everyone was excited about organizing the conference, but not everyone was happy about how the conference was being organized — and especially not the women. Although the Hat Creek Action Group was a mixed group, the women in it were feminists and keenly aware of the dynamics between themselves and the men. Our standards for male behaviour were high, in particular because we believed that the way in which we worked together as a group had to reflect the kind of society we wanted to achieve. We wanted equality, and if we couldn't get it in society at large, we were going to get it in the groups we worked in *now*. While the goal of the Hat Creek Action Group was ultimately to put the fate of the Hat Creek Valley in the hands of the people, not B.C. Hydro, we weren't willing to sacrifice our feminist ideals for our environmental ideals. We did not see the two issues as separate but rather as interconnected: the same thinking that objectifies women and places them below men in the social hierarchy also objectifies the natural world and places less significance on plant and animal life than on human life.

The women were not about to tolerate sexist behaviour in the group. The sexism in the Hat Creek Action Group was not the blatant kind in which women were expected to serve coffee and clean up after meetings, or referred to as chicks and used as the brunt of jokes for some comic relief. Rather, it was a more subtle sexism practised by well-intentioned men — men who, indeed, saw themselves as feminist. From the start, our feminist feelers picked up on the male members' domination of discussion. The decision-making around jobs always ended up with the men being assigned the more public tasks, such as being spokespersons at the conference or writing the leaflets, as well as the supposedly intellectual tasks. The women tended to sit quietly listening and then would volunteer for the more menial tasks such as postering, mailing leaflets, and phoning prospective participants.

The more we examined the dynamics of the group, the more we noticed the patterns. The files of information on B.C. Hydro and the environmental groups were located in one of the men's houses. The contact people for most of the environmental groups were men. During meetings the men's voices were louder, more assertive, and directed towards the other men; the women tended to be spectators that the men were trying to impress. We realized that the women had to take some responsibility for these dynamics, but eventually we decided that we would rather put our energy into changing ourselves than changing the men. This would be better accomplished for the time being if we had our own women's faction. That way, any women intimidated by men would be more likely to speak up and voice their opinions. Women would be able to write leaflets, control information, and be spokespeople. Maybe later on down the road, we thought, when our women's group had gained more skills and knowledge, we could reintegrate with the men without falling back into the position of passive spectators who only came to life when environmental secretarial work was needed.

The summer of 1981 was my awakening as a feminist. Between working with Angie in the Women Against Prisons group and the women's faction of the Hat Creek Action group, I was learning to implement feminist ideas that I had previously been exposed to only in books. I had found that in mixed groups all too often women tended to relate to the men more than to each other. It was as though they too were infected with the mistaken belief that men were smarter and more competent and therefore conversations should be directed at them. In our struggle to gain recognition from the men, some of us found ourselves competing against one another instead of relating to each other as allies. Once we started our own group we began to relate to each other as equals, not opponents. We became independent people with names, interests, and fears, instead of some man's girlfriend, talking incessantly about our man's occupation and accomplishments. In the end, taking on responsibilities made us feel stronger and more competent, and we felt better when we weren't just sitting back and letting the men do it all.

August was consumed with preparations for the fall demonstration and conference on B.C. Hydro megaprojects. Ironically, the Hat Creek Action Group was able to get government funding earmarked for environmental non-governmental organizations, and we used the money to help subsidize travel to the conference for people from northern British Columbia. We were able to mail cheques to the Native people from the Liard and Peace River regions to attend the conference. Brent and Nick wrote a pamphlet analysing B.C. Hydro's *Blueprint 1980*, basically providing a factual description of the various planned megaprojects and a political breakdown of the effect they would have on the province. These publicly funded megaprojects would provide the necessary infrastructure for the exploitation of British Columbia's natural resources, but the profits, we argued, would end up disproportionately in the hands of the private industry owners who extracted these resources, and in the hands of their shareholders. For example, the Cheekeye-Dunsmuir power line, funded by taxpayers, would provide the electricity for pulp and paper mills such as MacMillan Bloedel on Vancouver Island, and the resulting profits would benefit the company's owners and shareholders far more than they would the taxpayers. The Stikine-Iskut dam in northern British Columbia would provide electricity for the expansion of Alcan's smelter there. The plant would have a negative effect on the environment and way of life of the Native people of the area but provide huge profits for Alcan's owners and shareholders, who lived many miles away. The pamphlet called for a people's inquiry, independent of the government or B.C. Hydro, into the need for these megaprojects.

For the morning of the conference we had organized a demonstration that would go from Oppenheimer Park along East Hastings Street to the conference site at the Carnegie Community Centre, in the heart of Vancouver at the corner of Main and Hastings. This area, known as the Downtown Eastside, was Vancouver's ghetto, inhabited by drug addicts, prostitutes, and businesses that fed off the poor. The main artery servicing the area, Hastings Street, was lined with pawn shops, run-down bars, cheap restaurants, and flop houses.

Around sixty people showed up as the morning sun peeked over the low apartment buildings, warming up the demonstrators and the bodies lying on benches and under trees all over Oppenheimer Park — people still comatose from the previous night's attempts to escape reality. Our colourful placards and noisy morning laughter were in sharp contrast to the dark figures beginning to stir under their blankets and overcoats. I watched a Native man peek his scarred face out from under his coat and scowl at a couple of young women handing out placards — "DAM BC HYDRO," "POWER TO THE PEOPLE," "RED POWER NOT HYDRO POWER" — to the people arriving for the demo. He couldn't have cared less.

After milling around the park for about an hour, we were ready for our short march to the Carnegie Centre. Our small group of protesters, made up of young, white environmentalists, Native people from up north, and some farmers from the central part of the province, began walking slowly along Hastings Street chanting slogans. Even at ten in the morning a disproportionate number of Native people lined the street. Young girls, scantily dressed, hung around corners waiting for a trick. There were more dark, prone bodies on the pavement, people trying to sleep as long as they could to avoid facing the day. Drug addicts, gaunt and desperate, watched us pass by.

The Native people from up north looked uncomfortably at their urban counterparts — a testament to the future that B.C. Hydro had in store for their relatives who were still able to eke a traditional living from the rivers and forests left untouched in the north. No matter where you went in the city, there were no Native people working in the stores, or bustling down the streets in business suits. Native people there tended to work in drug rehab clinics, the Native Friendship Centre, or in social work offices, where they would desperately try to help at least a few people climb out of the ghettoes before they died from overdoses, alcoholism, or stabbings. Their chosen professions reflected the Native peoples' struggle merely to survive as opposed to get ahead.

The white people in the demonstration marched along happily, confidently angry. We all knew that if we ever chose to join mainstream society, that option was open to us. Those of us who were poor were so by choice. Not so for the Native people. They looked uneasy, perhaps sensing that the young Native man on the sidewalk turning his back could be them, only a megaproject away. It took a lot of effort for Native people to maintain a lifestyle off the streets, whereas for us white folk it took effort to be on the streets.

Bordering Hastings and Main streets was Chinatown. Many of the Chinese immigrants who had built the railways and worked in the mines of British Columbia, among a variety of other kinds of work, had settled in Vancouver and built a lively community of restaurants, stores, and other small businesses. The crossroads of Main and Hastings was teeming with the odd mix of traditional Chinese people going about their business — some of them carrying armloads of vegetables and other food home from the market — and young Native people milling about, most of them just trying to occupy themselves, some of them trying to score.

Our small demonstration was swallowed up by the crowd as we began filing into the Carnegie Centre, home of the Downtown Eastside Residents Association, a public housing organization and a place where poor people could hang out. In the centre's conference room we had set up seats in a huge half-oval facing rows of seats for spectators. The place filled up quickly, with many of the seats taken up by people who simply wandered in off the streets because they had no place else to go.

One by one, speakers from each area that would be affected by Hydro's future megaprojects spoke to the crowd about their region and the impact that the dams or coal-fired generating plants would have on them. Our group's paper on the people's inquiry proposal received a warm reception, but it soon became apparent that transforming the idea into a practical reality was another matter. Who would be members of the "board" or "inquiry," and how would they be elected or appointed? Once a mechanism had been determined to create the inquiry, how would its recommendations be implemented or even recognized? We had no illusions that the government would give the inquiry any credibility, because we were not only rejecting government involvement in the process but also investigating the government's role in the megaprojects.

Rather than being discouraged by these problems, we were inspired by the enthusiasm with which our idea was embraced. The next step was to figure out how to implement it. Valuable networking had been accomplished at the conference, and we now knew people from all over the province, people we could contact and work with over the next phase of our project.

After helping to put away the folding seats and sweep the floors, Brent, Nick, Saphie, Bridget, and I headed out to a Chinese restaurant with some Native people from Rivers Inlet, an isolated community about half-way up the B.C. coast. Sitting in one of the restaurant booths with us, Jeannie and Tom of Rivers Inlet told us about the reserve they came from, one of the smallest in the province. "There are no roads, trains, or planes, other than float planes that can reach us, so most of the year we are completely isolated," Jeannie said. She was twenty-eight years old and said her people had lived "traditionally" when she was young. They fished and hunted to survive, heated their houses with wood, and made their own clothing and other things they needed. "It was a wonderful life," Jeannie said. "The only bad thing was the drinking. Even then, there were people who would boat to Prince Rupert and pick up as much booze as they could afford, or they'd make it in stills."

"There's no industry around our reserve, so there are no jobs," continued Tom. "You can imagine the devastating effect it would have on our people if the fish died off from toxic mine tailings or if a lumber company clear-cut our area and the wildlife relocated. There would be nothing left but the booze."

"Our reserve is one of the last few to remain self-sufficient," added Jeannie, "but people my age leave anyway because they want the excitement of the city and dream of getting a job, earning lots of money and having a life like the one they see in magazines, with a house, car, and all kinds of junk."

"If the traditional way of life becomes impossible," Tom said, "younger people will have no choice but to go to the cities, and the old people will just stay in Rivers Inlet and drink themselves to death. As it is now, some young people do return when they discover the jobs in the city aren't for them and they didn't have the money for an education."

"That's why we're here," Jeannie told us. "I was a heroin addict a few years ago. I came to the city because I wanted the life I heard about on the radio — there are no TVs in Rivers Inlet. But I couldn't get a job and soon I met other Indian people who introduced me to drugs and I discovered an easy way to reach paradise. Luckily, I was smart enough to go back to the reserve and kick my habit. But I'm terrified that the so-called development projects they're planning for northern B.C. are going to make our traditional way of life impossible. Then there will be no place for us to go. I was lucky to be able to go home and clean myself up, but that option is not open to many of our people and is becoming less and less so."

"In the areas where these megaprojects are going to be built," Tom said, "the young people from the reserves will have to migrate to the city, and most of them will end up here." He looked around. There were no Chinese people in the restaurant. Most of the people there were Native prostitutes, drug addicts, or homeless people spending their last dollar on an egg roll. "They'll hire Indians in the construction phase," Jeannie said. "There's a lot of hard, unskilled labour required. But once the dams are finished, very few people will be needed to maintain them. Companies like Alcan don't end up hiring many Native people, because the Native people in the Stikine-Iskut region have lived traditionally, hunting and fishing, as long as we can remember, and just can't adjust to a nine-to-five lifestyle working in an aluminum refining plant."

We invited Jeannie and Tom to spend the night at our house so they could save their hotel money for something else. At home, late into the night we sat around under the loft swapping stories about our lives and making plans for the future. We learned more from them than we would have from reading a million pamphlets about the effects of progress on Native peoples. Our conversations became further fuel for my increasing passion to do something to help prevent the destruction of the natural world upon which their traditional way of life depended.

✳ 12 ✳

Our quest to find a robbery site intensified after the conference. One evening during rush hour I was standing at an intersection, waiting for the lights to change, when out of the corner of my eye I saw a guy in a small grocery store bending down in front of a safe in the front window. To my surprise, I saw him take money out of the safe and then scurry off towards the back of the store. Instead of crossing the street, I walked up to a phone booth right in front of the store so I could further case the situation.

The grocery store was part of a large chain — if it had been a ma-and-pa operation I probably wouldn't have stopped even to think about it. We were adamant about not robbing family-owned businesses, because we didn't want to take money from anyone struggling to survive. A place like a Cineplex or a large grocery chain store, we reasoned, had plenty of insurance covering robberies and made such huge profits that it was not at all immoral to rob them. From our perspective, a lot of these chain stores were already robbing people legally through inflated prices.

In the phone booth I pretended to dial a number and make a call while I waited for the guy to emerge from the store. Fifteen minutes passed before I saw him walk from the back of the store, down the aisle towards the front. If I hadn't had the phone booth for a cover, I would have been hard-pressed to find an excuse to be hanging around outside the store for such a long time. Finally he opened the door, locked it behind him, and walked casually past me, holding a brown paper bag. He seemed completely at ease. Why not? It was rush hour and a robbery would be foolish so close to wall-to-wall traffic. I watched him walk the block to the bank, drop his bag into the chute, and head off down the crowded sidewalk. Putting the phone back in its cradle, I looked at the line of cars a foot away from me, backed up for three blocks waiting for the lights to change from red to green. Damn! It was a perfect place except for all this traffic. No wonder he was alone and relaxed doing his deposit.

When I got home I phoned Hector and asked him to come over. After I had filled him in on what I had seen, in detail, we both decided it was risky but worth further investigation. The following evening found us walking down the sidewalk towards the same intersection. We scouted the area for a less conspicuous place we could use to case the situation. A bus stop on the other side of the road, at the intersection, met our criteria perfectly. As soon as the store was scheduled to close, we took up our position there. Since it was rush hour, a small crowd had congregated at the stop so we kept up a bit of chit chat to distract anyone from wondering about our true intentions. Taking turns keeping an eye on the store, we watched the few stragglers inside finish their shopping and line up at the only open cashier.

I recognized the same guy from the evening before restocking cigarettes at an empty counter. He went over and unlocked the door each time a customer was ready to leave. He looked quite young for someone I presumed to be the manager. When the last customer finally shuffled out the door, I watched the young guy go up to the cashier and exchange what I assumed were a few friendly words — even from across the street I could see the warm, affectionate smile she gave him in return. He seemed like a nice guy. I had already noticed the friendly smiles each of the customers gave him when he held the door open for them. I sure hoped that if we did a robbery, nothing would go wrong with it, because the more I watched this guy the less I liked the idea of terrorizing him — an inevitable consequence of robbery. When I had watched him the evening before I thought he had been alone when he opened the safe, but now when he went over and knelt down to dial the combination the cashier was still there, balancing her till.

As we took turns watching the store, Hector and I invented an imaginary world in our conversation. It was an interesting exercise because we had to concentrate on the story we were fabricating while trying to notice every detail about the events unfolding in the store, all without drawing undue attention from anyone else at the bus stop. When it was my turn to keep an eye on the store, I paced around for a minute and situated myself facing Hector and the store. Inside, the manager took the till from the cashier gently and gave her a tender smile. I bet they're in love, I thought.

Meanwhile, Hector was telling me that our imaginary son, little Ricky, had been in a fight in school yesterday. When I expressed disappointment that Ricky had confided in Hector instead of me, he voiced the opinion that boys were more open with their fathers. "What a sexist assumption!" I snapped. After the cashier handed the till to the manager, she put on her fall jacket and he accompanied her to the door, money in hand. While unlocking the door for her, he placed the till and money bags on a counter. She stepped out the door and for a split second placed her hand on his shoulder. Something's going on between them for sure!

In Hector's opinion, little Ricky would probably confide in me more if I wasn't so hard on him for fighting, and if I continued showing my disapproval Ricky would either tell me nothing or start lying. I reminded Hector of his own suggestion that I hide my pregnancy from my parents for six months, until after we were married. After the store manager disappeared in the back of the store to count the money, I watched the cashier walk across the street towards us. As she passed us, I noticed a small diamond ring on her wedding finger. Complicated.

The bus was coming and the manager had still not left the store. Wouldn't it seem odd to the other people waiting for the bus if we didn't get on it? On my own finger I had a gold band I had been given years earlier. Discreetly pulling it off, I dropped it on the pavement. Then I carefully put my running shoe on it and began shrieking to Hector that I had dropped my wedding ring. He acted pissed off but diligently began to search the sidewalk. So did a few other people waiting for the bus. As it pulled up in a cloud of dust and diesel fuel, I told the few people helping us that we'd catch the next bus. Grateful to be relieved of their duty, they boarded the bus. Just as it pulled away, I found my ring under my shoe.

Finally the manager came down the aisle, once again holding a brown paper bag, and left the store, locking the door carefully behind him. He followed the same route as on the evening before. Good.

As the store manager went along the street, I turned my back on him and continued elaborating on our outrageous story. It had come to the point where I had gained thirty pounds before the wedding but my family still didn't know I was pregnant. As another bus pulled up, a man who had been eavesdropping since we had begun the tale of my pregnancy asked how I had explained having the baby after only three months of marriage. "I rushed to the hospital and told my family I was having a miscarriage," I said. "They were so relieved that I didn't have a miscarriage but a healthy full-term baby that they never did question the time of conception."

After everyone boarded the bus, Hector and I decided to walk home. It was a beautiful cool fall evening, and the combination of casing for the robbery and making up the story about our phony marriage had brought us closer together. Hector was normally the kind of person who was difficult to get close to, but, perhaps in part due to his uncanny similarity to Doug, I felt warm and comfortable with him. Although he considered himself a feminist man, by nature he was not the kind of person prone to displays of emotion. Sometimes I felt sad for Hector because I felt as though he was a prisoner of his protective armour. Under the tough-guy veneer was a sensitive, vulnerable person, easily hurt by callous remarks from others. In my amateur psychoanalysis, I suspected the reason he lived such a solitary existence was because he feared the pain that accompanies close relationships. Inevitably situations come up where close friends squabble and say things to hurt one another. Hector was ill-equipped to let these run off his back like water off a duck. Instead, they would get under his skin and fester. The only way Hector had learned to cope with the inevitable emotional attacks that accompany friendships was to avoid them altogether. I was one of the privileged few whom he let into his little world — a privilege I held sacred. I knew that if I ever attacked him personally, he would retreat and it would be a long time before he would let me in again. The flip side of his apparent machismo was his tendency to be a fiercely loyal friend who would sacrifice just about anything for anyone he counted as being in his inner circle. A perfect partner for a robbery.

We stopped at one of the many cafés along the street to discuss the possible robbery. Tiring of the endless anxiety that accompanies months of casing, we decided to do it the following weekend. We just wanted to get it over with.

All of the following week was coloured with the dark thoughts of the robbery looming ahead. Though certainly not looking forward to it, I felt compelled to follow through on our plan — after all, we had invested so much time and effort in it. In retrospect, I believe my desire to do the robbery had more to do with my budding identity as an urban guerrilla than it did my need for the old van, which wasn't worth anywhere near the risk that the robbery would inevitably entail. But I was eager to test my mettle in a serious situation, not just some trashing or shoplifting experience.

Finally the weekend arrived. In our previous two attempts, Hector had been the would-be robber and I the getaway driver. This time I volunteered to be the robber. It was an unseasonably bitter cold day for September, but providential for my disguise. Until then, I really didn't know what to wear to disguise my appearance. Since I would have to stay in the phone booth from the time the guy opened the safe until he came out of the store to go to the bank, I was afraid my big black hair would draw attention to me. If he noticed me standing in the phone booth as he was opening the safe, he might later become alarmed when he saw me still standing there on his way to the bank. That outrageous hair would jump out at him. But the cold weather was a gift from the gods, providing a good excuse to be seen wearing an overcoat, a dark fedora hat, and gloves. I would still be overdressed but not peculiarly so. The other advantage of this attire was that the guy might assume I was a man, since he would probably have the preconceived notion that a robber would be male. If I capitalized on this probability by lowering my voice during the robbery, chances were that he would describe me to the cops as a man. Not only would he have almost no description of my natural features but he would also mistakenly describe me as male. Perfect!

A few minutes before the store's closing time, Hector dropped me off in the getaway car, a block away, and drove on to park in the store's lot while I began the long walk to the phone booth. We had left the Pinto parked about six blocks away on a quiet residential street. As I walked towards the dreaded phone booth, I ran over in my head the commands I was about to give the store manager. The fondness I felt towards him while we were casing was transformed into a steely determination to leave him in no doubt that he MUST obey me for his own safety. If he obeyed, the odds were that everything would go as planned. But if he disobeyed, the odds weren't in our favour. This was a busy intersection. In fact, as I approached the phone booth, I realized how crazy this was. If we hadn't already had two failed attempts, we would never be doing a robbery in this particular place, but maybe our frustration was making us reckless — the very thing we had plotted to avoid.

As I neared the phone booth, I noticed my focus narrowing, filtering out everything but the events and things relevant to the robbery at hand. I stepped into the phone booth and pretended to dial. I could see Hector sitting in the getaway car at the back of the store parking lot, slumped slightly over, probably to appear less visible. Out of the corner of my eye I could see the rush-hour traffic speeding by, alarmingly close. God, if I had to rob him while the cars were stopped at a red light, they couldn't help but notice. There were also lots of people walking along the sidewalk. I felt myself becoming even more aware of the insanity of this location.

I put my hand in my overcoat pocket to cover the obvious bulge created by Hector's .38 handgun. Like clockwork, the store manager appeared from one of the aisles, walking quickly to the front door to lock it. As soon as I saw him, I averted my eyes and started talking into the receiver, staring at the bank only a block away. But out of the corner of my eye I could see everything. One lone customer remained in the store, checking her purchases out with the cashier. Earlier in the day I had thought I looked normal, but now, as I glanced at my reflection in the glass of the phone booth, I felt as though the dark fedora looked almost criminal. But at least, I hoped, I looked like a male criminal.

The last customer was waiting to be let out just as the manager knelt in front of the safe. He glanced up, looking straight at me. I felt naked, as though he could see through my disguise and could see that I was carrying a gun to rob him. To compensate I laughed into the receiver as though someone had told me the funniest joke in the world. I hoped this would put him at ease.

He went back to the safe, opened it, and took out a tray. Then he went over to the cashier to get her till. She was not the same woman who had worked the weekend before. Just as he was about to walk down the aisle towards the back of the store, she put on her jacket and called out to him. He turned around and accompanied her to the door, locking it behind her. I turned my back to the store as she passed me on the sidewalk. When I turned around, he was gone, presumably back in the office to prepare the night deposit.

I couldn't believe how calm I felt. My hands were dry and steady. The whole situation seemed unreal, but at the same time I could not envisage chaos. The rush-hour traffic roared around me and exhaust fumes drifted into the phone booth every time the traffic backed up behind a red light. The wait for the manager to reappear seemed too long. I started to feel conspicuous, standing talking in the booth for almost half an hour, but then who would notice? Everyone around me was on their way home. Nobody was loitering at this busy intersection, and the phone booth was so noisy and full of fumes that only someone desperate would want to use it.

Then the manager reappeared. He wore a fall coat and was swinging his brown paper bag lightly at his side. Now my heart began to thunder. Time began to slow down. Once again I turned my back to the store, giving him time to unlock the door and feel reassured that I wasn't watching him. I knew my timing was critical. If I came out too soon, he would see me approach and perhaps run away. If I waited too long I would have to pursue him. I wanted to make my move from the booth just as he passed me. Rhythm was essential. I turned around slowly, just as he finished locking the door. Smiling, I casually hung up the receiver. He stepped out into the middle of the sidewalk just as I stepped out. I could hear the cars behind me coming to a halt. I knew that if anyone in those cars could see my face, they would be able to see the fear in my eyes, but I pushed that thought out of my mind.

I stepped in front of his path and the moment his eyes met mine, he knew. Before I had even opened my mouth to say a word, the blood drained from his face. It was so white that some pimples on his forehead stood out as clearly as his eyes. His facial features became embedded in my mind's eye forever. He had a plain face with short greasy hair and was much younger close up than from a distance. Deep inside, I wanted to put my hand on his shoulder and tell him not to be afraid, that I liked him and would never hurt him. But instead, in a deep, firm voice, I said, "Give me the money or I'll kill you." I had the handgun out, close to my body, pointing right at him. I was just out of his reach. I was a little surprised at just how frightened he looked. How could he know what I was really thinking? He handed me his bag. "Just keep walking to the bank and nothing will happen to you," I instructed him as I turned to leave. He did.

My life was in the hands of fate, and on that particular day the hands were on my side. The odds were not, because it would have been a good bet that someone waiting at the lights could easily have noticed the robbery and started beeping their horn, got out of their car, or something. I don't know to this day what went on behind my back at those lights except that nothing happened to me. I walked quickly to the stolen car and lay down on the floor.

Hector stepped on the accelerator and drove swiftly, but not recklessly, out the back entrance of the lot into the residential neighbourhood behind the store. "That was great!" he gasped. He had probably been more frightened than me, because he would have seen everything going on around me, including all the cars stopped at the lights only a few feet away from the robbery. As soon as I hit the car floor, I stuffed the hat, overcoat, and money into a duffle bag. Not more than three minutes after I got in the car, we pulled over and casually got out. Glancing around by moving only our eyes we scanned the neighbourhood for witnesses, then walked quickly to the Pinto. As soon as we began to drive off, I lay down on the floor again. Adrenalin coursed wildly through our bodies, giving us that odd high of exhilaration mixed with fear. Looking up at Hector's face for reassurance, I saw a big smile of relief plastered all over it. I let out the breath of air I had been holding in, giving a big sigh, when, unbelievably, a siren began wailing right behind us.

"What's happening Hector?" I cried.

"The cops are right behind us." His foot was still frozen at the same careful speed on the accelerator. "It's an unmarked car." I don't know why Hector didn't floor it and catapult us into a high-speed chase, but something intuitive told him to maintain our course. It wasn't rational, but that's what we did. The bright red light on the unmarked car's dashboard was whirling around rhythmically, reflecting in our rear-view mirror. For about sixty seconds the car rode on our tail while we debated what to do. Then it made up our minds for us. It veered into the passing lane and shot in front of us, disappearing into the traffic ahead.

"What's happening Hector?" My imagination was running wild.

"He passed us and is turning way up ahead," Hector said, craning his head to see as far as he could. For a few seconds neither of us said a thing. Then Hector came up with the answer. "I think the cops were responding to the robbery because he turned in the direction of the bank. That guy probably walked up to the bank and told someone to call the cops."

"What a twist of fate." I laughed uneasily. I wasn't completely convinced we were in the clear yet. Not until we were out of the neighbourhood did we begin to relax. After driving around for about twenty minutes, we decided to go home. We parked about ten blocks from the house and walked home, carrying the duffle bag with us.

Fortunately, no one was home and we didn't have to answer any questions. I felt a sense of elation, not because I enjoyed the robbery but because it was over and we were free and no one had got hurt. I could see why some people find robberies addictive. It is a situation in which you lose yourself completely in the moment. Each of the actions involved has an extreme consequence, dictating that the individual concentrate completely on the moment because any error is potentially fatal.

* * *

We didn't get a lot of money from that robbery — just enough to buy the van and to help Hector survive for a while. I worked off my anxiety over the robbery by hammering out rusty sections of the van's side panels and wheel wells. Probably because it was the first vehicle I'd bought myself, I took a certain amount of pride in fixing it up to look as good as it could. For hours I bent over the wheel wells, sanding the blobs of body filler and fibreglass until they were smooth enough to paint. Since I had spent all my money purchasing the van, I decided to paint it with a roller, which created a unique orange-peel effect. I couldn't have been prouder of my handiwork if I was showing off a brand new Corvette.

A few weeks after the robbery, I was having trouble with the clutch on my van. I decided to put in a new one on the side of the road outside our house when a familiar voice nearly startled me out of my skin.

"How's little Ricky, honey?"

I was smiling before I even turned around to see him. "He's just fine but he misses you," I said looking up at him affectionately.

"Is he still fighting at school?" Hector grinned back at me.

"No. When you didn't come back, he clammed up for awhile and then finally started talking to me. He explained that the kids pick on him because his mom and dad don't have jobs."

"I'm glad he's finally opening up to you. It's probably better that I'm not around so much. It gives you a chance to get closer to him." Hector paused. "I'm going away."

"What!" I exclaimed, genuinely surprised.

"I'm going to Nicaragua and see if I can't do something to help the Sandinistas. I know it sounds crazy but I get bored going to meetings and organizing all these liberal campaigns to change things. I want to work with real revolutionaries."

"What about us?" I asked. "You know that it's just a matter of time before we're ready to carry out some real revolutionary actions."

"That's great and everything but you'll be totally isolated. There's no mass movement behind you. You're only going to be representing a small group of a couple of hundred people. Once you're dead or busted, it'll die out quicker than a candle in the rain," he prophesied.

I remembered what Sabine Schmidt had told me in France, and I repeated her words, hoping that I would have the same effect on him that she did on me, but to no avail. "I don't want to waste my life and that's what I feel I'm doing here. I want to be part of a movement that isn't going to die out. I believe I can find that in Central America," he said with finality. "What I find the most aggravating here is all these white middle-class leftists who join support groups for the Sandinistas in Nicaragua or some other Third World liberation movement involved in armed struggle, but if you even hint at the possibility of doing the same thing here, they immediately come up with every excuse they can muster to avoid putting their own lives on the line. They'll say that a guerrilla group here would not represent the people but would be acting on its own. Well who are the *people*? Are we not the people too?"

"My belief is that most middle-class leftists have comfortable lifestyles they don't want to put at risk. It's fine and dandy to go out to meetings at night and demos on weekends, but there's no way they're going to lose their cosy little homes for prison or, worse yet, death, for the sake of some theoretical revolution," he went on. "Let the poor, starving peasants take the risks — they're dying anyway. So the leftists come up with all kinds of political justifications for their complacency. I don't think their political ideology of supporting armed struggle in the Third World but not here is based on sound intellectual reasoning — they just didn't want to lose their cushy lifestyles. Revolutions are rarely initiated and fought by people who have nice homes, good food, and lots of opportunity."

"Yeah," I agreed. "But then why are you running away?"

"I'm sick of the hypocrisy and I want action. Is it a crime to want some excitement and adventure?" He laughed. "If I was forty, I'd probably plod away here in some radical organization, writing pamphlets and organizing protests, but I'm young, I've got guts, I'm willing to risk everything for revolution now. So *adios amigos*."

I smiled and shook my head. The robbery had brought me close to Hector over the summer. We had put our lives in each other's hands, trusting our instincts and judgement in a situation in which any mistake would be potentially fatal. It had been one of the most intimate experiences I'd ever shared with anyone, although admittedly in a macabre sort of way.

There were people who were critical of Hector's motives for going to Central America, but I never could find fault with someone for wanting some excitement as well as political commitment in their life. I often thought that one reason so few young people in North America got involved in politics was because of the lack of adventure and excitement so necessary at that stage of their lives. I never saw Hector again, but I heard from some of his friends that he did make contact with the Sandinistas, and perhaps he did become involved in the revolutionary adventure that he so craved.

✳ **13** ✳

After the ENGO conference in the fall of 1981, Brent, Doug, and I began to escalate our guerrilla plans. We were coming to the conclusion that there were no other people ready to participate in any serious guerrilla actions, but we decided to begin at least acquiring the materials for future actions. That way when the people surfaced and the time was right, the infrastructure would be in place. The strategies developed at the conference to fight B.C. Hydro's megaprojects could easily be carried out by other environmentalists, without our participation, but there were no people around to actually stop the megaprojects if the political process failed. We could be those people.

While the rest of us were involved in organizing the ENGO conference by day and learning to steal cars by night, Doug had been preoccupied with research into explosives and weapons. He had learned that the Department of Highways used an explosive called Toval to blast rock from mountain faces alongside highways. Toval was manufactured in gel form and packaged in dynamite sticks about an inch and a half in diameter. The dynamite was detonated by blasting caps ignited through an electric charge. Doug had learned all about how to handle the explosive. Toval couldn't be detonated through heat — even if it was thrown into a fire, it wouldn't ignite — but the shock of puncturing the dynamite casing with a sharp object at a certain velocity could set if off. If we wanted to handle it we would have to be extremely careful.

Doug had devised a simple, yet ingenious way of breaking into one of the dynamite magazines that we had spotted on our target-practice runs. After taking another trip up the Squamish highway to verify that the magazine was still there, we decided to test his method. We built a small dynamite magazine from two-by-fours and plywood and painted it with camouflage colours so that we could hide it on some remote mountainside until we needed it. One Sunday afternoon we made the trip up the highway to another abandoned logging road. Eventually we got out of the van and hauled the walls of our homemade magazine up the side of a mountain through thick scrub brush to a place where it seemed unlikely anyone would go. Using a battery-operated drill, we assembled the magazine and left it to become overgrown and disappear from sight in the dense underbrush.

On another beautiful Sunday afternoon, carrying the necessary tools, we made the journey up to the place where we had seen what looked like a logging road blocked by a chain-link gate — which signified that a dynamite magazine was not far off. We snapped through the padlock on the gate with heavy-duty bolt cutters, then drove the van through and hooked the chain-link gate up again. Brent stayed behind, hiding up on some rocks overlooking the highway so he could warn us in case someone decided to stop and go for a walk up our logging road.

Doug and I lurched up the overgrown logging road in my van, and managed to get within a hundred yards of the magazine. We didn't want to have to carry the awkward fifty-five-pound cases any further than we could help it, and especially didn't want to risk dropping the dynamite on the sharp rocks protruding out of the ground.

The huge dynamite magazines looked like rusty steel obelisks, monumental reminders of humankind's omnipresence even in this remote wilderness paradise. Birds had left their retaliatory statements splattered all over the magazines in shades of green, grey, and white droppings. The magazine was roughly the size of a ten-by-ten room with a large, heavy-gauge steel door mounted on hinges guarding the entrance. The lock was covered by a similarly heavy-gauge steel plate to prevent thieves from picking or drilling into it. To overcome this problem, Doug had brought along an electric key-hole saw designed to drill through metal — which also called for a car battery and an AC/DC converter. For a good five minutes, we took turns holding the drill as it bit into the steel plate, throwing shards of shiny grey metal onto the ground. We had to keep stopping and spraying the bit with a cooling lubricant to keep it from expanding and binding in the metal. Finally, success: with a sudden jerk, the circular bit broke through the plate. With no time to celebrate, Doug quickly put in a straight metal bit and began the easy task of drilling into the soft tumblers of the keyway. Once they had been shattered and picked out of the keyway, we simply inserted a screwdriver and opened the door. It creaked open slowly, heavy on its hinges, exposing its cache of six neatly stacked cases of dynamite. For a minute we were awestruck. The whole exercise had gone so flawlessly that we half expected the magazine to be empty, but this was yet another of our lucky days.

While Doug peered around in the darkness of the magazine with his flashlight, looking for the important box of blasting caps, I began the slow, laborious, and nerve-racking task of transporting one case after another to the van. When we had finished the loading, we brushed away our footprints from the dusty magazine floor with a leafy tree branch and tried to erase any other evidence that could possibly help to identify us. As we made our final trip back to the van carrying our battery and tools, I realized that the whole time we had been working, the local birds had been screeching and cawing, warning other animals of our intrusion into their territory. Now that we were leaving, they could go back to their normal routine of foraging and hunting.

We drove even more precariously back down the logging road because this time we had an extra 330 pounds in the van. I held my breath until we put the chain-link fence gate back in place and Brent was safely sitting between us on the engine housing. On the drive over to our homemade magazine, we were on a natural high, laughing and talking over top of each other. Not every mission went so flawlessly.

* * *

Although we had no specific plans for the dynamite, just knowing it was in our possession inspired more discussions around possible future actions. After organizing the ENGO conference and being so absorbed in developing strategies to stop the various B.C. megaprojects, we were heavily favouring doing an action against one of them. The other issue that we were beginning to discuss was the cruise missile.

On the day after Remembrance Day, November 11, 1981, we were as usual having a morning coffee and reading the paper. One article in particular jumped out at us. It was a small piece about a group called the Cruise Missile Conversion Project, which had organized a blockade of the driveway into the Litton plant in Toronto. That was where the subsidiary of the giant U.S. multinational company Litton Systems produced the guidance system for the cruise missile, a twenty-foot pilotless aircraft, which could be outfitted with a nuclear warhead. At the blockade twenty-one people had been arrested and charged with trespassing. We decided to keep abreast of developments around the struggle to stop Litton from manufacturing the guidance system for the cruise. The Litton business placed Canada in a key role in the manufacture of nuclear armaments.

Ideal actions would be around issues that had attracted popular support but had exhausted all legal avenues of opposition. We figured in those cases critical members of the public would be able to understand and perhaps even support militant direct action, since they could clearly see that the political process had failed them. Perhaps over time we might inspire other people to take direct action, thereby beginning the slow process of developing a militant movement. If our actions were not favourably received, we could always resurface from our underground lifestyle, but that option would only be open as long as we made no mistakes and left no evidence behind.

We realized that if we were to carry out any of our vague plans, we would have to acquire handguns, false identification, and money in order to live an underground lifestyle. This phase was fast approaching. We were not deterred by the realization that our guerrilla group might be limited to just Brent, Doug, and myself.

None of us relished the thought of living underground, leaving behind lovers and friends, but if we were to carry out actions with serious consequences, we couldn't afford to be living in the community, where we would be easy targets for police surveillance and arrest in the event that we did leave evidence behind. Continuing on a low-profile course of acquiring money, weapons, and ID would give us the precious time we needed to reconcile ourselves to the inevitable loneliness and stress of an underground lifestyle. Once we took the step of carrying out a serious, illegal political action, there would be no turning back, so it was essential that we be mentally prepared for the consequences.

Our weapons were limited so far to the Ruger Mini-14 and a very unreliable Llama .38 handgun, which misfired so often we could only use it as a decoy. We didn't need an arsenal of weapons, but we did need some concealed handguns for protection during an action. The stringent criteria for buying a handgun made it difficult if not impossible to buy one legally — although we had ruled that option out anyway, since we did not want the police to be able to trace a handgun to any of us. We decided we had only one route open to us: a break and enter of a gun owner's home.

Brent had been periodically dropping in to the various gun stores in town just to look around. He had a peculiar talent for acquiring sensitive information using imaginative techniques, which turned out to be remarkably useful in the development of our little group. I call it a talent because it is not something that can be learned or developed, but a complex gift involving spontaneity, imagination, foresight, and daring. One day in late November he was browsing around a local gun store when he noticed a flyer advertising an upcoming meeting of the Thompson Mountain Shooting Association's executive committee. The flyer listed the names of the executives. Grasping the utility of this information, Brent scooped up the flyer, and on the way home he stopped into the government office that had voter registration information.

That evening, Doug and I were sitting in the kitchen sharing a supper of stir-fried vegetables on rice when Brent nonchalantly walked in and casually dropped the ad and a page of paper with the list of names on the kitchen table. Seeing the significance in his action, I quickly picked up the papers and scanned them.

"So what's up?" Doug said with a note of irritability in his voice. He didn't like these little games of innuendo.

I smiled over at Brent, who was helping himself to a huge plate of vegetables. "It looks like Brent has discovered some places where guns might be got." I pushed the papers across the table so Doug could examine the sections where Brent had highlighted the executive's addresses on the photocopies of the voters list.

"How did you get these?" asked Doug, holding up the pages from the voters registration list.

"Oh, I made up some story about owning a collection agency and needing some addresses, which made the government bureaucrat very accommodating."

For a few minutes Doug read over the names and then stared off into space, squinting his eyes as though reading a page printed in thin air in front of him. Then he pushed his chair back and disappeared downstairs into his room without explanation or finishing his meal.

Brent and I were in the middle of a discussion over the morality of doing break and enters when Doug returned looking almost excited. Now it was his turn to plop something down in front of us, a gun magazine opened at an article on home security. I leaned over and began reading an article that was part of a regular series on home security written by a Richmond man named Drew McClure, who just happened to be an executive member of the Thompson Mountain Shooting Association.

"Well, we can assume that he'd have a gun collection in his home, but he wouldn't be my first choice for a B&E," I said.

"No, but it's worth checking his place out," Doug said.

Over dinner we drew up plans to case out everyone on the gun club's executive. Drew McClure's home, in the suburb of Richmond, was especially inviting because not only was he a member of the executive but so too was his wife. This meant that the odds of no one being home at their place on the night of the meeting were high.

Unbelievably, we had still not ditched the Pinto. Every week we swore it was time to get rid of it, but there always seemed to be some small reason to keep it just a little longer. Now that we were close to doing a gun robbery, we decided that it would be a perfect vehicle for committing that crime. Then we would ditch it. We had always been meticulous about fingerprints, and we were all willing to stake our lives on never having touched it with our bare hands.

We had also managed to get a police scanner by way of a five-finger discount and had it pre-programmed to intercept a number of police and emergency broadcasts, including the RCMP from Burnaby, Coquitlam, and Richmond. This would come in handy during a B&E because someone could stay in the vehicle listening to the scanner and warn us if any emergency broadcasts related to our activities came across the air waves.

After a brief period of casing the other members of the executive, we settled down to concentrate on the McClures. We took turns parking a few blocks from their house in the hours when children usually head off to school or return home. Not only did it appear that they were childless, but also Mrs. McClure seemed to be missing. Either she was on vacation or they were no longer living together. Either way, we really didn't care, as long as she didn't turn up at home on the night of the executive meeting.

Aside from being a member of a gun club and a bus driver, Drew McClure was also a home security expert. Why his status did not deter us from deciding to break into his house escapes me, but we were attracted to the irony of breaking into the home of a security expert. We figured that he might learn some invaluable lessons in the process that might further his career.

On the night of December 7, at almost the exact time that the gun club's meeting was scheduled to begin, we pulled up in our trusty Pinto on a side street near Drew's house. He lived on a busy street lined with a single row of houses that had a large field spanning their backyards. We parked on the street behind the field, so that we could sneak through it and make our entrance through Drew's back door. We knew that we were taking a big risk, given his sideline, so we had come mentally prepared to abort the plan if the house really did turn out to be a veritable Fort Knox. But during our casing we'd never seen any sign of a guard dog, which was our biggest fear. Nobody relishes the idea of being confronted by a well-trained dog.

Leaving one person in the car listening to the scanner, I and my partner crawled across the field to Drew's backyard with our little bag of break-in tools in tow. Since the meeting was scheduled for late in the evening, we guessed it would include a Christmas party. This scheduling worked out well for us because most of his neighbours would either be going to bed or watching the news. Upon reaching Drew's backyard, we scanned his neighbours' yards and saw no one in sight. Although we weren't wearing balaclavas, which we deemed too conspicuous, we were wearing toques, gloves, and bulky clothes so no identifying features would be visible if we were noticed by a neighbour.

Drew's backyard wasn't enclosed by a high-security fence but by a small picket fence with an unlocked latch. Oh well, we thought, he would probably compensate for this lack of security by having a deadbolt lock and other security paraphernalia on his back door. Once again, Drew surprised us with a simple doorknob lock that any amateur criminal could open by simply gripping it with a wrench and turning it forcefully until the lock broke. Now we were on red alert. Surely this lack of security must be a set-up for something so sophisticated that we would be trapped at a point when it would be too late to escape. As we forced the doorknob open and slowly began to turn it, we looked at each other one last time, preparing for a net to drop over us from the ceiling or for bright lights and sirens going on — or a pack of Dobermans suddenly lunging at us from the darkness. But no, as we let the door slowly swing open on its own momentum, nothing happened.

We peered in sheepishly, still not believing that we weren't being lured into some super-tech security net. My partner gingerly put a foot across the threshold and entered the kitchen: no sign of laser-beam motion detectors or dogs. We pulled the door shut behind us, tiptoeing through the kitchen into a hallway. Our eyes were straining to see whatever they could in the darkness, looking out to see if there wasn't some security system in this security expert's home — apparently not. Whatever Drew had up his sleeve must be very cunning, because still it eluded us, although admittedly we were far from professional.

We began checking rooms along the hallway. One was the

bathroom, one the master bedroom, and one was *the gun collection room*. No lock, no motion detector, no nothing. Weapons of all kinds were strewn about the room, on racks, on tables, but not in locking gun cases. There were even gun powder and casings he was obviously using to make his own ammunition. While my partner admired the gun collection, I went back to the bathroom and grabbed a couple of laundry hampers, which I figured would make handy carrying cases. Then I went into the master bedroom and pulled a pile leopard-print bedspread off the bed to wrap the weapons in. Something about a pile leopard-print bedspread reeks of marital separation and wild bachelor sexual experiences.

My partner was so spellbound by the sight of all the weapons that he seemed to have forgotten that we were in someone else's home. "Come on!" I urged, nudging him into action. Quickly he began wrapping weapons in the bedspread and putting them into the laundry baskets. There were so many it soon became obvious we could not take them all. We certainly did not need an arsenal, but now that we had taken this risk, we thought we might as well take as many as we could carry in one go. Into the laundry baskets went a Dan Wesson .357 Magnum with all the attachments, a Smith and Wesson nickel-plated .44 Magnum, a 12-gauge Remington pump-action shotgun with a folding stock, a PO8 9-millimetre pistol, an M-1 carbine and scope, a Colt .45 pistol, and many more. We had piled the laundry baskets so full of weapons we could barely see over them to walk when my partner put his basket down and picked up an old single-shot Mossberg, which had to be manually loaded with gun powder to fire. It was a collector's piece with no practical use, but I could see by the affectionate way he handled it that we weren't leaving without it. Reluctantly nodding my approval, I finally led him out of the room.

Leaving the house was more risky than entering, because anyone spying us carrying heavy laundry baskets in Drew's backyard at midnight would think we were doing something suspicious. Once again, luck was on our side. When we got back to the Pinto, we carefully placed the laundry baskets in the trunk and drove a few miles to a deserted area where we'd left my van. After loading the laundry baskets into the van, we spent a few minutes staring at the Pinto that had carried us through a number of hair-raising adventures. "The stories that car could tell," smiled my partner. "It's been like a good luck charm. I almost feel sad letting it go, but we can't keep pushing our luck."

After unloading the weapons back at our home, each one of us picked out a favourite. I really didn't know much about guns but I picked the .357 because it had a detachable barrel so that you could screw in a two-, four-, six-, or eight-inch barrel. Even without statistical proof, I would guess a disproportionate number of men have a penchant for weapons. Doug and Brent were no exception, even though they had been raised in liberal homes where hunting was frowned upon and gun control was supported. They didn't like to see themselves as macho, but the long hours they spent reading magazines like *Guns and Ammo* and cleaning their weapons led me to believe they found something irresistible about the power of a gun.

Shortly after the gun theft it dawned on us that we could also be the victims of a B&E. Since we were not experts on home security and didn't have the money to outfit our slum housing with a high-tech security system, we decided on a low-budget solution — building a big heavy box that would be difficult to break open. There were only two ways of obtaining the contents of this box. One way would be to carry it out of our house, which would be difficult because it was the size of a coffin, very heavy when loaded full of weapons, and impossible to transport in a car. The second way would be to smash it open with a sledge-hammer or cut it open with a chainsaw, which would involve making a tremendous amount of noise. Since our box resembled a coffin, we decided to paint it black. We figured if anyone did break into our house, they might hesitate about trying to smash up or carry out something that looked like it just might have a body in it.

✳ **14** ✳

Christmas was coming. Having been raised in Ontario, I was used to the traditional white, snowy Christmas, but in Vancouver the holidays usually meant more rain. The lack of a traditional Christmas climate did not bother me that year because I was as alienated from Christmas as a Buddhist monk. We saw Christmas as just another capitalist ploy designed to get people out shopping. The only concession to Christmas I made was a brief phone call to my worried family.

Just before Christmas we were surprised one night by the sudden appearance at our door of Gerry and Julie. They had left as punks but now returned as mountain folk in plaid shirts and natural, longer hair. The mountain air seemed to have cleaned away the urban grunge. At first they were exuberant, talking over each other, telling us stories about Julie's job with Parks Canada as a flag-person on a road crew and Gerry's job at the Marmot Basin Ski Resort. The fall experience working in the mountains and living in a remote cabin seemed to have cemented their relationship.

But the Rocky Mountain high had gone sour. At first Julie had loved her job. Her boss, a Boy Scout leader who had been voted Man of the Year in Jasper, had turned out to be something quite different, a sexual predator. It had all started with his making sexual advances towards her whenever they were alone in his truck, which she was forced to be since he had to drive her to places where they needed a flag-person. She had clearly shunned his advances but he ignored her wishes and kept escalating his efforts until one day he grabbed her breast in his truck. When Julie confided in a female co-worker, that woman said the same thing had happened to her. Julie decided to charge him. The morning of his hearing, he didn't show up and when someone went to his house to get him, they found him lying in his garage with his mouth wrapped around a hose attached to his car exhaust.

Although Julie realized his suicide wasn't her fault, she felt traumatized because he had a wife and kids. She began to feel as though everyone in Jasper hated her, even though there were rumours that her boss had abused his children as well. And so the story concluded with Julie and Gerry returning from Jasper with a bit of money in their pockets, looking for work and a place to live.

Bridget and Saphie had moved out of our house a few months earlier because they didn't want men around anymore. They still enjoyed Brent and Doug's companionship but they weren't happy with the other frequent male visitors. We suggested Julie could stay with them, and Gerry said he could stay with his mother until they could find their own place together. His father had died when he was young and he had developed a close relationship with his mother, helping her out whenever he could.

They were at a crossroads in their lives, searching for new identities and dreams. We were there to fill the void and guide them down the road towards becoming urban guerrillas. In retrospect I can see that they were too young and politically naive to make an informed decision about becoming urban guerrillas, but at the time we were desperate for members. Gerry was a victim of his love for Julie. She was a wilful and passionate young woman who had a tremendous influence over him. Tragically, Gerry was quite willing to give up his life, not for a political cause, but for Julie, and if that meant becoming an urban guerilla, so be it. Our judgement was also swayed by Julie's unbridled enthusiasm, fuelled partially by the passions of her youth and partially by her fascination with us and our dreams. We were not guilty of consciously manipulating and pressuring them into becoming involved with us, but we were certainly guilty of blinding ourselves, in particular to Julie's obvious naivety and gullibility. At the age of eighteen, Julie was incapable of fathoming the depths of the hardships we would inevitably face. Her dreams of young people racing romantically around the country robbing the rich to fund the just causes of the oppressed ended just before the young revolutionaries were mercilessly gunned down, before they went to prison, or before they were living in isolation while a nationwide manhunt went on around them. Her dreams were fuelled by the stories of Robin Hood, Bonnie and Clyde, and Romeo and Juliet, but her youth did not allow her to dwell on her own mortality or the inevitable sad ending to all those old stories.

Admittedly, Doug, Brent, and I were also somewhat idealistic and unprepared for the consequences of our dreams. But we were older, we had done more political study, and we had given the whole matter a lot more thought. Who is ever prepared for the consequence of death or prison, which is the destiny of many revolutionaries? But we continued blindly on, refusing to acknowledge that once the going got rough, Julie and Gerry would be ill-prepared to withstand the repression and isolation that our plans would entail.

On New Year's Eve, Doug, Brent, Julie, Gerry, and I sat around our kitchen table, with a couple of bottles of wine lubricating our thoughts. Deeply embroiled in philosophical discussions, we were oblivious to the chimes of the clock ringing in the New Year of 1982. It was a typical conversation, one that, with minor variations, we had many times over.

"The chances of anyone doing anything militant that might get them in jail are zilch in this country at this time," predicted Doug, who, by the way, didn't drink at all.

"Then what the hell is the point of carrying out actions if nobody can relate to us or is ever going to join us?" yelled Gerry, who did drink and had downed half a bottle himself by that point.

"We do it because it's the right thing to do," Brent said, standing up and holding his glass in the air. "Not because we are going to succeed, which is the capitalist way."

"Yes," I agreed. "Revolutionaries are motivated by their ideals, not by practical consequences. If they are effective and something practical comes of their actions in the long run, great, but if not they at least get the satisfaction of basing their actions on truth and justice. To be effective or successful implies having popular support from the people, but unfortunately the majority are not always right. If we were to determine what is the right or wrong course of action by what the majority believe, then we would still have slavery and women would still have the same status as cattle. Historically, change has often been initiated by a few enlightened thinkers, and just as often they've been in the minority. They might not be effective in terms of having the support of the people and changing society in the short term, but history may prove them to be right in the long term."

"Alright then," continued Brent, still standing, "another big question. Does the means justify the ends? For example, are robberies and bombings justifiable to accomplish a revolution aimed at bringing in a new society where robberies and bombings are no longer necessary?"

"I think the means will determine the end," I pontificated. "The organizations and actions carried out during a revolution are the microcosm of the new society. If the organizations are hierarchical, then that's the kind of society that will evolve, and if the actions involve militancy, then no doubt the people will continue to use militant actions to maintain the new society whenever necessary."

"I don't see any contradiction between robbing the rich, blowing up destructive property, and a revolutionary society," Brent said. "In a just society, nobody should be wealthy at the expense of others, and if they are they deserve to have that wealth confiscated. And if people are building weapons of destruction to maintain their wealth and power, I see nothing wrong with destroying those weapons."

"Being a cynic," Doug said with a smile, "leads me to believe that there is no such thing as an idealistic society other than the ones we dream up in our minds. We have this wonderful capacity to imagine perfection and ideals, but if we look around us in the real world, these concepts only exist for fleeting moments. Perfect peace, love, and harmony are interspersed with episodes of violence, hate, and discord. Our role, as idealists, is to struggle for a world where *good* overshadows *evil*. So, to answer your question, Brent, I would say we should try to use the tactics of peace and love in order to attain a more perfect society, but if those in power are using violence and hate against us, we may have to use less than ideal tactics — or else we will end up standing passively by as they massacre the meek. Since human beings have an inherent capacity for evil, even in the best of all possible worlds, we will have to be vigilant against those who would use violence to oppress others."

"I heard this woman in a café the other day say she didn't want the kind of peace you find in cemeteries," said Julie, who had been quietly absorbing the conversation up until then. "To me that means we don't want peace at the expense of others. If peace means living quietly while powerful people are oppressing and killing the powerless, then I don't want peace. That's not peace, that's complacency."

"That's good," I said, impressed by the thought.

"It's time we descend from the clouds," Brent said, "and get down to reality. When are you going to Ontario, Ann?"

Before Christmas I had purchased a plane ticket so I could go and get an Ontario driver's licence in the name of Mary Milne. We had a couple of sets of ID with social insurance numbers and birth certificates from the surveys we had done the previous year, but no driver's licences. Our ID people lived in British Columbia, so it was probable that they had B.C. driver's licences. We had investigated how advanced cross-referencing was in relation to provincial driver's licences and had discovered that it was still possible to get a driver's licence from out of province without the licence bureau knowing that you already had a licence in British Columbia. We knew that it would not be long before it would be impossible to acquire two driver's licences from different provinces for the same person because computer technology was quickly making routine procedure of centralized information.

A year had passed since I had got a learner's permit in Mary Milne's name, so I was ready to take the driver's test. "I leave in a week." I raised my eyebrows to warn Brent not to go further with that topic in the presence of Julie and Gerry. Although we were steering them in the direction of joining our little group, we weren't ready to include them in our plans yet. They had still not shown any kind of consistency. One minute they were planning to move up to the Chilcotins to build a cabin and the next they were gung-ho for a heavy militant action. If we had more people, we would have ruled them out completely, but three people is a far from ideal number to carry out a militant action campaign.

"Where's Nick?" Julie asked.

"Home at his parents for Christmas," I said. "He'll be back just before I go to Ontario."

By the time we finished the second large bottle of wine, our conversations had degenerated to crazed laughter over Gerry's mimicry of some characters in the radical community. Eventually Doug made an exit for his bedroom while the rest of us continued to laugh into the early hours of the new year.

✳ **15** ✳

I landed at the Toronto International Airport and transferred to a bus headed for Ottawa, where an old friend, Victor Zuzek, lived. Even though I hadn't seen Victor in years, my vivid recollection of his yard came in handy because I had lost his address. As I turned down his street, I recalled that his house had stood out the last time I visited because it had been almost completely reclaimed by the native vegetation of the area. I remembered seeing at first sight only two front windows peering through a maze of vines climbing out of a once well-kept garden. When you got closer you could see the paint peeling off the wooden siding, and then his house number. To get to his door you had to make your way through patches of lush dandelions that had triumphantly broken through cracks in the patio stones. An unkept lawn had transformed itself into a small field of tall grasses interspersed with various flowering weeds. Compared to the other sterile yards with their well-manicured gardens, Victor's had been alive. An assortment of butterflies had flitted about from the vines to the wild flowers.

My memories served me well — the house looked deserted, but then it always did. I made my way around the side, where I was confronted by a three-foot wooden fence covered with dead vines. Compared to everything else in my life, a three-foot fence was not an obstacle. As I was climbing over it, I was suddenly faced with a

Bouvier dog who began half-heartedly barking at me. "Hi Bouchie!" He responded by wagging his tail so hard his whole back end wagged with it. As I bent over to pet him I heard another dog barking, but looking around all I could see was an old rusty car parked in an alley at the back. Then I spotted the familiar head of Louie, a yellow Terrier cross, peering over the car's steering wheel. I figured I better greet him in order to alleviate any fears he might have about intruders on his property. As I headed towards the car, Louie hopped out the open driver's window, scrambled over the fence, and trotted up to me with his tail wagging too.

The two dogs followed me quite happily up the stairs to the back door. I knocked once and yelled in for Victor, but only silence greeted me. The room just inside the house resembled a kennel with some conveniences added for human comfort. A huge bag of kibble surrounded by fur balls prevented the back door from opening completely, and doggy toys were strewn all over the floor. Walking in uninvited, I spotted a pot of coffee still plugged in and warming on a kitchen counter littered with dirty dishes. Despite the mess, the kitchen table had been cleared off.

As I perused the place the dogs followed me, wagging their tails enthusiastically the whole time. I was touched to find the spare bedroom meticulously clean, with what looked like fresh sheets on the bed and a vase of wild flowers adorning a clothes bureau, because house cleaning was the last item on Victor's list of priorities. I went back to the kitchen and poured myself a coffee and settled down at the table to wait for him. About three minutes before he appeared, the dogs started running back and forth from the front window to the back door, whining and barking and looking at me in an attempt to persuade me to open the door. I peeked out the window and was happy to see that Victor looked the same as ever. His hair and beard had greyed somewhat, but otherwise I would never have guessed that he was someone who, just that past year, had survived a double organ transplant.

As soon as he opened the door, my surprise greeting was thwarted by his dogs leaping up and licking him as though they had not seen him in months. His grey sweatsuit was about three sizes too big and covered in muddy dog prints. We talked about his dogs and our lives for a couple of hours, and then I began to wonder how I could broach the topic of borrowing his car to take a driver's test using phony ID. I trusted Victor implicitly, but I had promised Brent and Doug that I wouldn't tell anyone about our plans. Finally I just blurted out, "Do you think I could borrow your car to take a driver's test?"

He looked at me for a while with a little smile on his face, knowing that I was usually up to something. I smiled back sheepishly but didn't offer any more information, and he didn't ask. "Tomorrow, after I take the dogs out, you can borrow the car as long as you want," he said, and that was the end of it. We talked some more and then I made a phone call to book an appointment for Mary Milne's driver's test.

The next morning I got up early so that I would have plenty of time to shower and dress like an average student, which is what I guessed Mary Milne was. Over coffee I memorized her vital statistics.

"When's your appointment?" Victor had made a point of getting up early so we could spend some time together.

"In an hour?" I said, hoping he would put off his morning dog walk until later in the day. He read my mind.

"Well you better go and I'll take the dogs out when you get back." He smiled reassuringly. I went over to him and wrapped my arms around him, fighting back the tears that accompanied my sense of betrayal for having left him to pursue my political passions in Europe, years earlier. But my feelings were tempered by knowing that, had I stayed and not pursued my dreams, my regard for him would have turned to resentment, making his life miserable. Sadly, understanding these feelings didn't dampen the love and guilt I felt for a man who might well have been my lifelong partner if I had been a "normal" woman. Tears welled up inside me and escaped in quiet sobs as I held him. Why was I crying? Was it for me or for him or for both of us? Being close to him made me painfully aware of the emptiness in my life. Holding him stirred up memories of our former life, when we were both truly happy. Memories of walking together holding hands with our dogs to the local farmers' market to buy cheese and fruit. The smells and sounds of the market and the warm feeling of sharing that simple experience together were still vivid. After, we would go to a local swimming hole for the day, laughing and playing in the water, then basking in the warm afternoon sun knowing that when we got home we could make a wonderful meal with the market food. The little things that were right there for the taking had always made our lives worth living. Why had I turned away from a life that was so peaceful and good to pursue this revolutionary dream that would no doubt turn into a nightmare? Were my motives pure? Did I really believe that my actions could make a significant differ- ence in society, enough to justify the personal suffering that I — and everyone else I touched — would go through? My sadness turned to fear.

"Am I crazy, Victor?"

"Yes, but in a good way. You better get going or you'll miss your appointment."

By the time I was driving to my test, I had put sentimental thoughts out of my mind and was focusing on the task at hand. The driver's examination was uneventful, and I passed without problems. Victor would mail my licence certificate to British Columbia. We spent my last day in Ontario doing what we had always enjoyed most, just walking the dogs and talking.

* * *

Only a few weeks after my return from Ontario, our quest for qual- ity false identification took an unexpected turn for the better. So far we each had a set of false ID that we had obtained from the survey information. The problem was that those people still lived in British Columbia, which meant that we would all be implicated in each other's dealings with the criminal justice system. We had no solution to this problem until Brent stumbled upon it.

One cold January evening when he was walking home from a meeting he caught a glimpse of a large metal garbage container — a dumpster — the size of a ten-foot-square room, sitting in a far corner of the U.S. Consulate's parking lot. To most people this background object would not have stimulated any brain activity, but in Brent it sparked an inspirational thought. American Con- sulate — garbage — the relationship could be quite interesting. Brent's curious and imaginative nature, in combination with his unorthodox thinking patterns, could produce a brand of genius at times.

Brent knew that the entrance to the embassy parking lot, with its security attendants in a booth, was on the other side of the building. He quickly pulled himself up and over the low concrete retaining wall and into the parking lot. He had a talent for moving unnoticed inside stores and, in this case, parking lots. Within sec- onds he was poised back behind the garbage container, peering around its corner to be sure no one was around to spy on him. Across the cavernous expanse he could make out a couple of park- ing attendants talking together inside their heated glass cubicle.

Otherwise, there was no one else around. There wasn't much activity inside an embassy on a cold Sunday evening. Like a cat burglar, Brent slithered quietly over the side and down into the metal garbage container. To his relief, he was the only living, breathing thing inside it.

Brent had no preconceived notion of what he was looking for, but he had a hunch that the garbage of the U.S. Embassy had to hold something of interest. As he bent over to pick up some waste paper, he noticed a face on a photograph looking up from under his shoe. The face was on part of a form ripped in half. The other half was right beside it. The form was an application, filled out by one Annette Lillicropp, for landed immigrant status in the United States. Brent's brain immediately registered the importance of this find. Quickly he scanned the form and saw that it contained all her vital statistics — social insurance number, mother's maiden name, birth date, physical description, brief personal history. To make the find even more monumental, dozens of other forms, merely ripped in half, were scattered all over the place. For people like us, planning to live as fugitives, a find like this was akin to what the discovery of the first bipedal fossil, Lucy, was to the archeological community. The forms would provide us with the identities of real Canadians who had relocated to the United States; their activities, as documented through their identification, would never clash with ours. As quickly as he could, Brent scooped up the papers and stuffed them into a large box he also found in the garbage. When the box was full he proceeded to stuff the forms into his pants, shirt, and every other place he could find on his body. He had so many ripped-up forms hidden in the nooks and crannies of his clothing that as he slunk back out from the parking lot a few pieces of paper escaped and drifted harmlessly across the concrete floor.

Once he was safely back on the street he sprinted as fast as he could to our house and arrived, excited, at the door. As luck would have it, Doug and I were home to catch the full impact of his find. Dragging us down into Doug's bedroom, he put down his box of treasure and began tearing the forms out from all over his body.

"This is great!" Doug laughed. "I can't believe they don't shred this stuff."

Brent smiled. "If they ever discover what we've used it for, they'll invest in a paper shredder."

For hours we sat on the bed matching the pieces of ripped-up applications until we had dozens of complete application forms with all their vital statistics and information. We amused ourselves fabricating fictional histories of these individuals based on the information in the forms, but the best one was real: an application from a reverend and his wife who wanted to work in the United States. We figured that those particular IDs would be ones the police would never suspect.

During the rest of January and February, we busied ourselves mailing away for and picking up the new identifications. We had also managed to acquire a sizeable sum of money, enough for the three of us to live on for at least a year. Although there was really no pressing need for us to go underground and begin a militant campaign, now that we possessed all the prerequisite identification, guns, and money we had a false sense of urgency. Over a series of meetings at Bino's we decided to subject ourselves to a little experiment to see if we were psychologically prepared for the lifestyle of urban guerrillas. We suspected it would be difficult, but we had the foresight to realize it would be wiser to voluntarily isolate ourselves first rather than carry out a bombing and then be forced to live in isolation without being prepared for the consequences.

We decided that our experiment in living as fugitives would also give us the opportunity to articulate on paper a political philosophy and strategy upon which we could base our future militant activities. Doug hated writing political treatises, but Brent and I had been aware for quite some time that without an articulate political theory, our actions would be meaningless. Unless people understood why we were acting, they might mistake us for right-wing vigilantes, or mercenaries, or maybe even just kids carrying out dangerous pranks. In our case, we owed the radical community an explanation for our actions since, inevitably, they would bear the brunt of the consequences of our actions.

Where would we go? One of Doug's idiosyncrasies was a phobia about leaving British Columbia, but the whole point of living underground was to avoid meeting anyone we knew, even accidentally. After years of activism, Doug and Brent could easily run into someone they knew anywhere in the province. The closest big city outside the province was Calgary. Why not Calgary?

Moving there would be inconsequential for Brent and me, but for Doug it would be a real test of commitment. When Brent suggested Calgary, we scrutinized Doug's face for a reaction because we knew that he would never articulate his feelings. As much as he wanted to be a feminist man, capable of expressing emotions, Doug was by nature a repressed individual. As the idea of living in Calgary began to fester in his mind, his face took on a preoccupied look, his eyelids blinking rapidly. For a few minutes, Brent and I just unabashedly stared at him, waiting for some response. Finally he began to pace back and forth in front of the kitchen table.

"Okay," he said sitting down abruptly. "We'll give notice and leave March first. Somebody's going to have to stay here to pick up the ID we're still waiting for." He gave us a piercing look as though we had murdered someone in his family.

"Do you want to stay for that?" I asked him gingerly.

"No, I think Brent and I should go first. It's always better for a woman to go into those apartment buildings to pick up the ID. Men always seem more suspicious," he said in a sharp, clipped voice.

"That doesn't give us much time to see Angie, Rachel, and Nick, does it?" said Brent, acknowledging our various lovers.

"I think they know where we've been headed for the last few years," Doug said. "I'm just going to tell Rachel that I have to go away for a while. She'll understand. So will Nick and Angie."

Brent and I looked at each other with raised eyebrows, knowing that Doug had just made a stronger display of commitment towards becoming an urban guerrilla than either of us had done. We had often heard him say the only way he would cross the B.C. border would be in a box. Would we be able to make the same kind of psychological sacrifice when the time came?

When Nick came in later that evening, I looked at him with different eyes. Up until then I couldn't honestly say that I was in love with him — at least not the kind of "in love" where you imagine growing old together and making plans for more than a few months at a time. The only thing about our relationship that made us more than friends was sex, but I was often intensely aware that my feelings for Brent far overshadowed whatever I felt for Nick. But Nick either didn't notice or didn't care.

That evening he looked different. For the first time I saw what a kind, decent person he was, and not all that bad-looking either. Usually when he came in I wouldn't stop what I was doing to show him any affection, but that night I got up from my chair and wrapped my arms around him, squeezing him so tightly that he asked me what was wrong.

"Nothing. I just want you to know how much I care about you." I still couldn't bring myself to use the word "love." He pushed me back gently so he could look at my face, then smiled and said he cared a lot about me too. "I saw Brent up at the laundromat a little while ago and he said I could have all his files," Nick said with a puzzled look on his face. "I know how much those files mean to him and how valuable they are. What's up?"

Brent was an information man. Ever since he had relocated from his parents' home to Vancouver he had collected copies of every radical poster and pamphlet made in British Columbia. Sometimes he used them to make his own signature collage posters, but most of the time he kept them in a well-organized metal file cabinet. Every radical in Vancouver knew that if they needed some obscure information for some project, chances were Brent would have it. If there had been a dollar value on rare old posters and leaflets, Brent's collection would have been priceless.

I shrugged, evading his question. "Do you want supper?"

Nick laughed. "Something big must be up. Brent's giving away his most prized possessions and now you're offering to make me supper. Are you two dying or something?"

"No, but we're going away for awhile," I blurted out. I hadn't planned on telling him so soon, but he was making it hard not to. "Brent and Doug are leaving at the end of the month and I'll be leaving a few weeks after. But it's very important that you don't tell anyone."

Brent, Doug, and I had long accepted, and appreciated, Nick's role in our group of friends: an intellectual, putting out his quarterly booklet, *Resistance*, reproducing and analysing communiqués from different international guerrilla groups. Even though he identified as a militant, he wasn't actually very good at doing anything illegal, even shoplifting. But we understood that any political movement was strengthened by the diversity and talents of the characters involved. If there were no intellectual theorists or publishers, then how would the ideas that motivate the militants ever be propagated? We were hoping Nick would publish any communiqués or writings we might produce in the future.

Nick's face dropped as he digested what I had said. We so rarely discussed our feelings for each other that I really wasn't sure just how much he felt for me.

"So I guess we'll be giving up the house," he said, glancing around him.

"Yeah," I said, waiting for a reaction.

"Maybe I could move in with Corrie and Phoenix?" he said flatly.

"I'm sure you could. Maybe I could stay there with you for the two weeks before I go? Will you ask them?"

He nodded sadly. Even though we had never shared any of the details of our plans, Nick knew what we were up to, and he also knew better than to ask questions. He understood the "need to know" principle — in illegal matters, it was not in either his or our best interests for him to know anything other than what he needed to know. That way, if we ever got busted, there was nothing he would be able to tell the police. If he fell in love or got drunk or his loyalty waned with the passing of time, he would never be able to tell anyone anything.

We had as romantic a supper as we'd ever had, which simply meant we ate alone and talked about things other than politics for a change. I tried to draw him out by asking about his feelings and plans for the future. He mentioned a plan to get a job as a printing press operator and become active in the union. *Resistance* was still his pride and joy, but he was in dire straits financially so the union job would satisfy his needs for both money and activism as a member of the working class.

As is usually the case, the awareness that I might never see him again brought out my tender, sentimental feelings towards him. It also made me question whether I was doing the right thing in becoming an urban guerrilla, and was I really attracted to Brent after all? Without a doubt Nick would make a better partner — loyal, kind, supportive — but Brent was more exciting, charismatic, and brave. There would be a price to pay for Brent's more dynamic personality, though. He would be far more likely to stray sexually, inflict subtle emotional abuse, and pursue his own needs at my expense. Still, at that point in my life, romantic, revolutionary dreams filled my head at the expense of realistic plans for personal happiness.

It didn't take long for us to clear out our house. Brent and Doug didn't explain to anyone where they were going, just that they were travelling, and I moved with Nick to Corrie and Phoenix's house and subjected myself to the painful sight of Nick adjusting rapidly to living with the two sisters in unconventional domestic bliss.

By mid-March all the identification we had sent away for had arrived. It was time for me to go. I woke up early so that Nick and I could eat breakfast together, but when I rolled over and looked at him breathing deeply, I didn't have the heart to wake him. The morning sun played over his alabaster skin, beckoning me to wrap my arms around him. Down below the sounds of the city traffic beginning to hum broke the serenity of the moment, reminding me that I had to go. It would be so nice and safe to stay here. But I knew that in another hour a different kind of energy would be pulsing through my body, driving me on to another adventure. I just wasn't ready for a predictable, settled-down life yet. I had to pursue my dream no matter what the consequences. I gave Nick one last kiss on his cheek, then rolled out of bed.

✳ **16** ✳

Two hours later I was on a bus heading for Calgary, with nothing but the clothes on my back and a purse in my hand. I had already gotten over my reluctance to leave Nick and was looking forward to seeing Doug and Brent again. A new chapter in my life was about to unfold. Actually it was so much more dramatic than that: a new *life* was about to begin — a new identity, appearance, and lifestyle. Like a caterpillar, I was about to transform from one entity into something completely different. I would step out of this metal cocoon in Calgary to transform myself into a butterfly named Lillicropp; a very plain butterfly, though — one that could fly unnoticed down the streets, through the malls to whatever destinations I had in mind. I would not be of an exotic variety, with huge colourful wings, but rather a plain moth-like creature that nobody would notice.

From the bus terminal in Calgary I transferred to a city bus destined for the university, our prearranged rendezvous. Riding across the city, I watched the scenery go by, trying to get a feel for my new home. In comparison to Vancouver, Calgary looked like a bland city. Vancouver is surrounded by breathtaking mountains that could lift my spirits out of the city anytime I looked up. It is a city teeming with different ethnic groups that bring colour and diversity to whatever cold concrete buildings they keep themselves busy in. The brightly painted wooden suburban homes that sprawl from the city core on hillsides reflect the many alternative-lifestyle people drawn to the beauty of the west coast. Calgary's distant ridge of mountains seemed less compelling. The city, at first impression, appeared to be a flat, homogeneous place inhabited largely by white middle-class people who seemed to fear anything culturally exotic or eccentric — at least that was my first impression.

At the university I headed for the cafeteria, expecting to find my two friends waiting for me. Instead the place was near empty — which wasn't surprising, because it was late in the evening. But Brent and Doug's absence was alarming, because I couldn't think of any reason why they wouldn't be there to greet me. I got a coffee from a machine and retreated to a seat in the centre of the room. I sat for about ten minutes before I saw them. At first I was taken aback by the two men I vaguely recognized coming in the door. Doug had shorn his blond locks for a military-style haircut. Brent had a matching haircut and was not wearing his usual glasses. Could he be wearing contact lenses? Both were sporting dreaded polyester pants and shirts in neutral shades. Their metamorphosis seemed to have gone awry. In their case the personal transformation seemed to have reversed, turning colourful butterflies into ugly caterpillars. They had worked so hard at looking normal that they had gone over the edge to appear almost like military characters. Even the way they carried themselves had changed. There was a brisk cadence to their walk, and their posture was poker-straight, lending credence to the old adage "you look the way you feel" — only in reverse, "you feel the way you look."

"Well if it isn't the guys from Dragnet! I swear, if I didn't know better, I'd think you were cops." My excitement at seeing them was quickly dampened by their preoccupied and tense expressions.

"We're being followed," Brent said tersely, still standing. "We saw the bus arrive and watched you through the cafeteria windows to be sure you weren't being followed."

"You should have seen what we went through just to get here," Doug said. "We spent about an hour going in and out of malls and using all kinds of other anti-surveillance manoeuvres to shake any tails we might have."

"Why would you be followed?"

"We'll explain later, but let's just get out of here," Brent said.

I thought they had overactive imaginations and were jumping into this guerrilla thing way too fast. To my knowledge, they hadn't even done anything illegal yet. Maybe they were bored and had developed this paranoia just for something to do. As we walked across the parking lot towards a lone pickup truck, they kept peering around to see if anyone was following us. When we got to the truck, Brent took out a set of keys. "This is ours," he said with a surprising lack of enthusiasm.

I understood why when he turned over the engine and it began to run as though it was on its last legs. I could see they had been busy. "Well, fill me in," I said impatiently as we began the short drive back into Calgary.

"As soon as we got here," Doug said, "we rented a furnished apartment and decided to buy a truck. We needed one. Public transit here is the shits."

"Unfortunately, we got ripped off," continued Brent. "We don't know anything about vehicles. Neither of us have ever owned one so I guess we should've taken it to a mechanic first. But when we tried it, it seemed fine.

"The people you bought it off might have been professional rip-offs," I suggested. "If it ran fine on a test run, they might have used heavy oil or STP to disguise the sound of metal on metal from the lifters or pistons." I had heard of this ploy, but essentially I was no expert on vehicles either.

"Whatever happened, it's too late now to do anything about it — unless we want to get our money back with the help of an enforcer," he said with a sarcastic smile. "Anyway, after we bought the truck, we decided to buy some ammo since it's so much cheaper here than B.C. We read about this sale on 223 ammo for the Mini-14 at a place called the Klondike in Edmonton. So we drove up there and bought two thousand rounds of it."

"Two thousand rounds!"

"Yeah, they had a sale," he repeated in a quiet voice. Obviously it had dawned on him, after the fact, that the quantity was a bit over the edge. It seemed there were no half measures in our world.

"I'm surprised they could legally sell you that much," I said, still wondering what had ever possessed them. Did they think the three of us were literally going to wage a war against the Canadian army or what? I was a little alarmed, because I thought guns were to be used only as a deterrent during the commission of a robbery or political action.

"We need a lot of ammo for target-practice. If we ever do have to use guns, we need to be confident and in control enough not to shoot someone by accident," Doug said.

"We're going to have to do a lot of target-practising," Brent added.

I was becoming distressed because there I was, in Calgary barely an hour and already immersed in a cat and mouse game with the cops, apparently due to our own stupidity. I was beginning to wonder if our motive for carrying out political actions was to initiate a more militant movement or if it was just to have fun with guns and ammo. I had anticipated using this time in Calgary to develop our politics, but I was beginning to wonder if my companions were being sidetracked by their fascination with guns.

"I still don't understand why you think you're being followed?"

"After we bought all the 223 ammo, we decided to drive around to different gun stores and buy bullets for the .45 since the stuff was so cheap in Edmonton," explained Brent. "But we noticed the same guy we had seen standing around in the Klondike in another gun store we went to."

"We thought that was a bit weird but we wrote it off as coincidence until he reappeared at the next store," added Doug. "Then we started to get worried. We decided to try one more store on the other side of the city, so we drove over and bought one last box of .45 ammo, and who should appear outside the store on the sidewalk but our follower."

"Are you sure it was the same guy?" They both nodded, but I didn't detect absolute certainty.

"I just don't understand what the motive would be for anyone following you. You haven't done anything illegal. Granted, buying two thousand rounds of ammo was odd, but even then, there must be other people who take advantage of a sale."

"I know it doesn't make much sense," Brent agreed. "But we're pretty sure it was the same guy at each store. Maybe there's some law that gun-store owners have to report unusual purchases of guns or ammo, just like banks have to report cash transactions of more than $10,000?"

"Naw," said Doug. "I've never heard of that, and anyway that guy was in the store before we even bought the ammo."

"That would mean the heat must have originated in Vancouver," Brent said, somewhat excited about solving this riddle. "Maybe we've been under surveillance in Vancouver for a while, but why?"

"Maybe they've been following us since the Amax actions," I suggested. "But on the other hand, I can't see the cops spending that much money and manpower following us for such small actions."

We pulled up in front of a seedy-looking motel with a sign offering cheap rates. "We've been staying here ever since we got back from Edmonton," Doug said. "We didn't want to lead them to our apartment — to the guns, ID, and everything."

I shook my head in disbelief. The whole thing just didn't make sense. Either they were impatient to get the experience of being fugitives underway or they were totally paranoid. Regardless, their actions did not inspire much confidence. Suddenly I was filled with doubt about my partners' emotional stability. It was a bad omen that my first day living as an outlaw was consumed by what I thought was a surveillance phantom.

Their motel room consisted of a room with two double beds, a fake-wooden bureau, a coffee percolator, and a bathroom with tub and shower. This was not the kind of place to call home. I felt the weight of depression beginning to settle on my shoulders. I wouldn't have minded dealing with a problem resulting from a real political action, but this one seemed to be of their own creation, whether it was real or not.

"Are you hungry?" Brent asked softly.

"Yes," I said dejectedly.

"Let's go pick up some burgers, Doug, then we can talk some more," he said, picking up the keys.

I lay back on the worn bedspread and rested my head on my arms. The scattered stains on the faded wallpaper and rug were reminders of the many strangers who had spent their nights here, drinking, smoking, and arguing. Old coffee stains splattered across the wallpaper seemed to tell the story of a morning argument after a drunken night, climaxing in a couple of coffee cups being hurled across the room in frustration. Cigarette burns and liquor stains were testimonials to many late-night debaucheries, and the lack of any moveable decor attested to the poorest of clientele. This was not the kind of place that warmed the spirit. I closed my eyes, hoping to escape to a more peaceful place, and pictured Nick's skin luminous in the morning sun. Oh how I wished that I was curled up in his arms drifting off into a tranquil sleep. Already I regretted my inability to be content with a more predictable lifestyle.

I never did eat the burgers that Brent bought. I woke up in the morning still in my clothes, to the sound of cars and trucks beeping outside on the highway. I rolled over and saw Brent sitting up on the edge of the bed, lighting a smoke. He must be feeling anxious, I figured, since he didn't normally smoke first thing in the morning.

"I'm going over to the apartment," I announced after a while. "It just doesn't make any sense that you would be followed. What else are we going to do, just stay here and leave the coffin behind?"

Doug had been listening from the bathroom. "I suppose if you did some anti-surveillance manoeuvres, it would be safe."

"Yeah, I'll go over to the apartment, hang around there for a few hours, and if everything looks cool, we can go home. I'll meet you at that burger joint across the street in a few hours."

Perhaps the novelty of living as fugitives in this seedy motel had worn off and they were eager to get on with things. The more time passed, the more appealing became the possibility that they had been mistaken about being followed. I jumped into the shower, hoping that the cleansing would bring with it a new day full of hope and possibilities. I would have to get a new wardrobe, a new look, a new identity. What kind of caterpillar would I become? I smiled to myself.

After an hour of anti-surveillance manoeuvres, I arrived at a plain red-brick two-storey apartment building that looked just like every other building on the block. It would always be of utmost importance that we never stand out, that nothing about us be memorable. We had to become the kind of people whom the clerk at the corner store couldn't quite remember; the kind that blended into a crowd, whose voices did not rise above the din and whose shoes did not make a sound. Rather than caterpillars, perhaps, we had to become chameleons blending in perfectly with whatever environment we were in.

I walked down the hall and inserted my key into the lock. Only for a few seconds did I feel any fear. It seemed so implausible that we would be under heavy surveillance just for purchasing a lot of ammunition in Edmonton. I pushed open the door. Nothing happened. Nobody jumped out, and no suspicious shadows lay across the floor. Stepping inside, I shut the door behind me. After inspecting the place thoroughly, I concluded that no one had been there since Doug and Brent had left a week earlier. A hair that Doug had told me about — carefully placed in the seam between the coffin's lid and the box — was still there, proving unquestionably that no one had tampered with the apartment. Since the apartment was so sparsely furnished, with nothing but a bed, dining-room table, couch, and bureau, any intruder would immediately be drawn to the huge black coffin sitting in the bedroom. I made a mental note to rectify this situation by putting a table cloth on it so it could be used as a coffee table in the unlikely event that we had visitors, even if only the landlord.

I made a coffee and sat down on the couch, staring at the walls and floor to pass some time. The place was immaculate but so barren it felt like a small institution. I better make this place a little homey, or it would only add to the inevitable depression that would accompany getting used to being away from friends and lovers. My running shoes squeaked as I walked across the clean wooden floors. When I put my cup down on the kitchen counter, the sound echoed against the walls. The place was creepy. I had planned on spending at least an hour there but could only tolerate fifteen minutes. I put my jacket back on and opened the door.

I met Doug and Brent at the prearranged time in the burger joint. They were each carrying a large gym bag full of ammunition, which they'd been carting around since leaving the motel. Despite the good news that nothing was amiss in the apartment, they decided to keep their eyes open on our way back for any signs of the man they believed had been following them around Edmonton. As for the truck, we decided we'd look for another one in good condition that we could steal, so we could convert it into a seemingly legal one that would meet the description of ours.

On our way back to the apartment, we drove past a mall with a sign in an upstairs window advertising reduced rates for anyone willing to let student hair stylists perm, cut, or shampoo their hair. "Stop!" I yelled. "I'm going to go in there and get my hair done before people in the building see me as I look now." Brent turned the truck around and pulled up in front of the beauty school. I knew we weren't far from the apartment and reassured Brent and Doug that I would have no trouble getting back by bus.

As I walked by the mall's department store window I glanced at the reflection of the tall slim woman with long lank hair that matched my description walking in perfect step with me. I smiled and pointed at her as if to say "Gotcha," then marched up the stairs to the beauty school. Halfway up the stairs I faltered and decided the woman in the reflection needed a new wardrobe. I hadn't bought clothes in a department store since I had left high school ten years before. Surprisingly, I found myself a little excited at the prospect of developing a new image. I wished it could be someone exotic and beautiful instead of someone plain and normal, but nonetheless shopping for new clothes was fun when it was for a purpose more important than simply consuming.

I passed by the funky clothes that appealed to me and headed towards the section my mother would have chosen for me. I knew that if I bought the exact opposite of what I wanted, I would have the perfect look. Instead of the tight black leather pants in the boutique section, I bought green wool slacks with a slim cut. Instead of a black low-neck sweater, I bought a white blouse. I would have looked super cool in cowboy boots to set off the black leather pants, so I bought plain black pumps to set off my super-normal look.

As I stepped out of the store I smiled approvingly at the reflection of the woman in the plate-glass window, walking in perfect step with me. She was a neat, attractive woman who could easily blend in with the other women bustling about the mall. If this woman were to be spotted among a crowd at a crime scene, her only definable feature would be her long, ungroomed hair. That had to go.

Shedding my old clothes was invigorating. I took the stairs up to the beauty school two at a time, but that was the old me. Getting a grip on myself, I slowed down and took the last flight of stairs one at a time just like any other woman my age. I made a mental note that I not only had to look different, but I also had to act different. No more running up flights of stairs two at a time, no more joking around with clerks in stores or making sarcastic remarks to waitresses about food in restaurants.

I took a plastic seat in the waiting room. I looked over into a large room filled with rows of sinks and hair-styling chairs where students worked on clients, and others — their instructors, I assumed — watched over them with a critical eye. It was easy to spot the students: they were the ones holding up strands of hair for an inordinately long period of time before cutting them cautiously with a pair of shears. None of them were snipping away recklessly with that artistic look that I saw in the faces of hair stylists on TV and in movies. Yes, these were hairdressers, dressed in snippets of hair from their clients' heads, not hair stylists.

Even though the scene in front of me was far from inspiring, I was not afraid. Since no one came over to serve me, I preoccupied myself with leafing through a hair stylist magazine. Within minutes I came across the look I wanted in a photo of a woman with feathered hair, styled in a cut called "the cheetah." The woman with "the cheetah" cut was far too foxy-looking to fit into a crowd, but at the time I pushed this obvious truth to the back of my mind.

Once I had found the look I wanted, I became impatient to get the metamorphosis underway. I waved my hand in the air, flagging down an instructor who seemed annoyed that I wanted my hair done. "All our students have clients right now, except Maggie, and I must warn you that she's not very experienced and lacks confidence in her abilities."

I had always felt protective towards the underdogs of life, and Maggie certainly sounded like one, so I readily agreed to have her do my hair. "I'm not very fussy about my hair, so she won't have to worry about me complaining if she doesn't do a perfect job." I smiled and felt good about myself for potentially sacrificing a perfect "cheetah" hairdo so that this woman Maggie could build up some confidence.

"Alright," the instructor said dubiously. In a few minutes she came back with a slightly overweight, middle-aged woman in tow. "This is Maggie and you are . . . ?"

I paused. "Lilly."

The instructor left me with the anxious Maggie. "So what do you want?" she asked timidly.

"Can you cut and curl my hair like that?" I asked, pointing at the "cheetah" photo.

She took the magazine out of my hands and closely examined it. "Sure," she finally said. She pinned a plastic sheet around my body and proceeded to explain how she planned to wash, cut, and curl my hair. It was about two o'clock in the afternoon. I suspected I wasn't going to get "a cheetah," but I still harboured a faint hope. My hopes were dashed when she started to wash my hair. She turned on the hose and accidentally pointed it straight on my face, soaking everything *but* my hair. "Oh my God, I'm so sorry," she cried, looking around the room for an instructor to help her.

"It's alright," I spurted out. She was almost in tears already. "Let's do it," I said in a gung-ho tone of voice. "You can do this. If it doesn't work out quite like the picture, I won't be upset."

She did an excellent job of shampooing, although it took a lot longer than I would have expected. Then she began pulling long strands of my hair up in the air and carefully snipping them off. Each time she was about to snip she would pause just long enough for my eyes to get as large as quarters. Throughout the whole process I asked her questions about her life, to which she gave long, sad answers. By the time she had finished cutting my hair I was thoroughly convinced that she was an emotionally abused woman and that cutting my hair was a liberating experience for her.

The shampoo and hair cut went reasonably well, but in the curling stage she confessed that this was her first perm. We decided that an instructor might be helpful, so she flagged down the woman I'd met when I first arrived. The instructor was not a patient personality. Instead of hanging around to oversee Maggie's first perm, she quickly ran over the steps involved and then dashed off to continue whatever it was she was doing. Maggie was noticeably nervous and took a long time to roll each curler and spray it with the perm solution. After each time she had rolled up a curler, she would look around the room for help. Since no help was forthcoming she began asking me questions, for which I found answers even though I didn't know the first thing about doing hair. I had by then given up all hope of looking even remotely like "the cheetah." By the time all the curlers were in and Maggie was seating me under the hair dryer, I noticed other students beginning to pack and leave for the day. The instructor finally came over and began inspecting my curlers. Keeping a dead-pan expression on her face, she put a plastic cap over my head and pushed me under the hair dryer. For the longest time I sat under the hot hum of the hair dryer reading a fashion magazine and looking up once in a while to see the instructor sitting impatiently across from me smoking one cigarette after another. Every five minutes she would pop up and feel my hair, then go back and sit there smoking and kicking her leg back and forth. Maggie cleaned her hair station and swept the floor of the entire beauty school. Finally I was done. She pulled off the plastic cap to reveal a head of tight little curls closely resembling that of a poodle — certainly nothing like a cheetah.

I gasped in horror and exclaimed, "It looks good, eh Maggie?" Maggie knew that I was lying, but smiled thankfully at me and put on her coat. Unfortunately my goal of having a hair style that would allow me to blend in with the masses had not been met. I was far too young to have this kind of 'do.

"You don't have to pay," the instructor said.

On the bus back to the apartment, I tried to come to terms with

my appearance. Something good usually comes from a bad experience, and this was no exception. Before that a perfect stranger
could have deduced through my appearance — my naturally long
hair and second-hand clothes — that I identified as a rebel with
roots in the hippie subculture. I had come to accept that my identity was as grounded in my physical appearance as was the identity
of any woman who kept up with the latest in fashion.

Now, in my wool pants, black pumps, and poodle hair cut, I
was no longer Ann but Lilly. I truly felt alienated from the image I
presented to the world, and from now on each of the superficial
aspects of my life would be in keeping with this image. I hoped I
could come to terms with it but not lose my old self. Our identities
are made up of so many small things: the food we eat, the kind of
home we live in, our clothing, the way we walk, our friends and
partners. The only bond I would have with the old me would be
Brent and Doug. Our relationships would be so important. I could
already imagine how devastating it would be if they began to
crumble. With no friends to visit, no family to share the past with,
cut off from all the cultural events we used to attend, the pressure
on our mutual relationships would be immense. There would be
no one else with whom we could vent our frustrations, share our
fears, joys, and love. The enormity of our isolation dawned on me,
and I felt so alone.

I got off the bus in our nice neighbourhood of identical red-
brick apartment buildings, unblemished by trash or hookers on the
street corners. I hadn't lived in an area like this since I was a child.
I walked up the stairs, one at a time, to our apartment and
unlocked the door. Brent and Doug were sitting together on the
couch reading. When they saw me they burst out laughing, breaking the spell of depression that had settled over me.

"I can't believe how different you look!" Doug chuckled.
"There's no way anyone from the past would recognize you walking down the street. Where did you get the duds?" The story of the
beauty salon set them off laughing again.

* * *

Even though we knew each other so well, it was strange being
alone together in Calgary. We sat around that evening talking
about the phantom surveillance guy and the lemon truck, but
every now and then an uncomfortable lull in the conversation
would punctuate the fact that there were just the three of us with
no one else to visit and nowhere else to go. After a few hours we

ordered a pizza and focused the conversation around a more comfortable topic — our political strategy for future actions.

"I think an action against the Cheekeye-Dunsmuir power line would be popular and easily understood, at least in the province, because the legal struggle has failed, in the sense that the line is now under construction," said Brent.

"I like that idea," added Doug, "because a lot of people across the province fighting the other Hydro megaprojects can relate to the issues raised by Cheekeye-Dunsmuir."

"Yeah, that would be great," I agreed. "You can also make the connection between the power line and Canada's economic role as a natural resource base in the world economy. The line'll make it possible for Canada to export more lumber and pulp and paper products to the U.S. and Japan."

We started to talk about what we would call ourselves, and it was Brent who finally came up with the name Direct Action. "I know it sounds like that Action Directe group that was responsible for something like twenty bombings in France, but it's the most accurate description of us," he said.

"The cops could assume we're a cell and that could bring your name up as a suspect, Ann, if you were ever under surveillance over there," Doug said. "Didn't you go to some trial in West Germany?"

"Yeah, I went to the trial of a lawyer who represented some of the Red Army Faction. It was held in Stammkeim, in a special self-contained courthouse in a potato field beside the prison — a courthouse for so-called terrorist trials. He was accused of passing letters and a gun to the RAF during the legal visits. They checked my passport and took it away for a while at one point, so I guess they could have relayed that information to INTERPOL. Yeah, the name's similar enough to that French group, chances are they'll investigate links between us, but the name is so good I think we should take the risk. I don't really see that my name should come up, since the RAF is a Marxist group and isn't affiliated with Action Directe, which is more of an anarchist one."

Brent argued that the name Direct Action was perfect. "It implies we take political action into our own hands instead of relying on government representatives to change situations for us," he said. "Especially since the government usually represents the interests of big business." We looked at each other and nodded our heads — Direct Action it was.

Once again we fell into quiet introspection. If only I could have been as sure of our plans as I was about the suitability of our name. I thought it was really too bad that we were in Canada, because our plans would have been so much more effective in El Salvador or any Third World country with an active liberation movement. "There's virtually no revolutionary movement here," I said, "so how many people are going to be inspired to become militants when all they have to look forward to is social isolation, prison, or death?"

"I know," agreed Brent. "We were born at the wrong time and place in history for what we want to do." We had talked about all of this many times before — and especially about how militant movements had to start somewhere. "I'm sure even in the Third World, the first liberation movements didn't have many people or support," Brent said. "It takes a long time for political movements to develop." None of us were under any illusion that we were part of some huge revolutionary movement. Instead we believed that we were simply trying to inject militancy into a movement that already existed, and we hoped we would help it grow.

"I worry that the repression that will follow our actions might actually kill whatever tiny revolutionary movement there is," I confessed.

"Well, if they can't take a bit of repression, then they can't call themselves revolutionaries, can they?" Brent said.

✳ **17** ✳

The days and nights in Calgary seemed endless. We were used to an active social life in Vancouver, running around the city attending meetings, organizing benefits and demos, and planning our future urban guerrilla strategy. We were accustomed to a high level of tension and excitement. Now, all of a sudden, we were at a standstill, with very little to do other than plan, think, and write. Having all this time to think and talk was not necessarily good for our resolve to stay in Calgary. Each morning Brent and I would plan to carry out a few tasks such as food shopping, paying bills, or picking up literature to read. Shoplifting was out because now that we were developing bigger plans, it would be foolish to risk being busted for something small. The apartment could end up getting searched. Besides, we had lots of money to live on, so shoplifting was no longer a financial necessity.

Doug had his own routine, much like the one he had in Vancouver. He would only sit around with us in the evenings to discuss our future plans. His isolation was more profound than ours, because while Brent and I hung out together during the day, Doug was usually completely alone. At least in Vancouver he had a girlfriend, some friends, and his mother, whom he was very close to. Brent and I would spend time every day in restaurants feeding off each other's loneliness and dissatisfaction with our life in Calgary. I had harboured a deep bond and desire for Brent for a long time, but once we were alone in Calgary and the possibility of consummating our relationship was very real, surprisingly I found myself missing Nick and feeling distant from Brent even when I was in his presence.

One afternoon we sat in a mall restaurant, picking away at plates of fries and drinking coffee. For a few seconds our eyes met. In Vancouver, such an eye encounter would have revealed a spark of repressed desire, but now there was a glaze over our eyes hiding the discomfort and loneliness we felt in each other's presence. It was as though the fire and passion between us in Vancouver had been fuelled by its forbidden quality. Perhaps we'd been in love with a fantasy romance as unrealistic as our political goals. A romance that had never been tested by the frustrations and mundane activities of daily life. It had been wonderfully unattainable by our commitment to the lovers we saw every day, but at the same time the romance was kept alive through the plans to escape to another place where we could begin our romantic underground life and union as revolutionary urban guerrillas.

Now that we had finally escaped and were free to consummate the relationship and begin the underground life, we were profoundly disappointed by the reality of our situation. It was boring and we were terrified of touching each other. It could never match the fantasy. What if the first touch did not elicit a response? What if our flesh was dead? In my fantasy the earth moved and mountains tumbled to the sea. Here in Calgary, in that barren apartment, those fantasies could never happen. If the attempt failed we would not only be faced with a loveless relationship, but we would also have destroyed the possibility of returning to the ones who we knew loved us. In this case it might be better to have never loved than to love and lose everything.

We had left our lovers too suddenly. Normally, new relationships grow out of the ruins of old ones. As the squabbles and bickering of old relationships grow, they nurture the need for someone new without all the irritating characteristics of the old. But we had terminated our old relationships while they were still blooming and ripe. Our memories of our lovers were not wrought with images of arguments and silence but with tender moments and heart-wrenching goodbyes. Suddenly the reality of looking into each other's eyes was frightening in comparison to the beautiful memories of the loved ones we had left behind.

I dipped a fry in some gravy and looked at Brent's face surreptitiously. He was chewing on a huge mouthful of fries, with gravy dripping out of the corner of his mouth. Nick would never fill his mouth so greedily with food. He was always neat and clean. Memories of cutting, critical words Brent had launched at me during times of stress came to mind. Nick had never called me stupid. In fact, he would never criticize me. Granted, Brent had many good qualities, but he was also burdened with a lot of bad ones. In his own self-analysis he attributed his critical nature to his parents. He deduced that they had projected their own unhappiness and unfulfilled goals on him, so when he didn't meet their expectations, they would be cuttingly critical. Despite his awareness of this syndrome, he could not help perpetuating this critical personality trait that he had internalized from his parents. Although I gave him credit for having this self-awareness, it did not compensate for the cruel words that would sometimes cut me to the core. As a child, I had never been exposed to any kind of verbal abuse and so I was very thin-skinned. One critical word would send me reeling.

Brent looked up at me as he slurped his coffee, and he smiled. But it was an uncomfortable smile. Either he could sense that I was thinking bad thoughts about him or he was feeling guilty about doing the same about me. I found myself comparing Brent to Nick. Brent was much more charismatic, charming, extroverted, and exciting, but these were not qualities that made a good person. A good person was selfless, humble, generous, and kind. Nick was all these things. What was wrong with me? Why was I attracted to charisma, excitement, and charm?

"Do you miss Angie?" I said, egging him on.

He looked at me coldly. I would have bet he was thinking the same things about me as I was of him. "Yes," he said sharply. "But she probably doesn't miss me. She knew I wouldn't be coming back so she probably has someone else."

"She wouldn't be involved with someone else already."

"No. She's always preferred women, but for some reason I don't understand, she loved me and that's what held her back from having a good relationship with another woman. Now that I'm gone, her head will be free to pursue a woman and she'll probably be a lot happier."

"Yeah, Nick will probably be involved with someone else too, now that I'm gone," I wallowed in self-pity along with him.

"How do you think Doug feels?" Brent asked. "He hardly spends time with us during the day. He must be lonely."

"Does he ever say anything to you?"

"No. He's very stoic about all this," Brent said. "He's probably taking everything better than us. His lifestyle has always been very solitary, so maybe this is not as much of an adjustment. Anyway, are you done?"

"Yep." I got up as I spoke.

On the way home we decided to talk to Doug more about our feelings than about politics. Over dinner we talked about our loneliness and how to overcome it. There were no easy answers. Doug felt that with time we would grow closer and that as we began to prepare to carry out actions we would become so focused on our work that our loneliness would subside. Brent and I concurred that we would eventually just grow accustomed to this life and the memories of our lovers would slowly begin to fade.

Contradictions were developing between what we secretly hoped for and what we advocated. We agreed that celibacy was the only way to promote group unity and avoid the situation of one couple developing at the expense of the third person living in total isolation emotionally. For the sake of group unity, the idea of a communal sleeping room seemed like a good one. So we decided to start sleeping all in the same room, using the bed and two double mattresses on the floor.

After our evening discussion I went to bed early while Doug sat up in the spare room, which we had turned into an office, and Brent went out. I vaguely remember Doug going to bed several feet away later in the evening. It was a strange situation, three adults sleeping in the same bed with no sexual relations, but that's how it was. I must admit that the plan worked: knowing they were sleeping a few feet away did distract me from thoughts of Nick, and it did create a stronger group bond.

I was awakened even later that same evening by noises in the kitchen. I sat up and, seeing that Brent was still not in bed, tiptoed carefully over Doug. Brent was in the kitchen wolfing down a plate of Chinese noodles with some kind of Chinese fungus and soy sauce topping.

"Why are you up so late?" I asked.

"I have a confession," he whispered. "Do you promise not to tell Doug?"

"Yeah," I said eagerly.

"I phoned Angie," he said, looking at me hard.

"What!" I gasped angrily. We had agreed not to contact anyone unless it was an emergency.

"Don't worry. It's perfectly safe. I arranged beforehand to call her once a month at a pay phone in Vancouver where there'd be no tap, just to keep in touch with what's happening there and also in case we needed help."

"Well that's not fair," I practically spat at him. "Why shouldn't Doug and I have the same privileges?"

"You could," he tried to placate me. "Angie could arrange for you and Doug to phone Nick and Rachel too."

"You've got to tell Doug."

"She really misses me too," he said with a soft light in his eyes. "Ann, I don't think this lifestyle is healthy. I've been thinking about it and there's no reason why we can't plan and prepare for our first actions in Vancouver and go underground when we have to. We have everything we need."

I stood with my hands on my hips, looking at him with dismay. But it was an act. Deep inside I was bubbling with excitement at the mere thought of going back. I just didn't want to be the first to admit it.

"Well," I said, softening very quickly, "you know how much I miss Nick. It just feels so vacant here. Doug looks unhappy too. There's no rush to be underground. I think we left prematurely." Now that I had admitted it, I sat down on a chair and smiled softly at him.

We sat up late into the night scheming how to break it to Doug that we weren't happy here and should go back. In the end we decided to wait it out another week, and if we still felt as lonely we'd talk to him and give our landlord notice. After all, the apartment was in one of our good IDs' names, and we certainly didn't want to ruin that identity by doing something as stupid as not giving our landlord notice.

We tiptoed carefully back into the bedroom and lay down under the covers. It was strangely disconcerting sleeping so close to Brent and yet not touching or saying anything to him. Listening to his breathing did distract me from my loneliness for Nick. I wondered how Doug would react to the idea of returning to Vancouver. Surely he would be as eager to see Rachel as we were Angie and Nick.

* * *

The next week passed much like the previous ones. We got up early, made plans over breakfast, carried out errands, read, wrote, ate supper, and then talked until it was time for bed. It was difficult for Brent and me, in particular, to get used to a sedentary lifestyle holding no danger or excitement. Every day we managed to rendezvous privately to counter each other's loneliness and find further justifications for returning to Vancouver. A week in Calgary felt like a month in Vancouver. I realized that when life is rich in experience, time seems to pass much more quickly than when each day is no different from the next.

Finally our deadline passed and, predictably, we agreed to suggest to Doug that we return to Vancouver. That evening Brent and I were nervous over supper, saying very little. After cleaning up the dishes, we sat down in the living room.

Doug sensed something was up.

I found myself blurting, "Doug, we think it would be a good idea to go back to Vancouver."

"You're kidding," he said, knowing full well that we weren't.

"No." I figured it was best I do the talking because Doug had a softer attitude towards me than he did to Brent. "Are you happy here?"

"No, but we didn't expect to be happy. That's not the point," he said in his quick, clipped way of speaking when he was upset. "I don't think we came here to find happiness. We came to develop our politics, plan our actions, and be underground so the cops won't be able to find us if we're suspects once this all begins."

"I know," I said sheepishly, "but we could do all those things in Vancouver and then go underground after Cheekeye. To be honest, I want to spend more time with Nick and I'm quite sure Brent wants to see Angie again."

"So you two have been conniving behind my back."

"We have discussed the topic," admitted Brent.

"You two are pathetic. You know the dangers of living in Vancouver if we carry out an action."

"We won't be living in Vancouver after an action, just until we do one," we both said almost in unison. There was a long silence while we attempted to get our emotions under control. Doug looked at us as though we were traitors, then turned on his heel and retired to the spare room. He didn't come out for the rest of the evening. Brent and I hung our heads, feeling ashamed for backing out of this attempt to live underground, but we knew there was no turning back. Our minds were made up. We had to see Nick and Angie one last time.

* * *

Doug's disappointment in us was profound. On the ride back to Vancouver he said little. I had assumed he would be happy to go back to see his mother and Rachel, but he was one of those rare individuals who allowed reason to hold sway over emotions. He was convinced, and rightly so, that living in Vancouver was dangerous because we were known not only by the police but also by the radical community; so if we did anything illegal that was overtly political, we would be easily found and apprehended.

Our arrival back in Vancouver was without fanfare. Most people didn't even know we had left. The few we had told were under the impression that we had taken a vacation and weren't surprised to see us again. Brent and I rented cheap one-room apartments, a block apart, and Doug rented a basement apartment in the suburbs.

I had warned Nick of my return by telephone a week before we left Calgary. My feelings about returning were confused. On the one hand, I felt as though my relationship with Nick was unresolved and as such would always haunt me. On the other, I felt guilty about returning because it was not the strategically correct thing to do. Returning meant that we would be preparing to do an action against the Cheekeye-Dunsmuir line while living amongst the radical community, and thus we would be open to surveillance. We would definitely have to leave the community before we carried out an action. Until then we had time to resolve our emotional needs with our lovers and friends.

Knowing we would be leaving for good in the near future, not just as a trial run, set the stage for my relationship with Nick — a stage filled with obstacles and bound for failure. In a kind of déjà vu situation, I saw him in a critical light just as I had Brent in Calgary. I tried so hard to make love with all the passion and abandon that I had remembered in my dreams of him, but that love turned out to be an illusion. Nothing that he said or did was as wonderful as I had imagined in those lonely Calgary nights. He hadn't changed in a month, but my psyche had. I wanted him out. Out of my mind and my heart. He was a threat to my dreams and future. I continued to see him and spend nights with him, but slowly the relationship began to change as he noticed the distance in my eyes and the dryness of my flesh.

Our group had made a firm decision to carry out an action against the Cheekeye-Dunsmuir line sometime in the spring, while it was still under construction, but we first had to investigate the line and plan exactly what to do. At the same time, we were deeply immersed in discussions about other future actions. These preparations, combined with our decision to have limited contact with people from the radical community, led to relatively isolated lives. Since I was no longer involved in any political organizing, the only person I saw, other than Brent and Doug, was Nick, and that was only at night.

A few weeks after our return from Calgary, the confusion in my emotional life was resolved by the subliminal forces that, I believe, drive our rational life as well. It happened on a beautiful spring day, fittingly symbolizing new life and beginnings. I had to go over to Brent's to pick up some maps of the proposed Cheekeye-Dunsmuir line because I was planning a trip to view all the proposed construction sites for the new hydro substations. The moist, warm air and songs of the birds courting each other in the trees filled my spirit with joy. I felt so light and energetic that my feet barely touched the pavement. I pictured myself springing along, just as Brent always did when he walked. I sang a little song out loud and laughed to myself.

I ran up the stairs to Brent's room, two at a time. I had dropped the Lilly persona upon returning, so I no longer had to lumber up the stairs one at a time. My poodle haircut had relaxed somewhat, and I had packed away Lilly's wardrobe for some future time. When I reached Brent's door, I gave it my signature knock.

"Come in!" he yelled.

I could tell that the spring air had entered his lungs and bloodstream, affecting him much as it had me and the birds singing their love songs outside his window. His eyes were gleaming and his movements were smooth and relaxed.

"Do you have those B.C. Hydro maps?" I asked.

"Yep, they're right here," he said leaning over his desk, where he had neatly laid them out. I stepped up close to him and leaned over the maps as well. He began talking and pointing to the various sites, but I wasn't listening to his words. I hummed and hawed in agreement at the appropriate times, but I was distracted by a familiar churning sensation in my stomach. It wasn't hunger of the food variety. It was of the sexual kind. Perhaps the spring air was a perfect conduit for pheromones, I don't know, but I had stood beside Brent hundreds of times — in fact, I had slept this close to him — and never felt quite like this. My stomach began to ache, my breath was short, a thin veil of perspiration covered my body, and all my senses became acutely aware of his presence at the expense of all else, especially my sense of reason. That flew out the door.

Just at the moment when I felt as though I would lose all control and begin kissing him madly, he turned to face me and without a word wrapped his arms around me and began kissing me as I had never been kissed before. My knees went weak and gave out. Luckily he was holding me up or I would have collapsed on the floor. The passion between us was powerful, like a river that had been flowing into a dammed up reservoir for a long time and suddenly the dam could hold it no longer. Over the edge it poured in huge powerful waves, unleashing forces held back for far too long.

It seemed as though we kissed for hours. Our tongues wrapped around one another, one gently caressing the moist protrusions of the other. Softly I ran my tongue along his teeth, his lips, and into every last part of his mouth. I became the moment, losing all consciousness of myself and him.

We fell onto the bed and tore the clothes off each other. Like participants in an erotic dance, we established a rhythm that alternated between violent desperation and a tenderness so gentle that a butterfly's touch could not have been softer. Our hands and mouths tore and bit into one another's flesh, devouring each other in a love-starved feast in which our appetites could never be satisfied as long as we remained two separate entities. Damned to eternal frustration, our flesh would not meld into one. Time and again, we merged, only to lay back, frustrated by the impossibility of achieving our subliminal desire. In tender gestures of consolation we caressed each other's limbs so gently that our efforts would better be described as whispers than touches of the flesh. Finally our passionate dance was over and we lay there, spent and shaking from the sheer exhaustion of it all. Words would only destroy the moment, so we listened to the sounds of spring outside the window and the silence of the room around us.

Finally I got up and, still wordless, picked up the maps from the table. I dressed and left. I walked down the street, deep in thought, in shock over the morning's events. I had assumed since I first met Brent that we would someday consummate our relationship, but now that it had actually happened it came as a surprise. I had always thought I would see it coming. Now what? I felt as though I had betrayed Nick and Angie, but at the same time a deep satisfaction filled my soul. This was right. It had to happen. Now we could move forward. I was ready to live in the underground.

Doing Cheekeye-Dunsmuir and Litton

✳ 18 ✳

Brent and I realized the morning we first made love that we owed it to Angie, Nick, and Doug to tell them as soon as possible about the change in our relationship, but we were afraid of the repercussions. The next day we got together, supposedly to discuss how to handle the sensitive situation, but instead again succumbed to our passions. Not only could we not put the water back in the reservoir, but it continued to spill over the dam in torrents. Later, when we finally lay back in the bed again, exhausted, we began to talk.

"I wish this had happened after we had said our goodbyes to Nick and Angie, just before Cheekeye," I said feebly. "It seems so awful to hurt them before we leave for good."

"I know what you mean." Brent rolled over on his side to light a cigarette.

"And Doug . . . he probably won't even want to go ahead with Cheekeye if he knows we're lovers, because that will leave him as a single person living with a couple in the underground."

"But there's no going back." Brent smiled mischievously.

"Why don't we wait to tell Nick and Angie until after Cheekeye?" I suggested. "They'll never know if we don't tell them. Maybe the old cliché 'What you don't know, won't hurt you' is relevant in this situation."

Brent put his head back on the pillow and finished smoking his cigarette, deep in thought. "I hate not telling Angie something like this, but what's the advantage in telling her? All it will do is hurt her."

"Okay, so we don't tell Nick and Angie till after we're underground. But what about Doug?"

"Now that's the difficult question." Brent furrowed his brow. "Nick and Angie must suspect we'll end up lovers once we're underground. Angie has said that to me a few times already when she's been mad at me. But Doug won't like the idea of working with two people who are lovers who will back each other up intellectually."

"I don't think we'll do that," I said quite honestly. Brent and I had always had healthy disagreements. The chances of us agreeing intellectually just because we had a sexual relationship were nil. "Maybe we should keep our sexual relationship a secret from him," I offered. "We don't need to sleep together and act monogamous

183

around him. Really, I don't think it will affect our relationship or behaviour with other people at all. The only thing that's going to change is that once in a while we'll go off by ourselves and have sex. That's it."

In retrospect I can say that Brent and I were fooling ourselves. To avoid telling Doug we were risking our entire plan of carrying out actions as an underground guerrilla group. It was unethical to carry on without disclosing this important change in our relationship, but we took the cowardly route out of a difficult situation. The betrayal would ultimately cost us the trust and confidence essential for a good friendship. But for the time being we continued with our blinkers on, refusing to acknowledge that the breach of trust would cost us dearly in the long run. In the end, our reasoning and judgement were driven by our subliminal need to fulfil our sexual passions, and so we sacrificed our friendship with Doug for our sexual union.

We continued making plans for Cheekeye-Dunsmuir, continued seeing Nick and Angie, and in secret continued having sex. Sometime in April Angie told Brent that she was going to take a road trip to Ontario to visit her family. Since our proposed deadline for doing Cheekeye was not until May, Brent decided to accompany her and use the opportunity for casing out a possible future action against Canada's role in the manufacture and development of the cruise missile. Litton Systems in Etobicoke, Ontario, was manufacturing the guidance system for the cruise missile, and the United States was pressuring Canada to agree to test the unarmed cruise missile in northern Alberta.

The cruise was not a missile itself, but an aircraft four to six metres long with a computer for a pilot. Flying along at tree-top level and thereby avoiding radar, it could follow a course pre-programmed through a guidance system. It allowed for precision bombing attacks because it was designed to carry a nuclear warhead that would explode within forty metres of its target. One of the many reasons why a protest movement had developed around Litton Systems was because it was a subsidiary of Litton Industries of California and had received a $1.3 billion contract from the U.S. Defense Department to manufacture the guidance system in Canada — with the help of $48 million in grants and interest-free loans from the Canadian government's Defence Industries Production Department. In addition to the cruise guidance system, which comprised only 30 per cent of the plant's production, Litton was also manufacturing everything from microwave ovens to CF-18 cockpit display programs and security systems for nuclear power plants.

We had been closely following the development of the struggle against the cruise missile testing and the building of the guidance system. Doug had a particular interest in the issue because in April 1980, when he had been involved with the Pacific Life Community, he had helped organize the first anti-nuclear rally in Vancouver. Some five thousand people attended that rally. The Easter Walk for Peace of April 1982 had drawn thirty-five thousand people in Vancouver — the largest march ever in the city to that time — and conservative estimates claimed that more than one hundred thousand people had attended similar marches across Canada that day. The marches had taken place two days after Canada had agreed to test nuclear weaponry for the United States at the Primrose Lake test range in Alberta.

Officially the Pentagon argued that the region's vast stretches of snow-covered wasteland made it similar to Siberia, but some critics, including writer Peter C. Newman in his book *True North: Not Strong and Free*, were pointing out that flights to predetermined Soviet targets would be over industrialized Eastern Europe, not over land comparable to northern Alberta. Prime Minister Trudeau had argued that the tests were required to meet Canada's NATO commitments and that the flights could be used as a bargaining lever in disarmament negotiations with the Soviet Union. But, Newman argued, these cruise missiles were not connected to the weapons under discussion at the Geneva disarmanment talks. This missile was a second-generation strategic weapon under U.S., not NATO, command.

A protracted campaign in Ontario against the cruise missile, targeting the Litton Systems plant in Etobicoke, had been spearheaded by a group called the Cruise Missile Conversion Project (CMCP), which had been focusing on convincing management at the Litton plant to convert its war-related production to socially useful production. Every week the CMCP leafleted the employees at the factory gates with information about disarmament and the message that conversion of the factory to civilian technology would create more jobs as well as giving the workers a more socially useful occupation.

A CMCP vision paper described the organization's structure: "As a collective, we make our decisions by consensus. By struggling with this method, we are saying that every person should actively take part in formulating group decisions. We are striving for a non-hierarchial group process whereby no individual or small group dominates the whole; all participate equally in forming decisions; tasks and responsibilities are rotated." In terms of tactics and strategies, they used a combination of civil disobedience (CD) and education. Their CD techniques included everything from blocking the driveway of the plant and passively resisting removal by police, to pouring blood on Litton property. They planted white crosses on Litton lawns and painted green doves on Litton walls. They combined these activities with leafleting the workers at the plant and organizing public education in schools, community groups, and churches. Their work was grounded on Gandhian principles of non-violence, and by early 1982 they had about fifty members involved in the internal group process, ranging from radical Catholics and Quakers to artists and traditional anti-war activists.

A possible future action against the cruise missile fit in with our political opposition to nuclear weapons and the role of Canada as a puppet of U.S. military strategy. Politically, we believed, Litton would be a good target if the legal struggle failed to stop the testing and manufacture of the guidance system, because polls showed that the general public was opposed to Canada's role in the development of the cruise missile. Our only concern was that anti-nuclear activists in Ontario might interpret an action on our part as interfering with their legal struggle.

* * *

While Brent and Angie were in Ontario, Doug and I were going to do a preliminary casing of the entire Cheekeye-Dunsmuir line to verify if the construction of the line was going according to schedule and also to check the feasibility of the action. The only schedule we had was over a year old, and construction projects were notorious for being behind. We wanted our action to do substantial physical damage that would delay construction and make the line less financially feasible. We hoped that successful militant actions would cause investors and politicians to think twice about supporting projects that were politically controversial and costly to protect. We did not subscribe to the idea of symbolic actions intended for educational enlightenment alone. Why not carry out actions that might actually stop the megaproject from being constructed, or at least hinder other projects from being initiated?

There were a lot of factors we had to consider before carrying out the Cheekeye-Dunsmuir action. We did not want to sabotage the project after it went on-line, because we wanted to avoid causing power blackouts to residential areas. Ordinary people would feel the brunt of the action if hospitals, traffic lights, or other essential services were shut down, and we didn't want that. The best time to sabotage the line would be just before it was ready to go on-line. We also had to see what part of the line was the most expensive. Blowing up a few hydro poles or knocking over transmission lines wouldn't do much economic damage, and the poles and lines could easily be repaired. But if we could sabotage a substation just when it was being completed we would be hitting B.C. Hydro in its pocketbook. After considerable time spent in the library researching the components of hydro power lines, Doug had concluded that the reactors located at each substation were the most valuable equipment to sabotage. If we could explode dynamite under the reactors when they were filled with the oil used to cool them down, they would not only be damaged but would also burst into flames.

Timing would be critical. Too early, and we would not cause the maximum amount of damage. Too late, and we would cause a major blackout, which in turn would swing public sympathy against us. We wanted to pinpoint our actions against physical structures that were threatening the health and happiness of the general population. We did not want to do anything that could be viewed as terrorizing the public or even particular members of the power elite. We were strictly interested in sabotaging a project that ordinary people could clearly understand was a threat to their best interests. Perhaps an act of sabotage against the Cheekeye-Dunsmuir line would be a somewhat obscure target to people outside British Columbia, but people living in the province were familiar with the issue and would understand that we were opposed to the industrialization of Vancouver Island, not merely opposed to the flow of electricity.

We also had to case out the entire line to decide which substation was the most practical to carry explosives to and to escape from. We certainly didn't want to be trapped on a tiny place like Texada Island after the bombing, and we didn't want to be seen carrying heavy boxes of explosives into a substation in a heavily populated area.

After bidding Brent and Angie adieu before their trip to Ontario, Doug and I busied ourselves getting ready for our excursion along the route of the Cheekeye-Dunsmuir line. We loaded up our not-so-trusty truck with all the new camping equipment accumulated on our many shopping sprees. I was looking forward to our trip as a time for Doug and me to get closer, since we rarely spent time alone together. Brent and Doug had a much longer history as friends and were comfortable doing all kinds of things together.

The map we had to follow was vague, because it wasn't designed for road trips but rather to give the interested hydro customer a general idea of the location of the new line and its substations. As soon as we reached the first substation, Cheekeye, near Squamish, we discovered that following the route of the line under construction would be a challenge and take some tracking skills. We quickly eliminated Cheekeye as a possible target because we saw no signs of construction there. That substation was obviously behind schedule. After travelling back down to Horseshoe Bay, we took a ferry across to Gibsons Landing and headed up the Sechelt Peninsula, looking for the next substation, called Malaspina, which appeared to be in the middle of the peninsula. We were hindered in our task because we didn't want to be seen at any of these locations in case we were ID'd by some overzealous hydro employee on the lookout for environmental activists. So when we finally came to an innocuous Hydro sign indicating the future site of the Malaspina substation, we decided to make ourselves as invisible as possible.

The construction of the Malaspina substation seemed to be further along than work at Cheekeye, in that the area had a fenced-in gravelled yard and a parking lot, but other than that it was deep in a wilderness area with no sign of reactors or other hydro equipment. Surprisingly, the parking lot was filled with vehicles, even though there were no people to be seen. Our truck nicely blended in with the others, so we parked and then carefully disappeared into the bush to scout out the substation. As we made our way through the dense brush surrounding the apparently abandoned substation-to-be, we heard a faint drumming sound in the distance. The awareness of this sound had barely reached our consciousness when the sound became amplified a thousand times until it became a thudding roar that pounded right through our bodies. It happened so quickly that we had no time to consult each other. I looked over at Doug, and dove into the bushes just in time to avoid being seen by a helicopter landing somewhere so close to us that the wind from its blades spinning above the tree canopy sent all the leaves and debris on the ground funnelling upward in its wake, like the suction from a tornado.

By the time we had recovered there was only the silence of the bush again, minus the usual peeping of the birds, which were no doubt traumatized by this giant mechanical alien. Doug looked like a soldier in a state of siege. He lay face down on the forest floor, his face smudged with dirt and his hair filled with leaves. He looked up at me and said with a smile, "Too bad Brent's not here. He'd love this." I knew what he meant. Brent loved running around in the woods, dodging and diving to elude some imaginary enemy. He seemed most alive when we were target-practising in the mountains, running along a trail trying to hit paper targets in the trees.

No sooner had we regained our balance and were trying to figure out exactly where the helicopter had landed when the dull sound of whirring blades in the distance reached our ears again. This time we didn't wait for the sound to come closer. We dove into the underbrush and stayed there for about half an hour while a series of helicopters landed not far from where we were hidden. Finally, when the silence was no longer being interrupted, we stood up and moved around to get the blood circulating in our legs again.

"What the hell was that?" I asked, brushing dried leaves and dirt off my pants.

"My guess is we're right beside some kind of helicopter pad for Hydro," Doug said. He was also trying to brush the remnants of the bush off his clothes. "They must be using the copters to transport workers and stuff up and down the mountainside." The workers were probably returning from their shift just then, at the end of the day. He looked at his watch. "It's just after four. That's why there are so many cars in the parking lot, yet no people to be seen. I bet if we go out there now, they'll be gone."

I was sure he was right. After straightening ourselves up some more, we continued creeping through the bush, following the perimeter of the empty hydro substation. Once we'd satisfied ourselves there were no reactors there, we headed back towards the parking lot, keeping an eye out for people. We weren't surprised to find only our truck parked in the lot. Our curiosity to verify our theory about the helipad didn't override our caution about being seen. We jumped in the truck and headed on down the highway.

The drive along the Sechelt Peninsula was breathtaking, but it also illuminated the dark side of the B.C. lumbering industry. The lumbering companies had not attempted to hide their clear-cut logging practices, which they so carefully tried to conceal along major tourist routes like the Trans-Canada Highway. On one side of the coastal highway lay the Strait of Georgia, but on the other was the devastation that environmentalists likened to the rape of the mountains. The mountainsides had been stripped of trees, leaving their slopes exposed to the ravages of rain, wind, and snow. The protection that the forests normally afforded the soil and vegetation was gone. All that remained were stumps of trees sticking up out of the barren earth like the cropped hair of a holocaust victim. Now that there were no more trees to break their flow, the spring rains would send torrents of water down the mountainsides, washing away the soil in devastating mudslides. In this way nature would have its revenge — or should I say achieve its justice — in some universal, cosmic sense. All along the coastal highways, where clear-cut logging had been practised, the mudslides would desolate the lives of animals, children, and adults, regardless of race, creed, or class. We shook our heads sadly.

In Powell River we caught the last ferry of the day to Texada Island. Eventually underwater marine cables would carry the hydro transmission lines under the Strait of Georgia between Texada and Nelson islands to their eventual resting place at the Dunsmuir substation on Vancouver Island. When we reached Texada Island we had just enough time to find a camping spot before dark. On Texada Island Rachel owned a small cabin where Doug had vacationed, so he was familiar with the territory. He suggested we camp near a beautiful quarry so we could take a swim before bed. Now that was really fun! The cool, silky water that had welled up from the underground aquifers was refreshing, for both body and soul. After the swim we cooked up some horrible canned stew on our Coleman stove and devoured it with the relish normally saved for something more exotic.

Although we were enjoying ourselves, we didn't say much. Every time there was an uncomfortable silence, my conscience would obsessively fix on the nagging idea that this was the perfect time to confess my infidelity. My friendship with Doug was such that my sense of guilt about withholding the sexual nature of my relationship with Brent was growing increasingly. The internal debate raged on: should I confess or not? And so a heavy silence settled between us. Doug was not one to initiate conversation. I had always been the one to lead when it came to talk between us, but on this day the evil silencer, guilt, gagged me. To make matters worse, he probably thought my silence was caused by my discomfort in his presence. Why else would I be so quiet? We were having fun, and nothing else appeared to be going wrong. If only I didn't have to carry this heavy burden of deception for the entire trip. But if I confessed I would have to bear the repercussions on my own, because Brent was off with Angie. No matter what I did, suffering would be involved. If I confessed, Doug might be so enraged that he would decide to abandon our plans. That would leave only Brent and me. As it was, we could barely carry out our plans with three. If there were only two, we would most definitely appear to be criminals, using politics to justify some fantastic bombing spree. Somehow, two didn't make a political group, but three did. No, I was better off keeping my mouth shut and suffering the guilt of deceit than jeopardizing our noble plans.

The next day we managed to follow the route to the reactor station on Texada Island, but all B.C. Hydro had accomplished there was clearing brush for the installation of towers. After another short ferry ride to Vancouver Island, we stopped in Courtenay for a quiet fish and chips lunch at a seaside restaurant. Before heading down the coast to our final destination, the Dunsmuir substation, I decided to do some shopping at a Zeller's store. I don't recall what possessed me to do this — maybe my clothes were dirty — but it was uncharacteristic. I didn't usually shop unless it was absolutely necessary. Doug waited in the truck patiently while I ran in to see if they had any cheap pants. Even though I had $77 in my wallet, I found myself glancing around for potential witnesses in the jeans section as I debated whether or not to shoplift a pair of blue jeans. I knew we couldn't afford for me to get caught under the current circumstances. But I had internalized a value system that told me it was wrong to pay for anything from a big chain store. Besides, shoplifting had become a means of honing my criminal skills and nerve for more serious actions.

I glanced around surreptitiously but could only see an older man a few aisles over. I knew that Zeller's hired store detectives, but I rationalized that the store would never hire someone that old to be a detective because he wouldn't be able to outrun or subdue the young people who so often shoplift. I carefully picked up a pair of Levi's and leaned over so I could slip them into the sports bag I always carried with me. Then, before heading towards the door, I sauntered aimlessly around for a few minutes just to see if anyone was following me. I had only placed one foot outside the store door when a hand reached from behind me and grabbed my arm firmly. I spun around to face the old guy, inches from my face.

His hand closed hard around my arm. "What have you got in the bag, lady?" I would have pulled loose and run but I already knew I had nowhere to go, and there was Doug witnessing this sorry series of events from the truck. I certainly didn't want to implicate him. I hung my head and walked meekly back to the store office. I figured Doug would be furious. It didn't take long before local RCMP officers arrived and began to fill out the necessary papers. I gave them my real name, and immediately realized how stupid this move had been, in light of the future action we were planning, possibly just down the road from here, in a few months. Oh well, too late now.

When I finally got back into the truck, Doug didn't say a word. As we drove off I hung my head in shame, staring at the road map in my lap and only looking up occasionally to check for signs of where we were going. Finally I noticed a sign saying Nile Creek as we drove over a small creek emptying into the Strait of Georgia. "We've passed the station."

Doug put on the brakes to turn around and then he backtracked until we came to a newly gravelled road leading back to a spot that we assumed must be the location of the Dunsmuir substation. We didn't drive down the gravel road but parked by the ocean and began hiking into the woods that parallelled the road. The road ended about a quarter of a mile from the coastal highway in a large gravelled opening. There, behind a high metal fence, were four huge, black reactors. Not surprisingly, because it was late on a Saturday afternoon, there were no signs of human activity. Still, for a while we stayed at the edge of the woods, staring through our binoculars, to make absolutely sure no one was around. When we emerged from the shadows of the woods and walked out into the open, Doug took out a little notepad and began making copious notes and diagrams for future reference.

The substation seemed to be ideal for an action in every respect. There were no homes or buildings within view. The four giant, expensive reactors were attached by means of steel footings to large concrete pads, set in a perfect rectangle with a small control building located over one hundred metres from the closest reactor. I thought they looked a bit like small space stations, sitting ready for blast-off on their concrete landing pads. The only other items inside the enclosure were an oil-pumping plant for the reactors and a portable crane that had no doubt been used to put them in place. Otherwise the place was a huge barren enclosure, with the gravel preventing any plant life from taking root within its boundaries.

The reactors could easily be sabotaged by placing dynamite underneath them. Even though there was a construction trailer inside the fenced yard, no one appeared to be there during off-hours, although we would have to confirm that by coming back sometime late at night. We would have to verify whether or not Hydro employed a security guard in the trailer at night or had security patrols. Even as we surveyed the area we kept on our guard for vehicles, in case a security firm had been hired to do hourly patrols. This was a politically controversial power line, and opposition to it already had a history of civil disobedience. It only made sense to us that Hydro would have stepped up security for this substation so near to completion. After walking around the substation several times, we concluded we should return a week before the action and climb the fence to pace off distances and get a closer look at the reactors.

As the sun was setting, we sat back on our heels on the side of a hill to admire the golden hue spreading over the fields and forest. Not far from us, a doe and two fawns emerged from the woods and began quietly grazing, oblivious to our presence. The construction crews had cut a huge swath through the forest that led like a giant trail into the sunset. This swath would eventually be the route taken by the transmission towers and high-voltage power lines. For the time being, tall grass had taken root where the forest had been cut down, providing a good grazing spot for the local deer. While I was getting a closer look at the deer through the binoculars, I noticed what appeared to be an abandoned railway bed intersecting the trail. I followed its path into the forest and wondered where it went. I had always loved following old railway beds. When I mentioned this find to Doug, he took the binoculars from me.

"Let's follow it," he suggested. " It might lead us to a place we could park the truck and camp for the night when we do the action." We headed down the path, which made its way towards the coastal highway, then followed along beside the road. The spring air, and beautiful colours spawned by the sunset, fuelled our excitement as we found ourselves becoming deeply immersed in the details of our plans. About a mile down the railway bed, an old logging road crossed it. Nearby we found the perfect place to pull off the highway and park for the night without being seen by any passersby on the main highway.

"When Brent gets back, we'll have to come back here and camp so we can go into the substation yard," Doug said. "Let's jog back to the truck."

It felt good jogging on the soft bed of cedar bark covering the old railway bed and breathing in the moist spring air. When we got back to the truck, we timed our trip to the ferry and picked up a spring and summer schedule of the ferry run between Horseshoe Bay and Nanaimo. In light of all the other dangers and excitement going on in my life at this time, I didn't give the shoplifting charge much thought. After the Cheekeye-Dunsmuir action we would be living in the underground anyway, with far more pressing concerns than a failure to appear in court on a shoplifting charge.

✳ **19** ✳

A few days after Brent and Angie returned from Ontario, Brent, Doug, and I went out to Bino's for bottomless coffee and one of our long talks. It was such a perfect place to meet because the eating cubicles, surrounded by plastic plants, afforded each group of customers quite a bit of privacy. Brent had photos he had taken of the Litton complex and two other Atomic Energy of Canada buildings. Doug and I hunched over the stack of photos, examining each one meticulously. When we came to the series of the Litton plant, we were taken aback by a few showcasing Angie posing like a tourist in front of the buildings. Although it was an unspoken assumption that we had each revealed something of our plans to our respective lovers, it was still our duty to keep each other from opening up too much.

Doug asked the obvious. "Does Angie know we're thinking of doing Litton?"

"No," Brent said. "She just knows I'm interested in Litton but what for is still a mystery."

"What's with the workmen?" I wondered why he had included

a photo of Angie standing beside some city labourers repairing the cement on a sidewalk in front of the Litton plant.

"Well, I thought if they were suspicious of us taking photos of the plant, by including them in the photo I portray myself as a man without paranoia and thus disarm them." He smiled triumphantly. Doug and I couldn't help smirking at each other.

"So what did you think about the feasibility of doing an action there?" I asked.

"Great! It's a must-do situation."

"Man, you're in a good mood," I remarked. "Spending all that time with Angie must have done you good."

"Actually, we fought most of the way there and back."

"But that's the way you are," I protested. "You argue with everybody all the time. It's the way you communicate."

He just smiled at me mysteriously. "How did Cheekeye go?"

"They're way behind schedule," Doug said. "They'll have to pick up speed if they intend to have it on-line by October 1983. That's about a year and a half from now. From what we saw, they're mostly still just clearing brush for the right-of-way. Not much has been done on the substations and no cable has been laid. We didn't see any hydro towers."

Doug and I began talking simultaneously about our adventure at the Malaspina substation with the helicopters. "You're right," laughed Brent. "I would have loved to have been there. So what's the bottom line: is an action feasible in the near future?"

"We could do one at the Dunsmuir substation," Doug said. "It was the only one with reactors. I think we should go back there in a few weeks for a final casing, then do it at the end of May."

We told Brent about the place we had found to park the truck and camp not far from the substation. "We could take turns," I said, "watching the substation all night just to be sure they don't have night security patrols or a guard in the trailer." We wanted to make sure no one would accidentally get hurt during the bombing.

"Sounds like fun," agreed Brent.

"I want to go into the yard," continued Doug, "and check to see if the shunt reactors have oil in them yet, because if they do then they should burn once the dynamite goes off. That will really destroy them. The reactors are the most expensive part of the transmission line and therefore the best target." The shunt reactors, we knew, were there to compensate for the change in voltage that occurs when electricity has to travel for long distances in underwater cables. Since the iron-core inductors would get extremely hot from the increase in voltage, they had to be immersed in oil to cool them down.

Brent took out a cigarette pack and looked at the calendar on the back. "Let's set a tentative date for this action on May 31st. That's a Monday. Then we'll have something to shoot for. We'll have to work on a communiqué."

"Sounds good," agreed Doug. "But you two can work on the communiqué. I ain't into it."

"Come on Doug," I pleaded. "That's the most important part. We should all pool our thoughts on it and then one person write it."

"I'll read what you write and let you know if I want something added or omitted."

Brent and I knew we were fighting a losing battle. This was the best we could get so we accepted it. "Tomorrow morning, why don't you and I get together and write it," I said to Brent. "Then we can go over it with Doug and rewrite it later."

"Just don't make it long," added Doug. This time Brent and I shook our heads in dismay. "Oh, I ran into Saphie at the Granville Market yesterday," Doug said as an afterthought. "You know Julie is staying with her and Bridget until she can get a place with Gerry. Anyway Saphie says she's always asking about us and is pissed because she thinks the reason we don't see her is because Saphie is recommending against it."

"What are you talking about?" I said.

"Julie thinks Saphie is saying things to discourage us from working politically with her," Doug said. "I told Saphie that Brent will set Julie straight."

"He'll set her straight alright." I looked over at Brent suspiciously. "He'll invite her to go on the Cheekeye action with us."

"If that happens, don't count me in," Doug said firmly. "They just aren't politically sophisticated or experienced enough. They need more time to get ready."

"Well it might not be a bad idea to do some target-practising with them," suggested Brent.

"Speaking of which," continued Doug, "I almost forgot. I guess you were writing Julie when they were out in Jasper, suggesting she get a FAC. Well, apparently she went and got one, and a B.C. firearms licence." Brent grinned. "Great! See, she's the only person we know who's done that. She might be young, but she's into it."

"Let's get out of here," I said furrowing my eyebrows at him sceptically as I slid out of the cubicle.

* * *

The first light of dawn was just beginning to peer over the mountains when Doug pulled up in front of my apartment on May 30, 1982. I had a hard time waking up when the alarm clock went off because we'd spent the day before in the mountains north of Squamish, moving about 350 pounds of dynamite in fifty-five-pound cases down the side of the overgrown mountain into the truck. By the time we got back it was late, but I had foolishly offered to make sandwiches for the day so I had to stay up even later fulfilling my domestic duty.

I peeked out the window and watched Doug get out of our pickup truck. The dynamite was neatly stacked inside the truck and covered with boxes and blankets so it couldn't be seen by anyone nosy enough to peer inside the truck canopy. I grabbed the sandwiches out of the fridge and put them and some pop into a cooler waiting by the door. By the time Doug knocked on my door, I had my running shoes on and was ready to go.

As we headed over the Second Narrows Bridge towards the Capilano highway, we watched the sun rise in all its glory over Grouse Mountain. The sun's pink and purple hues were breaking through some light, scattered morning clouds, but fortunately it didn't look like rain. All the way to the ferry terminal at Horseshoe Bay, we rehearsed the upcoming night's activities, right down to the colour of our clothing.

Even though we had left very early, a long line of cars was already backed up waiting for the first ferry to Nanaimo. We were surprised that so many people wanted to take an early ferry to Vancouver Island on a Sunday. After we had turned off the truck engine in the bowels of the ferry, Doug suggested we take turns staying there, since we didn't want to risk anyone snooping around or breaking into the back of the truck. I volunteered for the first watch because I was still tired and figured I could get in a short snooze. Soon the soft rocking of the ferry lulled me into a light sleep. It seemed as though all the passengers had just disappeared to the upper decks when Doug knocked on the window beside me, startling me out of my dream. It was time for his shift.

I got out and walked along the metal floor of the ferry, noticing how spooky the clanging of my feet sounded echoing down the empty, cavernous space of the ferry hold. I passed a few people who had also chosen to stay in their vehicles, and I wondered if any of them could be cops following us. It was easy to get paranoid on an excursion like this.

By the time we reached Nanaimo the sky was overcast and dark clouds were rolling in. The forecast didn't call for rain, but on Vancouver Island rain was always a possibility. We waited in the truck for the ferry to dock. The ferry jolted as it hit the rubber tires lining the dock. Within minutes we were driving up the metal ramp and onto the road that leads into the city centre of Nanaimo.

For most of the beautiful fifty-five-kilometre drive north to the Dunsmuir substation we sat in silence. Each of us respected the other's need to prepare for this life-changing action, the biggest one we had taken so far, and the most dangerous. The weekend before we had spent two days camped out a mile down the abandoned railway bed from the Dunsmuir substation. Taking shifts, we had each sat on the hill overlooking the substation staring through the binoculars, watching for security patrols or any signs of life. Then, as the early light of dawn broke over the horizon, all of us had scaled the security fence and examined the reactors, pacing out distances in order to fine-tune our plans for early on the morning of May 31st.

As we rounded a bend in the highway, a break in the trees exposed the dark ocean waters of Qualicum Beach sparkling in the sun. It had been overcast most of the morning but now, as we neared the substation, the clouds began to clear. My stomach began to churn as the truck tires roared past the small creek, the Nile, that emptied into the Bay only a little more than a kilometre from Dunsmuir substation. I slowed down so we wouldn't drive past the logging road. There it was! I stared into the rear-view mirror to make sure no one was behind to notice us turn off the main highway. We bounced along the deserted logging road in a cloud of dust until we came to an overgrown trail that veered off to the left. A few hundred metres down the trail we pulled into a clearing and parked. We had rehearsed our plans so many times that there was no need to talk. Without hesitation we each grabbed a packsack from the truck canopy and began marching down the railway bed in single file, like soldiers on a mission. I was so immersed in my thoughts and emotions that for once I didn't notice the sounds of the birds or the wind in the trees. Between us we were carrying about 150 pounds of dynamite as well as a detonating cord, blasting caps, a timing device, and bolt-cutters, so, needless to say, the load was heavy. The thought of going back for a second load didn't make the task any easier. I did not want to appear weak, so each time I felt the need to rest I would tell myself to walk another one hundred metres, giving myself time to catch a second wind. We weren't in a big hurry, but it was already late afternoon and we wanted some time to relax and rest before the sun set and the time came to lay down the explosives.

When we reached the substation we hid our packsacks in the bushes at the edge of the woods and once again sat on the edge of the hillside above the huge seventy-acre enclosure. We took turns staring into the binoculars looking for any signs of human activity. The giant steel reactors looked like grotesque sculptures set in some misguided display in this beautiful island wilderness. I hoped the deer and her fawns would not be feeding on the grass surrounding the enclosure when the bombs went off. I found myself wishing that we didn't have to do this, but I pushed the thought out of my head. It was too late. The plan was in motion.

There was no sign of human activity at all. There was only a hawk soaring on the wind above, maybe scouting around for a mouse to kill. It was so serene and still that it was hard to imagine we were actually going to lay enough dynamite under these four giant monoliths to destroy them. Each reactor weighed a hundred tons and cost about $1 million. The cost of the oil-pumping plant had been estimated at $400,000. As the sun began to drop towards the horizon, Doug got up and went over to the bushes to organize the dynamite and other equipment. It would be almost dark when he would be placing them under the reactors, so he wanted to be totally prepared in advance. Only two things could go wrong with this action before we returned safely to Vancouver. One would be someone finding the dynamite before it was set to explode — but that possibility was remote, because we had not seen a soul on either weekend when we were casing. The only other problem could be something going wrong with the timing device, but after studying and building timing devices for the past year Doug had become an expert. He had tested the one he had designed hundreds of times and it had never failed to go off at the correct time. So I was not too worried about anything going wrong during this phase of the action. My biggest fear centred around the public's reaction. We couldn't realistically stop the Cheekeye-Dunsmuir line from being completed. We could make it more expensive and less politically viable, but the political part depended on the public's reaction to this bombing. In any guerrilla campaign, whether small or large, success is dependent on a broad popular support.

Finally the sun disappeared behind the trees on the horizon and within an hour the light had grown dim. My role would be to help carry the dynamite down into the enclosure, then to come back up on the hill and watch for intruders with the binoculars. I was to whistle if I spotted anyone. Doug got up and slipped on his gloves, then headed down the hill towards the security fence. I followed along behind, lugging a heavy packsack over my shoulder. Since the security fence was eight feet high with a row of barbed wire running along the top, we had decided to cut a large hole in it so we could just walk in with the heavy packs. While Doug cut through the fencing with the pair of heavy-duty bolt-cutters, I scurried back and forth up the hill, carrying down the other two packsacks. Within minutes Doug was walking purposefully towards the first reactor while I headed quickly up the hill to take my position as a lookout.

Doug carefully stacked the dynamite up against the steel base of the reactor, right underneath a control panel. Then he ran the detonating cord from that reactor to the next one, where he carefully attached it to another stack of dynamite. I was impressed with how efficiently and quickly he moved. It didn't take more than half an hour for him to place the dynamite and detonating cord under all four reactors. There was just enough light for me to see the detonating cord running like a long umbilical cord, connecting all four huge, black reactors, and Doug moving soundlessly between them like a shadow. By the time he was kneeling over the last reactor, presumably setting the timing device, the night sky was a deep purple and the stars were beginning to twinkle. There was not a sign of human activity otherwise — no lights in the distance, not even the distant sound of tires on the highway, which usually plagued even the remotest country retreats. I felt completely relaxed.

Throughout all this Doug had walked briskly but had never broken into a run. There was no need to rush because we had plenty of time to make it to the ferry before the timing device was set to go at 1:30 in the morning. In fact, we would be getting into bed when the blast would be going off. The first we would know about the results of our action would be in the news sometime the next day. When Doug was finished I could barely make out his form in the dark as he squeezed through the hole in the fence.

Then, for the first time, he broke into a light jog up the hill towards me.

"It went perfectly! Let's go!" he said, grabbing my arm and pulling me up. No time to talk now. Once again, I felt like a soldier on a mission as we jogged along the railway bed towards the truck. I drove back out without turning on my headlights. As we neared the highway, we could see that luck was on our side: again there were no vehicles. I switched on the headlights and sped towards Nanaimo. I had to concentrate on keeping the accelerator just below the speed limit. My nerves made me feel like speeding, but I knew that could be a deadly error.

Once we were safely heading towards the ferry, we excitedly went over every detail of the action, double-checking to be sure we hadn't left anything at the substation. This was far less scary than shoplifting, I thought, and safer. The possibility of something going wrong seemed very remote. I settled back into my seat and concentrated on driving perfectly.

"Don't forget to pull over to a postbox so I can mail these communiqués." Doug slipped on a pair of latex gloves before pulling a pile of envelopes out of a plastic bag from his packsack.

"I won't." I glanced over at the return address on the envelopes. We had written "B.C. Hydro, 13 Commercial St., Nanaimo." Brent had suggested we use B.C. Hydro's business address on the Island in case any of the communiqués were returned to sender.

We stopped at the first red postbox we could see and, with his gloves still on, Doug dropped in the communiqués. We were leaving no prints on anything, but our fate was sealed. Within twenty-four hours, fourteen organizations and media outlets would receive our communiqués claiming responsibility for the bombing of the Dunsmuir substation.

We arrived at the ferry terminal just in time to catch the second-last ferry for the night. The 9:00 p.m. ferry from Nanaimo to Horseshoe Bay was always busy on a Sunday night with cottagers and weekend visitors trying to get home at a reasonable time for work and school on Monday morning. We drove under the huge glass-walled control booth on the steel arch that spanned the metal ramp leading onto the ferry. This was where ferry security sat so they could spot the licence plates of suspects wanted by the police on either the Island or mainland. Although I knew it was unreasonable to expect anyone to know of our activities that day, I still felt a little paranoid as I glanced up at the two men standing behind the glass watching the vehicles board the ferry.

"I don't think we should leave the truck in case we run into someone we know on the ferry," Doug said when we came to a stop. I nodded my head, although I felt so hyper I could barely sit still. People were pouring out of their vehicles and heading towards the upper decks. To avoid being noticed Doug bent his head and began reading a book he had brought along, and I leaned my head against the truck door, pretending to be asleep.

Once the ferry had lurched out of its docking berth, the parking hold had emptied of its human cargo except for us and the odd persons sleeping in their cars. We sat and relived the evening's activities and made up funny stories about what might happen in the morning. It seemed so unreal that those little stacks of dynamite could potentially destroy the one-hundred-ton reactors.

The ninety-minute ferry ride to Vancouver seemed endless. The closer the time came for the blast on Vancouver Island, the more excited we became. We pulled into a Bino's to eat a late supper. It might be good if we were spotted sitting in a restaurant in Vancouver the night of the blast. At 1:28 a.m., I looked up at the tacky brass clock on the restaurant wall and felt my heart beat with the second hand. It seemed odd that at 1:30 a.m. the few people in the restaurant were continuing to eat and talk, cars were driving by slowly outside, and life was going on as though nothing special was happening. Without expression Doug and I looked at each other, then continued eating.

✳ **20** ✳

Violet Spankie was snoring under her down-filled comforter when an incredibly loud bang penetrated and rocked her little wooden bungalow, just thirteen kilometres from the Dunsmuir substation. She sat up poker straight and felt her heart pounding in her chest.

"Oh my God!" she thought. "Could this be the end of the world or an earthquake or what?!" She was about to get out of bed to see what the world outside looked like when the phone began to ring, making her jump yet again with fright. Her husband, Harold, was working nights and she was alone except for her cat, which was sitting with her on the edge of the bed. She reached over and grabbed the phone. "Hello!" she cried anxiously. "Harold?"

"No Violet, it's me, Jerry."

"Oh, thank God, Jerry," gasped Violet. Jerry was her next-door neighbour. "What on earth is happening? Did you hear that bang? Did you feel it?"

"Yeah, that's why I'm calling. I was wondering if you're alright?"

"I think so," Violet said. "But what was it?"

"I don't know. I'm calling the cops."

"Good," Violet said. "Phone me right back and let me know what they say."

She hung up the phone, then gingerly put her feet on the cold floor and tiptoed over to the window and peered out into the darkness. The dark outlines of the trees, her garage, and Jerry's house next door looked the same. No earthquake as far as she could tell. She fumbled around to make sure the window was locked, and the phone rang again. It was Jerry.

"Well, I called the cops and they said no one reported anything, and there's been no earthquake so they figure maybe it was just a car backfiring on the highway."

"I don't think so, Jerry," whispered Violet. "It shook my house."

"Mine too. But I guess we'll just have to wait for the morning to see what happened."

After she hung up the phone, Violet timidly tiptoed around her house to make sure everything was locked and alright. After that she went back upstairs and lay down with her cat and wondered what could possibly have caused her house to shake that way. If there was one thing she was sure of, it was that her house had shaken.

* * *

Around 9:00 a.m. on May 31, Wayne Fraser got the call at his Canadian Law Enforcement Unit office (CLEU) in Vancouver.

"Hold on to your seat, Fraser," said a familiar voice on the other end of the line. It was Fraser's superior, Detective Jean Despaireux, head of Vancouver's Integrated Intelligence Unit. "There's been a bombing on Vancouver Island."

"What?!" Fraser couldn't believe it. The most extreme activity he had to deal with as an intelligence officer in CLEU's political wing was minor property damage. Bombing! This was not a Third World country.

"You heard what I said," Despaireux said irritably. "At the new

Dunsmuir hydro substation. They're taking us by helicopter over to the Island as soon as we can get there."

"I'll be right over," Fraser almost shouted at his superior. He grabbed his note pad, tape recorder, and mobile phone, then told the receptionist to take his messages as he ran past her and out towards the parking lot. Once in his car he turned on the emergency siren and drove as fast as he could to the police helipad, not far from CLEU. Despaireux was already there, standing beside the helicopter, his shoulder bag slung over his arm. Fraser parked his car and jogged over to him.

"That was fast," Despaireux said with the kind of smile limited only to the mouth. "I bet you've been hoping something like this would happen for a long time."

"What are you talking about?" Fraser had never liked Despaireux's cynicism. It rubbed his natural optimism the wrong way.

On the flight over to the Island, Despaireux filled Fraser in with the few details they had. "There's no witnesses yet, only a couple of neighbours who phoned the local RCMP last night just after 1:30 a.m. to report a blast they said shook their houses. They live over eight miles from the Dunsmuir substation, so we can assume there was a hell of a lot of dynamite involved. The cops responded by sending someone down the highway to see if there had been a car accident or something, but there was nothing. At first they just figured a truck had backfired or something."

"Well, I've been following the protests against the Cheekeye-Dunsmuir line," offered Fraser, "but never in a million years would I have guessed that anyone would do something like this. Most of them are into civil disobedience, you know, pulling up stakes, blocking bulldozers, stuff like that. Certainly not bombing."

"Looks like one of your lunatic fringe types went right over the edge," Despaireux said sarcastically.

As the chopper cut its way through the sky towards the Dunsmuir substation, the passengers could see smoke furling up into the sky from a few miles away. Fraser speculated that it was from the oil burning inside the bombed-out reactors. The closer they got, the more grisly the scene became. Within minutes the giant blades of the chopper sent a cloud of dirt and gravel funnelling upwards as it landed a hundred yards away from the substation in the right-of-way, cleared for the future transmission line. What stood before them was like a scene from a movie: four burnt-out reactors, three torn apart; huge pieces of concrete and hunks of steel transformed into shrapnel and scattered all over the place; the perimeter fence in ruins, with bent, jagged holes torn open by pieces of flying shrapnel and concrete. One eighty-pound fragment had apparently been propelled through the fence for 120 yards before it slammed into an office trailer. The whole side of the trailer was covered in earth and gravel that had rained down hard upon it, smashing the windows.

Fraser could barely make out the firemen, hosing down the three mangled reactors, through the clouds of grey toxic smoke billowing out of the reactor orifices, where the oil was still burning. The fourth reactor was badly damaged but had not caught fire. He walked carefully through the debris and found the Island RCMP officer in charge.

"Did you make sure these men are aware they are not to disturb anything?" Fraser asked, referring to the firemen.

"Of course, corporal," the officer snapped. "But they do have to put out the fire."

"Of course," said Fraser, wishing they could just let the fire burn itself out. He was worried that the intense pressure from the chemicals they were spraying on the oil could damage evidence.

Despaireux was standing beside a group of RCMP officers. Fraser assumed they must also be from the Island. He and Despaireux were probably the first cops to arrive from the mainland. He strode over to Despaireux and asked, "Who discovered this?"

"Some construction workers, when they arrived first thing in the morning," Despaireux said. "I've instructed these guys to close off the area for about a mile around this substation and to begin looking for evidence. They've already formally interviewed the construction workers who arrived first."

Fraser, like everyone else, had already put on a special pair of plastic boot covers to distinguish his footprints from those of anyone who had been there before that morning. He began walking methodically around the fence perimeter, looking closely at the ground for footprints. As he walked, he began dictating into his tape recorder everything he had been told and seen since arriving on the crime scene.

"Over here!" yelled Despaireux. Fraser looked over, and through the grey smoke billowing up from the reactors he could just barely make out Despaireux, standing near the fence on the other side of the enclosure. He jogged quickly over to him and saw a large gaping hole in the fence. This hole hadn't been torn through by the effects of the explosion but had obviously been cut. Despaireux was busy taking photographs of the hole and of footprints marking where the intruders had stepped into the enclosure.

"There's two sets of prints, Fraser," Despaireux said. "The ones going in are deep, and the ones going out are shallow. So it looks like they carried something heavy in, and then left their heavy load behind them."

"When will the forensic guys get here?" asked Fraser, realizing how important it was that plaster casts of these prints be made before it rained. He looked up warily at the grey rain clouds above them.

"Any minute," replied Despaireux, deeply preoccupied with taking photographs and notes. Fraser took out his measuring tape and began jotting down numbers, but his main job was to come up with theories and possible suspects based on the daily intelligence gathering he had been doing for years. He paused and looked down the right-of way where the footprints were headed.

"Let's go!" he said to Despaireux.

"I want to, but I better report to the forensic guys and somebody should stay here as commander. I don't want these local Island guys screwing things up," Despaireux said.

Fraser began following the two sets of prints, walking a few feet alongside so he wouldn't disturb them. The footprints headed up a hill to a spot where the spring grass had been flattened. He yelled down his discovery to Despaireux, who quickly came up to see for himself. They began to search the area for evidence, but Fraser was eager to continue tracking the suspects. He took notes and talked into his tape recorder as he walked, noting that the suspects appeared to be jogging. A hundred yards further the prints turned down an old railway bed that intersected the right-of-way. Fraser stopped taking notes and began keeping an eye out for evidence, such as discarded cigarette butts, gum wrappers, anything. He couldn't help feeling the excitement of it all. At least no one had been hurt. Finally, about a mile down the railway bed, the prints suddenly headed off into a clearing beside an abandoned logging road. There in the spring mud were perfectly clear tire marks from a truck of some sort. Fraser smiled. This was great! Luckily he had brought along a roll of yellow police tape, and now he began tying tape to a tree. He carefully ran the plastic tape around the area, then walked down the road and put the tape across the entrance to the logging road. He had better get the forensic guy down here as soon as possible.

"Hey Jean!" he called into his walkie-talkie.

"Jean here, Fraser." Despaireux's voice crackled back through the walkie-talkie.

"Send somebody north on the highway. I'm about a mile down. I've got the location where the suspects parked their truck before they did the bombing," he said as unemotionally as he could.

"Done," said Despaireux.

Fraser turned off his walkie-talkie and looked up at the clouds. Looked like the rain was going to pass them by. Thank God. A police car was already speeding down the highway towards him. He waved and the car pulled over. A young cop jumped out.

"We need to have this whole area sealed off and guarded until the forensic guys can catalogue the evidence," Fraser explained. "This is the area where the suspects parked while they were setting the explosives. Be careful you don't disturb any tire tracks, footprints, or anything. Don't even touch the leaves!"

* * *

It had been a long day, but Fraser didn't feel tired. This was the most exciting thing that had happened to him since he had begun his career as a police officer. Late in the afternoon, Fraser and Despaireux flew back to the Vancouver office for a meeting with the other officers in the Intelligence Unit. They would summarize the day's events and begin planning the investigation. He grabbed a cup of coffee from the office's canteen and walked into the meeting room, where Despaireux was already beginning to brief the other officers on the information they had so far.

"Oh good, Fraser, you're here." Despaireux cut himself off in mid-sentence. "Most of these guys aren't familiar with the Cheekeye-Dunsmuir line and the protests surrounding it, so maybe you can fill us in. At this point, it would seem that the motive for this bombing would be related to the construction of this power line."

"That would be my guess." Fraser, taking a sip of his coffee, began a quick synopsis of the history of the protest. "B.C. Hydro announced plans to build this 112-kilometre, 500,000-volt power line from the B.C. mainland to Vancouver Island in 1979. Right from the beginning, people started protesting because they weren't given any say in whether or not this power line was needed or where it was going to run. Many people on the Island didn't want more pulp mills and mines, which is what they believed the electricity would be used for. They want to keep their pastoral way of life. They were also worried about the environmental effects because the transmission lines will emit electro-magnetic radiation, and herbicides will have to be used on the right-of-way to keep down the undergrowth. On the mainland, people were opposed to the $1 billion price tag that the taxpayer will be footing at a time when a lot of people are questioning the need for these Hydro megaprojects.

"Now, the B.C. government has refused to hold hearings into the need for this line or the route it will take so there have been a lot of demonstrations in front of the provincial legislature, plus letter-writing campaigns and protest meetings. On the illegal front, a small group of people have been organizing blockades to stop construction along the route, especially on Texada Island. These people have pulled up survey stakes and blocked the contractors from using their bulldozers to clear the land. Hydro got court injunctions authorizing the RCMP to arrest those who continue blocking bulldozers from clearing the land."

"What kind of people are doing the civil disobedience?" one of the officers asked.

"Mainly environmentalists and some local citizens," Fraser answered. "But there has been support in the way of letters from unions and Indians as well."

"So who do you suspect could have done a bombing like this?" asked the same guy.

"I've been to the demos and there's only a few fringe radicals that could even come close to being suspects," Fraser offered. "I'm going to check them out, but right now no one definite comes to mind. Anyone who has enough time and determination could acquire the dynamite to cause an explosion like the one we saw today. There's no foolproof way of storing money, gas, or explosives."

"B.C. Hydro has already decided to post a $25,000 reward for information leading to the arrest and conviction of those responsible," Despaireux added. "Which, by the way, I think is a good idea."

The meeting went on for an hour or more before Fraser remembered a note from the receptionist about a call from his sister, Rose. The memory stirred him out of his seat. He whispered to Despaireux as he left that he would get back to him before he went home for the night. He walked quickly down the hall to his office and picked up the phone. He glanced at the time on his wristwatch as he waited for someone to answer the phone: nine o'clock.

"Hello," said a soft voice.

"Rose," he said. "I'm sorry I didn't get back to you sooner, but as you could imagine, I've been very busy."

"I know," she said, "and I'm also sorry for interrupting you, but I just couldn't sleep without letting you know that no one I've been involved with would even think of doing something like this."

"I know," he said reassuringly. "But it would be of great assistance to me if you could let me know if anyone's name ever comes up that could know anything."

"Of course, Wayne," she said. "I just want you to know that this is the kind of act that people in our community don't support. It's counterproductive because it scares normal citizens from getting involved in protesting against these Hydro megaprojects. We believe in the democratic process and that with time the government will set up mechanisms for the people to decide what projects we would support."

"I know," he said again. "Anyway, Rose, don't worry. I'll be in touch. Just remember what I said. You can be of help."

He hung up the phone and leaned back in his chair, closing his eyes for a few minutes. He had better get going home soon or he would be too tired to drive. He felt himself beginning to drift off into sleep when a sudden realization flashed through his mind. Fraser had often found that hunches and answers to problems came to him in that semi-conscious state just before and after sleep. That guy at the university! In 1977 he had chased that guy who had pied Joe Clark, and then he had seen him at several demonstrations and political rallies over the years. He and his friends were known as graffiti artists — they obviously had no respect for the law. Of all the characters he had seen over the years, that was the one face that popped into his mind's eye. Now what was his name? He was just too tired. Tomorrow morning he would look it up in his notes or old newspaper files about the pieing. He let out a deep breath, then picked up his notebook and began jotting down his thoughts. It was just a hunch. Just a hunch.

✳ **21** ✳

I took the stairs to Brent's apartment two at a time, barely able to contain my fury. I turned his doorknob, too much in a hurry to bother knocking. He heard me and yelled through the door, "Try knocking!"

"Come on, open up!" I yelled angrily.

I could hear him push his chair back and walk slowly to the door. He could be so irritating. As soon as I heard the lock unfasten, I pushed it open impatiently. "Guess what that idiot did?" I turned the lock behind me.

"I'll never guess what idiot or what." He sat back down and casually continued taping newspaper clippings of the bombing into the scrapbook on the table.

"I had arranged to meet Nick for dinner," I said quickly. "So we're talking and he let it slip that he took all your files that you gave him and burned them!"

Now it was Brent's turn to freak. "That idiot! Why?"

"He's just too paranoid," I said, calming down now that Brent was upset.

"What . . . does he think that anyone who has any information about Cheekeye-Dunsmuir is going to be a suspect in the bombing?"

"I have no idea how his mind works, but I think he is superparanoid just because he knows us."

"That is a total drag," Brent said dejectedly. "Those files are irreplaceable. There were pamphlets from years ago on all kinds of obscure topics. Nobody has leftist archives like those. I trusted the guy! I thought he would be the best guardian, but I was wrong." He began leafing through newspaper clippings again.

I sat down across the table from him and began scanning the scrapbook he had made of all the articles about the bombing. I hadn't slept with Nick since the first time I slept with Brent. I'd never told Nick why. The topic hadn't come up. We didn't have the kind of relationship where we discussed our feelings, so it was not unusual for Nick to ignore the fact that we had not had sex for a month. Perhaps it disturbed him intensely. I really didn't know. But since he had known before we went to Calgary that our relationship would end, he had been prepared for a long time for the sudden death of our sex life. I also didn't know if he had another lover, but it wouldn't have bothered me if he did. Our relationship had been based more on satisfying each other's needs than on being in love. I'd needed him when I was lonely and isolated in Calgary, but now that I was occasionally sleeping with Brent, I no longer needed Nick. I suspected the feelings were mutual because the basic needs that our relationship satisfied — that it was comfortable and convenient — were no longer there. He was growing increasingly wary of spending time with someone whose activities could put his safety in jeopardy.

"So do you think there was much public support for the Cheekeye-Dunsmuir bombing?" I asked, changing the topic.

"I wouldn't say there was a lot of support or opposition. My impression is that the public is indifferent." He had apparently already adjusted to the burning of his files. "Cheekeye-Dunsmuir is not a megaproject that arouses a lot of public debate, like the issue of nuclear power or weapons. I think it must bother Hydro, though, that more people are not outraged over the bombing."

"Apparently Julie was impressed," I said. "I was talking to Doug yesterday, and he said he had heard that Julie was pissed because she thinks Saphie is stopping her from working with us. She wants to be involved."

"Well, that's great," he said in a distracted tone of voice. "Once the media dies down over Cheekeye, we'll have to invite her and Gerry target-practising."

"Doug won't like that," I reminded him.

"I don't care," he said.

I shrugged my shoulders. "Well, I'll ask Doug to see if Julie and Gerry want to go target-practising soon, okay?"

"Sure," he said, cutting out another article.

* * *

Almost a month had passed since the Cheekeye-Dunsmuir bombing, and Fraser was growing increasingly frustrated. When not a shred of information materialized from the $25,000 reward offered by B.C. Hydro, the company upped the reward on June 25 to $125,000 and publicized it in newspapers throughout the province and in notices added to the utility bills of its one million customers. Still nothing. Fraser could not remember a case where more money was offered or where more advertising was put out for information leading to a conviction. Even then Hydro continued to up the ante. It printed two thousand posters advertising the increased reward money, with a toll-free number for anyone interested in offering information. But as Despaireux told the federal solicitor general, this approach had not even led to "a whisper on the street." To rationalize the ineffectiveness of the reward money, RCMP Superintendent Thomas Gardiner told the press, "People's values are probably changing. Money doesn't mean as much to them any more." But behind the scenes the RCMP was embarrassed, because it appeared as though the bombers were harder to crack than the bikers. The Force hated to admit it had no evidence, no leads, no informers, no nothing. All its officers could do was sit and wait.

"You know what the problem is, Fraser?" Despaireux suggested one afternoon as they sat on opposite sides of an office table scratching their heads. "There are just too many people who hate B.C. Hydro. It would take years to interview and investigate everyone who has expressed resentment towards them." Fraser agreed. He had searched out the name of the pie-thrower — Brent Taylor — and included it in a long list of people who were possible suspects, but there was absolutely no reason to believe that Taylor had anything to do with the bombing. He hadn't even been involved in any of the groups organized to stop the Cheekeye-Dunsmuir line. Taylor's name remained just one of many on a growing list of hunches.

Fraser had even been flown to France to exchange information with the French police and INTERPOL on the French "terrorist" group Action Directe, but they could find no connection with the Canadian group of the same name. No one who had ever been arrested or a sympathizer of the French group had any Canadian affiliation, so that lead had led nowhere.

"I had a call this morning from Robert Bonner," Despaireux said. Bonner was Hydro's chairman. "He was asking if I thought it would help to state publicly that the disruption caused by the explosion could delay completion of the line. He said the delay could cause power shortages on the Island late next year."

"Is it true?"

"I don't know," Despaireux said. "I got the impression he was asking more if it would be a good means of turning public sympathy away from the terrorists."

"If it's not true, I don't think it's a good idea. Because there are a lot of environmentalists and consultants out there who do know the truth. If they know the power line is crucial for industry but not for maintaining residential power, they will tell the public that Bonner and Hydro are lying, and the announcement will backfire.

Hydro is already unpopular, and if they are perceived as lying, they will be trusted even less than they are now."

"I don't know," said Despaireux sceptically.

"The problem I'm having," revealed Fraser, "is informers. I don't have any. The political analysts agree the communiqué is not written by your typical environmentalists or local citizens. They all agree it sounds like an anarchist bit of writing. They're a very difficult group to infiltrate or get informers from. They don't have organizations or hierarchy but are loose-knit groups of people who work closely together. They've all known each other for years and often live in communes. We have no informers in that community so it makes information-gathering difficult. I hate to just sit and wait for the next bombing to happen, but that's what I'm afraid I'm doing."

Fraser looked over the table at Despaireux's face. His colleague looked older than his fifty-odd years. Was it the job or was it the drinking? He shook his head, partially over Despaireux and partially over his frustration at the lack of leads in the bombing.

"There's got to be some people out there who know who did this bombing," Fraser began again. "Surely $125,000 should be a sufficient sum to lure some anarchist out of the woodwork. I guess the problem is, they're fundamentally opposed to this society and its focus on money so it's not surprising the reward hasn't brought us any leads."

Despaireux shook his head as well, then pushed back his chair. "Well, Fraser, eventually some anarchist is going to become disillusioned and sell out. $125,000 is a lot of money."

✳ **22** ✳

After the Cheekeye-Dunsmuir bombing our group kept an extremely low profile in Vancouver. We were aware that we were living dangerously by staying there, but we weren't ready to take the plunge into the underground so soon after Calgary. Instead we applied as many safeguards as we could, using false identification to rent apartments, avoiding public functions where we might run into acquaintances, and limiting our social contacts to one friend each, plus Gerry, Julie, and Doug's mother. Even within this limited social sphere, we did not admit to doing the bombing. Despite these precautions, we knew that our days of living in Vancouver were numbered. We were just putting off leaving until after the next action.

One thing we had decided upon was to get another truck. It had become evident that the truck Brent and Doug had bought in Calgary was unreliable, which was certainly an unacceptable quality in the world of the urban guerrilla. We couldn't afford to be driving away from an action and have our truck break down, so we began the search for a new vehicle — not a new one off a car lot, but rather a new one off the street. We had become proficient in our knowledge of converting stolen vehicles into legal ones through reading obscure pamphlets ordered from the back pages of *Soldier of Fortune* magazine.

Through our reading we had learned that we could take the vehicle identification number from our truck and put it on a stolen vehicle of the same make and model, even if the two were not of the same year. As long as the trucks were within a few years of each other, only an expert would be able to tell them apart. Even a stolen vehicle of a different colour was not a problem because we would simply have to notify the insurance company that we had repainted it. No one would ever come out to verify that it had actually been painted. And so our search for another truck began.

Everywhere we drove, we scanned the trucks parked along the sides of the roads for one similar to ours but in better shape. Finally we found one — a nice, big, brown four-wheel drive we would eventually name "Bob." I suppose we gave it a human name because it was so important to us. It was more than a mode of transportation — it was a getaway vehicle. In many situations our safety would depend on Bob's reliability. We developed strong feelings for Bob; trust, a sense of comfort, and dependence.

Stealing Bob was easy. Getting rid of the lemon truck from Calgary was not. For that we had to rent acetylene tanks and torches so that we could take off its serial numbers before we disposed of it. We took Bob's vehicle indentification number off and replaced it with the legal one from our lemon truck. Then we drove the lemon up north of Squamish, found a hidden gully not far from our target-practice area, and began the procedure of stripping the old truck of parts we could use on Bob in the future. Then we began torching the serial numbers off the frame, the axle, and the engine, just in case someone found and reported the hulk to the police. After spending a day dismantling it, nothing was left but the skeleton. In another decade or two, the combined environmental elements of the area would break it down into the metallic compounds from which it had originated. Soon, we rationalized, it would be far less harmful to the environment than when we had been driving it around using up fossil fuels and belching out exhaust fumes.

I began to spend a considerable amount of time attending to Bob's needs, particularly since his well-being would have a great effect on ours. I read the Chilton manual on Chevy pickups and cultivated a bit of a friendship with a mechanic who could advise me if I ran into trouble. I decided to repair Bob myself, because he was stolen and we didn't want to risk a mechanic noticing the replaced VIN.

Meanwhile, Brent and I were still entertaining the idea of involving Julie and Gerry in our plans. Even though we felt that the weight of responsibility for their involvement would be on our shoulders, certainly Julie's ambitions and enthusiasm made it hard to resist her. When we heard through Saphie that Julie was angry at her for being excluded from our activities, Brent sent messages urging her to invest some of the money she had earned in Jasper into purchasing a Mini-14. Then we invited her and Gerry to go target-practising with us north of Squamish. When we learned that both Julie and Gerry had purchased Mini-14s, we took this as further proof that they were serious about becoming militants. Even though we didn't drop our reservations about involving them in serious actions, we arranged to go target-practising in July. Doug also wanted to go along — he said that they would need his help sighting in their rifles.

Finally, after passing messages back and forth through Saphie, the day came when we loaded up the truck with an assortment of weapons from the McClure robbery and went to pick up Julie and Gerry. Our security plans were inconsistent. Even though we had agreed not to visit them at their apartment, that day we picked them up. We told ourselves that it had been months since Dunsmuir and there was no reason to believe that their apartment, just below Saphie's, would be under surveillance.

As soon as we pulled up, Julie came out the front door carrying a large packsack and her rifle bag. Gerry came lumbering along behind her, with much less enthusiasm. He put his rifle bag and packsack in the back of the truck, then climbed in there beside Brent. There was only room in the front of the truck for three people, so Julie, Doug, and I shared the front seat. We hadn't even left the city before Julie began to air her concerns over our lack of interest in working with her and Gerry. She was not one to hold back her feelings. "I'm sure Saphie told you I was pissed about you guys never coming around to see me and Gerry." She looked pointedly at Doug.

"Yes, she did," Doug said carefully. "I've been meaning to straighten that out. You see, Saphie has nothing to do with that decision or, in fact, anything we do."

"Well, I'm going to get right to the point," she continued. "I felt really hurt that you guys just dropped me as a friend after we came back from Jasper."

"I can't explain everything to you, Julie," Doug said, somewhat nervously. "We like you, but there are good reasons we don't hang around, and you just have to respect that."

She didn't push the issue further, but her face told the story. I peeked over at her and could see she was pouting slightly. She was a determined person, and when she wanted something she did not take no for an answer. After that short conversation the relentless pounding of the large truck tires on the asphalt created a mesmerizing background to the atmosphere of silence that engulfed us. A couple of hours later it was a relief to see "Gary Gilmore's" cosy little gas station nestled at the foot of the mountains, coming at us as we rounded one of the snaking corners of the coastal highway. As usual, we stopped to stretch our legs and grab a coffee. While Brent, Doug, and Julie went inside to buy the coffee, Gerry came over to me and began eyeing the truck like a prospective buyer.

"Nice truck," he said. "Brent told me how you got it."

"Yeah. Wait till you see how easy he takes the hills up that logging road. A four-wheel drive is definitely the way to go."

"He?"

"I know it's weird but I guess 'cause I spend so much time working on it, I've developed a personal relationship with this truck and started calling it Bob. It's caught on with Brent and Doug."

"Your other truck wasn't a four-wheel drive, though," Gerry said. "If the cops stopped you, wouldn't they notice on the ownership papers that the description doesn't exactly match this truck?"

"If they're observant. But chances are they won't notice." I proceeded to tell Gerry about our risk-benefit analysis. The only thing indicating whether or not a vehicle was a four-wheel drive was a "K" in the VIN number. This truck had no "K." We figured that the benefits of driving a four-wheel drive far outweighed the minimal risk of being stopped and the cop noticing that the papers didn't match a four-wheel drive. We had thought all of that through. The important factor in the equation was that the driver must always abide by the rules of the road, and even more so do nothing to attract attention so the odds of being stopped become just about nil. How often do you get stopped for no reason? The cops almost always stop a vehicle if you're breaking a traffic rule or doing something odd, like driving too slowly or driving with no turning signals. There's a chance of being stopped at a drinking and driving checkpoint, but those checks are usually done at night, and if you haven't been drinking the cops don't usually check your ownership papers all that closely. It's too dark to see, and they're in a hurry because there are other cars to check. You could get stopped if the cops are looking for a vehicle matching your description that has been involved in something illegal — but the chances of that are low. As long as we obeyed the rules of the road and made sure all our lights were in working order, we believed the risk factor was very low.

"Very impressive," Gerry said — although I wasn't sure he really was all that impressed by the explanation. "Do you mind if I sit in the front seat with you and Julie? We were out late last night getting gas and I don't feel that great." I had noticed that he looked a little green.

"Sure. Doug won't mind sitting in the back with Brent," I said, relieved to have a less tense combination of personalities in the front seat.

"We were up in Shaughnessy siphoning gas — about five of those red ten-gallon containers — so by the time we were finished I was barfing and hallucinating from sucking up so many gas fumes."

"Is it worth it, for the amount of money you save?"

"Oh yeah!" Gerry was on unemployment, with all the lack of funds that state of existence implies.

The others were soon back with hot coffee and chocolate bars. Doug and Brent quite willingly piled into the back of the truck. Once we were on the road again, Julie put in a tape and cranked up the volume. She didn't seem any worse for wear from their gas-siphoning experience.

"Ger, you look terrible!" she said, placing her hand across his forehead. "Do you have a temperature?"

He shook his head. "I didn't suck up as much gas as you, but I feel like shit. I don't want to do that anymore."

"Did you tell Ann what we got last night?" she said excitedly. He shook his head again. "A canoe!" she squealed. "We were going down this back alley that runs behind the backyards, looking for cars to get gas from, and saw this canoe leaning up against someone's garage. Rich people — they had a pool and everything. We just put the canoe on our shoulders and took off."

"Great," I said. "But siphoning gas isn't a good idea. You'll get brain damage from the gas fumes. Do you need the money that bad?"

"No," Julie said. "We won't do it anymore. But the canoe will be great for camping." The two of them loved camping.

I turned off the highway at the logging road leading to the box canyon and marvelled at how easily Bob climbed the steep, twisting trail up the mountainside. We were able to drive all the way into the canyon and park. We pulled out the packsacks and Doug unwrapped the weapons. Julie's and Gerry's eyes seemed to widen when they saw the .357 Dan Wesson, the .44 Magnum, and the shotgun. They looked back and forth from Doug to the weapons, but they were streetwise enough to know not to ask questions. They probably assumed they were stolen. As Doug unpacked and organized the weapons, he suggested they use my Mini-14 and one of the handguns until he had sighted in their own Mini-14s, which would probably take the first part of the afternoon.

Julie immediately claimed the silver, nickel-plated .44 Magnum. "Hey, isn't this the same kind of gun that Clint Eastwood used in *Dirty Harry*?"

Doug was already so focused on what he was doing that it was futile to ask him questions. He put the handguns, my Mini-14, the shotgun, and some ammo on the tailgate for us and disappeared with the other Mini-14s and a small tool box down the trail.

"I drew a bunch of targets and set them up down that trail." Brent pointed to the opening of the box canyon. We had a game we had developed, where we took turns running down the trail and just before you reached a target someone would yell out "Stop" and the runner would have three seconds to aim and shoot at the bull's eyes. Whoever got the most shots nearest the bull's eyes was the winner. Soon we were laughing, talking, and taking turns running down the trail and shooting at the targets. We took turns using the .357, since it was a more useful gun than the .44

Magnum, which was quite heavy and powerful with its eight-inch barrel. I don't think either Gerry or Julie were all that attracted to guns, but they did enjoy being in the mountains and running up and down the trail playing the game. We felt like kids again, playing cops and robbers in the backyard, but instead we were using real guns. Making no attempt to be tough or cool, we let all our inhibitions go for the day, forgetting for the moment what these dangerous weapons could lead to.

I remember walking back up the trail after taking my turn shooting at the targets when a huge six-inch banana slug, sliding along the moist grass, caught my eye. Coming from Ontario, I was always struck by the size of these giant yellow slugs that are native to the rainforest climate of the West Coast. I picked it up carefully and continued walking up the trail towards Brent and Gerry. Just as we were about to pass one another, I held the mucus-covered slug in their faces. Screaming, they ran back up the trail, with me and my slug in hot pursuit. We were anything but the unemotional, fearless urban guerrillas commonly portrayed in the media.

When Doug had finished sighting in the Mini-14s, we joined up at Bob's tailgate for lunch. Brent uncrumpled some of the newspapers the guns had been wrapped in and began reading them. He found an article from July about how the Canadian government had recently signed an agreement allowing the air-launched cruise to be tested on Canadian soil. He read, "This action provoked an immediate response among North American disarmament groups which scheduled demonstrations for July 23 at the fourteen Canadian consulates in the United States."

"That's outrageous!" Julie said. "Why don't they test the missiles on their own bloody soil?"

"They could test it there just as easily. There's lots of places in the U.S. with terrain similar to northern Alberta, which is where they're going to test it, but the U.S. wants the world to see that Canada supports their nuclear policies," Brent explained. Only a few days earlier a U.S. Defense Department master plan had been leaked to the press. It caused a lot of flak because it said the United States should prepare for a protracted nuclear war and reject the concept of peaceful co-existence with the Soviet Union.

"I was reading in the paper that Trudeau says if we don't test the cruise we'll have to leave NATO," Gerry said.

"That's a pile of crap," Brent said. From our research we knew that Canada's NATO agreement did not include requirements to develop nuclear weapons or delivery systems. And we knew that Norway had refused to test the cruise, and that Scandinavian countries in general had refused to have the weapons on their soil and they were still members in good standing of NATO. "The air-launched cruise is not even a NATO weapon but a U.S. Air Force weapon," Brent said. "It's already been tested on reactivated Soviet Second World War battleships equipped with Tomahawks, the battleship-launched version of the cruise. Boeing Aircraft has even been contracted to manufacture them and is planning to turn out about forty a day by October of this year. They wouldn't be planning to make that many if there was any doubt they didn't work just fine. The most they want to do over northern Alberta is fine-tune the guidance system. Trudeau knows that, but he's saying whatever he must to convince Canadians to support testing them here."

Brent paused as though he was making a quick mental calculation. Then, in his compelling voice, he continued. "If they go ahead and test the weapon here and continue to produce the guidance system in Toronto, I'd like to blow up Litton and see if we can't stall the production of the guidance system and let the world know that Canadians are not going to sit by peacefully while they continue to test these weapons of global destruction."

"Me too!" added Julie quickly. I watched Gerry's reaction, but he didn't say anything. He just sat on the edge of the tailgate looking at the ground and watching Julie out of the corner of his eye.

"You know what really bugs me?" I asked without waiting for an answer. "The hypocrisy of the left in North America. If a revolutionary south of the Rio Grande picks up a gun, North American radicals are eager to demonstrate in their defence. But if revolutionaries next door do the same thing, they are condemned as misguided adventurists and they come up with all kinds of political reasons to persecute them. Myself, I think the real reason they defend the revolutionaries south of the Rio Grande is because it's too far away for them to feel guilty about not joining. But if it's the revolutionary next door, then their politics are put in question and they feel guilty."

"What about people who say a bombing changes nothing? It only brings down repression on the left?" asked Julie eagerly.

"Does a demonstration or act of civil disobedience change anything?" I answered. "No one act of protest, whether it's peaceful or militant, changes anything by itself. It's when you add up all the acts of protest over time that you see social change."

"I support guerrilla actions," Gerry said. "But I'm more into low-level expropriations that we can do locally. I'm not ready to do something really heavy."

"I respect that," Doug said. "Not everyone is cut out to do heavy actions. You have to be prepared to go to prison, or worse."

"I was planning on going up to the Chilcotins this summer and build a cabin where people could hide out when there's too much heat." Gerry looked over at Julie for support.

"Gerry, I want to do more than build a cabin," she said.

"I ain't travelling to Ontario to do an action," Doug said firmly. "There's enough I can do locally without going out of the province."

Brent and I smiled at each other — we knew all too well Doug's phobia about leaving British Columbia, and we weren't altogether sure that his Calgary experience with us hadn't become a contributing factor. All we knew for sure was that lately Doug had been making it perfectly clear that he was not prepared to travel outside of the province to carry out actions.

"Hypothetically speaking, what would you think of someone doing a bombing at the Litton plant in Ontario?" Brent asked Julie.

Julie frowned. "I just finished reading that book by Bommi Bauman you gave me, and it mentions a bombing the Red Army Faction in West Germany did in the Springer Press Building. Even though they gave the authorities three warnings that there were bombs in the building, nobody even tried to clear out the people. Maybe they thought it was a hoax. Maybe the Springer management thought it wasn't worth the money they would lose to clear the building, since chances were good it was a hoax. But when the bomb went off, seventeen people were killed."

"Yeah, the RAF said later that you can't rely on the cops to clear a building," Brent said. "But that doesn't mean a bombing can't be carried out safely. Hell, more people get killed driving cars every day than they do in any bombing."

"If we did decide to do Litton, we'd put a bomb in an area where no people were working, or we would set it to go off at night, so that no one would get hurt," I reassured Julie. "We would take every precaution we could imagine to make absolutely sure no one would get hurt. We'd learn from the RAF's mistakes and not rely on the cops clearing the building. Julie, if someone like you was involved, we could have you do something remote, away from the action. I wouldn't want you to do anything risky."

"I know," Julie said softly, looking up at me. I could see that she was absorbing everything I was saying, and I couldn't help feeling like her mother for a minute. I didn't like the feeling.

"Yeah." Brent jumped in. "If we were to do Litton, Ann and I would do the actual bombing and the only thing we would need someone else for would be to make a phone call warning security about the bomb. That person making the call would be perfectly safe because they wouldn't be anywhere near Litton when the bomb would be placed or go off."

"What do you mean — security?" asked Julie.

"I went to Ontario in April and took a look at the Litton plant, and there's this big glass-walled security tower at the entrance to the plant," explained Brent. "Besides the cruise guidance system, they manufacture a lot of sensitive stuff like security systems for Ontario Hydro nuclear power plants and cockpit display programs for the CF-18. There's a history of protesters blocking the gate and driveway that's been going on for two years now, so they have these security guards that just sit in that glass room and make sure the plant is secure. If we did a bombing, someone would have to phone security and warn them that a bomb is about to go off so they could block off the road in front of the plant. That way we'd be extra sure no one would get hurt."

"Wow," said Julie, obviously impressed. "I'd love to help. I could do the call. What do you think Ger?"

"You should think about it, Julie," cautioned Gerry, looking deeply into her eyes. "If anything went wrong, that would be a heavy, heavy action and you'd be in prison for a long time. Or dead."

"Well, what about you?" she said, suddenly looking at him as though he should be offering his services as well.

"I want to build the cabin this summer, you know that, Jules," he said, almost pleading with her. "Like I said, I'm not ready for this. All I want to do are low-level expropriations."

For a time Brent and I continued to reassure Julie that we would not let anything happen to her, at least as much as was humanly possible. "We'd do all the dangerous stuff," I said, "and we wouldn't even carry it out until we all felt it was absolutely safe." I sounded convincing. My conscience was telling me to shut up, because I knew we could never guarantee anyone's safety. Despite my reservations, my drive to continue on the road towards bombing Litton overrode my better judgement.

"I trust you guys," Julie said, adding to my burden of guilt. But at that moment she looked so innocent and trusting that I also truly believed I would do absolutely anything to make sure Julie did not go to prison or get hurt if anything went wrong.

At that point a silence fell over us as we fathomed the depths of the words that had just passed among us. In that silence I marvelled at the paradox of Julie's character. She was as independent, wilful, and rebellious a person as she was trusting and impressionable if she felt a person was worthy of her respect. In Brent and me she had found what she thought were trustworthy comrades. I was not altogether comfortable with her trust and dependence. The little voice inside me was uncomfortable with the responsibility of carrying out something like a bombing with someone whose convictions were not based on years of experience and analytical reasoning but instead on what I saw as blind faith and passion. Julie's character was not the only paradox. My spontaneous words and reactions were a mystery to myself as well.

We finished up our lunch and our thoughts in a lengthy interlude of silence, and then resumed our target-practice games. The thunder of the guns roared down the mountain. At times I worried that people driving on the highway below could hear us, but Brent and Doug reassured me that the sound travelling those few miles would be muffled by the trees and rocks. At worst, drivers would think some hunters were out target-practising. We soon forgot our conversation about bombing the Litton plant. The sounds of our laughter mingled with the gunblasts.

When the shadows of late afternoon began to stretch across the grass, we decided to call it a day. We walked around and picked up as many spent shells as we could find, then carefully wrapped up our weapons and set off in Bob down the logging trail to the highway below. Although we hadn't made any final decisions about Litton, we had laid the groundwork. It was clear that Gerry and Doug wanted no part of it. Brent and I decided to sleep on the idea and let it jell before talking to Julie about it again.

On our way home Julie and I were in the front seat with Brent, while Doug and Gerry sat behind under the truck's canopy. As we drove past a B.C. Department of Highways yard on the outskirts of Squamish, something caught Brent's attention. "Hey look," he yelled, pointing to a group of trucks parked in the Department's yard. "An explosives truck!"

"Cool!" said Julie.

"I bet if we followed that truck early in the morning, it would take us to a full dynamite magazine," Brent said.

"Yeah," gushed Julie. "We should do it."

The storage yard was a fenced-in area with a small office and one of those large teepee-shaped structures filled with sand used to spread on slippery roads in the winter. In the twilight we could see a dozen or so trucks parked in the lot, including the explosive truck's telltale black and yellow stripes, warning motorists of its dangerous cargo.

I had noticed signs on the way up the Squamish highway telling motorists about blasting going on in the area, a common occurrence in the summer. Road crews were constantly blasting loose rock off the mountainsides so it wouldn't slide down onto the road during heavy rains. "I'll go with you tomorrow morning if you want?" I said, thinking it would be good to spend more time getting to know Julie.

"Great!" She quickly took me up on my offer. "We can take my car. It's better on gas than this truck."

"We'll have to get up early because they probably leave the yard sometime between six and seven in the morning."

"We should dress *normal*," Julie said immediately. Her suggestion did not come as a surprise, because she had shown a real interest in disguises during our Amax actions.

When we stopped for a coffee in Squamish we told the others of our plans. Doug and Gerry weren't as enthusiastic as Julie. Doug's reaction didn't surprise me, since I assumed he didn't want to move too quickly with Julie and Gerry. I took Gerry's reaction as further proof that he was not interested in militant activity unless it would bring him closer to Julie. However, it seemed easier to proceed with our plan than to unravel it and risk upsetting her further.

The next morning I woke up at five and put on my best and cleanest clothes and waited for Julie. We still had dynamite left over from our first dynamite theft, but not enough to carry out another big action. Julie and Gerry had not been involved in the Cheekeye-Dunsmuir action, and I felt leery about doing this casing with Julie. Afterwards she would be compromised by any future action that involved the dynamite, whether she took part or not.

We got to the Department of Highways yard shortly after six, just in time to scout around for a place we could park and wait and watch unseen for the explosives truck to leave the yard. We went onto a side road, just a hundred yards away, and parked. I rarely had a chance to talk to Julie alone so I used the opportunity to draw out her ideas about militant actions. She told me she had taken up politics because she wanted answers to questions about poverty and suffering. At meetings on the conflict in El Salvador, she found herself attracted to Brent because he seemed to have some answers. She had noticed that the authorities were ignoring peaceful protests and legalistic appeals over issues like the cruise missile and violent pornography. So she had started studying the tactics of guerrillas in Europe by reading books Brent gave her. Finally, when she started trashing Amax-related buildings with us, she said, it gave her a sense of power and made her feel less helpless.

I had just begun to tell her how I became politically active when we noticed a truck turn out of the Department of Highways yard and, sure enough, right behind it came the explosives truck. We waited until it had gone a short way before we pulled out, and then we followed the two trucks at a respectable distance. Traffic was sparse on the mountain highway at six in the morning, but it wasn't unusual to have one car follow another vehicle along the winding roadway. Our surveillance was going so smoothly that I was a little surprised to see the turning lights flicker on the explosives truck soon into our mission.

"Memorize everything about this spot," I ordered Julie, as I also furiously took note of telltale landmarks around the turnoff spot.

"Don't worry," she said. "I set the odometer at zero before we left the yard area, so we'd know exactly how far up this highway we've gone." A little taken aback at this good idea, I wondered if perhaps I had been underestimating Julie's abilities.

We continued driving up the highway until we came to road signs indicating "Blasting Ahead." We turned around and drove back into Squamish and ordered breakfast to give the road crew time to do what we figured they were doing, which was load the truck up with explosives. We wanted to go back to the spot where the explosives truck had turned to verify the existence of a dynamite magazine, but we wanted to make sure we didn't pass the truck along the way.

After breakfast we headed north out of town. When the odometer read 11.7 miles, we found the logging road where the explosives truck had gone, and turned down it. A few seconds later we were confronted by a heavy chain hanging between two metal posts. Predictably it was locked, so we got out and began walking up the winding logging road. About a mile into the bush, we found what we had hoped for: two large, locked steel sheds that I immediately recognized as dynamite magazines. Mission accomplished. We jogged back to the car and drove back to Vancouver.

* * *

Doug, Brent, and I were still spending a lot of time studying and discussing possible future actions. Brent and I were keen on doing something around the cruise issue. We did not want Direct Action to be considered a provincial group but rather one with international politics, acting across Canada. Although we hadn't made any final decision on acting against Canada's role in the development of the cruise missile, we would need more dynamite no matter what we planned to do. We quickly decided to break into the dynamite magazines and take whatever was in them.

Despite our misgivings about Julie and Gerry, they did have a backyard where we could cut plywood and paint our magazine with green and brown camouflage colours. Once that was done we loaded it under Bob's canopy and drove up to the remote area not far from our target-practice area, where our other magazine sat, hidden in the woods on the side of the mountain. It was no small feat lugging up the plywood and assembling it on the side of that mountain. We had chosen an area that was steep, covered in dense, thorny underbrush and littered with sharp, jagged rocks. The natural features made it uninviting for hikers and hunters and very hazardous for us as well, even without baggage.

A few days after the magazine was in place we set off on a Sunday night, a time when most people would be in bed early for work on Monday morning. We were thankful Bob was a four-wheel-drive with a load-carrying capacity of about a thousand pounds, which would mean he could be loaded up with a lot of dynamite before the shocks would give out. We were just about to pass the Department of Highways yard that night when a combination of Brent's curiosity and boldness inspired an idea.

"Ann, pull over on that side street for a minute and turn off the headlights," he barked.

"Brent, this is not a good time to go exploring," I implored him. My cautious nature was a good check for Brent's natural boldness.

"I've got to check something out." His tone of voice left no room for questions. I pulled over and watched impatiently as he ran over to the high chain-link fence surrounding the yard.

"I can't believe he's doing this!" I sighed, exasperated, to Julie. "This is not part of the plan. There could be a security guard in the office, and if a cop drives by and sees us parking here he's bound to stop and check us out. It wouldn't look good with break-in tools, dark clothes, and all. It's obvious, we're up to no good." Julie did not share my misgivings. She idolized Brent and watched raptly as he scrambled over the top of the fence. The spotlights illuminating the yard silhouetted him clearly against the black night sky. Then, after almost rappelling down the other side, he disappeared into the darkness of the yard. I looked anxiously in my side-view mirrors, praying that I wouldn't see any headlights coming in the distance.

"Can you see anything?" I asked Julie.

"No, but I'm sure he'll be back in a minute," she whispered. I could tell by the gleam in her eyes that illegal activities excited her, much as they did Brent.

I was about to get out of the truck to call him, when we saw his silhouette again at the top of the fence. He climbed a few feet down, then pushed himself off and landed miraculously on his feet. He was lucky to be naturally athletic or he would have broken his ankle jumping down from that height. Arriving breathlessly in the truck, he pulled something out of his pocket. In the dim light I could just barely make out the shape of keys. He jangled them in front of my face to confirm that they were, indeed, keys.

"So what the hell are they?" I asked irritably.

"Keys from the explosives truck," he smiled as I started up the truck and began driving north again.

"Wow!" exclaimed Julie with unabashed awe.

"I just had a hunch," he said. I had to admit that he always had good instincts when it came to things like that. "I went over to the explosives truck, and sure enough it wasn't locked, so I got in and what should be sitting in the ignition but the keys."

"I'm surprised you didn't just turn it on and drive out," I said sarcastically.

"Oh, I would have, except the front gate is locked and I didn't want to fool around checking for the gate keys," he said, looking at Julie. He was definitely enjoying impressing his young protegé. I shook my head in disbelief but had to admit that this could be very useful.

"On the way back, I'll return them," he explained. "The beauty of this is that if there's a key for the magazine on here, then they'll never know how we got in unless the driver admits he was negligent in leaving the keys in the ignition. Or they'll think it's an inside job. Either way, I think it's cool." Julie agreed enthusiastically.

When we reached the logging road I checked for headlights in the rear-view mirror, then turned in and drove quickly up to the chain fence, which was not visible from the road. Brent hopped out and ran over to the gate. He motioned for Julie, which sent her scurrying out after him. A second later she shone a flashlight on the lock so he could try out the keys. Once again, Brent's instincts proved true. He thrust a victorious fist, with the open lock clenched tightly, into the air, then motioned for me to drive through. After locking the chain gate we drove slowly up the logging road with the headlights off. It was a cloudless night, so the moonlight was just enough to guide us up the trail. In a few more minutes the black silhouettes of the magazines rose eerily before us. We began unloading the tool boxes onto the dewy grass. The air was still except for the sound of crickets and bullfrogs in some woody marsh. There was not a sound coming from the highway below. We had chosen the right night for this. I had barely put the tool box down when I heard Brent give a little coyote-like yip of excitement, which I took to mean that he had found a key to the dynamite magazine. Yes, he was a lucky man.

He waited until Julie and I were by his side to open the door. It was a momentous occasion. Would it be empty or would it be full of the precious dynamite cargo we had come for? He pulled on the thick metal lip that covered the lock and the heavy steel door swung noisily open on its metal hinges. The groaning noise of the hinges sounded spooky in the night. The wilderness around us did not scare me, but opening up a metal door to reveal the unknown sent a chill up my spine. Maybe a dead corpse would fall out? The danger and darkness fuelled my vivid imagination.

As the door slowly opened, Brent shone his flashlight into the thick darkness of the steel room to reveal not cobwebs, dead rats, or corpses, but row upon row of boxes stacked neatly on metal shelves. The small round light roved around inside, exposing a metal room meticulously clean. He shone the light on one of the boxes to read the black, block lettering: TOVAL, a name familiar to us from Doug's study of explosives. This was the kind of dynamite used in rock removal, because it was powerful yet not volatile. It could not be ignited by fire or shaking.

We soon started carefully carting the fifty-five-pound boxes of dynamite from the magazine into the back of the truck. Brent also took some time to find a box of primer cord and three boxes of blasting caps, prerequisites for an explosion. After awhile the truck's frame was dropping lower and lower, until the wheel-wells were just barely clearing the tires.

It was a lot of dynamite to move. I had developed a rigorous exercise regime in the past few months that included jogging, weightlifting, and push-ups, but even that had not prepared me for the strain of carrying box after box of heavy material. In a short while my arms ached. I figured Julie must be exhausted, but being a real trooper she didn't complain or rest unless I did. Although she was about nine years younger than me, I knew she must be hurting, so I had to admire her grit.

"That's all we can carry in the truck this load," Brent finally said, as Julie and I gratefully sank to the ground. For a few minutes we lay on our backs in the wet grass, looking up at the black sky peppered with stars. Off in the distance we could hear the distinctive yipping of coyotes, warning each other of their territorial boundaries.

With what we figured was close to a thousand pounds of dynamite in the truck by the way it had dropped on its shocks, we drove very slowly down the trail to the gate. Once again, Brent locked the gate up after we had driven through so the scene was left exactly as it had been before, without a trace of intruders other than our footprints. Our homemade magazines were only about ten miles north up the Squamish highway. In the early hours of Sunday morning, we didn't pass one vehicle.

On the drive up the other logging road leading to our magazines, we held our breath as we lurched up and down the potholes, praying that the tires could withstand the weight and beating they were getting. Now the real work began. I soon realized I had never done anything before as exhausting as carrying hundreds of pounds of dynamite in awkward boxes up the side of that mountain. I remember picking up boxes and beginning the trek up in the dark, tripping over huge shards of rock that tore open holes in my blue jeans, leaving me even more vulnerable to the thorny bushes along the way. In the moonlight I could see Julie's white face covered in sweat and cuts from falling in the thickets and against the rocks.

As the night wore on, I became so exhausted that I stopped

caring about dropping the dynamite boxes on sharp rocks. I didn't care about anything. I couldn't see where I was stepping, with the sweat dripping in my eyes and stinging the cuts on my face. I couldn't feel my own limbs. I felt like some soldier in the jungles of Vietnam carrying out a search and destroy mission in the night. Towards the end I actually wished that if I did drop a box it would explode and the misery would quickly be over. I was sure that the force and speed of the explosion would be so fast that I wouldn't have time to know I was going to die. It would be instant. It would only seem like a horrid death to the living. In fact, death is what I thought about during that mission — how the fact of being dead is painless, but the thought of death is what is frightening and painful.

Unbelievably, we decided to go back for more. I don't know what drove us on. Well, Brent did. I knew that Julie would not initiate a call to stop for fear of losing his respect. I think I just went along with my practical side, which said that it was better to suffer a lot now and get it over with than to have to do it again. We would get so much dynamite that we could do a lot of actions and wouldn't ever have to repeat this torture.

By the time we were carrying the last boxes from the last load, delirium had set in. The thought of one of the boxes exploding if we dropped it made us laugh out loud. There would be no sign of the magazines or us, just a huge crater in the ground. They would have to identify us through the buttons on our shirts, which would probably land on the highway far below. As I carried one of the last boxes through the underbrush, dropping it periodically on whatever was underfoot, I noticed a sticky yellow goo all over my hands: the contents of a dynamite stick that I had punctured, no doubt. I couldn't have cared less.

When we finally headed home, shades of grey with pink washes appeared on the eastern horizon in the night sky. It took all my concentration to stay awake. I had forgotten about Brent's plan to return the keys, but he hadn't. As we drove up to the Department of Highways yard, he shattered my reverie by shouting "Stop!" Somehow he managed to get up and over the fence again and return the keys. All the time I was sure he would be seen. It was close to 5:00 a.m. and I thought the day's workers would arrive any second. Just as Brent slid into our truck and slammed the door shut, I saw a car on the horizon. I stepped on the accelerator and pulled out before it was close enough to identify our truck or licence plate. As we sped off towards Squamish, through the rear-view mirror I saw the car turn into the Department of Highway's yard. "Whew" was all I could say.

Driving into Vancouver, I managed a smile. Julie and Brent's clothes were torn to shreds. Branches and leaves were caught in their clothes, and scratches and bruises appeared wherever their skin was exposed. But the worst was the sticky goo that ran in blobs down their pants, arms, and even faces. It was probably filled with nitroglycerine. Better not smoke. What a trip!

* * *

That morning when I finally got back to my apartment it took hours before I was able to relax enough to go to sleep, but once I did I couldn't wake up. The next day the sounds of kids on the sidewalk below coming home for lunch told me it was past noon. I sat up in bed and looked at the yellow goo and red bloodstains all over my sheets and quickly recalled our excursion. Now that I felt well rested, I realized just how foolish we had been to try to carry so much dynamite up that treacherous mountainside in the dark. Only our good luck had saved us from a quick and untimely death.

I was in the shower when I heard Brent's knock on my door. I wrapped a towel around my body and unlocked the door. He came in looking chipper and waving a couple of morning papers in the air. "Well, it's already in the news." He walked over and put his arms around me, but I wanted to read the paper first and pushed him away.

"You're more interested in the paper than me?" he said, feigning hurt.

"Well, I'm curious and you can wait." I smiled and sat down at the table to read a short article about a record dynamite theft near Squamish. Basically it said the police were mystified by the theft of two thousand pounds of dynamite from a highway department powder magazine on July 28. There were no signs of forced entry to the steel shed housing the explosives, and another shed was untouched. The story concluded by saying the police believed the lock was either picked, opened by a key, or was left unlocked by a highway worker.

"I hope the driver of the explosives truck doesn't get fired over this," I said.

"Naw," shrugged Brent, "they won't do that. Why would he steal it and set it up so he would be the prime and only suspect?"

"I can't believe we took that much and there was more left!"

Brent was standing behind me, rubbing my shoulders with a deep, sensuous motion. It felt so good to have my sore, tight shoulder muscles massaged, but I knew he had other things in mind than a back rub. I relaxed and gave in to the erotic sensations. Soon we lay intertwined on my bed, feeding each other's hungry souls with passionate kisses and caresses that lasted long past the school lunch hour. It was through our bodies that we communicated our feelings for one another. We rarely talked about our feelings or engaged in any kind of relaxing activity. Our lives were consumed by politics. But at times like this we touched each other and communicated the deep feelings we held for one another. We relieved the stress that had built up during the days and nights of planning and acting. It was a strange life.

"Do you think we should get together with Julie today?" I said, sitting on the edge of the bed.

"Why?" Brent asked, still laying naked on the bed beside me.

"Just to see how she is."

"Sure."

"What do you really think about doing Litton?"

"I think we should do it, but count Doug out."

"Just the two of us?"

"No, we need the third person to make a phone call — Julie."

"I don't think we can make a precise plan from here. We'll have to go to Toronto and make the plan there."

"Yeah."

"Why don't you make some sandwiches while I shower?" I stood over him with my hands on my hips. He slowly pulled himself up off the bed while I gathered up some clean clothes and disappeared into the shower. By the time I had finished, Brent, still undressed, had placed a plate of sandwiches on the Arborite table in the middle of the room.

"Okay." I said, sitting down to eat. "Let's at least see if Doug supports us going and if Julie's serious about going along. Then we can put the dynamite in the truck and drive across the country. It would be fun." I looked over at Brent to see his reaction. He was now struggling to put his pants on.

"We'd need a lot of dynamite to cause serious damage to the plant." He had finally managed to get his clothes on and sat down across from me. "I don't want to do a symbolic action. It's got to cause some real financial damage and maybe stall the production of the guidance system. We'll have to find out which building is used to manufacture the guidance system. There's a bunch of buildings at the plant."

"If we did a bombing, it would make the Americans think twice about giving their Canadian plant the contract to build the guidance system," I said between mouthfuls of bread.

"Yeah," Brent added, "and it would show people in the anti-nuclear movement that militant actions can affect political decisions. The Americans don't want to waste money, and they won't like the publicity that blowing up their plant will draw."

"Well, should we just drop over to Julie's or what?"

"Let's go," said Brent, wolfing down the last bite of his sandwich.

That afternoon we drove over to Julie and Gerry's apartment and found them playing their guitars together in a scene of domestic punk bliss. Julie was still keen on going to Ontario, as long as her only involvement in the action was a telephone warning call. While we talked to her, Gerry sat quietly strumming on his guitar with a sullen look on his face. We tried to include him in the conversation, but he simply nodded his head one way or the other and said whatever decision Julie made, he would be supportive. He reiterated that he would be going up to the Chilcotins to start work on his cabin. I saw on his face his disappointment that Julie had chosen to go with us rather than travel with him to the mountains. As for Julie, she seemed confident about her decision and showed no signs of doubt.

We made plans to leave in mid-September, before the snow fell and the driving became dangerous. The only obstacle left to finalizing our plan was Doug. Surprisingly, he was supportive. Once again he expressed his misgivings about us taking Julie along, but since he didn't want to go and we would need someone to make the phone call, Julie was the only other possibility. His support rested on his belief that Direct Action should do something against the manufacture and testing of the cruise missile and that an action in Ontario would show we were not a regional group.

There were a lot of preparations to be carried out before we could leave. We spent August acquiring camping equipment for the trip across Canada, studying the anti-nuclear issue and the cruise missile in particular, and most importantly perfecting a timing device that would be one hundred per cent reliable. Finally, on a beautiful sunny day in the middle of September, we stood outside Brent's apartment to say our goodbyes. Gerry lifted the truck canopy window a few inches, peeked inside, and laughed.

"I can't believe there's 550 pounds of dynamite in there," he chuckled softly. "Whatever you do, don't get in an accident. If you did, no one would know what happened. All that would be left would be this huge crater in the highway and a few minuscule body parts spread for miles around."

"At least there wouldn't be any evidence left behind." Doug smiled as he said this. We had carefully stored the blasting caps in the back of the truck in a separate box, lined with insulation. The timing device was wrapped up so it wouldn't get damaged by any jostling around.

Julie and Gerry stepped a few feet away from us and kissed each other fondly. Julie's old dog, Rex, nudged them as though to say, "Don't forget me."

"Oh Rex," Julie sighed, kneeling down beside him. "How could I forget you?" Tears welled up in her eyes. "Gerry, you'll take good care of him?" Gerry nodded and ruffled the hair on the old dog's head. "You guys take good care of Jules for me, okay?" He looked up at us.

We had reassured them both, over and over, that we wouldn't do anything until we were sure the action would go safely — especially Julie's end of it. There was nothing left to say, so we piled into the truck and drove slowly down the road, heading east. I looked in my side-view mirror and watched Doug, Gerry, and Rex standing side by side on the sidewalk with sad expressions on their faces. Then we turned the corner.

✳ 23 ✳

Despaireux drove the green RCMP Jeep so quickly up the logging trail that Fraser began to worry they might lurch off into the dense underbrush growing along the sides of the road. "Slow down!" he yelled. "What's the panic?"

"I don't want those Squamish cops walking around wrecking evidence!" Despaireux yelled back.

Fraser reassured him that he had instructed them, first off, to seal off the area to protect evidence from being contaminated. Although there was no proof that the dynamite theft of the Department of Highways magazine was related to the Cheekeye-Dunsmuir bombing, the police suspected a link.

"I hope they can follow instructions then," Despaireux said irritably. "It's the only lead we've had in three and a half months, even with the reward."

"Yeah, it's remarkable no one has come up with any evidence," Fraser said. "Even if anarchists aren't interested in money, you would think someone involved would have said something to a family member or friend outside the anarchist community."

Just then they came to the police cars, cops, and yellow plastic ribbon marking off the area. As they pulled over into the brush and jumped out of the Jeep, a young officer with an air of authority strode over to them. He introduced himself as Sergeant Craig Fallows.

"So what happened here?" said Despaireux, dismissing formalities.

"We got a call this morning at the Squamish detachment around nine from a couple of men out hunting around here," he explained. As he spoke he glanced down every now and then at a notebook he had open in his hand. "They were walking along that ridge up there when they came across a couple of sheds painted with camouflage paint. They thought it looked suspicious and phoned us. Luckily they didn't try to break in. The sheds were locked. No windows, just small ventilation holes covered in a double mesh screen." When Fallows paused, Despaireux said, "Yes, go on." Fraser was writing down everything the sergeant said in his own notebook.

"So we sent a Jeep down here," Fallows continued. "They took photos and notes regarding the state of the sheds and their locks, then proceeded to cut through one lock."

Despaireux shook his head. "Why would they do that?"

"Sir, they had no way of knowing the relevance of these sheds. They thought they might be some hunter's storage sheds or huts to rest in," he said apologetically.

"Go on." Despaireux sighed.

"As soon as they saw inside, they realized the significance of the contents and immediately began to take precautions not to disturb any evidence," he continued eagerly. "The shed's full of dynamite, and we are assuming the other shed is as well. Presumably it's the dynamite stolen from the Department of Highways magazine approximately nineteen kilometres south of here."

"So nothing has been touched since the officers broke the lock on the one shed?" clarified Despaireux.

"That is correct, sir."

Despaireux went back to the Jeep and took a large tool box out of the back and slipped a pair of plastic boots over his footwear. All the police officers in the area were wearing them. He headed back to Fraser, slipping on a pair of latex gloves as he walked. "Okay Fraser, I want you to watch me, take notes, and make sure I don't make any mistakes."

The two men began the ascent up the mountainside in the direction of the sheds. The structures were well hidden and still not visible. The only thing indicating their whereabouts was a long strand of yellow plastic police tape pointing the way.

"I don't know how they managed to carry two thousand pounds of dynamite up this slope," huffed Fraser, struggling to keep his footing on the jagged rocks protruding out of the dense underbrush.

"Look!" shouted Despaireux. "Footprints! Those forensic guys are right behind us?"

"Yeah. They should be here any minute," Fraser said, stopping to place a small stake in the ground beside the footprints. "There's footprints all over the place. And they look fresh! I bet these perps were up here in the last day or so."

Despaireux had stopped again to mark another set of prints. "There's a small set that are probably a woman's. Or a really small guy. Then there's a set — obviously a big guy who is not light."

They continued the climb until they reached the sheds. They went up to the shed that had been opened and looked inside. Fraser began counting the boxes of dynamite, stacked neatly in rows. The cases were clearly stamped: 75 per cent Toval, manufactured by Du Pont of Canada, and the code D.2, which Fraser knew meant they had been manufactured in April 1982. The weight — fifty-five pounds — was also stamped on each box. "There's twenty-eight of them," Fraser said. "These are from the dynamite theft on July 28th, alright."

"These homemade magazines are well-constructed," Despaireux added, looking carefully at the wood joinery. "Everything's been screwed and glued together from the inside so no one could unscrew it from the outside, and it's put together to withstand a lot of weather. Even the camouflage paint job is effective. They aren't incompetent."

They walked over to the other magazine, taking care not to step on the perps' footprints. After examining the outside of the magazine, they looked at the lock and decided it would be wise to wait for the forensic police.

"I'd say these people were up here in the last two days," said Fraser, kneeling down to examine a set of footprints. "We had a heavy rainstorm two days ago, so my guess is they were here either yesterday or the day before."

Sergeant Fallow had followed them up and was standing behind Fraser. "We got a call from your forensic guys and they're on their way up the trail now. We've isolated a stretch of track to analyse the tire tracks. We've got the location where they stopped, got out, and probably loaded the dynamite in their truck. By the tire treads it looks like they must have been driving a three-quarter-ton four-wheel-drive. There's a noticeable difference in the depth that the tires sunk into the mud, before and after loading up the dynamite, so they must have left with a heavy load."

They turned in unison to watch a green RCMP Jeep lurch to a stop down below. Fraser yelled down to them and waved his arms in the air. The three officers laughed as they watched the two forensic detectives slipping and sliding as they navigated the treacherous slope on foot. By the time the officers joined them, their pants were blotched with mud.

"I'd like you guys to examine this lock before we open it, or suggest where we should cut it," Despaireux said. One of the forensic detectives began taking pictures while the other carefully cut off the lock. Within minutes, the door to the magazine was open, revealing more rows of dynamite.

"Damn!" exclaimed Despaireux. "No more Toval D.2, eh? I guess that means this stuff is from a different haul."

"Yeah." Fraser scratched his head in thought. "I'll have to get a list of all the dynamite thefts to find out where this stuff came from. It's definitely not from the Department of Highways theft. But now my biggest concern is that these guys left here either yesterday or the day before with 550 pounds of dynamite." His biggest fear was that sometime soon they would find out where that dynamite was — and he hoped it wouldn't involve casualties. "I pray to God, whoever stole this dynamite are not the same people who did the Cheekeye-Dunsmuir bombing. If they are, they're going to be acting real soon, and this time it's going to be one hell of an explosion."

"Too bad we don't know exactly what kind of dynamite they used in that Hydro bombing," Despaireux said. "Maybe this stuff is what's left from that?"

"I'll get some explosives experts on it right away," Fraser said. "They have been able to analyse the residue from the bombing, so they should be able to tell us how likely it is that this dynamite is from the same batch used there."

"While you're at it, you might want to replace the real dynamite in those boxes with sand, so if the culprits come back and somehow get it, they won't be able to blow anything else up." Despaireux gave Fraser a somewhat condescending look.

Fraser looked at Despaireux and felt a wave of intense concern surge through his body. The skill involved in the Department of Highways dynamite theft and the construction of these magazines were all part of a pattern that matched the work of the Hydro bombing. He was convinced that the jobs were all the work of the same people: Direct Action. With 550 pounds of dynamite missing, they'd better turn up the heat on finding these people before a more life-threatening bombing occurred.

For the rest of the afternoon Despaireux and Fraser supervised the gathering of evidence and co-ordinated the setting up of a motion detector to relay a signal to the Squamish detachment if anyone came near the homemade magazines. They also ordered replacement locks identical to the ones found on the magazines, to be purchased and delivered to the site. As the last rays of the sun disappeared over the purple Tantalus Range in the west, they sat together in the Jeep, going over a checklist of necessary work.

"Are all the footprints and tire tracks from the policemen and their vehicles removed?" Despaireux asked, referring to his list.

"Yes," answered Fraser.

"Is the motion detector set up and tested?"

"Yes, and they're going to do another test tomorrow."

"What's the response time, if the device is tripped?"

"Twenty minutes."

"Is there a guy permanently stationed in Squamish to monitor the device?"

"No, but there's a red light in the main reception area, manned twenty-four hours a day, which will flash if the motion detector is tripped. They're also going to go up every week and make sure it hasn't been disturbed."

"You've contacted the explosives experts to replace the dynamite with sand and analyse it to see if it's the same dynamite used in the Cheekeye bombing?"

"Yes."

"Have all the residents in the immediate area been warned to stay out of this area and to notify the Squamish detachment if they see anybody or anything suspicious?"

"Yes."

"Information about the missing dynamite put on the computer so every station across Canada and the Western states knows about it?"

"Yes."

"Arrangements for a helicopter to do a flyby on a daily basis until this dynamite and these bombers are caught?"

"Yes."

"Can you think of anything we've forgotten, Fraser?"

"No, sir."

"Okay then, let's get the hell out of here. They've got a copter waiting for us in Squamish, and I want to get home."

Fraser turned on the Jeep and looked back at the lone police car still sitting there. It would leave after them. As he drove down the bumpy logging trail, he ran through his mind all the things he had to do tomorrow. Now, he knew, he was in a race against the clock — and his level of anxiety would be increasing all the while.

✳ **24** ✳

In August Brent and I finally made the decision to tell Doug, Angie, and Nick about the change in our relationship. It was long overdue. I didn't ask Brent whether he'd continued to have a sexual relationship with Angie, because I didn't want to know. The guilt I felt over our own silence was weighing on me, and I wanted it lifted as soon as possible. I wasn't there when he told Angie, but according to his account her reaction was much like Nick's: accepting. I think Nick and Angie had assumed since we left for Calgary that a sexual relationship between Brent and me was inevitable. During that time they had dealt with the dilemma in their own private ways.

Doug was more disappointed, probably because he had never made the assumption that we would become a couple and because our union had a more direct effect on him. It would mean that if we were ever to live a completely underground lifestyle, he would be the only single person. Somehow it would have been different if all three of us were single. There would have been more pressure for us to satisfy each other's needs for companionship. But, as a couple, Brent and I would in theory be more likely to spend time alone together, be more likely to act as one when making decisions, and be happier because we would be able to fulfil each other's emotional needs. I'm sure our union tipped the scales in the direction of Doug staying in British Columbia when the time came to make decisions about leaving. Although we had been living in relative isolation since the Cheekeye-Dunsmuir bombing, life in Vancouver was still relatively fulfilling for Doug — and more so than if he left the province. In Vancouver his emotional needs were taken care of through his relationships with Rachel, Saphie, and his mother, whom he still saw from time to time.

Brent, Julie, and I were giddy with excitement about heading off towards Toronto in a van full of dynamite, a few clothes, and enough money to carry us through. Our plan at that point consisted of the vague idea of bombing the Litton plant, but since we couldn't work out any details until we got there, the enjoyment of travelling across the country overshadowed any fears we may have harboured over the seriousness of what we were about to do. This would be my first opportunity to have an open relationship with Brent — almost like a honeymoon — and for Julie it would be her first trip outside British Columbia, with the exception of a few short excursions to Seattle. We were very naive.

It took the better part of a day to get out of the Fraser Valley and into the Rocky Mountains. We spent most of the time laughing, talking, and listening to tapes we had made especially for the trip. Julie's selections reflected her involvement in the local punk scene: the Dead Kennedys from San Francisco, and DOA from Vancouver. Brent and I had taped a lot of tunes from the rock bands of the sixties and seventies. I liked the melancholy atmosphere of Bruce Springsteen's newest album, "Nebraska," with its ballads of the hope and despair inherent in ordinary people's pursuit of the American Dream. I also gravitated towards the Door's first album — its final song, "The End," became an anthem for our trip. In the beginning we amused ourselves by deriving meaning from the lyrics, until by the end of our journey, Jim Morrison's obscure phrases told the story of our trip to Toronto and its cataclysmic goal.

At the end of our first day we pulled into Mount Revelstoke National Park, on the western flank of the Rockies. We had brought along a small tent and other camping supplies to avoid having to rent motel rooms every night. As long as Brent and I had known each other we had hidden our feelings for one another to varying degrees, and so this sudden freedom to express ourselves would take some time to get used to. Certainly this trip would have been more honeymoon-like if Brent's attitude towards Julie's presence had not put such a damper on our expression of affection. The night before we left Vancouver, Brent had told me that we should avoid open displays of affection because he didn't want Julie to feel lonely. He believed that her age and her separation from Gerry, with her going away to do something very dangerous, could lead her to feel particularly vulnerable and maybe depressed, and a display of affection could accentuate these feelings. He suggested that we try to relate as a group at all times, rather than as a couple and an individual. I instinctively recoiled at his suggestions, because I felt that he was more concerned about Julie's feelings than mine. He reminded me that I was older and therefore should be stronger and have confidence in his love for me. Just one more sacrifice, Ann, I told myself. Surely when this trip was over, I would get a chance to be open in my feelings towards Brent. Anyway, what was more important: my relationship or carrying out this action? If I had to sacrifice my open expression of love for Brent to make Julie feel more comfortable, then surely I could make that sacrifice for the sake of our mission. And so I buckled down like a good little soldier.

But what Brent had not told me was just how far he intended to take his efforts to make Julie feel like part of the group. After we put up the tent that first night, he turned around casually and asked, "Who wants to sleep in the tent and who wants to sleep in the truck?" I had assumed that our effort to make Julie feel part of the group would be limited to daylight hours. Shocked and angry, I quickly said I would sleep in the truck — in a tone of voice that made it perfectly clear that I was acting under duress. I don't know what Julie thought, but she acted as though nothing was wrong. I climbed into the cab of the truck, furious, and hoped this was not an omen of what was to come.

After a sleepless night, scrunched up in the cab of the truck, I sat up and lit a cigarette. I didn't usually smoke first thing in the morning, but I was still upset. Sitting there, looking over at the tent, I wondered just how far Brent had taken his efforts to accommodate Julie. I had to stop myself from walking over and kicking the tent and its contents over. As I sat smoking, Brent came crawling out of the tent. One glance over at me and I knew he could tell what was on my mind. He sheepishly slunk over to the truck and defended his actions. He hadn't touched Julie, he wasn't interested in her, and he was merely trying to make her feel comfortable. As he spoke he changed tactics, assuming the offensive, and ended by admonishing me for being immature and lacking confidence in our relationship. I don't remember what I said in response, but I know it was something hostile. It was not a good beginning to day two of our trip.

Julie and Brent took down the tent while I watched them with armour-piercing eyes. When everything was packed away, we drove off in silence. I didn't know Julie well enough to be able to read her body language, but it still seemed as though she didn't notice anything was wrong and was just keeping quiet because it was so early. She must have noticed the wall of silence between Brent and me as the morning progressed, because it was so thick no amount of tape-deck music could penetrate it. I drove and chain-smoked with a dark scowl on my face. Brent stared at the road with a blank expression. By noon we had begun to tire of our anger and a few tidbits of small talk poked holes in the wall. I made a pact with myself that I was not going to let my insecurities or anger rule me. After all, I had an important task to carry out on this trip. But try as I might, I found this emotional triage impossible to sort out. I couldn't put my anger at Brent on the back burner.

Our second day of travelling took us through the mountains and across the prairies. The prairie landscape may arouse a wealth of feelings in anyone raised there, but for me, an Ontario girl, the prairies evoked loneliness and emptiness. My insignificance as an individual seemed particularly poignant when contrasted to the vastness of the landscape. As I drove along, watching tumbleweeds blowing across the highway, I often found myself questioning what I was doing. What was the point? Would a bombing do any good? Would attending a demonstration? Of course not. As an individual alone, I could only do a little, but over time there was a chance that the actions of many individuals could accomplish a lot. If not, I had no choice but to do what I thought was right — even if I was destined never to bring about social change in any significant way.

After setting up camp on the prairies that second evening, we sat up late into the night staring into our campfire and talking about deep philosophical questions — the meaning of life and the significance of individual acts. By the time I was ready to go to sleep, Julie had solved the problem of who was to sleep where. She went into the truck and curled up to sleep. Maybe she was more aware of the friction between Brent and me than I thought.

The next morning we got up much more light-spirited than the day before. We took turns reading passages to each other from a book on the Trilateral Commission, which inspired more serious political discussions that we interspersed with scenarios of what would happen if someone smashed into the back of our truck. Our dark sense of humour was a way of relieving the stress of driving a truck full of explosives across the country and a way of dealing with anxieties about what we were going to do when we got to Toronto.

By the end of the third day we had reached northern Ontario and decided to rent a motel room. After three days of sitting in a hot, dirty pickup truck, a nice, hot shower was an attractive proposition. I thought the issue of who sleeps with whom was behind us and so, with a sense of relief, I went into the motel room looking forward to enjoying the benefits of civilization. Even the sight of one double bed and a single didn't set off alarm bells. Graciously I suggested that Julie take the first shower. While she was showering, I went over to Brent and wrapped my arms around his neck and gave him a quick kiss. Everything was going great! He went out to make sure the truck was locked up, while I took my turn in the shower.

It wasn't until later, when Brent stepped out of the shower and came into the room with his towel still wrapped around him, that I realized my sense of relief was premature. He walked over to the nightstand where he had left his wallet, pulled a penny out of the change compartment, and said, "I'll flip a coin to see who sleeps in the double bed." It landed on "tails," which Julie had picked. "The single bed," she said without a hint of emotion. I couldn't tell whether she was aware of the conflict that this ambiguity of who sleeps with whom was creating for me. She didn't know us that well, but surely she must have known that it would bother me to have to "share" Brent with her. There was the distinct possibility that, in her mind, we were on such a high pedestal we were above succumbing to jealousy and insecurity. But I was not Superwoman.

As I crawled into bed beside Brent, I vowed that I wouldn't let my insecurities come between Julie and me, because if anyone was

at fault it was Brent. I couldn't forgive him for belittling our relationship and putting me in this situation, especially when we
needed all our emotional strength and focus for the Litton action. I
would have it out with him the next time we were alone. Unfortunately, the three of us were together constantly, so there was little
opportunity for us to iron out problems in our relationship.

The last day of our trip took us over the Great Lakes. Although
it was a long, gruelling drive, I always enjoyed driving through
northern Ontario with its sweeping rocky Canadian Shield, covered in coniferous forests and dotted with dark blue lakes — and
the wild, vast reach of Lake Superior below. I had found a moment
to make it clear to Brent that I wasn't going to have our sleeping
arrangements determined by a flip of the coin, and now I was
determined to put the issue behind me. Instead I focused on the
beauty of the land and put my energy into making our little group
work. Julie seemed to be thoroughly enjoying this part of our journey. I was convinced she was oblivious to the problems between
Brent and me. Her uninhibited and spontaneous nature would
make it impossible for her to hide any bad feelings she might har-
bour towards us.

We reached the outskirts of Toronto late at night, dead tired
from the long drive. The first cheap motel we saw drew us in, and
this time there was no discussion of sleeping arrangements. In the
morning, when the noise from the rush-hour traffic outside our
room made it impossible for me to sleep anymore, I got up and
bought a Toronto newspaper. I went through the ads and circled
apartments within our price range. Over breakfast in a donut shop,
we pored over my selections and decided to look at a furnished
one-bedroom in the east end of the city. We made a phone call and
arranged to meet the landlord. Besides an apartment we would
also have to rent a garage, because we figured that the bomb
would have to be rigged inside a van. The details of how, when,
and where had yet to be determined.

Driving across the city we passed through one ethnic area after
another. This was the aspect of Toronto I liked the most — the distinct ethnic communities that gave the city its life, colour, and
flavour. In the Caribbean community in the west end, there were
small dance bars and Jamaican meat patties everywhere. As we
drove through the heart of the city the narrow streets lined with
tiny stores teeming with smoked ducks, oriental vegetables, and
bald chickens hanging by their necks marked Chinatown. When we

reached the east-end neighbourhood where the apartment was located, the restaurants advertising moussaka and souvlaki told us that this was a Greek community.

The apartment, a few blocks off Danforth Avenue, was a basement flat in a house. The two main floors of the house were also taken up by rental apartments, so we wouldn't have to deal with an over-friendly landlord. Anonymity was important. The apartment had a separate entrance from the backyard and was furnished. Surprised by our good luck in finding a place so fast, we immediately paid the first and last months' rent and then, after the landlord had left, surveyed our home, only to discover that the kitchen was cockroach-infested. Other than that, it was perfect. The furnishings consisted of a sofa, chair, and TV in the living room; a table, chairs, and another sofa in the kitchen, and a double bed and bureau in the bedroom. After Julie had walked around and tried all the chairs, beds, and sofas, she announced that she would sleep on the long sofa in the kitchen. That statement put my mind to rest.

"So where should we put the dynamite?" Julie asked, looking around at the sparsely furnished living room. There was no closet big enough for it, and we decided to just plop it down on one side of the room, next to the TV. It wasn't as if we were going to have any visitors. "As long as we put the blasting caps and detonating cord somewhere else," Brent said, "I'm sure it will be just fine."

We moved in our suitcases, leaving our most important possession, the 550 pounds of dynamite, to be moved in after dark. We spent the next few days settling in, but not like most people. Julie had become something of a shoplifter, and bad habits are hard to shake. Although we had talked about giving up shoplifting, she seemed to like the excitement or challenge of it. Money was not a problem. We had reassured her before we left that we would foot the bill for this trip since it was our idea. But perhaps she felt guilty for not contributing financially. Quite often she had come home with little things like candles, cups, and expensive food items that weren't important but did lend atmosphere to our dark little apartment.

A couple of days after we had arrived, I was walking through Chinatown picking up food for supper when I noticed that the back alleys were lined with little wooden garages. I decided to take a stroll down some of those back alleys. They weren't visible from the main streets and would be a perfect location for a garage to rig up our bomb. Sure enough, one of the garages had a small "For Rent" sign attached to its door. I jotted down the phone number and hurried home.

"Nice," was all Brent said when the old Chinese man showed us the inside of the garage. It was immaculate. "Now all we need is the van," he said on the way home.

That night we climbed into the truck to case the Litton plant. It consisted of seven buildings enclosed behind a high wire-mesh fence, a stone's throw from Highway 427, a big freeway that went north-south near the Toronto International Airport. A glass-windowed room in a tower at the entrance to the plant gave away the high-security nature of the products manufactured inside. We parked on the shoulder of City View Drive, the street servicing all the manufacturing plants bordering the freeway. Other cars, probably belonging to factory workers, were parallel-parked in front and behind us. We had arrived about ten o'clock on a Friday night to see if there was a night shift. Everything about this action would have to be analysed, and nothing left to chance. A major concern was to ensure that no one would be hurt when the bomb went off, and we wanted to find out if there was a night when no one worked at the plant.

As we sat in the dark truck, I kept my eyes on the motionless landscape of the plant. Other than two employees moving about inside the illuminated security tower, there were no signs of life. "Looks like they're joking around and drinking coffee," said Brent, focusing a pair of binoculars on the security room. "What else is there for them to do on a Friday night?"

"Are there many cars in the workers' parking area?" I asked.

Brent shifted his view over to the parking lot. "Yeah. There's quite a few. We'll see when a shift changes, and if they all go."

I looked over at the floodlit lawn and hedges bordering the front of one of the buildings. I had already figured that we would have to drive the van up over the roadway curb and onto the lawn and park in front of that building. There were not a lot of options. Most of the buildings were behind the high wire-mesh fence surrounding the site, but that one building was outside. Anyway, we had no means, without jeopardizing our security, of verifying which building manufactured the cruise missile guidance system, so we were left with hope and opportunity as the only factors determining where we would place our van bomb.

"This has got to be the ugliest place in the world," Julie said, looking ghostly every time the lights from a passing car reflected off her pale complexion. "There's nothing but factories, highways, and concrete in this whole place." Sometimes we had trouble hearing each other talk over the roar of the traffic rushing by one hundred metres away on the freeway. But even the din from the freeway was drowned out every five minutes by a jet taking off from the airport, climbing off over the lights of the huge high-rise airport hotels.

"If we use all 550 pounds of dynamite in this bombing, it might blow out the windows in all those hotels," I said. "We better make sure they're all warned to stay clear of their windows before the bomb goes off."

"Yeah," agreed Julie. She seemed increasingly nervous with each passing day. Her youth was beginning to show. In Vancouver, when she had been enthusiastic and eager, she had seemed older than her twenty years, but here she seemed much younger. Even her voice sounded weaker and her physique more petite.

"What if people are working in these buildings all night?" she asked softly, her pale blue eyes wide open in the dim light.

"That's what we're here to find out," said Brent, not exactly answering her question.

Eventually a flood of people began pouring out of the plants and heading in long streams towards the parking lot. Within minutes cars jammed the driveway exiting the plant. "You can sure tell they're hourly workers," Brent said. "The second their shift is over, they're outta there." We smiled at each other.

I didn't like that the line of cars had to pass us, but we put down the binoculars and pretended to be looking at a map in the truck. I glanced up at the faces of the people inside the cars as they passed and noticed how intent they were on getting out of this neighbourhood. It was Friday night, and no one was dilly-dallying. As quickly as the floodgate had opened, it shut. Within ten minutes the river of people pouring out of the plant had dried up to a trickle, until by 11:00 p.m. there was not a soul in sight other than the same two security guards in the tower.

Brent picked up the binoculars again and strained to see if there were more cars left in the lot. "Damn," he whispered. "There's still about twenty-five cars in the lot. When me and Angie were here in the spring, there was definitely no night shift. Maybe they got a bigger contract. I don't know."

We stayed for another hour to make sure that the remaining cars weren't stragglers, but when they failed to leave we decided we would have to come back again because it looked like Litton had added a night shift. When we got back to the apartment, Julie lit the candles she had arranged all over the living room and I put on our morbid anthem, "The End." The candlelight flickering in the dark cast an eerie light across the room. I looked over at Brent and Julie sitting dejectedly on the sofa, lost in their own thoughts.

It was obvious that we would have to case the plant to determine whether there was a night when no one was working, but what if there wasn't? Would we go ahead anyway, and take whatever precautions necessary to make sure no one got hurt? Even though that little voice inside me said we shouldn't go ahead and take the risk, my sense of reason told me that we had come too far and invested too much to stop now. I knew Brent wouldn't turn around and go back and neither would I. Julie would probably jump at the chance of going back now, but if we proceeded she would go along with us regardless of her misgivings. Our situation reminded me of a friend who had worked hard to get a grant to fund an expedition to a mountainous region to film the nesting site of a rare bird. The expedition was the culmination of years of hard work. After assembling a film crew, climbing the mountain, and being on the verge of filming, they learned that the area had been designated high risk for rock slides. Should they go ahead or go back? Despite the danger, they had invested too much time and money into their expedition to turn back. I knew we wouldn't change course either.

As though she was reading my mind, Julie suddenly broke the silence with a question. "Don't you think 550 pounds is too much dynamite? And don't you think we should target somewhere else if there is a night shift every night? Remember when the RAF bombed the Springer building in Germany and the cops didn't take their bomb threat seriously so all those people got killed?"

I looked over at Brent for an answer.

"Anything less than 550 pounds would just be a symbolic bombing," he said. "We want to get the idea across that sabotage should be used to cause real financial damage, to deter investors from going ahead with their deadly projects. We can learn from the RAF bombing and make sure the cops and security know it's a real bomb. The RAF didn't use a van. We'll park the van where they can see it and leave a real stick of dynamite outside the van so they'll know we're serious. Don't worry, Julie. Everything is going to be fine."

Julie looked at him without emotion, then went to bed.

"We should go out and get a van tomorrow night," I suggested. "Because if we're going to go ahead, we should be working on the van while we're casing." Brent nodded, then brought in the electronic timing device from our bedroom and set it. We rewound the Doors tape and listened to it again, and as the prophetic song "The End" finished, the little red light on the timing device went on, signalling that the dynamite would be ignited twenty-five minutes after it was set. The little red light was so anticlimactic that I laughed, thinking it should set off blaring horns and a series of bright flashing lights when the bomb was symbolically supposed to go off.

Every time we tested the device, which was several times each night, it worked like clockwork. Nothing could be more fatal than a malfunctioning timing device. What if it went off as we drove the dynamite-filled van down the crowded freeway? Or just as the workers came pouring out of the plant at shift change? No, a faulty timing device would definitely put the brakes on this action.

We spent the next afternoon carrying out mundane household tasks and met in the evening for supper. Julie was putting a meatloaf in the oven when Brent came bounding down the stairs with news that he had managed to buy us tickets for a Who concert — probably their last.

"Who the hell are they?" laughed Julie. "Some geriatrics trying to milk the last few dollars they can from the baby boomers before they get too old to go to concerts?"

"Hey, they're great," Brent said. "It's going to be an outdoor concert at the CNE with seventy thousand people, so it'll be a trip no matter what The Who are like now."

I wasn't a big fan of The Who but it had been years since I had been to a concert. Besides, we needed to do something fun to take our minds off this bombing.

"Let's catch the news while that meatloaf is cooking?" suggested Brent, bouncing on to the couch. Julie jumped up and bounced on the couch beside him and Brent immediately began tickling her until she let out shrieks of laughter so loud I thought the neighbours might come down. As Julie's mood had become increasingly morose and withdrawn, Brent had taken up games of horseplay with her that usually involved some kind of physical contact, like tickling or lifting her up and swinging her around. For me, it was a pain to watch them tickle away at each other. I had been wrestling with confused feelings about these games ever since they had started. I was uncomfortable with the image of myself as the jealous "wife," uptight at my "husband" for rough-housing with the "kids." But Julie was not a child. She was a very attractive young woman who I sensed was infatuated with Brent — feelings that were inevitable, given her isolation and apprehension over this impending action. I didn't know what to think. I knew that if I confronted Brent with his behaviour, he would defend himself as an innocent man just trying to make a young, lonely woman happy by playing some silly games with her. He would charge me with being insecure and immature. But try as I might, I couldn't help feeling like screaming "Stop! Shut up!" whenever he started tickling or touching her.

I watched Julie lie back on the sofa, her black hair falling in long strands across her flawless pale complexion as Brent straddled her so she couldn't get up. He tickled her again until she screamed "Stop, please stop!" I looked at her full, moist lips and gleaming blue eyes, and my skin crawled with anger. "Stop!" I ordered Brent. "The neighbours are going to come down to see what's going on if you don't tone it down."

He looked at me reproachfully and got off her. I turned and tried to walk into the bedroom casually, although "stormed" might be more appropriate. He sensed my anger and followed me. "What's your problem?"

"She's infatuated with you and you are encouraging it!"

"You're crazy! She loves Gerry and she's lonely and depressed. I'm just trying to have a bit of harmless fun with her. You're right in the room with us. If I had ulterior motives, I'd wait until you weren't around."

"I wouldn't be surprised if you do the same thing and more when I'm not around!" I whispered so Julie couldn't hear us. "It's all for your ego, not for Julie. If anything, you're encouraging her to have feelings for you. At your age, it's not all innocent."

"You're crazy!"

Just then an ear-piercing ringing engulfed the apartment. "My meatloaf!" Julie shrieked. We ran into the kitchen, which was filled with smoke streaming out of the oven. Julie pulled her burnt meatloaf from the oven, opened the back door, and began frantically fanning the smoke outside while Brent fumbled with the smoke detector to shut off the alarm. The dynamite!!!

"My God, what if someone calls the fire department and we've got all this dynamite in here?" I hissed as I ran into the bedroom to get a blanket to cover the boxes of dynamite piled beside the TV.

Brent managed to disconnect the alarm from the smoke detector and for a hair-raising half-hour we fanned smoke out of the apartment and waited for someone to show up at our door. Fortunately, no one responded to the alarm. After it was all over, we disconnected the smoke alarm and vowed that avoiding anything that might turn it on must be a priority.

Not until the crisis was over did I notice that Julie was crying to herself. Overwhelmed by guilt, I rushed over to her and put my arms around her. "It's okay Julie. Nothing will come of this," I said in an effort to console her. Her vulnerability and spontaneous emotional reactions to everything brought out my maternal instincts. I was falling into a pattern of confusing emotional responses to her. Whenever she played with Brent, I would resent her presence and find myself fighting off hatred towards what I saw as her infatuation with him. After venting these feelings with Brent, I would be overwhelmed with guilt and end up acting motherly and protective towards her. In the end, my emotional dynamic with her was an unhealthy roller-coaster ride of resentment, guilt, and protectiveness.

After the smoke-detector fiasco, I went out for a jog with Julie, partially to alleviate my guilt, while Brent made something else for supper. There was a park a block away that we jogged around as part of our daily exercise regimen.

"Do you want to go out with us tonight and look for a van?" I asked.

"Sure," she said in a small voice.

"You don't have to."

"No. I'd like to."

"If you want, you could help me?"

"What do you mean?"

"Well, I'm going to steal a van but I'll need someone with me to shine the flashlight so I can see what I'm doing."

"What about Brent?"

"He'll keep watch. You could do that if you'd rather?"

"No. I'll go with you."

I wondered how aware she was of my insecurities surrounding her relationship with Brent. I had never confronted her with it because I felt so guilty and I figured it was Brent's responsibility. He was the one who initiated the tickling sessions, and he was older and definitely more in control of their relationship. I had to admit she didn't flirt with him. I think I felt so guilt-ridden because her only crime was being naturally attractive, something no one could fault her for. In the end I decided that living in such a socially isolated environment would inevitably lead to unhealthy personal relationships. To be so dependent on two or three people to satisfy all our social needs was bound to lead to jealousy and resentment.

Late that night, when most people in Toronto were going to bed, we drove slowly up and down residential streets looking for a van we could use in our bombing. What we wanted was a recent model that would be unlikely to have mechanical problems. In Vancouver we had been partial to underground parking lots, but in Toronto such lots usually had locking doors or attendants. We hadn't been searching long when Julie pointed out, "There's one." It was a dark blue van, probably only a few years old, with the logo "Gauley-Gage Cartage Co." written on its side. As soon as I saw that it was blue, I knew this was the one. I had become super-stitious about our anthem, "The End," and in the song they talked about a "blue bus calling us," although I had to admit that it could also have symbolized a police van.

We parked a half-block away on the old, tree-lined street. As I stepped out of our truck, I scanned the neighbourhood. This was a middle-class area of Toronto where the residents weren't the types to sit out on their porches drinking beer late at night. The big old homes, set back off the street, had dark windows, and the vegeta-tion in the front yards was thick and overgrown. This was the type of neighbourhood where it would be difficult to see someone sit-ting inside a parked van from your window late at night. Perfect.

Brent fell back behind Julie and me, because he was going to duck into some bushes near the van so that he could watch out for potential witnesses and warn us if the need arose. I was getting used to this sort of thing, but I could tell by Julie's face and voice that she was nervous, which surprised me because she was such a bold shoplifter. Later, when I asked her why, she explained that being enclosed in a vehicle made her feel claustrophobic and vul-nerable.

When we got to the van, I slipped the Slim Jim between the window and door frame and began probing at the locking mecha-nism inside. A dull click, and the door's lock button popped up. In a flash we were inside. Julie turned on the tiny flashlight and aimed it at the keyway. Her fear made her irritable, and she whispered "Hurry" to me. I had to conscientiously push from my mind all thoughts except those related to the task at hand. Finally, with the whole ignition pried out, I gasped, "Great!" and asked Julie, "Do you want to drive the truck?"

Shaking her head, she got out of the van and walked down the street to our truck while Brent came and slipped into the van beside me. I stuck the screw driver into the gaping hole where the ignition had been and turned it on. This was the telling moment. If the van stalled, or did anything out of the ordinary, we wouldn't use it, but instantly it turned over and purred like a kitten. I smiled over at Brent and stepped on the accelerator.

We drove across town to Chinatown and pulled into the alley. Julie was already there with the garage doors open. After we had pulled in and shut the door behind us, I finally let out a sigh and relaxed. We had boarded up the garage window so there was no danger of anyone knowing there was activity inside. Before Brent got out of the van, he opened the glove box and pulled out a beautiful folding pocket knife with a rosewood handle. He had a habit of taking trophies from car thefts, and this was to be no exception. I noticed him slip the knife in his pocket but I didn't say anything.

Now that the danger was over, Julie's spirits picked up. "Hey, this is great eh?" she said, looking the van over. "It's blue, just like the bus in the song." I smiled. She had picked up on that as well.

The inside of the van had been fashioned into something of a tool storage area with row upon row of boxes filled with tools and screws. "We'll have to rip out the tool boxes and run the detonating cord under a rug we can glue to the floor," said Brent, already planning how to set up the bomb.

"Why under the carpet?" I asked.

"So whoever drives it to Litton can turn on the timing device from the front seat, and then the cord will be under the carpet and not move around when you're driving. We can pile the dynamite in the back in such a way that it doesn't jostle around." We sat around in the garage for a while going over the details of building the bomb until we had unwound from the night's activities. Then, satisfied, we drove home.

* * *

Brent went back to the Litton plant every night of the next week, always to find a dozen cars in the parking lot all night long. We didn't agonize too much over it but resigned ourselves to devising as many ways as possible to warn security and the police of the bomb. To alleviate the tension of our mission we went to the Who concert and, later, to hear Johnny Rotten of the Sex Pistols at a smaller venue. The Johnny Rotten concert was a concession to Julie, since she wasn't a big fan of sixties rock. Although those evenings were a diversion from the Litton plan, I never could escape my identity as a stranger in town preparing to carry out this huge bombing. It was a strange feeling standing in a crowd at a concert watching all these kids moshing or dancing, knowing that they probably would go back home to school or work while we would go back to our apartment or the garage in Chinatown to continue preparing for the bombing of the Litton plant.

Our plans for the bombing were evolving. As we began work on the van, we decided to rig the bomb so it would be difficult to find the detonating cord and timing device. Even though we weren't going to booby-trap the bomb, because we didn't want anyone to get hurt, including the police, we wanted to create the illusion that it might be booby-trapped so that they wouldn't go inside and disengage the timing device.

Brent's idea of concealing the detonating cord, blasting caps, and timing device under a carpet that we would glue to the van floor created some problems of its own. When the night came to glue down the carpet, Brent returned from a hardware store with a couple of gallons of contact cement. "Okay, let's rock and roll!" he exclaimed, excited about his idea. "Carpet's cut and we're ready to glue!"

"So, according to the instructions," I said, after reading the glue can, "we'll have to work quickly because after we've painted the van floor and carpet with the glue, we should only leave it for a few minutes to dry, just until it gets tacky, before we stick them together. We better be organized, because once we press the carpet to the floor, we aren't getting it back up again, so the cord better be in the right place."

We each grabbed a big paint brush and began smearing the contact cement all over the floor and carpet. It didn't take long before we had used up both gallons. But the most critical section of instructions was the section I had just glanced over. Even before we had finished gluing, we began chuckling and making remarks that inspired gales of laughter like I had never experienced before. The jokes weren't memorable, but the laughter sure was. As I laughed myself into a state of hysteria, I vaguely recalled the warning about the effects of poor ventilation: fumes from the glue could cause lightheadedness or headaches. We sure enough were experiencing the lightheadedness.

We were pressing the carpet down over the detonating cord when Brent noticed that the carpet was a bit too big. Through tear-stained eyes, he took out his new pocket knife and pressed down as hard as he could, to cut off the extra section of carpet. "Ta da!" he sang, holding up the piece of carpet. At that climatic moment, through his glue fume-induced euphoria, he was struck by a terri-fying revelation. "Oh my God! We cut right through the electrical cord!" We chuckled. Brent's horrified expression instantly cracked, and he started laughing uncontrollably. "We better get out of here before we blow ourselves up," he said, struggling to think reason-ably through the fog of glue fumes enveloping his brain.

The dynamite was still in our apartment. We wouldn't hook it up to the blasting caps and electrical cord that ran to the timing device until the night of the bombing. We turned off the garage lights, locked the door, and stumbled out into the alley.

"I think we should go somewhere and straighten out before we drive home," Julie giggled. "I would do anything for one of those Jamaican meat patties." We put our arms around each other's shoulders and stumbled down the street towards a West Indian nightclub that sold Jamaican meat patties late into the night. We fit in perfectly with the largely drunken clientele. For hours we sat eating and laughing over the absurdity of gluing down the carpet over the electrical cord and then cutting through the cord with a knife. The implications of this disastrous mistake had not hit us yet.

The next morning we all woke up with the second side-effect from glue sniffing: headaches. "This is really a drag!" moaned Brent. "If we don't splice the wires properly, the timing device might not work." In silent penitence we sat marvelling at how we could have made such a stupid mistake.

When we got back to the garage, we could still smell the glue fumes from the night before. This time we felt like vomiting instead of laughing. We left the door open a crack and sat outside on chairs, going over how we would splice the wires together again. We lacked confidence in this area — none of us were trades-people, after all. Finally the air seemed breathable so we mustered up the courage to attempt to splice the sensitive wires together.

While Brent did the splicing, I supervised his movements with an eagle eye. We could not afford to fail. After a tense ten minutes, we hooked the timing devise to the electrical cord and set it to go off. We placed our chairs in a little semi-circle around the timing device and waited anxiously for the little red light to start blinking at the exact moment. After twenty-five minutes, the little red eye looked up at us and started its slow, reassuring blink. We let out a collective "Whew!"

* * *

A few days after stealing the blue van, we decided to steal our get-away car, so it wouldn't be so "hot" on the night of the bombing. The last thing we needed was the police pulling us over during our getaway because they remembered the description of a stolen vehicle. Again, we were limited to stealing older vehicles — we had never solved the problem of disengaging locking steering columns. Julie prided herself, though, on being able to guess a car's age, a skill she had learned from her older brother.

The early hours of October 4, 1982, found us once again cruising residential streets looking for a reliable car more than five years old. It didn't take long to find a 1975 Oldsmobile parked in a middle-class neighbourhood like the one where we found the van, and a few minutes later we were driving it off to another neighbourhood to leave it for the night. The next afternoon we went back and moved it. We had to keep moving it each day until the night of the bombing.

The night after stealing the Oldsmobile we went out again, this time to get a second vehicle so we would have two getaway vehicles to buffer our truck from the bombing. We found one and ended up parking it, ironically, in the lot of the Skyline Hotel only a block away from the Litton plant. But that 1974 Chevelle turned out to have problems with stalling, so the next night, when it came time to move it, Brent decided to just leave it in the Skyline parking lot and forget it rather than risk having mechanical problems on the night of the bombing. This meant we had to spend another might cruising the streets to find a suitable second getaway car.

The time was drawing near. I could almost hear the clock ticking in my head wherever I went. We set a date: Thursday, October 14, at 11:45 p.m. The night before the bombing, I sat one last time in the dark with the candles flickering, listening to "The End." Alone with my thoughts while Julie and Brent went for a midnight jog, I found myself wishing that I could just quit, buy a little farm somewhere with horses, and have a baby. I was getting tired of the stress and starting to feel afraid that something could go badly wrong. Was it worth it to go to jail for the rest of our lives? Or die? To carry out actions that the vast majority of people would think were insane? I never doubted my motives. I didn't feel insane, didn't feel that I was consumed with anger or had any other psychological problem. But I was profoundly disturbed by what I saw as the ongoing destruction of the natural world, at the wasting of human potential, and from everything I read and saw and experienced I couldn't see our society becoming a better place to live in as long as the prime motive was profit, ever-increasing material wealth at the expense of all else. Although I tried to imagine myself settling down on my farm in the country, I knew I'd get involved in community politics as soon as I learned of some injustice in the area. But why did I feel the need to go to such extremes? It seemed as though any other course of action that society offered could be co-opted by the system. I sighed. Maybe my need to act would be fulfilled after this bombing, and my conscience would let me settle down somewhere and learn to glean whatever joy I could out of this society. All I knew was that I was getting very tired and depressed. I needed joy, happiness, and peace in my life.

When the song ended, I got up quickly and turned the tape off. Why did I feel so moved by this morbid song? Was this some kind of death wish? I shuddered and blew out the candles.

✳ **25** ✳

The evening of Thursday, October 14, arrived all too quickly. As I forced a few tablespoons of mashed potatoes into my mouth, I felt like I was going to be sick. I couldn't recall ever being so nervous. My stomach ached and my hands were sweaty. I glanced up from my plate at Julie and Brent, who were eating in complete silence, and didn't dare put my terror into words. Somehow, verbalizing it would only make the others more nervous. Maybe they were harbouring the illusion that I was not afraid, just like I was doing towards them. Brent, in particular, did not appear nervous. He was stuffing huge mouthfuls of meatloaf and mashed potatoes into his mouth. Every time I lifted a spoonful of the white mush to my mouth, I noticed my hand shaking. I knew from past experience that anticipation was a lot more nerve-racking than the actual event. I wished I was driving the van to Litton right now. Every few minutes I looked up at the clock: 9:15 p.m. Time had slowed down agonizingly since yesterday.

Brent shoved his plate away from him. I jumped. My nerves were definitely getting the better of me. "Julie." He broke the silence. "I'm going to give you two hundred dollars just in case something goes wrong and you have to leave. Go to the bus terminal and catch a bus to Vancouver, the first one you can get — although I'm sure nothing is going to go wrong."

He pulled his wallet out and counted out ten twenties. Julie's face was pure white. She didn't say a thing, just pocketed the money.

"Well, we better get going," he said, walking off to the bedroom. I followed after him. In the bedroom I wrapped my arms around him, pressing him close. Perhaps this would be the last time I would ever feel him again.

I put my wallet with my false ID and driver's licence, along with my keys and gloves, in a small black purse I had bought for the occasion. Then I went back to the kitchen where Julie was waiting, dressed in her "normal" clothes. We got into the truck and drove in silence to Chinatown. It felt unreal, like we were actors in a movie.

The last thing we had to do was hook up the timing device to the detonating cord. This was a frightening step, because of the remote chance that an unexpected electrical current or charge could set off the blasting caps and therefore the dynamite, right there, in the middle of Chinatown. In such a heavily populated area that would mean a massacre.

We opened up the side doors of the van and Brent carefully took the positive and negative wires and twisted them onto the connectors of the timing device. We let out a collective sigh when nothing happened. 9:45 p.m. There was nothing left to do but the bombing.

"You have the phone number of the security tower, eh Jules?" Brent asked softly. She nodded. "So I'll get you on the walkie-talkie as soon as I see Ann get out of the van. Then make your call. Just be sure they hear and understand you. Okay?" She nodded again.

"Then, wait for us," he explained for the hundredth time. "If we aren't there within a couple of hours, you'll know something went wrong. Then you're on your own." Once again, she nodded.

"Okay, Ann, I'll follow you. Everything okay?" he asked. Now it was my turn to nod. I was afraid to speak because my throat felt so parched. Julie seemed to tiptoe on her way out of the garage to the truck. She closed the door so quietly we didn't hear it shut. It seemed as though the quieter we were, the safer we were.

Brent opened the door of the van and helped me in. We had bought new ignitions for the van and our two getaway vehicles so that we wouldn't have to use screwdrivers in the ignition holes. I inserted the key in the ignition and turned it on. The noise of the engine turning over made my stomach knot up even more. In seconds exhaust filled the garage with a purple haze. For the first time since we had brought the van here, Brent opened the garage doors all the way. The garage's yellow light cast a bright swath into the black alley and sparkled in the puddles that had formed in the potholes.

As though to form a perfect backdrop to a bombing, it had started raining. The rhythmic swishing of the windshield wipers seemed to be in perfect sync with my heartbeat and the metronome of seconds passing by in my mind. 10:15 p.m. I backed the van out of the garage and waited while Brent shut the doors and got into the second getaway car, which we had parked nearby. The water droplets on the windshield were like a hundred drops of oil, which the old wipers smeared across the glass, leaving a glaze that obscured all the objects in my line of sight. Damn! We should have replaced the wipers. I pulled some Kleenex from my pocket, got out, and frantically tried to wipe the glaze off the windshield, to no avail.

Finally we were ready to go. My every movement was premeditated and focused. Absolutely nothing was on my mind but the 550 pounds of dynamite stacked behind me and the process of driving the van. We had decided to take the freeway to the Litton plant because it would involve less stopping, starting, and interaction with other vehicles, thus minimizing the chances of something unforeseeable happening. I leaned forward into the steering wheel, peering through the greasy windshield. The oncoming headlights formed a blur of white lights streaming towards me, like the ones you see in time-lapse photographs. At first I gripped the steering wheel until my knuckles went white, then, consciously, I loosened my grip so that I would be able to react to any change in the traffic. In my rear-view mirror I saw Brent's car following close behind me. He was just a dark silhouette in the blackness.

We drove to the neighbourhood near the Litton plant where we had parked the Oldsmobile. I stopped the van and waited while Brent got out of the second getaway car and transferred into the Oldsmobile. 11:00 p.m. Within minutes we were turning onto City View Drive. I slowed to a snail's pace, fearful we would get there too soon, just as all the workers were leaving from the shift change. A couple of stragglers were driving towards us. 11:10 p.m. Looking back in my rear-view mirror, I could see Brent was driving so close to me that he was almost touching my bumper. Why would he drive so closely? If I stopped, he would hit me. I slowed down even more.

There it was: Plant no. 402. 11:15 p.m. I glanced back again and saw Brent pull over and turn off his headlights. Then I looked up and was surprised to see how close I was to the security tower. The bright fluorescent lights inside made it possible for me to see the expression on the men's faces. One guy was sitting down looking at a magazine while the other guy bent over his shoulder so he could see it too. Something like a *Playboy* magazine, I thought. Look up, you idiots! It was imperative to our plan that they see me park the van. How could they miss me?

The van lurched slightly as it drove up over the curb onto the front lawn of building no. 402. I prayed that my existence wouldn't be extinguished by that lurch, but I continued coasting slowly over the floodlit lawn towards the west wall of the building. I felt so vulnerable and naked, driving on the lawn, the van brightly illuminated by the floodlights. Once again, I glanced up at the security tower and still the men continued to gaze, smiling, at their magazine. Then I stopped, put the van in reverse and backed it up against the wall. The back wheels crushed the hedges that lined the building. The hedges would conceal the back of the van from the security guards' view, but if they looked they would see the front of it. I turned off the van and felt my heart beating even faster. If only I could go as fast as my heart.

Turning in my seat, I looked at the little toggle switch of the timing device and once more prayed that when I flicked it on, it wouldn't ignite prematurely. It clicked, then nothing. I reached over and took the fluorescent orange cardboard box with the stick of dynamite taped on top. I got out and set the box carefully beside the van, then locked the door. On the side of the box we had printed instructions in huge black block letters: *DANGER EXPLOSIVES — Inside this van are 550 lbs. of commercial dynamite*

*which will explode anytime from within 15 minutes to 25 minutes
after the van was parked here. The dynamite will be set off by two
completely separate detonating systems. Do not enter or move the van
— it will explode. Phone the police immediately and have them block
off Highway 27, City View Drive, Dixon Road and other roads surrounding the Litton Plants and have the workers inside the plants
moved to protected areas. Nearby hotels and factories should also be
notified so that no one will be hurt by the blast. On top of this box is
an authentic sample stick of the dynamite contained inside the van.
This is to confirm that this is a real bomb!*

The two sections of this warning that weren't true — the two
detonating systems and booby-trap — were only included to be
sure no one attempted to tamper with the bomb.

11:20 p.m. My legs felt like jelly as I jogged quickly over to
Brent's car. As soon as I jumped in, I told him that I was quite sure
the security guards hadn't seen me park the van. "I sure hope
Julie's phone call gets through alright, or this could be a disaster!"

For five minutes Brent drove quickly but within the speed limit
to the place where we had left our second getaway car. The further
away we got from the plant, the better we felt, but I could not
extinguish the panic welling up inside me. Everything had not
gone as we had planned, we thought, as we drove off in the second car. I soon saw Julie pacing back and forth at the bus stop
where we had arranged to meet, not far from her phone booth. We
pulled over and she slid into the back seat and began talking
quickly in a small but frightened voice.

"He couldn't understand me. I read the message and when I
finished, he said "What?" and asked me to repeat it. I couldn't
believe it. I started thinking that he might just want to record my
voice, so I just told him to go to the van and read the message on
the box. Then I hung up . . . I did what you said, but he just didn't
understand." She kept repeating the details over and over until we
told her we believed her and not to worry. For sure, he would see
the van, read the box, and call the cops. Usually when an action
was over, I would feel an overwhelming sense of relief, but this
time I didn't feel like it was over. I wasn't at all sure that it had
gone well, and if it hadn't, I didn't even want to think about it.

We ditched the second getaway car and transferred into our
truck. Some forty-five minutes later we pulled up on the side street
near our apartment. Still I felt panicky and my stomach churned
uncontrollably. Brent's and Julie's stony silence convinced me that

they shared my feelings. As soon as we got into the apartment, I went into the living room and turned on the TV. Anything to get my mind off this bombing. If only there was some way of knowing what had happened. I switched channels mindlessly looking for a diversion, when suddenly the screen went black and a sober voice boomed out of the speaker announcing that the program was being interrupted by an important news bulletin. I had never seen normal broadcasting interrupted like that before.

A newsreader announced that there had been a bombing at the Litton plant. The next picture showed a fleet of ambulances arriving at the plant, their emergency lights turning, sending a bright red light flashing across what seemed like a wartorn landscape. A reporter appeared on the screen, standing in front of a huge crater with smoke billowing out of it. Behind the crater stood the shell of a building with a huge gaping hole bombed out of it. Thick steel support cables were dangling out of huge slabs of concrete that had been violently torn apart. But worse of all — and especially from our point of view — was the sight of stretchers with bodies covered in white sheets being carried to waiting ambulances.

The reporter was talking to a man with blood pouring down his face from a wound on his head. He was telling her that he had just been told to clear the building because there was a bomb outside when a terrific explosion had torn apart the building and thrown him to the ground. Bright emergency lights illuminated a catastrophic scene of emergency crews, reporters, and injured civilians milling about the ruins of the Litton plant behind them. The van was nowhere in sight — only the crater and hunks of rubble all around it. If I hadn't known any better, I would have assumed that the unlikely scenario of a surprise bombing attack on Canada was underway.

Inside my head I could hear myself screaming. There was only one thing to do. Die. I could not live with this. That I was sure of. How many people were dead? We were mass murderers. How should I kill myself? We had a bottle of Valium that we had brought along in case of some emergency, and this was it. Was there enough for us all? I sat frozen, glued to the spot, eyes on the screen.

Julie was crying and Brent stared at the TV in profound disbelief. How could our plans have gone so horribly wrong? "We'll have to flee to the States," concluded Brent in a hushed tone of voice.

"No," I assured him. "I'm going to kill myself. I can't face this.

These people. We didn't mean to kill anyone, and I certainly wouldn't be able to stand up in court now and feel politically righteous about this action." Julie didn't say anything, but her expression spoke volumes. She stared at the screen as though looking at her own death — the grey and white images bouncing off her pale complexion.

The special news report seemed to go on forever. Although it didn't make sense that anyone could know we had done it or know where we lived, I kept expecting the door to crash down and a SWAT team burst in the room and mow us down in a rain of machine-gun fire. A fitting end to a terrible deed. What had we been thinking?

"It must have gone off early," Brent said in the same hushed voice. "How could that have happened? We tested it hundreds of times and never once did it malfunction." For a few minutes we sat in silence fathoming this possibility. "The security guards must not have cleared the building or blocked off the road."

"I made the call!" snapped Julie defensively, turning to look at Brent with angry eyes.

"I know you did," he reassured her. She relaxed noticeably after that, but I could tell she was already riddled with the guilty feeling that somehow this disaster had happened because the guard had not clearly understood her telephone warning.

For a solid hour the live television coverage of the Litton bombing continued. All the while the reporters apparently couldn't say exactly how many casualties or injuries there had been. They would keep the audience posted on later developments. I don't remember sleeping that night. We sat up until the sky was light and talked about the various possibilities. Should we commit suicide or should we flee to the States?

* * *

Terry Chikowski looked over his friend and co-worker Maxwell Spencer's shoulder at the *Mad* magazine and laughed. That *Herman* cartoon was his favorite. He liked the night shift, because there was little to worry about and he enjoyed spending time with his friend. It didn't even seem like a job to him.

When the phone rang, Max picked it up. Terry didn't think anything of it, until Max reached over and tapped him on the shoulder and motioned to the receiver. Something was going on. Maxwell pushed the button that records phone calls and then a few minutes later said to the person on the other end of the line, "I don't understand what you're saying. Sorry, but can you repeat that?" Then he looked up at Terry with a serious expression on his face. Apparently the caller did not want to repeat the call because Max hung up.

"What the hell? That was a bomb threat. Hey, Terry, do you see any van parked out there?" Max said, squinting out into the darkness. Terry stared out too. One problem with such a brightly lit room was that, in contrast, the night outside looked very black. It was almost impossible to see anything that wasn't illuminated by the ample floodlights aimed at all the building walls. After a few minutes of looking in every direction, Terry noticed the front end of a van parked against the west wall of building no. 402. The back end was concealed by the three-foot hedges that lined the building. It looked oddly out of place alright, backed up against the building like that — kinda spooky!

"You better call the cops, Max. This might not be a prank." Max dialled the number taped in front of the phone on the wall. "Hi, this is security over at the Litton plant on 25 City View Drive and we just received a bomb threat and there's a suspicious van parked against a building wall. The caller said the van is going to explode in fifteen or twenty minutes, so you better get someone over here in a hurry!" Maxwell listened to the response of the police, then turned to Terry. "Should we check it out?"

"You better stay here in case they call back, and I'll go over and take a look and meet the cops."

By the time Terry was going down the flight of stairs outside, he could see the emergency sirens of the cars responding from the bomb squad. He turned to look and sure enough there they were, three cars, with their red emergency lights flashing and turning, speeding down City View towards the plant. Less than ten minutes had passed since the woman had phoned in the bomb threat, and 23 Division station was all the way over in the northeast end of Etobicoke. As the police officers pulled up, Terry pointed over at building no. 402, where the front half of the van was shining in the floodlight. Three officers got out of their cars and began walking towards the van, while another stayed behind to report in on the car radio. Together the officers walked across the neatly manicured lawns of the Litton plant, slowing down ever so slightly as they neared the orange fluorescent box laying several yards from the van. From thirty metres away they could clearly see the stick of dynamite lying on top of the box.

"Don't go any closer!" The officer waiting by the cruiser yelled sharply at them. "It looks like it could be a real bomb!" For a few seconds the other officers paused while they tried to read the block letters from a distance.

Meanwhile Terry was running as quickly as he could to the side of building No. 402 and into the side entrance. He went down the main hall towards the middle of the plant where the workers would be. He only glanced briefly in each office he passed to make sure no one was there, but as he came down the hall towards the office of James Tayles, the precision inspector, he stopped and went in. The van was parked right outside that office. He called out James's name. No answer. Tayles must be on a cigarette break. Then Terry ran towards the middle of the plant. There they were — having a break!

He yelled, "Get out of the building as fast as you can! There's a bomb parked right outside your office, James!" Terry hadn't done that much running for a long time. He slowed down for a second, gasping for air, when the world came crashing down around him.

The blast knocked him over and tore apart the building. The deafening roar created such a force that it blew out his ear drums, leaving Terry's hearing damaged forever. For a split second he thought he was dead, then realized he was in the fight of his life. Pain ripped through his abdomen, and with every breath he took a sharp pain pierced his rib cage. He was pinned down by huge slabs of concrete that spewed up dust so thick he could swallow it. Fighting the pain, he tried to move, but his whole body was covered in rubble. The only parts of his body he could move were his arms, which he began frantically using to claw away at whatever concrete he could move. To make a bad situation even worse, the sprinkler system suddenly came on, pouring hundreds of gallons of water down on the rubble around him, making it impossible to breathe. Miraculously, the sprinkler system had survived the bombing intact. Terry looked up at the water pouring down on him and wondered if he was fated to drown in the sprinkler system after surviving the bombing. Pinned under the rubble with pain shooting in agonizing waves through his body, Terry tried to call out for help. But every time he opened his mouth it was filled with water from the interminable streams pouring from the broken pipes in the ceiling. He couldn't believe this was how he would die. Cancer or a car accident, yes, but a bombing? Even in all his pain, he couldn't believe this was really happening.

Gasping desperately for air, he clawed away at the rubble. The concrete slabs were far too heavy for him to lift, but he couldn't just lay there and die. Then he heard voices, and through the dust, water, and smoke he saw men in uniforms clambering over the rubble towards him. He waved his arms in the air and felt tears of joy welling up in his eyes.

"We've got you!" one of the men yelled as they scrambled quickly towards him. He fought the waves of pain that were making it difficult to breath while the men heaved and pulled at the huge slabs pinning him down. After what seemed like hours, he felt the final weight lift off his back. His strength was draining from him, but he fought to stay alert. A stretcher appeared beside him, and when they lifted him up he saw the bloody pieces of flesh that were his own organs hanging from the open wound in his side. As though in a dream, he could hear the men in white talking about the steel and concrete shards sticking out of his back. As they placed him on his side, he gasped for air, as something sharp stabbed him in the ribs. My God, would he still die? The pain in his body was so acute that the constant ringing in his ears was just a minor irritation.

"Don't worry Terry, you'll be alright," he vaguely heard his friend Maxwell say as they placed him carefully in the ambulance. Opening his eyes, he looked up at Max's kind face. Then, closing them again, he fell into unconsciousness.

✳ 26 ✳

"This hunt for Direct Action is making me feel like James Bond," Fraser said as he struggled to keep up with Despaireux for a change.

"How so?" asked the detective, his cliché trenchcoat billowing out behind him as he hurried up towards the Litton security tower on Monday, October 18.

"I've been on more planes and helicopters since May than I have in my whole life," he said, finally catching up to the normally slow Despaireux. "With the speed you're moving at today, I'd swear you've quit smoking." Despaireux didn't respond, but gave Fraser a condescending look.

They took the short flight of stairs to the security room, two at a time, in unison. Standing at the top of the stairs to greet them were Staff Sergeant Bob Kent, head of the Toronto investigation, and Joseph Green, the head of Litton security. After a round of handshakes and introductions, their meeting began. Kent led the way into the glass-walled security room from where they could get a good overview of the plant and the effects of the bombing.

"As you can see, this was a devastating bombing," Kent began. "Not just from a physical point of view but also in terms of human destruction." He swept his hand dramatically across the front of the huge plate-glass window, through which they could see the ruins of building no. 402. The whole front of the building had been blown out to reveal partial ceilings, floors, and walls among the guts of the interior. In front of the shell was a huge crater, two and a half feet deep by about twelve feet in diameter. Milling all around the bombed out building were hundreds of workers, clearing away debris and knocking down dangerous pieces of concrete and wire that clung precipitously to the remains of the building.

"We had a couple of hundred employees give up their weekend to help clean up this mess so we could be up and running by today," Green said with obvious pride. "In fact, the actual production line for the cruise guidance system is running and wasn't touched by the bombing. I don't think they had done their homework when it comes to the location of their bomb."

"You may be right, but intentionally or not, they certainly succeeded in causing a tremendous amount of damage, both in financial and human terms," Kent said. "It's a miracle that no one died." He paused for a few moments to let the severity of the situation sink in. "These people aren't a bunch of non-violent civil disobedience do-gooders. They are very dangerous terrorists. At this point we know virtually nothing about them — whether they're some of the people from the anti-cruise movement who have been carrying out civil disobedience around this plant for years, whether they are a local cell from this Direct Action group that first surfaced in B.C. this spring, or whether they're the same individuals who acted in B.C. But that's what we're here to discover. We do know they seriously injured ten people in this bombing."

Referring periodically to a sheaf of papers in his hand, Kent listed the names of the injured. James Tayles would have been dead if he had not left his office for a cigarette break only minutes before the bombing. Barry Blunden, in mid-plant when the bomb exploded, suffered a fractured skull, a broken collarbone, and a broken finger, had his leg broken in three places, and had to have a skin graft as part of his treatment. Security guard Maxwell Spencer suffered a back injury, and security guard Terry Chikowski, who was in mid-plant warning the workers to clear the building when the bomb went off, had four broken ribs, four cracked ribs, a shattered spleen, and a wound in his back so severe he had four pounds of muscle removed. Nehemiah Bailey was treated for smoke inhalation. As well, three police officers who responded to the call were also injured.

Kent looked up from his papers directly into Fraser's and Despaireux's faces. "By the way, it was only through the grace of God that these three officers weren't killed. Police Constable Mervyn Dennis has severe facial lacerations, a fractured leg bone, and is believed to have suffered permanent hearing loss. He was only thirty metres away from the explosion when it happened. Police Constable Bruce McKee was also only thirty metres away, and he also received numerous lacerations that had to be stitched up. And Police Constable Guy Courvoisier was left with a concussion when the blast knocked him unconscious. He was about seventy-five metres away from the van when it exploded. The force of this van blowing apart was so powerful that parts of it flew one hundred metres onto Highway 427, causing two accidents that resulted in a sprained neck, hearing damage, and serious headaches to the individuals involved."

Kent paused again. "Now those are the human injuries. In financial terms, preliminary reports estimate the damage of this explosion to be in the range of close to $4 million. This includes the damage to the plant and windows shattering in everything from a Safeway store, only 270 metres away, to the Skyline Hotel, 545 metres away. Once again, I must emphasize that it is only through the grace of God that many people were not killed in this terrorist act."

For a few minutes the four men stood side by side staring out over the bombed-out building, watching the Litton employees clean up the debris. Fraser looked west at the busy eight-lane freeway, only about one hundred metres from the crater, and marvelled that there weren't more casualties. Then he looked south, down City View Drive, at the wall-to-wall industries that culminated in the outline of the multi-storey Skyline Hotel, which serviced the airport only a few miles away. What an ugly area, he thought. Nothing but roads, industries, airplane noise, and cars. He could hardly wait to get back to British Columbia.

"So what do you have on this bombing?" asked Despaireux, cutting to the chase. He and Fraser were in Toronto to exchange information on the activities of the group calling itself Direct Action. Kent moved over to a table in the middle of the room and sat down, motioning to three chairs facing him on the opposite side. Despaireux and Fraser took out notepads and began scribbling as fast as Kent spoke. Green sat impassively, staring blankly at Kent's face.

"After our detectives questioned people in the neighbourhoods surrounding the plant, we had a number of people report that a 1975 Oldsmobile, which had been parked outside their residences, had been moved sometime after ten o'clock on the night of the bombing," Kent explained, once again referring to his notes. "We believe this is the same vehicle that an employee of Litton, leaving work at between 11:10 and 11:15 p.m., noticed travelling very, very slowly northbound on City View Drive, so close behind a van that he couldn't see the headlights. He remembered this incident because of how close the Oldsmobile was travelling to the van. But he didn't think it was peculiar enough to report until after the bombing."

"Then at approximately 11:20, security guard Maxwell Spencer got a phone call, which he began to record when he realized it was a bomb warning. By the way, the voice was a woman's. When she finished her warning, Spencer asked her to repeat it, but she sounded panicky and instead said to go to the van and read the sign. Then she hung up. The guards called the police, who arrived on the scene at 11:25 p.m. The caller said the bomb was set to explode in fifteen to twenty minutes, so that meant they had another ten to fifteen minutes to clear the building and roads. Instead the bomb went off at 11:31 p.m., shortly after the bomb squad arrived.

"Now we've already contacted the FBI on this one, and they said that if these people used an electronic timing device, the electronic frequency from the bomb squad's radio transmissions could have set the bomb off prematurely. Anyway, if we are to believe the bombers, it went off twelve minutes prematurely."

"Yeah, that's why they always warn motorists in B.C. to turn off their car radios when they're driving through blasting zones in the mountains," Fraser interjected. Kent just looked at him blankly. He didn't share Fraser's youthful air of open excitement. He was of the old school of jaded cynicism.

"Yeah, well that's just a theory," Kent responded blandly. "We really don't know why or even if the bomb did go off prematurely. However, we did recover a stick of unexploded dynamite, probably the one that was attached to the orange box, and wrappings from a stick of dynamite stuck to a piece of metal from the truck — stamped D.2, indicating it was manufactured in April 1982. The explosives experts have been working all weekend on this case, and they have come to preliminary conclusions based on the size of the crater and analysis of residue. They say over five hundred pounds of 75 per cent Toval dynamite were used. That means the make, date of manufacture, size, and chemical composition of the dynamite is identical to that stolen in B.C." Once again Kent paused, partially for effect and partially to let Fraser and Despaireux catch up on their note-taking.

"We have also been able to ascertain the ownership of the van used in the bombing through the serial number found on the axle," he continued. "It belongs to a Donald Frank, who reported his blue 1980 GMC van stolen from 71 Latimer Avenue in Toronto two weeks before the bombing. We're also checking into a suspicious 1974 Chevelle found in the parking lot of the Skyline Hotel a block from here, which was reportedly stolen on the night of October 4, near Memorial Park and Kinbourne in East York. We don't have any evidence that this vehicle was used in the bombing, but its location is suspicious. The most important piece of evidence to date, the voice recording of the telephone bomb warning, has been sent to the lab for testing. It should be a very incriminating piece of evidence when we find those responsible."

Fraser looked up from his note-taking and asked, "Why weren't the employees cleared out of the building as soon as the bomb threat was phoned in?"

Kent looked at him irritably. "They began clearing the building ten minutes after the bomb threat was phoned in. We don't know exactly why the security guards didn't begin clearing the building right away, but we're looking into that."

"Did the bombing screw up Litton's ability to manufacture the guidance system?" Fraser asked.

"I talked to the head of Litton Canada, Ron Keating," Kent said, "and he thinks the bombing will only set back production of the guidance system by two days, thanks to the help of the hundreds of employees who gave up their weekend to clean up this mess."

Fraser leafed through the pile of pamphlets Kent had given him and found that two groups were spearheading the civil disobedience actions at Litton: The Alliance for Non-Violent Action and the Cruise Missile Conversion Project. As though he had read his mind, Kent began to summarize the information he had about the latter group. "For the past two years, a Toronto-based group, called the Cruise Missile Conversion Project, which I'll refer to as the CMCP, has been leading the protests here at the plant. Their goal is to convince the workers and management to convert the plant to what they call socially useful production such as guidance systems for public transit. They claim to be non-violent and leaflet the factory gates every week with pamphlets like the ones you have in front of you.

"But we've noticed that their tactics have been escalating over the past two years. They started out with prayer meetings and leafleting, then moved on to pouring red paint and broken glass and painting doves on the plant property. The elements within this group that have moved on to property destruction could have moved on to bombing. It's not out of the realm of possibility. Anyway, I'm going to leave you guys to interview some of the employees and look around the place. If you have any more questions, you know where to reach me." With a quick smile, Kent walked out of the security room, presumably en route to his car parked outside.

Despaireux raised his eyebrows at Fraser as though to say, "Who the heck does he think he is?" Then he went over to Green to check on who was available for an interview. Green gave them some names, and then pointed to a couple of men standing outside by the bombed-out building. "Come on," Despaireux said, motioning for Fraser to follow. The two detectives walked casually over to two Litton employees engrossed in conversation. It was a windy October day and Fraser shivered under his flimsy trenchcoat. He reminded himself to bring winter clothes the next time he came to Toronto. After a short conversation with the men, the detectives decided to take a trip to a nearby hospital to interview two of the injured Litton employees.

Fraser hated the antiseptic smell of hospital rooms. They always made him feel faint, so when they entered the room where James Tayles and Barry Blunden were recuperating, he took a seat between their beds, leaving Despaireux to do the talking. Tayles lay propped up on pillows with a huge bandage around his head. The nurse at the reception area had told them he was recovering from surgery on his inner ear and had a foot injury that was not considered serious. On the small bed beside him, Blunden appeared in much worse shape. He also wore a head bandage, but his eyes were swollen shut and his face was black and blue.

"Yep, I'm the guy saved by a cigarette," joked Tayles, smiling painfully. "If I hadn't left my office for a smoke, I would've been dead for sure."

"Why's that, sir?" asked Despaireux gently. Fraser concentrated on taking notes.

"The van was parked right outside my office. I was in mid-plant having a smoke break when the bomb went off. The last thing I remember was Terry Chikowski running by us yelling to get out of the building because there was a bomb parked outside my office." Tayles gave the detectives a piercing look and said, "The police were outside looking at the van and we were inside not knowing a thing. I'm disgusted it took so long for them to tell us."

"What do you mean?" asked Despaireux, not letting Tayles's tone of voice get to him.

"Well, I was told by Max Spencer that security staff were warned about the bomb ten minutes earlier but didn't tell any of us until twenty seconds before the blast." He coughed, then seemed to reconsider his attitude. "I guess I could be bitter, but I'm just happy to be alive. You know it's funny but I was just saying to my wife, before the bombing, that I would give anything to take a year off work to be a father to my kids instead of coming home from work every night, a grumpy old man. I hate to admit it, but in a way I'm kind of happy. I'm more relaxed and less intense. If anything goes wrong, I just tell myself, I'm lucky to be alive. You know, I don't even feel bitter towards whoever did the bombing. They're foolish but I guess they did it because they believe in what they're doing and they'll pay the price whenever they do get caught."

"That's nuts!" his roommate rasped from the other bed. "They're a bunch of idiots and I hope they rot in jail!"

Despaireux turned towards him. "What do you remember about what happened?"

"They tell me I was hit by flying steel, but I don't know," Blunden continued through swollen lips. "That night is totally blank. It's right out of my mind. I don't even remember the security guard running in to warn us. It was just a reaction in my mind." Even as he spoke the last few words, he seemed to fade away, presumably from the effects of his medication. Despaireux looked over at Fraser, who motioned towards the door. It was obvious that the two injured men didn't have much more to offer. The detectives thanked them, then tiptoed out of the room.

"I think we should interview some of these so-called peace activists," suggested Despaireux. "Maybe they'll have more information than we got from the reward money in B.C."

✳ **27** ✳

In the days following the bombing we walked around the apartment in a daze, searching for a way out of a nightmare from which we couldn't wake up. No matter which way we looked, we couldn't justify or escape the horrible reality that we had screwed up, big time. My initial plan of escape, suicide, began to fade along with newscasts assuring us that no one had died or been critically injured, although this in no way absolved us of the inescapable guilt of having seriously injured innocent people.

Every time I looked at Julie, she seemed to be pacing and wringing her hands and moaning about how regrettable it was that we had used so much dynamite, that we had not bombed the plant when there was no possibility of anyone being inside it, and that the cops had her voice recorded. Brent spent a lot of time scribbling notes in a desperate attempt to find the perfect words of explanation and apology to add to our communiqué. I smoked and slept, hoping that the next time I woke up everything would seem all right again. Being awake was painful — I could never find a perspective that would bring peace of mind.

We had originally planned to mail our communiqué the morning after the bombing. But, given the injuries, we postponed that step until we came up with a satisfactory explanation. In a country in an imminent state of revolution, injuries would be seen as an inevitable repercussion of struggle between opposing forces. But in Canada injuries would be seen in a different light. They would certainly sway most people to support the police and government in whatever actions seemed necessary to quash the anti-cruise movement. Even without the injuries, we knew, it would have been difficult to gain the support of the general population for the bombing.

"I want to go back to B.C.," announced Julie, looking over at

Brent. He ignored her comment until he had finished carefully cutting out a clipping from *The Toronto Star* about the bombing. He was collecting newspaper clippings in a scrapbook, which I called his paper trophy collection whenever I was mad at him. I had reminded him that serial killers usually collected some keepsake from their victims and that police psychologists called the collections "trophies." He would counter by saying that my association of collecting newspaper articles with criminal behaviour reflected my disintegrating political identity. The stress from the bombing aftermath was beginning to undermine our relationship.

"What?" he said distractedly.

"I want to go back to B.C.," Julie repeated firmly. "I don't feel comfortable in Toronto and I miss Gerry."

Brent leafed through another paper, then said, "Me and Ann are going back too, you know, in a few days. We just have to mail this communiqué out. I'm just about ready with the apology section. You can't wait?"

"No. I hate it here and I'd rather just take a bus. I'm paranoid knowing they have my voice on tape. What if they play it on TV and somebody, like the landlord, recognizes it?"

"Nobody will recognize your voice on tape. It won't sound that clear."

"I don't want to stay." She was adamant.

"All right, take a bus back — it's your decision. You'll have to pay back the two hundred dollars it will cost."

It struck me as a cold response to Julie's needs and fears. I wondered if he was reacting this way because he felt Julie was rejecting him by leaving early. Secretly, I found myself feeling relieved that she wanted to go back by herself. The jealousy and insecurity I felt around Brent and Julie's physical horseplay were mounting and adding to a stress level I could barely cope with. Before the bombing, I'd argued with Brent over her again and again when we were alone and had come to the conclusion that I would not continue living with him when we got back to Vancouver if we had to live with Julie. He had sloughed off my accusations as crazy.

"Here," he said, pulling some papers from under the newspapers. "Read this and see what you think." He turned and handed me three pages under the heading "Apology." Then, as though to drive a dagger deeper into Julie's heart, he asked her, "Are you absolutely sure the security guy heard your warning?" He knew she was touchy about the phone call. We hadn't mentioned it since the night of the bombing. In the privacy of our bedroom, Brent and I had already discussed the possibility that Julie felt as though the injuries were her fault because she hadn't repeated the phone warning when the guard had asked her to.

"Yes!" she almost shouted. "I already told you that I read it once clearly and then when he asked me to repeat it, I just started and then hung up, but he heard me the first time for sure!" I glanced up from the "Apology" and saw that Julie was visibly shaken.

"Brent," I said softly in an attempt to get him to lay off. "The bomb went off early. There's nothing any of us could have done to prevent that."

Julie didn't waste any time leaving. She went down the block to the phone booth, and when she returned she announced she would be taking a bus that afternoon to Vancouver. When she came out of the bathroom, her black hair was piled up under a shower cap and reeked of peroxide.

"I have to go down to the university to type this up, so we'll take you to the bus station," Brent said in a feeble attempt at apology. Julie didn't respond but continued bustling about, packing her things and trying on different clothes that she thought might make her look more like a student.

"I like the apology," I said to Brent. "You admit we made mistakes that others could learn from, like don't count on the cops clearing buildings. That's an important one. And of course the list of things we did to ensure no one would get hurt is good. It's very important everyone knows we had no intention of hurting anyone, not even the cops."

"It's really a drag that all these activists are drawing a line between us and them. I thought we might get some support, but I guess the injuries guaranteed that wouldn't happen," Brent said, ignoring my compliments. "Hey, here's a cool comment." He held up an alternative newspaper. He began to read a statement by Philip Berrigan, a well-known U.S. Catholic priest and peace activist. Berrigan argued that the real terrorists were Litton and other corporations and governments threatening the lives of every person on the planet. Still, Berrigan said, "All things being equal, bombs should not be a strategy of non-violence because there is not only the threat of injury and the threat to life that is implicit in using explosives but there is the reaction of people who are in a state of emerging consciousness."

"At least he pointed out that we are not the real terrorists," I said, trying to find some consolation in this statement.

The same article also quoted Jim Douglass, who had helped found the Ground Zero Centre for Non-Violent Action. Referring to underground guerrilla groups, Douglass said, "I think the process is also contrary to non-violence. It involves extreme secrecy and not taking responsibility for the action. It is only through a growth and acceptance of responsibility that we're going to stop the war making." Douglass pointed to the danger of becoming what it is you were trying to stop.

I took the paper from Brent and found another Berrigan quote: "However benighted such an attempt might be, it is better than doing nothing against war preparations, especially the nuclear kind."

"What's she doing?" asked Brent, referring to the sound of a hair blower in the washroom.

"She's getting ready to catch the bus to Vancouver. You could be a bit more sensitive."

"You're one to talk. If she knew what you were always saying about her behind her back, she'd have left before the bombing."

"That's your fault," I scowled at him. Just then Julie came bouncing out of the washroom — a completely different person. Her hair was a mousy brown and she wore a pair of glasses that definitely gave her a studious air. The decision to return to Vancouver and change of appearance had noticeably buoyed her spirits.

"How do I look?" she said parading in front of us, making me feel like a parent with a daughter searching for approval.

"Great!" said Brent. "Just like a young university student."

"Are you guys ready to go?" she asked.

"In two minutes," Brent said, getting up and collecting his papers. "I'm going to type this at the university and then mail it out today. The media should get it on the 19th. There's nine pages altogether, six under the heading Direct Action and three are the Apology. Do you want to read them?" He looked over at Julie. She just shook her head and continued packing her bags.

We arrived at the bus station downtown just in time for Julie to buy her ticket and board the bus. Although the past month had been intense and our emotional bond had certainly grown, there was a great distance between Julie and me. In a sense, she was already gone. After a few quick kisses and superficial reassurances that we would see each other when Brent and I returned to British

Columbia, she boarded the bus, just like any other student going home to her family. I let out my mixed feelings of sadness and relief in a long sigh, then turned to Brent.

"Where to now?" I asked.

"The university," he said cheerily. There was no time to dwell on Julie. Typing and mailing the communiqué demanded focus. We typed it up in an isolated area of the university library, wearing latex gloves and putting our own paper in the photocopy machine so the cops wouldn't be able to identify where the document had been produced. Now that we were the subjects of an extensive manhunt, we couldn't afford to make one mistake. While Brent typed and photocopied, I acted as his eyes and ears, watching and listening intently for snoopy or accidental witnesses to our work.

"So where did you get all the facts in that communiqué?" I asked as we strolled down University Avenue towards a set of mailboxes.

"Mainly from a leaflet put out by the Toronto Disarmament Network that they distributed for this upcoming Refuse the Cruise rally they're having in Ottawa on October 30th," he said.

"Once the cops analyse the communiqué, they'll no doubt figure, at the least, that there's a Toronto connection with Direct Action because of the facts you lifted from that leaflet."

"I guess. So?"

"Nothing. Anyway, when do you think we should hit the road?"

"I think we should start cleaning up and make sure we don't leave the slightest hint of who we are, then leave."

"Sounds good to me," I agreed, then doubled over as a sharp pain in my gut engulfed me.

"What's wrong?" Brent asked, putting his hand on my back.

"I've been getting these sharp pains in my lower intestines. I'm going to have to see a doctor."

"Why don't we go to a clinic after we mail these things?"

Later, at the clinic, the doctor told me I had an infection in my uterus and should have my IUD removed the next day. It was a strange twist of fate, because it coincided with a growing desire to have a baby. Often when I was out jogging, I would make up stories to amuse myself that inevitably involved having a baby. This habit of making up stories that seemingly unravelled on their own had stayed with me for as long as I can remember. If I bothered to analyse them, they were often dreams of what I wanted for my future or my present. After all, when I was a child the main character in my fantasies had always been the girl I wanted to be, living in pioneer days on a horse farm with a couple of brothers and having lots of adventures with my horse. Before I'd met Brent and Doug, the stories had centred around being this totally heroic, courageous urban guerrilla, fighting selflessly for a world in which nature, animals, and people could live in peace and harmony without industrial destruction. Now the stories had taken a dramatic turn, moving away from being an urban guerrilla towards living this peaceful life on a small farm with horses, friends, and community, but most of all children.

The next day, after my IUD was removed, I gingerly broached the question of having children and beginning to wind down our armed struggle strategy. I was afraid Brent would see me as a sellout — but perhaps he harboured similar unexpressed thoughts. I was wrong.

"You want to have a *baby*?" he said with genuine surprise.

"I've been thinking about it."

"I really can't see myself living on a farm and having kids."

"Well, it wouldn't have to be permanent," I said, backtracking. I was as needy for Brent's love as I was for having a baby. "We could take a break for a few years and let the heat die down and give the movement a chance to develop. There's not a large enough revolutionary movement in Canada yet to sustain an ongoing campaign of guerrilla struggle anyway. After a while, it would become counterproductive. If the cops start raiding people's homes and arresting supporters, they might succeed in scaring people away from supporting us or starting their own cells. We're only introducing the idea of more militant actions into the radical community. There's no way that five of us could continue waging this kind of campaign by ourselves."

"This is my identity," Brent said. "This is what I've always wanted to do. I just can't see myself settling down and farming."

"You don't have to farm. I really just have this strong maternal instinct to have a baby. I want it even if you don't." This last statement surprised even me.

"Let's at least give it some thought," Brent said, with a note of reconciliation in his voice. But from that day on, he took it upon himself to wear a condom every time we had sex.

* * *

The Litton bombing had certainly not been well received by the disarmament groups. They not only denounced the bombing but also even speculated that it may have been an attempt to discredit the movement. Peace activists were particularly angry, because they claimed that the communiqué presumed that the bombing would have a positive effect on their efforts. The only impact that the bombing had on the peace movement, according to Juliet Huntley of the Christian Movement for Peace, would be to intimidate people from getting involved. As for any publicity value the bombing may have had, the general consensus of the peace movement seemed to be that the negative impact on the public's perception of the peace movement far outweighed the value of a few more people knowing about Litton's contribution to the arms race. If anything, peace activists believed that the bombing garnered more public sympathy for Litton and the police, giving them a green light to use whatever force they deemed necessary at future demonstrations.

The communiqué had also criticized non-violent strategies and called for more militant actions, inspiring Murray MacAdam of the Cruise Missile Conversion Project to write, "Society is violent enough and the cruise missile is just a horrible example of that violence. The Direct Action bombing is perpetuating this violence." Juliet Huntley wrote that the obvious rebuttal to Direct Action's strategy was the result of their own bombing: it was ineffective in stopping Litton and didn't inspire peace groups. In fact it scared the Litton workers and public, making it even more difficult to gain their support in stopping the arms race. Both Huntley and MacAdam wrote that it was important for peace groups to work together in solidarity with other movements for social change — a process that was clearly impossible for a group like Direct Action.

✳ **28** ✳

"Doug!" I wrapped my arms around his neck and held him close to me, breathing in his clean, natural smell. "Oh, we missed you!" I pulled back and looked at his smiling face. He seemed genuinely happy to see us. Brent stood back a little, a big smile on his face as well.

"Come on in!" Doug stepped aside so we could go down the steps into his little basement apartment at 3895 Windermere Street. The aroma of Earl Grey tea permeated the tiny white kitchen. Doug sat down on one of the plastic chairs, but we chose to stand. We had just spent a week driving across the country.

"I guess you read the papers?" asked Brent.

"Yeah. Not so good eh?" He smiled at us. Doug knew about the speculation that when the bomb squad arrived and turned on their radios, the electronic frequency must have triggered the timing device.

I stated the obvious. "We should have spent more time checking for a time and place where no one would be around. That was a big mistake."

I suggested a walk in Stanley Park. Doug loved walking in the big city park. We drove down and spent the rest of the afternoon walking and talking. It was invigorating to be able to talk to someone else again. For the past two months we had virtually spoken to no one other than Julie. It had dawned on me that our social isolation prevented us from discussing the pros and cons of what we were doing in any depth. Even though I was still committed to carrying out militant actions, during the times when I experienced doubts or considered taking a break I found myself hesitating to express these feelings. Most of the time I didn't want to be labelled a sell-out, and, even more, I didn't want to be one. The level of commitment needed to take actions carrying such extreme risks meant we had banished all doubts from our minds, or at least had resolved not to express them. Expressing doubt in situations of adversity can be like infecting people with weak immune systems. If expressed often enough, the doubt will begin to rot their resolve until they no longer have the commitment to carry on.

I often wondered if perhaps each one of us had doubts that we were afraid to express for fear the others would think us weak, afraid, or willing to sell out our militant politics for an easier life as a legal activist. Wouldn't it be ironic if we continued carrying out militant actions even though each individual would rather stop and live a normal life again? Even though these thoughts had occurred to me, most of the time I was still committed to continuing our work. Still, I had to admit, the Litton bombing had created cracks in my resolve to carry on as an urban guerrilla indefinitely. Every now and then, some light would make its way through those cracks and illuminate a different life: either the old fantasy of living on a farm or the newer one of living in Vancouver as a radical and perhaps carrying out a few small actions now and again.

For hours we talked, analysing our mistakes in the Litton

action and discussing possible future actions, but never once did we discuss the possibility of stopping. The closest I had come to this taboo topic was the baby issue with Brent, which he had quickly vetoed. For the time being, I wrestled with my maternal instinct on my own, vowing never to broach the topic again. I had felt embarrassed admitting that I wanted to have a baby more than to be a heroic warrior for the salvation of the planet.

After our reunion with Doug, we headed over to Julie and Gerry's basement apartment at 1947 Charles Street. I was not as genuinely excited about that reunion. I knocked lightly on the door. When Gerry opened it, I could see the anxiety in his eyes behind the wide smile that cracked his face.

"Heh, you guys!" he yelled, probably to warn Julie of our presence. She appeared behind him a few moments later, a feeble smile on her lips. Her brown hair was tousled almost as though we had interrupted them in bed.

I said the obvious. "I hope we aren't disturbing you?"

"Oh no," laughed Gerry. "Sex is always more exciting when someone is knocking on the door."

"Gerry!" Julie sighed.

Brent stepped in, uninvited. "Have you been back long?"

"No, just a little over a week," Julie said, straightening her hair.

"She sure gave me a scare," chuckled Gerry. "When I opened the door, I thought she was the librarian coming to get me for overdue books." He went off to get some beers.

Julie just shook her head. "It's been the best time we've had together," she said softly. "We've just been having fun for a change."

I looked around the apartment. The walls were covered in drawings and posters that Julie had made. It was a homey little place with a lot of attention to detail. Old lamp covers had been replaced with colourful pieces of cloth, dried gourds were piled in wicker baskets, and faded throw rugs covered the worn, wooden floor. Julie had obviously put effort into making this place a home — unlike myself, who usually treated a place like a hotel room I didn't plan on living in for very long.

"I guess you want your money back?" she said to Brent.

He looked somewhat taken aback. "That isn't why we came over."

"All we have is unemployment insurance, so it'll be awhile," she said, ignoring his comment.

"So how have you been doing?" I asked, trying to break the ice.

"Jules has been terrified about her voice being recorded," Gerry said. "We just didn't foresee that happening, which was pretty stupid."

"Yeah," agreed Julie. "I don't know why none of us thought of that."

I knew she felt bitter because she was only supposed to play a minor role, and as it turned out the only evidence they had, so far as we knew, was connected to her.

"So what are you going to do?" asked Brent, directing his question to Gerry.

"I don't know. I guess get a job. I'm kinda hard up for money. I can't finish the cabin with no money."

"You don't want to play in the band anymore?" I asked.

"No. I'm just burnt out from that," he said. Julie's old dog Rex came waddling out of another room, whining. Julie squatted down and wrapped her arms around him. There wasn't much to say so we excused ourselves, saying we had to get home before Doug went to bed.

At least Doug was genuinely happy to see us. He invited us to spend the night on his floor, and we accepted. Unlike Julie and Gerry, Doug had a spartan abode — clean and practical with no frills or knick-knacks. He had spent a lot of his time with his girlfriend, Rachel, and seemed in good spirits. I felt a little lost.

On the drive back to British Columbia Brent had suggested getting a house in Vancouver, where we could all live together like one big, happy family, but once there the reality was quite disillusioning. I did not want to live with Julie and I had the distinct impression that she did not want to live with us. Doug also stated clearly that he wanted to continue living alone at his Windermere address, and I was completely sure that Gerry would go wherever Julie was. I thought about Nick, but the memories did not inspire strong emotions. Brent expressed a desire to see Angie, which, surprisingly, did not bother me. I liked her and didn't feel jealous of her relationship with Brent.

I rolled over on the mattress Doug had put on the floor for us. Brent's breathing was deep. Somehow the whole idea of being a guerrilla seemed so much more righteous as a dream. Just like most dreams, the realization is often quite disappointing.

When we got back from Ontario, Brent and I did an accounting of our financial situation and determined that we could live another three or four months without any income. But rather than waiting until we were completely broke, we decided to begin casing for another robbery to finance our political plans. After the last robbery we had divided the proceeds equally, and Doug felt he would be able to go on for another year with the money he had.

Despite our cool reunion with Julie and Gerry, we began to spend a considerable amount of time with them again, probably because they were the only people, other than Doug, we could talk to. Surprisingly, when Julie and Gerry heard our plans, they were eager to participate. Their unemployment insurance was on the verge of ending and they wanted to continue working with us, or so they said.

The relationship between the four of us had become quite strange. In fact, there were two separate realities: the one in which all four of us participated, and the one that we experienced as couples alone in our bedrooms. When we were all together, we would reinforce each other's political morale and drive, urging each other on in our plans. When we were alone in our bedrooms, we expressed doubts and fears over both the idea of a robbery and carrying out future militant actions. No matter how much tension arose between us, we never broke down and exposed the private reality that we guarded so carefully. And so we carried on, harbouring this false belief that the other couple was committed to carrying out the robbery and future militant actions. Only Doug managed to remain apart without having to breach the sacred front of total commitment that we all managed to maintain publicly. He had quite masterfully managed to appear completely involved with us, while not being involved at all.

Julie, Gerry, Brent, and I decided to rent a small house on the outskirts of Burnaby, using false ID, so that we wouldn't be living in the same neighbourhood as our radical friends. I relented to living with Julie because it seemed the only logical thing to do, considering we were going to carry out a robbery together. But I vowed to myself and Brent that after the robbery I would live alone with him.

Even though we were clearly not living completely underground, we were trying to live as hidden a lifestyle as possible, which meant limiting our social contacts to a few close friends. In my case that meant no one beyond our group. I did not find it difficult to sacrifice my relationship with Nick, mainly because I had never been deeply in love with him. Brent still saw Angie on occasion, though only after engaging in counter-surveillance manoeuvres, and Julie and Gerry saw their families once in a while. Doug saw Rachel, his mother, and Saphie, but again only after taking extensive counter-surveillance measures. None of us ever took anyone home, and we had no phones. We were aware that our links with the outside world were weak points in our security, but our experience in Calgary led us to believe we would rather take this risk than be unhappy living in total isolation.

The house we rented in Burnaby was behind a large mall. One afternoon Brent came back from shopping and casually mentioned something he had witnessed. "I was walking through the main floor of the Woolco near the pet section when I spotted this Brink's guard coming out of the accounting area, carrying a money bag in one hand and his other hand dangling down near his revolver." We were all ears.

"So I followed him along a hallway to the exit, where the Brink's truck was waiting for him," he said, noticing that he had piqued our attention. "Anyway, I was struck by the fact he was alone and I figured that a large Woolco store at Christmas would probably have a hell of a lot of money. It would be easy to rob the guy in that part of the store and have a car parked in a different area of the parking lot."

"A Brink's guard!" I exclaimed.

"Why not?" he said. "If we're going to do a robbery, I would rather go for a lot of money and not have to do one again for a couple of years than do a smaller one and then have to do one again in six months."

"Yeah, I agree," Julie said. Her characteristic enthusiasm had returned. "What about a depot?"

"You've got to be kidding?" I said. I was still not reconciled to the idea of robbing a Brink's guard.

"Now that would be a challenge!" Brent laughed. From there the conversation took off into a flight of fantasy in which we began inventing hilarious stories of absurd robbery scenarios, but after a while we settled back down to the matter of the Brink's guard.

"Anyway," concluded Brent, "next time you're over in the mall, keep your eyes open for the Brink's guard and make note of the time."

Even though initially I thought the idea of robbing a Brink's guard was extreme, the more I thought about it the more sense it made. It would be less risky in the long run to do one big robbery every couple of years than a bunch of small ones more often. The odds of getting caught were probably higher in the second scenario. The next day I made a point of going to the mall. Brent said he had spotted the guard at around one o'clock. I got there at noon and sat around outside on a bench, smoking and reading a magazine when, sure enough at 12:45, a Brink's truck pulled up. Casually I got up and moseyed on down to Woolco's pet section. By the time I got there the guard must already have gone into the office area, which was good because I didn't want him to see me. It wasn't difficult killing time looking at the fish, and after ten minutes the guard came out. I glanced over at him without turning my head. He was a big, chubby guy who smiled and had a greeting for every employee he passed. The way he sauntered along gave me the impression that he was not the least bit paranoid or on red alert for robbers. He also carried a nice, big bag, which I hoped carried cash rather than cheques. But that's the thing about large department stores back then — the majority of transactions were in cash. In the early 1980s, credit cards and cheques and bank debits were not yet the most popular means of making small purchases.

I had found it irritating the way Julie had boasted about wanting to do a Brink's robbery — she had never before done a robbery — but I had to admit that the situation did look enticing. As I walked across the parking lot back to our house, I decided we should set up a casing schedule amongst the four of us to see if this place would be the best place to rob. Wouldn't it be a weird twist of fate to rob the mall right behind our own house?

* * *

"Hmmmmmm." Fraser scratched his head and stared at the name on the pad in front of him: "Francis Theresa Doyle." That was the name of the box holder for post-office box 790A, Vancouver, through which The Friends of Durutti got their mail. Yesterday morning, October 26, he had received an important call from Staff Sergeant Kent in Toronto asking him to follow up on a tip from a reporter in Toronto. Apparently a young reporter, Lorne Slotnick, who had once been associated with the radical left in Toronto, had brought a pamphlet he had found in a left-wing bookstore to Jock Ferguson, another reporter at *The Globe and Mail*. They had noticed the style of writing used in the pamphlet, *Resistance*, was very similar to that used in the communiqués distributed by Direct Action, and they decided to pass on this information to Kent. Their tip had elicited some interest from Kent, not only because there was some substance to the reporters' hunch, but because *Resistance* reprinted communiqués by armed struggle groups from all over the world and included editorials apparently written by a group called The Friends of Durutti, based in Vancouver. Since Fraser didn't have a clue as to who Durutti was, he had gone off to do a bit of library research. He found out that Buenaventura Durutti was a Spanish anarchist active in the Spanish civil war of the 1930s.

Now that he had obtained the name of the box holder, Fraser had to find out who she was and where she lived. Maybe, just maybe, she would lead them to Direct Action. As the RCMP undercover officer in the Vancouver Integrated Intelligence Unit responsible for gathering information on the radical community, Fraser had the best files on political activists in the city as well as a hands-on knowledge of these people, so it was only logical that he had been asked to find the name of the box holder. It had been easy — he had simply gone to the post office, shown them his badge, and told them why he wanted the information, and the clerk had handed him the form Francis Doyle had filled out. As a home address she had written 1947 Commercial Drive.

Fraser got up from his desk and walked over to his grey metal file cabinet, where he stored all his information on the radical left. The name Francis Theresa Doyle did not ring any bells. He opened the drawer with file headings A to D and ran his finger along until he came to a file headed Saphie Francis Doyle. Even as he pulled it out, he found himself instinctively suspecting that this little tidbit of information was the key to unlocking the identity of Direct Action. He carefully took the two-and-a-half by four-inch file card to his desk and sat down before looking at it. He used to practise this delayed response when he opened his presents as a little boy at Christmas.

As he began to read the little penned notations, he clearly recalled a fall day a couple of years earlier when he had chatted with Doyle about a spray-painting charge he had laid a few years before that. He could also recall in detail the time with the shopping cart filled with laundry, strewn all over the road, plus Doyle's dark-haired girlfriend and the tall woman with them. At the bottom of the card he had written in block letters, "KNOWN ASSOCIATES," and then the name Brent Taylor, and their mutual address of 2347 St. Catherines Street.

Now he was really excited. Taylor's name jumped out at him. He had suspected Taylor from the beginning. The pieing of Joe Clark, the demonstrations, the benefits — Taylor was one of the most notable anarchists in Vancouver. He jumped up from his chair and strode quickly over to his file cabinet and pulled out the file cards on Taylor. There were five of them. Reading them carefully, he noticed the address at St. Catherines Street was still the last known address for him. He dialled Despaireux's number.

"Jean," he said. "I've got the name and address of the box holder and another possible suspect. I have good justification, besides the *Resistance* pamphlet, to get permission to have them put under surveillance. Jean, I think this is the best lead we've had so far. I'm quite excited about this."

"Good," answered Despaireux flatly. He never got excited. "Meet me in my office as soon as you can with the info and we'll talk to Anderson."

Fraser hung up the phone without saying goodbye. He threw his trenchcoat over his shoulders and walked briskly down the hall to the elevator. Inside the elevator, he scanned the file cards on Taylor and shook his head. Of course. He had to be involved! Despaireux's office door was open. Fraser set the file cards on the desk in front of him, leaving Despaireux to read them himself. Despaireux sat back, lit a smoke, and read the cards, twice. "Saphie Francis Doyle is not the same as Francis Theresa Doyle," he finally stated.

"She just changed her middle name to the first and threw in Theresa. Probably after the saint," explained Fraser. "There is no other Doyle in my files, and Saphie has all the markings of a suspect. She's been charged with spray-painting lesbian and political slogans on walls, which means she has a propensity for crime and she associates and lives with a known anarchist, Taylor, who advocates violence and has a history of small-time illegal political activity. He pied Joe Clark in '77 and was kicked out of the military for insubordination. He's been charged with shoplifting and ticketed for spray-painting revolutionary anarchist slogans a number of times. It's all small-time stuff, but he may have graduated to more upscale activities."

"Well, I agree this warrants surveillance. I'll call Anderson," said Despaireux, picking up the phone. He got Corporal John Anderson of the Security Service on the line, explained the situation, and asked permission to put surveillance on the house. After a few minutes, Despaireux put down the phone and turned to Fraser.

"They're going to put the Watchers on them starting tomorrow. What is that? The twenty-ninth. He wants you to go down to his office now with everything you have on Doyle and Taylor, including photographs."

"Why don't they use CLEU?" asked Fraser, referring to his own section, the Canadian Law Enforcement Unit.

"At this point, we have no evidence these people have committed a crime so we can't justify CLEU. The Security Service is strictly an intelligence-gathering outfit and they can cover their butts with national security clauses, which we can't. Once they have information that proves a crime has or is about to be committed, they'll hand the surveillance back to us."

"Okay," Fraser said, getting up and collecting his precious file cards. "I'm going to drop into that leftist bookstore Spartacus on my way down and see if I can't find a copy of *Resistance*."

"Yeah, but don't be too long," advised Despaireux. "They want to get organized for this surveillance tomorrow."

* * *

Len Desroches was impressed with the turnout on Parliament Hill — an estimated fifteen thousand people. Even though he would never have been involved with a bombing, he had to admit that ever since the Litton bombing, attendance was up at all the protests associated with the anti-nuclear movement. He was a dedicated member of the Cruise Missile Conversion Project, but since the bombing that organization had more or less disappeared, so most of the organizing had fallen into the hands of the Alliance for Non-Violent Action (ANVA).

The differences between the two groups were fewer than their similarities, but essentially the ANVA situated its opposition to nuclear war in an anti-imperialist context, whereas the CMCP did not question the social order but simply wanted the prevailing powers to abandon the manufacture and use of nuclear weapons. At times Len wondered if he shouldn't change his allegiance to the ANVA, but as a member of the direct action collective, a subgroup of the CMCP, he felt his needs were better served there. He was instrumental in co-ordinating demonstrations, leafleting, and civil disobedience actions. In fact, he had been quite effective in organizing the busing of hundreds of people from Toronto to Ottawa for this Refuse the Cruise Rally.

He looked around with pride at the thousands of people milling about and standing listening to the speakers on the platform in front of him. A surge of adrenalin rushed through his body as he screamed, along with the rest of the crowd, "REFUSE THE CRUISE" over and over again.

"Brian!" he yelled, seeing his friend standing a few rows in front of him. The friendly face turned around and yelled back, "Come up here!" Len pushed through the crowds until he could reach his friend, Brian Burch. "Great turnout eh?"

"Yeah, better than a rock concert. I hate to admit it, Len, but I think the bombing did bring Litton and the cruise into the public eye. Before the bombing, when I talked to people about Litton, they'd say, Litton who? Now they immediately know what I'm talking about and jump right into the conversation with an opinion whether it's pro or con. How did the leafleting go last week?"

"Not good. The moderates in the group aren't even coming out, and the workers are pissed. I guess Litton's spent around two million dollars on added security, so they're not only mad about possibly losing their jobs but they blame us for the fact they don't feel safe anymore."

"I guess having a name like the direct action collective doesn't help, eh?"

"Yeah. The workers have to go in through a guarded gate and you should see the fence now. It's super high and covered in barbed wire. One of the workers that knows me said he heard Litton might not get to bid on the guidance system for an advanced version of the cruise missile. I guess the head honchos in California don't like the negative publicity from the bombing and don't want their company becoming a headline feature."

"So what do you think about this peace petition caravan that Operation Dismantle is organizing?" Brian asked. "You know the one they're sending across the country asking parliament to oppose the cruise missile testing?"

Len shrugged. "They might be distancing themselves from the bombing, but I heard they've tripled their membership in the past year to two thousand. You could say the bombing and the protesters have done wonders for their membership numbers."

The two friends smiled wryly at one another, then focused on the speaker trying to cut through the noise of the thousands of people milling about below her. For Canada, especially on the last cold day in October, this was a successful demonstration.

Under Surveillance

✳ **29** ✳

Fraser got up at the crack of dawn as usual on Friday, October 29, and that day he couldn't wait to get going. He had been asked to be integrally involved in the surveillance of Saphie Doyle and Brent Taylor, since he was the most familiar with the suspects. He rolled out of bed quietly so as not to wake up his wife and tip-toed down the stairs to the kitchen. He opened the curtains and looked out at the beautiful pink and purple hues that the rising sun cast upon the downy clouds. He sighed and marvelled at the majesty of the universe, then put the kettle on.

Sitting down in the dim light of the kitchen, he placed a page of typed notes in front of him to read while he ate his cereal. He wanted to brush up on the RCMP Security Service's Watchers, since he would be working with them for a while. The Watchers were a ten-member team supplied by the Security Service to gather information until the Force had enough evidence to be certain that a criminal act had been or was about to be committed. They would often be employed only for this task. It would not be unusual to find small Asian ladies, short fat men, old men with glasses, and women who looked like housewives working for the Watchers. The team of ten was usually split into five pairs, each with a vehicle so one person could work on foot while the other waited nearby to pick them up.

The Watchers Service originated in the 1950s as a single surveillance unit, but by the 1960s the service had been established in a number of cities. Vancouver got its first Watcher service to gather intelligence on Soviet ships suspected of carrying intelligence officers on board, using the city to gain access to Western Canada, because travel is restricted for Ottawa-based agents using diplomatic cover. One of their early cases involved a Vancouver post office clerk, George Victor Spencer, accused of feeding information, including names on gravestones, to the Soviet Union.

Fraser smiled and figured he would not actually be used in the field — he did look very policeman-like. The kettle was whistling furiously. After making a coffee, he grabbed the pages off the table and left.

When he arrived at John Anderson's office in the RCMP building, the Watcher team was already there, sitting around while Anderson prepared the photos of Taylor and Doyle that were to be projected on a large screen at the front of the room. What immediately struck Fraser was just what an odd assortment of people was in the room. Sitting at the front were an older Chinese couple, speaking in Chinese, who looked just like any immigrants you would see in the Chinese market area of the Downtown Eastside. A couple of young women with permed hair and polyester pants would have blended in perfectly in any mall. A large Italian-looking fellow got up and poured himself some coffee. He would definitely not pass the fitness section of the RCMP examination, Fraser thought. The remaining five shared the one common feature of the group: it looked like they would never pass a test to become a police officer.

After giving a short synopsis of the case, Anderson instructed the Watchers to be very careful and assume that the suspects could be armed and dangerous even though they might appear young and innocent. Then he handed the podium over to Fraser, who, after repeating everything he knew about Doyle and Taylor, displayed the enlarged photographs he had obtained of the suspects and their known associates.

It was well past noon before the Watchers headed off to the two locations where Doyle and Taylor had last been officially residing. Fraser spent the rest of the day with Anderson exchanging notes and ideas while they waited for communication from the Watchers. Finally, at 9:13 p.m., the radio crackled as the two observers at 2347 St. Catherines Street, where both Taylor and Doyle had resided, called in to report some movement. An unidentified white man was observed leaving and then walking to the bus stop on Broadway. According to the description, he didn't sound like Taylor, but that didn't discourage Fraser. For the next two hours, the Watchers followed the man from one Downtown Eastside bar to the next until finally they lost him heading south in a cab at 11:15 p.m. Exhausted, Fraser drove home and dropped into bed.

* * *

On October 30 the surveillance at 2347 St. Catherines Street observed the same man leave the house in the late morning, and later return. In the afternoon he came out again, but this time with a woman, who did not match any known description. The two of them headed off downtown to the bars again, returning home in the late afternoon. Fraser was beginning to wonder if either Taylor or Doyle still lived there. If they were responsible for the bombings, he doubted very much that they would still be living at a known address.

The surveillance at 1947 Commercial Drive was a little more rewarding. In the early evening a young woman arrived and entered an apartment in the building. While she was inside, the Watchers identified the licence plates on her yellow Toyota as belonging to Linda Power, listed as living at 2006 East 6th Avenue. At Commercial Drive the woman picked up another woman and a young man. They left the young man at East 6th and headed downtown to the Roxy theatre, apparently to watch a movie, then returned home to East 6th for the night. Fraser and Anderson decided to put the East 6th address under surveillance and continue watching St. Catherines St., although Fraser was convinced that the suspects no longer lived there.

The next morning, October 31, they got their first big break. A young man and two women left the East 6th address and headed to Richmond in the yellow Toyota. At this point, the Watchers asked a Richmond RCMP officer working in the area to approach the Toyota and come up with an excuse to ID the occupants. He came back with a positive ID of Francis Theresa Doyle, who matched the description of Saphie. The other two occupants were ID'd as brother and sister. Even though the Watchers officially described the occupant of the car as being someone other than Saphie, Fraser was absolutely convinced that Theresa and Saphie were one and the same.

Each morning Fraser found himself waking up impatient to get to work even though his working hours were running from nine in the morning to well after midnight. He didn't have to stay at the office all that time, but as long as the surveillance was going on, he wanted to be there. Each day seemed to reveal another piece of the puzzle, and he couldn't wait to find the next. His police instincts told him they were hot on the trail. He didn't think Saphie was a main player in the Direct Action group, but he felt sure that she would lead them there. The closer they got, the more excited he became. He laughed to himself, wondering if he had been a bloodhound in his previous life.

When he arrived at work on November 1, one of the Watcher teams radioed in to report that it was impossible to put surveillance on the post box used by the Friends of Durruti because of its location inside the post office. But this bit of bad news was overshadowed by a new identification of Theresa Doyle. That morning Doyle appeared to be doing errands until around four o'clock in the afternoon when she went to a new address, 1947 Charles

Street, where she remained until around seven o'clock in the evening. She departed in a green Volkswagen van, driving towards the outer suburbs of the city, around Nootka and 22nd, where she met up with a new man. She spent about an hour and a half talking with him in the backyard of a school. When the Watchers lost them, they began driving up and down the back alleys behind the residential homes of the area until they spotted the same man coming out of a basement door at 3895 Windermere Street. His behaviour appeared odd, because he ran down the back alley onto 22nd and Lillooet for no apparent reason, and once again the Watchers lost visual contact with him. A quick tour of the neighbourhood found Doyle and the man parked in the green Volkswagen. A short time later they left for downtown Vancouver and went into the Capitol 6 Theatre on Granville and watched a movie. Afterwards, Doyle drove him back to the same neighbourhood. He must have left the car without the Watchers witnessing his exit, because one minute they could see him in the car but the next, after the car made a turn, he was no longer in the car with Doyle. The Watchers searched the neighbourhood but couldn't locate him. Since it was past eleven in the evening, they decided he had probably gone indoors for the night and discontinued their surveillance.

Questioning the Watchers thoroughly after their shift, Fraser concluded that the unidentified man with Doyle that evening had been making a conscious attempt to shake the surveillance. How could they know they were under surveillance? The Watchers were positive they had not been spotted, yet the young man and Doyle had appeared to be doing counter-surveillance manoeuvres. Fraser instructed them to be especially careful from now on and to change personnel frequently to avoid a positive identification. Despite his disappointment that the suspects seemed to be on to them, he was thrilled to have discovered this young man in Doyle's company. He was certainly acting suspiciously. Fraser couldn't wait for tomorrow.

In the first four days of surveillance, then, four pieces of the puzzle had emerged. Theresa Doyle had been located, or so Fraser believed. Addresses for her and her close friends had been found. A man with suspicious behaviour had been located, along with what might be his address, and two vehicles used by Theresa had been identified. Fraser could not have hoped for more.

November 2 did not disappoint either. The Watchers set up surveillance on both 1947 Commercial Drive and 1947 Charles

Street. The two street addresses had the same number, which was a weird coincidence, Fraser thought. Doyle was not an early riser. Around noon she headed out in the Volkswagen to a new address at 44 West 14th Avenue, where she picked up another young woman and man. They headed over to Pinky's Coin Laundry, presumably to do laundry — probably the same laundromat Doyle had been leaving the day Fraser had talked to her after she had tipped over her laundry cart. Afterwards she dropped off her friends and drove back to 22nd and Nootka, where she had been the night before. After parking the green Volkswagen van, she walked to the rear of 3895 Windermere and stayed inside for about three hours. At 6:30 p.m., a couple of people the Watchers couldn't identify as either male or female got into the van, but, the Watchers observed, there were more people in the van than they had witnessed entering it. They drove to a Wendy's restaurant, where the Watchers were able to confirm that Doyle and another woman and two men were inside. After they had eaten Doyle dropped the three people back at Windermere, then returned alone to 1947 Commercial Drive with a large green plastic bag.

Fraser was elated. Once again his bloodhound instincts told him that the people at Windermere were close to, perhaps even part of, the Direct Action group. Any activity around this address was accompanied by suspicious behaviour, which could only be interpreted as counter-surveillance manoeuvres. Only guilty people would act as though they were being followed. Now they had Doyle, another woman, and two men associated with that address. What would November 3 bring?

Surveillance that day began at 1947 Commercial Drive, where Doyle, they believed, lived in apartment no. 4. Doyle's day began around 11:00 a.m., when she drove off to the house at 44 West 14th where a number of women appeared to live. Throughout the day much activity revolved around that house. Vehicles came and went. By day's end, the Watchers had five new vehicle's ID'd, all belonging to women, two of whom kissed on the lips. This kiss drew a lot of attention from the surveillance teams — apparently they had never before witnessed two women kissing for any length of time on the lips. Even Fraser couldn't help noticing this. Lesbians, he thought. Radical, anarchist lesbians. Probably radical, anarchist, terrorist lesbians!

The next morning Fraser arrived at the RCMP building to go over the results of a large number of freshly developed photographs taken by the Watchers the day before. Using the photographs, they wanted to see if they could identify the suspects at Windermere and the women at all the other addresses frequented by Doyle. Anderson had already prepared, for Fraser's use, a photo lineup of all the radicals under thirty with criminal records in Vancouver. Fraser also had his own photos, with the subjects already identified, from his work as an intelligence officer. In the six days of surveillance so far they had enough photos of known associates of Doyle's to cover an office desk. The problem would be that many of these people would not have criminal records and thus would not be identifiable.

As soon as Fraser looked down at the photospread on the desk, Brent Taylor's picture jumped out at him. He picked it up and set it aside, writing Brent Taylor underneath. Then systematically, he picked up one photo after another and carefully tried to match it with one in the photo lineup of people with criminal records. An hour later he stood quietly in front of a line of photos that he had managed to match up with identifications. He held up the photo of the first young man Doyle had contacted at the Windermere address: Doug Stewart. Then he held up a photo of a tall, blonde woman with a record of shoplifting: Ann Hansen. Using his personal photo files compiled during his surveillance of political benefits, he identified another young man seen at Windermere: Gerry Hannah, a punk musician.

Fraser was struck by the large proportion of suspects who were women — this was possibly because Doyle was a lesbian, or so he thought — but many of the women could not be identified because they had no criminal record and, as a consequence, no photo in the police files. Oh well, at least they had names to go with many of the faces, and this was a big accomplishment.

On November 4, surveillance began again at 1947 Commercial Drive. Around 12:30 p.m. Doyle left her apartment and got into the green Volkswagen with Ann Hansen and headed out of the city to Marine Drive. Doyle parked on the street while Hansen got out and walked around, apparently looking at a Red Hot Video outlet. After staying there for only a short while, and without going into any stores, they went back into the city and parked in a lane between West Hastings and Alberni streets. Once again Hansen got out of the van and seemed to be interested in the back door of 4439 West Hastings, which also turned out to be a Red Hot Video outlet. Without going into any establishments or purchasing anything, Doyle and Hansen proceeded on, this time driving to the Barnet Highway heading towards Port Moody. In Port Moody they stopped in the parking lot of the Carpetland Centre and walked together to yet another Red Hot Video outlet, at 2215 Coquitlam Avenue. Again, they did not go into any stores but headed south to New Westminster, where, to no one's surprise by now, there was also a Red Hot Video store. They passed by the store, parking a few blocks away. Following a by now well-established pattern, Hansen walked past the front of the Red Hot Video outlet at 7705 6th Street and continued to the end of the building, where she seemed to be checking it out. After she got back into the van with Doyle, the two drove directly to a Red Hot Video store on New Westminster, at Scott Road and 95th Avenue. This time they parked in the store lot, staring out at the store for about three minutes before taking off. Their last stop of the day was in the parking lot of the Langley Hotel. Hansen got out and walked past the local Red Hot Video store, giving it a good once-over. After an afternoon of cruising all over the lower mainland, Doyle dropped Hansen off a few blocks from 3895 Windermere and returned home to her apartment on Commercial Drive. The time was about 5:30 p.m.

When Fraser and Anderson got these reports from the Watchers, Anderson asked Fraser, "Do you see a common thread here?"

Fraser laughed. "I suspect they are not fans of Red Hot Video."

"We should do a check on RHV and see why all the fuss."

"My wife has a friend who works at the North Shore Women's Centre," Fraser said. "I'll give her a call and see if she can find out." Anderson nodded his head. Fraser reached over and dialled his wife. He rarely asked his wife for help, but he couldn't see what harm it could do for her to ask her friend about RHV. "I'm still here at the office," he told her. "I want to ask a favour. Could you call your friend Janice and ask her what she knows about the Red Hot Video stores? Don't mention me when you ask her. Just ask as a matter of personal interest. Thanks, honey. See you when I get home. Yes, it'll probably be late."

Fraser had assumed that the day's activities for his suspects was over, but he was wrong. The Watchers reported that Taylor was seen entering 3895 Windermere after Hansen, around 5:30 p.m. At 7:00 p.m. Taylor and Hansen got into a brown pickup truck with Alberta plates and headed down the Kingsway until they reached the Kingsway Mall. There the Watchers lost them, but meanwhile another team was following Doyle to the Van Auto Villa

Motel at 3090 Kingsway near the mall. Although visual contact with Taylor and Hansen was broken, the surveillance team believed they were also in the motel. Soon another older orange pickup truck arrived, driven by an unidentified female. Hansen left the motel briefly to retrieve a stuffed animal from the Alberta pickup. She returned to the motel, where two more people had arrived — obviously some kind of meeting or party was in progress. For several hours, no one came or left the motel room, but at 11:00 p.m. three people left in the orange pickup. They dropped one person off at the Windermere address, then returned to the motel. At midnight Doyle and two other women left the motel in separate vehicles. The two other women headed for 44 West 14th in a car with California plates, which had been ID'd the day before. The brown pickup with Alberta plates did not leave the motel that night.

It was just after midnight when Anderson's phone rang. "It's for you, Fraser. I think it's your wife."

Fraser sat and talked for awhile with her, then turned to Anderson and smiled. "Good news. My wife talked to her friend tonight and got some info on the Red Hot Video chain. Janice says Red Hot Video has been targeted for closure by women's groups since they first emerged in Vancouver in the early part of this year. Since then the chain has expanded to fourteen outlets, porn outlets. Women, including those in Janice's group, have been petitioning the B.C. Attorney-General's office to close them down under the obscenity laws for combining explicit sex and violence, but they've been ignored. Specifically, they submitted a Red Hot Video catalogue that contains pictures of violent pornography, but the A.G. refused to take legal action and stop its distribution. Janice says that someone not associated with her group threw a firebomb through the window of the RHV store on Main Street, but it didn't ignite. She says she's been afraid that some of the more radical elements within the women's movement would take the law into their own hands because women are very upset about the videos this chain sells. She says the videos show women being beaten, raped, tortured — forced to have enemas by armed intruders — and learning to enjoy it or begging for more."

"Sounds like a likely target then," Anderson said. "Also looks like Direct Action is quite a large group."

"Yeah," agreed Fraser. "Disturbingly large."

The next couple of days — November 5 and the early part of

November 6 — weren't notable, with the exception of Doyle picking wild mushrooms in a Richmond field with a number of female
companions. The surveillance teams found some comic relief in the
probability that the mushrooms were hallucinogenic. Back at the
Windermere address, Taylor, Hansen, and Stewart were seen getting into the Alberta pickup and driving to the Terris Video Shop in
Richmond around 4:30 p.m. They went into the store, and upon
leaving Taylor was observed feeling the bottom of the hinge side of
the main entrance door.

The next day, November 7, Gerry Hannah met up with Taylor
and Stewart at a Wendy's restaurant, then left in Hannah's orange
pickup to travel to the Marine Drive Red Hot Video. For fifteen to
twenty minutes the three men stood in front of the store talking
and pointing to various locations inside the store. They walked all
around the store before getting into the pickup and driving behind
the store, as close to it as possible. Afterwards they drove directly
to the Red Hot Video store at 44 East Hastings Street. Once again
they peered into the front window and talked and walked all
around the store before leaving. Hannah dropped the other two off
at the Windermere address before returning to the 1947 Charles
Street apartment.

After two days of reports indicating the men were casing Red Hot
Videos, Fraser commented to Anderson that they were much less
cautious about their behaviour than the women had been. Besides
this mundane observation, Fraser and Anderson were beginning to
wonder what they would do if it became obvious that this group of
people was about to bomb a Red Hot Video store. They were worried
that it would be premature to arrest them without any concrete evidence they could use to lay charges for the Litton bombing.

Monday, November 8, was uneventful, but the 9th marked
another turning point in their investigation. At 11:00 a.m. the Watchers observed Taylor and Hansen loading household goods from Windermere into the back of the Alberta pickup. The suspects drove to a
side street in Burnaby, where Hannah was parked in his orange
pickup truck. They parked behind Hannah, who got out to talk to
Taylor. Hansen got into the orange pickup and then Hannah and
Hansen drove to Hannah's presumed address of 1947 Charles Street.
Along with another young woman, they loaded up his truck with
household goods. Meanwhile Taylor drove to 9866 Sullivan Street in
Burnaby and unloaded the Alberta truck. Not long after, Hannah,
Hansen, and the young woman arrived and unloaded their truck at

the same address. They continued moving household goods from the two addresses to Sullivan Street until mid-afternoon, at which time Hansen and Taylor picked up Stewart and then dropped him off at a Fine European Foods store, before going to the Lower Mainland Mini Storage Room Self Serve on Richards Street and loading a number of boxes into the truck. They then proceeded to the Downtown U-Lok Mini Storage on Cambie Street and loaded more boxes into the truck. They took these boxes to 9866 Sullivan Street and unloaded them. This process of moving went on all day until Hannah, Hansen, Taylor, and the young woman finally shut out the lights at Sullivan Street at two in the morning.

After almost two solid weeks of sixteen-hour days, Fraser slept in on the 10th. He was exhausted. When he arrived at the RCMP building around noon, he was relieved to hear he hadn't missed much. "They're sleeping in with you, Fraser," chuckled Anderson. "There's been no movement so far this morning. If my guess is right, there won't be much happening today. They just moved, so they'll probably spend the day emptying boxes. I'd love to see what's in those boxes from the storage places."

Fraser agreed. "I think we've got our Direct Action group. We'll have to find out who owns this Sullivan Street address and ask what name they rented the place in."

"Done," said Anderson. "Not finished, but we're working on it."

"I'm impressed," said Fraser genuinely. He liked Anderson's efficiency. He wished he could have a partner like him instead of Despaireux, who he felt was too much of the old school. In his opinion Despaireux was a cowboy who was more comfortable with his gun than a computer.

"Don't jump to conclusions, Fraser," cautioned Anderson. "There could be a number of cells in this Direct Action group. Remember the FLQ? They had cells made up of three or four people who worked independently of each other for the same cause. That house at 44 West 14th could be another one. Then there could be Doyle and her friends and more cells in Toronto. We just don't know yet."

"I'm terrified they're going to act before we get evidence to lay charges on Litton and Cheekeye-Dunsmuir."

"I think we'll have documented enough evidence to justify our suspicions that a crime is about to be committed," Anderson said. "And then CLEU can take over surveillance and we can fill out an affidavit for a room bug."

"When?"

"Soon." Any more suspicious behaviour around these Red Hot Video stores and I'm sure we can convince a judge to give us the room bugs. I'm just as concerned as you are about these yahoos jumping the gun on us. But if we don't dot our i's and cross our t's, we won't get a conviction in court."

Fraser was well aware that to get a room bug they would have to produce a sworn affidavit, free of fraud and non-disclosure about the investigation to date, and show that all other means of investigation had been exhausted. In other words, the sworn affidavit had to be honest and disclose all the pertinent information regarding the investigation. This was the kind of police work he enjoyed but Despaireux hated. Despaireux liked the pursuit and arrest, not the slow, meticulous investigation.

"Anyways, Fraser, why don't you take the day off, and I promise I'll call you if anything happens."

Fraser sat down and thought about it. He was tired and couldn't think straight anymore. His reactions to events had become more emotionally extreme than normal. Probably he was more of a hindrance than a help to the investigation in this frame of mind, but Anderson was too kind to tell him. His wife could certainly do with some time off from the kids. If he went home he could nap and be there for the kids when they got home from school, and his wife could do some shopping. Without explaining, he got up and shuffled some papers into his briefcase. "I'll see you tomorrow, John," he said as he walked out.

✳ **30** ✳

Len Desroches took a deep breath and focused on the eight-foot barbed-wire fence in front of him. Behind it stood a thick line of cops, no less than four hundred, dressed in full battle regalia — robocops in black — completely intimidating with shields, helmets, nightsticks, two-foot flashlights, bulletproof vests, and knee-high leather stompin' boots. Scattered amongst them were the horsemen on their formidable beasts, the horses sweating and champing on their bits, straining to rear and buck like the wild creatures they might once have been.

In a short line on either side of Len stood twenty young people dressed in frayed blue jeans and running shoes, with bandannas around their noses in case the cops unleashed tear gas. Len wished he had at least brought his leather gloves so he wouldn't have to worry about the barbed wire piercing his hands. Behind and around them milled seven hundred others, hoping to act as a diversion at the moment that the twenty front-line troops stormed the Litton factory fence.

It was Remembrance Day, November 11, 1982 — thirty-eight years after Len's grandfather had stormed the beaches of Normandy. When he heard a woman's shrill voice scream "GO!" his mind flashed back to a scene he had never witnessed but had heard about so many times from his grandfather. How they had slogged out of the boats onto the beach, heading slowly towards the cliffs where they knew the German soldiers would be firing down on them, trudging hopelessly into the gunfire with nothing but God or fate between them and a violent, painful death. When Len focused on this scene, he felt a surge of strength and courage run through his body. He would live to see another day. Nobody would die, and tomorrow he would wake up in his warm, clean apartment, listening to the sounds of traffic on Queen Street.

He ran as fast as his thin legs would carry him towards a part of the fence that looked no different from the rest. As he scrambled up the wire mesh, he could see the huge hands of several cops extended out to him from the other side. It was truly hopeless. He grasped the top of the fence and felt the sharp barbs penetrating the flesh of his hands, but he felt no pain. Quickly he slung his leg over the top and poised there, looking down at the sea of black leather and helmets just below. As he was about to thrust himself as hard as he could over the side, he turned his head to see Carie Stearns, silhouetted against the grey sky, clinging with both hands to the top of the fence, weaving back and forth, as she struggled to maintain her balance. A huge cop jumped up and pushed as hard as he could, flinging her like a rag doll back to where she came from. He heard the thud as she hit the ground below, landing in the mud. A crowd of bandanna-clad supporters enveloped her like a pod. Len froze. Two young men no more than sixteen years old had managed to hit the ground on the other side. He recognized them as part of the gay affinity group or troop, as the images his grandfather had created in his mind began to blend menacingly in with reality. Before they could get on their feet they were swarmed by a dozen cops. Two of the policemen grabbed them by their hair and pushed their faces into the mud. He heard the boys gasp for air and try again to scramble to their feet, but instead the huge leather gloved hands grabbed their collars as though they were dogs and dragged them through the mud towards one of the waiting convoy of paddy wagons.

He had done the mathematics before they stormed the fence. Twenty cops to every person trying to get over the fence. Dotted here and there on the other side were a few pathetic protesters who had successfully gotten over the fence. They were either lying in the mud being prodded by nightsticks or flashlights, or being dragged through the mud and gravel and dumped like dead meat into one of the paddy wagons.

Once again, Len snapped out of his reverie and was about to jump, when he saw his friend Dave being grabbed by the scruff of his neck and then being smashed, face first, into the pavement. A trail of blood oozed from his forehead. Len grabbed the barbed wire for balance. Not yet. Then another person, a woman, just below him, struggled to stand. She had just got her balance and appeared to get ready to walk on her own to the paddy wagon, when one of the cops pushed at her and then grabbed her and began dragging her across the ground.

Fuelled by anger, Len hurled himself down into the enemy below, screaming at the top of his lungs as he flew. It was a spine-tingling sound that caused the sea of black to part below. Instead of landing in the leather-gloved hands, he landed with a painful thud on the grass. As quickly as he landed, he sprung up on his feet, marvelling that nothing appeared to be broken. Then a long nightstick came out of the black leather mass and, with a slam on his shoulder, knocked him back again onto the slippery grass. Len tried to get up but once again the nightstick knocked him down. Now Len tried to grab the stick but instead it was lowered at groin level and then met its mark. Len saw stars, then blackness. Soon in agonizing pain, he was lying on the floor of the paddy wagon with his hands cuffed behind his back. He looked around and felt a sense of relief to see a friendly face looking down from the metal bench above him: Ivan LeCouvie, a friend from Peterborough, Ontario.

"Are you alright?" Ivan asked without moving. Len could see that Ivan's hands too were cuffed behind his back, which made it difficult to move in the swaying paddy wagon.

"I think so." Len took a moment to concentrate on his body. He could feel everything. He still felt the pain in his groin but other than that he didn't think he had sustained any serious injuries. "Do you think many people made it over?" Len asked.

"I didn't have time to count, but I would guess about ten or twelve out of twenty. That's not bad."

"It was hopeless, but worth the try. We would never have been able to get to the main gates and stop the afternoon shift."

"No. Five of us came from World Emergency, but I think I'm the only one that got over."

When the paddy wagon stopped for a few minutes, Len managed to scramble onto the seat. He was sitting trying to gather his thoughts when Ivan broke the silence.

"I know it seems hopeless, Len, but at least we tried and stuck to our principles. You can get some satisfaction out of that." He was trying to cheer Len up a little. "We're bound to come up against police repression if we stick to our principles. The whole point of civil disobedience is to make a moral statement. It's not a competition or game to see who wins or loses. It's all about doing what's right and screw the consequences."

"Yeah, that's right," Len said. "It had nothing to do with actually stopping the workers or deliveries from entering the plant. It had everything to do with principles." He squirmed around on the metal seat so that he could look back over his shoulder at his hands, cuffed behind his back. When he clenched his fists, his palms felt sticky and hurt. There were very distinct puncture marks in the middle of his palms where fresh blood was still oozing. That was where the metal spikes at the top of the fence had penetrated.

When Ivan saw him looking at the wounds, he smiled knowingly. "You know, I bet most of the people who climbed the fence have the same wounds. It would have been impossible to climb with gloves on and just as impossible to grab the top without being pierced. Crucifixion marks." Len puzzled over his friend's remark.

When they reached the police station there was a huge backlog of people waiting to be processed, and Len and Ivan were put in holding cells with a number of other protesters waiting to be formally charged, fingerprinted, and photographed. The twelve affinity groups that had participated in the action had all anticipated being arrested, and had decided that each individual would in turn decide whether to co-operate in the booking procedure.

"How many protesters did they arrest?" Len asked one of the demonstrators sitting on a bench with his pant legs rolled up, checking his wounds.

"I overheard one of the cops say over sixty," he said without looking up.

Len looked around for Ivan LeCouvie and spotted him in a corner by himself. He walked over and sat down beside his friend. Len was starving. At 6:30 in the morning, he had wolfed down a sandwich when he first arrived at the plant with the other 150 blockaders, but hadn't eaten anything since then. They had warned the Litton workers to arrive at work early so that they wouldn't be prevented from reaching the plant by the blockade, which was intended to stop deliveries. But the police had shown up in full force, four hundred strong, and had set up metal barricades half a mile from Litton's main gate, on both the north and south end of City View Drive.

When about seven hundred demonstrators showed up, they broke up into two groups at each end of City View Drive and peacefully sat down in the road to block traffic. The police were obviously prepared, and when the protesters refused to get off the road the cops began to drag them off, some by the hair. By early afternoon, the protesters were becoming frustrated about not being able to get near Litton, and some affinity groups decided to climb the fence near the company's main gate. Twenty people, Len among them, stormed the fence. At that point he hadn't felt much like eating.

"How are you doing, Ivan?" Len asked.

"Fine, except I stupidly brought a calendar with me in my knapsack, which the cops took. Now I'm a bit worried because it chronicles a trip I took in the summer of '81 to Prague, where I went to the peace conference of the World Federation of Democratic Youth."

"So? What's the big deal about that?"

"Maybe I'm just being paranoid but I remember I made some notes about some communist youth organizations I was interested in making contact with when we had a stopover in Moscow."

"You mean Moscow, as in the Soviet Union?" asked Len, still not seeing any significance in this.

"Yeah. I know it doesn't seem like anything, but the cops were really going overboard today, and when I think about it they might have planned to make a lot of arrests, hoping that somebody at this demo was involved in the Litton bombing and they would have evidence on them. I wasn't involved in the bombing in any way but I know how paranoid they are about Russia and they would assume that anyone with a Soviet connection must be, at the very least, sympathetic to the bombers."

"Naw, Ivan, now you *are* being paranoid," Len said, putting his arm around Ivan's shoulder supportively. "There's no way they're that dumb. Just because you went to Russia over a year ago? I don't think so."

"We'll see. That was stupid of me. Please don't tell anyone."

"I won't," Len assured him. "One thing you're right about is the cops being more than ready for this demo. Without a doubt, they'll use the Litton bombing to justify their show of force today."

"Just like the Liberals are using the bombing to justify the new Security Service bill they're introducing in the House of Commons," added Ivan. "They were working on this Security Service Bill long before the Litton bombing, but no doubt they'll try to get public support for its passage by saying the Security Service needs more power to prevent things like the bombings, and even the opposition parties will be afraid to criticize it."

Just then a cop came up to the holding cell and pointed at Len. "You! Come with me!"

Len figured he would co-operate with the fingerprinting and mug shot, since he had no plans of agreeing to the bail conditions. He had overheard some hostile remarks coming from people who had not been involved in the demonstration, people who had been brought in on more everyday charges. They were getting angry at waiting to be processed because some demonstrators refused to co-operate.

When they got into the processing area, Len saw the woman he had witnessed being dragged through the puddles. She was being forcefully fingerprinted and photographed. She just sat on the floor while a female police officer picked up her fingers, placed them in the ink, and rolled them on a paper. Then two cops picked her up and held her so they could take her mug shot. Her clothes were soaking wet and her arms were cut up. Len tried to talk to her, but after they gave her a blanket they hustled her off towards a different area of the lock-up. When Len asked the cops where she was going, he was told she was being taken to the bullpen to spend the night since she was refusing to co-operate.

After being processed, Len was led off to a cell for the night. It wasn't until he heard the heavy steel door shut behind him that he realized he was really in jail. The angry noise from the other prisoners enveloped him. His first thought was of food. It must be around 7:00 p.m., and they still hadn't been fed. He looked around his eight-by-five-foot cell with its metal cot, toilet, and sink, all attached to the concrete wall, and wondered how people could survive in a space like this for years and years.

* * *

At 7:00 a.m. two guards opened Len's door and told him they were going to court for a bail hearing. When they arrived, he was put in a holding cell with a large number of people, both protesters and people being held on other matters. Len looked for Ivan, but he wasn't in with this group. He noticed across the aisle another large holding cell for women. He walked over to the bars and saw the woman who had refused to co-operate in the booking procedure. She didn't look well.

"Hey!" he yelled out. "I'm with the Litton demonstrators. Are you?"

"Yes!" she yelled back and pressed herself close to the bars. She told him about how she had been left all night alone in the bullpen, with nowhere to sleep but the concrete floor and only a blanket and the wet clothes she was wearing. Apparently another woman had been strip-searched five times the day before, and another woman who had cut her hands badly had been refused medical treatment.

"I'll see what my lawyer can do," Len told her. He looked over and recognized the woman with the badly cut hands — she was the one he had seen being pushed back down off the eight-foot fence. He had to admit that the women had been pretty hard core. He gave her a feeble smile and turned back to his bullpen. Finally he found Dave Collins, another friend, the one who had had his face smashed in the pavement. By the look of the dried blood, he hadn't received any medical attention either.

"You know what's weird, Len? Those cops must have had instructions to arrest certain people and not others, because there was this guy right beside me from the high-school affinity group who was cut real bad, but he didn't get over the fence so they didn't charge him. I was looking for him because he was beside me just before I went over. He didn't make it, but that woman over there who got pushed back got charged. I've noticed they seem to have picked on the most active political people, the women and gays. They seemed to have left the young folks and less active political people alone."

Len looked around. The two main event organizers were from

the Alliance for Non-Violent Action, and most of the blockaders were from its eighteen member organizations. He saw one of the organizers in the cell — the other was a woman. Len walked over to the young man. He found out that he and his partner, Sue, had been arrested early, before the protesters had even stormed the fence. They hadn't even been active in the blockade when the police arrested them, but just standing on the edge of the demonstration near the people sitting in the road. "My guess is the cops were instructed to arrest leadership early, perhaps to disorganize the blockade," he explained. Len had to agree. He found his way back to Dave and spent the rest of the morning waiting. He found out that no one had been fed since they had been brought in.

As the hours ground by, Len started noticing a distinct scowl on most of the regular prisoners. Dave agreed. When the guards brought everyone a greasy hamburger for lunch, Len overheard one guard telling a regular prisoner that he shouldn't be surprised if he was remanded in custody because there were so many of these "damn" protesters that the judge would never be able to hear all the bail applications. The "regular" seemed to know the guard and muttered something about "a bunch of goofy idiots," which Len took as referring to the protesters. It dawned on him that the regulars, who were probably in and out of this court every month, might resent the protesters taking up so much court time and thus causing themselves to be held in prison overnight. No doubt the guards and court officials would divert any tension from the regulars to the protesters rather than blame themselves for being understaffed.

One by one the protesters were called into court and read the charge of "resisting the police in the execution of their duty." After pleading not guilty, which all the protesters had agreed to do, they were let out on their own recognizance on two conditions: that they stay away from the Litton plant and not associate with any co-defendants.

Slowly the bullpen emptied as the protesters agreed to the bail conditions and rushed out onto University Avenue to reunite with friends and family after a night in jail — all, that is, except Dave Collins, Joanne Young, and, of course, Len Desroches. They stubbornly refused to agree to the bail conditions on the grounds that they had the constitutional right to demonstrate peacefully on any public land or road, whether it is in front of or beside the Litton plant.

After the bail hearing, Len and Dave were returned to the bullpen until the paddy wagon arrived at the end of the day to take them to the East Detention Centre with the rest of the "regulars." After being admitted, Len was taken to a cell with concrete walls covered in prophesies and revelations written in everything from pen and pencil to blood. As in the cell in the lock-up, the metal cot, toilet, and sink were firmly fastened to the cement walls with metal bolts to prevent any hostile prisoners from using them as weapons.

The silence in the cell was broken by the crackle of a radio speaker fastened to the wall above the door. It was not a welcome sound. Len looked up and couldn't see any dials to control the volume or station. The endless drone of Muzak, broken up by intermittent static, filled the air. It occurred to Len that this could be a form of torture. There was no escape. It entered his head and disrupted his thoughts. Every attempt he made to think pleasant thoughts was sabotaged by the staticky sounds of Muzak. He went to his door and yelled through the bars for a guard. After what seemed like hours, one arrived.

"Could you please turn this thing off?" asked Len.

"No," the guard said flatly.

"You mean I have to listen to this thing all night?"

"No, it goes off at eleven along with the lights." The guard turned away to indicate the conversation was over.

Len focused on his stomach rumbling and regretted he hadn't asked the guy about something to eat. For about an hour he sat on his cot thinking about his request for a call to his lawyer, and supper, but no matter what he did the Muzak seemed to dominate his consciousness. Something about his inability to control his surroundings made the radio's constant Muzak particularly irksome. Finally he stood on his tiptoes and reached up towards the speaker. It was too high. Then he tried banging on the wall, thinking that perhaps the radio's static meant that it had a short-circuit, and perhaps a bang or two would somehow shut it off. Miraculously, the speaker suddenly fell off the wall and dangled in the air, suspended by its own wires. But it still managed to continue playing, although more staticky than before. Len laughed. The Muzak didn't bother him so much now that the radio was hanging from the wall like a dying prisoner.

Finally a guard appeared at the door and told him he could make a call to his lawyer. Len didn't bother mentioning the radio, but just followed the guard down the hall to a phone booth. He had barely hung up the phone when another guard appeared to accompany the first in escorting Len back to his cell. When they herded him down the hall in a different direction, Len asked what was going on. They informed him that he was being escorted to the solitary confinement area.

"What?" gasped Len. "Why?"

"You know why," the first guard stated.

"I really don't have a clue," Len said, becoming increasingly alarmed.

"You tore the radio from the wall in your cell," the guard said.

"I did not!" exclaimed Len. "I just banged my fist on the wall and it fell off! It must have been just sitting in there in the first place. Somebody who was in there before me must have pulled it out of the wall. I couldn't even reach the damn thing."

"Tell it to the judge," the guard said without emotion.

"I want to call my lawyer," said Len hotly.

"You've already had your call, and there's absolutely no extra calls."

By then they had reached the solitary confinement cell, which was windowless with nothing but a toilet. For twelve restless hours he remained without books, paper, pencil, socks, shoes, or underwear. He found himself wondering how anyone could keep their sanity in conditions like this. Finally an official came and announced that Len's hearing for being placed in solitary confinement was going to be held on the spot. For Len, twelve hours of angry festering had created a backlog of remarkably clear thoughts, but just as he was about to offer them up, the official interrupted him. "I don't believe you. I'm finding you guilty, and I'm leaving you here indefinitely and I'm putting you on a special diet."

As the door slammed shut behind him, Len vowed that he would not eat again until he was released from his unjust solitary confinement. He feared that he would go mad if he didn't focus his anger into some constructive action. He thought about his grandfather and the courage it took to charge up that beach knowing that row upon row of German soldiers were firing down on him. How did he muster the courage to go on?

He had no power in this situation. He couldn't force them to do anything, but he could refuse to co-operate, just like that woman who had refused to lift up her hands or body to be fingerprinted or photographed. He would refuse to eat. He would not participate in this fraud. He had not broken the radio, so he would refuse to eat until they put him back in the general population. It was the only power he had.

At night they put a mattress into the cell for his comfort. By then Len's spirits had sunk almost as low as he thought they could go — until he was ordered to remove all his clothing and in return was handed a thick, asbestos tube, without sleeves, which went from his shoulders to his knees. "What the hell is this?"

"It's called a baby doll," the guard told him. "You'll have lots of time to think in here before your trial." He walked away before Len could ask any more questions.

It was midnight when he finally drifted off to sleep. The next morning he was awakened by the harsh words of a guard. "Get up, your lawyer's here to see you." Still with nothing on but his asbestos tube, Len simply got up off the mattress and told the guard he was ready. He was surprised when the guard told him to put his hands behind his back so he could be handcuffed, but at that point Len would have done anything to have contact with the outside world.

He was led upstairs to a room with a lot of glass windows that was used for legal visits. After his unsuccessful bail hearing, he had arranged to see Clayton Ruby, a prominent yet left-leaning lawyer, a rare combination within the legal community. Len explained what had happened with the radio in his cell, and Ruby promised to take his case up under the new Charter of Rights and Freedom.

"There was a woman who also refused to sign the bail conditions," Len said just when Ruby was about to leave. "Did anyone see her?"

"Yes, one of my colleagues saw her last night," Ruby answered. He settled back down to talk some more. "Normally I wouldn't be able to tell you about her case because of client confidentiality, but in this case she told me to let everyone know what's happening. She's a teacher from the Exeter area. She was protesting peacefully by sitting on the road by the barricades, and the police came along and dragged her to the side of the road through the puddles. When she returned to the barricades, they charged her with 'resisting the police in the execution of their duty.' We're going to challenge the charge on the grounds that she has the constitutional right to demonstrate peacefully, which she was doing. It was the police who were guilty of using force. Then they punished her for not co-operating during fingerprinting and mugshots by leaving her in her wet clothes with just a blanket, alone all night, on the floor of the bullpen. There's a number of cases where people were handled in a very heavy-handed manner."

"Do you think the cops had certain people singled out to be arrested?"

"We don't have any proof, but it is odd that the organizers were arrested early on without participating in the blockades, and some people were handled more forcefully than others," Ruby explained. "The morning papers said there were close to four hundred police involved and forty of those were on horseback. The taxpayers will be billed $400,000 for the police operation at Litton on November 11 alone and that doesn't include the money spent on bail applications, the court time fighting the charges, and the expense of holding you and a couple of others in prison for who knows how long."

"How do you think the public is interpreting all this?" asked Len.

"Unfortunately, I think the public is behind the police," said Ruby sadly. "The police are using the bombing to justify their use of force and I think the public is eating it up. A lot of people can barely see the difference between yourselves and the bombers. They see pictures of young people with earrings and dirty blue jeans trying to climb the fence and sitting on the road and they think they are the same kind of people that did the bombing." He rose to leave.

"Yeah, well, thanks for everything," Len said, standing up as well. He watched the lawyer disappear down the hall — his only contact with the outside world — and waited for the guards to take him back to his cell.

For five days Len kept up his hunger strike, spending his time mostly exploring his thoughts and feelings. After a couple of days without food, he noticed a change in his emotional state. He felt a calmness settle over him that seemed to give him greater clarity of thought and vision. He wondered if this state of mind was one of the reasons many religious people fasted as part of their spiritual practice.

On the fifth day, a guard woke him up and told him to gather up his belongings, because he was going to general population. Even though this had been the goal of his hunger strike, Len was secretly disappointed that it had to end before he could experience the full effects of fasting. After five days in solitude, the noise and overcrowding of general population prison conditions were jarring on his nerves, but his disappointment at ending his hunger strike stopped with the first smell of food wafting up from the kitchen. It was probably a good thing he was starving, because after that first meal of prison food, he could barely stomach it again.

✳ 31 ✳

Fraser didn't realize how tired he had been until he woke up on November 11. His concerns, which had seemed so insurmountable the day before, seemed insignificant in retrospect. He told himself that he would have to start working no more than ten hours a day for six days in a row or else he would make mistakes that would negate all the hours he was putting in. He called the office to let Anderson know he was coming in, only to be told that nothing notable was going on so he may as well take another day off. For a moment he had the paranoid feeling that they didn't need him on the case any more, but pushed the thought out of his head so he could concentrate on studying the surveillance notes to date.

When he returned to the office on the 12th, he reviewed the surveillance notes from the 11th to discover that nothing eventful had happened until around midnight, when Hannah, Stewart, and Taylor had taken the Alberta pickup to Langley and parked a half-block away from a Red Hot Video store. They walked past the store, and in passing one of the men had grabbed the front door and given it a hard pull to find it was locked. Then they tried pulling on the door of a vacant store right beside the RHV, as well as the door to the nearby Timber Mill Restaurant. After eating a pizza at a back table of another nearby restaurant, the Pizza Palace, they walked around the RHV before returning to Windermere with Stewart and then going home for the night to the Sullivan Street address.

When Anderson arrived he saw Fraser reading the surveillance notes. "Sure looks like these guys are just as interested in the Red Hot Video stores as the women, eh Fraser?"

"Yeah. I guess as soon as we see some evidence to believe a crime is about to be committed, we'll hand it over to CLEU, eh?"

"Of course," Anderson said with an edge to his voice. He had already assured Fraser that this would happen. "Anyway, we've already had a report today that the unidentified female, who we figure is Hannah's girlfriend, went shopping this morning in Port Coquitlam at the Second Step Society for Physically Disabled Adults, and asked a clerk if they had any wine bottles with caps. When she was told they had the bottles but no caps, she bought a knitted item but didn't pick up any bottles. After this, she drove over to the Timbermart and bought some silver electrical tape and light bulbs."

"Hmmmm. Could be preparing to make Molotov cocktails?" speculated Fraser.

Once again the rest of the day was uneventful until Fraser was about to leave the office. At 6:30 p.m. they got a call from one of the surveillance teams reporting that Hansen was meeting with Doyle and two other unidentified females in the Ho Tak Kee Won Ton House downtown. Two hours later Fraser was still sitting in his office — his new resolve to leave early had gone out the window. When the meeting was finally over and Hansen had dropped the three women off at 44 West 14th and returned home herself, Fraser went home.

Since their suspects seemed to be most active at night, Fraser decided to start working the night shift. On Saturday, November 13, he arrived at the office around 5:30 p.m. to be briefed that Hannah and his girlfriend had just left 9866 Sullivan Street and were having Chinese food at the Ho Inn on West Pender with a young woman described as "short, chubby, and baby-faced with short, brown, thinning hair."

While the suspects were busy eating, Anderson went over the day's activities. It had been a typical day for Hansen and Taylor. They left the house before noon, with Hansen starting her day with a jog in nearby Bell Park. Taylor spent a lot of his time, as usual, at the Lougheed Mall, making a few phone calls — they didn't have a phone in their house — and playing video games in the Krack-A-Joke shop. After her jog Hansen had puttered around with the trucks. "The activity that the surveillance teams find the most irksome so far," Anderson said, "is the amount of shoplifting this group does. Almost daily, one of them is seen shoplifting, as though it's a hobby or something. Often the items are cheap. They couldn't be that poor, so I'm left to conclude that they enjoy it — almost a group kleptomania kind of thing."

"If only it was that innocent." Fraser smiled. "By the way, if they have police scanners, could they listen to our communication with surveillance?"

"No," Anderson assured him. "It's on a special channel that's scrambled so even our own people can't tune in." Just then the radio crackled, signalling a call from one of the surveillance teams.

"They've just gone into the Commodore Night Club with their friend and are sitting at a table listening to a couple of punk bands," Anderson reported. "The Watchers must be enjoying themselves."

When Fraser arrived at work the next afternoon, Anderson greeted him with a knowing look. "Well, all four of them spent the afternoon shoplifting at health food stores. You'd think, being so-called political people, that they'd draw a line at the kind of stores where they'd shoplift, but no, it seems to be a fairly mercenary kind of decision based more on the facility with which they can pick things up than whether it is ethical."

"Maybe they just prefer health food," Fraser said sarcastically.

"Yeah, but you'd think they'd want to shoplift at politically correct places. Here's my notes on the day's activities so far." Anderson handed Fraser a page of handwritten notes. "Around 1:30 p.m. Hannah, his girlfriend, Taylor, and Hansen left 9866 Sullivan St. and drove to the Life Stream Natural Health Food Store on W. 4th Ave. They entered the store carrying various gym and tote bags but left the store separately, putting the articles from the store in the rear of Hannah's pickup truck. Then they drove to another Life Stream store on Broadway, three entering the store with tote bags and one with an Adidas bag. A Watcher entered the store and witnessed Hannah's girlfriend filling her bag with frozen foods and leaving the store without paying. Taylor is also observed taking toothpaste and vitamins and leaving the store without paying. Hansen and Hannah are still in the store. Hannah's girlfriend goes back inside the store with her bag empty and comes out moments later with her bag full and empties it in the back of the truck. Finally Hansen and Hannah come out with their bags full and also empty them in the back of the truck. After leaving the store, they stop for gas, at which time, Taylor and Hannah go down an alley and pick up an empty cardboard box and two two-litre empty wine jugs which they put in the rear of the truck. After paying for the gas, they head to another Health Food Store on E. 9th where they, once again, go in with empty tote bags and come out with them full and empty them in the rear of the truck."

Fraser spent the rest of the evening beside the radio, waiting for a call from the Watchers and catching up on his notes. Finally, around 7:30 p.m, the radio crackled, signalling a call. The Watcher gave Fraser a synopsis of the suspects' evening activities, which Fraser recorded.

"Around 2:30 p.m., Taylor and Hannah, in his orange truck, picked up Stewart at 3895 Windermere St. and parked in a Safeway parking lot in Langley. They walked past the Langley Red Hot Video store and stopped to look in the window of a nearby store called Guns and Stuff. Then they drove to Port Coquitlam and parked in the Chevron Service Station and left the truck but Hannah returned to the truck and moved it 20 to 30 yards out of the station parking lot and walked back carrying a red 5-gallon jerry can. While Hannah put some gas in the jerry can, Taylor rummaged around in a blue Smithrite garbage container while Stewart remained standing in front of the office, hands in pocket, looking around. Taylor returned with two empty plastic anti-freeze containers and Hannah with the jerry can, and at that point, a large glass jar appeared in Stewart's hands. They put all these items in the rear of the truck. Their next stop is Bino's. Taylor goes in alone and comes out a few moments later with a large glass jar with a screw-on lid. Then they drive to the rear of Mother's Restaurant and rummage around in the garbage container and return with unidentified objects which they place in the rear of the truck. Next stop, the garbage container at the rear of the Corkscrew Restaurant where they rummage around again and Taylor comes back with two white type containers. They drop Stewart off in the vicinity of 3895 Windermere. They never drop Stewart off right at Windermere but we always see him entering the back of that address shortly after they let him out in the area."

It was getting close to one in the morning and Fraser was preparing to leave when the radio crackled again with a report that Hannah's truck was leaving 9866 Sullivan with an unknown number of occupants. "These people must sense that I'm about to go home when they decide to go out," thought Fraser irritably. He hated to leave when there was activity at this time of night. He took off his coat and settled into his chair. At least that was the last thing he remembered doing when the crackle of the radio woke him up. He picked up the receiver and heard the agitated voice of the Watcher on the other end of the line.

"Hannah and Taylor picked up Stewart at Windermere in Hannah's truck and then they went to the Coquitlam area and cruised a residential neighbourhood. We couldn't tell who was who anymore. They were wearing toques and dark clothes, as though they were trying to hide their identities. Anyway, finally they park and two targets disappear, leaving only the driver sitting in the truck. After a while he starts driving and before you know it, all three of them are in the truck heading back to Sullivan Street. While they were out, the green van with someone besides the driver in it arrives at Sullivan Street. Around 3:00 a.m., three men, who we couldn't positively ID, got into Hannah's truck and drive back to the same residential area. Now we ID Hannah letting out Stewart and Taylor and then turning off the lights and motor of the truck. Suddenly, Hannah starts up the truck and pulls out onto the road directly behind another vehicle. There's two people inside the vehicle but Hannah's driving about ten to twelve feet behind this vehicle so we can't read the plates. That's where we are now, trying to follow this pair. I'm calling because we suspect they stole the vehicle. We were told to phone in if any criminal activity is suspected."

Fraser felt his heart racing. He had to make a decision. He didn't have a clue where Anderson's night-shift replacement was, and he had no time to find out. "Give me your location," Fraser directed in a firm voice. He decided to keep the surveillance on them but not make a bust yet.

"We're following them east on the Lougheed Highway towards Gilby," said the Watcher.

"Good. Can you keep on the line and let me know what's going on?"

"Sure thing, boss," said the Watcher cheerily. "Oh, they're turning into a residential area. We're having trouble keeping with them because they're using a criss-cross pattern, which makes it just about impossible to follow them at this time of the night without blowing our cover." The next thing Fraser heard was "Lost them, damn!!" He shook his head. A few minutes later the Watcher came back on the line.

"We got them again but now there's three people, with Stewart in next to the passenger door. They must have ditched the other vehicle they were following. Looks like they're heading back to Sullivan Street. Yup, that's where we're heading. Once we get there, we'll just park and see what happens."

Some forty-five minutes later the Watcher called to report that three people had gone out to Hannah's truck and were driving towards Stewart's neighbourhood. The last report of the night was that the truck had returned to Sullivan Street with two occupants. At five in the morning all the house lights went out.

Fraser leaned back in his chair. He had only slept about an hour but he decided to lay down on the couch in the staff room until Anderson arrived to tell him first-hand about the night's activities. Should he have called for uniformed cops to make an arrest for the possible car theft and risk blowing their cover, or did he do the right thing? He'd get the day shift to find that vehicle. It had to be parked in the residential area where Hannah had lost them last night, but for now he had better get a few hours sleep until the day shift arrived at eight. Three hours' sleep was better than none. He trudged into the staff room, pulled off his shoes, and stretched out on the plastic couch. He fell asleep as soon as he put his head down.

"Fraser!" Anderson's stern voice sent him into a bolt-upright position. "What the hell are you doing?"

"What do you think?" said Fraser irritably. He explained what he had been doing all night. "I slept here, and this is what I get for my dedication. A rude awakening! Where's my coffee?"

"I'm way ahead of you, as usual Fraser." Anderson handed him a coffee. "I've already been here an hour and read over the notes from last night's Watchers, and I've already contacted the Coquitlam RCMP to look for the vehicle Hannah was following."

Fraser sat up and sucked back his coffee. Just after 10:00 a.m. the Watchers called to report that Taylor had left 9866 Sullivan Street for the mall, where he made a couple of phone calls at the Krack-A-Joke shop. Meanwhile Hansen was repairing the Alberta pickup truck.

"Hey Fraser," Anderson called in through the door of the communications room, where Fraser was waiting for calls. "They found the vehicle and it is stolen — so what do you suggest?"

Fraser had already been thinking about it. "They're bound to go back, so I think the uniformed guys should do a normal car theft bust and our targets will get out the next morning and then we hand the investigation over to CLEU."

"I agree," Anderson said. "The car's going to be under surveillance until somebody comes to get it."

In the early afternoon Taylor and Hansen left Sullivan Street in the green van and visited a number of car parts shops before heading over to Windermere, where they picked up Stewart. From there they went to a rental place, the Mini Store All, and rented an acetylene torch and two tanks. Then they returned Stewart with the acetylene torch and tanks to his Windermere address. Hansen and Taylor went on to visit a couple of other car parts shops before dropping the green van off at Doyle's apartment on East 6th, and catching a number of buses to Sullivan Street.

"Looks like they're having mechanical problems with the Alberta truck so they borrowed Doyle's van," observed Fraser. "What's with the acetylene torch?"

"I don't know," said Anderson. "Maybe they're going to use it on the stolen vehicle? I have no idea."

"Aren't you worried that they'll take off if we bust them for car theft?"

"Not if we do it totally above board," explained Anderson. "Not even the judge will know they're under surveillance. He'll let them out, because they don't have any records to speak of."

Fraser was not as confident about the outcome of this course of action, but he was not about to go home if it looked like their targets were going to go out and get the stolen car tonight. When he started feeling really tired later in the evening, he pulled out a book and read. Just after 10:00 p.m. his patience was rewarded. Taylor had reportedly got into Hannah's truck with an unidentifiable male and headed off in the direction of the stolen car. At that point, Anderson came into the communications room.

"Fraser, we're not going to officially transcribe the surveillance notes of the Watchers when we bust these guys eh?" stated Anderson, in a strange way.

"Why not?" The suggestion took Fraser by surprise.

"Because we don't know if we'll get in trouble later on for admitting we knew they were stealing a car."

"But we didn't actually see them steal the car."

"Down the road, a defence lawyer might argue that we should have charged them with conspiracy to commit arson of the Red Hot Video stores or something," said Anderson. "We have to go further and find out if they did the Litton and Cheekeye bombings, so it would be premature to arrest them for anything serious yet. Just trust me on this. Sometimes being a competent cop means being a bit of a visionary. We don't just want to arrest these characters — we want to convict them and have them spend the rest of their lives in jail. That won't happen if we aren't visionaries at times."

Fraser had never been involved in a case of this magnitude before. "What do you mean by a visionary?"

"There's a good chance that we won't get enough evidence to support a conviction on the Litton and Cheekeye bombings before these people do, let's say, an arson of a Red Hot Video Store. So what would you want? We bust them for a Red Hot Video arson and they get off the other two bombings, or would you rather let them do a bit of damage to a Red Hot Video store while we sit tight and get them later for the other bombings as well?"

"What does that have to do with me deleting Security Service's surveillance notes?"

"Okay, let me explain it to you," said Anderson patiently. "Later on, we might have to apply for an authorization from a judge for a room bug in order to get evidence about Litton and Cheekeye. In order to get that authorization, we will have to fill out a sworn affidavit outlining our investigation so far, and saying that we have exhausted all other means of investigation and that we have reasons to believe a crime is about to be committed. If we have surveillance notes of the car theft and, let's say, an arson, and don't disclose them, then we will be open to accusations of fraud for non-disclosure of our investigation to date, but if there are no surveillance notes of us witnessing these illegal activities, then we can't be accused of fraud. Do you see what I'm getting at?"

Fraser nodded, and Anderson continued. "If their defence lawyers can prove we witnessed these illegal activities, then in a future trial they'd be able to get any wiretap evidence thrown out, which could be the basis for our entire case against them on the Litton and Cheekeye bombings. So I want you to blank out references in your notebooks to Security Service involvement in monitoring car thefts and any future illegal activities, especially once CLEU takes over. The Security Service is strictly an intelligence-gathering outfit. Once we determine a criminal act, such as that an arson is about to be committed, then we are supposed to hand over surveillance to CLEU, who are also equipped to make arrests."

Once again Fraser nodded. Anderson smiled. "So you see, Fraser, we have to be visionaries who can see the future and tailor our police investigation techniques accordingly. And by the way, if you have any pangs of conscience about deleting Security Service surveillance notes, just think about the Direct Action group in France, which has been linked to assassinations of U.S. and Israeli diplomats in Paris. Do you want that to happen here? I repeat, we must be visionaries who aren't just making arrests but are making convictions and putting bad guys in jail." Fraser finally understood.

* * *

When Hannah and Taylor didn't return to Sullivan Street that night, one of the women got into the Alberta pickup and drove to a phone booth around midnight to make a call. Fraser wrote in the official transcripts of the surveillance notes for November 15, 1982: "At 22:15 p.m., Taylor enters 7704KG with U/K occupant. They travel to Guilby [sic] and on to Edgar. Surveillance is terminated. At 00:16, observe ALTA SVB82 northbound on North Road. U/F in a phone booth at North Road, near Cochrane. 2:00, discontinued surveillance."

The next morning Fraser transcribed the Watchers' notes into an official version. The targets had been arrested during the night and held in jail. They had called their lawyer, Stan Guenther, and Taylor had used false identification under the name of Benjamin Romanin. But all Fraser said in the official transcript was, "Taylor and Hannah observed inside courtroom, 2165 Kelly Avenue, Port Coquitlam. Taylor and Hannah leave courtroom. Hansen is sighted in the Westwood Mall. Her U/F#1 and Stewart meet and travel via SVB982 to courthouse. Hansen gets out at the courthouse. U/F#1 takes the wheel with Stewart as passenger. Hansen, Taylor, and Hannah leave courthouse together and walk to Shaughnessy St. All three enter Dairy Queen together. Hannah inside speaking to U/F waitress. Taylor, Hansen go to bus stop on Shaughnessy. Hannah exits and stands at bus stop on west side of Shaughnessy. Taylor and Hansen board a bus and get off at the Kootenay Loop. Taylor and Hansen board a 10th Avenue bus."

Just as Fraser was finishing typing up the official transcript, Anderson came in. "I guess our targets are a little paranoid," said Anderson. "Hannah's girlfriend drove Stewart home from court in the Alberta pickup but the rest took the bus home, maybe thinking we might ID whatever cars they left the courthouse in. We just filed the charge in the name of Romanin and told the Coquitlam RCMP to just leave it for now. By the time the car theft comes before the courts, hopefully we'll have them for something much bigger."

"Are you preparing to hand the case over to CLEU?" Fraser was reluctant to continue editing surveillance notes.

"Yes," Anderson assured him. "By the 18th, the investigation will be in CLEU's hands. Then we won't just have the Security Service's Watchers on them but, if my guess is right, we'll eventually have four different police organizations at work — the RCMP's National Crime Intelligence Unit, the Vancouver Integrated

Intelligence Unit, the RCMP Security Service, and your beloved B.C. Canadian Law Enforcement Unit. By the 19th we'll have cops following every one of these suspects at Sullivan Street and Windermere and all the people they come into contact with." Anderson smiled from ear to ear, and Fraser couldn't help thinking that his partner looked like an alligator waiting to chomp down on an unsuspecting prey.

Fraser went home early that afternoon and slept in the next day, Wednesday the 17th. When he arrived that day in the communications room, surveillance reports revealed that Stewart was taking a bus back from Sullivan Street to his Windermere address, where he met Doyle and went out for breakfast. Hannah's girlfriend was driving the Alberta truck, and Hannah's truck was still parked in the residential neighbourhood where they had been busted the night before. At 10:00 p.m. Hannah and his girlfriend, plus Hansen, Taylor, and Stewart spent the evening at Sullivan Street, but other than that, nothing much happened. Fraser speculated they were probably trying to figure out what to do, but with no informants or room bugs he had no way of knowing.

Finally, in mid-afternoon of November 18, Fraser got the call he had been waiting for. He typed the last sentences in his official transcript of the surveillance notes: "14:30. Discontinued surveillance. At this time, hand over to Criminal Branch completed."

✳ **32** ✳

The cold wind blowing wasn't enough to stop the sweat from dripping in my eyes. One more lap. Of all the parks I had jogged in during the past few years, Bell Park was the worst. It was so small I had to jog around it about a hundred times to run five miles, but it was worth it. According to articles I had read, strenuous exercise stimulated the brain to secrete natural endorphins that acted much like the synthetic chemical morphine, as a pain killer. I always felt great after a good jog; energetic, relaxed, clear, and at peace. For me, jogging served two purposes. On the one hand, it helped maintain a high fitness level that could be useful if I ever had to run from the police or escape from a building or simply outrun a security guard while out shoplifting. On the other hand, jogging helped me deal with the stress that came with our unnatural lifestyle. Jogging was an almost religious ritual for me. Every morning, after we got up and had our breakfast get-together, I always went jogging, no matter where we lived.

After finishing my last lap that day I broke into a walk to cool off before I got home. Our house on Sullivan Street was a run-down clapboard affair, concealed from the small residential street by trees and overgrown shrubbery. Right behind the house was the Lougheed Mall, which quite conveniently had a large Woolco store where Brent had witnessed an inviting Brink's pickup. Almost every day one of us would have to go to the mall to use the phone or pick up groceries, which we would time to coincide with the daily Brink's pickup sometime just after noon.

When I got back to the house, Brent had assembled the timing light, new spark plugs, and tools to help me set the timing and change the spark plugs on our truck. I didn't want his help, but I guessed he didn't have anything better to do. I never enjoyed his help because I found that Brent, like most men, tended to take over and tell me how to do everything before I had a chance to think it through myself. Before I got involved with the Hat Creek women's group, I had never quite been able to put my finger on why I always felt irritable whenever a guy was helping me do traditional male tasks. Through our talks in that group, I had become aware of the dynamics that all too often took over men's and women's relationships when they worked together. It seemed to me that the male ego was often disturbed when a woman took control or knew more about tasks that were traditionally male terrain. Most men seemed threatened by the possibility that a woman might be better at auto mechanics, woodwork, plumbing, or any other jobs of that nature, and they felt compelled to come up with suggestions or take over the tools to show her how it should be done. I don't think that men in general have bad intentions when they do this; it's just a consequence of gender. Brent was no different, in my opinion.

Resigning myself to working with him, I resolved that I would not let him take over, either mentally or physically. With an air of determination, I picked up the tools he had organized on the kitchen counter and went out to the truck, with Brent trailing along behind me. I popped the hood and began putting the fluorescent markings on the fan blades, while Brent found an outlet to plug in the timing gun.

"So is Doug coming over soon?" I asked when he returned.

"Yup," he said, plugging the gun into the extension cord.

I turned on the engine, then loosened the distributor cap so I could turn it to the right position while Brent aimed the timing gun on the fan blades. "I called Stan too," he yelled over the roar of the engine.

I turned the distributor cap this way and that until the marks on the blades flashed in unison with the light on the timing gun. "There!" I yelled triumphantly. "Now we can change the plugs." Brent unplugged the gun and took the new spark plugs out of their wrappers while I stood up on the bumper and struggled to unscrew the old ones. I vowed that I would not ask him for help even though I knew he was stronger.

"Stan said they set a trial date for April 6," Brent said calmly, watching me with a faint smile. After quite a long time he said, "Want me to try?"

I looked at him disdainfully. "Sure." I didn't like it, but it was totally irrational not to let him unscrew the plugs considering his superior physical strength. He calmly picked up a sparkplug wrench and put an extension on the handle, giving it greater leverage. I hated him for thinking of this obviously superior way of handling the situation.

"We're going to have to ditch the Romanin ID," he said, handing me the old plugs. I got back up on the bumper and screwed the new plugs in.

"What a bummer." I tried to keep my voice from exposing my fury at his sparkplug finesse.

"Yeah, I went downstairs this morning and did my notes on the Romanin ID. Now that it's associated with a car theft, it obviously can't be used again. Luckily we have lots more. I guess I'll use the Steve Sturrick one now."

"Don't you think it's a bit dangerous to keep all those notes on where you use the ID and copies of the communiqués? What if we got busted? Then the cops would have all this evidence to convict us."

"The way I see it, we get killed during a bust or die in prison. Either way we're dead. I really don't see a life after being busted."

Just as I finished closing the hood we saw Doug walking along from the bus stop. When we got inside, I yelled upstairs for Julie and Gerry, who soon came downstairs for our meeting.

"I wonder what they'll do when they find out you're not Benjamin Romanin," laughed Gerry, when we had all settled down in our chairs in the living room.

"Probably, not much," said Brent. "Most criminals use false ID or give a phony name when they're busted. Anyway, Stan will let us know."

"That was pretty hairy, eh?" chuckled Gerry. "I was just sitting there in the truck minding my own business, waiting for Brent to get back from moving the stolen car, when faster than a speeding bullet a bunch of cops run up with guns drawn and pull me out of the cab with guns to my head. The next thing you know, I'm on the street. I thought, 'What the hell did Brent do for me to deserve this?'"

"So do you really believe they just found out the car was stolen from someone on the street noticing the ignition was ripped out?" Julie asked. Obviously, she didn't find the situation amusing.

"I don't have a clue how they got onto it," Gerry said.

"I told you guys yesterday, but nobody seems to believe me," Julie said. "I'm quite sure I've been followed. Remember about a week ago, I went to Port Coquitlam to the handicapped store for wine bottles but bought that stupid little knitted thing for under a buck just as an excuse to be in there? I told you guys I saw the same car following me for a long time. It's a long drive to Port Coquitlam and the same stinking car, an undercover car, was following me the whole time. How do you explain the same car being behind me when I stopped at the Timbermart in Port Coquitlam and then still following me after I left?" she repeated angrily. "Nobody believes me."

"I believe you, Jules," Gerry said tenderly. Julie gave him a harsh look.

"Well, what do you want us to do about it?" asked Brent.

"I don't know," she said. "But at least listen to me and keep your eyes open. I don't think it's a good idea for you and Gerry to do a firebombing. There's enough women already."

"I agree," Gerry said. "I think it's a little weird to begin with for a couple of guys to do a Red Hot Video action anyway, and now that we've been busted with the car I think we should cool it."

"Yeah, I agree," Doug said. "We won't have a vehicle to do an action in, and I don't think it would be wise for anyone to go out and steal another one for a while anyway. I could still deliver the communiqué if the women want."

"Yeah, that's not a bad idea," I piped in. "We have enough women to do the firebombing anyway. Three places is enough, and we do need someone to deliver the communiqué. I'll ask my group if they want a guy to deliver it, and you can ask yours, Julie, and Doug, you can ask your friend if she thinks it's cool. If so, go for it. We'll write it and you can deliver it."

"So that's it then, eh?" asked Gerry. "We'll cancel the Langley firebombing. I don't see how this firebombing fits in with our politics around the Litton and Cheekeye thing anyway."

"This is a society run by a relatively small group of white guys who determine all the social relations we have with one another and nature." I was warming up for a small sermon. "And the value placed on these relationships is based on profit. A beautiful piece of wilderness land on Vancouver Island is seen as undeveloped and useless unless a profit can be turned from it. This value system is the same as the one that values women's bodies for the money they can make selling everything from cars to sex. Nothing on this earth is worth anything if it can't turn a profit, and these powerful white guys are willing to use nuclear weapons, like the cruise, to maintain it no matter how much land or how many people have to be sacrificed. At least that's how I see it."

At the end of this short speech, Gerry stood up and clapped.

"Yeah," agreed Brent, "we're not a one-issue group. We're revolutionaries with a new vision of society. We want to change the values that this society is based on, so of course our work is going to touch on a number of issues."

"Well, I think the Red Hot Video action would be stronger and easier for people to relate to if it's done by women," Gerry said.

"Okay, we've agreed that we're going to cancel the Langley action and just do support work for the women," concluded Doug.

When the meeting ended, I volunteered to drive Doug home. He was strict about his bedtime. He liked to get in at least ten hours of sleep per night or he didn't feel well rested. When I got to Doug's neighbourhood I stopped a few blocks from his house to let him out. Before leaving, I arranged to pick him up in a couple of days before the Red Hot Video action to give him a copy of the communiqué. Then I sat for a few minutes and watched him disappear down an alley as he made his way towards Windermere.

The next evening I had a meeting scheduled with two other women who were part of a group we had formed to do something about the emergence of the Red Hot Video chain, which had become a hot issue in British Columbia by the time we returned from the Litton bombing. The chain, established in the early part of 1982, had expanded to thirteen outlets by that fall. The North

Shore Women's Centre had lobbied the B.C. attorney general's office to charge Red Hot Video under the hate propaganda section of the Criminal Code to stop the distribution of its catalogue. That section of the code dealt with publications depicting or advocating violence and stated that "everyone who advocates or promotes genocide is guilty of an indictable offence." It defined "genocide" as an act "committed with intent to destroy in whole or in part any identifiable group." The attorney general, Allan Williams, had refused to take legal action, claiming he was stymied by the definition of "identifiable group," which was defined as a section of the public distinguished by "colour, race, religion, or ethnic origin." The North Shore Women's Centre then tried to get the provincial government to charge the chain under the Motion Picture Act, but again the government said that was not possible because the act was passed before videotapes were available and only referred to film or "moving pictures" and not to the magnetic storage of images on videotape. Not surprisingly, the women's community took this to mean that the government was simply not interested in stopping the proliferation of violent pornographic video tapes.

Even though we had few contacts with the community, the women whom we did speak to were universally outraged at the government's inactivity. One evening in mid-November I had met with eight other women, including Julie, to devise a strategy of action. We decided to call ourselves the Wimmin's Fire Brigade. I don't remember how we ended up making a decision to firebomb some Red Hot Video outlets, but by the time the meeting was over we had divided into three groups of three women each. The groups were each going to plan and separately execute firebombings of Red Hot Video outlets in North Vancouver, Port Coquitlam, and Surrey. The three groups of women would remain autonomous except to write a communiqué and co-ordinate the exact timing of the actions.

Direct Action itself had not come up with the plan for the firebombings, but our original group had no trouble justifying its involvement with the Wimmin's Fire Brigade. The action harmonized perfectly with our politics. When Julie and I told the men about the Red Hot Video plans, they were supportive and suggested doing a firebombing in Langley themselves. It would show that men were also opposed to pornography.

On this particular evening, on my way to the meeting, Julie's dire warnings of being followed had sown a seed of paranoia in my mind. Normally, when driving a vehicle that could pass as legal, I would be lulled into a false sense of security by using standard counter-surveillance driving techniques. Looking in my rear-view mirror, if I didn't see any cars following me, I would take a deep breath and relax, believing that as long as I continued to push through yellow lights, do quick U-turns on side streets, and drive down one-way streets, the wrong way — I would be safe. However, Julie's phantoms, as we called them, were bringing back memories of articles I had read about police surveillance techniques. I recalled reading that the police used grid patterns to follow targets as they travelled down a road, criss-crossing back and forth in front and behind them, keeping in contact with each other by radio. That way, even if one cop lost them, another would be somewhere in the area to find them. Maybe that innocent little Toyota in front of me with the young woman inside, or that green Pinto up ahead passing through the intersection, could be a cop. The seeds of paranoia had taken root, and I could see the enemy everywhere. The businessman jaywalking, the couple laughing as they got in their car, the cab driver parked in front of the hotel — were they apparitions? Cops disguised as real people? I felt like I was going crazy. I finally calmed myself down with the fatalistic thought that it really didn't matter anyway, because if they were following us, it was too late now. There was nothing we could do.

I parked and walked into a restaurant and right through it, out the back door, and ran down the alley towards the Chinese restaurant where I had arranged to meet my two friends, Andrea and Gale. I walked in the back door of the restaurant and saw them sitting at a back table, the only Caucasians in the restaurant. I felt some peace of mind, thinking that the cops couldn't have followed me into that joint. I smiled at my friends, sat down, and glanced quickly around the place, wondering how easy it was for the cops to find Chinese people to work on surveillance. Luckily my friends had chosen an isolated table with no one sitting within earshot.

I got straight to the point. "Gerry and Brent got busted the other night trying to steal a car, so they aren't going to do a fire-bombing."

"Really!" they said in unison, wide-eyed and genuinely shocked. No one in their circle of friends did car thefts. "How did it happen?"

"We don't know how the cops discovered the car was stolen, but after the guys stole it they went back the next day to move it.

While Brent was in the car, the cops busted both him and Gerry, who was waiting in his truck."

"Wow," said Gale. "I hope they'll be okay. Will one of the guys still want to deliver the communiqué?"

"Sure," I said. "I'll give it to him and he'll deliver it shortly after the time we set for the firebombing."

"Did you hear about what happened to Renee?" Andrea leaned across the table towards me. I shook my head. "Somebody broke into her house and ransacked her files and left them scattered all over the floor," she whispered. "They didn't take anything from her house and only targeted her files, where she kept her information on the Red Hot Video stores." I raised my eyebrows. These women didn't know I was involved with Direct Action.

"Sounds like the cops or somebody paid by the cops?" suggested Gale.

"Or somebody affiliated with Red Hot Video?" said Andrea.

Once again I raised my eyebrows. A little Chinese lady came over and asked in broken English if we were ready to order. As soon as she left we settled back down to business.

"I did a little investigation myself the other night," Gale said proudly. "Well, actually, I had some help from a friend." Then she paused, perhaps for effect. "Anyway, I asked Rob to rent some videos at the RHV store on Main Street late one night. He goes in and there's a line of guys in there waiting to rent tapes. He says there were never less than six guys in the place the whole time. The layout is simple, just a long counter with two cabinets behind it, filled with tapes. There's some catalogues with an adult title list of over three hundred tapes. It has a warning: 'these movies are uncut and sexually explicit' and are 'not to be shown in public.' He asked the clerk if they had anything in the way of rape, bondage, incest, or basically anything violent — I thought that was too straightforward, but he's an amateur." We smiled at her comment.

"They handed him a RHV directory," she continued. "Which he took to the end of the counter and made notes so it looked like he was just writing down titles he wanted." At this point, she pulled out a rumpled piece of paper, which we assumed was Rob's. Then she began to read from Rob's notes about the directory: "Reference no. 2, Bondage and Discipline — Sadism and Masochism — Bizarre video specializes in this genre. Write to them for a catalogue. The films listed have outstanding S&M or B&D scenes but are not solely of that genre. Reference no. 4, First Sex Experience

— includes both willing and unwilling virgins. Reference no. 10, Rape and Gang-Bang — rape and gang-bangs are pretty much standard fare in bondage films. Reference no. 12 — Young Girls — most films try to have youthful looking girls. These are thematic films about pubescent females."

She turned over the paper. "Rob ended up renting three films, and I had the misfortune of having to watch them. I couldn't believe it. They definitely inspired me to go on with this action. I have no doubt in my mind that we're doing the right thing."

She gave us a piercing look, then described the content of the films, referring to her notes on the back of Rob's paper. The first movie, *Bad Girls*, was about four women taken hostage by an all-male cult. The women were hung from the ceiling by chains and whipped until they begged for mercy. They were sexually abused and beaten. The object of the cult was to teach the women that men are their masters. The next film, *Young and Abused*, was about a teenage couple who ran out of gas while driving in the country. When the sixteen-year-old girl was left alone in the car, two adult men came by and dragged her into their van and beat her and both raped and sexually abused her while she screamed in pain. One man ejaculated in her face. While they were torturing her, they repeatedly asked her if she enjoyed being tortured, and all she did was scream for mercy. "I was almost sick watching that one," Gale said.

The third video they watched was called *Water Power*. In it women were slapped, whipped, raped, and had their hair pulled before being forced to accept enemas. That one, Gale said, was definitely the most violent and obscene of the three.

"Where do they get these films — or do they produce them right here in Canada?" asked Andrea.

"I wouldn't be surprised if some are made in Canada," Gale said. Then we talked about an article we had all seen in the women's magazine *Kinesis*. The article explained how Red Hot Video had managed to dodge a loophole in Canadian copyright laws and was offering pirated copies of hardcore porn from other countries. The owner of the video store on Main Street was making a three hundred per cent profit on the tapes he sold and over four hundred per cent profit on rentals. Rumour had it that a local distributor to RHV had a bunch of video machines in his home and used them to copy tapes from ones he got in the United States. We all knew that the porn industry was way bigger than the conventional film and record industries combined — that there were four times as many porn shops in the United States as there were McDonald's and that 260 periodicals in the United States devoted themselves to child pornography.

"What I don't understand," I said, "is how people think looking at porn is harmless and should be an individual freedom. It flies in the face, as they say, of a universally recognized educational theory of rote learning — meaning if you expose children to ideas over and over again, they begin to incorporate or learn them. For some reason pornography is supposed to be the exception to this theory."

"Yeah. If teenagers manage to rent those films," Andrea said angrily, "how can anyone think they won't learn that it's acceptable to rape and torture women?"

Our dinners had arrived, and we sat eating in silence, each of us consumed, no doubt, by different visions of young women being raped and tortured. After reading our fortune cookies, we paid for our meal and pushed our chairs back to go. "I parked out back, so I'll just meet you guys at that gas station in North Van," I said. I didn't want to have to explain my paranoia about being followed. They agreed and, after paying the bill, went out the front door.

Moments after they left, I casually walked out the back door. In the alley I sprinted down to the other restaurant, went in the back door, and exited through the front to our truck. I got in quickly and glanced around nervously. There were no cops in sight, but that didn't mean anything to me. I drove over to North Vancouver using every counter-surveillance driving manoeuvre I could think of.

By the time I arrived at the gas station in North Van, my friends were just getting out of their car. Together we walked to the Red Hot Video store at 965 Marine Drive, taking our time in front so we could get a look inside. Like most of the outlets, this one had its front window covered up so pedestrians couldn't see inside. At the end of the block we turned down the alley that ran behind the store. When we reached the back of the store, two of us acted as lookouts while the third went over to the only window, a small one high off the ground. She stood on her tiptoes and with difficulty peered in, then returned to us. As we continued walking, we took mental notes of everything in the immediate area.

The plan would be to arrive late at night and park down this alley. One person would wait in the running car, with the head-lights off, while the other two went to the back of the store. We would have to make sure we had something to stand on — a crate, maybe — to make it easier to reach the window. With a cloth over a rock we would break the window, pour a red plastic container of gas in the window, throw in a torch to ignite the gas, then run to the car and leave the area as quickly as possible without speeding. It seemed simple and foolproof.

"Where does the window lead to?" Andrea asked, as we headed back to our vehicles.

"Looks like a bathroom," Gale said. "If we use enough gas, the fire should spread quickly to the rest of the store."

"Could you see if there were any living quarters in the back of the store?" I asked. After the Litton bombing, I was very cautious about the possibility of injuries.

"No way," she said. "It's too small a store to have living quarters in there. Plus the sound of the window breaking would wake anyone up in the remote chance somebody was spending the night."

We figured out who would get what we needed for the action, then arranged a time to meet on the night of the firebombing. That done, we parted.

When I got back to Sullivan Street everyone was in bed except for Julie, who was sitting on the living room floor brushing Rex. He was groaning with pleasure. "How'd it go, Julie?" I knew she'd had a meeting with her group as well.

"Fine," she said softly. "After our meeting I went back to Coquitlam by myself and knocked on the front window real hard to make sure nobody was inside. I even yelled. There's no other store beside it. I didn't hear anybody, but just to be sure I threw some pebbles against the window."

"Haven't you been there a few times now?"

"Yes," she said defensively. "I've cased almost every night since we decided to do this. There's no way I want something like what happened at Litton to happen again."

"You know what, Julie? At first when you told me about being followed by an undercover, I thought you were being paranoid and just needed to relax because it's probably nothing. But I'm getting a little paranoid myself. I'm sorry for not believing you."

She smiled weakly but didn't acknowledge my apology. "I'd rather do smaller actions like the Wimmin's Fire Brigade stuff."

"Yeah, me too," I said spontaneously.

"They're not so heavy and I like working with more people," she added.

"Yeah. These actions are probably more in line with what people in this country can relate to," I said, thinking out loud. "We should be heading in this direction, more like the Amax style stuff than the Litton bombing."

"Yeah." She went back to brushing Rex.

"Well I'm going to bed. I'll see you tomorrow," I said, heading towards the stairs.

* * *

November 20 was a typical day for that period of our lives. I got up around nine and went for my morning jog in Bell Park. By the time I got back, Julie, Gerry, and Brent were up and putting a hearty breakfast of bacon and eggs on the table. We made our plans for the day, which consisted of Julie and Gerry running some errands in town and Brent and me casing the Woolco Mall. Later Doug was coming over for dinner to pick up the final copy of the Wimmin's Fire Brigade communiqué.

After breakfast I had a shower and changed into what I called my "bourgeois outfit." I brushed my long, straggly blonde hair until all the knots were out, and then pulled it into a neat pony tail. I put on my nylon sockettes, green wool pants, white jacket, and velveteen black pumps. These were the same clothes I had bought in Calgary, but since I only wore them to case they were still in good shape. I looked in the mirror. What a transformation!

When I got downstairs, Brent was still polishing his beloved shoes, a pastime that had inspired Julie and me to christen them "Guccis," even though they were a generic version of the famous brand name. After he bought these shoes in Toronto, he had spent so much time caring for them that one day Julie had bought some chicken feet in the Kensington Market and, as a joke, put them carefully in his shoes. When he opened his closet the next morning and saw the chicken feet sitting neatly inside his shoes, instead of laughing he had spent hours decontaminating the footware and chastising us for such poor taste in humour.

We walked over to the mall and took turns hanging around in Woolco's pet section. Since I was first watch, Brent headed over to the Krack-A-Joke store to play video games. Playing video games had become something of an obsession with us. We would spend anywhere from ten to fifteen dollars a day on games all over the city. I took it as a sign that our lifestyle was not very healthy. We had too much money and the games were so quick that they demanded one hundred per cent focus, so that for our fifteen-minute intervals of play it was impossible to worry about whatever illegal action we were working on at the time.

I wandered around the pet section, feeling sorry for the little caged creatures, until I was almost run over by the Brink's guard. He had arrived early, catching me off guard. I was bending over looking at some hamsters on the bottom shelf when I saw him out of the corner of my eye, turning down my aisle. By the time I stood up, he was a foot away from me and our eyes met magnetically. I knew it was a fundamental rule of casing not to look your target in the eye. Not only was I looking him in the eye, but I was mesmerized. I could sense from his unguarded expression that he was a kind, trusting person. In my paranoid frame of mind, it felt like our eyes were locked for half an hour, but in real time it must have been a fraction of a second. He flashed a quick, warm smile and moved around me to pass. He was an overweight guy who couldn't pass by me without changing his course a little. As he passed I dropped my eyes, only to find them resting on his .38 revolver with a real wooden handle piece. Once again I found myself breaking the rules, this time locking my eyes on his revolver. I saw he did not have the leather strap closed, which would make it easier for him to pull the gun out of his holster. I tried to avert my eyes as he shifted sideways in passing, but as his revolver disappeared on the other side of him, the bulging money bag came into view. Unable to move my eyes, I couldn't help noticing that the shape of the bulges coincided remarkably to the shape of wads of bills. As he continued on down the aisle, his huge back safely towards me, I finally managed to pull my delinquent eyes out of the danger zone and look towards the hamsters again.

After an acceptable period of time, I went back to Krack-A-Joke and told Brent about my encounter, minus the eye contact part. We made a mental note to start coming earlier, since the Brink's pickup was not always at the same time. Then I left him in the mall playing video games and went home to make a big roast beef dinner. I had the better part of an afternoon to prepare a meal before Doug was expected.

Roast and gravy were my specialty, bringing back childhood memories of cosy family dinners. It was always a special occasion whenever Doug came over for dinner, probably because we had so few social contacts. By the time he arrived, we were all in good spirits. "Where did you get that?" he asked, pointing at the huge roast, surrounded by roast potatoes and carrots and drowning in lumpy gravy.

"At an Overwaitea."

"Shoplifting?"

"Yep," I said, placing plates down on the table. "We went out last week sometime. I guess we should be eating less meat, but not everyone wants to be vegetarian."

"I think it's fairly risky for you people to be shoplifting," he stated.

"I know, but Julie and Gerry don't have any money and they don't want to borrow any more." We kept our finances separate instead of pooling our money like a commune.

"For the amount of money you save, it's not worth the risk," said Doug practically. "Are you still shoplifting in Lifestream stores?"

"Yep," said Brent, helping me set the table. "They're owned by Kraft Foods now."

"It's still uncool," Doug reiterated. "If you got busted in there, I don't think many people in the radical community would be supportive."

"I don't give a fuck," said Brent, not looking at Doug. That little interchange set the tone for the evening. It was fairly cool between Brent and Doug, while the rest of us managed to ignore them. Doug decided to leave shortly after dinner, and I volunteered to drive him home.

When I got back, Brent was up in our room, making one of his collages. "I guess we better not mention shoplifting at Mountain Equipment Co-op?" I said by way of bringing up the touchy topic again. Doug was a member of the co-op and without a doubt would have been strongly opposed to shoplifting there. There was no ethical justification for shoplifting at Mountain Equipment Co-op. The only reason we had ever shoplifted there was because it was easy. I knew it was wrong, but justified it by telling myself that I was just going along with the group. That was no excuse.

"Selling Lifestream to Kraft Foods makes it no different than any other subsidiary of a conglomerate except they sell health food," said Brent again.

"It's different," I said. "They don't overpackage everything and they provide an alternative source of healthy food. Anyway, there's lots of places to shoplift that aren't seen as part of the alternative community. Plus I feel as though we're taking advantage of the fact that they don't call the cops when they do catch someone shoplifting." A friend of mine had been caught in there and all they did was lecture her.

Brent just snorted and continued working on his collage. I lay back on the pillows and tried to read, but I couldn't concentrate. I kept thinking about the tension between the five of us. The side effects of our unhealthy social isolation were beginning to surface. There weren't enough social outlets for our emotions, and we didn't have other friends who could act as sounding boards for our ideas and behaviour. If I had doubts about what we were doing, I could only discuss them with the converted — us. This situation of not being accountable or responsible to anyone was leading to questionable political decisions. I knew that Brent would not be proud of admitting that he shoplifted at Mountain Equipment Co-op. It was not part of a chain, it was a true co-op, run by its members. It sold high-quality camping and outdoor gear for reasonable prices. Even the decision to use 550 pounds of explosives at Litton would probably have been different if we had to get approval from a larger community of people involved in the anti-nuclear movement.

In places like El Salvador, I knew, thousands of people were supporting the guerrillas. There was an interplay between the guerrillas and the people they represented. The liberation movement funded medical clinics and schools in remote mountain villages. In return the people would hide fugitives and give them food and shelter when they needed it. Here, the five of us lived in total isolation from our community, accountable to no one, doing things on our own initiative. Emotionally we were all just about ready to explode.

In frustration I threw my book on the bed and went downstairs. Julie was making herself a pot of tea. "Do you feel good about our shoplifting, Jules?"

"Sure, why not?"

"I don't know. I think Doug's got a point about Lifestream. I think if we would be embarrassed to admit shoplifting at a place, then we should go with our instincts and not shoplift there."

"Yeah. If I feel nervous, I don't do it." She had missed my point, but I couldn't be bothered going over the whole issue again that night.

Gerry was sitting in the living room where he could hear us. "Brent was telling me you boosted a toboggan the other day," he chuckled. "What did you do, just pick it up and walk out?"

"Yeah," I said without enthusiasm. "That's the biggest thing I've ever taken but the bigger, the easier. When you put something like a toboggan over your head and just walk out, they figure you must have paid for it since it's so obvious."

"This punk, who makes a living boosting," Julie said, "was telling me that if she catches a store dick following her, she just turns around and starts chewing him out real loud in front of everyone, like 'Why are you following me around this store, what do you think I'm doing, shoplifting?' And sure enough, he scrams so she can shoplift without being hassled." This inspired another story from Gerry. I went back upstairs. I was in no mood to listen to boosting stories.

✳ **33** ✳

On the eve of the Wimmin's Fire Brigade arson, November 21, I felt cool as a cucumber. It seemed like such a simple, foolproof action that I really didn't have anything to worry about — at least not until we were half a mile into it. We had barely got out of Gale's neighbourhood when a heart-stopping red light started whirling around on the car behind us.

"Oh my God," whispered Gale. "It's the cops! I'm not speeding! What the fuck would he be pulling me over for?" I glanced over my shoulder and, sure enough, a police car was tailing us. "You better pull over," I whispered back.

When we stopped a tall cop came strolling up to the driver's door and asked for Gale's licence, ownership, and insurance. Luckily we weren't driving a stolen car. Maintaining a polite attitude, she rummaged around in her bag and pulled out her ID. He took it and walked back to his car, presumably to run her ID through CPIC, the Canadian Police Information Centre, a centralized computer information system that listed anyone with a criminal record. "Is there anything wrong with your car?" I asked.

"Not that I know of. It's old, but last time I looked all the lights were working."

A few minutes later the officer came back and simply explained that her brake lights had flickered, so she had better get them checked out before she drove around any more. He paused and asked what we were up to. We were completely unprepared for this. "Just heading out for some donuts," Gale improvised.

"I don't think it would be wise to drive around with a possible short-circuit in your brake lights," he advised. He glanced quickly around inside our car and then walked back to his patrol car. Luckily he hadn't asked to look inside the trunk, because that was where we had a five-gallon jerry can filled with gasoline, plus the rock and torches.

We sat frozen where we had parked. "Maybe we should cancel?" suggested Andrea from the back seat.

"Yeah, but what about the others? We have no way of getting in touch with them and they'll be heading out to do theirs," Gale said.

Maybe Julie was right. Maybe we were being followed and this was their way of trying to stop us. But on the other hand, maybe this was just a total fluke. If we were under surveillance, why would they send a uniformed cop to ID us? Why wouldn't they do something to stop us from carrying out the firebombing? I wished I could discuss these thoughts with my partners, but I couldn't. If we were under surveillance, they would just bust us as soon as we lit the torch. I looked at my friends and decided to leave the decision up to them, even though they didn't have all the facts.

"Get out and see if there's anything wrong with my brake light," instructed Gale. I got out and stood behind her car while she applied the brakes. They worked just fine. I didn't detect any flickering or signs of a short-circuit. "Nothing."

"Well, there's three of us. Who wants to cancel?" Gale asked. A dead silence was her answer. "It was probably just a coincidence that he pulled us over. I didn't get any weird vibes from him." She put the car in drive.

* * *

Around 1:00 a.m. we pulled into the alley behind the Red Hot Video store on Marine Drive. According to our plan, Gale turned off the lights but left the engine running and then stepped out of the car so she could act as a lookout while we did the firebombing.

We walked quickly up to the back window. Earlier we had left a crate nearby, and now we put it under the window. I stood on the crate and smashed the window with the rock. The shattering of the glass was deafening in the silence of the night. Then I heaved the heavy jerry can up and rested it on the window sill and let the gas pour in.

I remember being aware of how calm I felt. The only concern I had was that if we were under surveillance, the cops might suddenly appear. As the last bit of gas dribbed out of the spout, even that concern vanished. I put the can down and reached over to get the torch my friend was carrying. I smiled at her confidently, and pulled out a book of matches and struck it.

BOOM!!! The air exploded around me. I vaguely remember my coat being on fire and the smell of singed hair, but other than that I don't remember much. Later I was told the flames on my coat went out almost instantly. We ran to the car and jumped in. I do clearly recall the expressions on my friends' faces when they looked at me — shock, which was also the state I went into shortly after.

When we got back to Gale's house they told me to lie down on the couch so they could swab the burnt skin and ashes off my face. After they finished this painful procedure, I asked if I could look at myself in the mirror, but they adamantly shook their heads. It must be bad. Then Andrea brought some long, slimy, green strips she had taken from a plant and placed them all over my face. She was studying herbal remedies and was administering strips from an aloe vera plant. She left them on for about half an hour, then took them off and replaced them with more. They were soothing and made me feel as though everything was going to be alright.

All night I lay on the couch, half dozing, while my friends continued putting aloe vera on my burns. By the time the early morning light broke through the window shades, my face was beginning to swell. I sat up a little and could feel the heavy sensation of fluid building up under the skin. I had still not looked in a mirror and did not feel any acute pain, which is weird because I had always heard that burns are one of the most painful injuries a person can have.

I got up and walked into the bathroom. My friends didn't try to stop me. They knew I would eventually have to look at myself. What I saw almost knocked me off my feet. I looked like an old, Black woman, because the first layer of skin had been burnt right off my face, leaving pieces of parched, black skin flaking off all over. My eyebrows, eyelashes, and about four inches of hair from my head were completely burnt off. Because I had been lying down all night, the second layer of skin was beginning to ooze a clear fluid and swell from fluids that couldn't escape.

Julie had arrived sometime during the night. When I hadn't returned home, she had assumed I would be at Gale's or in jail. She was shocked and insisted I go to the hospital, but I was afraid that the doctors would call the police. "If we go to the hospital before the newspapers come out, nobody's going to think you got burned during an arson," she explained. "You could say you were lighting a gas stove and it exploded." It wasn't a bad idea, but I wanted to talk to Brent first to see what he thought.

The sky was washed in pinks and purples as Julie and I thanked our friends for everything. Andrea placed a couple of baby food jars filled with herbs in my hands and handed Julie the remains of the poor aloe vera plant. I can only remember "witches' root" as one of the herbs that she gave me, but I had every intention of following her instructions. I was already beginning to worry about permanent facial scarring.

Brent and Gerry had suspected that something was wrong when I didn't come home, but they didn't know what until I walked in the door. As soon as Gerry saw my face, his eyes filled with tears and he left the room. It wasn't until months later that he told me he had almost fainted when he saw how badly I was burned. They did not hesitate in insisting I go immediately to the hospital emergency ward with Julie. It was only 6:00 a.m.

After I was quickly admitted into the hospital with my Lillicropp ID, the staff shuffled me into an examination room and a young doctor appeared within minutes. I didn't wait for him to ask what happened but explained that when I struck a match to light our old gas stove, it had exploded in my face. He didn't question me but concentrated on cleaning and examining my face. Now that the shock was beginning to wear off, I was beginning to feel frightened of permanent facial burn scars and asked him what the outcome would be. He had managed to keep a poker face throughout the examination. "Miss Lillicropp, I must be honest with you. There's a 50 per cent chance you'll have permanent facial scarring. These are second-degree burns, which means the first layer of skin has been burned off or damaged. If the layer of skin underneath becomes infected, then you will inevitably have facial scarring. But if we can prevent infection, there's a good chance it will clear up. The important thing is that you go to your family physician every day to have your burns cleaned and new bandages put on." He looked me straight in the eye to see if I had digested this information. I had.

Without a word, he continued to clean off the dead skin and pus, then took out a tube of ointment and administered it to my whole face. As he put the cap on the tube I got up to leave, but he put his hand on my shoulder and explained that a nurse would be putting a full facial bandage on my face. I would have to change it every day for about six weeks. I sat back down. By the time the nurse was done, I looked like a mummy from a horror movie. Except for a tuft of hair at the top of my head, two slits for eyes and one for my nose and mouth, the rest of my head was wrapped in a hood of white gauze. Even I was horrified when I looked in the mirror. When I returned to the waiting room, Julie smiled, but her eyes were as big as saucers.

"That's great!" she said soothingly. A couple of kids sitting nearby with their mother were more honest. I couldn't help over-hearing them giggle, "Look Mommy, a monster!" Their mother sympathetically tried to shepherd them away from me, but no matter where she took them their little eyes remained transfixed on me. They hadn't seen anything like this except on TV.

That little incident became standard fare in my daily life for the next six weeks. Everywhere I went, little children would shriek, in fear or amusement, at my head mask. It didn't take long before I felt like a monster and started hunching over to minimize my exposure. Unfortunately, my posture didn't make me disappear but made me look even more like the hunchback of Notre Dame. What's worse, in the first few weeks yellow pus would ooze out of the slits of my eyes and mouth, making me look even more hideous. Although the doctor kept reassuring me that it wasn't infection, but rather fluid, I still felt a shiver of fear run down my spine every time I looked in the mirror.

Besides fearing permanent facial scarring, I was also afraid of losing Brent's love. Could it be skin deep, as they say? The answer came the next day. I was sitting on the edge of the bed dressing when Brent came in. I didn't look up because I felt so ugly, but I could feel his eyes on me. Without a word, he walked up and looked deeply into what he could see of my eyes, through the slits. Tenderly he ran his hands along my neck and down my arms, stopping to caress the vulnerable area inside my elbow. I melted in his arms and felt tears welling up in my eyes that he couldn't see. He made love to me in such a tender yet passionate way that I never doubted his love for me again. Indeed, never before, or after, did he show his love for me more than during that time. He even spoon-fed me my meals because I had a hard time getting the food between the slits. Most importantly, he never expressed pity or even an inkling of fear that when the bandages came off I might be a monster of facial scars.

I was able to use Lillicropp's health card for my daily doctor's appointments, since we assumed she was living in the United States. Religiously I took the herbal remedies Andrea had given me. I applied aloe vera to my wounds whenever I could and got my bandages changed daily at the doctor's office. No one ever questioned how I had been burned.

Shortly after the accident, I remember making an unemotional but unwavering decision to kill myself if the outcome of this burn was extensive facial scarring. This wasn't because my life hinged on my physical appearance; rather, because of my experiences with the facial bandage I knew I couldn't go through life having people pity me or shielding me from children who would stare at me in horror. In retrospect, I'm sure I could have had a meaningful life with facial scarring, though no doubt everything would have turned out differently. I am also quite sure that if I had suffered permanent burn scars, I would have driven out to the mountains and blown my head off.

* * *

When I left for the hospital the morning of the gas explosion, I was so consumed by the burn that I had given little thought to the fire-bombings. When I got back to Sullivan Street with Julie that next morning, my first thoughts were of the other women.

"How did it go?" I asked Julie, after we'd finished talking about the burn.

"We threw a rock through the front window and then a couple of jars filled with gas, but I didn't hear them break. I had my torch — you know, that stick I showed you, wrapped in gasoline-soaked cloth. Anyway, I was about to light it when this car comes around the corner. I just barely had time to light it so I don't think it really ignited, but I threw it in anyway and we took off. All that happened, I think, is the window got broken and the Molotov cocktails went through."

"You told me, you thought the car was a cop," added Gerry.

"I said it *might* be a cop," said Julie irritably.

"I wonder how it went for the others?" I said. "I guess we won't know till we get a paper. Hey, why don't we turn on the tube?"

Gerry hopped up and turned on the TV, but the morning news was over and had been replaced by the morning talk shows. "Brent went out to get a paper," Gerry said. We watched some television mindlessly until Brent burst through the door, holding the morning paper in the air.

"It made the morning paper!" he smiled. We crowded around him over the kitchen table, all trying to read it at once.

"Holy moly!!" gasped Gerry. "I can't believe it! They really burned down the Surrey store good!" The news article stated that a letter delivered to the Canadian Press bureau at 1:40 a.m. alerted police to the firebombings, but it was too late. The fire at 9440-120 Street in Surrey was detected at 2:00 a.m., and it completely destroyed the Red Hot Video store as well as a neighbouring shoe store and two other vacant stores that were part of a small mall. The result was hundreds of thousands of dollars' damage. The fire in the North Vancouver Red Hot Video store was discovered at 1:31 a.m. It destroyed a back bathroom and damaged the rear of the store, resulting in two to three thousand dollars in damages. A patrolling police car found a broken window and a homemade torch soaked in gasoline at the Coquitlam store. Looking inside the broken window, he found various gasoline-filled glass containers with tape hanging from them apparently waiting to be touched off, but none of them had been ignited. Although we were pleased with the results of our efforts, we weren't happy that the Surrey firebombing had also burnt down three other stores in the small strip mall.

Doug showed up unexpectedly later that morning. Just like the others, he was shocked to see my head wrapped up in gauze. After we explained what happened, he said, "I can't believe that no one thought to warn you of the dangers of gasoline fumes. Didn't you know that if you pour gallons of gasoline into a small room, the fumes will collect and explode as soon as you light a match!?" I must admit, I did feel stupid. He looked over at Brent and Gerry. "Didn't any of you fools know that this would happen?"

Everyone looked at their feet in shame, including myself. Finally, Brent came up with a defence. "I didn't know the details of their plan," he said sheepishly.

"It's true, Doug. We didn't go over the details with him so we really should shoulder the blame," I said in Brent's defence. In retrospect I was perplexed how this basic safety precaution had slipped past those of us involved. It was common knowledge that gasoline fumes are highly explosive.

"I have some interesting news," Doug said, changing the topic. "This morning, as soon as I got back from delivering the communiqué, one of your cohorts from the Surrey action came by. She didn't know who to talk to, so she chose me. Anyway, she said that when they got in her car to leave last night, she discovered that her brake lines had been cut. It was too late to take another car, so they went anyway."

"How did they stop?" asked Julie with surprise.

"Since it was late, there were few cars on the road, so they drove slowly and managed to make it using a combination of slowing down and gearing down. They chose roads that had very few intersections or stop signs. It's a miracle they made it there and back, but they did. Very brave in my estimation." We all agreed.

I told them about our experience in being stopped for a faulty brake light, which we found suspicious, and then Julie remarked how the newspaper article had verified her feeling that the car she had seen coming had been a police car. "Pretty coincidental, eh?" said Gerry. We just looked at each other in silence.

There was more than one miracle associated with the Wimmin's Fire Brigade arsons. For the next six weeks I continued going every day to appointments with my doctor. In the beginning I avoided asking her the question foremost on my mind. Would I have permanent facial scarring? Instead I would stare into the mirror each time she unravelled the long gauze strips, praying that I wouldn't see any yellow pus. When I didn't see any, I would turn and stare into her face, but she wouldn't give anything away. As the weeks turned into a month, she began to smile reassuringly at me. The swelling was almost gone, and still there was no sign of infection.

By the end of the six-week period her reassuring smiles had turned to elation. "This is truly a miracle! When I first saw you I thought the best we could hope for was minor facial scarring, but for reasons I don't fully understand, it appears you may not have any scarring!" I didn't tell her that this minor miracle may also have saved my life. I attributed it to Andrea's herbal remedies, which I faithfully took every morning, and thanked her profusely on the day that my facial bandages came off forever.

✻ **34** ✻

F raser and Staff Sergeant Kent from the Metro Toronto Police had just arrived at the CLEU building to be briefed about the latest developments in the Direct Action investigation. John Anderson picked up a media release from his desk and held it in the air. "This is the kind of stuff we have to contend with in B.C. The day after this group calling itself the Wimmin's Fire Brigade burnt down three Red Hot Video stores, we get a barrage of phone calls to local radio phone-in shows, from citizens *supporting* these crimes. To top it off, the B.C. Federation of Women sends out this news release which, to no one's surprise, shows up in all the papers the next day, basically advocating similar crimes. It's hard to believe, but I'll read you this crap so you'll have a clear idea of what we're up against in this province."

Anderson read from the press release: "While we did not participate in the firebombings of Nov 22nd in the Lower Mainland, we are in agreement with the frustration and anger of the women who did. We noted and appreciated their efforts to see that no one got hurt. Thirty-six women's liberation groups of the B.C. Federation of Women have made a decision to close the Red Hot Video outlets this year. We insist that B.C. Attorney General Allan Williams take action immediately to prevent rich men from profiting from Red Hot Video's hate literature about women and children. The women of B.C. are being driven to desperate acts. The Canadian and B.C. governments have failed to use the existing laws to defend more than half the population from the horrors of the pornographic industry. Pornography is the theory — rape is the practice."

Anderson looked up at Kent and Fraser for a few seconds before going on. "About a week after the arsons, more than thirty women's groups laid complaints with us about videotapes depicting violence against women. We sent a guy down to talk to some of the store owners and see if they wouldn't comply by getting rid of the worst videos without legal intervention. Only Tricolor Video in North Van complied. Now, today, what is it — the second of December already?" Fraser nodded.

"Anyway, this morning I got a call from the B.C. attorney general's office saying they've got thirteen women's groups pressuring them to investigate the video porn outlets. They gave the office a copy of a film called *Filthy Rich* to preview because they say it shows women being raped and learning to enjoy it. So what do we do? Our hands are tied by the law. Women aren't included as an 'identifiable group' in the hate propaganda section of the Criminal Code, and we've never had much luck getting convictions under the section prohibiting combining explicit sex and violence. We've got the women on one side, pressuring us to lay charges, and we've got the civil liberties folks on the other saying it's an infringement of personal freedom to censor what people watch in the privacy of their own homes. And both sides have well paid lawyers."

"I'm assuming this Wimmin's Fire Brigade is Direct Action?" asked Kent.

"We've had the Direct Action people under surveillance since the end of October and transferred the investigation from the Security Service to CLEU on November 18th, once we were quite confident something was going to happen around the Red Hot Video stores," Anderson explained. "The Wimmin's Fire Brigade has a lot of players. It's too early to tell how many of them were involved in the Litton or Cheekeye bombings. All we know is that there were nine women participating in the arsons and one of our original suspects from Direct Action, Doug Stewart, delivered the communiqué. The bad thing about this latest attack is that it's getting one hell of a lot of support. With all the injuries the Litton bombing was not popular. The Cheekeye bombing, back in the wilderness, was too obscure and local to get much support. But this Red Hot Video thing is a PR disaster for us. You wouldn't believe it, Bob. Dozens of women's groups have published letters of support for these arsons, and there's been demonstrations in a dozen towns all over the province calling for the closure of these porno stores. Unfortunately, in the public's eye the Wimmin's Fire Brigade has been much more effective in closing Red Hot Video than law enforcement has been. To date the Surrey store is closed because they burnt it down. Another store closed for fear of getting hit. Two others moved to different communities, and two more changed their names. That kind of success could spawn a small army of Wimmin's Fire Brigade groups."

"If you had them under surveillance, why couldn't you stop them?" Kent asked.

"We don't have any room bugs yet, so we weren't sure of what and when," explained Anderson. "But on the night of the arsons, we had ten people on Stewart, watching him deliver that damn communiqué and grab a cab home. We also made attempts to stop the women, but they kept going. We had a uniformed guy pull over the one vehicle and ID them, but they kept going. Another uniform passed by the Coquitlam store right at the beginning of the arson, so we did save that store. They panicked and didn't light their Molotov cocktails. The brake lines were cut in the third vehicle, but they drove to Surrey anyway. What were we supposed to do? If we had arrested them beforehand, we would only have had circumstantial evidence on the possibility of arsons against Red Hot Video, but we would never have got convictions — and we would have blown any hope of evidence on the Litton or Cheekeye bombings. If those two cases remain unsolved, you and me will be manning the phones in the front office for the rest of our lives." Kent nodded his head in agreement.

"So we made the decision to watch them and try to discourage them from carrying out the arsons, but we couldn't afford to blow our cover this early in the game," Anderson continued. "Now we know who most of the main players are, but there's a bunch of minor ones we aren't too sure of so we've been putting some heat on them. We picked up some of them and showed them long, detailed lists of women's groups and their members and told them who we knew were involved, and all they had to do was verify our information and we'd go light on them. A couple of our Mounties visited the boss of one woman and told her that her employee was not who she appeared to be, that she was in fact a terrorist. We picked another one off the street and told her we'd lay arson charges against her if she refused to give evidence against one of her friends who we know was involved."

"So what came of that?" asked Kent.

"Zip. A great big nothing," said Anderson. "Like I said before, these people are more tight-lipped than the bikers."

"What about room bugs?" suggested Kent.

"That's what we're working on," Anderson said. "But we also have to appease the public *now*. If the public doesn't see some action, we're going to find their support behind the Wimmin's Fire Brigade instead of the police and attorney general's office. So we've got our undercover guys renting videos and the AG's office is viewing them and preparing obscenity charges. Once we've got the evidence and a hard case, we'll orchestrate a raid, which, I hope, you'll see happening sometime in the next few weeks."

"Oh, that reminds me, John," interrupted Fraser. "I was talking to the owner of the Port Coquitlam store, Brian Trent, and he's planning on closing it down December 7th because he's afraid of another firebombing attempt. I think you're right about the public. If we don't do something soon, it's going to look like the Wimmin's Fire Brigade is more effective in closing them down than us."

"Yeah, but getting a conviction on the Litton and Cheekeye bombings is going to take more time, so we can't just arrest these women now," Anderson continued. "Okay, so what we are doing is writing up an affidavit, listing the evidence we have so far, showing the involvement of the people at Sullivan Street and Windermere in the Wimmin's Fire Brigade, minus the surveillance of the car theft and arsons. We've had to delete any surveillance notes that show us witnessing the arsons. Obviously if we admit witnessing the arsons and not making arrests, the affidavit will be fraudulent. We have to show that we have good reason to believe these people are involved in the Wimmin's Fire Brigade, but that we need room bugs in order to get more evidence against them. If we admit we witnessed the arsons, we wouldn't need the room bugs, would we? As I was explaining to our friend Fraser here, we have to look ahead to a court case, and the last thing we want happening is some fancy defence lawyer getting our wiretaps ruled inadmissible because the affidavit we used was fraudulent." Kent and Anderson smiled at one another.

Fraser sat with his eyebrows knitted, trying to fathom the whole complicated situation. Finally he said something. "If I remember correctly, there's a case going before the Supreme Court challenging the automatic right to enter a private home to install an authorized room bug."

"Yes, you're right Fraser," agreed Anderson. "But we'll have room bugs in before that case is anywhere near finished." He glanced over at the calendar on the wall. "I've got Corporal Larry Wilkinson working on the affidavit and application for the judge's authorization as we speak."

"Why didn't you just get me to do it, John?" Fraser felt somewhat slighted, because Larry was a colleague in the RCMP intelligence section of CLEU and wasn't as familiar with the case as he was.

"Don't be getting jealous on me," smiled Anderson. "You know that Larry specializes in preparing affidavits and organizing the installation of room bugs. I need your brain with me." Fraser blushed a little. He regretted questioning Anderson's choice of personnel, a question that would be interpreted as a sign of emotional weakness.

"Well, I hate to break up the party," Kent said, getting up, "but I have to catch my flight back to T.O. It looks like you guys have the core group of our terrorist organization, but we all know there must be a Toronto link or cell. There's no way they could have bombed the Litton plant without help in Toronto. My feeling is there's another hardcore group there as well as a band of supporters just like your Wimmin's Fire Brigade. After those trials for the Remembrance Day demonstration, we should have the public's support and the information we need to do some searches and hopefully come up with some suspects and hard evidence."

"What do you have so far, Bob?" asked Anderson.

"All we really have is a calendar we got off this guy from Peterborough who got arrested at the November 11th demo," Kent said, organizing his papers.

"And . . . ?" asked Anderson.

"Okay," said Kent, putting his papers in his briefcase, "but keep this under your hats. When we picked this character, Ivan LeCouvie, up at the November 11th demo, he had a calendar in his knapsack that we kept to look over. Well, lo and behold, if it doesn't document a trip this guy took to Prague, Czechoslovakia, last summer in order to attend a peace conference of something called the World Federation of Democratic Youth. In this calendar, he's got all kinds of references to communist youth organizations and a stopover in Moscow. The way I see it, he could be some kind of Soviet agent — we don't know, but it's possible. Most of these terrorist organizations have Soviet connections to get training and ideas. We don't have hard evidence that he actually is a Soviet agent, but the stopover in Moscow and his obvious interest in communist organizations are circumstantial evidence at the very least."

"We have to get the public on board. There's trials coming up for some of these protesters on December 7th, and so before the trials our Crown prosecutor Norm Matusiak is going to give a little press conference and let the public know we have this calendar, which proves that some elements of the peace movement have been infiltrated by the Soviets."

"Are you serious?" Fraser asked.

Kent turned and looked at Fraser like the RCMP officer was some kind of alien. "Of course I'm serious," he said sternly. "Would I joke around about something like this?"

"How could this kid be a Soviet agent?" asked Fraser incredulously.

"It's an expression," explained Kent in frustration. "LeCouvie is a follower of Soviet politics and philosophy and is using whatever he learns on his trips to Russia and Czechoslovakia to influence his friends in the peace movement. From what we know, he is very influential in these circles and we have *no* reason to believe he does *not* have a Soviet connection.

"Now, you guys are going to be putting a bug in your suspects' homes soon," he continued. "But we aren't that far along yet. We're going to use LeCouvie's calendar and other information we have to get a warrant to search the offices of the main anti-nuclear organizations and come up with more information so we can search the homes of people we suspect could have been involved in the Litton bombing and are perhaps members of Direct Action. It's a double-edged sword." Kent closed his brief case and looked at Anderson and Fraser to let them know he had to go. "On the one side, the searches might reveal information about those involved in the Litton bombing, and on the other side it will divide the peace movement into two camps — those who support the bombing and those who don't. We want that. Divide and conquer. We want to isolate those who support violence from the rest. The movement will be preoccupied arguing amongst one another over who supports and who doesn't support violence, and they'll have less time to organize as one body against Litton. You might think I'm an idiot, Fraser," he said, looking directly at him. "But I've taken some night courses and I do have a strategy. You don't get to be an inspector and head an investigation by being an idiot, you know." He opened the door and nodded his head at them. "Gentlemen, I'll give you a call in a week."

After he left, Anderson looked at Fraser and said, "it would be a smart move on your part to respect your superiors and not ask so many questions if you want to get ahead."

✳ **35** ✳

Ivan LeCouvie loved the films of Costa-Gavras, the renowned Greek filmmaker who specialized in political thrillers. He particularly liked *State of Siege*, about the CIA's involvement in training the secret police and helping to prop up a dictatorship in Uruguay — and about how the Uruguayan urban guerrilla group, the Tupamaros, kidnapped a U.S. Agency for International Development official. Now Ivan had just been to see *Missing*, the new Costa-Gavras film about the bloody U.S.-engineered coup in Chile.

As he and his friends were about to leave the Lansdowne Mall theatre in Peterborough, Ivan told them he would meet them out front after he had gone to the washroom. As usual, the washroom was filled with people, buzzing about the film. Ivan walked up to a urinal and watched the yellow liquid spin in circles down the drain. Out of the corner of his eye he noticed the man beside him glance over. Blushing slightly, Ivan hurriedly zipped up his pants, hoping the man had not taken his sidelong glance as a come-on. Walking over to the sink, he saw the same man whispering to another man standing against the wall, apparently waiting for him.

Ivan gave his head a shake. The movie was over. These were not CIA agents and he was not in South America, but just to be sure he decided to go into a stall to see if they would leave. He was in luck. The stall closest to him was empty so he darted in. He stood there and counted to sixty, then opened the stall door and, definitely, caught the same two men standing against the wall watching him, but this time without guard. Ivan stared back at them, then held his head high and marched out, vowing to tell his friends about this even if he did seem paranoid.

He had walked about twenty feet along the plush theatre carpet heading towards the exit door when he decided to glance back to see if the men were following him. His heart skipped a beat when he saw them walking ten feet behind him but speeding up and unabashedly staring at him. Ivan picked up speed but so did the men. He could almost hear them breathing down his neck when he made the decision to bolt for the door. Why, he didn't know. He hadn't done anything wrong but after watching a movie like *Missing*, the atmosphere almost demanded a state of apprehension.

Unfortunately his escape was foiled by a large, firm hand on his shoulder. "Ivan LeCouvie?"

"Yes?" said Ivan in a surprisingly weak little voice.

"You are under arrest."

"What?" Could this be real? Ivan felt as though he had gone into a time warp representing the virtual reality of the movie world. Ignoring his question, the men told him to put his hands behind his back and snapped a pair of cuffs on him. The stream of theatre stragglers had stopped flowing towards the exit door to witness the arrest, which was pretty exciting for a small city like Peterborough. Just like him, Ivan thought, they must be wondering if this was part of the movie. He flashed a reassuring smile at the small crowd of gawkers staring at him in horror. If he could have drawn a cartoon caption above their heads, it would have read, "He must have done something awful to be arrested in a public place." He looked around frantically for his friends, but they must have got tired of waiting for him and gone to their car.

When they got outside, one of the men placed his hand on Ivan's head and pushed him down into the police car. Ivan had always wondered why they did this in movies, and here it was happening to him. It must be to protect the top of his head from being hit by the top of the car door opening. It had always struck him as odd that they took such care to protect the prisoner's head when, moments later, they might be someplace in private beating him up.

He was driven to the Peterborough RCMP building, where he was placed in a small room with one wooden desk and several chairs. No windows. With *Missing* still in his mind, Ivan's imagination was running rampant. He envisioned himself being dangled from the window. Thank God there wasn't one. Or being pummelled with a thick telephone book that wouldn't leave marks, or made to balance in a chair at the top of a long cement staircase going down.

He didn't have to wait with his imagination for long. Moments after arriving, the same two plainclothes policemen came in the room and sat down across from him.

"So, Ivan, you must know why you are here," said the taller of the two.

"No, actually, I don't," said Ivan politely.

"You are being charged with attempted murder and the bombing of the Litton plant," the same cop said, watching for Ivan's reaction.

"You've got to be kidding!" Ivan gasped in true astonishment.

"Yes, Ivan. We have information written in your own hand from your calendar, which we seized at the Litton demonstration on November 11th. And we have the testimony of the other people involved." The cop continued to stare intently at Ivan's face.

"What people?" Ivan racked his brain trying to figure out who they could be referring to.

"The others involved in the Litton bombing," the cop said mysteriously.

"I don't know what you're talking about," Ivan said. "I wasn't involved in the Litton bombing in any way, shape, or form."

"Come on Ivan," the cop egged him on. "There are others who are testifying about your involvement, and if you don't confess you'll never see the light of day again. But, if you help us, we could help you."

Ivan shook his head in disbelief. "I want to see a lawyer," he stated emphatically.

"We'll let you call your lawyer in a few minutes. First, we just want you to help us with a few questions about notes you made in your calendar," said the tall man. Damn that calendar, thought Ivan. He knew it would lead to trouble. Why had he taken it with him to the Litton demonstration?

"If you answer a few simple questions, we could make sure your bail is reasonable. Otherwise it will be astronomical and you'll be in jail for years even before a court date," the tall man said when Ivan didn't respond. "There are frequent references in your calendar to the phrase 'non-violent direct action.' Explain what that means."

Ivan took a deep breath. At that moment he envisaged all the heroes he had ever seen. He had a vision in his mind of the brutal police interrogation of the Uruguayan revolutionaries in *State of Siege* and how the radicals sat there tall and strong and explained their revolutionary principles to the police, knowing that they would be tortured for these beliefs. Ivan did not see himself as a hero, but at that moment felt that inner surge of strength that comes from carrying out a mission more important than himself or his feelings.

"Ivan, tell us what 'direct action' means to you?" said the tall man gently.

"The essence of direct action," Ivan said, "is people fighting for themselves, rejecting those who *claim* to represent their true interests, whether they be revolutionaries or government officials. It is a far more subversive idea than civil disobedience because it is *not* meant to reform or influence state power but is meant to *undermine* it by showing it to be unnecessary and harmful. When people, *themselves*, resort to violence to protect their community from racist attacks or to protect their environment from ecological destruction, they are taking direct action." He could have skirted the issue of violence in his definition, but this evening Ivan was feeling brave.

The tall man appeared to be not at all moved by Ivan's speech. Instead he said, "Ivan, if you don't help us, we are going to have to transfer you to Toronto and there you will be interrogated by the head of the Litton investigation, even if it takes all night and all day tomorrow."

"I can't help you because I don't know anything," Ivan said in exasperation. "I told you everything I know, so if you don't mind I would like to call my lawyer."

"Since you obviously don't want to help us, we'll have to transfer you to Toronto. You'll be able to contact a lawyer there," said the tall man, getting up. He stood for a few minutes, looking at Ivan, giving him one last chance to talk, but Ivan just sat there looking back at him.

Ivan was transferred to Toronto that night. His friends, after finding out what had happened to him, quickly gathered a small group of supporters, including a local Roman Catholic priest who knew Ivan, and went to the local police station. They were not allowed to see Ivan and were not given any information. Later that evening they got in touch with Ivan's lawyer, who told them Ivan had been arrested by Metro Toronto police and was being questioned, pending charges related to the Litton bombing.

In Toronto Ivan was indeed questioned by the chief of the Litton investigation, who basically asked him the same questions as the cops had in Peterborough. When Ivan failed to give him the answers he wanted to hear, Ivan was told that he would be held in jail for at least four days. In criminal investigations, police have the option of detaining suspects an additional three days beyond the normal twenty-four hours before laying charges or having a bail hearing. After twelve solid hours of questioning in Toronto alone, the police finally released him.

Ivan was exhausted. He hadn't slept in twenty-four hours. He imagined that this was how it felt to be on acid. Exhaustion made everything, from colours to smells, seem different. Barely able to walk, he looked down at the slush on the front steps of the provincial courthouse, from which he had just been released. Concentrating so he didn't slip, he could hear a ruckus coming from the sidewalk below but didn't dare look up until he heard his name being used. Looking up, he saw a man in a suit, surrounded by reporters and photographers, giving what could only be a press interview. Ivan froze and listened to what the man was saying. Ivan gathered that the man at the centre of the scrum was the Crown prosecutor, Norman Matusiak, giving the press information about the outcome of the Remembrance Day protest trials. Between the banter of the reporters, the flash of cameras, and the cars splashing through the slush, Ivan managed to glean that his friend, Dave Collins, had been convicted of obstructing police in their line of duty. Dave was apparently being released with time served since he had been held in prison without bail since November 11. Then, to Ivan's surprise, the prosecutor held up Ivan's own calendar, using it as a prop to back up his accusations that the peace movement had a "Soviet connection." Ivan was almost blinded by the cameras as Matusiak brandished his calendar and flashed his pearly white smile in this photo opportunity for the six o'clock news.

Pulling his toque low over his face, Ivan bent over and headed towards the side of the courthouse, avoiding the pack of press hounds who were now racing up the courthouse steps after Matusiak.

"Ivan!" someone called out from a small crowd coming down the steps from the side door. Ivan couldn't believe his eyes. There was his mother, uncle, sister, and a small group of his friends, including Len Desroches, bunched together, rushing towards him. Unable to hold back his sobs, he ran across the slushy cement and wrapped his arms around his mother's neck. He could feel her chest heave under her heavy coat, and big tears rolled down her cheeks.

"Oh Ivan," she cried, "I was so afraid they were going to keep you here. We drove all night from Montreal, hoping to see you. But they wouldn't let us in. They told me that you were one of the Litton bombers, but I knew it wasn't true. You are my good boy." She held him back so she could see his face, and smiled.

"The prosecutor that just went in the courthouse was on the news last night, showing the world your calendar and saying the peace movement was infiltrated by Soviet spies!" said his sister, stroking his head. Ivan looked over his mother's shoulder and managed a smile at his friends.

"Thanks," he said. "It's frightening to think these people have the power to arrest! Soviet spies!" He had to laugh. "Let's get a coffee." Ivan, his family, and Len Desroches headed over to a little coffee shop nearby and found a booth. After talking to his family for awhile, Ivan asked Len how his trial had gone. Len told him that he had been acquitted of resisting a police officer, but Joanne Young wasn't so fortunate. "She was hardcore, eh? And a teacher too! She refused to co-operate in the booking procedure and wouldn't sign the bail conditions, so they kept her in the West

Detention Centre for five days. Some lawyers volunteered to help her and appealed her bail conditions to a higher court, arguing that the condition she stay away from Litton was unconstitutional. She won but lost her court case and got a discharge on the condition that she keep the peace and be of good behaviour for three months."

"I must admit," Ivan said, "I was impressed with the women at that demo. What happened to her teaching position? Did she lose her job?"

"No," Len said. "But she lost half a month's pay. Apparently there's a clause in her teaching contract that allows her special leave at the discretion of the principal. She thought that would cover her time in jail, but the principal wouldn't let her use it. He said it was just for teachers who had to appear in court for divorce actions." Which left Ivan thinking about how tough it would be to face the students and other teachers after all the publicity around the Remembrance Day demonstration.

Later Ivan decided to find a hotel for his family and himself for the night. They were all exhausted. His family had spent most of the night driving from Montreal and then trying to get in to see him at the jail. After finding some rooms Ivan decided to make a quick phone call to Peterborough to let his good friend Jack Kern know everything was alright. It was late afternoon, and he called the World Emergency offices at Trent University, where he guessed Jack would be. To his surprise, a strange voice answered the phone and then put Jack on the line.

"Hi Jack, it's me, Ivan," he said puzzled. "Who was that answering the phone?"

"The cops, Ivan," said Jack in a distressed voice. "They raided our offices about half an hour ago."

"Wow! Did you call a lawyer?"

"Yep," Jack whispered, "but it's legit. They've got a search warrant and went right for what they wanted. They've been going through our files and taking out anything relating to non-violent direct action. You know we've got a file under that heading. Well, that's the one they're most interested in. They're also going through the minutes of all our meetings, and took the photocopy of the Direct Action communiqué. It's obvious they think we were involved in the Litton bombing. You know we weren't, but I'm afraid they might try to set us up so I'm keeping a close eye on them. I've got a feeling they're going to be here for a while."

"I can't believe this, Jack," Ivan said in a tired voice. "I'm out now and they didn't lay any charges, but I've been up all night and my family drove down so we're in a hotel room. Listen, I better let you go but I'll be home first thing in the morning. Talk to you then."

* * *

When Ivan got back to Peterborough on December 8, Jack told him that the police had searched the offices of World Emergency for three hours, taking boxes of files and leaving the peace movement to ponder, in their wake, the meaning of the raid, Ivan's arrest, and the outcome of the Remembrance Day protests . . . but not for long. Early on the morning of December 14, Brian Iler, a lawyer who represented both the Cruise Missile Conversion Project and the Alliance for Non-Violent Action, got a call from the ANVA offices saying that they were being raided and searched by the police. From the ANVA the police confiscated, among other things, a list of members of the Society of Friends, a pacifist group more commonly known as the Quakers. Iler had just returned from the ANVA offices when he got a call from Murray MacAdam, who had been working at his desk in the tiny CMCP office, on the third floor of a church, when the police arrived. Iler hurried down to the office but found the door locked. After pounding on it, he was finally let in by what he described as a "testy and obviously uptight officer" who had taken the phone off the hook. The police had a search warrant, but Iler stayed to observe the search and to witness any possible attempts to interrogate MacAdam. For three and a half hours the police systematically went through every document and piece of paper in the office, looking specifically for the words "direct action." They wouldn't let Iler watch what they were doing or examine anything they took. Later Iler discovered that the press had been told about the raids three hours before they happened, leading him to conclude, "It's obvious at least one police officer sees his role as somewhat more political than just investigating crime."

After their searches the police used material relating to the CMCP's "direct action collective," a subgroup that co-ordinated demonstrations, leafleting, and civil disobedience actions, to obtain search warrants for the homes of at least two members of the subgroup. When Iler investigated the requests used to get search warrants from a justice of the peace, he found they simply fabricated statements, such as "so and so is a member of Direct

Action" or "so and so is a principal member of the group which claimed responsibility for the bombing." Unlike the affidavits for a room bug, requests for search warrants are a fairly simple procedure.

The day after the raids on the CMCP and ANVA offices, the police paid a visit to the home of Len Desroches. Even though they did not produce a search warrant, Len decided to let them in anyway "for a brief period of time." During this time the police quoted minutes from a CMCP meeting that Desroches had attended and asked him to explain some of the comments he had made. He refused to answer their questions because he didn't want to inadvertently give them information they could use against other people.

Later in the evening, when he learned that they had raided the home of another CMCP member, Ken Hancock, Len decided to pay him a visit. Murray MacAdam was already there, helping Ken clean up the mess from the raid. Ken was still visibly upset. "When I opened the door, there were four policemen with a search warrant. It gave them permission to take any material from my house related to Direct Action. When I tried to use the phone, they stopped me. I kept demanding my right to call my lawyer and they kept stopping me until finally they gave in."

"Wow!" Desroches exclaimed. "Luckily, they only questioned me and when I refused, they just left."

"I must be one of their prime suspects," Hancock said indignantly. "At one point, they pulled out a typed copy of what they said was the message telephoned into Litton shortly before the bombing and asked me to read it. Before I could even refuse, they put this tape-recorder on the table to record my voice. When I did refuse to co-operate, they pulled the whole trick of what-have-you-got-to-hide and said if I was innocent, then why not prove it? They were here for hours and eventually left with eight shopping bags of material, including my personal phone book and an appointment book."

"What do you think they're trying to do?" Len asked. "If the police really believe we did the bombing, then why did they wait two months to raid our office? I mean, the Litton bombing happened in mid-October — now it's mid-December. What's their trip?"

"I think the raids are part of a harassment campaign against the disarmament movement," Ken said. "The police are selecting a very narrow group of people within the peace movement to harass, basically, the vocal, activist-oriented groups. I think this will cause divisions within our ranks between those who co-operate with the police questioning and those who don't. The people who co-operate don't see any harm in trying to explain their innocence. These are the same people who want to build links with the New Democratic Party and other reform-oriented organizations. They want to appeal to a broad segment of the population and have very little overall critique of the state or of society as a whole. Their major focus is to stop the manufacture and testing of the cruise, but they don't identify as revolutionaries who are trying to change the values and institutions that created the cruise to begin with. When these people co-operate with the police, it makes those of us who have refused look guilty. I think when you co-operate with the police, it legitimizes the police's objectives. It's like trying to prove you're not a communist and going around saying 'We're not communists, we're nice, we don't deserve to be raided.' It's very liberal. Well, there are communists in our society. Do their houses deserve to be raided? Let's not get into this elitist 'Don't raid us' position.

"Ultimately, this harassment can either make us stronger or weaker; either way, it's up to us. It forces us to take our political differences more seriously. It puts to the test the liberal idea of putting our politics aside in order to stop the cruise. Besides," he added, picking up papers the police had left on the floor, "there's a practical element to the raids that goes beyond the psychological intimidation of peace activists. Part of it is to simply disrupt our work. All that stuff they took of mine, including my phone book and appointment book, is going to make it a lot harder for me to get things done."

"I think the intent of the searches is to keep asserting publicly that those of us who are being investigated must be involved in something," Murray MacAdam said, helping Ken clean the floor of papers. "Hey, what happened to the charges against Ivan LeCouvie?"

"With all the hoopla that the prosecutor made of his so-called Soviet connection, Matusiak ended up withdrawing the charges laid against him at the Remembrance Day protests," Len said.

"You guys want a beer?" asked Ken, walking into the kitchen. Len and Murray followed him and took a seat at the kitchen table. Ken put some bottles of beer on the table and sat down. "I agree with you, Murray. Part of their objective is to discredit us in the public eye. So what do you guys think of the bombing anyway?"

"It's a difficult topic," Murray said. "I don't want to be in the camp with Litton and the police by co-operating with their investigation, but I also don't want to be considered a supporter of violence because I refuse to co-operate. There's a big grey area here. I think many people in the peace movement distinguish between violence to people and violence to property, especially in the case where the property is being used to threaten the lives of millions of people. In that particular case, I think damage to property can be justified, but I don't think violence should be used against property unless it is absolutely the last resort because so much can go wrong. It's not the same as painting peace doves on walls or denting missiles with hammer blows. Aside from the issue of violence, as political activists, it is important for peace groups to work together and to work in solidarity with other movements for social change. I think it's clearly impossible for a group like Direct Action to do this."

Len and Ken nodded their heads in agreement. "Well, let's get this place cleaned up!" said Ken, pushing his chair back. "Time for us to get our working-class hands dirty and save the arm-chair politics for later!"

✳ 36 ✳

"Hi Bob, good to hear from you," said John Anderson, pointing at another phone on Fraser's desk. "I hope you don't mind if Fraser takes the extension?"

Fraser hurried over to his desk and picked up the receiver. Anderson put his hand over his receiver and whispered to Fraser, "Bob Kent."

"Sure, I read about the raids in the paper," Anderson said into the phone. "Yeah, there's nothing more disappointing than going on a fishing expedition and not catching any fish, eh? . . . Nothing? Hmmm." Fraser and Anderson sat quietly, listening intently to Kent on the other end of the line.

"Yeah, I agree, Bob, there's got to be a Toronto connection," Anderson said, staring blankly out the window as he concentrated on the conversation. "No, so far nothing has turned up here, but as soon as we have the bugs installed, I'll give you a call. I'm quite confident that we'll find a group of your peace freaks were involved out there. . . . Yes, Judge Lee Skipp of Vancouver County Court signed the authorization on December 6th. One of our surveillance guys had the good fortune of overhearing our suspects mention going camping on the weekend of the 21st and 22nd, so if all goes well, we've got a tentative plan to enter their house on that weekend. We'll be sending a couple of our veterans from the RCMP on the 21st to see if there's any booby traps and, if not, the bugs will be installed on the 22nd. You know we'll keep you posted.

" . . . Not much. It takes a while to prepare for our raids on the video stores. The Crown prosecutor's office has to review them and pick out the worst ones for prosecution. There's no point doing raids if we don't think we can get convictions." Anderson looked over at Fraser and smiled as he listened to Kent ranting and raving about the outcome of the raids in Toronto.

"There's been a bunch of women's groups picketing all the Red Hot Videos on the . . . " Anderson ran his finger over his calendar. "December 11th, but they were peaceful. . . . No, they weren't there. They've been too busy hanging out at malls. It looks like they're planning a robbery now. It's serious alright. Every time they're at a mall, there's a Brink's delivery and quite often they're in the area. . . . We haven't seen any activity to believe they're going to burn down any more video stores, but this possible Brink's robbery is a real problem." Once again, Anderson looked over at Fraser. "There's no way we can let them go through with it. We're doing as much as possible to get the room bugs in fast."

Fraser cut in. "Our main suspects have moved. To New Westminster. Yes, it's a little out of town. A suburb of Vancouver. I think the address is 1414 Tenth Avenue, New Westminster? Is that right John?"

Anderson nodded, then picked up the conversation again. "Oh, before you go, we've got a seasoned member of the Crown prosecutor's office working on our team now, Jim Jardine. He's the guy that encouraged us to use electronic surveillance — our other surveillance so far has given us zip in the way of hard evidence. He'll know what kind of stuff we can use to collect evidence that will fly in court. . . . Okay, Bob, if you find any new evidence about the case, let us know. Bye now." Anderson and Fraser put down the phones.

"Well, Fraser, whoever helped them out in Toronto has covered their tracks pretty well, eh?" Anderson said.

"Thank God we'll have that room bug in soon," Fraser said, as he settled in to making more notes on the surveillance teams' observations that had come in the day before.

"You know what's bothering me, Fraser?" Anderson asked after a while. "You remember that *Globe and Mail* reporter, Jock Ferguson, who gave Kent that pamphlet, *Resistance*?"

"How could I forget that?" said Fraser.

"Well, that was essentially the lead that broke the case, eh?" Anderson said in a tired voice. "As you know, sometimes reporters and cops have cosy relationships, in which they exchange information to get leads for stories and investigations, whatever the case may be. The important thing is, they trust each other and never reveal their sources. What's bugging me is a call I got from a BCTV reporter, Alyn Edwards, who's working on a story that claims the police were watching some people set fires in the Red Hot Video case. According to Edwards, Kent had another meeting with the *Globe* reporters, Ferguson and Lorne Slotnick, and Kent allegedly told them the police watched some people set fires. I don't know, but Kent might be dropping this information in hopes that they give him more leads on who's involved in the Litton bombing. I don't like the idea that this news about the police witnessing the arsons is out there and could be the subject of a TV newscast somewhere down the line."

"We'll have to deny it," said Fraser adamantly.

"Yeah, but it could be too late," Anderson said dejectedly. "I'm going to have to remind all our guys to watch what they say, especially to the press. The last thing we want is our wiretap evidence, once it comes in, being thrown out of court because the press have information that we watched the arsons and didn't make arrests."

"I think we should divert any questions from the press to Jim Jardine from now on," suggested Fraser. "It's the Crown's job to field questions from reporters, isn't it?"

"Good idea, Fraser," said Anderson, perking up somewhat. "I'll warn him. So you've got a meeting with their landlord this morning, don't you?"

"Yep," said Fraser, looking at his watch and getting up from his desk. "Yeah, I'm meeting with him and his wife so I can take some pictures of the house. If our suspects see me taking photos and ask about it, I told the landlord to tell them I'm a real estate agent. Do I look okay?"

"Just like a real estate agent," smiled Anderson. "If you looked any better, I'd ask you out myself."

"Thanks," Fraser said, putting on his coat. "I better wear a hat because, if Taylor's at home, he might recognize me." He went over to the coat rack and took a fedora-style hat from a hook and put it on his head at a slight angle.

"Now you look like a high-class pimp," laughed Anderson.

Half an hour later, Fraser pulled up a few blocks from 1414 Tenth Avenue, New Westminster and found the restaurant where he had arranged to meet Enrico and Suzanne Vizza, the landlords. As soon as he walked into the Italian restaurant, a short, stocky couple got up out of their seats and began waving their arms enthusiastically at him. They didn't both need to be in attendance, but obviously were quite excited at the prospects of being involved in an undercover operation, even if their roles were minor. Fraser had not divulged what crime their tenants were involved in, but Enrico and Suzanne were more than willing to co-operate in any way they could.

After introducing himself, Fraser explained that there might come a time when the police might have to tour the house, so it was important they tell their tenants that they were thinking of selling the house sometime in the future. The Vizzas were in no hurry to leave the restaurant, but Fraser explained that he wanted to take photos before his suspects got out of bed. The Vizzas shook their heads in disgust when Fraser told them that their tenants rarely left the house before ten in the morning.

They got up and walked down Tenth Avenue towards the house. The Vizzas said they had only met Steve Sturrock and his girlfriend, Suzanne Milne, when they first came to see the house. The two had said they wanted to rent the house with another couple and their dog. They gave the Vizzas the first and last months' rent in cash and assured them they would get their rent money at the beginning of each month. The Vizzas apparently didn't bother questioning them too much. "They had a truck, the cash, and looked clean, so we took them," Enrico said. "We don't want drug dealers. They aren't drug dealers are they?" Fraser shook his head and they looked at each other with relieved smiles.

Tenth Avenue was a busy main thoroughfare in New Westminster, lined with run-down rental housing that would eventually end up being sold as commercial property. The Vizzas' property was no exception. At some earlier point in history, the two-storey clapboard was probably somebody's dream home, but the years and location had taken their toll. What Fraser photographed was a green wooden house in bad need of a paint job, surrounded by a faded white picket fence. The large front yard, which set the house back off the busy street, would have been an ideal place for gardens and trees, but in the absence of an ambitious tenant, it lay to waste in a sea of brown crabgrass.

Fraser tried to open the picket fence's gate, but the rusty catch wouldn't budge. The undisturbed grass around the front stairs and the curtains drawn across the windows would have led Fraser to the conclusion that the house was vacant, if he didn't already know otherwise. "I assume, there is a back entrance?" he asked after he had taken a number of photos.

"Oh yes. All the tenants use the back entrance. There's an alley running behind the houses and a garage back there," Enrico explained in his heavy Italian accent.

They walked down the back alley until they reached a dilapidated garage, running parallel to the paved alley. The backyard had all the signs of daily wear and tear, with a well-worn path leading to a back staircase. Fraser was startled when his eyes travelled up the staircase to the back window, only to discover the curtains were open and a tall, young woman was bent over doing some household task. He stepped behind the protection of the garage. "You should probably step back here too!" he said to the Vizzas. "I'd rather they not see me," he explained.

"We understand," they said, looking perplexed.

Looking out, Fraser could see the woman moving around in front of the window, talking over her shoulder to persons unknown. Enrico, following Fraser's gaze, explained that this was a kitchen window over the sink and that she was probably doing the dishes. "As soon as she disappears, we should go," Fraser said, watching her intently. The second that she moved away from the window, he led the Vizzas out and along with him down the alley.

"I should probably talk to some of the neighbours so they aren't alarmed if they see us go into the house," Fraser said. "Are there any neighbours nearby who own their homes?"

Enrico looked at Suzanne. "There's William Dundas. He's a pensioner who lives right there," he said, pointing to the house next door. "Then across the street, there's Irene Berg. She's nice." Fraser explained that he was going to visit briefly with the neighbours and then had to be on his way. After shaking their hands profusely, he headed up the street to William Dundas's house, while Suzanne and Enrico shuffled off in the direction of the restaurant. Fraser pulled his fedora even lower over his face as he climbed William Dundas's porch steps. He glanced over at the green clapboard house and was relieved to find that he could not be seen from its side windows. A wizened old man opened the door and looked up from his stooped-over frame at Fraser. "Can I help you?" he asked in frail voice.

"Yes," said Fraser, pulling out his badge. "I'm with the RCMP, and unfortunately your new neighbours are under investigation so I am here to request your co-operation."

"Why, of course. Come in."

Fraser stepped into the hallway and took off his hat. "Your neighbours at 1414 are going to be under surveillance and so it would be advisable if you didn't get too friendly with them."

"There's been ten different people living in that house over the past ten years, so I don't bother getting friendly," the old man said with a chuckle.

"Have you noticed anything unusual going on next door?" asked Fraser.

"I think they moved in the end of November, but they're quiet," offered the old man. "The only time I see them is when they go in and out through the back way there. Otherwise their curtains are always closed. Day and night."

"There'll be some police officers entering the house on the weekend of the 21st and 22nd," explained Fraser. "So don't be alarmed. It's the only way we can install electronic surveillance." The old man didn't appear to be too interested so Fraser shook his hand and left.

Fraser paid a quick visit to Irene Berg, who lived across the street, repeating what he had said to Dundas, and then decided to approach the neighbours who lived directly behind his suspects' house, because they had the best view of their back door. Part of Fraser's mission was to scout around for a possible home where the police could set up an indoor observation post and maybe even a remote-control TV camera. As it turned out, the neighbours were very co-operative and showed Fraser a back bedroom that the police could use as an observation post and set up a closed-circuit TV camera. Fraser explained that it was equipped with night vision and would be able to record movement in their suspects' backyard at night even if the officers could not make visual contact. After reassuring them that their suspects were no danger to the home-owners in the area, he returned to the office.

After he briefed Anderson on his morning excursion, Anderson surprised him by saying, "How would you like to be part of the entry team going into the suspects' house on the 22nd? We need someone to take photographs of the interior and our regular photographer has another assignment. Plus I think you'd be good to have along — you're so familiar with the case." Fraser smiled thankfully, knowing that Anderson had gone out of his way to include him. "I'd love to!"

✳ **37** ✳

On December 21, once the investigation had been formally handed over to CLEU, RCMP criminal investigation officers known as the Special Observation Team took over surveillance from the Security Service's Watcher unit. Although these "Special O" officers were observations specialists, they were still police officers and more predisposed to be identified as such than their Watcher counterparts. When members of the Special O team watched the couples from 1414 Tenth Avenue cross the Capilano Bridge in their brown four-by-four pickup truck, they radioed the go-ahead to the entry team. The planned weekend of winter camping was giving the RCMP the perfect opportunity to go in and install the room bugs they so desperately needed to build a case.

The first entry would include only two members of the RCMP's Special I Section, which was providing technical assistance to the Force's criminal investigators: Paull, a specialist in picking locks, and Corporal Kuse, a "bug" expert. This first entry would be a reconnaissance mission aimed at finding a good location for the bugs, scouting out any possible booby traps, and picking locks. Once they had made their initial entry through the back door, using a key provided by the landlord, one officer crawled on his hands and knees while the other one walked tall, both of them looking for possible trip wires or detection devices. They found neither.

Early the next day Fraser arrived in New Westminster along with the other members of the Force who would make up the two teams entering the house. The first team, led by Paull, would again check for booby traps and make sure nothing was locked that the second team might need to get into. Fraser was part of the second

team, which would install the bugs. The two teams arrived in separate unmarked RCMP vehicles, parked a safe distance from the
house, and got out and began to assemble their equipment. Kuse
pulled a couple of bulletproof vests out of the car trunk and
handed one to each member of the team. Earlier Kuse had
explained the procedure to Fraser, whose only thought at first was
how cumbersome it would be to wear a flak jacket while taking
photographs. "Considering what I saw in that house yesterday,"
Kuse said, "I'm not going in without a vest and you aren't either.
I'm telling you, I've done about a hundred entries but this was the
scariest. Considering all the weapons, ammunition, balaclavas, and
camouflaged overalls these people have, I've come to the conclusion that they know what they're doing and when it comes to
shooting, they're probably better at it than I am!" Fraser, who considered Kuse to be one of the bravest men on the Force, quickly
donned his bulletproof vest and took the .38 revolver handed to
him.

They didn't have to wait long for the first team to come out,
after which Fraser, Kuse, another bug expert, and a police security
guard quickly walked up the back stairs into the house. As soon as
they opened the back door, two things struck Fraser. One was that
Kuse had pulled his .38 out of his holster and kept it drawn. The
second was the faint sound of whining coming from under the
door of a room just off the kitchen. He walked over and could
make out the dark shape of a dog nose sniffing along the bottom
of the door and the floor. Fraser felt a pang of sadness as he
remembered Kuse warning him that there would be a dog locked
in one of the rooms. The entry team must have controlled the dog
through the use of a very high frequency sound that had hurt his
ears to the point he backed off in the direction in which they
manipulated him.

For a moment he forgot who he was and knelt over by the door
and whispered, "It's okay, old boy. We'll be outta here soon and
then you'll be alone again." As he glanced around the kitchen he
noticed a huge bowl of kibble and water in the corner.

In the few minutes that Fraser had been preoccupied with Rex,
Kuse had already taken the plate off the electrical outlet on the
kitchen wall and was busy connecting wires so the electricity from
the outlet could run the bug. Fraser took his camera from its case
and began snapping pictures of the kitchen, although there was
nothing out of the ordinary in the room. It was a barren kitchen

with no pictures or knick-knacks anywhere. The only object that Fraser zeroed in on was a small radio that most likely was normally plugged into the outlet that Kuse was working on.

Fraser moved along into the hallway and living room. He was instantly taken aback by the dazzling gold tinfoil and red felt-textured wallpaper that the Vizzas had apparently used to adorn the living room. Before taking photographs of the room, Fraser adjusted the focus on his camera lens to compensate for the glare that this intense wallpaper would no doubt create. Perhaps the Vizzas had been short of money when they decorated and were forced to use Christmas wrapping, he chuckled to himself. Then he shifted his camera lens to the fireplace, another example of extraordinary gaudiness. The entire wall that housed the fireplace had been inlaid with stones of all shapes and sizes, overwhelming everything else in the room except the wallpaper. Other than the interior decorating, there was nothing else out of the ordinary in this room either.

Fraser went back to the kitchen, where Kuse and his partner were packing up and preparing to go downstairs to install bug number two. With guns drawn, all of them went down the stairwell into a finished basement, where Kuse immediately turned and opened a door. The light from the stairwell dimly illuminated what appeared to be a bedroom. In the eerie lighting, Fraser involuntarily jumped when his eye caught sight of four heads sitting on a bureau. His trigger finger clicked off the safety as he spun around and stopped, his pistol straight out in front of him, pointing at a long, black coffin. He could hear his own breathing. Kuse flicked on the ceiling light. In the glare of the light bulb it became apparent that the four heads were white, featureless mannequins, each adorned with identical Dolly Parton-style hairdos in red, blonde, auburn, and black. The coffin was a black, wooden box, with a heavy lock on its hasp.

Kuse had put his pistol back in his holster. He looked at Fraser and the others before walking over to the coffin and carefully pulling on the lock. It snapped open. Probably Paull had unlocked it during the earlier entry. Kuse signalled for Fraser to come over. Slowly he opened the heavy lid to reveal an impressive assortment of handguns, rifles, shotguns, and boxes and boxes of ammunition and gun-cleaning equipment. As Fraser started snapping photographs, he noticed that the coffin was actually a homemade box, designed to be difficult to break into. Upon a more careful inspection, he noticed that all the screw heads were on the inside, making it impossible to disassemble the box from the outside. The whole box, including the locking hardware, was designed to be impenetrable with anything but a sledgehammer — or a good locksmith, like Paull. After taking all the photos he could without disturbing anything, Fraser carefully closed the lid. Kuse and his helper were already busy installing another room bug in an electrical outlet near the bed.

By this time, Fraser had judged the bedroom to be worthy of meticulous documentation. He began taking photos by slowly rotating in a 360-degree circle. The room had a carpet over the cement floor. Its small basement window had a closed curtain. Near the foot of the double bed a small table supported an old black and white television. There were no posters or pictures on the white stucco walls, but a series of bull's-eye targets in various stages of completion were leaning against one wall. It appeared as though several people had been working on the design of the targets using a black Magic Marker on cardboard. Some of the targets had ominous caricatures of pig faces scrawled in the centre. Others were more obviously human faces but had the word "PIG" written across the forehead. Most frightening to Fraser was a pile of used bull's-eye targets from some previous excursion. They had black burnt-out bullet holes in them, expertly pinpointed in the centre of each target. Fraser shuddered. No wonder Kuse had warned him about their shooting proficiency.

He took some shots of a pile of *Guns and Ammo* magazines strewn across the bedside table, with an overflowing ashtray on top. In the clothes closet, which had no door, hung a wide array of coats, jackets, and pants, many in camouflage colours. Hanging on a hook behind the door was another assortment of balaclavas, mainly in dark colours.

By the time Fraser had finished shooting, Kuse had finished his installation. He led Fraser down the basement hallway to another room, which housed an office of sorts. Inside were a couple of typewriters, boxes of files, and a wide variety of books. Fraser adjusted his lens and began taking close-ups of the literature. At a quick glance Fraser couldn't spot any fiction, but there was a healthy assortment of non-fiction material: *The Trilateral Commission and Elite Planning for the World*, B.C. Hydro plans, various government brochures on future megaprojects, literature on the cruise missile, Peter C. Newman's book *True North: Not Strong and*

Free, Bulldozer, Resistance, and Andrea Dworkin's *Pornography: Men Possessing Women*. Then there were the stacks of *Soldier of Fortune* magazines. Kuse picked up a few pamphlets with his latex-gloved hands and set them up so that Fraser could photograph them: *Trashing, In the Steal of the Night, Night Writers, Getaway Driving Techniques, A Thief's Primer*, and many more.

While Kuse was rearranging the pamphlets in the way he had found them, his partner had been looking through a file box and had come upon something interesting. He carefully pulled out some papers from the "M" section, which turned out to be notes on how to convert a Mini-14 into a fully automatic rifle. Another gold mine of information in the file boxes proved to be loose-leaf folders containing information on when certain phony identification was used. The final treasure was a dog-eared scrapbook containing newspaper articles from all over Canada pertaining to the Litton explosion. After photographing all this material, they carefully arranged everything back in the way they had found it and decided to make one last stop in the garage.

Conveniently, Paull had left the garage unlocked for them. It was empty except for miscellaneous tools, garbage cans, and a few cardboard boxes stacked under a wooden workbench. After quickly scanning the area they were about to leave when Fraser decided to snoop inside one of the boxes. Another treasure. Lengths of green plastic garden hose had been cut in eight- to twelve-inch lengths and punctured with three-inch spikes at different angles. The policemen were familiar with these homemade tire-puncture hoses. Criminals drop them out of a getaway car when fleeing a robbery so any police car pursuing them will end up with flat tires on the side of the road. The investigators took these as a clear sign that a robbery was being planned.

It was time to go, but Fraser had one more question for Kuse. "Did you let that dog out of the other bedroom?" Kuse nodded. Quickly they walked down the alley towards their waiting vehicles. Kuse had been right. Fraser had seen more tragic and depressing places, but this was the scariest.

❋ **38** ❋

Bob lurched and his tires spun as he struggled, even in four-wheel-drive mode, to make it up the slippery mountain logging road. We hadn't planned on driving too far up, but the heavy snowfall in the mountains was making it harder going than I had imagined. Finally, after skidding dangerously close to the precipice of a cliff, we decided to pull over and drag our camping gear and firewood the rest of the way on the toboggans. We loaded our tents, sleeping bags, guns, and firewood onto the toboggans in huge swaying piles that constantly threatened to topple over as we made our way at a snail's pace through the thick mountain snow. Even though we were soaked in sweat, within minutes the huge downy snowflakes and breathtaking vistas buoyed our spirits.

Luckily we had the best camping gear that money could buy, although in this case it was stolen. We had Gore Tex everything: wonderfully dry and warm Gore Tex coats, boots, sleeping bags, and tents. It was a miracle waterproof material, newly on the market at the time, with tiny air holes just big enough to allow perspiration to escape but small enough to prevent rain droplets from getting in. We were laughing and talking all at once, free at last from the dirty urban streets and, at least temporarily, free from the incessant casing and planning of the robbery that seemed to go on day and night. Every now and then we would stop pulling to get our breath but would end up in a drag-'em-out snowball fight that was even more exhausting than pulling the toboggans. At last we reached the box canyon that was such a perfect spot to camp and target-practise.

Since it had taken the better part of the day to get there, we decided to set up a target range before setting up camp. "I'm going to use the .357," I said, unpacking my favourite handgun, the Dan Wesson. Brent was busy rummaging around for the P08, which was the one he favoured. "Did you phone the landlady before we left?"

"Yes," I said. "I phoned her last night. What made you think of that?"

"I was so busy getting everything ready last night, I forgot to ask," he said.

"Yeah. I told her I saw someone taking photos of our house the other day and she said it was probably some real estate people because they're thinking of selling the house."

"Great. That's all we need, a bunch of nosy real estate people snooping around our house. Did she say when they're going to sell it?"

"No, but she said they'd give us plenty of warning if anyone wants to see the place."

Brent shook his head, then looked over at Gerry, who was rummaging around in the rifle bag. "Hey, what are you doing, man?"

"I told you, I want to practise with my Mini-14. I've been having problems with the clip and I want to make sure it's working perfectly before the robbery."

"Okay, so you want to practise with the Mini, and we're going to practise with the handguns, right?" asked Brent.

"Right." Gerry held up the Mini-14, which he had finally found in the bag. After Gerry had organized his rifle, ammunition, and targets into his carrying sack, he trudged up through the snow to an area higher up the mountainside to set up a target range. I watched him ploughing his way through the snow and figured it would take most of the afternoon just to set up the targets and sight in his rifle. He probably wouldn't have much time to practise, but there would still be tomorrow.

Julie, Brent, and I had a blast. It didn't take long to set up a combat range, and once we had gone through a few runs, there was a fairly good trail we could use. Even though we were concentrating on improving our shooting skills in case something went wrong during the robbery, it was serious fun. We took our shooting skills seriously, because if we did have to shoot we wanted accuracy: if we were aiming at someone's legs we didn't want to accidentally shoot them in the chest.

It was Julie's turn. "Go!" yelled Brent, running along about six metres behind her. She was in her heavy snowmobile suit, and her gait was more of a lumber than a run. When she got close to the first target, she fell laughing into the snow just as Brent yelled, "Stop!" Luckily she had the safety on and the pistol didn't go off.

"Get up! Get up!" he yelled frantically, trying to create the panicky atmosphere of a robbery scenario. "The guy's pulling out his revolver and you're going down in one second." Stretched out in the snow, where she had fallen, Julie rolled over on her stomach and held her pistol out in front of her. Using the snow for support, she steadied her pistol, squinted her eye, and clicked the safety off. *BOOM!!*

The kickback from the gun firing noticeably raised the pistol off the snow. Miraculously, she had hit the target — not a bull's-eye, but she had managed to hit a twelve-inch-square piece of cardboard at twenty yards. Not bad, considering she had just fallen.

"Go!" Brent yelled again. No time to rest. She got up, and Brent yelled, "What about your safety, Jules?!"

"Damn!" She clicked the safety back on and again began running down the trail between the boulders towards the next target. This time when he yelled "Stop," she didn't fall but simply froze and clicked off the safety. While I counted to three in my head, I watched her steady her outstretched arms, slowly squeeze the trigger, and fire. *BOOM!!*

This time the black bullet hole was close to the middle of the target. "Great!" yelled Brent, and they disappeared around a bend. A few sonic booms later, they came marching back through the snow, smiling with exhilaration in the fresh mountain air.

"You're next!" ordered Brent. During these target sessions, I thought, he reverted back to his army cadet days. But I appreciated the discipline he inspired. Even though we were having fun, this was no joke. "Go!" he screamed in my ear. I ran through the snow, huffing and puffing almost immediately. Trying to move quickly with heavy winter clothing and carrying a heavy revolver wasn't easy. As I neared the first target, I consciously kept my trigger finger out of the trigger guard until he yelled "Stop!" Then I turned towards the target and supported my outstretched trigger arm with my other arm. A ten-pound revolver is harder to hold still in an outstretched arm than one would think. My arms were quivering, and I had to slightly bend my elbows and relax to keep them still so I could get a steady fix on the target. My breathing was so heavy from running that the gun was moving up and down with each breath. The count in my head was already "two." I held my breath so the sight on the end of my gun barrel was perfectly still, then slowly squeezed the trigger. A .357 has a double-action trigger mechanism that makes a safety switch unnecessary, unlike the so-called hair-trigger of a pistol, which can fire with just the slightest pressure.

BOOM!! Even though I had heard the blast of a gun so many times before, the sound never ceased to shock me. To muffle the sound somewhat we were all wearing ear silencers, which looked like huge plastic earmuffs. My ears rang as the sound reverberated throughout my inner ear, leaving a ringing in its wake. I stopped noticing it when I saw that I had almost hit the centre of my target. "Yeah!!!" I screamed as I headed, sweating, down the combat range towards the next target.

The sun was low over the mountains when we heard Gerry yell a warning to us as he approached from the upper combat range. We stopped and waited for him. As his dark silhouette loomed larger and larger with his approach, I took a few minutes to absorb the beauty of the landscape. The setting sun cast a pinkish hue on the billowy snow that covered the deep purple of the coniferous trees and the rocks protruding from beneath this soft blanket. If only we could spend more time appreciating what it was we were trying to save. Brent was sitting on a rock, admiring the vista with me. "How'd it go, Gerry?"

"Frustrating." He grinned and gave Julie a bear hug. "It's a nightmare getting that Mini sighted in properly. I spent almost the whole day just putting up targets."

"Yeah," Julie said. "I only heard a few shots coming from up there about an hour ago."

Gerry sat down with us until he got his breath back. "You might think I'm paranoid, but did you guys notice a helicopter fly by this afternoon?" The three of us looked at each other and shook our heads in unison.

"Hmmm," he said, "I definitely saw a blue and white helicopter fly right over us, and I could swear it was checking us out. I mean, it could have been anyone. Maybe it was just some private guy curious as to why these crazy people would be up in the mountains in the dead of winter shooting off guns, or maybe it was some forest ranger. Whoever it was, I don't like it." Although he seemed concerned, he was smiling, which was Gerry's way.

"Tomorrow I think we should do some target-practice with the shotgun, since that's the most useful weapon in a getaway scenario," Brent said, passing over Gerry's observation. He didn't like to encourage what he saw as paranoia.

"Yeah," agreed Gerry. "I'd like to try it out cause I'm a bit nervous about it. I've only fired it twice before. I'm always a bit afraid of guns until I fire them about five times."

"Definitely," agreed Julie.

"Yeah, I could explain the shotgun to you and show you how to load it and all that kind of shit," said Brent, getting up. "Well, I guess we better put up our tents and light a fire before it gets too dark to see." We had been sweating all afternoon, and there was a distinct danger of getting cold by sitting around too long. We got up and began setting up our tents.

Winter camping is much more comfortable and warmer than most people might think. With a good sleeping bag, winter clothes, and dry firewood, it can be just as fun as summer camping. Setting up the tents is no different than setting up tents in the summer, except that instead of tent pegs we tied pie plates to the tent ropes and buried them under the snow for support. At night, if it snowed, someone would have to get up and knock the snow off the tent so the weight wouldn't bring it down.

While the others set up the tents, I shredded some newspaper and cut some kindling from the dry logs we had brought up on the toboggans. More experienced winter campers could gather wood from the area, but we had decided to bring our own, which we thought was a safer and easier way of guaranteeing a good fire. In no time I had a roaring fire going, which could keep us warm for hours and dry our wet clothes. Once it had been going for a while, we let it die down slightly so we could lay a grill across the hot coals and cook up some cans of stew.

It was dark after we had eaten but still early, so Gerry suggested we try tobogganing down a clear slope not far from our campsite. The children inside of us weren't dead yet. When he suggested the idea of tobogganing, our eyes gleamed and I added the word "races." We jumped up from the fire, grabbed the toboggans, and headed towards the slope. My memories of that night are still vivid, because it was one of our last truly joyful times of freedom. A full moon reflected its soft light on the white snow, creating an almost dawn-like lighting. There were no rules for the toboggan races, they were pure anarchist competition where anything goes. It was the "girls" against the "boys." We started at the top of the hill standing in pairs beside the toboggans until someone yelled, "Go!" Then down we went, using any tactic imaginable to get to the bottom first. Julie and I quickly discovered the easiest way to victory was to sacrifice one of our team in order to make a kamikaze leap off our toboggan in an attempt to knock the boys off their toboggan like bowling pins. There was no rule saying that two people had to make it across the finish line, so we reasoned that if even only one of us got across first, we would be victorious, and victorious we were! We beat the boys thoroughly that night, and that sweet victory sent us to bed with content smiles on our faces.

The next morning, when I stepped out of the tent, the first thing I noticed were dark ominous storm clouds hanging low over the mountains: a harbinger of things to come. I threw some kindling on the firepit so we could have some coffee and breakfast before shooting. By the time the fire was crackling and popping, everybody else was up, searching for their coffee cups in the snow. We sat around in an atmosphere of early morning silence, warming up around the fire, drinking coffee and eating muffins. Brent pulled the rifle bag out of the tent and started getting the shotgun and ammunition organized. Julie and Gerry looked over at him, then looked at each other quizzically and started getting their handguns and ammunition organized.

"Are you guys going to clean your handguns already?" Brent sounded puzzled.

"No," Julie answered brusquely. "We're going to use them."

"Oh." Brent glanced over at me as though to say, "That's weird," but instead said, "Okay, but we're going to use the shotgun, since that's what me and Ann would be using during the getaway."

"Are you going to use it down here?" asked Julie, referring to the combat range we had used yesterday.

"Uh-huh." Brent wasn't paying much attention.

"Okay, well, I'm going up to the other range then, 'cause there's no point in four people using the shotgun together, 'cause then we'll all be standing around waiting and stuff," Julie said.

I didn't really care which gun I used, but I had hardly ever used the shotgun and I figured I would shoot with Brent because he was quite proficient with it. So while they got the guns ready, I went down to the combat range we had used the day before and put up some new targets. By the time I got back, Julie and Gerry had already begun the ascent to the upper range and Brent was ready with the shotgun. Brent and I spent the better part of the morning using the shotgun on the combat range. Around one o'clock I mentioned to Brent that I was getting hungry.

"Yeah, let's go up and talk to Julie and Gerry and see if they want to have some lunch and then use the shotgun," Brent said. "I can show them how to use it. They can fire off some shots, then we can put the thing away so the combat range will be freed up again." When a shotgun is fired, the pellets are sprayed over a wide radius, making it unsafe to use any other weapon in that area at the same time.

"I figured they'd come down when they wanted to use the shotgun," I said, placing it carefully back in its bag. "It's been a long time. Maybe they thought we'd come up and get them." We began making our way up the trail towards the upper range, when a dull thudding sound came from the sky. I looked up, but since it was so overcast I couldn't see anything. Brent looked up as well. The sound was getting louder and louder until suddenly a helicopter appeared, flying low just below the dense storm clouds. It was unmistakably blue and white.

"There's Gerry's helicopter." Brent strained to make out its markings. It was too late to hide from its view. It flew low over the box canyon, then continued on its course.

"It doesn't look like it changed course to fly over us," I observed. "Maybe it's just some government chopper doing a routine flyby through the mountains."

"Hopefully nobody's complained about all the shooting up here," said Brent. We stood for a few minutes watching it disappear over the mountain ridges in the distance, then continued our ascent. "Hey, you guys, want to come down and have some lunch?" Brent yelled as we approached Julie and Gerry.

"Yeah, I'm starving," Gerry said. Julie didn't respond. "Are you coming?"

"No," she snapped. "I'm going to shoot off some more. I'll be down in a minute."

By the time we had eaten a few sandwiches she appeared from the upper range, still looking quite irritable. The atmosphere during lunch was heavy with repressed emotions. Finally Brent began to speak with a slight stutter, which only appeared in situations in which he was apprehensive. "Why d-don't we all go down to the combat range and use the shotgun together for awhile, so we can put it away and use the handguns like we did yesterday?" He looked around at everybody. "We had a lot of f-fun yesterday and with Gerry, it would be great!"

"I agree with using the shotgun down here for a few minutes, since Gerry and I don't know how to use it, but then we should just switch," Julie said assertively but calmly. "We used that upper range almost all day and I think it's just fair that we get a chance to use the combat range."

"By the time we finish with the shotgun, there's not going to be much time left," said Brent. "Don't you think it would be sorta fun if we all use the combat range like yesterday?"

"I don't necessarily see the point in sharing the combat range down here." Julie was becoming noticeably agitated. "I don't want to waste time waiting around for four people to shoot on the combat range. I'd rather just get the shotgun over with and switch ranges. You can use that upper range. I found it useless because you basically have to shoot uphill. It's nothing like shooting on a flat surface."

"Well, if you didn't want to go up there, then why didn't you say something this morning?" I said, also in an irritable voice.

"I did," said Julie defensively, "but obviously nobody was listening so I basically just said okay, forget it. I'll go shoot there, but I was really mad that I'd given in, 'cause I didn't think it was the fairest method. I don't even see why you had to use the combat range with the shotgun in the first place?"

"I thought we'd all use the shotgun on the combat range and get it over with so we could concentrate on the handguns, but then you and Gerry just got your handguns ready and marched up top," Brent said.

"That's just an assumption you made," said Gerry. "We didn't want to use the shotgun for more than a few shots. Julie wanted to just use the combat range down here with her handgun, since that's what she'll be using in the robbery."

"Well, I couldn't have cared less where I went," I said. "I certainly wasn't plotting to monopolize the combat range and force you to use an inferior range. The problem is that there was no discussion. Everybody just went off to separate ranges without a proper discussion."

"For me, the upper range was a total waste of time. I spent the whole morning setting up targets and walking back and forth," Julie said defensively. "By the time they were set up, I only had about fifteen minutes left to shoot so I fired them off fast. I wasted fifty rounds!"

"If it was so useless, then why would you shoot off fifty cartridges?" said Brent offensively. "Did you just fire them all off to make a point?"

"Fuck off!!!" hissed Julie in his face. "I was obviously shooting off those bullets to get better, and anyway, who are you to judge?" She stormed off towards the tent and Gerry, Brent, and I looked at each other nervously. The situation had escalated so quickly that none of us were sure exactly what had gone down. After a while Gerry went over to the tent to see if he couldn't convince Julie to come out and talk. An hour later they came out of the tent. Julie appeared madder than ever and Gerry looked very much like a lamb being led to the slaughter. As soon as I saw Julie's face, I felt my blood pressure rise and knew that I was in no shape to be conciliatory.

Gerry initiated the discussion by appointing himself the arbitrator, because he felt he was the most neutral, in that he had no strong feelings one way or the other about where we practised. When no one disagreed, he suggested we begin by taking turns going over the sequence of events because Julie felt that would reveal the injustices that had occurred. After Brent and I went over our version of the events, Julie ended her account by saying, "When we finished lunch Brent started saying what he thought we should do, and that's when I calmly explained why I didn't think it should happen that way and why, and you two started saying to me that we should do it your way and I just had no vote, right?" Brent and I looked at her with astonishment.

"I remember giving real strong reasons why we should just switch ranges since Gerry and I had already shot up there, and now it was our turn to use the combat range down below," she said angrily. "But you people were just getting real agitated when I was saying this, almost like you were thinking, 'I'm not going up there. You're not pushing me out of this range.' "

"I don't even agree with this way of dealing with it," I said. All the resentment I had harboured towards Julie since our trip to Toronto was beginning to surface. "As far as I'm concerned the sequence of events doesn't even matter, because let's say you and Gerry want to do something one way and Brent and I want to do something another way. If we don't agree on something, is it fair for me to just yell, 'Well I think our method's better' and if nobody agrees, 'Fuck you!?' "

"I never did that," said Julie hotly.

"I thought you got mad because we didn't do things your way." I was feeling slightly out of control.

"I was mad because it was completely unfair for you and Brent to arrive at decisions the way you did!" she yelled. "You didn't even listen or hear what I was saying!"

The discussion degenerated to a point where Julie and I were simply yelling at one another until Brent and Gerry stepped in and explained that nothing could be accomplished this way. We decided to pack up and go home. At some other point in time, when we had calmed down, we could talk again and try to get at the underlying issues.

I had plenty of time to think on the drive home, because nobody was talking. Once I had calmed down I realized that although Brent and I hadn't intentionally made all the decisions about where and when we did things, regardless of our intentions we were still dominating and controlling events. Obviously Julie was becoming aware of this and resenting it in a big way. In retrospect I realized we should have discussed where we would do our target-practising as a group and really listened to what everyone was saying instead of just making unilateral decisions. The issue of Brent's and my domination and control of Julie and Gerry became a major underlying theme in our relationships and would resurface time and again during the next month, causing endless, and unresolved, anxieties.

* * *

When we got back from our camping trip on the evening of December 23, we pulled up behind our house in New Westminster to unload the truck. Before we even began to carry things in, Julie ran to the back door, unlocked it, and, from the sounds of Rex's whining, had a happy reunion with him. I struggled up the back stairs with as many packsacks as I could carry and dumped them just inside the kitchen door. Julie was not on speaking terms with any of us, including Gerry, but her concern for Rex overrode her anger at the rest of us.

"Something's wrong with Rex," she cried, running her hands all over his body. "Whenever we leave him for a few days, he whines, but this time, he was real distressed!" In fact, Rex was still whining. I patted his head and looked at him. He didn't seem to have any visible signs of injury. I figured he was probably just more lonesome than usual and went back to the truck for another load. After three trips to the truck, Rex was still standing in the kitchen door whining pathetically.

"Yeah, he's really trying to tell us something," I noted. "Even I know he doesn't usually cry this much." By now Gerry was also trying to console Rex.

I carried a bunch of stuff down into the basement with Brent and decided to put some frozen meat pies in the oven for supper. By the time I went back up to the kitchen, Gerry was sitting forlornly at the table, stroking Rex and muttering sweet nothings to him. "How is he?" I asked. He was still whimpering every time anyone paid attention to him.

"I don't know, but if he's still like this in the morning, we'll

have to take him to the vet," Gerry said. "Next time we go away —
if there is a next time — Julie's going to leave him at her mom's.
Maybe he's just old and insecure about being alone. He has
enough food. He didn't even eat all his kibble, and there's still
water in his bowl."

"Do you want a meat pie?" I asked, arranging the frozen pies
on a cookie tray.

"Yeah," he said dejectedly. "Don't put one in for Julie, she left."

"She left?" I repeated.

"Yeah," Gerry said. "I don't know for how long but she took off
in the Scottsdale as soon as we got home."

"She'll be back," I reassured him. "Rex is here." Gerry smiled,
and Rex whined.

"What's wrong?" I asked Gerry, thinking he might want to talk.

"She's mad at me because I didn't instantly see this as a domination trip by you two and jump into the fray," he opened up. "I
wouldn't do that even if I thought you two were being really
fucked up about it. What she was saying makes a lot of sense, and
maybe I should have been more forceful in backing her up, but I'm
not going to start crying and yelling about it." He sighed. "It's
really sad. I don't know if I could live without her because I do
need that kind of relationship. Usually after a short period of time,
I'm fucked up without a relationship and there's not many women
in this small circle of people we know who I could relate to."

"I know," I said softly, pulling out one of our old plastic kitchen
chairs.

"If I don't work with her, then what am I going to do?" he said,
scratching Rex's back. Rex whined. "I couldn't work at a regular
job. Even the coolest, hippest job sucks, and I wouldn't be happy
sittin' around playin' the guitar while people are out fighting. If I
had a cabin and could live there and just hunt and stuff, that'd be
cool, but it takes money to live in the woods. It's ridiculous but
true. The way I feel right now is there's nothing else for me to do
but this, 'cause it's the only thing I can do where I feel like I've
done something."

Gerry began to philosophize. "In this world sanity is insanity,
and insanity is sanity. Is it more rational to go blow up some
weapons plant and get killed than it is to go down to the pub, get
stone drunk, and get killed driving home in my car?" He seemed to
be dwelling on his last few sentences, then jerked up. "It's too bad
we can't be more mellow. If you're in a collective, you can't be

flippin' out at people all the time." I nodded. Eventually the oven timer rang, signalling that the meat pies were done. I stuck my head down the stairwell and yelled for Brent to come up.

After eating, Brent and I went down to our bedroom. We were exhausted after shooting, arguing, and driving home from the mountains. It felt like our little guerrilla band was already disintegrating, and we had only been living together for a few months. Brent was watching the eleven o'clock TV news. "What would you do if we weren't living in this house with Gerry and Julie, doing this guerrilla trip?" I asked, sitting on the edge of the bed.

"I don't know," he said absent-mindedly. "Out of all the many options in life, this is actually what I want to do. If it all fell apart, it would be a big letdown." I looked at him and could tell that, for him, what he had said was profoundly true. Of the five of us, Brent was probably the most truly dedicated to being a revolutionary. Then, as an afterthought, he added, "Well, I guess the second thing I'd want to do other than this would be just to live with you, and then once that happened, I'd think of the third thing." He paused for a few seconds. "What would you do?"

"I'd go to Vancouver and figure out how to get the ID I would need to move to West Germany. There's no way I'd live in Vancouver until I got old and died," I said without hesitation.

"Well, you've talked about that before," said Brent, getting up and flipping the channels.

"Right, because you've told me you wanted to go to the States and live by yourself if this all fell through."

"No."

"Yes."

"No — that's what I say half the time when you say you'd probably go back to West Germany."

"No."

"Yes."

"Well, whenever I feel like it's hopeless here, then I want to run off to someplace where the potential for revolution is higher," I said passionately. "I have this real identity to be a guerrilla, and when I met you my whole world changed. I thought, 'Great, here's somebody who's a kindred spirit and he knows other militants.' But it feels so hopeless these days. It's just not working out with Gerry and Julie, and there's no other people to replace them. It seems as though there's hardly any radicals and no revolutionaries in this country. You're probably the only man around who I know I could do anything with. I don't know of any other women to work with who would actually be interested or serious about the guerrilla. I don't just want to do one Red Hot Video action a year. I want to do militant stuff on a full-time basis. I'd move to West Germany because I know there are a lot of militant radical people working there."

"Why wouldn't you move to San Francisco or something?"

"It's a different country, but it's the same objective conditions as Vancouver, if not worse. If I'm going to go to the trouble of moving to another country, I'd go somewhere where there's more potential for revolution."

"You threaten to go to Europe every time nothin's gonna work out." He turned up the volume on the TV.

"It's not a threat, 'cause it really is the only alternative I can see." I got into bed and lay quietly beside him, wrapped up in my own thoughts until sleep finally came.

* * *

Fraser could hardly contain his excitement about listening to the first recordings from the bugs installed at the New Westminster address. In fact, in his haste to reach the intercept room he almost tripped running down the stairs at CLEU headquarters. Just before opening the door he redeemed himself by pausing to catch his breath and straighten his shirt. He opened the door and casually walked in. In order to reach what was called the "slave room," he had to pass through the master intercept room, where a master tape was made of all the conversations being recorded. In the slave room each police officer sat in front of five UHER 4000 tape recorders, listening for legal evidence. In Fraser's vivid imagination, the rooms resembled a NASA control room, the forty-eight tape recorders all whirling away with tiny red lights flashing and bright digital displays logging the date and time of each recording. He walked up with an air of authority to the policeman sitting in front of the two slave tape recorders picking up all the sounds from the kitchen and Taylor and Hansen's bedroom. The officer was wearing a pair of padded headphones, so Fraser tapped him on the shoulder. "How's it going?"

"Good," said the guy. "The reception's not bad as long as they aren't playing the radio in the kitchen or the TV in the bedroom." Fraser's heart sank. He had feared that would be a problem, but there had been nothing they could do.

"We've got special amplifiers and isolators that raise voice levels when necessary and cut out taping noises in these babies," he explained, patting the large UHER 4000 tape recorder. Fraser nodded, then asked if he could listen for a while.

"They aren't up yet so there's nothing going on," the policeman explained. "I'm listening to another recording from another case."

Fraser glanced around the room, then decided to come back later in the morning when he figured his suspects would be up and about.

❉ 39 ❉

When we came upstairs on the morning of Christmas Eve, Gerry was alone in the kitchen even though Julie had returned sometime during the night. Before she got up, Gerry suggested that we postpone, until after Christmas, trying to resolve the issues that had surfaced so explosively during our camping trip, in the hopes that a short separation might ease the tension. He and Julie were going to spend Christmas Eve and Christmas Day with their families.

"Christmas Eve!" announced Gerry, as Julie came in the room. "We better take Rex, 'cause my mom said she never sees him and I think he needs to get out of this house." He looked over at Julie nervously. The atmosphere was polite, yet restrained. "Do you think it would be cool if we took Rex over in the truck and parked it a ways from my mom's?" he asked, looking over at Brent and me. "Once we get to Burnaby, we'll go down a bunch of back alleys and make sure we're not being tailed."

Brent was reading the paper. "Fine by me."

"Sure," I said, taking out a heavy cast-iron frying pan. "Does everybody want bacon and eggs?" I was hoping we could have a friendly breakfast before separating for Christmas.

"Sure," said Brent and Gerry. Julie said nothing, but I made some for her anyway. Breakfast was a quiet affair, interspersed with small talk designed to break up the uncomfortable silences that would build up between mouthfuls of food. After eating, Julie, Gerry, and Rex made a quick exit, leaving Brent and me still sitting in the kitchen, browsing through a pile of radical newspapers strewn all over the table. Since my family was in Ontario and Brent wasn't on speaking terms with his, we were going to spend

Christmas alone at home, with no plans other than cleaning the guns from our camping trip.

The only concession I made to the holiday that year was to phone my mother just before supper. I hadn't talked to her in months and I thought she would be worried sick if she didn't hear from me. I told Brent I was going down to the pay phone. "Wait! I'll go with you and we can eat at the Italian restaurant on the corner." We hadn't eaten in a restaurant for ages. It would be our Christmas dinner.

When I looked around at all the Christmas lights on the houses on our way to the restaurant, I realized how out of touch we were with everyone else's reality. People driving by in their cars were smiling and exuding that warm feeling known as Christmas cheer. In our zeal to change society, we were indiscriminate in our criticisms of everything it had to offer, including its traditions and trappings. Our alienation from society was absolute. Our denunciations left nothing unscathed: the nuclear family, marriage, owning a home, and Christmas were all capitalist institutions, earmarked for annihilation.

While Brent went into the restaurant, I went to the pay phone on the corner and made my Christmas call. I felt a pang of sadness, more for the pain I knew I was causing my mother than for the absence of a family Christmas dinner in my life. When she answered the phone, I put on my cheeriest voice and made up a story that I thought might bring her some peace of mind. But no matter how cheerful I tried to sound, I could hear the concern in her voice and I knew she didn't believe the feeble explanation I gave regarding my whereabouts and my activities. At that point in my life, even if I had to sacrifice seeing my family and friends in order to make a significant contribution to revolutionary change, it was all worth it.

The restaurant owners must have thought we were a rather sad couple, sitting alone and sharing a bottle of wine with our lasagna on Christmas Eve. But we were actually quite content, enjoying each other's company and talking about our plans. Since we were the only customers, they brought over a candle to light up our solitary table in the middle of that huge, cavernous room, dimly illuminated by a few pot lights and a single strand of multicoloured Christmas bulbs draped loosely over the bar. Afterwards we walked home hand in hand and spent the rest of the evening watching the TV news in our garish living room.

When Julie and Gerry returned on Boxing Day, it seemed as though all the tension had dissipated. They didn't say much about their Christmas, but I could tell they had enjoyed spending time with Gerry's family. Coincidentally, when they came in, Brent and I were again sitting at the kitchen table, browsing through the newspapers that were always lying strategically in piles beside the toilet, on the coffee table, and all over the kitchen table. "Hey, Jules," I said cheerily, "did you read that article in *Kinesis* about the women in London, who call themselves Angry Women?"

"No." She picked up *Kinesis*," a Vancouver feminist newspaper, and read about a group of women in London, England, who had attacked Anne Summers' Sex Shop. They had tacked a notice on the door saying "Closed for Renovations" and then broken inside and poured and sprayed paint all over. They had also destroyed video machines, magazines, rubber dolls, and other women-hating materials — a kamikaze-like attack in the daytime. According to the article, they had tried to burn down the same shop four times before. The sex shops were part of a chain with 138 stores, just like Red Hot Video, and they were also trying to become part of the family entertainment industry and appear harmless. The women activists in London were trying to take the porn shops out of the closet and onto the street and expose them for what they really were.

"That is so cool!" Julie sighed after finishing the article.

"If we were real gutsy and practised, we could be in and out within a minute," I said, my imagination beginning to take flight over another possible Red Hot Video action.

"I know," said Julie, watching me.

"I think we'd get a huge bucket full of Javex bleach and just drop the tapes into it. That would destroy them!" I said excitedly.

"Really?"

"Well, I don't know, but I think it would," I said, slowing down a little.

"I don't know anything about bleach but it probably would, though." She was obviously thinking this scenario through.

"We'd have to do it at around nine in the morning when there weren't too many customers," I suggested.

"It's so direct." She sounded a little perplexed, probably wondering if I was serious.

"We'd need some kind of weapon — otherwise, the owner or someone could just grab us." I looked over at Brent and Gerry for help. "If we carried in a knife, we could be charged with armed assault."

"You could go in with a baseball bat," suggested Brent.

"Yeah," said Julie.

"We'd have to wear balaclavas and smash the surveillance video camera with the baseball bat as soon as we got there," I said, continuing on my flight.

"That'd be cool," said Julie.

"We could also take a stopwatch with us so we wouldn't get carried away and stay too long. Yeah, one person could be smashing everything while the other two put videos in buckets of bleach," I said triumphantly.

"Closed for Renovations! That is so funny!" Julie laughed.

"And they wouldn't be able to prevent these trashings in the future either," I added. "They wouldn't be able to identify us because we'd be wearing balaclavas and we'd smash the video cameras right away! The primal release you'd get from smashing up a porno store would be great. It'd be so therapeutic to release all the anger we feel towards the porno industry!"

"Yeah, I even got a thrill out of smashing the windows with that huge rock," agreed Julie. "It's so beautiful. You just throw it and then you turn around and see all this glass falling out."

"It's a great idea, but I'm not so sure the other women would want to do something that risky and open." I was coming down to reality again. "I don't even know if they want to do another Red Hot Video action."

"Yeah," said Julie quietly. I wasn't even so sure she wanted to do another Red Hot Video action.

I looked over at Brent and Gerry. "Besides casing, what do we have to do this week? I guess everybody's going shoplifting?"

"Shoplifting for what? Our consumerism?" Julie said sarcastically.

"Whatever camping shit we want," I said, ignoring her remark.

"I want to get a new sleeping bag," Brent said. "My old one isn't very warm."

"I guess I should get some boots," Julie added.

"I wouldn't mind going camping again," said Gerry unexpectedly.

"I would too 'cause I'm getting worried about this robbery. I didn't get in enough practice on my handgun, and I don't feel confident about using it if anything goes wrong," revealed Julie. After the weekend arguments, I was genuinely surprised that Julie and Gerry were eager to go again.

"Someone should definitely go down to Bellingham or Seattle before we go because Gerry won't even be able to practise with that Luger if the magazine doesn't work," I said, referring to a German Luger Gerry would be carrying during the robbery.

"Well, I'll phone around beforehand and see if I can locate a gun store that carries Luger magazines, but someone else can go down and pick it up," said Brent.

"Me and Gerry could go down," offered Julie.

"And then it'd be nice to find out from Customs beforehand if it's legal to carry a magazine across the border, 'cause if it's not, you might want to put some effort into hiding it," I pointed out.

"Operation Luger Magazine," chuckled Gerry. "And what other stuff do we have to do this week?"

"Gerry's got to get an address for his driver's licence." Brent was referring to an address where Gerry could pick up a phony driver's licence, for which he was planning to be tested.

"Does anyone want to go swimming tonight?" I asked.

"I do," said Brent.

"I'll go swimming for sure," said Julie.

"Yeah, I think I'd be interested in swimming myself," agreed Gerry.

"So you're going to do the laundry now, right Ann?" asked Brent.

"Yes. So we're going to case this week and somebody's going to go down to the States and then we're going to do the postbox thing and maybe go camping, plus shoplifting, right?" I tried to summarize our plans for the upcoming week.

"Ummm, I wouldn't mind just going shooting for one day, let's say Friday, if we can get a magazine for the Luger by then," suggested Gerry, "because I won't have had any practice on the handgun I'm going to be using for the robbery and it's getting late."

"Okay, but my concern nowadays is, we are getting low on money and it costs at least two hundred and fifty dollars every time we go target-practising in the mountains," explained Brent.

"Because of all the ammo we use?" asked Gerry.

"Yeah, and the gas."

I got up and put on the kettle. "I think I'll have one more coffee and then I better head out and do the laundry."

"So . . . how can we do another cruise action?" asked Brent.

"Not here, that's for sure," said Julie.

"How about in Ottawa, right after the robbery?" suggested Brent.

"What were you thinking of — in Ottawa?" asked Julie.

"The U.S. Embassy," Brent said casually. "The American and Canadian governments are in the middle of making agreements to test the cruise in Alberta. I think the only way to affect reality is to do an action before the agreement happens. Because if we do a bombing after they make the agreement, then we can't stop anything. But if we do it before, then it's in the realm of possibility that the Canadian government might just say, 'Sorry America, like we're just not into having these direct action bombings in our country so you can go back and test your missile in Utah or someplace.' "

"They won't do that," countered Gerry.

"Well, there's a slight possibility," said Brent.

"I don't know," Gerry said. "Have all the RAF actions in West Germany influenced the Americans to take out any of their army bases?"

"Well, they're starting to move their headquarters out now and relocate them in England," Brent said. "If we did do the Embassy it would be even more of an international action, which does tend to have that galvanizing effect throughout the whole movement."

"Is there a U.S. Embassy in Ottawa?" Julie asked.

"Yeah, it's outrageous," exclaimed Brent. "You got the Parliament buildings on one side of the street and directly across from the front door is the U.S. Embassy. So you have this Parliament building that is actually controlled by this American building across the street with these hardcore Marines guarding it in ceremonial uniforms!"

"Wow!" said Julie in her wide-eyed way.

"I'm not totally serious about it, you know," explained Brent. "But it's a possibility."

I made coffees for everyone and sat down at the table again. "Do you ever write much, Gerry?" Brent asked unexpectedly.

"No, I'm a shitty writer," he laughed.

"But you're a good talker," added Julie.

"Well, if I had a Dictaphone, I could rant and rave and then have it transcribed," he joked.

"At some point you might try writing something, because communiqués should be statements from the whole group," explained

Brent. "So it's real important that everyone is completely happy with what's being written."

"I remember being so frustrated in high-school English because I had so much to say but I couldn't write," said Gerry.

"But you can write songs," added Brent.

"Most of the songs I wrote, I didn't like," explained Gerry. "But I'd like to be able to write, because at some point I may not be an active guerrilla and might just want to be a political activist. . . . This is a little off the topic, but I don't feel we should rush off to Ottawa right after the robbery to do a cruise action. I think there would be a lot of room for sloppiness. We need to do more long-term planning — plus I'm somewhat concerned about alienating Doug any more than necessary. There's no way he'd go to Ontario to do an action."

"Yeah, but there's going to be a fair break between the robbery and Cheekeye, 'cause Cheekeye isn't actually going to happen till sometime in June and if we do the robbery in February, then we got March, April, and May," countered Brent. By that time we had made a definite decision to bomb another substation on the Cheekeye-Dunsmuir line before they electrified the line in October 1983. "We haven't even lived here a month and we're working on a robbery and half the time it feels like we're just sitting around. So if we're not even working on a robbery for those three months, what are we going to be doing?"

"I don't feel like we're sitting around that much," said Gerry.

"I don't know if I want to be really international. I don't know exactly," said Julie meekly. "I'd rather do another women's action, more like the Red Hot Video action. I don't really have the need to always move, you know. I don't feel stagnant. Working on this robbery takes a lot of energy and moving a lot just throws me off, but I'm not absolutely against it."

"Do you think we should move out of here on the first of February?" Brent looked at her with an expression of bewilderment.

"Yeah, I'd say so for sure," said Julie more confidently. I looked over at her as well. It was becoming increasingly obvious that her doubts and indecisiveness were symptomatic of her waning interest in our little guerrilla group.

"I'd just as soon give notice at the end of January and stay here through the month of February," added Gerry.

"Really?" Julie looked surprised.

"Yeah, that'll give us some leisurely time to move our stuff out of here and we could go rent a new place," suggested Gerry.

"Probably your idea is best because we won't be rushed, walking around tripping over our shoes because we have to get out fast. How do you feel about that, Brent?" Julie asked.

Brent appeared not to hear her question. Instead Gerry said, "I could easily fill up those so-called periods of nothing happening with reading the stuff that the three of you have collected over the past year. It is actually necessary that I do some reading on that technical stuff so I'm on the same level as everybody else."

"I'm feeling really insecure about the whole thing," revealed Julie suddenly. "I just know that rather than jumping into something right now, I just have to have time to really get my space together and figure out if this is what I'm going to do and how I'm going to proceed, right?" Now she had caught Brent's attention. His head shot up and he stared at her.

"Like we all have doubts, right?" added Gerry, jumping into the fray while the opportunity existed. "Every now and then, like, we all turn around and go, wow, man! What am I doing with my life? I'm basically throwing it away. For a good reason, but I'm throwing it away. Everybody stops and takes a double-take every now and then, and sometimes they're more severe than other times. Sometimes they last for a couple of days and we get out of it and say, 'I'm doing what I want to do,' and other times they're more severe and you decide that you don't want to do it anymore."

"Right," agreed Julie.

"I think all of us probably go through that stage sometimes, and when people do then they should be given a lot of space and leeway to make up their minds, right?" continued Gerry passionately. "Because it is a weird trip we're into. Like, we're not in El Salvador where there is a possibility of a big breakthrough someday and of our country actually being liberated. If people really believe we're going to have some big revolution, they're kidding themselves. There's no way that we're going to see any direct result from what we're doing for quite some time, if ever."

"I keep having this major contradiction coming into my head," Julie said earnestly. "I really, truly believe inside that I can't make people change to believe what I believe. It's almost like being a Jehovah's Witness, trying to get people to believe in your religion. Sometimes I feel really freaked out by it, and other times I believe in doing the actions and that's all I want to do."

By that point in the conversation Brent and I should have opened our eyes and seen the writing on the wall. It was obvious that Julie and Gerry were having major doubts about being urban guerrillas, and in light of the seriousness of our actions this would have been a good time to stop and reconsider. Unfortunately, our passion for commitment to our revolutionary dreams blinded us to the storm brewing around us. That's why, fifteen minutes later, the conversation turned back to future actions.

"What about Comox?" I suggested, oblivious to the cracks in the wall. Comox was a Canadian air force base on Vancouver Island.

"If you're looking for an anti-cruise-type action, one against Comox would get Doug's support, but it would bring down heat on Vancouver Island, which would not be too cool because our next Cheekeye action would also be on Vancouver Island," Gerry pointed out. "And there's another thing we're going to be doing between the robbery and Cheekeye, and that's the court trip for the car theft."

"Too bad we couldn't figure out a way to do an action at Cold Lake, because that wouldn't be so far away for Doug," I said. The Primrose Lake air force base was near the town of Cold Lake, Alberta.

"I'd really be into that, if we could get away," agreed Gerry. "I'd rather do that than the U.S. Embassy."

"Even if it is just symbolic," I thought aloud.

"Yeah, I would like Cold Lake better than Ottawa too," agreed Julie. "Would Doug go there?"

"He'd be more likely to go there than Ottawa," I said. At the mention of Cold Lake Brent went downstairs and quickly came back up with a map of Alberta. He opened the map on the table and we huddled over it. "I wonder how long it would take to do an action up there?" I asked.

"It would probably depend on what we did. If we wanted to blow up a parking sign it'd probably only take a week," joked Gerry. "How about blowing up the head honcho who runs the damn place in his car?" We smirked at Gerry's morbid sense of humour.

"Or some of the planes up there?" I said in a more serious tone. "Just like we were gonna do in Comox?"

"So you think Doug would go along?" asked Julie again.

"He's already going off trying to plan an action by himself," said Brent. We just looked at one another. "So anyways, we're agreed that we're going to give notice on the first of February then?"

"Yeah." Gerry glanced over at Julie, who was nodding. "And then we either do something or split up for a while and get back together and do Cheekeye."

"If I'm going to get the laundry done before we go swimming, I better get going," I said, pushing my chair back. "Brent, how would you like to help me carry the bags out to the truck?" He folded his map up and followed me downstairs to our bedroom. After shoving a few armfuls of dirty clothes into a bag, he sat down on the bed, looking discouraged. "In a lot of ways it's kind of frustrating working with Julie and Gerry."

"Why?" I was still gathering up dirty clothes up off the floor.

"They're just not together enough," he said. "Months ago Gerry said he was getting an address where the ID could be mailed, and he still hasn't done it. And I know if I didn't phone about the magazine for his Luger, he'd never get around to it. He says he's so busy all the time but he's not busy at all. Numerous times he's said he's going to do some reading but he hasn't read one thing."

"It'll make me very happy to give notice February 1st," I added, hoping that somehow Brent and I would not be living with Julie. I was still struggling with feelings of jealousy.

"Maybe in Europe people could be more together politically at Julie's age because the whole society is so much more politicized, but here it's just not possible for someone who's twenty to be an urban guerrilla," he said bitterly. "Julie's definitely into moving out, but she doesn't even know how much she's really into this stuff. I don't think we should even be doing this Brink's thing in such an artificial situation, you know what I mean? We get these people who sort of dig the idea of the guerrilla but really aren't together enough to do it. Gerry says how nice it would be to learn to write, because after he's done the guerrilla, he would like to be able to inform the community! So why is he doing this? He says because it's a contradiction to advocate the guerrilla but never do it. So basically he's saying he's doing this so he can quit later and advocate it without being a hypocrite!"

I stopped picking up laundry and sat down on the bed beside him. "Julie's starting to sound like she's not into it either," I added softly.

"I'm starting to see the guerrilla as the ideological glue that's holding us together, but it's not a reality," he said dejectedly. "It's a convenient excuse to justify carrying out the robbery. After the robbery, everyone will have all this money and then it will be much easier for people to say, 'I'm not really into working on the guerrilla that much.' How can we really get deep into planning a guerrilla campaign when Gerry is thinking of quitting for sure?"

"Yeah, I think he plans on building his cabin after the robbery. You know, we don't have to do the robbery," I said in a consoling voice.

"If we don't, it's poverty city. Even Cheekeye . . . it's not that cool to do an action and then put out a communiqué advocating that we build a militant movement and then two months later, we quit."

"If only there were more people, then it wouldn't be so bad. Right now, we're so dependent on our own little world, eh?"

"The situation is so depressing. I'd feel like putting out if there were more revolutionaries committed to doing this. I fear that Julie and Gerry are using the situation to do the robbery. Unfortunately, I'm starting to think that what you used to say is true. There's no possibility of the guerrilla in Canada."

"It's terrible to admit, but I often think it's completely ridiculous, yet I carry on because it just seems horrible to stop after putting so much of my life into it."

"And then there's this problem you have with me and Julie that also creates bad vibes. You just seem to be seething at each other half the time."

"I can't help it. It's just something that's happened and I don't know what to do about it. I've felt like this for months and months and I can't seem to shake it."

For a few more minutes we sat side by side on the bed, each wrapped up in our own dark thoughts until finally I gave my head a shake and finished picking up the laundry. This problem was too big to solve in one day, and in the meantime the laundry still had to be done. I began carrying the laundry up to the truck and soon Brent came up behind me, carrying the last few bags. He gave me a peck on the cheek.

"I'll see you later. I'm sure we'll feel better if we go swimming tonight," he said, shutting the driver's door for me. As I drove off I watched Brent in my side-view mirror as he shuffled slowly towards the house. I remembered a time, not long ago, when he sprang.

* * *

The next morning we gathered in the kitchen, as usual, for our morning discussion. The possibility of doing a cruise action in Alberta was still very much on our minds. "Blowing up some jets would be a great idea," said Brent enthusiastically, referring to the planes on the Primrose air force base. "But how would we do it?"

"It would be good if we could attach some dynamite to a magnetic device that could be stuck to the gas tank of the jet and then have it set to go off in five hours, giving us enough time to get back to Edmonton," suggested Julie. It seemed as though the swim the night before had cleared all doubt from her mind.

"We'd have to run detonating wire between all the jets or else have forty separate timing devices if we were going to do forty planes," Brent said.

"There's probably around two hundred and fifty jets on the whole base. There's no reason why we'd have to do forty of them," said Gerry, just as enthusiastically as Julie.

"They probably have CF-18s there," Julie said. I had noticed that the evenings we swam at the local New Westminster pool always seemed to wash away the stress and tension that had built up amongst us during the week.

"They do," said Gerry assertively. "They're worth about $5 million apiece." Gerry was something of an amateur airplane buff. "The cruise is only worth something like $2 million apiece and it's powered by a jet engine, not a rocket like most of them. Do you know where the fuel tanks are on the CF-18s? They're on the tips of the wings and look like bombs. They're streamlined like a bomb but built as part of the jet. Those are the things to go for unless they drain the kerosene from them."

The night before Brent had found a defence book with photographs of the Primrose air force base. Gerry opened the book up to a map that showed the entire perimeter of the air force range. "Look at the size of it!" he exclaimed.

"It's huge!" said Julie in awe.

"Yeah, it goes all the way into Saskatchewan!" Brent ran his finger over the map.

"We better get going, Gerry," Julie said, getting up. They were going to case the Sears mall, while Brent and I were going to case the Brentwood Mall. We were still in the process of narrowing down the best mall in which to rob a Brink's guard.

"Yeah, I just have to grab the binoculars," he said, heading towards the downstairs bedroom.

"What about the stopwatch?" yelled Brent. "Last time I cased the Sears mall, as soon as the Brink's guard opened the truck door, I timed how long it took for him to get back to the truck."

"Good idea," agreed Julie.

"Do you have any questions about what you're supposed to watch for?" asked Brent.

"I'm gonna see where the guard goes inside and see if the latch is done up on his gun holster," reported Julie, seemingly unfazed by Brent's question.

"You're gonna go in, then?" I asked.

"Yeah. I should've talked to you about it, but how would you feel if I just stood real far back and watched the guard, real cool like?" asked Julie.

"I think it's okay," I agreed. "But I'm more concerned with what they do from the outside."

"Yeah, and then you two are gonna go to the Brentwood Mall, eh?" asked Julie.

"Yeah, Brent's gonna go first and I'm gonna meet him there later and take over," I explained. They were standing by the door, ready to go. "Okay kids," I joked.

"Bye, bye," said Julie in a baby voice.

"Au revoir," said Brent, without looking up from his paper. "This is a great article about an action carried out by a Puerto Rican guerrilla group. They bombed $45 million dollars worth of U.S. military jets on this well-guarded base in Puerto Rico. During the Second World War, there were tons of actions against these guarded bases. So, if people can do it during military situations, we should be able to do it here during peacetime."

He passed me the newspaper. "Limpet mines would be the coolest, if we had them. They're about an inch thick. We could just walk up to each plane and stick one on it. If we were gonna do ten planes, we'd need a package of five sticks for each plane, laid flat between pieces of tin plate or plywood or something. Then each one would have a detonating cord coming out of it, running to the next plane, so we wouldn't need ten timers, right?"

"But how would you even reach them? Aren't those planes pretty high to reach standing up?" I asked. Brent shrugged. "I guess we'd rent a place in Edmonton and then just drive to the base from there. We could improvise, just like in Toronto. Doug might be more willing to go too, if we're in Edmonton."

"He'd probably be more willing to go if we just send him a letter when we're ready to do the action and then he could catch a train to Edmonton and stay for a few weeks," Brent speculated.

"Besides hurting the Defence Department financially, the beauty of this action would be that it shows they are vulnerable and can be attacked right where they plan to test the missiles," I said. "If we lived in Edmonton, the whole thing would probably only take about a month because all we'd have to do is case, then devise some sort of carrying case and write the communiqué." I looked over at Brent to see if he was listening. "Or we could write it before we go. Everyone could contribute to it through discussions and then, if you want, you could write it?"

"Yeah," he said unenthusiastically, "but it could be slightly shorter than the last one. We could write it while we're working on the robbery, then leave for Edmonton right after. If Doug is hesitant, he could just come out for the two weeks before the action."

Most of the afternoon was spent casing at one of the four malls we had identified as being possible robbery scenarios. By seven in the evening we were again congregated in the kitchen, discussing our casing observations. Besides exchanging information informally, we also made copious notes detailing all the times, dates, and locations of the various Brink's pickups. Still, that evening plans for a Cold Lake bombing action dominated our discussions.

"I was thinking," Gerry said. "We don't have the right clothes or gear for this expedition. Our tent and clothes should be white. But if all our clothes were white except for our snow boots, and somebody was scanning the range from a distance, then our feet would look like stumps or rocks."

We looked at Gerry as though he was from another planet. "When we do get up there," Brent said, ignoring Gerry's concerns, "someone could drive a car around the base and dump people off so they can walk around. We should be prepared to spend about twelve hours just walking around in the snow. We'd probably want to do it at night."

"It would be nice if we could charter a plane and fly over the area to do aerial reconnaissance. Didn't the RAF do something like that?" asked Gerry.

I was the resident RAF expert. "Yeah, but it was a prison they were going over. When I visited Vancouver Island, you could watch the jets in the air, preparing for landing, but you couldn't actually see where they parked. I would assume they're parked near a populated area with buildings and stuff. You'd have to be very daring to sneak in there and place bombs on the jets."

"Dead and daring," chuckled Gerry. "They have the right to shoot, you know. If they see somebody deliberately sabotaging the railway, they can actually shoot them, so I would imagine it's the same thing with the air force. I'd much rather be shot than go to prison anyway. It sounds like my kind of action." I interpreted Gerry's morbid sense of humour as his way of releasing his fears and anxiety about what we were doing, or planning to do.

"I don't think they actively look for intruders on the base unless they have reason to believe someone is actually there," I said.

"No, but if they do find a bomb, they're gonna comb the whole area," countered Gerry. "It doesn't scare me off doing the action, but if we have both the bombs and ourselves well camouflaged, then there's a reasonable chance we could get back to Edmonton before they go off."

"If we used a magnetic device to attach the explosives to the jets, wouldn't the magnet screw up the timing device?" I asked.

"I guess it would depend on what kind of timing device we used," speculated Brent. "What if we put a clock beside a magnet?"

"I think it would upset the time," I guessed.

"I think the blasting caps would be most affected by a magnetic field," said Gerry. "Whether we use magnets or not would also depend on what material the jet fighters are made of. I think it's some kind of aluminum alloy, which magnets don't stick to."

"Well, we could tie the explosives underneath them," I said.

"Do you think they keep the jets outside or in a big hanger?" asked Brent.

"They keep them outside," stated Gerry with certainty. "I just don't know about getting to the jets. They may watch them more carefully than we think. We should plan on making a few reconnaissance trips, but it would be a bit weird to be caught walking around on the base."

"Yeah," I laughed. "I'm sure nobody normally goes up and walks around in forty below temperatures. So why are four young people walking around with snowshoes in a blizzard or something?"

"Well, it wouldn't be so weird if we were carrying cameras and taking pictures of the prairies in the winter," Gerry said, with another chuckle.

"That's something I never thought of . . . but we could pose as photographers," said Julie earnestly.

"We could bring along a bunch of bird books," I suggested, half-seriously.

"Alberta has snowbirds and special breeds of ducks," said Gerry. "We could study the area and find out what birds are particular to it and then, if asked, say we're doing some kind of report. We could make it sound like we know what we're talking about. You wouldn't want to be caught and taken into some office and interrogated and say we're looking for a speckled chickadee and then find out it doesn't even exist. We'd have to have a good story."

"Do you think Doug would come?" asked Julie again.

"There's no way he'd come for the whole period," stated Brent emphatically. "Do you honestly think he wants to be cooped up in some room with us in Edmonton?"

"What if we had a big house?" I suggested. "It could be like a vacation for him."

"Can you really see that as being a vacation for Doug?" asked Brent incredulously.

Gerry was browsing through the Defence Department book on air bases in Canada. "We're going to have to get a book on jets. We have to find out the distance from the ground to the fuel tanks and figure out if there's any fuel in them or just enough to taxi over to the fuel depot where they fill up before take off. Without fuel in the tanks, we'd just blow off the wings."

"My major reservation about this action is moving there," Julie said. "I just can't handle moving all my junk everywhere. After the robbery, me and Gerry could rent a cheap place and leave all our stuff there and just pack a couple of suitcases."

"I didn't plan on moving all our belongings," said Brent. "I thought we'd take the kind of stuff we took to Toronto."

"Yeah, but it'd also be real hard on Rex," said Julie.

"Would it be that horrible for him to stay at Gerry's mom's?" I suggested.

"That's an idea," said Julie. "I'm into doing Cold Lake in a big way. It would help get Direct Action established in every province of the country." I looked at her curiously. The inconsistency of her commitment was dramatic. One day she seemed full of doubt and then the next completely gung-ho. I couldn't help thinking that I should take the initiative to nip this Cold Lake plan in the bud. If anything went wrong, the consequences were so dire that the action should only be carried out by people who were 100 per cent aware of and committed to what they were doing. Yet my drive to carry on still far outweighed the pangs of guilt that were beginning to trouble my conscience.

✳ **40** ✳

On December 28 Julie and Gerry once again spent the after-noon casing, but this time they cased both the Sears and Brentwood malls while Brent and I cased the Lougheed Mall and the Woolco in Burnaby. By 7:30 that evening, I was putting a roast in the oven when Julie and Gerry came in, looking a little tired. Brent had not yet returned.

"So, how'd it go?" I asked.

"By the time I found a good place to park the truck, the win-dow facing the Brink's truck was all fogged up," Gerry said in a worried tone. "Normally, I like the windows foggy because when you wipe a little away from where you're going to look, you can see out but they can't see in, right? But today, unfortunately, if I'd wiped the fog from the window, the Brink's driver could have seen me, so instead I had to watch him through this foggy window and I couldn't see clearly at all. Plus the gap in the curtains wasn't big enough." Gerry was referring to curtains we had put across the windows in the canopy of the truck.

"What happened at Brentwood?" I asked.

"Nothing," said Julie dejectedly. "No truck at all. We cased it till it closed too."

"I was very suspicious of these young women at the Sears mall," said Gerry.

"Oh yeah," said Julie.

"Before the Brink's truck came, there were these young women, standing eating ice cream sundaes. I looked through the crack in the curtain towards the loading bay to see if the truck was coming and I noticed this woman standing quite a ways away, looking right at me, and then she pointed at me," said Gerry, imi-tating the woman pointing, "and said something to her friends and then they looked right at me too. They might have been pointing at something over on the other side of my truck but it sure looked like they were looking at me. I was freaked out about that because right after that happened, Julie came and we left and then we saw the Brink's truck coming up the Kingsway so we pulled right around and came back. If they were still standing there when the Brink's truck arrived, they might have thought, 'You know, that's interesting. That guy was looking right in this direction and here's a whole bunch of money in this truck, right.' I couldn't be sure one way or another if they were still around because of how the truck was parked when we returned."

I thought he was being paranoid but kept my thoughts to myself. "How did you like the meeting at Doug's today?"

"Good!" "Great!" said Julie and Gerry respectively.

After breakfast that morning we had driven over to Doug's for a meeting. He had expressed a serious interest in bombing an ice-breaker being constructed at the Burrard Yarrows. He was so serious, in fact, that he had already taken an excursion in a little boat he owned to the Burrard Yarrows shipyards on the North Shore of Vancouver and in Victoria. The *Terry Fox* icebreaker, as well as its sister ship, the *Kulvick*, in Victoria, was being built by Gulf Canada. The *Terry Fox*, which was being built at the North Shore shipyard, was scheduled to be completed in March 1983. The icebreakers would be two of the most powerful privately owned icebreakers in the world and would be used to escort oil drilling units to the Beaufort Sea. Doug had also showed us his casing notes, which included a description of the North Shore Burrard Yarrows dry dock, the time of the Pinkerton security guard shift change, and points about the vulnerability of the electrical transformer. As well, he had a detailed plan of the Victoria dry dock, including infiltration routes and descriptions of the guards' routes, with times marked at various locations. The time and energy he had invested reflected the seriousness with which he approached this project.

"I'm a little bit nervous about doing both actions," I revealed.

"I don't blame you," said Julie sympathetically.

"By actions, which ones are you referring to?" asked Gerry.

"The robbery, the icebreaker, and the air force base," I said. "The main reason I don't like doing three actions in a row like that is because I don't think the people will appreciate all these bombings happening one after the other. Besides, I think the odds of getting busted greatly increase if we do that many actions in such a short space of time." Julie and Gerry nodded their heads in agreement.

"And you know what else?" I held up a copy of the Defence

Department's magazine, the *Sentinel*. "It says they've just finished building an $8 million radar and computer type building at Cold Lake, and it says the CF-18 and other fighter jets have fuel tanks that are basically uninflammable. Here," I added, pointing to the article in question. "It says safety features include self-sealing fuel tanks and fuel lines, fire suppressant foam within the fuel tanks, built-in fire extinguishers, foam in the fuselage to protect against the spread of a fire, and a system that detects all the fuel leaks and then isolates that section of the plane." While they were reading the article, I added, "Rather than just leaving it up in the air, I would like a commitment from Doug. It only seems fair, if we commit to helping him with the icebreaker action, then he should commit to helping us do Cold Lake. Oh, Brent found out that the fuel tanks are in the wings."

"Right." Gerry put down the *Sentinel*. "The whole wing holds fuel."

"I went through every National Defence Department magazine from 1980 through 1982 and none of them had any photos of Cold Lake, just photos of planes that are at Cold Lake. So, do you like the idea of doing the *Terry Fox*?" I asked.

"Yeah, I do." Julie said. "Besides being fun and adventurous, doing an action against oil exploration in the Arctic would have an international impact. It should be done immediately since they're going to go to the Beaufort Sea this spring. I was even thinking that if no one else is into helping Doug, then I could do it with him. Doug and I could come up to Cold Lake two or three weeks before the action up there."

Gerry frowned at Julie. "I would be against people breaking off into little groups and working on separate actions." It was obvious that this was the first time she had expressed this idea to him. "It would mean that you wouldn't be as available to help case and plan the robbery. It's so dangerous and out in the open, if we got caught, we could easily get killed. If one of us is helping Doug plan the icebreaker action, it would subtract from the overall collective work going into the robbery. Anyway, I don't think this is our last chance to act against the issue of oil exploration in the Beaufort Sea."

"But I think the icebreakers are extremely vulnerable right now," Julie said, looking at Gerry. "It's important that we do some damage before the summer, because that's when the oil exploration is done. I like the idea of opening up this vision of preserving the North and the way of life of the northern people. I want to show them that there's another way of dealing with this issue, through direct action. These icebreakers are owned by Gulf Oil and are very technological and we could inflict a lot of damage to them now, while they're dry-docked, without too much energy or risk."

Gerry just looked at Julie with a scowl on his face but didn't respond. Even though I wasn't keen on doing both Cold Lake and the *Terry Fox*, I was impressed that she was thinking independently and that she appeared unafraid to express her views even if we didn't agree. Before we had the chance to address this topic any further, the back door opened and Brent came in. Even before he had taken off his boots and coat, he turned to Julie and Gerry. "So, what did you two see today?"

"At the Sears, we waited until 3:30 and left, assuming the Brink's truck had made its pickup earlier in the day. Then we passed it coming down the Kingsway so we turned around and followed it back to Sears," said Julie eagerly. "The guard made two trips into the store with carts. While he was in Sears, he had both hands on the cart, but outside we noticed that he seemed to keep one hand on his gun. Inside, he goes through a door that says 'Employees Only.' In that area I noticed there are tons of employees going in and out of that door constantly, but they don't have any badges that say they are employees. It would be interesting to go through that door to see if the guy goes around a corner and takes a service elevator down or something."

"So maybe he just avoids the staircase because it's a likely place to be robbed," speculated Brent.

"I wouldn't want to rob him in that area because there are so many employees around that it would be impossible to control them and easy for someone to jump in and be a hero," said Julie.

We continued going over our casing observations for awhile, but when Brent's eye caught sight of the *Sentinel* magazines on the kitchen table the conversation quickly turned to political actions again. "I guess Ann told you the fuel is actually in the wings and those things that look like bombs hanging under the wings are actually auxiliary fuel tanks," Brent said.

"I also read there's about four hundred people on the air base," I said.

"Hmm, that's not very many," said Brent. "These guys are living and working together, so they probably recognize just about everybody that lives on the base, which makes it a problem for us to be wandering around casing the place."

"Yeah," I smiled, "It does make it difficult to explain why five weirdos are marching through a blizzard towards the air base with packsacks on their backs."

"We can just say we're on a secret mission for Colonel Gordon and we can't divulge anything more," laughed Brent.

"A mission from God," added Gerry, laughing out loud.

"You know there's this private firm in Edmonton that has been subcontracted to do all the maintenance work on the planes at the base." Brent became serious again. "Canada has all these jet fighters, like 104 Starfighters, stationed in Europe — they're Canada's contribution to NATO's jet tactical forces — but every time they need maintenance they have to be flown back on these huge Hercules transport jets to Edmonton to be fixed. It's unbelievably mindless!"

"Maybe it's America's way of controlling Europe," I suggested. "If Europe can't maintain the jets, then we will always have control over them."

"The British military advertising magazine, *Jane's*, is another interesting magazine," Brent said. "It's full of slick advertising for military equipment that you never see in *Time* or *Chatelaine*. All these huge companies, like Ford and General Electric, make military equipment and list all their latest weapons in *Jane's* for sale to governments. See, here's an advertisement by Ford for sidewinder missiles."

"So if Doug agrees to come along, do you think we should go up target-practising on Tuesday?" I said to no one in particular.

"Yeah," said Julie, half-heartedly. She was looking through the *Jane's* military magazine.

"Well, he should fucking come," I surprised even myself with the bitterness in my voice. "He isn't a very collective person at all!"

"I know," agreed Julie, looking at me.

"And if we do the icebreaker with him, he should really come to Cold Lake if for no other reason than out of a sense of obligation to the group," I added just as bitterly as before. Obviously there was a considerable amount of resentment building up inside me towards Doug. "I would be really upset if he said no."

"I know," said Julie compassionately.

"The scene here is so limited," I continued on my rant. "If you weren't happy with Gerry or if I'm not happy with Brent, there's no alternative to this group. There's no other group of women or guerrillas like ourselves to work with."

"I know," said Julie with sincerity. I'm sure the same thoughts had crossed her mind. Gerry and Brent were so engrossed in the *Sentinel* and *Jane's* magazines that they didn't appear to hear us.

"There's the four different Canadian fighter jets," said Gerry, pointing to some photos. "And there's a photo of one with the extra fuel tank. It's only a couple of feet off the ground."

"Whoa!" exclaimed Brent. "Look at this woman! It says she's an air weapons technician working on a twenty-millimetre cannon on a CF-104 Starfighter. She's just standing there at ground level fixing this cannon on the side of the jet. Read this, Gerry! It says Northwest Industries Ltd. has been awarded a multi-million-dollar contract to carry out all repair programs of the CF-104 aircraft. 'Aircraft from Cold Lake will fly directly to Edmonton while European-based 104s will be ferried two at a time aboard Pacific Western Airlines' Hercules leased to Northwest Industries.' That's what I was trying to explain to you earlier."

"Ohhh!" sighed Gerry. "Did you know that Smith and Wesson makes handcuffs?"

"Oh yeah," said Brent. "You can buy them downtown."

"We got to get them," said Julie urgently. "We got to get a pair."

"Smith and Wessons are the most expensive handcuffs on the market," explained Brent. "They're about thirty-six bucks a pair!"

"Canada hasn't made a jet since the AVRO," stated Gerry, changing topics again. We were all over the place that evening.

"Canada did make some 104s through some company called Canada Air or Canadair," said Brent. "Well, they actually contracted them out and made quite a few parts under the Defence Sharing Agreement."

"The AVRO was considered to be the best fighter jet in the world at the time," explained Gerry. "Canada made four, I think, and we were supposed to manufacture enough for our own air force and some for France, and other people were thinking of buying them as well until Diefenbaker had it scrapped. Some of his buddies in the States probably said 'Don't build it or we'll get uptight.' "

"You know," continued Brent, "military manufacturers are the biggest industries in the world, yet they are clandestine in the sense that society knows very little about them."

"Yeah!" said Gerry excitedly, leafing quickly through the *Jane's* magazine. "Look at this! Renault, Fiat, and Mercedes make armoured vehicles. When I worked up at Marmot Basin, they had this four-wheel-drive vehicle that you could hook up to a back hoe or a winch or a blade or anything you wanted. It had these monstrous all-terrain tires that could go so slow the wheels would only turn around once an hour. We heard that they'd used these vehicles in West Germany and France for troop carriers."

"Hey, did you want to see what I got today?" I said suddenly. Everyone looked up from their magazines. I ran downstairs and came back upstairs holding a brand new Makita cordless drill. Expressing the general anticlimactic feeling, Gerry asked, "What did you want a cordless drill for?"

"With this," I said proudly, holding it up for everyone to see, "we could drill anywhere without power. They have really strong, rechargeable batteries so we could drill right through the metal plate on a dynamite magazine, or we could take it into an underground parking lot and use it to steal a car. We simply insert a metal bit and drill out the tumblers in the ignition, then stick a screwdriver into the keyway, turn on the car, and we're outta there. This way we can steal any model — a Dodge, GM, Ford, you name it."

When I squeezed the drill trigger, a low humming sound came from it, noticeably quieter than the plug-in variety. "This is cool," I purred. "I love it! Yeah, the first time we stole dynamite, we had to plug our drill into an AC/DC adapter and a car battery. From now on we'll be able to steal cars without a car battery or adapter. I'm so happy because the car theft thing has been getting me more and more freaked out. Now we won't have to drive all over the neighbourhood looking for the only few models we can steal using those stupid little fingers that keep falling all over the floor. Now, all we'll be looking for is good theft locations. It also means any of us can use it. You don't have to practise picking or using an extractor."

"It'll also be great if we have to break into an office, because it's so quiet," added Brent, taking a turn using the drill. We took turns playing around with the drill for awhile until I turned the conversation back to the robbery.

"So, it seems as though the Brink's guard at Sears is into random patterns?" I observed, looking at Julie and Gerry.

"It seems so," said Gerry, "and he doesn't even park regularly. He parks completely weird."

"I don't want to spend the month of January on that place," I said. "If you write down everything you saw, Brent and I will go tomorrow and then we can decide whether we want to continue casing the Sears or concentrate on the Brentwood and the Guild-ford. The Sears could be a hopeless cause."

"I honestly do feel scared in there 'cause there's so many peo-ple," revealed Julie. "I think it's a big waste of time."

"There's been a dramatic increase in Loomis robberies lately," said Brent, using the word Loomis and Brink's interchangeably in reference to any armed security company. "There was one today and there was one last week that wasn't even in the paper except that they referred to it in today's article."

"Where? In Vancouver?" I asked.

"In Edmonton — half a million dollars cash," Brent said. "There's been so many robberies lately that by the time we get around to it, the guards will be on red alert and blow us away. We should have taken advantage of it when the time was right."

"Yeah, I guess we should have done the Woolco, but we really weren't ready," I said. "How much did they get today?"

"A hundred thousand dollars," Brent said. "They think it's the same gang, but I doubt it. Today there were four masked men. It's the eighth one this year in Edmonton."

"That roast will be another half an hour," I said. "Can you guys call me when the timer goes off? I'm going to go downstairs and organize these magazines."

"Sure," said Gerry, smiling at Julie. Every opportunity to be alone as couples was treasured these days. I could tell by the expression on his face that even half an hour alone with Julie would make his evening. Brent must have noticed as well because, without saying a word, he gathered up a pile of magazines from the table and followed me downstairs.

For a while we sat together on the floor, organizing the *Sentinels* into neat chronological piles. I could see by the furrow in his brow that he wasn't thinking peaceful thoughts. When he noticed me staring at him, he remarked, "This group of people are so com-pletely fucked. I really do toy with the idea, at times, of just saying forget it. At that meeting this morning at Doug's, it sounded like he wants to run around bombing stuff by himself. What's that all about? What does he want to do? Just get killed?"

"I've always felt it would be wacko for individuals to go around and bomb on their own, but I keep saying to myself that he won't actually do it."

"The idea is to create a political force, not just a few people who can blow up a couple of things until they get caught," Brent said. "So at times I just toy with the idea of saying 'Well this is a nice try but why sacrifice ourselves trying to get some stuff happening?' You know how you're always saying that maybe we're just doing it because we put so much energy into it over the past two years that it's a shame to not carry through with it? But it's way more of a shame if we carry through with something that's completely fucked and end up in jail for it."

"Yeah, I know what you mean. It's so frustrating, because I don't think we can stop any of this shit, really. Hopefully, we'll just inspire more people to be militant. We live in too small of a world, you know. In a normal situation, if you have something you don't like about a person, you don't have to be with them day in and day out, unless they're your lover or something. Normally you can also see other people or move out. All we can do is move to another place. I have to somehow learn how to shake these bad feelings I have or else I have to completely quit. There's no other cell to join. There's no other people to visit other than Doug. I can't really move into another place by myself, because there's constantly better reasons why we should all be living together, even though I find it an incredible strain. I have no solution to the problem other than to remain here for another two months plus March and April, but it's a horrifying thought for me." For a few minutes, I sat there staring at the piles of *Sentinels*, trying to find a solution to our problems, but nothing came to mind. "Probably, the best thing is to just plough through this year mentally, then take a break."

✳ 41 ✳

Anyone dropping into our little house in New Westminster would assume, based on outward appearances, that we led a normal life with predictable routines. But what distinguished us from everyone else were the activities that made up that routine — at this particular time, casing various malls and shoplifting all over the Lower Mainland. I would often find myself standing in some mall, waiting for the Brink's guard, wondering which mall I was in. They were all the same and none of them felt safe. Either the getaway route involved driving past the Brink's truck, or the guard followed a random pattern, or the possible robbery site was too busy. By early January, all I could think about was robberies. We woke up talking about them and went to sleep talking about them. There was no escape other than getting the damn thing over with.

Finally we decided on the Woolco at the Lougheed Mall — not so much because it was safe, but because the other malls were less safe. The only reservation I had about the mall was based on an incident that happened one afternoon when Doug and I were at the Woolco so that I could case and he could get a ride to the bus stop. It was when we were living on Sullivan Street, just behind the Lougheed Mall. We were about 50 per cent positive that a woman had been watching us as we were sitting in our truck outside the Bay store area, before the stores opened. A woman parked right in front of us had stared at us and then written something down on a piece of paper. We thought it might have been our licence number, and we left the parking lot right away.

Still, it had been two months since we had been living on Sullivan Street, and we managed to convince ourselves that we were okay now. We continued to make elaborate plans for the Woolco robbery. Of the stores we had cased, it seemed the best. The big problem was, the Brink's truck never arrived at the same time — sometimes it was between 10:30 and 11:30 in the morning, and sometimes it was between 11:30 and 12:30. We couldn't be all hanging around, either in the mall or in a stolen car, for a couple of hours at a time. We had decided that Brent would be the one to draw on the guard, and he would do it in the pet shop. We thought maybe the two women — Julie and I — would be in the car and Gerry and Brent would hang around somewhere outside where they wouldn't be noticed. When Julie and I saw the truck arrive, Julie would get out of the car, be joined by Brent, and they would go into the mall as a couple. Gerry would walk in separately. I would stay behind and have the car running. Inside, in the pet shop, Julie and Brent would meet the guard head on, and Gerry would approach him from behind. Gerry would take his gun and handcuff him, while Julie would pick up the money bag. Brent would keep watch on things while this was going on.

"There are problems," Gerry insisted at one meeting. "All they gotta do is show our mug shots later on to the Brink's guard and we're up shit creek!" We knew this possibility had to be taken seriously. "Except the Brink's guard might not see me," Gerry said, looking like a light bulb had gone on over his head — but then it went out as quickly as it had gone on. "But certainly there'll be some witness who will see me. There were a lot of people in that pet area when we went there today."

"I never noticed a lot of people," Julie said, glancing over at Gerry irritably. "It's outrageous for you to say that because I was in there for about two hours and there weren't many people at all!" Sometimes her temper flared up unexpectedly with Gerry.

"When I say a lot of people, I mean during the whole time I was there," Gerry said defensively. "During the whole time, there was at least one person in each one of those aisles. Now, that's not a whole lot of people but it's enough for somebody to see something if something goes down."

"Well, I expect there to be people," Brent said matter-of-factly.

"Yeah, I do too," said Gerry. "I'm just adding it in so everybody's aware of it."

"It's not a high-traffic aisle," Brent said. "You don't get a lot of people strolling down an aisle in the pet department in Woolco's lower level."

"We're never gonna find a deserted place unless you find the guard in a stairwell, which is very unlikely," I added.

"I was wondering," Julie said seriously. "Do you think it would be possible to handcuff this guy to those huge fish aquariums? Do you think he'd actually pull over a fish aquarium full of fish in order to get loose?"

"Uh-uh," I said, after thinking about it for a few seconds. "It would be cool but it might be better if we had him on the ground with his face down as fast as possible so he can't see you anymore. You don't want him standing there getting this real good description of you. The best move might be to get him down on his knees, like this." I got up and mimicked the guard falling forward onto his knees. "Although you have to be careful that he doesn't go for his gun on his way down, right. See, you want him to freeze and put his hands up in the air right behind his head." I proceeded to mimic my own instructions. "Like you get him like this, so you can handcuff his hands behind his back and then Julie takes his gun from his holster and then you have him lie down on the floor, like this. See, now he's having a nice rest."

"Okay, try to stand up," ordered Julie. I struggled to get up, but it was almost impossible to do so with my hands cuffed behind my back. We talked about getting the handcuffs the next day and then practising the robbery scenario every day, timing how long it would take from the moment we said "Freeze" to the moment we would begin to leave.

"As soon as he puts his hands over his head, you tell him to drop the bag," added Gerry.

"Yeah, if Julie's gonna pick up the money, then she has to have her own bag to put it in," suggested Brent.

"No, she could just put it in my bag," said Gerry, "because I'll just put it on the floor."

"So I tell the guard to put his hands up and then lay down," said Brent, going over the robbery scenario. "As soon as he's lying down, Julie's holding the gun on him, right, and, Gerry, you hand-cuff him. If he starts to do something, like grab Gerry, then Julie just kicks him in the head."

"Remember, you're going to be real nervous," I cautioned, "and he might just involuntarily flinch and you don't want to shoot him accidentally. I do think you should disarm him before you handcuff him."

"I agree," said Gerry firmly.

"Yeah," added Brent. "It's a way better idea for Gerry to take the gun, then handcuff him. I also think it would be easier for Gerry to pick up the money bag as well since he'll already be bending over. He's got to pick up his own bag anyway, so why not just drop in the money bag in one motion. That way, we avoid Julie and Gerry getting in each other's way. Plus, this frees up Julie to concentrate on holding her gun on the guard while I keep watch of the store."

"What makes you think the guard is going to just drop the money bag at Julie's feet?" asked Gerry. "He might not. He might play dumb and put the money up in the air with his hands when you say 'Freeze.' Then it will be more obvious to cashiers that there's a holdup going on, because here's this money bag going up in the air with the other hand, right? Okay, so here's the thing. He comes walkin' along with the money. Brent says 'Freeze' and points the gun at him. Then Brent says, 'Throw the money at her feet.' The guard has the bag in one hand and throws the money at Julie's feet, right? And then you say, 'Okay, put your hands up over your head,' and he puts his hands up over his head like this. Then you say, 'Lie down on the floor face down with your arms stretched out in front of you,' and he does that. Now the money's down there safely clear of his arms at Julie's feet. So he's lying there stretched out. I come up from behind and take his gun away. As soon as Julie sees that I've got his gun in my possession, right, with one hand on her gun, trained at his head on the floor, she picks up the money. Then she puts the money in the bag, all the while keeping her gun trained on his head. Meanwhile, I'm handcuffing him. That will save time."

"I'd prefer not to have to tell the guard what to do with the money bag and just let him do it," said Brent. "I'll have enough on my mind. He can't put the money any place that difficult. He could put it here or here and the difference is basically insignificant."

"Well he might drop it at his feet, not knowing that you're gonna make him lie down on the floor," said Gerry, "and then when he lies down, he may lie right on the bag!"

"I don't think he'll do anything ridiculous like lie on the money," I laughed, "because he wants to save his life, I'm sure. If he does, just tell him to roll over." We reminded ourselves, once again, to reassure the guard that he wouldn't get hurt if he did what we said — above all, we didn't want him to do something outrageous in a desperate move to save his life.

"Another thing I was thinking about — during the robbery, what should we use as our names?" asked Julie. "Because I can't go, 'Hey Gerry.' "

"What about our nicknames?" suggested Gerry. "We never use them except on the radio. I like Julie's idea of using the French accent. When we're done, we'll just say, with a French accent, 'Holy sheet! It's eleven-thirty, we gotta get outta here fast! Au revoir!' " We broke into laughter and began talking all at once with French accents.

"We should practise these scenarios over and over again," I suggested. "And we should probably steal a couple of cars on Monday night." We didn't want to leave anything to chance, not even our emotional reactions to spontaneous events. For instance, we spent hours discussing how we would react if the guard didn't react the way we expected — all to avoid the possibility of one of us shooting him. We spent endless hours going over details I would never have imagined until we embarked on this robbery.

By January 9 we had the location of the robbery nailed down but still had a few other details to take care of. "We should go over the getaway route and look for a place to steal a car," Brent said over his morning coffee.

"And we don't have any handcuffs, so we should get them tomorrow," added Julie.

"Are we definitely going out to steal cars tomorrow night?" asked Gerry.

"Yeah," said Brent.

"Are we gonna steal both or one?" asked Gerry again.

"I'd like to do both," said Julie.

"Probably both," said Brent.

"What are you going to do about your appearance, Brent?" Julie asked.

"I'm just gonna wear a hat and some heavier rimmed glasses."

"I'm gonna wear a wig that I can just whip off immediately." Julie always enjoyed figuring out disguises.

"The most visible person after the robbery will be Ann, because we'll be lying down in the back of the car the entire way home. She's the one who's gotta look completely normal when she's driving. She could easily be passing by cops parked watching all the cars go by," Brent said, anxiously. "The only wig that's remotely passable is that long, black-haired one, and even that's abnormal."

"She can't wear that!" exclaimed Julie. "It would look outrageous! Black hair is a bit too bold. I'm gonna try to steal a couple of shoulder-length sandy brown ones."

"Yeah, that wig does look poor," agreed Gerry. "It might look normal in Texas, but up here you don't see many women with black Dolly Parton-style hairdos. What about the classic housewife's look, hair up in curlers?"

"That would be outrageous too," laughed Julie.

"What if we got one of those baby seats and strapped a doll in it?" chuckled Brent.

"Yeah, the cops will be drivin' by and see this car go by with this baby upside down in the baby seat!" Gerry laughed.

"Gerry, let's buzz over and get those handcuffs today," Julie said.

"Do you think it's a good idea for you to get the handcuffs if you're going to be identifiable after the robbery?" I asked.

"Not if I go as Vivian?" Vivian was a false identity that Julie assumed during illegal activities. She had an uncanny ability to transform herself, both physically and mentally, into this alter ego, who was completely the opposite of Julie Belmas. Vivian was soft-spoken, mousy, and nondescript, unlike the sparkling and vivacious Julie.

"It doesn't matter to me as long as you don't think they would be able to recognize you from a photograph?" I wanted her to weigh the consequences.

"They're not going to ask for my name or anything when I buy them, are they?"

"No, but they can usually trace where any piece of merchandise was sold."

I was doodling a plan of the pet department layout on a piece of scrap paper and examining it. I had drawn the four possible aisles in the pet department from which the Brink's guard would have to choose after exiting through the office door with the money bag. The fourth aisle was closest to the cashiers who handle all the purchases on Woolco's lower level.

Brent glanced over my shoulder to see what I was doing. "I was just making some notes on the aisles in the pet department. If he goes down that first or second aisle, closest to the door, then the cashiers will hardly be able to see him because the high shelves and plants obscure their view, unless they make a really conscientious effort to stare at him. The only thing I don't like is that last time the guy went down aisle number four."

"When I was there the other day, I counted three clerks going in and out of that door in five minutes," said Gerry, putting a damper on my enthusiasm. "That's a fair amount of traffic flow. What if one of them goes down the aisle where we're holding up this guy?"

"I would just be real heavy with the clerk," said Julie assertively, "and say 'Get down on the floor!' "

"Would you make them get down?" asked Gerry with surprise. "I wouldn't even bother worrying about it."

We let that issue rest for the time being. "The getaway's really scary," I said. "Actually, I don't know why I even said that. I don't really feel that scared at all. It's just this thing about the time. Last night, we timed it from the moment we begin the robbery until the time we get into our second vehicle and it's about four minutes. For the first minute, the cops won't necessarily even be notified. In the second minute, they will probably be getting mobilized because they'll have got the call, and after two minutes they're gonna be responding. So that means they have two minutes to find out where the getaway car is and be at that intersection in order to find us. After four minutes we'll be in a different car and only me and the baby seat will be visible."

Brent pulled out a road map of the area surrounding the Lougheed Mall. We spent the next half-hour or so meticulously going over the possible routes out of the mall, but no matter how we looked at it they all involved passing through a busy intersection about two minutes after the robbery had begun. I had been designated the getaway driver through group consensus, because everyone felt that I was the best driver in terms of being able to maintain my wits even if the situation were to deteriorate into chaos. "Once we have it worked out, I'm going to drive over it again and again until I know it really well," I said, more to reassure myself than anyone else.

"The guard I saw yesterday was definitely not the same guy I saw last Monday," I continued. "He was sorta short, had a pot belly, brown hair, and, surprisingly, he had his hand on his gun. Maybe that's part of their preventative security plans. I don't think it means they're trained or told to draw, but it's just good preventative security because, if every time people see the guards walking like this, it'll deter them from thinking of robbing them. In Montreal they always have their guns drawn — there's been so many Brink's robberies and guards killed that they just routinely come out of the banks with their guns drawn."

"Have you been in Hunter's buying ammo before, Julie?" asked Brent.

"Yeah."

"It'd be better if Gerry went in, just in case they remember you after the robbery."

"It's not normal to be getting nine-millimetre handgun ammo unless you've got a handgun, and you're supposed to have a restricted weapons permit to get that," explained Gerry.

"I could say it's for my boyfriend," said Julie. "I think it's weirder for you to get it. Are you going to say you're getting it for your girlfriend?"

"No," Gerry said with a smile, "for my uncle, who's living in Argentina. He can't seem to get any ammo down there. Uncle Herman."

Brent was still staring at my little drawing of the aisles in the pet department. "I've been thinking. If Julie and I aren't in aisle number one, then the guard will probably go down that one but if there's someone else in it, then he'll probably take aisle number two. I think it would be best if you're blocking aisle number three and four, Gerry."

"What if he tries to walk past me to aisle three or four? Should I trip him?"

Brent smiled and continued, "It's true, if he goes down four, he's too close to these fucking cashiers. I'd say forget it, but if he goes past you, down aisle three, just start rotating his way and go with him, right, and if I see him turn down three, then I'd probably go in and yell 'Freeze.' "

"If we have to cancel it, I'd say forget Woolco for another year," said Gerry. "If we follow him over to four, it's likely he might be on to us and have his gun drawn by the time we get over there."

"He can't do that, I don't think," said Julie.

"What, take his gun out?" said Gerry. "They do it in Montreal. They have their guns out when they come out of any place. Anyways, we could feel it out. If we're calm and relaxed, we could feel if he's onto us, but if we're tense it's going to be real nerve-racking trying to make a quick decision as to whether we're gonna do it or not, while all this is happening. By the time we get to aisle four, he'll have had time to think about it and go 'To hell with regulations' and get out his gun."

"Definitely we go for it if he goes up aisle three, but if he goes up four, then we play it by ear," concluded Brent. Soon after that we put on our casing clothes and left for the day to buy ammunition, find a place to steal a car, and, of course, the main staple of our lives, went to case the Woolco store.

* * *

The next morning I got up before everyone else and walked groggily into the kitchen with coffee on my mind. Normally nothing could deviate me from my coffee-making ritual, but that morning I was stopped dead in my tracks by the sight of all the kitchen chairs sitting upright on top of the kitchen table, each facing out in opposite directions. The sight of those chairs placed so neatly, yet so oddly, sent a chill up my spine. It was the kind of thing I associated with occult worship or a mental breakdown. I half-expected to find a cat dangling from a noose in the next room. I continued on towards the coffee-maker, determined that nothing was going to stop me from making a coffee, but blocking my path were three dirty pots, neatly arranged on the floor, upside-down. This I could not ignore. I picked up the three pots and placed them in the sink and started to make coffee. While it was brewing, I put the chairs back on the floor in the more familiar yet chaotic pattern that I found comforting. I was just about back to normal after drinking my first cup of coffee when I had to go to the washroom. There, once again, objects placed in an irregular pattern sent me reeling. This time it was no less than forty rolls of toilet paper arranged meticulously in a huge pyramid in the middle of the bathroom floor. I can tell you from this experience that it doesn't take blood, weapons, or the thought of death to strike fear in the heart. Totally irrational behaviour definitely shocks the mind out of its usual complacency.

When Julie, Gerry, and Brent got up I didn't say anything but decided to find out who the culprit was by waiting to hear their reactions to the toilet paper pyramid, which I had not disassembled. The first person to enter the bathroom was Julie. She shrieked, which told me that she wasn't the insane party. When I heard her shriek, I examined Gerry's and Brent's faces. Brent looked worried and got up to see what the problem was. Gerry just smiled peacefully.

"Gerry!" I said, "What the fuck is going on?"

"It's a message," he said. "I'm sick and tired of getting up in the morning and finding the chairs spread all over the kitchen like an obstacle course, and no one bothers to rinse out the pots after a late supper. The toilet paper — I know you guys like to shoplift lots of it but you don't have to open a new roll every time you go to the washroom."

I had to laugh. Being a particularly good natured, easy-going person, Gerry had decided to deal with his angst over the mess and chaos of our housekeeping habits in his own way, which happened to be much more effective than the usual nagging and arguing that accompany complaints of this nature. After that morning, I don't recall more than one roll of toilet paper ever being open at one time again.

* * *

We had found a good area with low apartment buildings and easily accessible underground parking garages in which to steal the two cars we would need for the robbery. At 1:00 a.m. we congregated in our kitchen to go over a few points before leaving to do the thefts.

"What kinda car do we want for our first and second getaway car?" asked Brent.

"What about a not-too-weird-looking four-door, that's reliable," suggested Gerry.

"And the newer, the better," I added.

"If they don't start up right away, then fuck it," said Gerry.

"Yeah," I agreed. "If it sounds weird when you start it up, just drop it. Forget it. There's no point even bringing it home. Both have to be completely reliable and should be completely different colours and models."

"Yeah, bright yellow and dark blue would be nice," Gerry said. "Stealing these cars tonight is small potatoes compared to what we're going to be using them for."

"I'd like to do the robbery tomorrow," I said anxiously. "I just want to go and do it."

"I know, I know," agreed Julie, nervously. "I just want to forget about it. It's really, really dominating our whole lives, right?"

We got the walkie-talkies, our car-theft tools, and dark clothes ready and headed out to the pickup truck for a night of slinking through underground parking garages. The car thefts went exceptionally smoothly and by four in the morning we were back at home, sitting around our kitchen table once again, trying to unwind before we went to bed.

"It was quite the experience getting that blue Buick Skylark," said Gerry excitedly. "It was filthy but I like it. I know that action's gonna go good now that we got that car because it's so fucking cool!" Gerry laughed. "It's got a nice-sounding engine too. When I came out of that parking lot . . . " He mimicked the sound of a rumbling car engine.

"It sounds like an outboard motor." I laughed as well. It felt good to release the tension from the night's experiences.

"Instead of getting a doll for the baby seat," Gerry said, with a laugh, "I think we should stick Rex in there with a bonnet on."

"I don't want that dog in there whining away at me when I'm driving," I howled. "When we steal cars for a political action, we should leave a bit of money or a note or something. That'd be sorta cool eh?"

"Very little bit of money," joked Gerry.

"Fifty bucks!" roared Brent.

"We could leave 'em a bus fare card," laughed Julie.

"Or a ticket to Hawaii or Acapulco," added Brent.

"We could even leave 'em a box of dynamite." This from Gerry, who was not to be outdone.

"I'm glad that went well tonight," I said, calming down a little.

"I know," said Julie warmly.

"I'd like to drive that first getaway car around a bit," I said, finally turning serious again. "It's got about a quarter of a tank of gas so I should put some more gas in it."

"Maybe you should try and get the ignition for it, then you

could drive it around and start and stop without looking really weird," added Gerry.

We continued joking and laughing for a while longer and then went to bed feeling relaxed for the moment, knowing that we had cleared one more hurdle in our race to get the robbery over with.

I didn't get up until almost noon the next day, when I found Julie alone in the kitchen. It was a rare occasion. "We will be so happy when this robbery is over!" I said, breathing a deep sigh of relief.

"I know. All our problems will be over! I feel as though we're pretty much home free now."

"I don't think you ever get really relaxed about stealing cars," I confessed.

"Yeah. I'm just terrified of the thought of sitting in the car and having some guy come out and look at us, right?"

"And run after us," I added. We were thinking about a time when we were chased by a huge man who caught us stealing a spare tire from his four-by-four in the middle of the night.

"I know. I dread that more than being taken in by the cops, believe it or not."

"I'd like to take a break from being completely underground and go back to living normally for awhile." The words just came out of my mouth spontaneously. "We could hide every little piece of evidence and just hope that maybe there would be possibilities of doing more for the people . . . " I trailed off. "There's certain things about the four of us. It really is just the four of us. Doug is sort of in a different situation. The idea of spending the rest of our lives together, just the four of us, and not ever working with other people seems sorta weird."

"That's true. It would be really cool if other people learned how to do this."

"If I was living in Vancouver again, I'd do actions that might not be super-duper heavy but could be done with more people, eh?" I was exposing my doubts gingerly to Julie, but shortly after that Gerry and Brent came in the room and all doubts disappeared, at least for the moment.

"I was wondering what would be the best day to rob the Woolco?" Brent said as soon as he sat down.

"The best day to rob it would be the day the guard walks down the right aisle," quipped Gerry. "I'm going to move that car we stole last night. Ann, could you give me a lift and hang around a distance from the car so if I have trouble starting it, then maybe you could give me a hand?"

I went to get my coat. I drove Gerry to the place where we had parked the stolen car and sat a block away while he started it up, then left. Since he was going to drive home and leave it in our garage, I headed back so I would be there to open the door for him when he returned. Two hours later Julie and I were still waiting and beginning to worry. Finally the back door opened and Gerry came in, looking rather sullen.

"What's wrong, Gerry?" asked Julie anxiously. He was looking pale.

"We have to steal another car tonight. It stalled at the corner of Twelfth and Main."

"And you couldn't get it started?" I asked, surprised.

"And I couldn't get it going again," he said, looking very depressed. "I was blocking traffic and all these people were honking at me and stuff. I was on a hill so I couldn't push it by myself, but there's this woman behind me. I thought about running away but there's too many people and I was afraid they would call the cops if I just took off so I went back to this woman and said, 'Hey, I'm sorry I'm blocking your way but can you help push me into that gas station?' Well, she gets out of her car and helps me push it into the gas station. So then, I thought, maybe I should sit here and try and get it running again but then the gas station attendant comes over and wants to help. He says, 'Do you want me to help you figure out what the problem is?' and I said, 'Oh no, I know what the problem is. The ignition has all its guts torn out.' I said that just in case he decided to take a look at it. I expected him to say, 'Okay,' and then go back to work but, oh no, he starts bugging me about it so I said, 'Oh look. Let's put it over here. I've got a friend that just lives about six blocks from here so I'm going to get him.' So then we push it into this parking spot and I said, 'I'll be right back' and he turned away and goes 'Okay.' It was terrible! I was just making up lie after lie. Finally, I went up the road and I was gone."

"Good," sighed Julie.

"There was a car dealership," continued Gerry, "just up the road beside a bus stop so I went into the car dealership, kinda nonchalant, and stood there between the cars and looked at them as though I was interested until the bus came. It was only two blocks away when I arrived so I didn't have to wait long. I was sweating, though, and I was a little bit nervous for sure, quite nervous, actually. If the gas station had been a self-serve, it wouldn't have been such a hair-raising event."

"I hope you didn't freak out and split the scene!" Julie said.

"No, Julie," Gerry said, making an effort to stay calm. "I didn't look like a fugitive who just finished robbing a bank, running around, hiding behind these cars. That's not the way it was."

"You didn't touch the car with your bare hands, though, eh?" I asked.

"No," he said with certainty.

Gerry had barely finished telling us his story when Brent came home from parking the first stolen car in a garage we had rented in Surrey. He accepted losing the Buick Skylark with good humour, but after a brief discussion we decided it would be best if we went out that night to steal another one. Late that night, after another uneventful car theft experience, instead of parking on a side street we drove our newly acquired stolen car directly home and parked it in our garage in order to avoid a repeat of Gerry's unfortunate experience.

The first thing we did the next morning was examine the ownership and insurance papers from the stolen vehicles, like pirates admiring their booty. "What year is that car?" I asked Gerry, referring to the stolen car parked in our garage.

"Seventy-eight Malibu!" he said excitedly. "That's cool. Pretty new eh?"

"Here's a B.C. Automobile Association card," Brent said. "It belongs to a John Mellis. He's been a member for twenty-five years." We figured that Mellis must be a retired man with a few bucks, given that he owned a '78 Malibu and was a member of the BCAA. The other stolen car belonged to a woman, Joanne Robson.

"Don't forget the landlord is bringing more people over to the house tomorrow night to look at it," Gerry reminded us.

"Charming," said Julie sarcastically. "We've got to do something with that car in the garage, because it looks too rich."

I agreed, but, "We can't tell them not to go in the garage . . . "

" . . . because our dog just had a litter of puppies," interrupted Gerry. "Nah, one look at Rex and that won't work."

"If we got a big tarp, threw it over the car and put a bunch of spray paint cans in there and spray a bunch of wood, we could say I'm an artist," I suggested.

"Yeah," agreed Julie enthusiastically. "You could say it's nouveau art . . . but why would we cover up the whole car?"

"Because it's brand new and paint floats around in the atmosphere," said Gerry.

"When they go through our house, they'll see that we're not really rich," pointed out Julie.

"The reason we don't have any money," I explained, "is because we bought this really expensive car."

Gerry laughed. "I'll agree to it, Ann, if you turn up at the front door with a beret and a paint pot."

"Doug's coming over Sunday night for supper," I announced. "I'm going to rip off a roast somewhere."

"And we could all go swimming," said Gerry, who was particularly fond of swimming.

"Maybe," I said slowly, "but I was thinking more like doing Brink's guard scenarios. He could play the guard and we could time it."

"Good idea," agreed Gerry.

"The next time we go target-practising, I'm just gonna practise on the Mini-14 at seventy five and a hundred yards," I said, changing topics. "Because I think that's the most likely distance I'm gonna have to shoot at. Don't you? I won't have to get out of the car and run towards the driver with a gun, do you think?"

"You might," said Brent.

"Yeah, but if I do have to shoot at him, it'd probably be at about seventy-five yards, don't you think?"

"I don't know," said Brent. "If you saw the driver get out, you should run up to one of those pillars for cover." He was referring to the huge pillars that supported the overhanging roof on the Woolco façade.

"Wouldn't he notice me?"

"He might," said Brent, cautiously. "And then the thing is, he could shoot at you and take cover."

"What do I do if you guys are already on your way out and the driver is on his way in?" I asked.

"Let him go in."

"But how do I know if you're on your way out? From the outside, I won't really know what's going on in there. There's this grave possibility that it could be a really bad scene. For instance, you guys have finished robbing the guy and are on your way out and then the driver steps out of his truck because somebody notified him that his buddy has been robbed. I guess I'd have to shoot him."

"They don't just get out of their truck," stated Brent firmly. "They have to have a person in the truck at all times, so if he gets out of his truck then he's breaking that rule for some reason, right?"

"But what if he's just going into the store to see if his buddy's okay? In this instance, you guys are already on your way out and everything is fine so if I shoot at him then he's gonna stay out and shoot back. And now there's this big firefight which wouldn't be happening if I hadn't started shooting at him."

"He's not just going in to see if his buddy's okay. I don't think he'd walk into a store full of armed robbers to see if his buddy's okay unless he's gonna do something. So I'd say if he gets outta his truck, it's a really weird scene."

"If we go target-practising next week, we should make targets with bodies as opposed to bull's-eyes because this time we should go for speed and accuracy, with a bit more emphasis on speed. You know, in a real shootout, if we start taking aim, he's gonna shoot first. I'm gonna draw torso figures and shoot at them as fast as I can."

Gerry had gone off to the washroom for a few minutes, and now he came back with a new thought in his mind. "I wouldn't mind some reassurance about that guy at the gas station not being asked to identify me after the robbery. That car we have in the garage was stolen less than two blocks from the place we stole the car I ditched at the gas station. If the cops bring photos of me and Brent from the car theft bust and ask the guy at the gas station to identify me, I'm sure he could. I'd like to go through the chain of events and try to figure out exactly what the cops know and if they did their damnedest, could they connect me to the robbery?"

"Well, the guard probably won't see you because you'll be behind him the whole time," I said, trying to reassure him.

"But the clerks will see me," he said, shakily. "It might only be for a few seconds, but they will still see me. Okay, first the cops find the two getaway vehicles and figure out what nights they were stolen. Since they were stolen one night after another, the cops would have to wonder if other cars were stolen on those nights by the same robbers. Now that's a bit obscure."

Brent jumped into the fray. "They might assume we have a third getaway vehicle since they don't know we are going home in our truck, but they'll write off the car you ditched because it was found the next day in the gas station. How could we have used it in the robbery?"

"I hate to say it," I said carefully, "but there is the remote possibility that they'll notice that the car in the gas station was stolen on the same night and less than two blocks away from the getaway car. Plus they both had their ignitions pulled out with an extractor. The same M.O."

"There's no way you can steal cars without taking the ignition out," Brent corrected me. "However, they could show the gas station attendant photos from their car theft file. But they probably won't have us in their file since we haven't been convicted in court yet. Plus, even if we had, we've only stolen one car. They wouldn't have a file identifying everybody who's ever stolen a car."

I began to laugh. "If for some obscure reason they did have your photo in some car theft file and, again, made the connection with the robbery, they'll think, 'Those boys are in the big times now!' "

"They'll say," said Gerry, as the conversation began to degenerate, " 'These boys have said to hell with car theft, they're going for the big one! Put an APB out on those Taylor and Hannah guys. Book 'em Danno!' "

"By the way, Gerry, are you gonna dye your hair a completely different colour before the robbery?" I asked.

"Not completely different, but lighter."

"Well, I'd suggest quite different, because if the cops get a composite picture of you from the clerks at the Woolco, you want a picture that looks as little like you as possible."

"I can't dye it blond because it'll look too phony, and I don't want to freak out the guard."

"Why can't you dye it black, the kind you can wash out?" suggested Brent.

"I dyed it black when I first got into punk. After that I dyed it green, but black looks really bad and blatantly obvious. We don't want the guard to be on edge, otherwise we might not even get a chance to rob him."

"So you're gonna shave your moustache off as soon as you get home?" I asked. Gerry nodded. "Hey, I just thought of something," I added. "I'll have the walkie-talkie with me in the getaway car so I could radio you if the driver gets out of the truck or if a cop drives into the mall. Julie could have an earphone in one ear so she could listen to me even if she can't actually pick up the walkie-talkie to communicate. We could arrange a code in which I only say something if the driver gets out or a cop arrives on the scene, and Julie could just press the button on the walkie-talkie when you're finished the robbery."

"There's no way a cop would have time to respond to the robbery before we've finished handcuffing the guard," explained Brent. "If a cop drives into the mall before Julie presses the button on her walkie-talkie, chances are it's just pure coincidence."

"Yeah, don't bother calling us if the cop is not connected to the robbery," added Gerry. "It will just make us all the more nervous when we come out, and then we'll look more fucked up. But if a cop arrives and hurries over to the guard and he gets out of his truck, then I'd say we're in trouble. But Ann shouldn't shoot at the cop or guard unless she sees them actually getting into position to assault us coming out of the door."

"All right, all right. I don't want to talk about shooting any more this morning," I said, flipping through a small pamphlet lying on the kitchen table. "This pamphlet from *Soldier of Fortune* on getaway driving techniques is really useful. I'll read a bit for you. It says here, 'In practising bootlegger turns, it is recommended that you learn how to manoeuvre on rental cars. Avis, Budget, etc, etc, offer all kinds of cars so that you should be able to find something similar to what you now drive. Needless to say, don't tell the rental agency people what you're planning to use their car for.' " I looked up at the others and we laughed. "Okay, this is the description of the bootlegger's turn, which you use if confronted by a road block. The idea is for the driver to evade the road block by doing a 180-degree turn right in front of the block. It says you go twenty-five to thirty miles per hour as you near the road block, as though you're about to stop. Then you crank the steering wheel, a quarter to half a full turn. At the same time, you slam on the emergency brake which controls your back wheels so they're gonna lock and the car is going to spin around about ninety degrees and then you fucking step on the gas and go back from where you came. I'll have to practise that."

"If we're being chased by the cops or some gung ho citizen," I continued, "we should huck our hoses out the car window in order to blow out their tires. And I was also thinking, at the same time we could lean out the windows and huck jars of paint at the pursuit car and if they hit their windows, of course, they won't be able to see. The important thing is to throw out hoses with nails in them or jars of paint rather than firing at a pursuant vehicle, because once we fire at the cops, the scene will escalate and that would be really wild! I mean, if we can give them a flat tire, then we should just keep right on moving and they won't know where we are.

Gerry's mind had wandered back to the topic of disguises. "You know, I'm gonna wanna look like this real bourgeois jock with a real expensive gym bag. I'm gonna have a Vancouver Canucks hat and my hair is gonna be perfectly feathered."

"I think you gotta be real careful about how you look, Gerry," I cautioned, "because the guard's gonna see you the minute he opens the door. I think this single guy, no matter how you look, with a big bag is definitely gonna make an impression. Even if he turns down the first or second aisle, it's still not cool if he's a bit freaked out . . . "

Gerry cut in, "They must see guys with bags all the time."

"So, if you're wearing something sporty with . . . " Gerry finished my sentence with the words "running shoes." Then I added, "It'll look like a getaway type outfit." We smiled at each other.

"Gerry's got to wear gloves, right?" asked Julie. We nodded. "It could put the Brink's guy on guard seeing Gerry standing there holding onto this bag with his hands hidden in his pockets because he's got gloves on." There were no reassuring words for this problematic vision.

"Whatever you do, Gerry," I advised, "don't look at the guard until you hear Brent say 'Freeze,' because, it's true, if you look at him, he might see the fear in your eyes."

"Maybe you could really get into what you're lookin' at," suggested Brent.

"There's not exactly a hell of a lot to really be into, unfortunately," chuckled Gerry. "There's those twelve-inch flower pots I could look at for two hours. . . . You're gonna dress like a Jehovah's Witness, eh Brent?"

"I guess so," said Brent.

"On a real paranoid level, those ski jackets aren't the best thing for us to wear," said Julie, "because they look sort of criminal with those big pockets."

"A thick tweed wool jacket with leather patches on the elbows that you could have your holster underneath would make you the least likely looking robbery suspect — namely a young professional or academic type," I suggested to Brent. "You're gonna have to look at him, aren't you?"

"Well, no. I'll just sort of glance up and see his hat start coming down the aisle."

"Julie should be slightly behind you so that you have freedom of movement. You could be standing, talking to Julie and see him without looking directly at him like you drive if someone's coming at you with their high beams on. If you're talking to Julie, you'll see him coming out of the corner of your eye, then when he hits the right spot, say, 'Freeze.' "

"You know what would be really funny?" Brent said. "If Gerry makes a bunch of noise to distract the guy . . . when he turns around again, the gun's pointing at his face."

"Why don't we have a little thread going over to the aquariums," said Gerry, always eager to joke, "and yank on it so that all the aquariums will come tumbling down."

"Gerry should be as cool as possible," I said putting a damper on the laughter, "because he's the first person the guard's gonna see and the most likely person to make him nervous. The minute the guy turns down the aisle so his back is towards you, look up, to see what's happening."

"There's one important question, we still haven't answered," said Brent, with a smile. "The date. Should we wait till the 31st or should we go for Monday, the 24th?"

"The sooner, the better," said Julie. "The 24th."

"Does anyone object?" asked Brent. An air of solemn silence was his answer. "The 24th of January, it is."

* * *

Setting a date for the robbery created an atmosphere of finality to our lives. We could no longer pretend it might not happen. There were a certain number of days, hours, and minutes until this dangerous, potentially deadly act was to take place. I imagined it felt something like a diagnosis of terminal cancer. There was the possibility that the illness might go into remission, but there was an even greater possibility that it might end in death. In our case, there was the possibility of the robbery ending in one of two equally unpleasant outcomes: death or prison. The first outcome meant facing the uncertainty of life after death; and the second meant facing the certainty of a living death. The best possible outcome, which would be to get through the robbery unscathed, was the one possibility we rarely celebrated.

I trudged down into our basement bedroom to get ready for a getaway route practice run, but as I pulled on a sweater my eye caught sight of a calendar hanging on the wall across from our bed. I walked over to it mechanically and marked a large red X across the 24th of January with red marker. Today was the 15th, and I couldn't help morbidly thinking that I had nine more days to live.

What a way to live! Instead of going to the mountains or beach, I would have to spend most of the next nine days living and reliving every moment of the robbery day: analysing and experiencing every movement and emotion associated with pulling a gun on that short, chubby man. Driving over and over again through the residential streets and intersections surrounding the Lougheed Mall, walking through the pet department, and up a short flight of stairs to the automotive department to emerge into the bright light of day under the busy façade of the Woolco store. Parked, only yards away, would be the huge grey armoured truck with the armed driver sitting inside, potentially facing us or perhaps not. I envisioned myself sitting there in the crowded mall parking lot, assault rifle in hand, focusing on the unsuspecting driver and the possibility of a patrol car cruising into the mall. Then driving for two minutes in a stolen car to a residential area where we would get out and walk purposefully to a second stolen getaway car and off again to our truck. Maybe, just maybe, we would make it home, where we could sigh a deep breath of relief. I really couldn't take too much more of this life.

<h2 style="text-align:center">✳ 42 ✳</h2>

The next day, Sunday, January 16, I almost forgot to mark an X through the date until early in the evening, but I didn't forget the robbery. Only eight more days of living or, more precisely, enduring this virtual robbery reality before it would finally become real. Even though I was in our downstairs bedroom, the sound of chatter and laughter seeped through the floorboards above me, interrupting my thoughts and beckoning me to hurry upstairs. As I went up the stairs a steady mantra — one that had begun plaguing me daily — beat through my mind with every step: *robbery, robbery, robbery*.

Doug was upstairs talking to everyone excitedly. I had gone downstairs to get the handcuffs so we could do some robbery scenarios after eating the roast-beast dinner I had prepared. There was a reason I called it beast as opposed to beef. Every Sunday evening I found myself being driven by childhood memories of warm, cosy family gatherings, to make a traditional roast beef dinner with carrots, potatoes, onions, and gravy, in a vain attempt to transform our stressed-out lives, filled with talk of robberies and shootings, into something comforting, if only for an hour. The main obstacle to re-creating this Rockwellian scene was not the fact that we were urban guerrillas, but rather that my roasts invariably turned out to be beasts, too tough or too raw to enjoy; my gravies, too lumpy or runny; my potatoes, undercooked on the inside. Yet I could always count on my comrades to make the most honourable oohs and ahhs in complimenting my meal, no matter how beastly the outcome. The only one I suspected of genuinely appreciating my Sunday dinner was Rex, who would gobble up the ample leftovers with gusto.

In the kitchen Doug was embroiled in the tail end of a conversation with Julie. "There's lots of actions that two or three people can do as long as you got a vehicle."

"But it would be outrageously great to have twenty people doing continuous actions, eh?" she exclaimed.

"Oh yeah. In that case, you'd have to split up on a semi-permanent basis. You couldn't afford to be in constant contact. It would be dangerous. If they ever busted one of your cells, then they'd be able to connect all the cells. To a large extent the different cells would be independent because the actual degree of strategic interaction you would need would be small. A couple of times a year, all you'd need would be an exchange of writings on your ideas and how things are going."

"Yeah, I also like the idea of each cell being responsible for its own safekeeping," added Julie with her characteristic enthusiasm.

"We've got the handcuffing down to sixteen and a half seconds," Gerry was saying to Doug. "That's why you were invited over to eat, because after eating, you're going to do plenty of work!" Doug chuckled, but he really burst out laughing when Brent came in the room, looking like a nerdy professor, sporting a tweed wool jacket and casual wool pants. During the past month Brent had also grown a full beard so his appearance would be very different from the mug shot taken after the car theft arrest in November. Like a model, he waltzed past Doug, flashing his .38 automatic pistol slung inside a leather shoulder holster concealed under his jacket. He tipped his navy-blue beret, saucily. To complete the ensemble, he had donned a pair of thick horn-rimmed glasses, which he took off for a second in order to give Doug a wink and a nod, before bowing.

"Can you see without your contacts?" asked Doug, laughing.

"Oh yeah, these are my old glasses. Besides, I don't like to wear contacts if I'm nervous."

"That's an excellent disguise!" said Doug enthusiastically. "You can't even see the pistol. The only bad thing about it is the beret. It will make you more noticeable in the aisle. It's not as straight as the rest of your outfit."

"When the guard goes up the aisle, he won't imagine that Brent is going to rob him," observed Julie.

"Oh no," agreed Doug.

"But the thing is, he's not going to see me until I pull a gun on him," explained Brent.

"If you're standing in a police lineup dressed totally different — no hat, no glasses, no beard — they'd never be able to match your face with how you look now," Doug pointed out. "By the way, Rachel and I were boating in Deep Cove yesterday. Rowing, actually, because the engine on my boat wasn't working so well, but fortunately right outside the launching ramp there was about half a dozen MacMillan Bloedel barges — all different kinds, like log barges and pulp barges. We managed to board these barges the whole afternoon. It was easy because they have these ladders hanging down about four or five feet above the water line so you just grab onto them and climb up the side."

I couldn't concentrate on anything but the robbery. "We did a walkie-talkie test in the mall the other day, Doug. They work great. I sat out in the parking lot with one and Julie was in the mall wearing an ear phone on hers."

Julie giggled. "Yeah, me and Brent were walking in the mall, and all of a sudden this woman's voice comes out of nowhere saying 'This is yellowbird, this is yellowbird!' It was so loud I had to put my hands over my ears."

"Ann should have said 'This is God, do you hear me?' " said Gerry. "All these people would get down on their hands and knees in the store and start looking around at the ceiling and say 'Give that woman in the red wig all your money.' "

"I think you two will stand out too much," I said to Brent and Julie.

"Yeah," laughed Doug. "Mr. and Mrs. Rich. What are you doing in a Woolco when Eaton's is down the mall?"

"The bombshell and the brute," I joked.

"All these sales clerks are going to come running over and try to sell you stuff," added Gerry.

"Gerry will be invisible," I smiled. "He looks like a typical Woolco person."

"And Ann's been getting all these getaway driving techniques from a book!" laughed Gerry. We were all in good spirits now. "Oh God! There won't be a fucking car without a dent in it for miles around. I can just hear the news . . . a robbery that netted $35,000 in cash and $45,000 in damages!"

"Central Dispatch!" I yelled, mimicking a police radio call, "it appears that Corporal Brown received a brake shoe in the head at a 180-degree wipeout and now the suspects are heading down the Kingsway backwards."

"Holy shit!" continued Gerry on this flight of fancy, "they were last seen abandoning a brown Chevrolet pickup truck with the driveshaft lying beside it and both back wheels burnt out. Now they've just expropriated a Dodge Challenger, but don't go after them. Leave them alone!"

The timer rang on the oven, signalling that the roast was ready. I could almost feel the others smiling at each other behind my back while I got the roasting pan out of the oven. As I struggled with the gravy and set the table, the conversation continued, although on a more serious note. "We put ignitions in our stolen cars, Doug," said Julie.

"Do they work?"

"Oh yeah. You'll be able to start them up and you don't have to worry about using those little needle-nose pliers or anything!"

"Here's some interesting reading," said Brent, laying a copy of the *Criminal Code* on the kitchen table.

"Yeah, I was reading it in the bathroom yesterday. If it's your first offence and you point a firearm at somebody for an undue purpose, or something like that, you get two years. That's not much," pointed out Julie.

"If you pull the trigger, it's forever," I quipped. "That's another good reason not to shoot unless we have to, because if we did get caught it certainly would be a lot different than if we just throw robber hoses with nails in them on the road."

Doug was leaning over Julie's shoulder, reading sections of the *Criminal Code*. "Here's a couple of minor charges. 'Everyone that carries or has in his possession a weapon or imitation thereof, for a purpose dangerous to the public peace, or for the purpose of committing an offence, is guilty of an indictable offence and is liable to imprisonment for ten years.' "

"That's every time we go up the road to Squamish," said Brent.

"All right," continued Doug, taking the book and holding it in one hand and his fork in another. " 'Everyone who carries a concealed weapon, unless he is a holder of a permit under which he may lawfully so carry it, is guilty of an indictable offence and is liable to imprisonment for five years.' "

"Well, that's every day," I said, thinking of the guns stored in the black, coffin-like box in the downstairs bedroom.

"Concealed," corrected Doug, "means carrying a concealed weapon when you're in some action." He read on while we ate. " 'Everyone who is an occupant of a motor vehicle in which he knows there is a prohibited weapon is liable to imprisonment for five years.' "

"Say you're not a 'he,' " asked Brent. "Would that mean women aren't subject to that law?"

"I'm certain it says somewhere here that legally, 'he' means 'anyone,' " explained Doug.

"Do you think it does?" I asked doubtfully. "I bet it doesn't."

"Oh, there's no way you'd get away with a loophole like that," stated Doug emphatically.

After dinner we got ready to do some robbery scenarios with Doug, even though he wasn't going to be involved with the robbery in any way. Gerry went downstairs to get the handcuffs, handguns, his gym bag, and stopwatch to time the scenarios. When he came back upstairs he had changed into his robbery clothes: a pair of jeans, running shoes, eye glasses, and baseball cap. Unfortunately, Doug was not impressed. "Yeah, he does look like an armed robber," he said to Julie.

I agreed. "I don't even know if he should wear that cap. Take it off for a second. Yeah, but you don't want your hair showing, do you?"

"Not particularly," said Gerry, looking glum.

"You know what I think would be better?" I suggested. "One of those little caps or a knitted toque with a tassel on top. Something about the way you look does make me feel more like an armed robber. Don't you think the guard's gonna become suspicious when he sees Gerry, you know, more on edge?"

"If Gerry's not looking at the guy or paying any attention to him, let's say, looking at some item on the shelf and if he's a fair ways away, then he probably wouldn't trigger anything in the guard's mind," said Doug authoritatively. We always gave Doug's opinions considerable weight. For a few minutes, poor Gerry stood there while we stared and assessed his appearance. "I mean, it is true that if Gerry looks slightly suspicious, it could make the guy more likely to turn up an aisle, rather than pass him," Doug added after a spell.

"Yeah, but hopefully not so suspicious that he thinks he's going to be robbed," I said. "But it could help channel him down into aisle one or two."

"Yeah," cautioned Doug, "but it's a fine balance."

"It would almost be better if he saw Julie first," I suddenly realized, "because he'd never associate a young woman with a robbery."

"Are we going to have the police scanner in Bob?" asked Julie.

"Yeah, we're leaving it in Bob so we can hear what's happening on our getaway," I said.

"Gerry," said Doug, still examining him, "it's something about your hair."

"Take off the hat and glasses," I told Gerry.

"Even without the glasses, he truly looks criminal," smiled Julie. "Look at those beady eyes."

"Try on your gloves," suggested Brent. "They seem too loose for you. Driver's gloves are the best."

"You can do anything with the black stretchy pair I have," I stated.

"If you're going to have the scanner in the truck," said Doug, "why don't you tape the whole thing?"

"Yeah," exclaimed Julie, "I'd love to hear it!"

Brent had gone down to the basement to retrieve the scanner — it would scan all ten channels, he told us. Doug lifted it up. "And it's got the crystals in it too. Let's fire it up and see what the reception's like." They turned it on and fiddled around with it for a while before Brent concluded, "It's the shits."

"Yeah, that's what I recall," Doug said, thinking of his past experiences with the scanner.

"Anytime we're ready to begin the scenario?" Gerry said impatiently.

Doug picked up an unloaded .38 revolver and hip holster. "I'm ready."

"I'll do the timing," I said, picking up the stopwatch. "Unfortunately, you're the best guard, Doug."

Gerry picked up his gym bag and gun. "Yeah, anytime Doug." Brent, Julie, and Gerry were all wearing jackets and carrying their unloaded handguns concealed, much as they would on the robbery date. Gerry was also carrying a pair of handcuffs in his gym bag. We marched into the living room and decided the hallway would be the Woolco aisle through which Doug would have to pass. Doug walked briskly through the living room, then turned into the hallway, where Brent stood with Julie just slightly behind him. Gerry stood poised in their bedroom doorway, ready to do the handcuffing as soon as Doug was on the floor.

As Doug turned into the hallway, Brent said in a stern voice, "Freeze right there! Put your hands out in front of ya. Okay, drop the money and get on the floor! Get down. Keep your face down. Don't look up!"

"Put your hands behind your back. Now don't fuck us around or you'll be dead!" ordered Julie. Gerry knelt over Doug from behind, took his handgun, and placed it in his gym bag, then handcuffed his hands behind his back. Meanwhile Julie picked up the money bag and placed it in Gerry's gym bag.

"Let's go!" she said. They ran down the hall into the kitchen.

Twenty-one seconds. We practised the scenario a few more times, then tried a new one in which Brent and Julie would wait at the top of the aisle, close to the office door that the guard would come out of. The major difference between the new scenario and the old one was that they would rob him before he went down any of the aisles. This would eliminate the possibility of having to rob him in aisle three or four, both of which were close to the cashier checkout line. In the new scenario Brent would be crouched down looking at something on a lower shelf while Julie watched for the guard. Gerry's position would remain unchanged.

"Okay, I'm in front," Brent said, "and you're right there, Julie."

"Okay," she said, standing tall behind him.

"I'll get down and you tell me what's going on with the guard," Brent instructed Julie, while crouching down. "I'll be looking at this display, peering through a little crack sort of thing."

"That'd be nice, if you could do that."

"You can come out whenever you're ready, Doug," I yelled. The robbery was in progress.

"Freeze!" said Brent again. "Put your hands in front of you. Get down on the floor. Keep your face to the ground."

"And don't try anything," added Julie. "Put your hands behind your back. Don't do anything wrong and nothing will happen to you."

When it was over I suggested to Brent, "If he's actually drawing to shoot, then you may be able to duck before he pulls the trigger rather than shooting back, right?"

We went over and over the robbery scenario until Julie slumped down in a living room chair and sighed, "It's just gonna be horrible!"

"Right," said Brent, getting ready to do it again.

"Is everybody ready?" asked Doug, sliding his revolver into his holster again.

Julie obviously wasn't ready. "What are you saying?" said Brent.

"I'm scared, is what I'm saying."

"Right. Just don't be too scared at the time, because it'll be real bad to walk in there and then somebody decides they can't take it."

"It's good to be scared now, right?" I consoled Julie. "The more scared you are now, the more you'll be getting accustomed to the fear. Instead of blocking it out and then suddenly, on the day of the robbery, being too scared to even think. At least that's my theory."

"I know," she said weakly.

"It's normal to be scared," I added. "I'm really scared too, you know."

"Yeah," said Brent sternly, "but the thing is, you have to learn to deal with it and realize that we're gonna do it. You're going to walk into that store and go through with what we planned, rather than freaking out when you're actually in the middle of it."

"I know," said Julie irritably. "But I think that if we're scared, we should be able to talk about it, not freak out and say 'shut up about it.' I know that I can go through with the robbery and do it without falling on the floor and saying 'Oh God, I can't do this!'"

"No," said Brent a little more sensitively. "I don't think you're going to do that either, but it's just the way you were saying you're scared."

"Ever since we saw the guard go down aisle three and four on the weekend, I've been feeling nervous. I don't like the idea of pursuing him down either of those aisles."

"Why don't we try this once more," Gerry said impatiently. "I hate standing around with a coat and stuff on if I don't have to."

"The reason we're practising this new scenario is so we won't have to pursue him down those aisles," Brent said, looking over at Julie. Instead of answering him, she got up and walked into the hallway.

"Okay," repeated Gerry. "Let's go!"

"Form an image in your mind of the real scene," Doug told her. "Really picture yourself standing in that scene for a couple of minutes, waiting for it to happen."

"This is Yellow Bird," I said, mimicking what I would say into the walkie-talkie. "The flight is on its way! I repeat, this is Yellow Bird! The flight is on its way!"

"Okay," Brent said. "So we walk downstairs. We walk through the pet department and come up to the hamster cage and I lean over to look at them. 'Freeze right there! Put your hands in front of you! Get down on the floor! Get down!' " Doug put his arms forward, then lay down on the floor.

"Please, put your hands behind your back," ordered Julie. "Nothing will happen to you if you do exactly what we say!" Doug obediently put his hands behind his back, at which point Gerry again took the revolver from him, placed it in his gym bag, and handcuffed him. Simultaneously Julie dropped the money bag into Gerry's gym bag while Brent scanned the store for problems.

"Keep your head down!" Brent reminded Doug.

"Nineteen seconds!" I said as they walked briskly into the kitchen. "If I see a cop pull up and go over to the Brink's driver, I'll let you know on the walkie-talkie. If you're in the middle of the robbery, you'll be able to scram."

"I'll be completely relying on you to let us know if there's going to be cops waiting outside for us," Gerry said nervously.

"If something like that happens before the robbery starts, you can call it off," I reassured him.

"Right," agreed Julie.

"You can make your own decision whether to finish it or scram," I repeated. "One more time."

They got into their positions again. Over and over again we practised the same robbery scenario, until 1:30 in the morning, way past Doug's bedtime. After winding down over tea in the kitchen, I volunteered to drive him back to Windermere.

✳ **43** ✳

When I woke up the next morning, the first thing my eyes fixed on was the damn calendar hanging on the wall across from our bed. I got up and marked a big X through the 17th, even though my day had hardly begun. As I headed for the kitchen, the same old mantra accompanied my steps on the staircase — *"Robbery, robbery, robbery . . . "* — but, alarmingly, a new refrain was involuntarily added to the repertoire. *"Freeze. Hold it right there. Put your hands in front of you and get on the ground. Get down. Keep your face on the floor. Put your hands behind your back, slowly. Nothing will happen to you if you do what we say. Just be cool. . . . Freeze. Hold it right there. . . . "* Thank God the robbery was only seven more days away. I prayed that doing the robbery would purge my troubled mind of these disconcerting chants.

After everyone had congregated in the kitchen, the first thing Gerry brought up was putting off the robbery for another week. "Since we just introduced this change last night, I don't feel particularly comfortable doing the robbery so soon without having a chance to see if there's any flaws in this new plan." He was referring to the new plan in which Brent and Julie would be waiting at the end of the aisle, closest to the office door where the guard would come out.

"What would we gain?" I moaned. "Another week of tension, another week of casing. Unless there's chores we won't have time to complete, I think we're just going to get more and more nervous."

"Ann was in there," added Brent, "and she seems to think it's a great plan. She checked out the layout and she thinks it will be fine, and she's not the type to be overly spontaneous about saying it's good. In fact, she's more the type to emphasize the dangerous aspects than I am, for instance."

"Yeah, okay then," said Gerry reluctantly. "My role won't be any different with this new plan, so if you three are happy, I'll go along with doing it on Monday."

"The guard won't have time to run or take cover when he comes out of that office door, 'cause Brent's going to say 'Freeze' as soon as the door is shut behind him," I explained.

"He might be tempted to go for cover, whereas in the middle of the aisle, there is none," Gerry countered.

"If he does do something stupid, we'll be quite willing to use our pieces if we have to, right?" added Julie, using the word "pieces" instead of "guns."

"No," said Gerry quite emphatically. "I'm not willing to use my piece at all."

"I am," Julie snapped.

"There's all these different things that people say that make me nervous," said Brent, "like 'willing to use our guns' and stuff makes me real nervous. The worst thing that could happen would be if we had to use our guns."

"It's the constant switching back and forth that bothers me," Julie said. "I'm not concentrating on using my gun, but people say 'If he shoots Brent, you better shoot him.' Like this could happen. I'm not saying if the guy flinches or fixes his hair that we should shoot him, but if he goes for his gun, we have to be willing to shoot him."

"Yeah," Brent said to Julie, "but you were responding to Gerry saying that if he moves or tries to take cover that you would shoot him."

"Well, he could hide and shoot at us."

"That's why I'm concerned about this new plan," said Gerry, "because it's of the utmost importance that we don't get into a situation like that. Our chances of pulling off the robbery successfully drop about forty per cent once we've fired a shot."

I tried to bolster Gerry's confidence. "There's pros and cons with both scenarios, but why would it be preferable for Julie and Brent to be waiting in the middle of the aisles, setting themselves up for the possibility that the guard might head down aisle three or four? If he does do that, he could easily see Brent peering over at him and then walking along at the end of the aisles to intercept him. I think Brent and Julie have a real advantage if they're waiting at the end of the aisle where they don't have to go anywhere to rob the guy. I just think that if they are more comfortable with that plan and they're the ones who gotta draw, then it's probably a better plan."

Julie looked at Gerry. "Well, if you feel like you're being dominated into this position, then I'd rather wait for another week."

"No," he said hesitantly. "If you three want to do it on Monday, I'm willing to go for it."

"But you're not very enthusiastic about it . . . " said Julie, still unsure about Gerry's commitment to Monday.

"Enthusiastic about it?" said Gerry with a sudden change of

heart. "I'll run like hell and put those handcuffs on the guy as fast as I can, regardless of whether we do it this Monday or next Monday. I'm just wary about rushing into things. I always am. Now my version of rushing into things is probably different than other people's version, but I want to make sure everybody feels completely good about it. I may have misunderstood you, Julie, but last night you said to Brent that you might suddenly get a surge of fear or something like that, and not be able to pull it off. I just said, 'Julie, you're one of the staunchest people in the robbery and you're not going to freak out. If anybody freaks out, it'll probably be me,' sort of jokingly at the end."

"But you said a couple of times before, that you're not even sure that you can do it, and that's freaking me out," Julie said.

"It's like that 'I'll love you forever stuff,' " he explained painfully. "Saying, 'I'll love and stay with you forever' is a real nice thing to say and it's beautiful to mean it at the time, but it's really a stupid mistake because you may not. You don't know for a fact that you will, right? Well it's the same thing with this. I feel real confident. I feel I can go in there and put the handcuffs on the guy. If something happens, I'll be able to respond, but I'm not saying that I'm Superman. Who knows, maybe I'll get in there, my legs will give out, I'll pass out and fall down on the floor. Maybe that'll happen. I don't think it will but it could."

"Well, that freaks me out completely!" said Julie tersely.

"Well, it could happen to you too," said Gerry sharply.

"I'm not letting that enter my consciousness."

"It's not doing anything to me by admitting that it could happen."

"I think it is."

"I don't think it weakens me at all," said Gerry confidently. "In fact, it makes me more relaxed and able to deal with the situation. I also admitted to myself that we may get shot or we may go to prison."

Brent went into mediator mode. "Yeah, everybody has different ways of dealing with it. Maybe it helps Gerry to think of all the different things that could happen, but I'm sure we're going to go in there and everything's going to go real smooth."

"I'm sure we're all going to be freaked out, but we have to force ourselves to keep going until it's over," I advised stoically.

"You have to start at one end of the tunnel and make it to the other end," suggested Brent, "and you gotta run like shit to make it to the other end. You can't turn back if you think you can't make it, but you just have to take a deep breath and fucking go till you get to the other side. We also have to be flexible over the issue of shooting. We're not going there to shoot and we're not going there *not* to shoot. We are only supposed to shoot in a life-threatening situation."

"Anyways," added Julie, "it's important for me to think of myself as a very heavy person. If the guy jerks me around and tries to shoot at me, then I gotta shoot."

"If he's *trying* to shoot at you, yeah," said Brent reassuringly. "But it's like you get vibes from Gerry when he says stuff, right? I must say I feel like you're the most trigger-happy person in the group. I feel it's more likely that you might shoot in a situation where you don't necessarily have to shoot than anybody else in the group, and that would be really bad."

Julie seemed to be on the verge of tears. "I just really feel like I'm probably the most scared person."

"That's why you might shoot, right?" said Brent compassion-ately. "If you don't have real confidence about when you're sup-posed to shoot or what you're supposed to be doing with the gun, you could have a tendency not to do it properly. And that's okay too, but just call me or something if you're not sure about what to do."

"You know what I was thinking last night?" I said suddenly. "If the guard grabbed Gerry, it would be bad if Julie shot sponta-neously, because she might end up shooting both the guard and Gerry. So I was thinking we should all try to be the guard some-time when we're doing scenarios, because you'd realize how vul-nerable he is. He isn't going to shoot or jump you. When you pre-tend you're the guard, you find out he can't even see. As the guard, you feel completely horrible."

"That's true," agreed Gerry. "I should try to be the guard. But if he does try to grab me, I'll probably kick him as hard as I can somewhere so he lets go, right? It's not the end of the world if he tries to grab you."

"Yeah, until he's getting his gun out or something like that, I don't think we should shoot him," continued Brent. "Like if we say 'Freeze' and he starts to move, I'll just repeat it again. The whole key to robberies is to use intimidation as a threat and verbally con-trol the situation. That's where our heaviness is supposed to come out. We would only use our guns in a life-threatening situation, but until that happens the whole thing is to control the situation through our presence. So if I go 'Freeze' and he moves or something, I'll just go 'Freeze buddy. I told you not to move!' "

"Just tell him that you'll kill him if he moves again," I suggested.

"Obviously I have my weak points too but I have confidence that when the robbery happens that everybody will react just fine," Brent said reassuringly. "I wouldn't do this with anybody if I didn't have confidence in them."

"I wouldn't worry too much about the guard being suspicious when he sees us," I said. "Because he must encounter young criminal-looking types hanging around in the aisles all the time. How often is he going to encounter only bourgeois people in the aisles anyway? I think he will only be on red alert if he sees three guys standing real strategically in front of him."

"Yeah," agreed Julie.

"One thing Doug pointed out last night," I continued, "is that the next time we go target-shooting, we should draw larger outlines and go for speed instead of drawing bull's-eye targets and trying to shoot them in the centre, because if you do have to shoot, you only have to aim for his body."

"I think we should use silhouette targets, because silhouettes represent figures that we will actually see," said Brent.

"I'm sorry about getting everyone upset," Julie said apologetically.

"Oh, it's alright," said Gerry, smiling tenderly at her.

"I'll be so glad next Tuesday when it's all over," I sighed.

"You know what, Ann?" Julie said. "If we have the scanner on, we'd know immediately if the robbery is called in." Now, thankfully, she seemed in a more upbeat mood.

"Hey, did we show you the car seat and doll we got yesterday?" Julie ran off into her room and came back a few minutes later with a car seat and life-like baby doll.

"Oh, that is nice." Brent gently picked up the doll.

"I felt really sad because it looks so much like a little baby," Julie said, looking at the doll maternally.

"That doesn't look like a little baby to me," laughed Gerry.

"Sure it will," said Julie, grabbing the doll from Brent and sitting it in the car seat.

"It sure sits up good for a little baby," chuckled Brent.

"Its forehead is way too big for a baby," Gerry said, with mock concern. With that, we decided to practise our robbery scenarios for another hour in order to shave some more precious seconds off the handcuffing procedure.

* * *

The next morning I marked a big red X through January 18. Perhaps this was a sign of my impatience for the days to pass quickly. Again, as I went up the stairs the silent mantra in my head accompanied me: *"robbery, robbery, robbery . . . "* By 10:30 we were assembled in the kitchen, ready to discuss the day's activities.

"After the robbery, other than the police force, about fifty other people in the whole world will know about it and those fifty people will all be at the Woolco," Brent said.

"Yeah?" said Julie, quizzically.

"So there won't be one person on the street that we pass, other than a police officer, that even has the faintest idea of what went down. For them, it's a normal Monday morning, right?"

"Right," agreed Julie.

"Entirely. So during our getaway, if anybody, even a big semi-trailer drives up and looks inside our pickup truck and thinks it's weird to have all that cardboard inside, they won't think it was for a robbery." He was talking about an idea he had that involved putting a pile of large cardboard sheets in the cap of the truck so that two people could hide under it during our getaway.

"Yeah," agreed Julie. "I also strongly believe that no matter what happens before, during, or after the robbery, that we should not make eye contact with anyone. Not in the store, on the street, nowhere — not even if people look at you weird. Just keep on walking, because if you do look up at them, then you're liable to get intimidated and they'll want to know why. The expression in your eyes will stick in their minds. Just keep doing your own thing and don't give anybody nothing, because that was my problem in Toronto. I figured out that the reason I was so paranoid after the bombing was because I was just too much into people and other things. I gave them my vibes. For sure people pick up on that very easily."

"It's true," agreed Brent, "if you don't notice people, they usually don't notice you. Just keep your energy directed into yourself."

"Right," said Julie with determination. "I hope we get more than fifty thousand dollars from this robbery."

"Me too, but it's real hard to say. I'd guess anywhere from eighty thousand down," said Brent. "We've really got all the angles to this robbery covered in a big way. But if I'm walking downtown and a Brink's truck pulls up after this, I'm not gonna bother walking past them for a little while."

"I felt so nervous when my sister said this guy she met was a security guard," Julie said. "I said, 'For what company?' and was thinking, 'What if she says, Brink's!' That would freak me out because I can just see my photograph hanging around the house and stuff and he visits and goes, 'That women there, I recognize her!' "

"I'm sure this'll make TV, if for nothing else but the hoses," laughed Brent.

Julie laughed as well. "Yeah, and I'll be the first woman in an armed Brink's robbery eh?"

We continued talking for a while longer, then headed off to carry out our various tasks. Brent and I spent most of the afternoon going over getaway routes until we decided on the one we felt the most comfortable with. After that we tried to foresee any possible problems we might encounter and to devise alternative routes. Late in the afternoon we headed down the Kingsway for a prearranged meeting with Angie for dinner. We rarely saw her, but since the outcome of the robbery was not written in stone, we had decided to have dinner with her in case the outcome was not good. On the way down the Kingsway, we stopped at Beaver Lumber for a few things Brent needed and then, since we were early, we dropped into a pool hall a few blocks away from the restaurant to play video games.

But a series of strange events occurred on the way down the Kingsway, and so after our dinner with Angie we phoned Doug and stopped to visit him on the way home. At his apartment, before mentioning our strange experiences, we talked about the possibility of the women doing another Wimmin's Fire Brigade action and then discussed the next Cheekeye-Dunsmuir bombing.

"People thought we were somewhat funny for putting B.C. Hydro as the return address on the envelopes for the Cheekeye communiqué," Doug said.

"We didn't do anything funny at Litton, though," I said. "That was a very, very serious action."

"Speaking of Cheekeye, I thought we might want to look into the possibility of doing Dunsmuir again, rather than the reactor station on Texada Island," suggested Doug.

"They just finished rebuilding Dunsmuir, didn't they?" I asked.

"Yeah," Doug said with a smile.

"That would really bug them in a big, big way." I smiled back.

"Last time they didn't have the transformers in there, but now they do and this time we could do the transformers, which would definitely shut down the line."

"Well, what about doing both?" said Brent. "On the same night."

"We don't have enough people to do that because they're both pretty personnel-intensive actions," Doug explained. "We could always save the reactor station for later."

"If we did the reactor station, it wouldn't necessarily shut down the line. It could continue operating, eh?" asked Brent.

"There's just a slight possibility it wouldn't shut down, but that's not the major reason for doing Dunsmuir again instead of the reactor station."

"The reactor station is on Texada Island, and I'm worried about how we'd get home on time," said Brent. "We'd have to take a ferry to Vancouver Island and then another ferry back to Vancouver. Anyway, we've got time to think about it. Hey, we had a weird situation happen tonight."

"Yeah. What?" Doug settled into his chair.

"It's quite weird," repeated Brent, who was the least paranoid of the group. "We were coming into town and stopped into Beaver Lumber, and on the way in I held the door open for this woman who came after me. Then I'm in this aisle and she's in another aisle on the other side of the store but she can see me, right? I was thinking of shoplifting and I noticed that she was positioned so she could see me. On my way out I looked back and there she is coming out the door a little ways behind me. Okay, so then we go downtown and we have half an hour to kill before we're going to see Angie, so we went in this pool hall to play video games, right at Main and Broadway, which is a twenty-minute drive from the Beaver Lumber on Royal Oak Avenue. We played a video game and were taking a break, sitting at a table by the front window, when I notice the same woman standing straight across the street, near the bus stop at Main and Broadway, but she wasn't actually standing at the bus stop. She's just sort of behind it, leaning up against the wall of the building there. Ann and I decided to go out across the street and stand beside her, like we were waiting for the bus, just to see what she would do. As soon as she saw us crossing the street towards her, she starts walking up Main Street and through the intersection. Now we decide to follow her. We walk right behind her for a few blocks and then she turns down Tenth Avenue. This doesn't make much sense so we continue following her, but two blocks down Tenth she stops and stands there for a second and seems to be muttering something into the lapel of her coat. Suddenly, out of the blue, a pickup truck comes zooming down Tenth, pulls up, and she runs across and jumps in and the truck takes off. She was walking briskly, almost running by the time she turned down Tenth. She looked visibly scared. We ran to the back alley that runs behind Mendo's and went in the back door of the restaurant. Angie was waiting there and we told her about it. All three of us got in her car and as soon as we started driving around the neighbourhood of Tenth and Main we see the same lady and a man in the pickup, still tearing around the area, as though they were looking for us. They didn't realize that we were now in Angie's car, so they couldn't find us. But it was weird!"

"Maybe she made a call at a phone booth for her boyfriend to pick her up?" Doug suggested.

"She was never out of our sight long enough to make a phone call," I explained.

"No, but she could have done it before you came out of the pool hall?" said Doug, searching for a reasonable explanation for this odd series of events.

"She had no idea we would be coming out of the pool hall, and if she did, why didn't he just pick her up at the bus stop where she was standing?" Brent said. "You'd think, if she'd called her boyfriend, she would have said to pick her up at Main and Eighth, instead of down Tenth."

"Yeah, people do weird things," said Doug. "But I agree, it is strange."

"Yeah, we should keep our eyes peeled for a while, because it wasn't too cool," I said.

"I can tell you," said Doug, looking for ways of reassuring us, "that if you go around looking for undercover cars behind you, you'll see them everywhere you look. Remember what happened in Calgary? It was a patently incredible series of coincidences. Yet it turned out, almost for sure, to be nothing. I would say, unless something ultra-blatant happens, it's not the cops."

"Yeah," I said, although I didn't feel any more reassured that the woman wasn't a cop than I had felt before we visited Doug.

"Years ago, I had an undercover car follow me around all day with uniform cops in it. The same one," said Doug, grasping at straws. "It's too expensive to freak out."

I knew that Doug's last statement was the bottom line. Unless we had one hundred per cent proof that we were under surveillance, we had put too much time and money and, most importantly, our lives into this to pack up and quit.

"The way it's going, I don't think they're going to actually figure out who we are until they catch one of us," Doug predicted.

"Well, that car theft. It was the worst thing that could have happened," Brent said, thinking of Gerry and his imminent car theft trial coming up in April.

"Plus all this shit with Gerry and that stolen car," I added.

"What car?" asked Doug.

I told Doug about Gerry's experience with the stolen car and the gas stations. "A bunch of people got a perfect ID of him," I said. "Unfortunately, the first getaway car was stolen from the same area as the car that Gerry deserted at the gas station." Once again we went through the ins and outs of the problems with the getaway cars and the likelihood of the police making a connection, either with the cars or with us. "The cops really do seem more incompetent than you think," said Doug. "There's so many things that we think they'd figure out because they're so obvious but they still don't seem to."

It was almost midnight and Doug was beginning to look sleepy. We told him we were going to go target-practising the day after next, Thursday the 20th. He said he would come. Brent and I said goodnight and drove home. The experience with the woman apparently following us had given us an extra shot of adrenalin so we were far from ready to go to sleep when we got home. Fortunately Julie and Gerry were still up, talking in the kitchen about — what else? — the robbery. We walked in on the tail end of a conversation about prison sentences.

"Julie, you're only twenty. You would never get that much time," I said. "I think you'd get the least time of all."

"I know," said Julie sadly, "but I don't care about that."

We were all very tired, and that's probably what led the conversation down a depressing path. It eventually degenerated into a brief discussion about the possibility of getting killed or going to prison forever, at which point Brent and I looked at one another and decided to hold back on the story about the woman following us. Events seen through the eyes of a well-rested individual always seem to have a more positive spin than they do when seen through the eyes of someone who is exhausted. However, in this case, no amount of sleep could totally erase the catastrophic implications of this woman following us from Beaver Lumber to the pool hall at Main and Broadway. Try as we might, we couldn't rationally explain the experience. Even explanations involving coincidence and the laws of random physics couldn't provide convincing justifications for the series of events. The only explanation that made sense was the one we really didn't want to face — that she was an undercover agent following us, and when she realized that her cover was blown she called for help on a transmitter in her coat and was subsequently rescued. To face this explanation meant we would have to immediately get rid of all the evidence of our past actions and give up plans for any future ones. If we had been under surveillance for any length of time, it might now be too late no matter what we did.

❋ **44** ❋

After listening to the tapes from Doug Stewart's residence on January 18, Fraser, Anderson, and Jim Jardine, the Crown Prosecutor, were elated.

"We've got it! We've got it!" yelled Fraser, as excited as a little boy catching the biggest fish of his life. All three men broke into crocodilian smiles. On the evening of the 18th, from 11:00 p.m. until midnight, Hansen and Taylor had dropped in for an unplanned visit at Stewart's apartment and had unwittingly mentioned doing the Cheekeye-Dunsmuir bombing, the Litton bombing, and the Red Hot Video firebombing. That tape alone, out of sixty-four unedited tapes, would give them a fighting chance in court of a conviction.

"My God, I can't believe it," Fraser said, unable to contain his relief. "In six more days, they would either be doing that robbery or we would have to bust them without the evidence for a conviction on the bombings."

Jardine smiled. "Yeah, and I really wasn't looking forward to letting them go through with that robbery." Jardine had been chosen to head the prosecution of the five suspects but would also have been perfectly typecast in a movie as a prosecutor with a villainous kind of handsomeness. He was tall with jet black hair and eyes, yet had been bestowed with a sharp nose and the stern facial features of a Hollywood bad guy. He looked like he could sleep in his neatly pressed dark suits and get up in the morning without a wrinkle in his starched shirt or a hair out of place on his impeccably greased head.

"I was having a hard time finding a recruit to act as the Brink's guard," Jardine revealed with a smile. During the weeks proceeding this miraculous tape, the team had debated replacing the real Brink's guard with an RCMP officer in order to let their suspects carry out the robbery, in a desperate bid for more time to acquire the necessary wiretap evidence on the Cheekeye and Litton bombings. This course of action was fraught with unpredictability, which was a feature the police particularly hated. What if one of the suspects shot the guard or one of the employees? What if a citizen decided to be a hero and tried to jump one of the suspects? Could they replace all the people in the store with police officers and still pull it off? If they did end up in a shootout with the suspects in the store, could they guarantee nobody would get killed? "I haven't been able to sleep for days," was Jardine's answer to those questions. "There were just too many variables in that plan."

"Thank God we have a wire in Stewart's place," Fraser said with a sigh. Two weeks after getting the authorization for the bugs in the New Westminster residence, they had applied for an authorization for a bug in the Windermere apartment from Judge D.B. MacKinnon of the Vancouver County Court. They were getting only unsatisfactory conversations from the New Westminster residence. The four suspects spent a great deal of time discussing the imminent Woolco robbery but rarely referred to Cheekeye or Litton.

When it became obvious that the robbery date was being firmed up for January, the RCMP pulled out their full arsenal of surveillance techniques. Their most creative operation took place one afternoon in a yuppie-style cafe that Stewart and his girlfriend, Rachel, frequented in the West End. One morning the Special O team spotted Stewart and Rachel touring around the Burrard Yarrows in a small boat, binoculars in hand, focusing in on the construction of the *Terry Fox* icebreaker. When they were overheard at a bus stop planning a lunch break at a West End café, the RCMP sprang into action. They quickly arranged to have a bug planted in a large rubber plant that adorned the front window of the café. After obtaining the co-operation of the owner, they also arranged to keep the table near the plant free and to substitute one of the regular waiters with a Special O officer. When Stewart and Rachel arrived, they were shepherded by the Special O officer over to the empty table beside the beautiful rubber plant. Feeling comfortable and relaxed, the couple sat at their table with a view, chatting away for hours, completely unaware that their every word was being picked up, as in some Orwellian nightmare, by the innocuous plant beside them. Unfortunately for the RCMP, most of their conversation meandered off into alternative culture and ended in a discussion of movies that they wanted to see. All their efforts had been in vain. Frustrated, the police had decided to plant a bug in Stewart's apartment. Maybe that would be the place where the terrorists would go to reminisce.

There was only one dark cloud to dampen the three men's spirits that day. "Now, I just hope we didn't blow our cover with that Beaver Lumber fiasco," Fraser said, his face turning from a smile to a frown. "We've got to tell those Special O people to be more careful."

"But it sounds as though they still aren't sure they're under surveillance," speculated Anderson. "I'm going to get those two officers in here today and see what happened. That can't happen again. We'll have to instruct them to cancel their surveillance the minute they have any eye contact at all with one of the suspects. That woman was foolish to continue following Taylor after he clearly had contact with her on the way into the Beaver Lumber. It's mind-boggling that she would be so incompetent — to continue following him after he held the door open for her in the store. I've a good mind to fire her. And can you believe the arrogance of Stewart, saying we're incompetent?"

"Well, based on the work of that Special O officer, I would have to agree," Fraser said.

Anderson shot him a glance. "They won't be so arrogant and boastful once we've got them in cuffs. If there's one thing I hate, it's an arrogant criminal."

"You should learn to appreciate the irony of the situation," laughed Fraser.

"What are you, an English major or a cop?" said Anderson, feeling belittled.

"Actually, I did major in English, and I do appreciate the irony of these people talking about our stupidity in complete ignorance of the fact that we're actually one step ahead of them."

"Enough," said Jardine. "We're going to have to act quickly." They made plans for an arrest as soon as possible. They would have a meeting with the Joint Forces and decide where and when to take the suspects down, and then organize the arrests. They knew they would have to call in reinforcements from the various Vancouver detachments and the Integrated Intelligence Unit. They needed to be well prepared — the suspects were "armed and ready to kill," and it would take considerable manpower to carry out the operation effectively and, most importantly, out of the eye of the media. "Don't forget that these people have their supporters," Jardine cautioned Fraser. "They aren't just your garden variety criminals. There are people who will be very angry if they are hurt or killed. And I, for one, am also very concerned that none of our own guys get killed either."

* * *

It was almost noon before I woke up on the 19th. Rolling out of bed, I was surprised to see that Brent was already up. I knew that he was having a hard time relaxing, with the robbery only five days away. Like a robot, I walked over to the calendar and marked my red X through the 19th in anticipation of having the day over with, then up the stairs . . . "*robbery, robbery, robbery . . .* "

Over coffee we described to Julie and Gerry the strange events surrounding the woman we had encountered at Beaver Lumber. Predictably, they were alarmed, but in the end we agreed that without conclusive evidence there was nothing we could do except carry on. We made a firm decision to "keep our eyes peeled" and, until we saw more evidence of surveillance, to carry on, business as usual. We made a quick decision to go for one last shooting practice in the mountains north of Squamish, leaving early the next morning on the 20th.

We separated for the first half of the afternoon so that Julie and Gerry could pick up some more ammunition while Brent and I went over the getaway route. We arranged to pick them up on our way home. The only other stop we had to make, after picking up Julie and Gerry, was the grocery store to buy a few items and pick up cardboard for silhouette targets.

We burst breathlessly through our back door, laughing and talking on top of one another in our excitement over what we had just witnessed. "I was just sitting in the truck waiting for you guys to come out of the grocery store with the cardboard when I saw this really young guy come running out of the store," I said for the hundredth time. It had been so exciting we couldn't stop reliving it.

"Yeah," Gerry said excitedly. "I saw him go up to the exit doors. He peered out of them and then stopped and looked like he was thinking for a second. He was thinking, 'I don't wanna get shot today.'"

"Is that what he said or something?" asked Julie seriously.

"No," scoffed Gerry with a smile. "I just thought he was thinkin' that."

"When I was waiting for Gerry and Brent to go through the checkout line, I was over by the magazines, just lookin' through them," Julie explained quickly, "and he was standin' beside me, real nervous-like. I thought maybe I was making him nervous because he wanted to shoplift a magazine. I even thought of reassuring him that I wouldn't call the clerks if he did pick one up. Then after a few minutes he walks over to the checkout line."

Then Gerry impatiently jumped into the conversation. "The cashier said, 'Excuse me,' and I turned around in the line and there's this fucking big money bag going by right underneath my nose. I looked right at it and then I looked at Brent and he's looking right at me and we both wink at each other. And then about five seconds, six seconds after, that guy robs her! He waited until she was walking towards the office with her bag and all that cash in it. It fuckin' blew my mind, I'll tell ya. My hair stood on end for about two seconds and my stomach sorta churned! I'm glad he didn't rob that cashier when she was right beside me! That would have been a blood-curdling experience."

"So that probably was a good till sweep, because it was about 4:30 or something, eh?" I said. A "till sweep" refers to a grocery store's practice of having a cashier routinely collect all the cash from each checkout cashier and deposit it in the office safe to deter would-be robbers. Normally there is a till sweep every day just before the store closes so the manager can count the money and do the books. Coincidentally we had arrived just before closing time.

"I bet he cased it," Gerry said. "Just think if Brent and I had taken the money from the clerk as she passed us. That guy would probably have held us up."

"You're lucky he didn't shoot you anyway," Julie laughed. "Because you two sure look like cops with those short haircuts!" They had cut their hair very short for the upcoming robbery.

"I wonder if he had a real gun?" I said. "He had it out when he was running, you know."

I didn't actually see any gun." Gerry started to laugh again. "That was priceless though, the way that guy got out of that store. What really amazed me was how fast he went after he went through the door."

"He was just a blur!" laughed Julie.

"When I saw him, I thought he was just shoplifting and some-body was chasing him," I explained. "He ran all along that front part real fast. Maybe he had somebody else waiting for him in a getaway car behind the store. It's cool that you carried all those cardboard boxes out, because that made you look completely inno-cent. Once our robbery is over, thank God, we won't have to do another one for at least a year."

"I ain't never doing another robbery again," said Gerry with conviction. Just then a good song came on the radio, creating a lull in the conversation. After the song ended, in a blatantly paradoxi-cal statement, to which the rest of us seemed oblivious, Gerry said, "I wouldn't mind doin' a smaller one."

"Yeah, I don't think that'd be bad," I agreed.

"But I'm not into bustin' into the Brink's depot or anything," he said, putting some kind of bizarre boundaries on what he consid-ered "small."

"I'm not yet, anyways," I agreed, qualifying my limitations in an equally bizarre way.

"Unless we're gonna use the money for something like . . . " He paused and searched his mind for a cause worthy of a Brink's depot robbery. " . . . Giving it away to all those poor children in Surrey." I completed his sentence for him. Surrey is a suburb of Vancouver noted for its high proportion of East Indian immi-grants.

"Surrey?" smiled Gerry, pondering the meaning of my state-ment.

"Yeah," I repeated. "Or maybe giving it away to the poverty-stricken on East Hastings." East Hastings is the poorest area in Vancouver's downtown core.

"Yeah," said Gerry, still smiling, "or give it to some righteous Native movement. Or what about the Karl Marx Foundation?"

Then I remembered something Brent and I had witnessed ear-lier in the day. "I don't know what it is, if it's because we're so focused on robberies or if it's just that there are more robberies happening, but we almost forgot to tell you. We actually walked right by a bank robbery today, right after it had happened."

"Where was it?" asked Julie.

"Right at Commercial and First. There were a whole bunch of cops inside the bank and they're standing around these two incredibly shady-looking guys. One of the cops was measuring distances inside so they could write down their little statistics about what happened."

"Weird," said Julie using our favourite expression, which seemed to capture just about every range of emotion we experienced.

"Anyway, tonight, let's cut out some silhouette targets for tomorrow and do a few more robbery scenarios. I'll be the guard," I said on a more serious note.

"I thought we were going swimming tonight," said Gerry with a disappointed look on his face. There was no response. "Well, I guess we won't have time to do everything, so maybe we could go on the weekend?"

"Yeah," said Julie, getting up. She disappeared downstairs for a few minutes, then returned to the kitchen with some cardboard, black Magic Markers, and scissors. Soon we were deeply immersed in drawing faces and silhouettes on the cardboard for target-practice.

I looked at a target depicting Porky Pig. "We better destroy these when we're finished 'cause they're not very good to have around."

"What if the cops found all our weapons and these targets?" Gerry said with a laugh. "They'd really be upset."

"I already thought about that, but then I realized that it didn't really matter." I chuckled. "If we got stopped in that truck, with the guns and everything, that's a bad scene as it is."

"Let's do some robbery scenarios before it gets too late," said Julie. "Where's Brent?"

He was down in the basement getting the guns packed up for our trip in the morning. "Brent!" I yelled. We heard a faint response through the floor boards. After about fifteen minutes, he came trudging up the stairs. It didn't take long to get ready for a short robbery scenario rehearsal. We were in good spirits that night, probably because we all looked forward to a day in the mountains, even if it was only for target-practice.

"Everybody ready?" I asked, poised to click on the stopwatch.

"Yeah!" said Julie enthusiastically.

"Feel your heart pounding. Feel the sweat dripping off your brow. The moment is arriving!" I said dramatically. "Everything in your life hinges on this moment!" Then I pretended to be the Brink's guard.

"Freeze! Hold it right there! Put your arms out and turn this way! Now put your face flat on the ground. Keep down . . . " Brent ordered.

"Be quiet. Don't move. This'll be over soon. Do what we say and nothing will happen to you. Put your hands behind your back. Just stay cool and nothing'll happen to you." Julie put the money bag in Gerry's gym bag. Quickly, Gerry put my handgun in his bag, then handcuffed my hands behind my back.

"Okay, friend, let's go!" Brent jogged lightly into the kitchen.

"That's not bad." Even with the handcuffs on, I managed to click off the stopwatch. "A little more than twenty seconds."

"I should practise keeping my voice low," Julie said.

"Julie, why were you turning this way so much?" asked Brent.

"I'm pretending that people are in this aisle."

"I think both of us aren't conscious enough about where the guard's hands are," Brent said. "His hands are right at our feet. Maybe he could grab our feet and pull them out from under us. We should be watching that more maybe." He turned to Gerry. "Do you think I should say something like, 'Hey Roger, let's go'?"

"Well, yeah. Ray, Roger, Johnnie. Any name but Gerry."

"What about Richard or Jacques?" asked Brent, using a French accent. He still wanted to create the impression that we were French Canadian in order to throw the police off.

After another hour of robbery scenarios, we headed towards our respective bedrooms in order to get a good night's sleep before our trip to the mountains. It was going to be very hard to get up in the morning because we were more accustomed to a schedule of late to bed and late to rise. I always said, "Who wants worms anyway?" whenever anyone said "The early bird gets the worm."

* * *

Brent had already done most of the packing, so that it didn't take long to carry everything out to the truck that morning. The guns were always unloaded and wrapped carefully in rags so they wouldn't get damaged. They were packed away in the bottom of large gym bags, with the ammunition and cleaning equipment stacked on top. We laid the cardboard targets flat on the floor of the truck bed so they would create a cushioning and insulating effect for whoever had to ride in the back. Gerry had volunteered to ride in the back of the truck until we reached Doug's place, at which point Doug and Brent would take his place. Even though British Columbia has a relatively temperate winter climate, it was still a long, cold ride for whoever had to sit in the unheated canopy of the truck for the two-hour ride to the mountains.

I lifted a heavy cooler filled with sandwiches and drinks into the back of the truck. "Is that it?"

"Yeah." Brent glanced back at Julie and Gerry, who were affectionately fawning over Rex before leaving. "I'm glad Doug's coming today. I want to be sure the Mini-14s are sighted in perfectly before the robbery."

"It's going to be a great day!" I prophesied, looking towards the east where the first morning rays of the sun had cast a pink and yellow hue on the night clouds. For a few minutes, I stood marvelling at the beauty of the sky, wishing we were going up to the mountains forever instead of just for a day of target-practice. But the sound of Julie shutting our back door broke my reverie. It's all worth it, I thought, if we could only contribute to stopping the destruction of the natural world.

As I bent over into the back of the truck, I scraped my finger on an old rusty screw sticking out of the canopy, and a gush of blood ran down my finger. Brent noticed it. "You better put some disinfectant and a Band-aid, on that or it'll scar forever." I scoffed at his prediction. "Forget it! Then I'd have to go back in and we'll be late. You know how punctual Doug is."

Brent grabbed my finger and took a better look. "I bet that will scar you for life."

Ignoring his prophesy, I shut the canopy door on poor Gerry, bundled up in a sleeping bag for warmth. And so we drove off with serene smiles on our faces, completely oblivious to the preparations taking place in the grey light of dawn on a sharp mountain turn — preparations that would end our lives as we knew them.

Epilogue

As is always the case during any militant political campaign, a corresponding campaign of police repression followed in the wake of the bombings. The campaign served a number of purposes. The police were able to use the frenzy of fear that the mass media had whipped up over the so-called terrorist threat to justify the raids and arrests of community political activists, without fear of impunity. The campaign was used to gather intelligence on the radical community, but was also part of a well-planned counter-insurgency program with the express purpose of criminalizing and repressing that segment of the left involved in any kind of direct action. In today's global economy, this strategy is no different from campaigns in other parts of the world.

Immediately following the firebombings of Red Hot Video, some women in the feminist community were singled out for questioning by the police and threatened with arrest if they did not co-operate. They were shown lists of women's organizations and asked to single out women they believed to be involved in the fire-bombings. Fortunately, none of the women co-operated, and the police did not follow through on their threats. However, after our arrests some of these women were picked up and once again threatened with charges if they didn't give information. Although the women never did co-operate, the intimidation had a strong impact on their lives.

In Vancouver, after our arrests a support group, Free the Five, was formed to help us with our legal defence. The police singled out people from this group — people who, they suspected, were more vulnerable and perhaps less informed of their rights — and tried to force statements from them. Once again the attempts to find informants failed, but the police continued to follow and photograph our close supporters. The surveillance was so intensive that it involved watching our close friends in their homes, work-places, and meeting places and following their vehicles, as well as tapping their phones. Two Mounties visited an activist's boss and told her that her female employee was suspected of "terrorist" activity. Another woman was picked up off the street and black-mailed with the threat of criminal charges if she didn't inform on a friend they suspected was a member of Direct Action.

On February 16, 1983, after a meeting of supporters, police raided the homes of four women who had attended the meeting. At one home police told two women, "We know you are lesbians," implying that this was a criminal activity. At another home the

461

police kicked in a door. From these homes the police took diaries, posters, letters, notes, address books, photos, typewriters, legal rifles, flak jackets, a clarinet, earrings, locks, boots, running shoes, ammunition belts, and logo paper. The items confiscated in these raids are striking in their legality.

After our arrests the police also tried to get the co-operation of the Community Congress for Economic Change (CCEC), a Vancouver credit union, in order to check the bank accounts of Doug Stewart and Brent Taylor. The CCEC refused to comply because the police did not have an authorized search warrant.

In Toronto the campaign of repression was not much different. On June 13, 1983, the police raided a house on Cambridge Avenue where most of the support work in Toronto was centred. The political offences listed on the search warrant were seditious libel, sabotage to undermine national security, procuring an abortion, and the firebombing of armouries in Montreal. Police overzealousness was apparent in the use of the seditious libel charge, a charge so outdated it had not been used in fifty years. Seditious libel means advocating the use of force to overthrow the government without proper authority. Perhaps to provide evidence for this obscure charge, the search warrant specified a number of items, including the *Bulldozer*, the *Trial by Media* videotape, and any correspondence with the accused. At the time of the search an issue of the *Bulldozer* was in production, and the search warrant specified seizure of this copy. The police carried off the typeset galleys, along with the original articles and the mailing list.

During the raid the police made it clear that the house had been under electronic surveillance for some time. They laid charges against a woman who had no direct participation in the political activities for which the surveillance was supposedly legally justified. These charges were very serious: procuring an abortion, procuring instruments for an abortion, and two theft charges. The police offered to drop the charge of procuring an abortion if she agreed to inform on any of the Litton bombers. She did not — and could not — co-operate, because she had no knowledge of the Litton bombing. After finding a few joints the police also charged four others with possession of marijuana.

The police used the raid on the Cambridge Avenue house to lay an exaggerated number of charges in a vain attempt to gain information on the political activities of others. Following a consistent pattern, the people living in the house did not inform on other political activists, despite being threatened with a total of eighteen charges.

Even before our arrests yet another episode of harassment (in addition to those mentioned earlier in the book) occurred involving Brian Burch, a member of the Cruise Missile Conversion Project (CMCP). He was picked off the street by police in an unmarked car on January 11, 1983. He was falsely accused of a driving charge and then questioned for half an hour about the bombing, the peace movement, and the *Toronto Clarion*. The police picked him up and drove him around downtown Toronto, telling him they were looking for someone with his name who was wanted for traffic violations in British Columbia. He said, "They asked me if I supported the bombing and I gave qualifications."

In June 1983 another Toronto supporter was charged with welfare fraud over $200. It was one year after the alleged offence had taken place, and it was during a time when he was part of a support group — leading one to believe that the charges were politically motivated. He had received a $700 welfare cheque while being registered with a vendor's permit for owning a business called the Focus Books and Art Store. He was also called in for questioning on August 9, 1983, by the same police who raided the Cambridge Avenue house. They told him he could be charged with conspiracy in the Litton bombing if he refused to testify against the five people imprisoned in Vancouver.

The harassment, raids, and charges in Vancouver and Toronto were part of a continuing campaign of repression that began in 1982 with the raids at the offices of the CMCP, Alliance for Non-Violent Action (ANVA), and the homes of the anti-cruise activists in these groups. Many of these raids took place after our arrests, during a time when the police knew they had ample evidence against us, which again suggests that the point of the raids was to intimidate and criminalize people supporting our cause. The police repression undoubtedly instilled fear in the radical community — psychologically deterring some people from doing support work and especially setting back work such as publication of the *Bulldozer* and pro-choice organizing. The repression also created division amongst the left as people began to focus energies on defending their support of the militant activists or criticizing those who did.

* * *

Many months after our arrests the Crown began to disclose its case to our lawyers during a *voir dire* — a streamlined form of preliminary hearing used to save time in cases in which both the defence and Crown agree that the evidence justifies a case going to trial. The Crown was obligated only to disclose the surveillance evidence it had gathered after November 18, 1982, the date on which the criminal investigation was officially handed over to CLEU. Before that date the RCMP Security Service's investigation was strictly classified as intelligence-gathering and was not intended to be used in court. But, ironically, while the prosecutor, Jim Jardine, was on honeymoon the Crown prosecutor's office accidentally released to the defence surveillance notes from the Security Service dated October 29 to November 18. Later, during the trial, our lawyers tried to bring out the evidence from these surveillance notes, which would show that both Direct Action and certain members of the Wimmin's Fire Brigade were under intensive surveillance before, during, and immediately after the November 22 Red Hot Video firebombings.

Under cross-examination by our lawyers, the Security Service officers who had worked with CLEU admitted they had been instructed to blank out in their notebooks incriminating references made before the official criminal investigation began on November 18 — that is, references to surveillance of illegal activities. Often complete pages were blanked out. When our lawyers called Corporal Andrew Johnston, the Security Service officer in charge of their part of the investigation, to the stand to answer questions regarding the names of Security Service personnel involved in surveillance both before and after November 18, he was accompanied by a lawyer, Harry Wruck, from the Justice Department, and Chief Superintendent John Venner of the Security Service. They had been flown in from Ottawa along with Michael Spooner, an assistant commissioner of the RCMP, to block evidence of the surveillance prior to November 18 and during the night of the firebombings.

The Justice Department lawyer, Wruck, told the court that when Corporal Johnston had been subpoenaed as a witness, his superiors had anticipated he would be asked questions touching on national security. In fact, Wruck warned the court, Chief Superintendent Venner was in court for the purpose of complying with sections 36.1 and 36.2 of the *Canada Evidence Act*, legislation dealing with the refusal of a witness to answer questions on grounds of "public interest" or of "national security." This was indeed the case.

Almost every time our lawyers asked Johnston a question about the surveillance in the delicate time period just before, during, and after the firebombings, Venner would jump to his feet and read a little speech that essentially excused Johnston from answering the question on the grounds that it was "prejudicial to national security." When pressed further, Wruck said the Security Service was reluctant to identify its members because it takes several years to train a member and maintain that person's cover. He also said that disclosure, because of the type of work the Security Service does, might result in harassment of the officer or his family.

According to the RCMP testimony, only one of the Direct Action group, Doug Stewart, was under surveillance — by no less than five surveillance personnel — on the night of the firebombings. Considering that the surveillance notes prior to November 18, despite the blanked-out parts, showed that all five of us were under intensive surveillance while carrying out suspicious activities surrounding Red Hot Video, this testimony was highly suspect, to say the least. The RCMP offered no logical explanation as to why so much surveillance was on Doug the night of the firebombings, and on no one else. But without being able to cross-examine the Security Service officers who carried out the surveillance prior to and after November 18, our lawyers found it difficult to expose the truth surrounding the surveillance of the firebombings.

Why would the Security Service not admit to witnessing the firebombings? Although the main reason would seem to be the controversy arising from having allowed the police to witness a major crime, I believe the real reason was the police's fear that the wiretaps would be ruled inadmissible in court, which would have crippled their case against us in regards to Litton or Cheekeye. If the police had admitted witnessing the firebombings, then the sworn affidavit they used to get authorization for room bugs would have been fraudulent, because it would not have disclosed the full extent of their case to date. Our lawyers would then have had grounds for getting the wiretap testimony thrown out of court.

Without evidence of the police witnessing the firebombings, our lawyers were faced with two problems in regards to getting the wiretap evidence thrown out of court. One was the Catch-22 situation in which they weren't allowed to view the sworn affidavit because it was sealed to everyone but the judge. The other problem was Venner and Wruck using national security clauses to block concrete evidence that could prove the police had witnessed the firebombings. In the end our lawyers were unsuccessful in their bid to have the wiretaps thrown out because the Justice Department and RCMP blocked their efforts to prove that the police had witnessed the Red Hot Video firebombings.

Members of the media privy to confidential police sources also bolstered the theory that the police had witnessed the firebombings. A BCTV broadcast written by Alyn Edwards stated that the police were watching some people set fires. In court Alyn Edwards testified that he had been given his broadcast information by a reliable source and that prosecutor Jardine had later implied to him that it was at least partially correct. *Globe and Mail* reporter Jock Ferguson also testified with certainty in court that Staff Sergeant Clarke of the Metro Toronto Police had told him the same thing.

If the police witnessed the firebombings, why didn't they arrest us immediately after? At that time the police were loath to make arrests without any concrete evidence to get convictions on the Cheekeye and Litton bombings. Even after they installed room bugs in the New Westminster home and the Windermere apartment in December 1982, it wasn't until the evening of January 18, 1983, that they had even the tiniest piece of evidence. That was when Brent, Doug, and I had an inadvertent discussion about the bombings in Doug's apartment. At that point, with the Brink's robbery looming days away, they had no recourse but to make plans to arrest us.

* * *

After the *voir dire* we were ordered to stand trial on more than one hundred charges. At first we debated using the trials as a political forum to expose the issues of environmental destruction, nuclear technology, and pornography, but we soon realized the futility of trying to accomplish that goal during a legal trial so completely controlled by the justice system.

The Crown broke our charges down into five separate trials. The Brink's conspiracy would be the first. We anticipated that this trial would effectively criminalize our actions, because it was unlikely that either a jury or the public would understand any of the charges — stealing cars, weapons, and conspiracy to commit a robbery — as being political in nature. We understood that once the media coverage of this first trial tainted the public's attitude, it would be almost impossible for any jury in British Columbia to fathom the political motivations behind the other charges.

In March 1984, even before the Brink's trial was over, Julie and Gerry decided to enter guilty pleas to five counts each: conspiracy to rob a Brink's armoured car, possession of weapons for "a purpose dangerous to the public peace," theft of three cars, possession of stolen property, and arson of Red Hot Video in Port Coquitlam. Julie also pleaded guilty to an additional two charges: possession of explosives for a dangerous purpose and causing an explosion at Litton Industries, Toronto. Julie was sentenced to twenty years and Gerry to ten.

When the jury for the Brink's conspiracy trial brought back their verdict, they found Brent and me guilty on all counts. Doug was found guilty on a weapons charge. By then we had already spent fifteen months in prison and were facing four more trials. When our lawyers advised us that our trial judge, Sam Toy, had no intention of ruling any evidence admissible that he did not consider relevant, we realized that there would be no possibility of politicizing the Cheekeye, Red Hot Video, or Litton trials. Now that we were in prison and facing trials, our actions and abilities to politicize events were extremely restricted. We were no longer playing in our court. We were playing in theirs, and they would determine all the rules. Judge Toy made it abundantly clear that if we used a defence of necessity — in which a person argues that the "crimes" they committed were necessary in order to avert an even greater crime — his rulings would define a narrow legal boundary for the admissibility of evidence. He would thereby render this type of defence impossible. We also believed that if we continued to present legal defences we would in essence be giving the judicial system credibility, which would be in stark contrast to our politics before our arrest. Even pleading innocent during the Brink's trial was a mistake, I believe, because that plea gave people the message that we held out hope for an acquittal and that we were willing to play by the judicial system's rules in order to gain some personal freedom. Rather than continuing to send out confusing messages to the left and, on a personal level, allowing ourselves to be dragged through years of trials, we decided to plead guilty and make political sentencing speeches. In the end these statements were the only political gestures, other than non-participation in the trials, that we were allowed.

A few months after the Brink's trial, we pleaded guilty to the charges that we had no hope of beating, while some charges were either dropped or stayed. Doug Stewart was sentenced to ten years after pleading guilty to the B.C. Hydro bombing and a weapons charge. Brent Taylor was sentenced to twenty-two years for unlawful possession of explosives and weapons, robbery, conspiracy, break and enter and theft of guns, possession of stolen property, theft of three autos, and the Litton bombing. I was sentenced to life imprisonment for conspiracy to rob an armoured-car guard, the B.C. Hydro and Litton bombings, arson at Red Hot Video, unlawful possession of explosives and weapons, auto theft, and possession of stolen property.

* * *

After years of cascading from the maximum- through the medium- to the minimum-security prisons, by January 1990 we were all out on full parole, even though some of us were still in halfway houses. Although we made it out of the prison system without physical scars, no one ever gets out without emotional and spiritual scars that essentially transform him or her into a different person from the one who went in.

Are those scars worth it? Did the bombings contribute in any positive way to stopping the construction of the Cheekeye-Dunsmuir power line, the expansion of the Red Hot Video pornography franchise, or the production and testing of the cruise missile in Canada? These are not easy questions to answer, because the effects of the bombings can't be isolated from the combined efforts of the many people involved in the various movements around these issues.

The first circuit of the Cheekeye-Dunsmuir power line was originally scheduled for completion in September 1983, but was finished in November 1983. B.C. Hydro was able to re-order new reactors and an oil-pumping plant, which were shipped out fairly quickly. The two-month delay was not significant, and can't in any case be conclusively attributed to the effects of the Dunsmuir sub-station bombing.

In sharp contrast to the dire warnings made by B.C. Hydro about possible electricity shortages on Vancouver Island if the line was not completed on time, B.C. Hydro was actually selling millions of dollars of surplus electricity to California by November 1983, fuelling the arguments of Hydro's opponents that its megaprojects were not needed for the domestic consumption of electricity.

Another major criticism of Hydro's opponents was the lack of public participation in the decision-making process and that environmental assessments of megaprojects were not mandatory, but rather up to the discretion of the B.C. Utilities Commission. Much later, in June 1995, the B.C. *Environmental Assessment Act* was proclaimed, which institutionalized environmental assessments and allowed for public participation and access to documents pertaining to the development of megaprojects. Still, despite public participation, the Environmental Assessment Board makes its recommendations to the B.C. cabinet, which, once again, decides whether the projects will receive approval.

In Ontario the Litton plant resumed production only two days after the bombing due to a show of support for their employer by many of the Litton workers, who used their weekend to help clean up. However, Litton Systems of Canada was not invited by its parent company in California to bid on the guidance system for an advanced version of the cruise missile. On April 17, 1984, Litton President Ronald Keating lamented in a *Globe and Mail* article, "They (the protesters) are an irritant. They get a lot of publicity and the Americans read every damn bit of it. The Americans assure us they understand but nobody else has been bombed. . . . Pressure from these people is making the Americans look twice at secondary-sourcing (military investment) in Canada." After the bombing and the demonstrations of 1982, Litton also spent $2 million dollars on additional security for the Toronto factory, which Keating said "was money which could be put into our business to help make us more competitive and further insure the future for all of us." The combined effects of the civil disobedience protests and the bombing appear to have influenced the Americans to award their contract elsewhere.

After the Litton bombing, Canadians continued to oppose the idea of testing the cruise missile in Canada. A Gallup poll in January 1983 showed that 52 per cent of those polled were against cruise testing and only 37 per cent in favour. Despite the obvious lack of popular support, the United States and Canada signed a five-year "umbrella" agreement in March 1983 to allow the testing of U.S. weapons on Canadian soil. Since their government did not appear to be listening to them, more than a hundred thousand Canadians took to the streets of Vancouver, Toronto, and Montreal in April 1983 to protest Canada's agreement to test nuclear weaponry for the United States. On July 15, 1983, when Canada signed the specific agreement allowing the air-launched cruise to be tested, North American disarmament groups scheduled demonstrations for July 23 at fourteen Canadian consulates in the United States.

Although the Litton bombing could not be credited for the growing opposition to the cruise, it certainly was not scaring people away from the issue. Days after the Litton bombing, fifteen thousand demonstrators marched in Ottawa at an anti-cruise rally. Operation Dismantle, one of Canada's largest anti-nuclear groups, tripled its membership to two thousand in the year of the bombing. In December 1982 leaders of the five major churches met with Prime Minister Trudeau to express their "deep concern over the idea of bringing the missiles to Canada." In April 1983 the two-million-member Canadian Labour Congress pledged to support the anti-cruise movement. Even within the reigning Liberal Party, a survey in April 1983 found that of 146 Liberal MPs, 6 opposed the cruise tests and another 115 refused to state their position. Their silence spoke volumes.

In British Columbia the expansion of the Red Hot Video franchise came to an abrupt halt in the wake of the Wimmin's Fire Brigade firebombings and the persistent pressure from the women's community. On January 3, 1983, forty-five women's groups filed a complaint with the B.C. Ombudsman over Red Hot Video. The coalition spokesperson said, "It is women and children who are the victims of violent hard-core pornography. We insist the laws be upheld." On January 7, 1983, in a co-ordinated effort between the RCMP and the Vancouver and Victoria police, twelve video stores were raided and over one hundred tapes seized from four Vancouver stores. The B.C. Federation of Women hailed the raids as a victory.

On January 20, 1983, the day of our arrests, the B.C. Attorney-General's office charged RHV in Victoria with three counts of obscenity. The Crown counsel, Barry Sullivan, said, "This isn't so much a test case as it is the first store to be charged. We're going to review each case as it comes along and proceed from there. There could be more stores charged, sure. We'll look at all of them." The obscenity trial against the Victoria store ended in a conviction and a nominal fine, but RHV complained it was being crippled with legal fees.

At the time of the firebombings RHV had thirteen franchises in the B.C. Lower Mainland. One firebombing immediately closed down the Surrey store. The Port Coquitlam store closed down for fear of getting hit again, two others moved to different communities, and two more changed their names. In the year following the firebombing, three RHV stores closed permanently and the remaining stores went on to pay thousands of dollars in legal fees to fight obscenity charges.

* * *

When Direct Action began its militant campaign, we had no illusions about being able to change society on our own. We knew that no single demonstration or bombing would bring any substantial change. But we did hope to inject a more militant political philosophy and action into the movement for social change. We hoped to show people that we should not allow the legal boundaries defined by those in power determine how and when we would protest.

There are many different forms of direct action, some more effective than others at different points in history, but in conjunction with other forms of protest, direct action can make the movement for change more effective by opening avenues of resistance that are not easily co-opted or controlled by the state. Unfortunately, people within the movement weaken their own actions by failing to understand and support the diverse tactics available. Instead of forming a unified front, some activists see the sabotage of destructive property by protesters as being on the same level as the violence of the state and corporations. This equation is no more accurate than saying that the peace of a concentration camp is the same kind of peace that one finds in a healthy society. If we accept that all violence is the same, then we have agreed to limit our resistance to whatever the state and corporations find acceptable. We have become pacified. Remaining passive in the face of today's global human and environmental destruction will create deeper scars than those resulting from the mistakes we will inevitably make by taking action.

Appendices

Communiqué Regarding the Cheekeye-Dunsmuir Bombing

This is the communiqué from the Cheekeye-Dunsmuir bombing, taken from *Black Flag*.

Direct Action — May 31, 1982

On May 31, we bombed four 500 kV transformers at the Dunsmuir substation on Vancouver Island. This substation is part of the $1 billion Cheekeye-Dunsmuir transmission line project being built by British Columbia Hydroelectric. This project, if completed, will provide electricity for a wave of industrial development planned for Vancouver Island.

It was in rejection of both the ecological destruction and the human oppression inherent in the industrial societies of the corporate machine in the West and the communist machine in the East. In the last two hundred years industrial civilization has been raping and mutilating the earth and exterminating other species at an ever increasing rate.

Already in this province, half the forest has been logged and many rivers dammed. The valleys are littered with highways and power lines, the estuaries are paved and polluted, the water is poisoned, mills and smelters belch noxious fumes, and nuclear power and acid rain are soon to come.

While being in complete opposition to further ecological destruction, we also oppose the human oppression resulting from the economic and political systems throughout the world that are based on profit and power. In fact, ecological destruction is directly related to the human oppressions of sexism, racism, hierarchy and imperialism. The desire for power, the insensitivity to the suffering of others and the need to feel superior are the sinister bonds that underlie all these oppressive human relations.

Canada's historical role has always been that of supplier of cheap resources to the industrialized world. As this role becomes more critical internationally, the development of energy and resource mega-project projects in Canada has become a government priority. As well as serving a strategic function within the international capitalist economy, the Canadian capitalists see these mega-projects as a means of overcoming the ongoing economic crisis nationally.

We must make this an insecure and uninhabitable place for capitalists and their projects. This is the best contribution we can make towards protecting the earth and struggling for a liberated society.

Appendix 2
The Litton Bombing Communiqué

The following is a direct transcript of the original printed Litton communiqué — including the title. It includes spelling and grammatical errors.

Statement Regarding the October 14 Litton Bombing

We claim responsibility for the bombing of a Litton Systems of Canada Ltd. Industrial plant in Toronto, Ontario where the guidance system for the Cruise Missile nuclear weapons is being produced.

We sincerely regret that any injuries occurred as a result of this action. We never intended any harm to come to anyone — especially the workers at Litton — but instead, we took great care in preparing what we seriously assumed were adequate precautions to insure the safety of all people in the area. Unfortunately, this did not turn out to be the case.

We do not regret, however, our decision to attempt to sabotage the production of the Cruise Missile's guidance "brain". We only claim in all honesty that this action was never meant to be an act of terrorism. We were not trying to threaten or kill the workers or executives of Litton Systems. We were attempting to destroy part of an industrial facility that produces machinery for mass murder. We wanted to blow up as much of that technology of death as possible.

Accidents happen; no systems or people are infallible. For us, however, this fact of life in no way excuses us for the mistakes that we made which contributed to causing injury in this action. We only pose these simple questions to put this tragedy into proper perspective. How many thousands will suffer from cancer-related diseases because of breakdowns at nuclear power plants? How many thousands are maimed and killed every year in industrial

478 / Direct Action: Memoirs of an Urban Guerrilla

accidents? And isn't it a fact that millions of people starve to death annually because so much money and human effort is put into systems of war rather than developing the means to feed the people of the world?

Although we still firmly believe that it is right to attack the technologies of death, we identify our mistakes in this action as the following:

1. The bomb exploded 12 minutes before it was supposed to, assuming that it did detonate at 11:31 p.m. as stated in the media. The bomb was set to go off at 11:43 p.m. If it had exploded at this time, we feel that it was reasonable to have assumed that the Litton plant and the surrounding area would have been safely secured. It is a mystery to us why it exploded early, as we had checked and double-checked the accuracy of the timing system many times.

2. The warning call was not repeated. The van was left on the lawn in front of the Litton building at 11:17 p.m. We telephoned a warning to Litton Security just one minute after the van was parked. This was to ensure a quick reaction by authorities, even though we felt certain that the van would have been seen as it was being driven across the lawn and parked. The van was parked 100 meters directly in front of an exposed glass-walled security guard's booth. In fact, the driver of the van could see 3 guards in the booth at all times during the approach and, as a result, knew that the van had not been noticed. Unfortunately, the Litton guard did not completely understand the instructions of the telephone warning. When he asked that the instructions be repeated, he was only told to go out front and look at the van. We see now that the telephone warning should have been carefully repeated. However, if the warning had been understood, and even the police have said it was "meticulous", then the authorities would have had approximately 25 minutes to clear the plant, the area, and surrounding roads — if the bomb had detonated on time. This was certainly a reasonable length of time to have left the authorities to evacuate the plant and secure the area. Even though the bomb went off early, it seems obvious that even 13 minutes was enough time for the plant to have been safely emptied had the instructions been understood.

3. We made errors in judgement about the "orange box" which was left in front of the van. This box was meant to be a back-up

warning system to the telephone warning — again to help authorities understand the situation and ensure prompt and knowledgable action on their part. The box was painted florescent orange so it could be easily seen and taped to all four sides of it was a sheet of paper with information and instructions. On top of the box was taped a stick of unarmed dynamite. We felt certain that the Litton guards, either by seeing the van being parked or by being alerted to it by the telephone warning, would quickly come upon the box — thus having written information in their possession to guide them. Unfortunately, we wrote "Danger Explosives" on top of the sheets of instructions. As well, it was not a good idea to leave an unarmed stick of dynamite visable on top of the box. Although these two things were done to prove that this was a real bombing, they actually frightened the Litton guards and police away from the box so that the instructions were never read. Because we left evidence of real explosives, and because the instructions contained the information that there were 550 pounds of explosives inside the van, we assumed that the authorities would have undertaken a massive emergency response and evacuation. This is what we were hoping would happen to make sure that no one was hurt. It was specifically stated in the telephone warning that the box contained important instructions and that the dynamite attached to it was harmless in both the written instructions and the telephone warning, we stated that the van would explode in approxiately 15-25 minutes. We said this to insure that everyone, including bomb squad members, would clear away from the van well before it exploded.

4. We were mistaken in believing that the Litton guards and police would be on top of things. The image of cops and guards as "super heroes" caused us to believe that they would have security and safety matters underway very quickly. This obviously did not turn out to be what happened. The Litton guards did not observe the van being parked even though it occurred essentially right before their eyes. A Litton guard did not understand the phone warning even though it was given clearly. It seems that the Litton guards did little or nothing to evacuate the workers until after the police arrived. As the workers have said, they were only told to leave the building seconds before the explosion. The police took a very long time to arrive after they were alerted — approximately 10 minutes — and even

then they only sent one car at first to investigate. Finally, neither the police, but especially Litton security, even took a close look at the orange box. We did not expect this kind of slow and indecisive response from the authorities.

We are very disturbed and saddened that injuries occurred as a result of this action. We have gone over what went wrong time and time again. Most significantly, the bomb exploded 12 minutes too early. But nevertheless, we feel we must strongly critisize the Litton security guards for the way in which they "handled" this incident. We know that there were at least 3 guards in the security booth where the van was parked and when the phone warning occurred. We feel it is undeniable that all injury to the workers could have been avoided if the guards had promptly evacuated the Litton plant, as they obviously should have. Although we had no knowledge of the previous false bomb threats (in fact, we oppose the use of fake bomb threats precisely because they do cause the authorities to be sceptical of the authenticity of real bomb attacks), we put effort into making sure that the authorities would quickly understand that this threat was real. It is not as if we said that a pipe-bomb was hidden somewhere within the entire Litton complex, so evacuate everything. We informed Litton security of where the van and box were. They were both completely visable to the guards simply by looking straight out through their booth's window, and the fact that they were there at all obviously indicated that something was definately amiss. We would like to know why a Litton guard went running into the plant to evacuate the workers only seconds before the explosion — instead of at least 10 minutes earlier? And we would like to know why the two other Litton guards were standing around on the front lawn, instead of informing workers in the other plants? As well, it is irresponsible of Litton to have never informed the workers of past bomb threats, and to not have a loudspeaker system combined with evacuation plans so that workers could be quickly moved to safety in the event of any danger, be it a bombing or otherwise.

The position where the van was parked was chosen for two reasons. One, so that it could be easily and quickly seen from the guard's booth. It would have been much less conspicuous, and therefore far less risky for the driver of the van, if it had been parked in front of the other two Litton buildings, as neither of these are within direct view of the guard's booth. Secondly, the van was parked in a corner of the building in order that the two walls of this corner would prevent debris from being cast in a southerly or south-westerly direction where the two nearby hotels are located. This position was the only such corner at the front of the three Litton buildings. Again it was at the risk of being apprehended on the spot that we chose to park the van in a location which provided the least risk to public safety.

We have written the above not to redeem ourselves, as we did commit inexusable errors, but simply as an explanation of our motives and intentions for those people who may feel threatened that there are crazed terrorists on the loose against the Canadian people. Again, we repeat, that we took great care in preparing what we seriously assumed were adequate precautions to insure the safety of all people in the area. Understand and remember, the terrorists are those who have set the world on the brink of nuclear war, not those who are fighting this insanity and inhuman madness!

Finally, we wish to state that in no way was this bombing the work of the Cruise Missile Conversion Project, or any other public peace movement organization in Toronto.

Direct Action
October 17, 1982

Direct Action

We claim responsibility for the bombing of a Litton Systems of Canada Ltd. industrial plant in Toronto, Ontario where the guidance system for the Cruise Missle nuclear weapons are being built.

There is every reason imaginable to tear down the systems and makers of nuclear war: for the survival of all life on Earth, for people's hopes and visions, for the possibilities of a liveable future. We dedicate this action to the spirit of the people, which if awakened, will overcome the threats to our survival.

Nuclear war is beyond question the ultimate expression of the negative characteristics of Western Civilization. Its roots lie deep within centuries of patriarchy, racism, imperialism, class domination and all other forms of violence and oppression that have scarred human history. As well, nuclear war expresses, in the most horrendous way, the general trend of modern technological civilization towards extinction — either by war or ecological destruction. It points out, with terrorizing finality, that unless people can stop the men that dominate societies around the world — the men who use science and technology for war and power and profit — then the intricate natural world as we know it will cease to exist.

The insanity of nuclear war, and the continuing development of the weapons for nuclear war, stands as a horror for all to see. In the industrialized world more resources, scientists and engineers are engaged in creating the armies and weapons systems for nuclear war than for any other single pursuit. Three to ten new bombs are added daily to the arsenals of global annihilation and over $300 billion is spent every year increasing and upgrading an overkill stockpile of more than 55,000 nuclear weapons. In the U.S., Reagan has asked for a 31% increase in the Pentagon's present $1.7 trillion five-year budget and has also announced a new $1.5 trillion arms program. Who can doubt that the dictators and militarists in the Kremlin are far behind?

The terrorism of this relentless nuclear arms buildup, the nightmare of witnessing the Earth being transformed into a giant doomsday bomb, and the realization that things are out-of-control because those in power are greedy and violent madmen has shocked billions with fear and concern. Yet in the industrialized world, many of the same people who profess their abhorrence at the idea of nuclear conflict are nevertheless unthinkingly, and often willingly, participating in the actual processes which are bringing about global nuclear genocide. People of the Western and Eastern empires must wake up to the reality that it is the same governments and militaries that they support, the same ideology and rationalizations that they believe in, the same materialistic, technological and consumeristic lifestyles that they adhere to, and the same corporations or industries that they work for that are directly responsible for the ongoing nuclear insanity that they claim to reject.

We believe that people must actively fight the nuclear war systems in whatever forms they exist and wherever they exist. Although, in total, the nuclear militarization of the world is a vast and seemingly unfathomable and omnipotent network, it can be understood and effectively resisted when we recognize that it is designed, built and operated in thousands of separate facilities and industries spread throughout the world. By analysing the interests and institutions in our own regions that are contributing to the nuclear buildup we find the smaller component pieces of the nuclear network that are realistic targets for direct confrontation and sabotage. Our opposition to the insanity of nuclear war must be transformed into militant resistance and direct action on a local and regional basis. It is not enough to only theoretically oppose the idea of nuclear war. We must take responsiblity for what is going on around us!

In Canada we must specifically fight against the production and testing of the Cruise Missle. But more generally, and strategically, we must recognize that the Canadian State is committed to, and actively involved in, the nuclear war preparations of the U.S. and the rest of the capitalist Western Alliance. As one of the seven Western Summit nations and through its military alliances, the Canadian State is directly participating in the desperate and deadly drive by the Western Alliance (primarily spurred on by the U.S. ruling class) to re-assert capitalism's hegemony globally through the attainment of total nuclear superiority and first-strike capability. The new nuclear weapons systems, such as the Cruise and Pershing II Missles, the Trident Submarines and the Neutron Bomb, are designed for offensive first-strike use, and are seen by the military strategists and leaders of the Western Alliance as a force to contain or defeat any threats to the security of capitalist interests or strategically important regions around the world — be it from the Soviet Union or liberation struggles in the Third World attempting to establish independent economies.

Canadian economic, foreign and military policy is not committed to peace or global justice, rather it is completely emersed within the genocidal nuclear strategy of the Western Alliance to wage nuclear war, if necessary, to maintain the multinational corporate economy throughout the world. Through membership in the NATO and NORAD nuclear military alliances, the Canadian State is fulfilling an active supporting role in maintaining and developing the nuclear fighting capacity of the Western military forces. Primarily, Canadian support systems for nuclear war involve communications devices which supply targetting information to U.S. nuclear weapons systems or detection of incoming attacks; as well as the deployment of nuclear missles at Canadian Forces bases at Bagotville, Quebec, at Comox, B.C. and at Chatham, New Brunswick. The ongoing complicity of the Canadian State with nuclear warfare strategies was re-affirmed recently by renewed committments to both NATO and NORAD, and by the government's support for NATO's nuclear modernization program.

Hand in hand with the government's military involvement in the nuclear operations of NATO and NORAD, Canadian capitalists are making profits from producing components for U.S. nuclear weapons systems. Current government policy places no restrictions on Canadian industrial involvement in the building of U.S. nuclear weapons. Litton is building the Cruise Missle's electronic guidance system, Hawker-Siddeley Canada Ltd. of Toronto is building launchers for the Lance Missles designed to carry the Neutron Bomb, Vickers of Montrail is building the hull cylinder torpedo tubes for the Polaris, Poseidon and Trident nuclear submarines, Heeds International of Port Moody, B.C. built the cranes to load nuclear warheads into the Trident subs, and a Canadian plant is working on a component for the MX nuclear missle system.

Industries in Canada that produce nuclear weapons components are fully integrated with the military and nuclear policies of the U.S. through the U.S./Canada Defense Production Sharing Arrangements. These arrangements cover the production side of the NORAD agreements for a continental defense policy and set out the division of labour between Canada and the U.S. for weapons production. The federal government directly assists and subsidizes Canadian armament manufacturers through a myriad of programs designed to help these death merchants win U.S. Defense Department contracts available under the Production Sharing Arrangements. Through the Defense Industry Productivity Program, the federal government has given Litton $26.4 million to subsidize production of the guidance system for the Cruise Missle. In addition, the government has given Litton a five year $22.5 million interest free loan for the same program.

Giving financial aid for the manufacture of components for the Cruise Missle and the agreements to test the Cruise Missle in northern Alberta and Saskatchewan attests to the complete hypocracy of Trudeau and the other government officials who proclaim that Canadian policy strives for suffocation of the nuclear arms race. In the grim light of reality, the "peace" pronouncements of Trudeau amount to nothing but enticing lies and illusions designed to con us into believing that the Canadian State is an ally in the struggle for disarmament, and therefore, a workable vehicle in which to direct our energies.

We've got to realize the implications of the government's decisions and actual policy. We must come to see the Canadian State as an active enemy to be fought, and not as misguided humanists open to our enlightenment. Far from listening to the growing protest from the Canadian public to withdraw its involvement in nuclear war, the government has done just the opposite. It has boosted military spending, re-affirmed committments to NATO and NORAD, publicly defended the U.S./NATO nuclear strategy, given free money to Litton to build part of the Cruise Missle, and agreed to let the Pentagon warmongers use Canadian territory for the testing of the Cruise Missle, as well as other newly developed U.S. weapons systems. Counting on these officials to solve our problems is rediculous. Any belief in the "democracy" of the system to save us is simply a belief in the democracy of lambs being led to the slaughter. We must stop our futile attempts at trying to transform the consciousness of the capitalist slime who make up the Canadian State and begin transforming ourselves and the strategies by which we operate. We will not survive if, in the final analysis, the success of our undertakings is determined by whether the nuclear enemy can be persuaded to change its sickened mind.

While we have no illusions that direct action, such as this one, can by themselves bring about the end of Canada's role as a resource based economic and military functionary of Western Imperialism, we do believe that militant direct actions are valid and necessary. Militant direct actions can have a constructive function both as a springboard to the kind of consciousness and organization that must be developed if we are to overcome the nuclear masters, and as an effective tool of resistance now. Whether they will or not depends on the integrity of the existing movement to develop the committment and courage to carry the struggle beyond legality and the personal security and privilage of comforatable lifestyles still aspired to, and attainable, by middle-class dissidents in North America.

We believe that it is critical that the already radical sectors of the movement for liberation and nuclear sanity recognize that direct action and militant resistance can have positive effects now, can weaken the enemy now, and that this possibility to sabotage the enemy's undertakings complements the movement's strategic long-term efforts to transform the consciousness of the people. We believe that, if undertaken seriously and well-supported throughout the existing movement, widely practised militant resistance and sabotage will become effective in slowing down the clock of death and inspire the people to respond to the threats to our survival with urgency, vitality and clarity.

The global situation of nuclear holocaust and extreme ecological disaster is rapidly becoming reality. The new Western Alliance weapons systems for first-strike nuclear war are to be in place by 1983-86. This destabilizing, ever-encroaching reality should compel us all to move beyond protest and work hard to develop a movement with the collective means and ability to actually do something directly to stop the realization of the enemy's life-threatening madness. In the absence of widespread popular refusal to participate any longer in the war projects of the ruling class, we believe that militant direct actions must be used as an attempt to keep uncompleted, or at least slow-down, the programs and technologies which are bringing about our own destruction. For us, this is where the impetus to act lies.

Historically, those in power have always used warfare and repression in order to maintain their control over other people's lives. And today this situation is no different. For the corporate owners and political rulers nuclear weapons are the ultimate tool in the repressive apparatus — the key to maintaining their power. Thus they will never voluntarily disarm or stand aside and watch their power be peacefully taken away. Instead, they will use whatever weapons are necessary to battle those who are threatening their rule. We are certain that only through revolt — not referendums or protest alone — can we stop the powercrazed from launching their W.W. III. It is with an eye towards the generalized development of an actively militant resistance movement that we have undertaken this action.

Appendix 3
Wimmin's Fire Brigade Communiqué
November 22, 1982

We, the Wimmin's Fire Brigade, claim responsibility for the fire-bombing of three Red Hot Video outlets in the Lower Mainland of B.C. on November 22, 1982. This action is another step towards the destruction of a business that promotes and profits from violence against wimmin and children.

Red Hot Video sells tapes that show wimmin and children being tortured, raped and humiliated. We are not the property of men to be used and abused.

Red Hot Video is part of a multi-billion dollar pornography industry that teaches men to equate sexuality with violence. Although these tapes violate the Criminal Code of Canada and the B.C. guidelines on pornography, all lawful attempts to shut down Red Hot Video have failed because the justice system was created, and is controlled, by rich men to protect their profits and property.

As a result, we are left no viable alternative but to change the situation ourselves through illegal means. This is an act of self-defense against hate propaganda!

Appendix 4
Ann Hansen's Statement to the Court before Sentencing

When I look back on the past year and a half, I realize that I have learned a lesson. Not the kind of lesson that some people would hope I had learned, but rather through direct life experience I have re-learned what I once only understood theoretically — that the courts have nothing to do with justice and prison is where they punish the victims of this society. For many years now I have understood that the justice system was actually a system of injustice when seen in the broader social context. I was aware that parliament is where men make laws to protect big business, wealthy individuals and the status quo. Police were employed to enforce the laws, courts were created to prosecute those who broke the law, and prisons were built to punish the guilty.

My faith in the justice system began to erode as I grew up and saw the big businesses ripping off people by selling poorly produced products at high prices, resource companies gouging and raping the earth, governments producing nuclear arsenals capable of destroying life on earth many times over, pornographic magazines that normalized and glamourized rape, incest and sexual assault, and Indians being herded into reservations to die. All these crimes against humanity and the earth are legal. They are protected and sanctioned by Parliament, the courts, the law and the police. This was all very wrong.

In Oakalla, where I have spent the past sixteen months, I have found that 70 percent of the prison population are Indian womyn, even though Indian people make up only 1 percent of the total outside population. This disproportionate number of Indian people in prison is reflected in prison populations across the country and reflects the racism of our society.

Everyone I have met in prison is poor. No one owns cars, homes, land or anything. They are there because they were forced to commit crimes to survive in a society that has no place for them. They have never owned forest companies that rape whole mountains of their forests, or handled nuclear murder weapons or stolen oil from Arab lands to be sold at scalper's prices in North America.

In the beginning when I was first arrested, I was intimidated and surrounded by the courts and prison. This fear provided the basis for the belief that if I played the legal game, I would get acquitted or perhaps less time. This fear obscured my vision and fooled me into thinking that I could get a break from the justice system. But this past eight months in court has sharpened my perceptions and strengthened my political convictions to see that the legal game is rigged and political prisoners are dealt a marked deck.

From the beginning in January 1983, the police illegally orchestrated press conferences and furnished the mass media with evidence, photos and information that became the basis for nation-wide news stories convicting us as terrorists. We were portrayed as dangerous, psychotic criminals without politics.

Then our charges were seperated into four separate indict-ments, of which the first was the Brink's conspiracy, so that we would be criminalized. This would make it harder for people to understand us as political people for our future trials.

During the voir dire, it became obvious through police testi-mony that the different police departments had committed illegal acts during their investigation. The Security Service in all probabil-ity watched the WFB (Wimmin's Fire Brigade) do the firebombings since Julie and I had been under intensive twenty-four-hour surveillance by the SS for days prior to and during the day of the firebombing.

CLEU (Co-ordinated Law Enforcement Unit) had committed illegal break-ins to plant the bugs in our house and in Doug's apartment among other illegal activities. But despite this, the judge permitted the wire-tap evidence. This taught me that there is one law for the people and none for the police.

But the event during the court proceedings that has had the most politicizing effect on me was Julie's sentencing. The judge ignored the fact that she had plea bargained and slapped her with the maximum prison sentence suggested by the Crown — twenty years. During the sentencing, the judge said that this case is crimi-nal not political, yet the twenty-year sentence contradicts this view and instead reflects the real political nature of these proceedings. The twenty-year sentence was justified by the judge as a necessary social deterrent, which indicates that the court is so threatened by the potential of social upheaval that it takes a twenty-year sentence to deter others. That is political. It seems that the severity of the prison sentence is in direct proportion to the perceived level of discontent in society.

I understand why I have participated in the legal system up to now, but, in retrospect, in order to be honest to my political principles, I should have refused to collaborate in this legal sham and instead simply stated my political reasons for doing what I did.

Since I didn't then, I have the opportunity to do so now. Over the last couple of days we have heard witnesses who are activists around the different issues. They have spoken at great length about their efforts and the efforts of other groups to prevent the testing of the Cruise and the construction of the Cheekeye-Dunsmuir line and to stop Red Hot Video. I think it has become fairly obvious through their testimony that in each case they had exhausted all the legitimate channels of social protest in order to stop these projects and businesses. It was because there was no legal way to stop these crimes against humanity and the earth that I felt I had to use illegal actions to do so.

I didn't just feel that I should; I felt I had a duty and responsibility to do everything in my power to stop these crimes. At this dangerous point in human history, we have a moral responsibility to stop the arms race, violent pornography and the destruction of the earth. This moral responsibility far overrides any obligation to adhere to man-made laws.

I would prefer to live in peace but, when I looked around me, I couldn't find it anywhere. Everywhere I looked, the land was being destroyed, the Indians were victims of genocide, Third World peoples were oppressed and massacred, people lived in industrial wastelands and womyn were being raped and children molested. I could never live in peace, only quiet — the kind you find in cemeteries.

Even though I knew that a few militant direct actions would not make the revolution or stop these projects, I believed that it was necessary to begin the development of an underground resistance movement that was capable of sabotage and expropriations and could work free from police surveillance. The development of an effective resistance movement is not an overnight affair — it takes decades of evolution. It has to start somewhere in small numbers, and whether or not it grows, becomes effective and successful, will depend upon whether we make it happen.

I believe these direct actions of sabotage complement the legal radical movement and serve a purpose that it can't fulfil. Not that the legal movement is ineffective: although its efforts often fail to stop a project, its work will increase people's consciousness. The important thing is that the above-ground and underground support one another because our strength lies in unity and diversity.

Although I did do these three political actions, they were the result of the culmination of a legal struggle around the respective issues. In fact, the point of an underground resistance movement is to develop a strategic political analysis and actions that are based on an understanding of the economics and politics of the corporate state. Instead of reacting to every issue that pops up, we carried out actions that were based upon an analysis. This way, if an effective resistance movement does develop, we can be subjects who determine history instead of reacting to every singularly obvious sympton of the system's disease.

The politics of Direct Action saw the interconnectness of militarism, sexism, environmental destruction and imperialism. We saw that all these problems are rooted in the value system and way of thinking called capitalism and patriarchy. These values are passed on from one generation to the next through the institutions of this society — the mulitnational corporations, schools, mass media, church and commercial culture.

The main value of this society can be boiled down simply into one word — money. All life on this earth is reduced to its profit value by the capitalist economic system. Women, animals, Third World people, and the environment are reduced to a product and thus are objectified. Workers are valued for their productivity, women as sex objects, animals for food or furs, the environment for its potential as a natural resource base. If some living being is of no economic value in relation to the capitalist system then it is valueless. Consequently, traditional Indian people become victims of genocide and huge areas of the earth are designated as "Natural Sacrifice Areas." So the Litton action, Cheekeye-Dunsmuir action and WFB action, at least for me, were not issue-oriented actions but were our resistance politics transformed into action.

Contrary to the Crown's and police's theories, Direct Action and the WFB were two different groups. Of the five of us charged with the Red Hot Video fire-bombings, only Julie and I did the firebombings. There were no men involved with doing the firebombings. Doug, Brent and Gerry just happened to either live with Julie and me or visit us. The WFB was not an ongoing underground group, it was simply a group of womyn who came together for the purpose of firebombing Red Hot Video because we felt there was no other way for us to stop the proliferation of violent pornography.

Direct Action carried out the Litton and Cheekeye-Dunsmuir actions. I do sincerely regret that people were injured in the Litton bombing. All precautions were taken to prevent these injuries and an explanation as to why it happened was released almost immediately after the bombing. But I must also add that I criticize the Litton action itself because it was wrong for Direct Action to place a bomb near a building that people were working in, regardless of the number of precautions taken to ensure that nobody got hurt. In carrying out actions, revolutionaries should never rely on the police or security guards to clear out buildings and save people's lives.

There is no excuse for these mistakes, and I will always live with the pain that I am responsible for, but these mistakes should never overshadow the incredible amount of pain and suffering that Litton contributes to every day and the potential for planetary extinction that the Cruise missile embodies. Every day millions of people are slowly starving to death because so much money and human effort is diverted into the international war industry instead of being used to feed the people of the world. In Canada, essential social services are cut so that the government can pour more money into the war industry and megaprojects. For example, the federal government has given Litton $26.4 million in subsidies to build the guidance system of the Cruise.

The use of 1984 double-think has become an important part of today's psychological warfare against people developing radical consciousness. We experience it every day, even in this courtroom. I am called a terrorist — one who tries to impose their will through force and intimidation — by the court and press. But I am not a terrorist. I am a person who feels a moral obligation to do all that is humanly possible to prevent the destruction of the earth. Businesses such as Litton, B.C. Hydro and Red Hot Video are the real terrorists. They are guilty of crimes against humanity and the earth, yet they are free to carry on their illegal activities while those who resist and those who are their victims remain in prison. How do we, who have no armies, weapons, power or money, stop these criminals before they destroy the earth?

I believe if there is any hope for the future, it lies in our struggle.

Between the Lines (Toronto) is an independent publisher of non-fiction books on politics, social issues, international development, history, education, the environment, health, gender, sexuality, labour, technology, media, and culture. Our books promote critical analysis and inform struggles for social justice and equity. For more information, visit our website: www.btlbooks.com.

Between the Lines
720 Bathurst Street, Suite #404
Toronto, Ontario
Canada
M5S 2R4
btlbooks@web.ca

AK Press is the publishing arm of AKA Books Co-operative Ltd., a workers' co-operative wholly owned by its members. AK's branches in the U.S. (Oakland) and the U.K. (Edinburgh) also distribute radical books and other materials published by other independent presses. To receive a free catalog, please contact us at the address below, or check out our website and online catalog at www.akpress.org or www.akuk.com.

AK Press Distribution
674-A 23rd Street
Oakland, CA 94612
U.S.A.
akpress@akpress.org

AK Press Distribution (UK)
PO Box 12766
Edinburgh EH8 9YE
Scotland
ak@akedin.demon.co.uk

DIRECT ACTION

Ann Hansen stood trial as one of the so-called "Squamish Five." Sentenced to life in prison, she served seven years. Now she tells her story for the first time.

Direct Action captures the excitement and indignation of the counter-culture of the early '80s. Missile tests were fuelling a new arms race. Reckless megaprojects threatened the global environment. Alienation, punk rock, and militancy were on the rise. Hansen and her fellow urban guerrillas believed that sabotaging government and corporate property could help turn things around. To prove their point, they bombed the Litton Systems plant in Toronto, where components for Cruise Missiles were being made.

Hansen's book poses unresolved ethical dilemmas. In light of the recent explosion of anti-globalization protests, *Direct Action* mirrors the resurgence of militant activity around the world.

"Damn, Ann Hansen can write! Her first career was clearly a mistake. Beautifully written and thoughtfully reflective of her analysis of the limits of violence as a force for social change."
  – Clayton C. Ruby, Barrister

"Hansen's story is an intense, articulate rendering of her motivations and desire to be part of an effective revolutionary force for social justice."
  – *Quill and Quire*

"Whether you agree with their tactics or not, Hansen's story is one that needs to be told. Read the book and debate the issues."
  – Jen Chang and Darryl Leroux, co-editors of
    RESIST! Grassroots Protests in Quebec City and Beyond

Ann Hansen lives on a farm near Kingston, Ontario. Formerly the co-owner of a cabinet-making business, she is now a freelance writer.

BETWEEN THE LINES
ISBN 1-896357-40-7

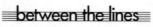

between the lines

AK
PRESS

9 781896 357409